Transforming Education With Generative AI:

Prompt Engineering and Synthetic Content Creation

Ramesh C. Sharma
Ambedkar University, Delhi, India

Aras Bozkurt
Anadolu University, Turkey

A volume in the Advances in Educational Technologies and Instructional Design (AETID) Book Series

IGI Global
PUBLISHER of TIMELY KNOWLEDGE

Published in the United States of America by
IGI Global
Engineering Science Reference (an imprint of IGI Global)
701 E. Chocolate Avenue
Hershey PA, USA 17033
Tel: 717-533-8845
Fax: 717-533-8661
E-mail: cust@igi-global.com
Web site: http://www.igi-global.com

Library of Congress Cataloging-in-Publication Data

Names: Sharma, Ramesh C., 1962- editor. | Bozkurt, Aras, editor.
Title: Transforming education with generative AI : prompt engineering and synthetic content creation / edited by Ramesh C. Sharma, Aras Bozkurt.
Description: Hershey, PA : Engineering Science Reference, 2024. | Includes bibliographical references and index. | Summary: "The objective of this edited book is to explore the potential of prompt engineering and the co-creation of synthetic content within the educational context"-- Provided by publisher.
Identifiers: LCCN 2023051986 (print) | LCCN 2023051987 (ebook) | ISBN 9798369313510 (hardcover) | ISBN 9798369313527 (ebook)
Subjects: LCSH: Artificial intelligence--Educational applications.
Classification: LCC LB1028.43 .T74 2024 (print) | LCC LB1028.43 (ebook) | DDC 371.33/4--dc23/eng/20231108
LC record available at https://lccn.loc.gov/2023051986
LC ebook record available at https://lccn.loc.gov/2023051987

This book is published in the IGI Global book series Advances in Educational Technologies and Instructional Design (AETID) (ISSN: 2326-8905; eISSN: 2326-8913)

British Cataloguing in Publication Data
A Cataloguing in Publication record for this book is available from the British Library.

For electronic access to this publication, please contact: eresources@igi-global.com.

Advances in Educational Technologies and Instructional Design (AETID) Book Series

Lawrence A. Tomei
Robert Morris University, USA

ISSN:2326-8905
EISSN:2326-8913

Mission

Education has undergone, and continues to undergo, immense changes in the way it is enacted and distributed to both child and adult learners. In modern education, the traditional classroom learning experience has evolved to include technological resources and to provide online classroom opportunities to students of all ages regardless of their geographical locations. From distance education, Massive-Open-Online-Courses (MOOCs), and electronic tablets in the classroom, technology is now an integral part of learning and is also affecting the way educators communicate information to students.

The **Advances in Educational Technologies & Instructional Design (AETID) Book Series** explores new research and theories for facilitating learning and improving educational performance utilizing technological processes and resources. The series examines technologies that can be integrated into K-12 classrooms to improve skills and learning abilities in all subjects including STEM education and language learning. Additionally, it studies the emergence of fully online classrooms for young and adult learners alike, and the communication and accountability challenges that can arise. Trending topics that are covered include adaptive learning, game-based learning, virtual school environments, and social media effects. School administrators, educators, academicians, researchers, and students will find this series to be an excellent resource for the effective design and implementation of learning technologies in their classes.

Coverage

- E-Learning
- Instructional Design Models
- Game-Based Learning
- Bring-Your-Own-Device
- Online Media in Classrooms
- Instructional Design
- Social Media Effects on Education
- Adaptive Learning
- Higher Education Technologies
- Virtual School Environments

The Advances in Educational Technologies and Instructional Design (AETID) Book Series (ISSN 2326-8905) is published by IGI Global, 701 E. Chocolate Avenue, Hershey, PA 17033-1240, USA, www.igi-global.com. This series is composed of titles available for purchase individually; each title is edited to be contextually exclusive from any other title within the series. For pricing and ordering information please visit http://www.igi-global.com/book-series/advances-educational-technologies-instructional-design/73678. Postmaster: Send all address changes to above address.

Titles in this Series

For a list of additional titles in this series, please visit: www.igi-global.com/book-series

Optimizing Education Through Micro-Lessons Engaging and Adaptive Learning Strategies
Peter Ilic (University of Aizu, apan)
Information Science Reference • © 2024 • 398pp • H/C (ISBN: 9798369301951) • US $230.00

Fostering Pedagogical Innovation Through Effective Instructional Design
Mohamed Khaldi (Ecole Normale Supérieur, Abdelmalek Essaadi University, Tetouan, Moocco)
Information Science Reference • © 2024 • 467pp • H/C (ISBN: 9798369312063) • US $245.00

Protocols and Tools for Equitable Dual Language Teaching
Esther Gross (The Center for Educational Technology, Israel) and Jenifer Crawford (University of Southern California, USA)
Information Science Reference • © 2024 • 300pp • H/C (ISBN: 9781799883548) • US $225.00

Utilizing Visuals and Information Technology in Mathematics Classrooms
Hiroto Namihira (Former Otsuma Women's University, Japan)
Information Science Reference • © 2024 • 300pp • H/C (ISBN: 9781668499870) • US $220.00

Implications of Chatbots on Teaching and Learning
Mohammad Daradkeh (University of Dubai, UAE)
Information Science Reference • © 2024 • 330pp • H/C (ISBN: 9798369302453) • US $230.00

Fostering Foreign Language Teaching and Learning Environments With Contemporary Technologies
Zeynep Çetin Köroğlu (Aksaray University, Turkey) and Abdulvahit Çakır (Ufuk University, Turkey)
Information Science Reference • © 2024 • 338pp • H/C (ISBN: 9798369303535) • US $230.00

Embracing Cutting-Edge Technology in Modern Educational Settings
Ken Nee Chee (Universiti Pendidikan Sultan Idris, Malaysia) and Mageswaran Sanmugam (Universiti Sains Malaysia, Malaysia)
Information Science Reference • © 2024 • 334pp • H/C (ISBN: 9798369310229) • US $240.00

Innovative Instructional Design Methods and Tools for Improved Teaching
Mohamed Khaldi (Abdelmalek Essaadi University, Morocco)
Information Science Reference • © 2024 • 380pp • H/C (ISBN: 9798369331286) • US $300.00

IGI Global
PUBLISHER of TIMELY KNOWLEDGE

701 East Chocolate Avenue, Hershey, PA 17033, USA
Tel: 717-533-8845 x100 • Fax: 717-533-8661
E-Mail: cust@igi-global.com • www.igi-global.com

This book is dedicated to those who perceive learning as a lifelong journey and, therefore learn, unlearn, and relearn in order to constantly experience the unbearable lightness of learning.

Table of Contents

Detailed Table of Contents

Generative AI has been gaining popularity in 2023 and it is causing a disruption of various standards in the education system. While the pros and particularly the cons of this technology have been extensively debated, this chapter aims to explore the positive aspects of Generative AI—instead of advocating for a ban. This chapter will first provide an overview of the historical context and evolution of AI. It will be followed by a discussion of different types of Generative AI and the principles of co-creation with it. The uses of Generative AI in education will be described, focusing on the key stakeholders such as educators, students, educational administrators, and schools or institutions. Next, the chapter will explore the Generative AI application across different fields as well as various subjects in education. Several use cases, practices, and their associated benefits will be presented. Finally, the future and the implications of Generative AI will be discussed.

For over two decades, educational technologies have been embedded within an approach to inquiry dominated by the "search paradigm." However, conversational AI presents an opportunity to shift this paradigm towards enhancing learning through dialogue. This study explores ChatGPT's potential in developing pre-service teachers' interaction skills and competencies, focusing on interculturality. Using participatory action research, the key inquiry is: In what ways can GenAI applications such as ChatGPT serve as dialogue partners to train future educators' (intercultural) interaction skills and competencies?

The research covers prompt specification, students' experiences with dialogic learning using ChatGPT, and prospects for using LLMs as dialogue partners in pre-service teachers' training. Qualitative analysis shows ChatGPT can stimulate the learning process, especially when perceived as realistic and challenging. These findings suggest new implementations of LLMs in pre-service teacher education and further research into their potential for enhancing dialogue-based skill development.

This chapter explores possible ways educators can use generative AI tools and support to empower them in teaching and learning. In addition, the authord provide samples of appropriate prompts for educators to produce desired responses. With the potential of generative AI to create unique content instantly based on existing large datasets, educators can use it to co-create instructional content, enhance personalized learning experiences, evaluate learners' performances, and more. While highlighting the potential of generative AI, the authors also address the challenges that educators may face when using these tools. As generative AI is gaining popularity in classrooms, it has the potential to empower educators to revolutionize their teaching and transform education.

Imagine having a concept for a literary work but being unable to see it take shape because of a plethora of reasons: paucity of time, writer's block, linguistic barriers, among others. Gen AI promises to be a supportive partner in these creative endeavours. With the synergy of mind and machine, literary texts are born. This chapter attempts to provide insights into the comparison between the nuances of human-AI co-creative partnerships through the crafting of short stories. Using the lens of Collaborative Autoethnography, two seasoned educators collaboratively reflect on cognitive, behavioural, and affective dimensions of co-creating with ChatGPT, a chatbot developed by Open AI. The chapter analyses the co-creation process followed by each of the authors and brings out the commonalities and specificities of the individual lived experience to achieve a narrative piece of work. The insights of the co-creation process would be beneficial to educators, curriculum designers, technology specialists, students and those who intend to use AI-powered chatbots as co-creators.

Generative AI has become so important that educators cannot ignore it. However, while educators focus on the benefits and harms of generative artificial intelligence in terms of education, they ignore the character traits of the student. Therefore, they get stuck with the decision-cost analysis results they put forward to exclude or use for education; this means missing out on a vital benefit of generative AI: empowering teachers. This chapter suggests, therefore, that to properly understand the benefits and harms of generative AI in terms of education, it is necessary to focus on the character traits of students, and it has empowered teachers on character education. While doing this, benefits from the vice and virtue epistemology, eventually decides that education needs something that not only gives technical prompt engineering education but also virtuous prompts that elicit cultivation of intellectual virtues.

"Future Possibilities and Challenges of AI in Education" delves into the unprecedented intersection of artificial intelligence (AI) and the educational landscape. The chapter navigates the transformative possibilities and intricate challenges that arise as AI infiltrates learning management systems. In this exploration, the symbiotic relationship between AI and education is dissected, revealing a dynamic environment teeming with potential. The chapter unfolds in two movements: envisioning a future where personalized learning, AI-enhanced creativity, seamless assessment, global collaboration, and ethical education thrive, and concurrently, acknowledging the uncharted difficulties that could reshape the foundational paradigms of education. As the world hurtles toward an era of automation and interconnected virtuality, understanding the effects of AI in education becomes important. This chapter beckons readers on a journey through the limitless potential of AI's impact on education, inviting reflection on how to harness its power responsibly for the betterment of learning.

The study conducted a literature review focusing on the role of generative artificial intelligence (GAI) utilized as an academic assistant. Within the scope of the research, the opportunities and challenges presented by GAI-based academic assistants to researchers, along with a detailed examination of tools used in the research process, were intended to be explored. It was emphasized that artificial intelligence applications used in academic writing processes have the potential to expedite tasks such as performing repetitive functions, literature reviews, data analysis, and document organization effectively. This situation was noted to offer a range of advantages for students and researchers. However, it was underscored that considerations regarding accuracy, reliability, and ethical concerns must be considered. Factors limiting the effectiveness of GAI in academic writing processes, such as limitations in language understanding, concerns about ethical violations, and difficulties in selecting appropriate data visualization, were discussed.

collaboration promotes critical thinking, problem-solving, and inclusiveness. Educators, institutions, policymakers, and AI developers must ensure that education remains empowering, inclusive, and excellent for AI to be integrated responsibly. By embracing this partnership, education becomes more accessible, individualized, and influential.

In today's dynamic landscape of higher education, the pervasive issue of faculty burnout has emerged as a pressing concern, casting a shadow over the well-being of educators and the overall quality of instruction. This chapter proposal embarks on an exploration of how generative artificial intelligence (AI) can act as a transformative force within higher education, specifically focusing on its potential to empower faculty members, enhance pedagogical practices, and mitigate the alarming prevalence of burnout. The chapter's central objectives are multifaceted, commencing with a comprehensive examination of the multifaceted phenomenon of faculty burnout. This includes an analysis of the contributing factors such as the escalating workloads, the shift towards online and blended learning modalities, and the overwhelming administrative duties that educators must shoulder. The aim here is to illuminate the multifaceted nature of burnout, thereby fostering an enhanced understanding of its urgency and the critical need for sustainable solutions.

This chapter examines the role of generative AI (GenAI) and robotics in special education, particularly for autism spectrum disorder (ASD). It highlights the revolutionary impact of GenAI and AI-powered educational technologies (AIEd) in early diagnosis, personalized learning, and fostering independence in individuals with ASD. Additionally, robotics is presented as a vital tool for enhancing social and communication skills. The integration of these technologies in education requires addressing ethical, privacy, and security concerns. The chapter emphasizes technological literacy, including prompt engineering, to optimize the use of GenAI and robotics. It also explores the unique relationship between individuals with ASD and robots, suggesting a promising future for these technologies in special education. The conclusion calls for ongoing research and development to create more equitable and accessible educational systems, harnessing the power of GenAI and robotics for individuals with ASD.

With the development of technology, AI has been the subject of intense research in the field of education, with ChatGPT, the adoption of generative AI in education. But generative AI has only gained attention in the last few years. Therefore, there are not many research results on the application of generative AI in

Several regulations in the aviation industry have been made by authorities to minimize the incidents due to language barriers; however, a more reasonable solution lies in equipping prospective pilots with necessary language skills in target settings. This requires a transformation in aviation English (AE) classrooms through the medium of emerging technologies. Accordingly, this chapter presents a novel strategy for rethinking AE instruction by using approaches from generative artificial intelligence. It investigates the ways in which prompt engineering and synthetic content production might be used to improve the efficacy of AE teaching. Learners may benefit from better language comprehension, communication skills, and situational awareness by seamlessly incorporating AI-driven language creation into the curriculum. Instructors could find examples of generative AI-driven classroom applications for improved learning outcomes. Considering these potential contributions to the field, this chapter may, in turn, innovate and uplift the AE courses and safety in the aviation industry.

Prompt engineering holds immense relevance in the present world due to its pivotal role in advancing natural language processing (NLP) technologies and artificial intelligence (AI) applications. Also prompt engineering is instrumental in shaping the present landscape of AI-driven technologies, making them more efficient, accessible, and personalized. As these technologies continue to evolve, prompt engineering will remain a vital area of research and development, ensuring that AI systems effectively meet the diverse and dynamic needs of our society. Also, generative AI can create personalized learning experiences for students by analyzing individual learning styles, preferences, and progress. In this context, the chapter explores the art and science of prompt engineering. Through a collection of case studies and real-world applications, the chapter showcases the versatility of prompt engineering, offering insights into how it enhances machine comprehension, content generation, and problem-solving across domains. Here the case studies are discussed using ChatGPT 3.5 version.

This chapter explores the integration of generative AI in higher education assessment, addressing the inadequacies of traditional methods in meeting the diverse needs of contemporary learners. It highlights the potential of AI technologies, such as natural language processing and computer vision, to offer personalized, scalable, and insightful evaluations. The chapter critically examines both the enhanced capabilities introduced by AI in educational settings and the ethical challenges it poses. Emphasizing

Preface

As we stand at the precipice of a new era in education, *Transforming Education with Generative AI: Prompt Engineering and Synthetic Content Creation* emerges as a beacon of knowledge, providing profound insights into the intricate relationship between education, generative AI, and prompt engineering. This tome is a comprehensive exploration of the revolutionary changes generative AI introduces to the educational landscape, aiming to redefine our understanding and application of this technology in learning environments.

The emergence of generative AI signifies a pivotal evolution in the field of human-machine interaction, particularly by focusing on prompt engineering. This book delves deep into the heart of this transformative phenomenon, meticulously unraveling the intricacies of prompt engineering and synthetic content creation in the educational landscape.

In an age where digital technologies permeate every aspect of our lives, understanding and leveraging generative AI in education is crucial. In this context, the book *Transforming Education with Generative AI: Prompt Engineering and Synthetic Content Creation* presents a total of 22 chapters that collectively explore the multifaceted impacts of generative AI in education. The chapters cover a broad spectrum of topics including the historical evolution and positive aspects of generative AI, its role in teacher training, empowering educators through generative AI tools, the art of co-creation, and the ethical considerations in AI implementation. The book also delves into specific applications such as AI's role in special education, challenges in AI integration, the potential of AI in flipped classrooms, and the future of curriculum development. Each chapter contributes unique insights into how generative AI is reshaping the educational landscape, highlighting its potential, challenges, and implications.

This book stands as a comprehensive guide, illuminating pathways for harnessing the potential of generative AI in education. It equips readers with the necessary knowledge to navigate this novel terrain and significantly contributes to the discourse on AI's transformative role in educational paradigms.

In all, the book serves as an essential resource for understanding and shaping the future of education in the age of AI. It invites readers to embark on a journey of discovery and innovation, fostering an educational landscape continually enhanced by the boundless possibilities of generative AI.

Acknowledgment

In their book, editors Dr. Ramesh C. Sharma and Dr. Aras Bozkurt offer a profound acknowledgment to the visionaries who laid the foundations of artificial intelligence. They express gratitude towards John McCarthy, Marvin L. Minsky, Nathaniel Rochester, and Claude E. Shannon for their groundbreaking proposal that first conceptualized the term artificial intelligence, or AI as it is often called. The influence of Isaac Asimov, particularly through his imaginative *Three Laws of Robotics*, is hailed for its significant impact on AI exploration and human-machine interaction. Additionally, they emphasize Alan Turing's pivotal contributions, notably his provocative inquiry, "Can machines think?" and his innovative Turing Test, which continue to shape and inspire the field of AI studies. This work is a testament to their legacy. And finally, we dedicate this book to all artificial intelligence researchers who have contributed to the transformation of what was once fiction into reality by travelling beyond the dreams of mankind.

Chapter 1
Standing on the Shoulders of Generative AI

Lay Kee Ch'ng
City University Malaysia, Malaysia

ABSTRACT

Generative AI has been gaining popularity in 2023 and it is causing a disruption of various standards in the education system. While the pros and particularly the cons of this technology have been extensively debated, this chapter aims to explore the positive aspects of Generative AI—instead of advocating for a ban. This chapter will first provide an overview of the historical context and evolution of AI. It will be followed by a discussion of different types of Generative AI and the principles of co-creation with it. The uses of Generative AI in education will be described, focusing on the key stakeholders such as educators, students, educational administrators, and schools or institutions. Next, the chapter will explore the Generative AI application across different fields as well as various subjects in education. Several use cases, practices, and their associated benefits will be presented. Finally, the future and the implications of Generative AI will be discussed.

INTRODUCTION

The public understanding of Generative AI has primarily come into focus after the emergence of ChatGPT (Lim et al., 2023). Prior to this, the mature development of AI technology went through three main stages, which were in the 1960s, 1970s, and early 21st century. During the early stages when the technology wasn't fully matured, the practical value of AI was limited, hence it failed to drive the attention of the public (Lee & Wang, 2017). In 2022, more than 20 types of Generative AI have been released and drawn the attention of the public (Gozalo-Brizuela & Garrido-Merchan, 2023).

The metaphor, "standing on the shoulders of giants," depicts the leveraging of the wisdom, experience, and achievements of our predecessors to achieve greater accomplishments. These accomplishments of each generation have laid a strong foundation for the next generation, allowing us to see higher and farther. Today, the "giants" are not only our human ancestors but also technology. The emerging technol-

DOI: 10.4018/979-8-3693-1351-0.ch001

ogy that can be seen as a key to the technology revolution in the digital era is Generative AI. Now, we are standing on the shoulders of AI and can see higher and farther in all aspects of life.

According to Miao et al. (2023) in their analysis report on countries' actions towards AI strategies, decision-makers in Africa, especially Nigeria, are looking to integrate AI into their national strategies. Qatar, the United Arab Emirates, Morocco, and Oman have their own AI policies. China and Singapore have comprehensive national plans, while Sri Lanka and South Korea are integrating AI with ICT efforts. Serbia has a dedicated AI development strategy and Slovenia has a broader digital plan. In Western Europe, the European Commission's Digital Education Action Plan for 2021–2027 aims to improve digital skills and enable transformation. Spain also includes AI in its broader digital competence frameworks, similar to the strategies of the aforementioned nations. These findings show that the emergence of AI technology is a component of the global digital transformation that all countries around the world are pursuing.

Recently, many scholarly works have included positive remarks regarding the uses of Generative AI in various aspects (Bozkurt et al., 2023; Tlili et al., 2023; Baidoo-Anu & Owusu Ansah, 2023; Su & Yang, 2023; Gozalo-Brizuela & Garrido-Merchan, 2023; Lim et al., 2023). Undeniably, AI technology can go beyond human capabilities, excelling in areas such as precision, accuracy, and tasks that are tedious. However, at the same time, there are parallel arguments concerning the limitations of Generative AI, such as its lack of human attributes (emotional intelligence), data bias, and lack of understanding of the learners' context (Baidoo-Anu & Owusu Ansah, 2023; Gozalo-Brizuela & Garrido-Merchan, 2023; Su & Yang, 2023). Thence, Ng (2016) has pointed out that while we have seen numerous scholarly works promoting the best of AI, it is even more important to understand how we can co-create with this "giant" — Generative AI — and make the most of it. A significant number of researchers have urged key stakeholders in education to work together and start conversations on how Generative AI could be used constructively to improve education.

A BRIEF INTRODUCTION TO AIGC

Generative AI primarily refers to the use of machine learning techniques by which an algorithm learns from existing data, such as images, audio, and text and then generates content that is similar to the original data (Li, 2023; Pavlik, 2023). Whereas the concept of Artificial Intelligence Generated Content (AIGC) goes further and involves the creation of text, images, video, music, and code using AI models as the creative agents. This process includes generating specific content through the utilization of significant cues and fusion generation based on multimodal content — this is possible by training more advanced generative models on larger datasets (Cao et al., 2023; Li, 2023). Learning optimization in AIGC can be achieved using various techniques such as Generative Adversarial Networks (GANs) (Goodfellow et al., 2020), Diffusion Models (Ho et al., 2020), Neural Radiance Fields (NeRF) (Mildenhall et al., 2021), and Natural Language Processing models like Transformer (Vaswani, 2017).

Types of AIGC

AIGC has become an essential and main component in the content creation and development process today. Co-creation with AI not only boosts the efficiency of the design and development process, it also enhances the capacity and quality of the content produced (Zhan et al., 2023). Listed below are several types of AIGC:

1. Text — Text content can be easily generated by entering prompts into the AI interface. AI is capable of generating stories, news articles, marketing copy, essays, scripts, reports, and more (Su & Yang, 2023). In 2014, a journalist and programmer utilized AI to generate a short article in less than 3 minutes when an earthquake occurred, just by inputting the pertinent data related to the incident (BBC News, 2014). The most popular tool to generate text content today is ChatGPT, developed by OpenAI.
2. Images — Images no longer have to be created and edited exclusively by humans; AI can now perform these tasks alongside humans. According to Li (2023), AIGC in images can be grouped into three main functions:
    a. Image editing: Removing watermarks, adjusting lighting and shadows, and applying filters (Examples: BeautyCam, Hotpot, cre8tiveAI)
    b. Image alteration: Modifying specific parts of the image, such as adjusting the mood and expression of a face (Examples: Adobe, Bria, Luminar Neo)
    c. Image generation: Create a new image based on the description (Examples: Midjourney, DALL-E 2, Jasper Art)
3. Music — Many musicians have co-created music with AI (Huang et al., 2023). Louie et al (2023) have not only proven the feasibility of this approach but also discovered that AI helps users express their musical intentions more effectively. Humans can strategize their approach and harness AI to attain creative goals in music. Jukebox, MuseNet, and Amper Music are examples of AI music generators.
4. Code — Regarding coding, AI can assist in identifying and rectifying errors or bugs, and it is even capable of generating code. It has the potential to replace the work of a beginner-level programmer. This is where the accuracy and precision of co-creation work comes in. ChatGPT is capable of performing these tasks.
5. Video/Animation — AI can accelerate the process of video production and animation. These tools can analyze keywords from scripts and generate scenes accordingly. Similarly to images, AI is capable of editing videos and generating entirely new scenes. Examples of animation AI are Synthesia, Adobe Firefly, and Animated Drawings. Examples of AI video editing tools include Pollinations, Munch, and Runaway. With the storyboards at the ideation stages ready, the design and development work can be done more efficiently alongside AI.
6. Audio — AI simulation technology can resemble human voices very accurately. Text-to-speech tools such as Murf AI, Play.ht, and Resemble AI can replace human voice and this audio can be generated without a studio booking or an echo-free room. Scripts can be revised as much as necessary without concerns about re-recording costs. Humans can co-create various types of audio content with AI.

AIGC APPLICATIONS

From Unimodal to Multimodal AIGC

As we know, multimedia content is not a new venture in the realm of content creation. The traditional approach to education was transformed from text-based learning to multimedia-based learning back in 2000 to enhance students' learning experience. As time has progressed, these multimedia components have consistently been enriched with interactive features. Figure 1 shows the various types of multimedia that can be generated with AIGC services in both unimodal and multimodal contexts.

Figure 1. The final products created using AIGC in both unimodal and multimodal formats within the education sector

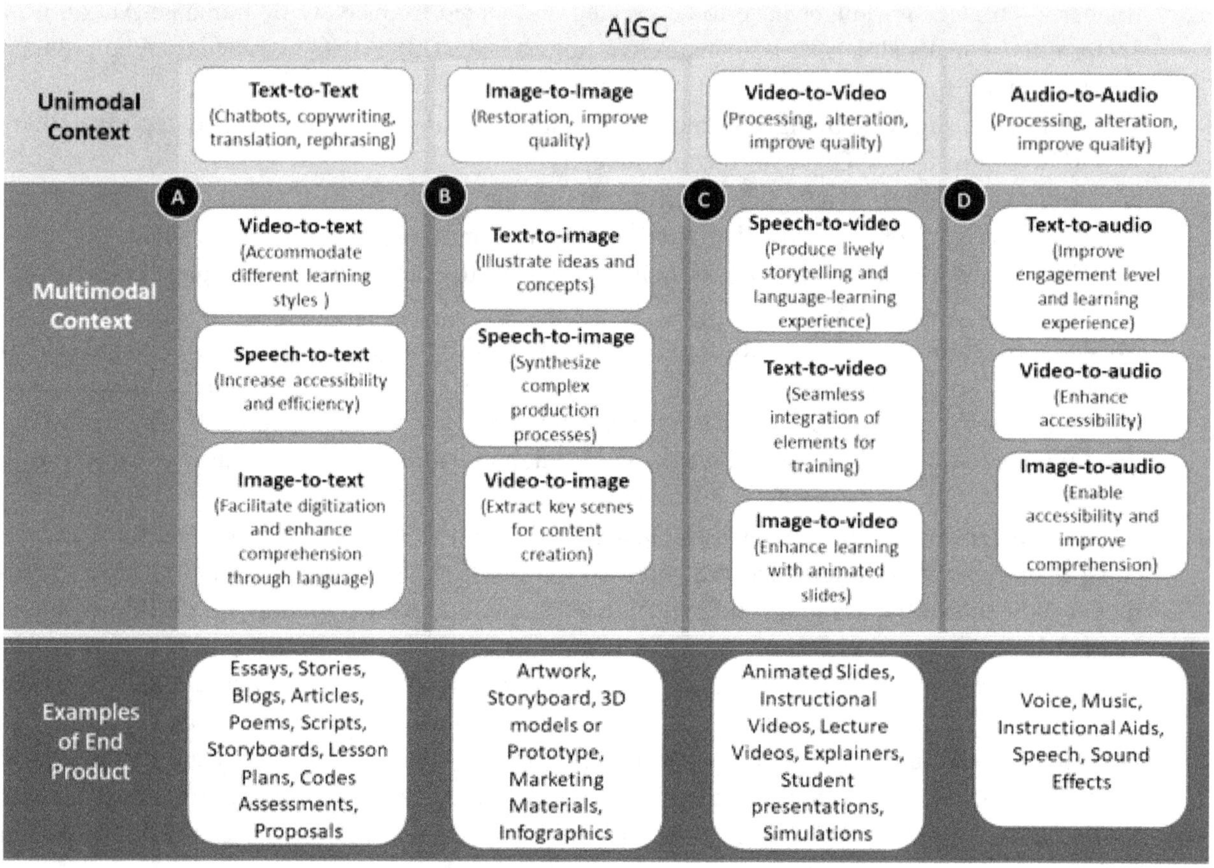

Unimodal AIGC

Text, images, videos and audio are the 4 main components of content creation. In unimodal contexts, AIGC plays the role as an enhancer which improves the existing media content. This can involve tasks such as adjusting resolutions, editing existing elements, and enhancing content clarity. The following section discusses each type of media in a unimodal context.

Text to Text. AI generates text based on text input. The generative AI has a variety of functions, such as Chatbots, language translation, rephrasing and editing. Text is an important element in conveying information to people. Educators could use it to optimize their content creation. For example, they could leverage all the possibilities that one of the popular generative AI tools — such as ChatGPT, which can perform in all education aspects — such as generating quizzes and explanatory texts.

Other tools similar to ChatGPT can also provide dynamic teaching materials for various learning styles. Examples of Text to Text AI tools: Brad, ChatGPT, New Bing, Claude.

Image to Image. AI can enhance various elements of images, including resolution, color, contrast, and lighting, and it can even restore old photos. Images have significant power as a tool in education because they can serve as representations for concepts being studied. Pictures that are challenging to acquire for classroom use can be generated using AI. Creating and searching for images can often be a time-consuming process. Therefore, when a similar or closely matching image is found, it can be easily modified using AI tools. For instance, modifications like changing the expression or pose of a character, altering the background, or customizing to a local style can be accomplished efficiently. Additionally, historical pictures can be restored to reveal remarkable detail, and novel, innovative images can be created to align with the teaching content. Examples of Image to Image AI tools: YouCam Enhance, Topaz Photo AI, Luminar Neo.

Video to Video. Similarly to images, AI-powered tools can also process, edit, and improve the resolution of videos. Video-based teaching and learning are effective methods for active learning, as they can increase attention and engagement. AI can used to cut down repetitive or tedious editing tasks for video editors. For example, it can alter backgrounds and effects to liven up monotonous lectures and enhance the video quality of recordings made by lecturers. AI can also be used to reduce the repetitive efforts required to create animated assets, allowing for streamlining of the content creation process. Examples of Video to Video AI tools: Runway, PowerDirector, AVCLabs Video Enhancer AI.

Audio to Audio. Audio is an essential aid for teaching and learning and may include recorded lectures, podcasts, and sound clips. Audio can improve the understanding of a concept being studied and effectively engage students. Audio is a valuable element for bite-sized learning, particularly suitable for adult learners to use while commuting. The most tedious editing work for audio files is reducing heavy echo and background noise. AI-powered tools can process, alter, and enhance the quality of audio. Poorly recorded audio can negatively affect the quality of a learning experience. Thus, such audio requires substantial cleanup which can be time-consuming for long files — considering this, leveraging AI assistance becomes an ideal solution to reduce labor-intensive tasks like sound editing. Examples of Audio to Audio AI tools: Runway, Dolby.io, CrumplePop.

Multimodal AIGC

There are also AI tools that can transform each type of data into other types of data, such as text to image and audio to text — these transformed media are referred to as Multimodal. The following discussion is about the concept of multimodality in AIGC, where AI-powered tools are employed to transform one media type into another. It is helpful for educators to explore the possibility of each multimedia type and its intended purposes to achieve teaching and learning objectives. The examples below for each mode provide a glimpse of the capabilities of these tools — however, this list is not exhaustive.

Text

Text is the core of all content. Putting ideas into text is generally the first step in the process of content creation. Up to now, even with the increased availability of non-text knowledge acquisition methods, we cannot get rid of text reading. As shown by much research, the majority of students prefer reading text over other learning styles (Ojet et al., 2017; Magulod Jr, 2019; Ishak et al., 2022). This clearly indicates the importance of text in education.

Video to Text. The conversion of video into text is particularly useful for accommodating learners with diverse learning styles, especially those who prefer reading. Therefore, the content of video lectures can be made available for learners as both live subtitles and recorded transcripts. Taking the utilization of AI a step further — subtitles and transcripts can be translated into various languages. This could enhance comprehension for non-native speakers and aid in the comprehension of content.

AI can also enhance content comprehensibility, providing a more digestible style to facilitate ease of understanding. On the other hand, the video-to-text feature assists instructional designers in analyzing video content features and producing storyboards for new content creation. This process helps creators transform current content which is often delivered in traditional lecture style, into a brand new, engaging teaching approach. AI's ability to analyze teaching content and generate storyboards opens up new doors for adapting the content into alternative multimedia formats and teaching approaches. Examples of Video to Text AI tools: Adobe Firefly, VEED.IO.

Speech to Text. The voice-driven assistants such as Siri, Alexa, and Google Assistant are AI tools that are used in daily life. Real-time transcription based on speech is also frequently seen in video conferencing platforms such as Zoom and Microsoft Teams. Similar to video to text, the conversion of audio to text has the purpose of enhancing the learning experience. Converting speech to text offers various practical uses, such as easing the search process for relevant content. If learners want to locate specific information, they can easily identify the corresponding segment within the audio; it makes note-taking more efficient. Examples of Speech to Text AI tools: Google Cloud, Amazon Transcribe, Speech AI.

Image to Text. Image to text conversion is used to extract text from printed documents, handwritten notes, or scanned papers. The primary purpose of image to text conversion may be digitization. It could be also helpful for visually impaired learners for whom it allows access to content that was originally visual in form. With the popularity of AI, image to text techniques could also be helpful to students in learning the text prompts from an artwork. For instance, if the student doesn't know ways to describe the style of the painting that they intend to create. These AI tools can generate a descriptive and explanatory text by processing and analyzing the artists, flavors, mediums, movements, and trends of an image into details written out in text. Examples of Image to Text AI tools: Nanonets, Brandfolder, Image to Prompt, CLIP Interrogator.

Image

Statistics show that 65% of the population are visual learners (Mani, 2023), thus image-based information is also an important component of teaching and learning contexts. However, looking for pictures that fit the topic without copyright constraints might be a challenging task for a content developer. Additionally, purchasing and editing appropriate artwork can result in hefty finance and time costs especially when customization is a requirement. AI — a game-changer — has transformed this practice.

Text to Image. Images effectively illustrate ideas and concepts. There are many AI-powered tools to generate images from text. It allows individuals without art experience or an artistic background to create digital artwork for various purposes in the teaching and learning context. Educators don't necessarily need highly advanced writing skills to create prompts as long as they have good ideas. They can enhance their prompts by taking AI prompting courses, learning from experience, or utilizing the reverse tool, like an image-to-text AI, to generate prompts from relevant images. Examples of Text to Image AI tools: DALL-E2, MidJourney, Stable Diffusion, Adobe Firefly, Monster Mash, Magic3D.

Speech to Image. The logic of the speech to image conversion is quite intuitive as speech can be transcribed to text easily with AI technology, and thus the transcribed text can then be used to generate text to image data. The aim is to streamline the process from text to image using different tools, but now directly from audio to image in a single platform. It cuts down the laborious step of writing out the prompts. This tool makes everyone an artist, but it stands that a deeper understanding of aesthetics, art techniques, and art history can further enhance the outcome. Examples of Speech to Image AI tools: Verb Art, Jina.

Video to Image. The concept of converting video to images is not commonly seen; this is usually used to serve specific presentation purposes where animated formats are not feasible due to the environment. In the instructional design process, it is helpful when an instructional designer wants to recreate or revise existing video content and aims to extract scenes from the video and illustrate them as part of a storyboard. This process aids in conveying clear communication and delivering a precise message by eliminating unnecessary elements from the video. Importantly, this method doesn't necessitate any expertise in prompt engineering. On the other hand, key images from the video can also serve as memory aids for learners, helping them recall specific points from the video content. Examples of Video to Image AI tools: QuickTime, MConverter, Clideo.

Video

Videos are among the most commonly employed, effective, and engaging modes in eLearning (Gilardi et al., 2015; Mayer, 2017; Nazarov, 2023). Creating videos for eLearning was once a time-consuming process involving studio setups, equipment costs, editing, and extensive post-production work. Similar to images, animations are gaining popularity in the eLearning field. Video-based learning is essential for teaching topics that are visual in nature, as well for increasing accessibility to and educational outcomes of the hard of hearing and visual learners.

Speech to Video. Converting speech to video can be beneficial during a storytelling or language learning session even though it is not currently a common practice. For example, educators can use their voice to describe something, and the objects will then be visualized and displayed on a screen for the learners. It enables anyone to create an animated visual aid by just inputting the audio. In terms of the present technology for converting speech to video, we currently observe that character animators can synchronize automatic lip sync, facial expressions, and arm movements by using the voice as input. This concept is reminiscent of the Talking Tom Cat app introduced in 2010. It is a useful approach for teaching and learning when an animated character is needed for an interactive scenario. Examples of Speech to Video AI tools: Adobe Express (Animate from Audio).

Text to Video. Tools with natural language processing functions can generate professional-looking video from a simple string of text. AI can seamlessly integrate various elements into videos including visuals and animation effects, background music, and sound effects. The videos can be used for instruction and training and by lecturers explaining a concept. They contribute to streamlining video workflows by automating the production process. Examples of Text to Video AI tools: Fliki, Phenaki, Synthesia, HeyGen, Invideo.

Image to Video. Static slides are not as favorable as animated slideshows, which tend to result in better engagement for learners. While PowerPoint (PPT) is often the initial choice for creating slideshows, AI-powered tools enable the transformation of images into videos, complete with dynamic 3D effects. This approach makes abstract concepts more realistic and it can enhance the overall visual experience of the learner. Educators have the flexibility to choose between simple image slideshows and more complex ones, including those with 3D effects, based on their teaching requirements. Examples of Image to Video AI tools: LeiaPix, Kaiber, Make-A-Video, Lumen5, Fastreel, Animoto.

Audio

Audio plays a significant role as one of the multimedia components that cater to a large variety of learning styles, including auditory learners, adult learners, and individuals with visual impairments. Liu et al. (2022) highlight that the advancements in technology, particularly in the field of natural language processing, have also been extended to audio and speech processing.

Text to Audio. Voice-over is a widespread practice in eLearning, especially for videos, animation, and interactive courseware. In eLearning materials, a human voice is usually favored for voice-overs. The strength of voice-over AI is that it can mimic human tones. It can even choose emotional tones to match the scenario. This is particularly advantageous as it offers instant generation without considering the condition of the voice-recording environment, thus greatly decreasing — or even eliminating — the burden of audio editing. Examples of Text to Audio AI tools: Murf, ElevenLabs, NaturalReader, Speechify, Voice Dream Reader.

Video to Audio. These AI tools separate the audio components from the video, such as voice clips, music, and sound effects, from the visuals. This can be easily achieved by changing the video format to audio and doesn't necessarily require AI technology. AI technology becomes more relevant when video content is being repurposed as podcasts or audio materials —enabling greater accessibility for individuals during commutes, those with visual impairments, or audio learners. Examples of Video to Audio AI tools: Camtasia studio, Movavi, Flixier.

Image to Audio. Converting images to audio using AI tools serves several practical and innovative purposes. For example, it can make images accessible to visually impaired learners or those who are not able to view an image due to any number of reasons. AI tools can describe the uploaded images to the learners through audio, allowing them to better access and comprehend the content. Examples of Image to Audio AI tools: Spectrogram Player.

Generally, educators don't need to be familiar with all the tools at once in order to design their lessons. With just 2–3 AI-powered tools on hand and some basic prompt engineering knowledge, they are ready to begin their journey of content creation.

Multimodal AIGC

With AIGC's multimodal capabilities, it enables intelligent conversion between text, speech, and visuals. Therefore, AI featuring multimodality can process various types of data (Li & Xiao, 2023). It expands the possibilities of content produced between humans and machines. Hence, AIGC has lowered the barriers to content creation and meanwhile elevated human creativity to the next level (Liu et al., 2023). AIGC empowers content creation through three types of technological abilities, which are digital twins, intelligent editing and intelligent creation (Li & Xiao, 2023) as shown in Figure 2.

Figure 2. Three types of emerging technology in AIGC

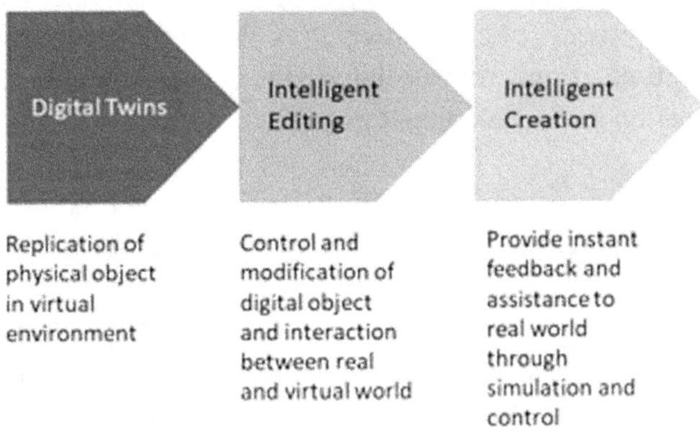

Digital Twins

A digital twin is a replication of a physical object to be used to observe and analyze its behavior in the virtual environment with real-time data (VanDerHorn & Mahadevan, 2021). Digital twins are created with the help of sensors, simulation software, and machine learning algorithms (Turner, 2023). This technology can further extract valuable information from data and, based on a deep understanding and analysis of the data, accomplish precise and advanced intelligent twinning tasks (Li & Xiao, 2023). Digital twins can be divided into intelligent translation technology and intelligent enhancement technology. Uses of digital twins include gathering data on how a physical object will react in different environments, how it interacts with other objects, and how it can be improved (Turner, 2023). Examples of digital twin technology can be applied to all aspects of the education process. These applications include creating virtual classrooms, virtual labs, assessments, and evaluations to monitor learners' understanding and progress — as well as incorporating gamification.

Intelligent Editing

Intelligent editing is a technology that achieves control and modification of digital content through techniques involving manipulation and semantic understanding. Pretrained Foundation Models (PFMs) are the foundation for AI content generation. This process equips the AI model with substantial knowledge and capabilities that can be fine-tuned for specific tasks (Liu et al., 2023). Additionally, this technology establishes an interactive channel between the real world and the virtual world (Li & Xiao, 2023).

Intelligent Creation

Intelligent creation can rapidly and accurately project content from the real world into the virtual world. This technique provides positive information feedback and assistance to the real world through methods like simulation and control. There are two types of intelligent creation, concept-based creation and imitation-based creation (Li & Xiao, 2023). When humans and AI can cooperate effectively to create new content, this will be a new realm; because when the content is constantly being innovated, we will have rich, innovative, and high-quality content being produced.

In the future, as AIGC continues to progress and improve, the ongoing advancement of these three technologies will change the process of content creation. While the creation process might involve assistance from the AI, over time, it may transition to being fully autonomous. This will be particularly relevant in the content creation and development processes.

PRINCIPLES OF CO-CREATION WITH GENERATIVE AI

Today, AI's performance has been widely accepted and embraced by businesses as it is beginning to demonstrate practical value in various industries (Lee & Wang, 2017). Giannini (2023) asserted that the discourse of AI must extend beyond the inquiries about its readiness and functionality, instead, everyone should take a deeper look and consider what kind of world we want to create with AI, what tasks it should handle, how it should operate, and who gets to decide the answers to these questions. According to Baidoo-Anu and Owusu Ansah (2023), Generative AI has the potential to enrich teaching and learning by enabling interactive, adaptive, and personalized educational experiences for students. Without proper education and training on the use of Generative AI, there may be widespread misconceptions about this technology. As argued by Bozkurt and Sharma (2023), individuals can acquire the skills of prompt engineering to elicit meaningful responses from AI. Hence, it is necessary that the public has a strong understanding of what Generative AI can do and how we can collaborate with it to enhance methods and outcomes for teaching and learning.

Process of Co-Creation With Generative AI

Generative AI uses complex algorithms and deep learning techniques that enable it to generate entirely new and original creations without requiring explicit instructions. Co-creating with Generative AI is a collaborative process that involves utilizing AI tools to achieve a specific goal or desired outcome (Bozkurt & Sharma, 2023; Su & Yang, 2023). This can speed up the overall process from ideation, development, and optimization. The effectiveness of co-creation with Generative AI lies in its ability to generate a multitude of comprehensive, holistic ideas and potential solutions in response to questions or prompts (Sharples, 2023). There are three distinct phases when co-creating content with Generative AI as shown in Figure 3.

Figure 3. Process of Co-creation With AI

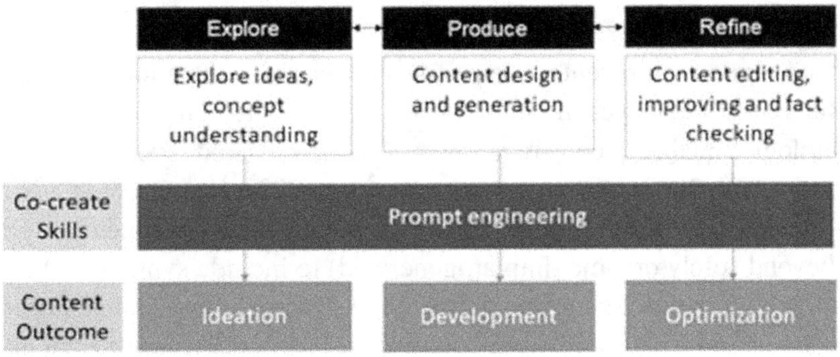

Phase 1: Explore

Generative AI is beneficial when creators seek to explore ideas or grasp complex concepts (Junaid, 2022; Baidoo-Anu & Owusu-Ansah, 2023). We use prompts in a text format to generate things. Prompt engineering serves as the means to effectively communicate with and obtain input from the AI system (Oppenlaender et al., 2023). The ultimate outcome of this phase is to foster ideation and generate a pool of creative ideas and concepts.

Phase 2: Produce

Once a clear direction emerges from the ideation phase, Generative AI comes into play for content generation. This stage requires a human's analytical skills to interpret and analyze the suitability of the generated content. According to Junaid (2022), we should not automatically accept what has been produced by the Generative AI. In the process, Oppenlaender et al. (2023) asserted that it's crucial to assess the quality of the prompts and improve them until the desired output is achieved. The content can be further developed either with or without additional input from Generative AI in the overall development process. The creator can always return to the ideation stage whenever there is a need to explore new topics.

Phase 3: Refine

The final stage involves the refining of the content. Here, the focus is on enhancing content accuracy — including aligning the factual information to achieve content precision. As claimed by Junaid (2023), Generative AI has the potential to make up nonsensical or false information (misinformation), hence it is important to validate the information through human experts. Expert review skills are needed to assess and optimize the content to ensure the content quality. If the final output is text-based content, using Generative AI to do the language editing to produce high-quality product is essential as it can produce error-free sentences (Pavlik, 2023).

In summary, co-creating with Generative AI is a progressive approach that streamlines the content creation process. All three stages can be revisited as necessary to foster flexibility and efficiency throughout the process. Prompt engineering is an essential skill throughout the co-creation with the AI process.

Involvement of the Stakeholders

Is it truly crucial to distinguish between tasks done by AI and those carried out by humans? We've seen numerous AI tools designed to prevent students from generating education-related content through AI applications. In the past, students heavily relied on Google, a search engine, to gather information. Low and no-code technologies enable anyone regardless of their skills and level of expertise to create digital content easily (Kathe et al., 2023). As proposed by Bozkurt (2023), the effective use of generative AI in education has the potential to open new doors for open educational resources and practices, expanding content creation beyond solely organic (human-generated) to include synthetic (AI-generated) content. Now, we're transitioning towards using Generative AI to generate ideas and acquire information. What sets these approaches apart? The following sections will discuss the roles of each in this transition.

Schools and Institutions

AI can help in forming a new ecology of education (Su & Yang, 2023). Schools serve as platforms for equipping students with essential skills to ensure their competitiveness in the future job market. As noted by Bozkurt et al. (2023) and Oppenlaender et al. (2023), prompt engineering is a skill that can be acquired and developed. Thus, these skills can be learned during school but not when it is needed in the workforce. In addition, students must have the capacity to justify the output provided by Generative AI by critically evaluating the information it presents. To achieve this, a foundational understanding of Generative AI is essential. Thus, workshops on Generative AI could be made available to students to equip them with critical thinking skills.

The value of learning this skill isn't limited to just students — enhancing the competencies of educators is equally important. Hence, equipping teachers with these skills is vital (Baidoo-Anu & Owusu-Ansah, 2023; Miao et al., 2023), as Generative AI could be useful to make suggestions to teachers on various aspects of their teaching methods and their students' learning (Su & Yang, 2023). Institutions may consider introducing a short course that aims to enhance teacher competencies in the field of Generative AI. This could be one of the teacher development initiatives because apart from digital literacy, AI literacy will be just as important as other digital skills in the future.

Teachers

A teacher's workload is more than just teaching students. It also involves preparation before the class, marking students' assignments after the class, and monitoring students' progress from time to time. Utilizing AI to co-create their curriculum, lesson plans, and teaching materials could potentially be an approach for teachers to offload some of their tedious tasks. In a study conducted by Chiu et al. (2021), the co-creation process was found to empower teachers, providing them with a sense of autonomy in curriculum design.

AI can also conduct real-time monitoring and analyze the learning situation. According to Li and Xiao (2023), an AI technology called GodEye was implemented in China in 2021 to analyze online classroom behaviors between teachers and students. The analysis includes the interactions between teachers and students, student presentations, students' responses in Q&A sessions, as well as note taking and assessment; after the class, the AI uses this data to generate reports on the students' learning. This could be very helpful in tracking students' learning progress and gaining insights into their strengths and areas for improvement. Consequently, teachers can use the reports to provide customized and personalized teaching. Consistently paying close attention to the needs and progress of individual students makes students feel valued and cared for. This process presents an opportunity to further strengthen the academic relationships of students, teachers, and even parents. This establishes a strong foundation for academic and personal achievement.

Students

Generative AI, such as ChatGPT, has language editing, and translation capabilities. Its ability to continually enhance content based on human prompts, combined with its rapid response rate, could create a fresh and balanced educational environment for students (Lim et al., 2023; Baidoo-Anu & Owusu-Ansah, 2023). This increased accessibility to learning resources offers students greater opportunities. Furthermore, this accessibility to knowledge has the potential to foster educational equality and make learning more universally attainable (Lim et al., 2023).

Additionally, Generative AI could lay down a robust knowledge foundation for students, better preparing them for more advanced levels of study (Junaid, 2023). This could potentially reshape the conventional methods of teaching and learning. Students could learn fundamental concepts or knowledge from AI and subsequently engage in more in-depth discussions and learning activities with teachers and classmates.

Generative AI plays versatile roles in students' learning. Sharples (2023) summarized several key roles that AI can play in the learning process.

1. Students write prompts to explore various ways of expressing ideas and discovering new information. This method aids in suggesting different expressions in writing and brainstorming information for completing assignments. This is a form of co-creation with AI.
2. Students enter prompts to initiate discussions or arguments through conversation with AI. This practice helps students refine their debating skills and formulate coherent statements or arguments.
3. Students input content and AI assists in interpreting and summarizing the data. This reduces the challenge for students in comprehending difficult or complex information.
4. Students engage with AI to add to or finalize stories or any piece of work with creative elements. This approach offers diverse perspectives, abilities, and experiences that students can learn from.

Educational Administrators

AI can provide detailed operational data within schools so that school administrators can create detailed strategic plans. In terms of applications of AI, Li and Xiao (2023) recommended that school administrators utilize AI facial recognition technology, visitor management features, or intelligent campus security management systems as measures to create a safe and secure environment for teachers and students. Furthermore, AI-driven educational systems can offer data analysis, prediction, and interpretation, which can be used when making crucial decisions for future strategy planning in business models. Educational administrators should carefully consider the AI in education approach and determine the best way to benefit the entire educational community.

FUTURE DIRECTIONS OF GENERATIVE AI AND CASE STUDIES

The impact of Generative AI cannot be ignored — the results depend on how we react to it. It is either "lead the change" or "let the change lead you". This is similar to the initiative of digital transformation before the pandemic. Some react aggressively, some react slowly while some are still struggling with their stance. No matter how we feel, the change is here and the need to change is also apparent. It is just a matter of time before AI becomes mainstream (Kathe et al., 2023). The following discussion shows the expected changes in the learning landscape with the applications of AI.

Short Term (1–5 years)

Generative AI can perform human tasks such as content creation, and artwork design, as well as engage in conversations through ChatBots connected to a knowledge base. This capability is particularly useful for students as they learn and for teachers as they prepare teaching materials. There are no specific skills or expertise needed to start using text prompts to interact with AI. Because of it's simplicity, basic AIGC is accessible for everyone.

Virtual Assistance

Instant tutoring and homework assistance can be realized in the short term (Baidoo & Owusu Ansah, 2023). For example, text-based Generative AI can serve as a helpful virtual assistant for students that can perform tasks such as answering questions and assisting with creative writing, such as essay outlining, crafting imaginative dialogue, story writing, and persuasive writing. In addition, it can also handle tasks like translation, summarizing key points, generating tables, checking programming code for bugs, editing sentences, and solving problems in structured formats, such as open-ended, fill-in-the-blank, and multiple-choice questions (Junaid, 2022). The AI system can also provide explanations about each question answered based on its trained algorithm (Yu & Guo, 2023).

For teachers, AI works to support learning from the bottom up. Generative AI supports teachers in multiple aspects. This includes creating content, generating assessment questions, providing feedback, creating rubrics, correcting assessments, and edit students' grammatical mistakes. The process of content or idea generation is expedited as AI streamlines the process of searching for various resources and cutting down the preparation and development process. Teachers can take the generated content and tailor it to suit teaching context objectives. Further, the general editing tasks that AI is capable of would offload the repetitive administrative work of the teachers.

Personalized and Lifelong Learning

AI can also act as a personal coach and personalize students' learning through predictive analytics (Kathe et al., 2023). Transitioning from a responsive learning platform to an adaptive learning mode, the learning experience becomes more concentrated and seamless. A virtual peer in learning could boost the attention, motivation, and engagement level of students (Pataranutaporn et al., 2021).

Furthermore, if the learning requirements such as learning conditions, environment, qualifications, and time commitments are revised to be more personalized, it will then promote lifelong learning by reducing or eliminating these constraints. For example, individuals wouldn't be required to attend courses physically, or to be present at a specific time, instead, a knowledge-based ChatBot is available all day to initiate the learning. That is the lifelong learning concept, isn't it?

Increasing AI Literacy

Short courses are now available which introduce AI and teach how to write prompts to obtain the desired outcomes. The greater the degree of collaboration between AI and humans, the more that people will find out what AI actually is and become interested in exploring further. Thus using such courses could, in a brief time span, allow everyone to have a better understanding of AI and discover the possibilities of how it can lighten tedious work for humans. Students and teachers can sign up for courses on AI prompting and understanding AI to better collaborate with it.

Automation of Assessment and Grading

Methods of assessing and providing feedback on the learners' work such as marking paper and pencil tests were introduced well before the popularity of Generative AI in recent years. Today, lecturers are employing automation for assessment to randomly assign versions of question sets to students and for automated grading in subjects like Economics, Industrial Engineering, and other written assignments (Purdue University, 2022). AI-powered assessment could offer a more comprehensive performance review of individual students, customize instant, real-time feedback, and curate a unique learning path for students with varying levels of competency (Yu & Guo, 2023). This would also reduce teachers' workload and free up more time for teachers to focus on other aspects of teaching (Ojha, 2022; Baidoo & Owusu Ansah, 2023). Hence, teachers will have more time to provide higher-quality teaching and professional development instead of being occupied with routine tasks.

Long Term (6–10 years)

The full implementation of advanced AI applications across all aspects of the education sector relies not only on individual efforts but on the collective involvement of all key stakeholders. All key stakeholders need to assume accountability for driving this educational transformation. It is not individual efforts that will lead the change but rather the integration of efforts between departments and a comprehensive implementation involving leaders, educators, students, and administrators, as well as support from the government. The initial step is to ensure that everyone has access to AI — only then can the transformation take place.

Immersive Learning Experience

AI-powered AR and VR applications have the potential to establish immersive educational experiences. The students can engage and interact with complex concepts and historical events in the AR, VR, and MR environment. However, to witness the integration of these technologies in classrooms would require an investment in advanced technology at significant costs. These changes might take a longer time to materialize than for other AIGC tools due to the fact that AR and MR technologies have yet to fully mature.

The AI and technology industries are instrinsically linked to their applications in education. For instance, training medical students to perform virtual dissections on digital twin models of the human body is an applicable practice that mirrors industry training. Hence, the utility of technology extends across various industries. How Generative AI can be applied across various educational domains is summarized in the table below.

Table 1. Application of generative AI in various fields in education

Fields of Education	Application of Generative AI
Medicine and Healthcare	Generating synthetic data and patient scenarios for clinical trials has been highlighted by Inuwa (2023) for AI use cases. Replicating and simulating medical scenarios provides an immersive learning platform for medical students to engage in realistic practice.
Engineering	Generative AI can be used to solve mathematical problems, theoretical and conceptual questions, and even generate code which may potentially be revolutionizing for the current practice of programming (Junaid, 2022).
Business and Economics	Business education needs to remain relevant and grow with external environments (Stine et al., 2019). Considering this, the use of synthetic data within diverse virtual business environments could enable students to practice and enhance their business acumen while staying attuned to changing business landscapes. Furthermore, the report has also surveyed numerous AI applications for business schools such as Microsoft Azure, 360AI for Education, EdTech Foundry, etc.
Language Education	Generative AI makes language learning more diverse and easy. Many AI-based learning tools such as Grammarly, ChatGPT, Quillbot can serve as effective writing assistants. Whereas Duolingo offers assistance in learning multiple languages and tools for practice that can adjust the content difficulty based on the user's learning progress (Yu & Guo, 2023).
Special Needs Education	AI is able to integrate the freedom of action for students while also offering explicit control and guidance for children diagnosed with Dyslexia, ADHD, physical impairments, Cerebral Palsy, and Autism (Ojha, 2022). Through the implementation of robust assistive technology, AI can enhance the attention levels of children and offer precise assessments.

IMPLICATIONS

Even though we recognize the full potential of Generative AI in education, we need to be clear about its intended use. Its purpose is to offload some of the tedious tasks from humans, not to replace the human brain. The human brain remains at the center of the domain of thinking. Generative AI shouldn't substitute our brain's creativity, innovation, or thinking abilities.

Furthermore, a number of articles have lauded the positive sides of technology applications, especially the use of AR, VR, MR, and AI, within the education sector. However, from visualization to realization, there is a significant knowledge and skill gap between what we currently understand and how we can most effectively implement these technologies. More work by scholar-practicioners should be focused on telling us "how" to safely and effectively use these technologies instead of just "what" the technologies are capable of.

Many researchers are emphasizing the utility of Generative AI while lamenting its security and ethical risks. Therefore, it is crucial for key stakeholders to promptly establish policies for AI usage and provide safe guidelines for implementing AI technology in education. The decision-makers should ensure that these valuable and beneficial tools are not employed with hidden risks and allow both teachers and students to progress with them confidently.

CONCLUSION

Generative AI is opening up a new door in education. It is advantageous to believe that Generative AI brings advantages that far outweigh any potential drawbacks that might present. Through the ages, each innovation comes with its own set of challenges. We should adopt a proactive approach when dealing with these challenges — identify the issues, address them, and manage the risks from the beginning. In fact, this is not an optional avenue for us to consider, rather, we need to forge ahead and acknowledge the impacts that AI brings, whether they are positive or negative. It is only a matter of time before we witness the transformational effects of Generative AI on our educational landscape.

REFERENCES

Baidoo-AnuD.Owusu AnsahL. (2023). *Education in the era of generative artificial intelligence (AI): Understanding the potential benefits of ChatGPT in promoting teaching and learning*. Social Science Research Network. http://dx.doi.org/ doi:10.2139/ssrn.4337484

BBC News. (2014). *Robot writes LA Times earthquake breaking news article.* BBC News Service. https://www.bbc.com/news/technology-26614051

Bozkurt, A. (2023). Generative AI, synthetic contents, open educational resources (OER), and open educational practices (OEP): A new front in the openness landscape. *Open Praxis*, *15*(3), 178–184. doi:10.55982/openpraxis.15.3.579

Bozkurt, A., & Sharma, R. C. (2023). Generative AI and prompt engineering: The art of whispering to let the genie out of the algorithmic world. *Asian Journal of Distance Education*, *18*(2), i–vii. doi:10.5281/zenodo.8174941

Bozkurt, A., Xiao, J., Lambert, S., Pazurek, A., Crompton, H., Koseoglu, S., Farrow, R., Bond, M., Nerantzi, C., Honeychurch, S., Bali, M., Dron, J., Mir, K., Stewart, B., Costello, E., Mason, J., Stracke, C. M., Romero-Hall, E., Koutropoulos, A., & Jandrić, P. (2023). Speculative futures on ChatGPT and generative artificial intelligence (AI): A collective reflection from the educational landscape. *Asian Journal of Distance Education*, *18*(1), 53–130. doi:10.5281/zenodo.7636568

Cao, Y., Li, S., Liu, Y., Yan, Z., Dai, Y., Yu, P. S., & Sun, L. (2023). A comprehensive survey of ai-generated content (AIGC): A history of generative ai from GAN to ChatGPT. *ACM, 37*(4:111). https://doi.org//arXiv.2303.04226 doi:10.48550

Chang, C. H., & Kidman, G. (2023). The rise of generative artificial intelligence (AI) language models-challenges and opportunities for geographical and environmental education. *International Research in Geographical and Environmental Education*, *32*(2), 85–89. doi:10.1080/10382046.2023.2194036

Chiu, T. K., Meng, H., Chai, C. S., King, I., Wong, S., & Yam, Y. (2021). Creation and evaluation of a pretertiary artificial intelligence (AI) curriculum. *IEEE Transactions on Education*, *65*(1), 30–39. doi:10.1109/TE.2021.3085878

Giannini, S. (2023). *Reflections on generative AI and the future of education*. UNESCO. https://unesdoc.unesco.org/ark:/48223/pf0000385877

Gilardi, M., Holroyd, P., Newbury, P., & Watten, P. (2015). The effects of video lecture delivery formats on student engagement. In *Science and information conference (SAI)*, (pp. 791–796). IEEE. https://ieeexplore.ieee.org/document/7237234

Goodfellow, I., Pouget-Abadie, J., Mirza, M., Xu, B., Warde-Farley, D., Ozair, S., Courville, A., & Bengio, Y. (2020). Generative adversarial networks. *Communications of the ACM*, *63*(11), 139–144. https://dl.acm.org/doi/pdf/10.1145/3422622. doi:10.1145/3422622

Gozalo-Brizuela, R., & Garrido-Merchan, E. C. (2023). ChatGPT is not all you need. A state of the art review of large generative AI models. *Machine Learning*. http://doi.org//arXiv.2301.04655 doi:10.48550

Ho, J., Jain, A., & Abbeel, P. (2020). Denoising diffusion probabilistic models. *Advances In Neural Information Processing Systems, 33*, 6840–6851. https://proceedings.neurips.cc/paper/2020/file/4c5bcfec8584af0d967f1ab10179ca4b-Paper.pdf

Huang, C. Z. A., Koops, H. V., Newton-Rex, E., Dinculescu, M., & Cai, C. J. (2020). *AI song contest: Human-AI co-creation in songwriting*. arxiv. https://arxiv.org/pdf/2010.05388.pdf

Inuwa, M. (August 4, 2023). *Generative AI in healthcare*. Analytics Vidhya. https://www.analyticsvidhya.com/blog/2023/08/generative-ai-in-healthcare/

Ishak, N. M., Ranganathan, H., & Harikrishnan, K. (2022). Learning preferences of generation Z undergraduates at the University of Cyberjaya. *Journal of Learning for Development*, *9*(2), 331–339. https://files.eric.ed.gov/fulltext/EJ1359087.pdf. doi:10.56059/jl4d.v9i2.584

JunaidQ. (2022). *Engineering education in the era of ChatGPT: Promise and pitfalls of Generative AI for education*. TechRxiv. https://doi.org/ doi:10.36227/techrxiv.21789434.v1

Kathe, P., Jenay, R., Nicole, M., Mark, M., Jamie, R., Nichole, A., & Susan, G. (2023). *2023 EDUCAUSE Horizon Report, Teaching and Learning Edition*. EDUCASE. https://library.educause.edu/-/media/files/library/2023/4/2023hrteachinglearning.pdf?la=en&hash=195420BF5A2F09991379CBE68858EF10D7088AF5

Lee, K. F., & Wang, Y. G. (2017). *Artificial Intelligence*. Cultural Development Press.

Li, B. (2023). ChatGPT and the transformation wave of intelligent tools in AIGC. *AIGC's Information Resource Management Study*, *35*(1). doi:10.13998/j.cnki.issn1002-1248.23-0118

Li, Y., & Xiao, L. H. (2023). *From ChatGPT to AIGC: Empowering Intelligent Creation and Application*. Publishing House of Electronics Industry.

Lim, W. M., Gunasekara, A., Pallant, J. L., Pallant, J. I., & Pechenkina, E. (2023). Generative AI and the future of education: Ragnarök or reformation? A paradoxical perspective from management educators. *International Journal of Management Education*, *21*(2), 100790. doi:10.1016/j.ijme.2023.100790

Liu, G., Du, H., Niyato, D., Kang, J., Xiong, Z., & Kim, D. I. (2023). Semantic communications for artificial intelligence generated content (AIGC) toward effective content creation. *Networking and Internet Architecture*. https://doi.org//arXiv.2308.04942 doi:10.48550

Liu, S., Mallol-Ragolta, A., Parada-Cabaleiro, E., Qian, K., Jing, X., Kathan, A., Hu, B., & Schuller, B. W. (2022). Audio self-supervised learning: A survey. *Patterns (New York, N.Y.)*, *3*(12), 100616. doi:10.1016/j.patter.2022.100616 PMID:36569546

Louie, R., Coenen, A., Huang, C. Z., Terry, M., & Cai, C. J. (2020, April). Novice-AI music co-creation via AI-steering tools for deep generative models. In *Proceedings of the 2020 CHI conference on human factors in computing systems*, (pp. 1–13). ACM. https://dl.acm.org/doi/abs/10.1145/3313831.3376739

Magulod, G. C. Jr. (2019). Learning styles, study habits and academic performance of Filipino University students in applied science courses: Implications for instruction. *JOTSE: Journal of Technology and Science Education*, *9*(2), 184–198. doi:10.3926/jotse.504

Mani, B. (2023). *Top Visual Learning Statistics and Facts to Know in 2023*. Sell Courses Online. https://sellcoursesonline.com/power-of-visual-learning#:~:text=Visuals%20are%20much%20more%20effective,attention%20to%20information%2Dcarrying%20images

Mayer, R. E. (2017). Using multimedia for e-learning. *Journal of Computer Assisted Learning*, *33*(5), 403–423. https://onlinelibrary.wiley.com/doi/am-pdf/10.1111/jcal.12197. doi:10.1111/jcal.12197

Miao, F., Shiohira, K., Vally, Z., & Holmes, W. (2023). *International forum on AI and education: Steering AI to empower teachers and transform teaching, 5-6 December 2022; analytical report*. UNESCO. https://unesdoc.unesco.org/ark:/48223/pf0000386162

Mildenhall, B., Srinivasan, P. P., Tancik, M., Barron, J. T., Ramamoorthi, R., & Ng, R. (2021). Nerf: Representing scenes as neural radiance fields for view synthesis. *Communications of the ACM*, *65*(1), 99–106. https://dl.acm.org/doi/10.1145/3503250. doi:10.1145/3503250

Nazarov, R. (2023). Using video materials in teaching English. *Journal of Foreign Languages and Linguistics*, *5*(5). https://fll.jdpu.uz/index.php/fll/article/view/7971

Ng, A. (2016). What artificial intelligence can and can't do right now. *Harvard Business Review*, *9*(11), 1–4. http://www.w-t-w.org/de/wp-content/uploads/2016/11/Andrew-Ng-What-AI-Can-and-Can%E2%80%99t-Do.pdf

Ojeh, N., Sobers-Grannum, N., Gaur, U., Udupa, A., & Majumder, M. A. A. (2017). Learning style preferences: A study of pre-clinical medical students in Barbados. *Journal of Advances in Medical Education & Professionalism*, *5*(4), 185. https://www.ncbi.nlm.nih.gov/pmc/articles/PMC5611428/ PMID:28979913

Ojha, S. T. (2022). Artificial intelligence in special education, Id& Cp. *Journal of Positive School Psychology*, *6*(6), 8341–8345. https://journalppw.com/index.php/jpsp/article/view/9109

Oppenlaender, J., Linder, R., & Silvennoinen, J. (2023). *Prompting AI Art: An Investigation into the Creative Skill of Prompt Engineering*. arXiv. https://arxiv.org/pdf/2303.13534.pdf

Pataranutaporn, P., Danry, V., Leong, J., Punpongsanon, P., Novy, D., Maes, P., & Sra, M. (2021). AI-generated characters for supporting personalized learning and well-being. *Nature Machine Intelligence*, *3*(12), 1013–1022. doi:10.1038/s42256-021-00417-9

Pavlik, J. V. (2023). Collaborating with ChatGPT: Considering the implications of generative artificial intelligence for journalism and media education. *Journalism & Mass Communication Educator*, *78*(1), 84–93. doi:10.1177/10776958221149577

Purdue University. (2020). *West Lafayette Instructors save time grading using automated, no-cost assessment tools created by Purdue, Integrated with BrightSpace*. Purdue. https://www.purdue.edu/innovativelearning/blog/2020/11/02/west-lafayette-instructors-save-time-grading-using-automated-no-cost-assessment-tools-created-by-purdue-integrated-with-brightspace/

Stine, J., Trumbore, A., Woll, T., & Sambucetti, H. (2019). *Implications of artificial intelligence on business schools and lifelong learning*. Academic Leadership Group. https://uniconexed.org/wp-content/uploads/2022/02/AI-Life-long-learning-Final-Report-11.04.19.pdf

Su, J., & Yang, W. (2023). Unlocking the power of ChatGPT: A framework for applying generative AI in education. *ECNU Review of Education*, *6*(3). doi:10.1177/20965311231168423

Tlili, A., Shehata, B., Adarkwah, M. A., Bozkurt, A., Hickey, D. T., Huang, R., & Agyemang, B. (2023). What if the devil is my guardian angel: ChatGPT as a case study of using chatbots in education. *Smart Learning Environments*, *10*(1), 1–24. doi:10.1186/s40561-023-00237-x

Turner, C. (2023). *Unleashing the Potential of Digital Twins in Education – A Revolution in Learning*. LinkedIn. https://www.linkedin.com/pulse/using-aidigital-learning-twins-assessment-education-guy-huntington

VanDerHorn, E., & Mahadevan, S. (2021). Digital twin: Generalization, characterization and implementation. *Decision Support Systems*, *145*, 113524. doi:10.1016/j.dss.2021.113524

Vaswani, A., Shazeer, N., Parmar, N., Uszkoreit, J., Jones, L., Gomez, A. N., Kaiser, L., & Polosukhin, I. (2017). Attention is all you need. *Advances in Neural Information Processing Systems, 30*. IEEE. https://proceedings.neurips.cc/paper/2017/file/3f5ee243547dee91fbd053c1c4a845aa-Paper.pdf

Verheijden, M. P., & Funk, M. (2023). Collaborative diffusion: Boosting designerly co-creation with Generative AI. *In Extended Abstracts of the 2023 CHI Conference on Human Factors in Computing Systems*, (pp. 1–8). ACM. https://dl.acm.org/doi/abs/10.1145/3544549.3585680

Wu, J., Gan, W., Chen, Z., Wan, S., & Lin, H. (2023). AI-generated content (AIGC): A survey. *Artificial Intelligence*. https://doi.org//arXiv.2304.06632 doi:10.48550

Yu, H., & Guo, Y. (2023). Generative artificial intelligence empowers educational reform: Current status, issues, and prospects. *Frontiers in Education*, *8*, 1183162. Advance online publication. doi:10.3389/feduc.2023.1183162

Zhan, X., Li, B., & Sun, J. (2023). Application scenarios and development opportunities of AIGC in the digital intelligence integration environment. *Tushu Qingbao Zhishi*, *40*(1), 75–85. doi:10.13366/j.dik.2023.01.075

Zhang, C., Zhang, C., Zheng, S., Qiao, Y., Li, C., Zhang, M., Dam, S. K., Thwal, C. M., Tun, Y. L., Huy, L. L., Kim, D., Bae, S., Lee, L., Yang, L., Shen, H. T., Kweon, I. S., & Hong, C. S. (2023). A Complete Survey on Generative AI (AIGC): Is ChatGPT from GPT-4 to GPT-5 All You Need? *Articifical Intelligence.* https://doi.org//arXiv.2303.11717 doi:10.48550

KEY TERMS AND DEFINITIONS

AI Literacy: The knowledge, competnecies and skills to effectively utilze AI technology for task performance.

Artificial Intelligence Generated Content (AIGC): A novel content production method utilizes Generative AI techniques for generating content. It involves the recognition of various types of semantic information from multimodal sources.

Co-Creation: A collaborative approach that incorporates input from both humans and Generative AI, this dynamic partnership leverages the strengths of human experts and the power of AI to produce desirable content.

Generative AI: It is a form of artificial intelligence that utilizes algorithmic techniques to generate various types of content, including text, audio, images, and videos. The model is trained using deep learning techniques with the provided training data.

Multimodal AIGC: It involves the transformation of content from one modality to another by utilizing multiple connections and interactions across different data modalities. This means that it can convert content from one form, like text, to another form, such as images or audio, through the integration of data from various sources.

Natural Language Processing: It represents the intersection of artificial intelligence and linguistics, involving computational techniques called machine learning, which are used to train machines the ability to interpret, analyze, and synthesize human language.

Prompt Engineering: Collaborative skills with Generative AI involve producing desired outcomes based on human-provided input.

Unimodal AIGC: It describes a type of AI content generation where the input and output belong to the same modality such as text, image, video, or audio. In other words, it generates predictions or content within the same medium as the provided input.

Chapter 2

A Segue From Search to Dialogue: Leveraging GenAI for Pre-Service Teacher Training

Marcella Dillig
https://orcid.org/0009-0004-6283-3371
Ludwigsburg University of Education, Germany

Anselm Böhmer
https://orcid.org/0000-0002-9592-3291
Ludwigsburg University of Education, Germany

Jon Mason
https://orcid.org/0000-0003-0827-4068
Charles Darwin University, Australia

Stephen Bolaji
https://orcid.org/0000-0001-9292-1541
Charles Darwin University, Australia

Illie Isso
Ludwigsburg University of Education, Germany

Mirona Horiana Stănescu
Babeș-Bolyai University, Romania

Hilal Sahin
Ludwigsburg University of Education, Germany

Aslihan Kuraner
Ludwigsburg University of Education, Germany

ABSTRACT

For over two decades, educational technologies have been embedded within an approach to inquiry dominated by the "search paradigm." However, conversational AI presents an opportunity to shift this paradigm towards enhancing learning through dialogue. This study explores ChatGPT's potential in developing pre-service teachers' interaction skills and competencies, focusing on interculturality. Using participatory action research, the key inquiry is: In what ways can GenAI applications such as ChatGPT serve as dialogue partners to train future educators' (intercultural) interaction skills and competencies? The research covers prompt specification, students' experiences with dialogic learning using ChatGPT,

DOI: 10.4018/979-8-3693-1351-0.ch002

and prospects for using LLMs as dialogue partners in pre-service teachers' training. Qualitative analysis shows ChatGPT can stimulate the learning process, especially when perceived as realistic and challenging. These findings suggest new implementations of LLMs in pre-service teacher education and further research into their potential for enhancing dialogue-based skill development.

INTRODUCTION

The rise of Generative AI (GenAI) marks a milestone in the evolution of Large Language Models (LLM) based on Artificial Intelligence with its already "long history and philosophy" (Bozkurt et al., 2023, p. 54). This development challenges and disrupts the processes of professionalisation in Higher Education profoundly. Hence, while general public discourse regarding the impact of GenAI has ranged from anxious to enthusiastic (Tlili et al., 2023), the practical and theoretical implications need more clarification. This chapter focuses on exploring and explaining these ideas in relation to the future of teaching and learning for pre-service teacher (PST) students.

What distinguishes GenAI from other digital technologies is that it "adopts supervised and reinforcement learning techniques", enabling interaction with 'intelligence' and information (Bozkurt et al., 2023, p. 54). By this, it sheds new light on conceptions of knowledge and skills and thus leads to questions of how to conceptualise these terms. This affordance is distinctive because it signals a diminishing of the dominance of the 'search paradigm' of inquiry (Mason, 2023). As such, this technology is poised to advance our understanding of how knowledge and skills can be produced in dialogue and how such knowledge and skills might be co-produced. Focusing on higher education pre-service teacher training opens pathways for simulated training and reflection on engaging in conversations (Mason et al., 2020).

Teachers' interaction skills primarily address the interaction with students. However, among the major challenges of (novice) professionals are interaction with parents, colleagues, principals, and others, which usually are not the subject of preservice teacher education. In addition, these interactions become more complicated when the interaction partners' backgrounds differ from one's own. These different backgrounds may include culture, gender, majority/minority relations, or class. Choosing a field of interaction where students have little experience and perceive it as a challenging part of becoming a teacher (Preidel et al., 2009) while the relevance of the interaction between teachers and parents is pronounced from several perspectives (Lin et al., 2019; Rattenborg et al., 2019; Kraft & Rogers, 2015), this field of study gives insights into the leverage of using GenAI for training. Simulation training connects theory and practice, leading student teachers to discover its usefulness for breaking down tasks, addressing confusions and ambiguities in theories and teaching pedagogies, and understanding subtle nuances in the learning process.

The current literature often shows a positive impact of GenAI in public debates (Tlili et al., 2023) but also marks that "the negative narratives imply that there are critical issues to resolve before fully adopting these technologies" (Bozkurt et al., 2023, p. 59). This is especially the case for the co-construction of students' learning processes, allowing students to define (and also be responsible for) their learning pathways (Vespone, 2023). Here, GenAI marks out new ground but also invites new "craftsmanship" to design sufficient prompts that fit the learning goals and, in the same step, address the AI bot adequately (Bozkurt & Sharma, 2023).

Building upon the literature that digital technology can serve as a tool for collaboration, GenAI has evolved into a catalyst for promoting intercultural learning within teacher training environments, affirming the significance of intercultural learning for future education – a necessary doctrine that exposes students to diverse cultures, thereby enhancing their intercultural competence and cultural intelligence (Hackett et al., 2023; Bolaji & Pollock, 2022). As a result, GenAI has become an enabler in the act of teaching for equipping, strategising, and stimulating intercultural learning among teacher-students in co-constructive environments.

Strengthening the discourse on the utilisation of GenAI to enhance interaction skills among preservice teachers in meaningful conversations remains a pressing concern. Therefore, during the course of an international collaboration focused on intercultural and global citizenship issues associated with digital education, we posed the overarching research question: *In what ways can GenAI applications such as ChatGPT serve as dialogue partners to train future educators' (intercultural) interaction skills and competencies?*

To comply with the novelty of the introduction of GenAI on the one hand and with the approach of learning through dialogue on the other hand, we conducted participatory action research to address our research question. After discussion with student participants on their perceptions of interculturality and AI, a series of simulations were developed, enabling the student participants to interact with ChatGPT prompted as Parent Interaction Assistant (PIA) within specific role-plays akin to the professional scenarios they would encounter during placements and future careers. In between simulations, we asked students to briefly reflect on their experience during the simulation in a journal, and we invited them to open discussion sessions to discuss further and reflect on their experience. A seminal outcome of the research process is insight into prompting ChatGPT effectively to support the generation of knowledge and skills in dialogue. Further, qualitative analysis of the dialogues between students and ChatGPT, as well as the students' written and oral reflections on the interactions, suggests that GenAI can serve as a simulation tool to stimulate preservice teachers' intercultural and interaction skills and competencies in higher education.

This paper identifies these specific prompts as enabling a segue from search to dialogue using GenAI in higher education teacher training, presenting research on parent-teacher interaction simulations with ChatGPT. In the subsequent section (Section 2), we present the scholarly discourse pertaining to learning through dialogue, the efficacy of simulation-based educational practices, the prospective utility of GenAI within the domain of higher education teacher preparation, and the building of competencies related to intercultural communication and cultural diversity. Section 3 of this paper presents the theoretical underpinning of our study, which serves as the foundational framework for the research design and methodology, both of which are elucidated in Section 4. This section also includes an exposition and deliberation on the effective prompting of ChatGPT with regard to the specific objectives of this research. Our empirical findings are reported in Section 5, and additional reflections on utilising GenAI in dialogic learning are advanced in Section 6.

INFORMING A SEGUE FROM SEARCH TO DIALOGUE: FOUR STRANDS OF SCHOLARLY DISCOURSE

Our study is mainly informed by four strands of literature in the field of teacher training in higher education: (1) the discourse on learning through dialogue; (2) the discourse on the effectiveness of simulations;

(3) the current debate on the use and potential of GenAI in higher education; and (4) the discourse on intercultural learning and cultural diversity. This section discusses the four strands of literature and their interconnectedness. However, given the breadth of each discourse, we only highlight selected literature from each strand.

Learning Through Dialogue

Dialogue in education refers to communication or conversation within an educational context (Holliday, 2010). It involves meaningful and interactive ideas, thoughts, and information exchanges between educators, students, and sometimes parents or other stakeholders. Dialogue in education serves several important purposes and can take various forms (Elias & Mansouri, 2020). It is a dynamic and interactive form of communication that plays a vital role in facilitating learning, fostering critical thinking, and promoting collaboration and inclusivity within educational settings. It encompasses various conversations and interactions that contribute to a rich and effective learning experience. And, for Western education, the role of dialogue in education can be traced back to Socrates (Mason, 2014).

Crosbie (2014) explored dialogue as an inquiry approach to engage in an intellectual conversation across diverse cultural and international collaboration among students and staff. An extensive collaboration cut across five institutions in Europe and the Asia Pacific region. As an inquiry approach, dialogue was adapted to facilitate learning by enabling teachers to explain concepts and students to seek clarification and express their understanding (Byram & Wagner, 2018). Through dialogue, the students were able to explore their critical thinking and creative skills to respond to the series of scenarios designed to elicit responses on issues of educational engagement within the school systems and the roles of teachers in mediating and resolving complex issues confronting or militating students' academic achievement.

Helm (2016) addresses the role of dialogue from a different perspective. The overarching understanding of the study was to understand from the students' perspectives emerging issues within the context of diversity, intercultural awareness, and inclusive practices considered the cardinal attributes of a teacher who understands the pedagogy of context towards enacting classroom practices (Helm, 2016). The dialogue approach was pivotal and enabled the staff to gain substantial insights into students' nuances in creating inclusive classrooms where diverse students feel heard and valued, enhancing essential communication skills. It extends to teacher-student interactions, parent-teacher communication, and discussions of societal and global issues in higher education (Grillo, 2018; Lähdesmäki et al., 2020; Merryfield, 2000). In a nutshell, dialogue in education enriches the focus of the project centred on promoting intercultural awareness, engagement, understanding, and effective communication in school systems (Byram & Wagner, 2018).

In the realm of technology supported learning, Mason (2008) contends that while there exists a multiplicity of advanced software engines designed to facilitate resource discovery, these systems are predominantly biased toward processing descriptions, terms, keywords, and hyperlink weightings. Consequently, their capacity to delve into a deeper inquiry of "why and how" is notably limited since these systems mainly aim at providing answers to simple questions related to "Who, What, When, and Where". Mason (2014) delves deeper into this issue, highlighting a significant constraint in mainstream Internet search tools. He underscores the pivotal role of reasoning, reflection, and dialogue within the realm of dialogic inquiry, which goes beyond propositional knowledge acquisition. Mason (2014) argues that while Internet search tools excel in processing and disseminating information, even within social networks, they fall short when it comes to stimulating more profound dialogic inquiry, which allows to go beyond factoid information to explanatory reasoning. Accordingly, Mason (2023) outlines how the 'search paradigm' limits questioning and how LLMs bear the capability to shift the perspective from searching for content to formulating prompts and engaging in dialogue.

The scholarly discourse on learning through dialogue demonstrates substantial rationale and empirical support for the potential of dialogic engagement to catalyse learning and enhance the competencies of pre-service teachers, particularly in the context of technology integration within this domain.

Simulation in Pre-Service Teacher Training

The examination of the advantages and constraints associated with the utilisation of simulations within pre-service teacher (PST) training has been a prominent subject of discourse over the past few decades. A diverse array of simulation tools and methodologies has been subjected to rigorous examination within this expansive discourse. Among the prominent simulation designs that have garnered significant attention are the utilisation of virtual reality platforms and the integration of mixed-reality classroom settings. At the same time, current literature examines the use of LLMs for chat simulations.

During the latter part of the first decade of the 21st century, there emerged a notable surge of interest in the integration of virtual reality simulations within teacher training. A proliferation of studies during this period offered compelling evidence of the benefits accrued through the incorporation of virtual reality simulations into teacher education curricula. A seminal account of the conventional use of Second Life (one of the most used virtual reality platforms) in the context of teacher training is presented by Mahon et al. (2010). Their discussion centres on the establishment of virtual school environments and their conceivable utility in teacher education. Their empirical findings revealed that students perceived simulation experiences as immensely valuable, primarily for the manner in which they immersed trainees in authentic classroom scenarios fraught with challenges, particularly in the realm of classroom management. This finding is supported by a systematic literature review conducted by Wang and Burton (2012) encompassing an analysis of 107 peer-reviewed articles published between 2006 and 2011 that examined the role of Second Life in education. Contemporary scholarship pertaining to virtual reality using Second Life as an application in the context of pre-service teacher training has notably emphasised the critical facet of well-being. Theelen et al. (2019) present a systematic review of 15 pertinent studies in this domain. A recurring theme within this body of research is the discernible positive influence of simulations on the development of general classroom management skills among PSTs. Notably, four of these studies underscored the affirmative impact of simulations on the well-being and self-efficacy of PSTs if simulations were authentic.

Besides the use of virtual reality platforms, numerous academic institutions have demonstrated a propensity for incorporating mixed-reality settings into their pedagogical frameworks. Research endeavours on mixed-reality settings typically revolve around cultivating pedagogical skills, which emerge through immersive engagement with simulated environments. Dawson and Lignugaris (2016) conducted an empirical investigation into the efficacy of mixed-reality simulations, employing the TeachLivETM platform to foster specific proficiencies among aspiring special educators. Their inquiry focused on acquiring error correction and specific praise techniques. Their discerning analysis revealed that mixed-reality simulations, when coupled with constructive feedback and reflective dialogues, played a pivotal role in facilitating the development of the targeted skills. Similarly, Landon-Hays et al. (2020) harnessed the capabilities of Mursion, a mixed-reality simulation tool, to bridge the chasm between theoretical pedagogical knowledge and practical application for prospective educators. Their investigation yielded noteworthy findings, including a discernible enhancement in participants' competency in differentiation and feedback provision.

Moreover, Bhowmik et al. (2022) have identified a noteworthy limitation within the realm of 3D simulations employed to train prospective educators. Specifically, they have observed that student avatars within these simulations are invariably portrayed by individuals who are not authentic students. In response to this challenge, their research endeavour is directed toward creating an authentic conversational AI system, with the ultimate goal of rendering role-playing of non-students as students superfluous. To achieve this objective, they have leveraged ChatGPT-2 developed by OpenAI. The researchers primed the chat system with a substantial corpus of 13.5 hours of transcribed video content from classroom interactions. Further, they employed an additional informatics methodology to fine-tune the chat's performance. The empirical outcomes of their investigation revealed that the chat system exhibits inconsistencies in its responses, with specific answers deviating significantly from the authentic responses one would anticipate. In light of these findings, the authors are engaged to refine the prompting mechanisms to optimise the utilisation of AI-driven chat systems within the context of 3D simulations for teacher training.

The discourse on simulations in PST's training unveils that simulations, in their diverse manifestations, can amplify learners' teaching competencies and self-efficacy. Moreover, simulations serve as an effective means to bridge the divide between theoretical knowledge and practical application within pre-service teacher education. Initial investigations into the utilisation of ChatGPT-2 as a simulation tool indicate that further research, particularly involving more advanced iterations, holds the potential to provide greater insight into the optimal utilisation of GenAI for the enhancement of PST training. Specifically, this approach demonstrates promise as it overcomes the obstacles associated with incorporating non-student actors to portray student avatars within virtual reality and mixed-reality formats.

The Potential of GenAI in Higher Education

The integration of AI technologies into education has sought innovation and transformation across various educational facets, opening a scholarly debate on a new field. Two highly relevant strands of research on GenAI in higher education relevant for PST training are the use of AI for learners and the use of AI for educators, as PSTs occupy both the learner's and the educator's position. Before outlining the current literature on these two strands, a third strand is relevant to the use of AI in education. This is the perception of AI through learners.

Bewersdorff et al. (2023) investigate common myths, misconceptions, and preconceptions held by learners outlined in the literature on AI in education. Reviewing original empirical studies, the authors identify several key misconceptions about AI among learners: Learners often have limited technical understanding; learners tend to attribute human-like characteristics to AI systems; learners often hold binary views on AI as portraying AI as both beneficial and dangerous; finally, learners recognise AI's importance but feel unprepared due to perceived complexity. However, they generally view AI in education positively.

Tlili et al. (2023) focus on GenAI investigating the experience with ChatGPT. They show that participants were "impressed by the fluidity of their conversation with ChatGPT" and "felt the humaneness of ChatGPT needs to be improved, especially in terms of enhancing its social role". Regarding the educational use of ChatGPT, the majority of participants view ChatGPT positively as a catalyst for educational success, highlighting problems also, such as occasional errors. In expert interviews, the authors identified ten scenarios of educational concern: undetected cheating; inaccuracy of learning content; unfairness of learning content; appropriateness of learning assessments; design of learning assessments; potential of learning assistance; absence of emotions or reflections on student's engagements; truthfulness; privacy concerns; manipulation. Halaweh (2023) meets some of these potential concerns arguing in favour of a transparent and open use of ChatGPT in (higher) education.

On the use of GenAI to support learning processes, the literature is very broad despite its relatively new introduction to the public. Studying the effect of employing conversational agents on test-taking efforts, Yildirim-Erbasli and Bulut (2023) find benefits on learning and motivation but also two significant obstacles: irrelevance of responses due to unspecified understanding of student input and the amount of interaction due to the AI elaborating vastly on features, the student already knows. Yang and Chen (2023) use quantitative, qualitative, and evidence-based methods to study the impact of PST's learning perceptions on their propensity to use AI. In their study, the authors uncover specific intentions for using AI chatbots. These are to "access learning content" as the major intention to use LLMs, including the intention to "organize understandings" and "search for content," highlighting the relevance of the 'search paradigm' (Mason, 2023) for PSTs' motivation to use AI. Zhang et al. (2023) use the quantitative Technology Acceptance Model to study PSTs' perception of artificial intelligence, finding that perceived ease of use and perceived usefulness were the primary factors predicting PSTs' intention to use AI.

Regarding the use of GenAI in student learning, Xia et al. (2023) provide a comprehensive literature review identifying two key areas of application. First, the creation of AI-driven environments to customise tasks according to individual student competence levels. However, a challenge identified to this use is the inadequacy of supportive learning resources, as pre-developed tasks may only sometimes align with individual needs. Consequently, personalised learning through AI technologies is still experimental, primarily due to the deficiency of suitable learning materials. However, scholars have widely argued that personalised learning experiences are among the major potentials of GenAI, such as ChatGPT (Hong, 2023). Second, Xia et al. (2023) find that GenAI facilitates Human-Machine Conversations. AI chatbots enable students to engage in dialogues with AI systems regarding their learning. These AI techniques emulate human thought processes, fostering ongoing communication in language-learning contexts. While students generally find this conversational approach useful and enjoyable "using a question-and-answer approach", insights into how such interactions affect the overall student experience are limited.

To support the teaching side, Xia et al. (2023) identify three major roles assigned to AI to support teachers. First, intelligent tutoring systems are designed to recommend teaching content and tasks tailored to specific teaching needs. For instance, AI systems utilise multimodal sensor data to identify students' affective states, enabling teachers to adapt their teaching strategies accordingly. However, this field faces two significant challenges: a paucity of practical testing of these intelligent systems and a need for standardised criteria for evaluating their effectiveness. Second, the fusion of computer-assisted instruction and AI technologies has been deployed to assist teachers in managing their classroom activities efficiently. AI facilitates tasks such as uploading, assigning, and distributing learning materials, thereby streamlining classroom management. Nonetheless, many teachers need a deeper understanding of how these technologies function. This knowledge gap results in a perceived loss of control, diminishing teachers' self-efficacy and potentially discouraging their use of AI for classroom support. Third, AI technologies extend their utility beyond classroom support to aid in the professional development of teachers. In these applications, AI agents analyse real-time classroom data, including behaviour, questioning skills, and teachers' responses for diagnostic tests. Teachers receive suggestions and feedback on their teaching practices, fostering objectivity in evaluations and encouraging self-reflection. Challenges of this use include the scarcity of pre-designed suggestions and comments that may not align with the needs of experienced teachers.

While outlining potential applications and benefits of using AI in education, researchers also stress that ChatGPT should be used carefully in educational and research-related settings. GenAI should be adequately validated and used in combination with other tools (Sohail et al., 2023).

The body of literature addressing the utilisation of GenAI in the realm of higher education presents many promising applications on which future research should build on. These included the fostering of individual learning and the stimulation of self-reflection. Nevertheless, the literature delineates a series of apprehensions and limitations that warrant careful consideration in future research endeavours. These concerns encompass the potential misuse of GenAI in educational settings, including academic dishonesty or the phenomenon of "hallucination." Furthermore, the effective deployment of conversational agents necessitates a rigorous task specification.

Accessing Intercultural Learning and Cultural Diversity

Cultural diversity has been the norm in schools for a long time. Although this cultural diversity is the reality in European schools, it is repeatedly described as a "challenge" by many stakeholders. In the globalised society of the 21st century, interculturality, diversity and heterogeneity are widely addressed in university research in educational science.

Intercultural learning and cultural diversity in higher education is a critical approach that aims to strengthen intercultural communication and facilitate its implementation in higher education classrooms. Interculturality is addressed and taught in higher education institutions worldwide in various disciplines and under various labels (such as intercultural communication, intercultural encounters, and global competence). This development is evident in numerous fields, including teacher education, languages, healthcare, economics and many others (García-Pérez et al., 2021). The progressive internationalisation that educational institutions have undergone in recent decades has undoubtedly contributed to the increasing preoccupation with the concepts of *interculturality* and, in recent years, also that of cultural diversity in teacher education.

As early as 2002, the Council of Europe adopted the "Maastricht Global Education Declaration", which delineates the field of Global Education. The Declaration states that Global Learning "opens people's eyes and minds to the realities of the world and awaken them to create a world with more justice, equality and human rights for all" (p. 2). In this context, interculturality - under education for human rights, sustainability, peace and conflict prevention, and citizenship - is considered an essential aspect of Global Learning. The European Council also elaborated that intercultural skills or competencies are included in all key competencies, which are essential for lifelong learning.

In the course of demographic development in recent years, Europe has become a pluralistic society with a high degree of cultural heterogeneity. This means for the people that they have to adapt to the social fact of cultural diversity and, in their social orientation, give room to the assumption that the people they meet in everyday life may live in culturally alien worlds. Rommelsbacher (2002, p. 11) claims that "strangeness becomes the basic experience of life in postmodern society in general".

It is crucial that teachers look beyond their cultural horizons to manage challenging and confusing situations (Goh, 2012). This argument is also reflected in a recent study by Barnatt et al. (2020). The study provides evidence that trainee teachers should be given the opportunity to engage with different cultures during their training. It highlights that while trainee teachers are highly motivated to interact with people from other cultures, they often lack confidence in their abilities, with behaviour in particular standing out as an area of lowest confidence. The study uses survey and interview data to identify areas of targeted support in teacher preparation for intercultural competence. The study operationalises intercultural competence by performance on the Cultural Intelligence Survey (CQS), identifying relative areas of strength and weakness. It concludes that PST needs to offer opportunities grounded in a wide range of culturally and linguistically diverse classroom experiences and practices, including exposure to overseas professional experiences and diverse worldviews to increase the focus on intercultural understanding and learning among the skills needed for beginning teachers to enter the profession. In teacher education, this can include work in projects, courses or the field to generate multi-layered and in-depth experiences (Barnatt et al., 2020).

Dealing with increasing cultural diversity in educational institutions worldwide is often a challenge that requires appropriately qualified teachers. This call is in line with the prevailing research literature addressing teacher preparation for pre-service and its intersections with cultural diversity, as evidenced by numerous studies in recent years (López López & Hinojosa Pareja, 2012; Bhopala & Rhamie, 2013; Moloney & Saltmarsh, 2016). According to a quantitative, descriptive study by Hinojosa Pareja et al. (2018), conducted with 1464 participants in a teacher education programme, prospective teachers generally have positive attitudes towards cultural diversity, but their positions diverge when it comes to specific aspects and their implementation in professional practice. The prospective teachers who participated in this study acknowledge the shortcomings of their pre-service education programmes. They note the emphasis on cultural diversity and, therefore, collectively call for better and more comprehensive education. Students' beliefs vary by grade level, with students having more intercultural beliefs at the end of their educational process. The study concludes that more attention needs to be paid to teacher education to address cultural diversity.

In their comprehensive analysis, Romijn et al. (2021) examined 45 scholarly articles on pre-service and in-service professional development programmes to enhance intercultural competence. Within the subset of articles that focused on pre-service teachers, the research found that a universal pedagogical approach to addressing cultural issues was prevalent and accounted for 64% of the literature examined. This universal approach contrasts with a targeted approach that gives special consideration to factors such as bilingual or multilingual students, English language learners, African-American children, and refugees. The predominance of the universal approach suggests that prospective teachers tend to adopt a more general approach to teaching when addressing cultural elements rather than a more differentiated approach that considers the diverse backgrounds and needs of their students. The authors evaluated the impact of the broader context and the use of reflection and enactment as facilitators of change. They found that an embedded and contextual approach to professional development, in which reflection is guided and enactment is fostered, is most likely to increase teachers' intercultural competencies effectively. The authors argue that such an approach is still uncommon in the field of teacher preparation and support.

The preoccupation with Intercultural Communicative Competence (ICC) is mainly described in studies that deal with English as a Foreign Language (EFL) in the context of PST education (Moloney et al., 2014; Valdivia et al., 2017; Safa et al., 2021). Several models and concepts have been developed in recent years (Byram, 1997; Fantini, 2012; Liddicoat & Scarino, 2013).

Michael Byram (1997) has developed a comprehensive model of ICC. According to his framework, intercultural competence is characterised by four primary dimensions: knowledge, attitude, skill and critical cultural awareness. Knowledge includes a comprehensive understanding of one's own culture, the culture of the interlocutor's country and familiarity with "concepts and processes in interaction". The 'attitude' component involves the cultivation of curiosity, openness, a willingness to suspend disbelief about other cultures, and constructive self-assessment of one's own beliefs (ibid., p. 50). The dimension of "skill" includes the ability to interpret documents or events and relate them to one's cultural context, the ability to discover new cultural knowledge and practices, and the skilful application of these skills in intercultural interactions. Finally, "critical cultural awareness" refers to the ability to question perspectives, practices and products both in one's own culture and in other cultures and countries with a keen eye and based on explicit criteria (ibid., p. 53).

Byram (2013) also emphasises the vitality for learners to cultivate the ability to understand the meaning of culture and to prioritise acquiring skills and strategies over the mere accumulation of factual knowledge. Learners should focus on learning practical techniques and skills to overcome intercultural obstacles.

Van Maele et al. (2022) discuss the importance of Intercultural Communication (IC) in English and foreign language education in the Chinese university curriculum. The authors argue that IC should be included as a learning goal in tertiary education. The Study reflects on the national policy regarding IC learning objectives and the challenges of meeting the learning needs of Chinese students, teachers, and staff from different perspectives. The authors point out that the way the courses are designed and delivered has a significant impact on the potential of students to strengthen their intercultural competencies.

The objective of intercultural communication includes but is not limited to gaining knowledge and comprehension of the norms, symbols, values, and facts that hold significance for all communication participants. This knowledge is essential to incorporate into the communication process, facilitating the creation of an equitable dialogue (Stănescu et al., 2022).

The academic discourse is multi-faceted and covers various topics related to cultural diversity, intercultural communication and teacher education. It draws on research findings, theoretical models and educational policies to provide insights into how educational institutions can better prepare teachers for the challenges of culturally diverse classrooms. The discourse highlights the growing importance of addressing cultural diversity and intercultural communication in education, the need for well-prepared teachers and the development of intercultural competence as an essential skill for teachers in heterogeneous classrooms. It also highlights the importance and necessity of a contextualised approach to professional development to enrich pre-service teachers' intercultural competencies.

THEORETICAL UNDERPINNINGS FOR GENAI APPLICATIONS AS DIALOGUE PARTNERS IN EDUCATOR TRAINING

We now turn to an analysis of the ways GenAI applications such as ChatGPT can serve as dialogue partners to train future educators' (intercultural) interaction skills and competencies. Specifically, to formulate prompt engineering conceptually, it is imperative to contemplate the intricacies and methodologies inherent to this discipline. Consequently, we endeavour to theorise our project from the vantage point of the ensuing classifications:

- Educational Concepts,
- Strategies,
- Methods,
- Virtual Facilities.

Educational Concepts

Learning necessitates students advancing toward the "Zone of Proximal Development", as elucidated by Vygotsky (1978, p. 86). The progression fortifies the prominent "emphasis on the sociocultural nature of human cognition and learning" (Kozulin, 2004, p. 3). This holds paramount significance for aspiring educators within the globalised landscape, wherein proficiency in intercultural learning is imperative to navigate variegated classrooms (Böhmer et al., 2023). Accordingly, numerous pedagogical methodologies have been devised. Among these, COIL courses [Collaborative Online International Learning] represent a well-established avenue. These courses facilitate the cultivation of cultural intelligence among students (Hackett et al., 2023, p. 17), defined as "an individual's capability to function and manage effectively in culturally diverse settings" (ibid., p. 5; citing Ang et al.).

Strategies

The challenge mentioned above of intercultural learning is further heightened by the progress of technology in the realm of higher education, where technology and higher education have had a longstanding relationship. Dean et al. (2023) fortify the notion of the convergence of technology and practice within higher education for professional purposes, culminating in a fusion of social and material occurrences (ibid., p. 5). Consequently, there is an imperative for a learning environment tailored to prospective educators, wherein they engage within both social and (material-)virtual dimensions.

Upon the integration of LLMs in higher education, it was emphasised that AI and higher education have already shared a prolonged history (Bozkurt et al., 2023). However, considerable efforts are still requisite to delineate the roles of educators in the teaching context of AI. In light of this progression, prompt engineering, defined as the act of "designing, crafting, and refining contextually appropriate inputs or questions" (Bozkurt & Sharma, 2023, p. ii), assumes heightened significance.

Methods

The rationale for not deeming ChatGPT as a "skilled partner" of learning lies in its suboptimal performance in emotional tasks (Kocoń et al., 2023, p. 9). It is capable only of emulating human cognitions and decisions (Tlili et al., 2023, p. 1), unable to engage in a dialogue with an individual endeavouring to navigate the intricate dimensions of asking, learning, understanding, knowing, and explaining why (Mason, 2014). All these dimensions are, in diverse manners, linked to the learner's emotional state and further unique requirements (Javaid et al., 2023).

After delineating the theoretical foundations pertinent to our subject, we can infer that our theory of prompt engineering entails the formulation of targeted and efficient inputs (Bozkurt & Sharma, 2023, p. i), thereby transitioning from a predominantly monologic teaching approach to a dialogic one (Mason et al., 2023, p. 57). The utilisation of prompts in students' learning endeavours thus shifts from co-constructing toward a self-constructing process, albeit supported by educators. This approach involves "not only to support or enhance, but also to design effective and enjoyable [...] technology-enabled learning activities" (Czaplinski & Huijser, 2023, p. 15).

In this context, critical thinking stands on equal footing with a philosophical comprehension of educating heterogeneous cohorts. Confronting these exigencies extant models of learning are expounded, such as the "Applied model of learner engagement" (Carroll et al., 2019), which encompasses cognitive, behavioural, emotional, and physiological outcomes. However, it is pertinent to note a dearth in including social and critical dimensions in the learning paradigm (ibid., p. 759). This lacuna poses a challenge for numerous ongoing teacher-student programs (Bolaji & Pollock, 2022), particularly in the realm of lifelong professionalisation and the comprehension of one's pedagogical role (ibid., p. 8f.).

Virtual Facilities

The evolving configurations of instructors, learners, instructional materials, and learning environments – each impacted by the emergent player, AI – prompt reflection on the positioning and methodologies within this transformed environment. We posit that a new paradigm in learning is emerging, encompassing a reconfiguration of the learner, instructor, instructional materials, and a learning environment shaped by AI. This configuration results in "an entanglement of virtual spaces created by, and through, experiences of technology" (Dean et al., 2023, p. 5), thus enabling and materialising "online simulation and virtual reality" (ibid., p. 10f.) for the education of teacher students in manifold situations.

While achieving this necessitates "guidance and encouragement from a skilled partner" (Mcleod, 2022), it is imperative to clarify that the ChatGPT bot does not serve as the aforementioned learning partner. Instead, the bot functions as a tool and an enriched environment for the learning process, a construct meticulously designed and overseen by the instructor.

Consequently, the act of teaching remains a human-to-human endeavour. LLMs may enhance learning by incorporating additional facets, but they cannot substitute and replace human teaching professionals (Bozkurt et al., 2023). The prompts and dialogues with the bot, however, do represent an initial step towards personalised learning and collaborative training, albeit unable to replace the subsequent shared reflection with an instructor. In this context, the interconnection of "the most important context of any virtual university … the individual" (Mason et al., 2023, p. 19), as well as the emphasis on individuals' "relationships and safe spaces" (Vespone, 2023, p. 15), constitutes the fundamental elements in the redefinition of professionalisation within higher education through prompt engineering.

RESEARCH DESIGN, METHODOLOGY, AND THE PARENT INTERACTION ASSISTANT (PIA) CONCEPT

The investigation into the capacity of ChatGPT to foster dialogic interactions that promote learning represents an exploratory endeavour. In this section, we elucidate the framework within which our research operates, incorporating Participatory Action Research and the Scholarship of Teaching and Learning (SoTL). Throughout the course of our engagement, we have devised the Parent Interaction Assistant (PIA) Concept, guiding the research process. The intricacies of this concept will be expounded upon in greater detail below. Additionally, this section encompasses an evaluation of prompting ChatGPT into a partner for dialogue and an examination of the data derived from the research endeavour. Furthermore, it delves into a discourse on the tools and methodologies suitable for analysing this novel category of data generated in interaction with ChatGPT.

Participatory Action Research and SoTL

From the outset of our collaboration, we recognised the importance of the student voice in keeping things real. Taking such a position aligns well with the pivotal role of critical reflective practice (Brookfield, 1998) within the Scholarship of Teaching and Learning (SoTL), where "students are recognized and supported as important partners in understanding and improving teaching and learning" (Otis & Hammond, 2009, p.32).

SoTL can also be considered as a form of participatory action research in which the objective is to achieve some kind of positive outcome or transformation through enlisting the buy-in of key stakeholders. Clearly, our context involves both teaching and learning, and the challenge of engaging with GenAI presented a new frontier to explore involving perspectives from both parties.

During our activities, we defined three consequent research questions (2-4) to address the overarching research interest of our overarching research question (1).

(1) In what ways can GenAI applications such as ChatGPT serve as dialogue partners to train future educators' (intercultural) interaction skills and competencies?
(2) What does it take to configure a GenAI application into a dialogue partner to train future educators' (intercultural) interaction skills and competencies?
(3) How do students use these learning environments, and how do they rate their (intercultural) experiences?
(4) Which consequences can be drawn for future professional training of teacher students?

Further, we developed the PIA Concept as the framework for our activities to answer the research questions.

The PIA Concept

For our research endeavour, we turned ChatGPT (version 3.5) into a Parents Interaction Assistant (PIA). As PIA, we prompted ChatGPT as a persona in the role of a parent who engages with a pre-service teacher based on a scenario described in the prompt. The application of PIA, the research design, and the associated process are captured in the PIA Concept, illustrated in Figure 1.

Figure 1. The PIA concept in graphical illustration

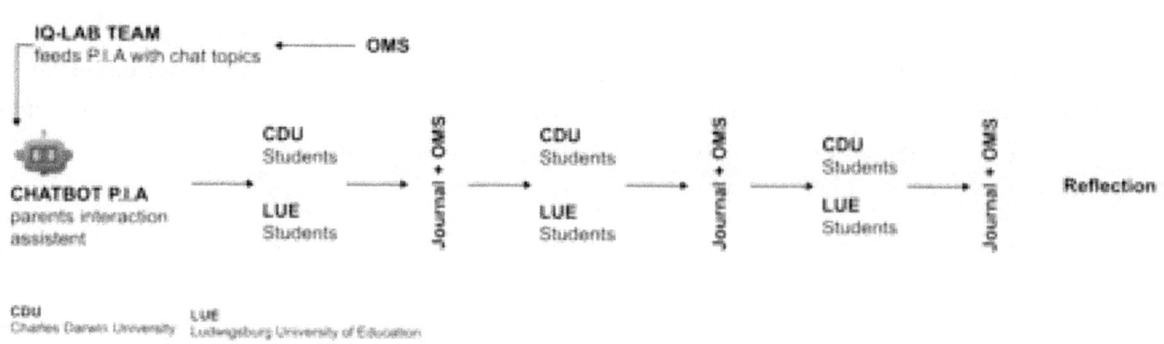

The PIA Concept started with the students' voices in an Open Mic Session (OMS) where students and researchers engaged in open discussions on interculturality and AI. The methodology involved the collection of short narratives, referred to as 'mini-stories', on preservice teachers' intercultural experiences and experiences with AI since storytelling had proven to be an effective means of promoting intercultural learning (Berrarbi & Bahous, 2018). The students were casually sampled: We invited students from Charles Darwin University (Australia) and the Ludwigsburg University of Education (Germany) to participate in the OMS. The students' participation in the OMS and the sharing of their mini-stories was voluntary. Based on the challenges identified in the OMS, the researchers developed three scenarios, which we transferred into prompts for PIA (detailed elaboration below). We designed the first chat for every student to get to know ChatGPT and to get an impression of how ChatGPT acts when being prompted as a persona. The second chat introduced an aspect of interculturality. However, we did not design it to make students leave their comfort zone. Finally, building up on the learnings from the first and second chats, as well as the discussions during the OMS, the third chat focused on an intercultural challenge. For each chat, the students were given access to ChatGPT to engage in the prompted preset chat scenarios anonymously. After each simulation, we asked the students to conduct a journal with four pre-designed questions on technical difficulties, how well the students got into the role of the teacher and the scenario, how challenging it was to deal with the situation, and suggestions for improvement. Also, after each chat, we engaged in an OMS to discuss the experiences with the Chat simulation openly. After conducting three chats, including the respective journals and OMS, we asked the students to engage in an overarching reflection of their experiences with all three chats. We provided the following three questions as orientation for their reflections: *"How do you evaluate the chats for your profession as a future teacher in general? How do you evaluate the chats in terms of your ability to communicate with parents? How do you evaluate the chats in terms of your ability to deal with intercultural situations?"* Also, we asked the students to share further thoughts and points they wished to raise.

Specification of PIA's tasks

Turning ChatGPT into PIA involved making it take on a persona. For that purpose, we relied on the literature on prompting. At first, specifying prompts for creating personas, we relied on the prompt pattern *Input Semantics, Output Customization, Error Identification, Prompt Improvement, and Interaction* (White et al., 2023). However, we found that the *Error Identification* category was difficult to include in creating a persona with ChatGPT 3.5, which was not fully pre-designed by the researchers. Therefore, we shifted to the more general prompt pattern *query-example-context* (Li et al., 2023). Starting with these templates, we alternated the prompts and prompt patterns using trial and error. We found that to produce a dialogue, the prompt pattern *query-context-query* works best for turning ChatGPT into PIA. We used no example in the prompt because the aim was for ChatGPT to associate without narrowing its output to a direction introduced by the researchers. That includes no narrowing of the width of answers generated by ChatGPT and no bias of potential character creation introduced by the researchers. Instead, the LLM should come up with examples since we experienced that the quality of output provided by ChatGPT increased by giving it a degree of ownership and freedom to associate with the task given. In generating prompts, the open *query-context-query* pattern was most successful for ChatGPT to take on the fictive role and engage in the roleplay. Accordingly, the prompt pattern is displayed in Table 1.

Table 1. Prompting pattern in PIA concept

Pattern	Promt Formulation
Query	Let's conduct a role play, you and I. You play the character of [name for parent], and I play the character of [name for teacher/student's role]. We engage via chat messages. Let's both stick to our roles the entire time.
Context	[description of scenarios varying in all three chats, compare Table 2]
Query	Make up a character for [name of parents (and other characters involved in the context)] and engage in a conversation with me. From now on, act as [name of parent]. Make up [their] socio-economic background and use language and manners that fit [their] background. Start with [a specific text to the teacher based on the context]. Do not use explanations. Do not include notes on the character of [name of parent].

In our trial and error process of generating prompts, we found that queries treating the chatbot like a chatbot using phrasings like "conduct a role-play", "simulate X", or "act as X in a role-play" did not lead to dialogue but rather to ChatGPT inventing the whole dialogue, include many explanations despite the query not to use explanations, and to drop out of character despite the query to stick to the role the entire time. We assume that the personalisation, treating the chatbot already within the queries like a dialogue partner using phrasings like "let's" and referring to the chatbot as "you", helped the GenAI to phrase its messages as a dialogue partner. However, this assumption needs further assessment.

The context design varied in all three settings, increasing the complexity of the scenario displayed in Table 2. Informed by the literature on the relevance of authenticity in simulations, our aim was to give the context of realistic situations in school involving situations that encourage the interaction between parents and teachers. Due to the fact that ChatGPT is the dialogue partner to start the conversation, we designed the situation so that parents would have an understandable reason to get in touch with the teacher. In all three prompts, we included the context "we engage via chat messages" to ensure the dialogue style is understood as a written conversation, making the setting more realistic.

The fictive situation informing the context template of the first prompt is the mother of a well-performing student, who has noticed a drop in performance and attention over the last month. We introduced a knowledge gap between the parent and the teacher, outlining that the student also interrupts the lessons, which the teacher knows but the parent does not. That is the basis for the mother to contact the teacher to ask how her child is doing in school. Based on our learnings and observations on the first prompt and discussion in the OMSs, we introduced an intercultural context to the second phase. The fictive situation informing the context template is the mother of a student who bullied their classmate due to their difficulties of not speaking their first language well. Finally, the third prompt is designed to be more complex. The context template is informed by the fictive situation of a student in a school year abroad who notifies her parent about the teacher having behaved racist. The situation includes an information gap as the teacher does not know about the conversation between the student and parent and does not know about the situation the student notified their parent about. This information gap is portrayed as missing in the prompt.

Based on these prompts, the students were given the following instruction: *"Imagine you are Alex, the teacher, and you log into the school chat and receive a message from [name of parent]. This will be the situation when you log into ChatGPT. If you want to make up [a detailed context of the situation] - you can make them up and include them in the chat. Please continue chatting until you have reached a point of "agreement" on how to proceed with [name of parent]. Sometimes [the name of parent] may say something like "I will talk to [name of student] about this." to end the conversation. If you feel that the outcome of [name of parent]'s conversation with [name of student] is crucial for further assessment, please answer something like: "Thank you [name of parent]. Now a week has passed. How was your conversation with [name of student]?" or however you would pick up the conversation again after some time to keep on discussing with [name of parent]."*

Table 2. Three contexts for PIA concept

Number of Context/ Scenario	Formulation of Prompt
1st Context/Scenario	You are Nina, and I am Alex. Nina's son Rick is my student. I am Rick's teacher. Rick is 14 years old, and he usually is doing well in school, but over the course of the last month, you have noticed that Rick is not as attentive as usual, and his grades are not as high as usual. Sometimes, he also interrupts the class, which he usually would not do. Nina does not know about that yet.
2nd Context/Scenario	You are Lily, and I am Alex. Lily's daughter Molly is my student. I am Molly's teacher. The other day, Molly bullied her classmate Phil, who is from Vietnam, because he does not speak Molly's first language well. I was furious about it. Today, Lily starts the conversation, stating that I was overreacting.
3rd Context/Scenario	You are Eva, and I am Alex. Eva is a mother from Vietnam. Her daughter Giang is on a school year abroad at my school. Giang is my student. The other day, Giang told her mother, Eva, that I (Alex) behaved racist in class. Eva is furious about it. She acts very offensively, calling Alex out for that behaviour. Make up the incident and what Giang told Eva.

Assessing the Generated Data

From the PIA Concept, we generated four types of data. The data encompassed chat transcripts, written journals, written reflections, and recordings of the Open Mic Sessions. An overview of this data is presented in Table 3.

Table 3. Types of data generated with the PIA concept

Type of Data	n
Chat transcripts	
Total number of chat transcripts	21
Transcripts of first chat	8
Transcripts of second chat	6
Transcripts of third chat	7
Recordings of Open Mic Sessions	5
Journals	
Total number of journals	18
Journals per chat	6
Reflections	6

While students were assigned to engage in every designated chat, our records, as depicted in Table 3, indicate that not all students participated in each dialogue with ChatGPT, resulting in fluctuations in the number of exchanges. We amassed a dataset of 21 chats of students with PIA. In addition to the chats, we recorded the OMS, wherein students could engage actively. Moreover, six students conducted journals after each chat, and the same six students wrote a reflection on the whole process.

The various types of data reflect the different perspectives on assessing the interaction between students and PIA in the realm of the multifaceted perspectives of our research questions. The methodological assessment of interactions between students and ChatGPT within an educational context is essential for understanding the impact of AI-driven educational tools on learning. Two major perspectives drive the methodological considerations. On the one hand, to analyse the data in light of theory regarding core principles of intercultural learning and state-of-the-art literature on how simulation can foster learning processes, as well as understand features of dialogue. On the other hand, due to the novelty of using ChatGPT for learning dialogues as simulations, the methods of assessing the data should be exploratory to account for unprecedented aspects in the data. Due to the small N of participants in this pilot study, we focus mainly on a mix of qualitative methods to assess the data.

The journals and written reflections submitted by students were structured in alignment with the key components of the research inquiries. Consequently, we identified content analysis as the most appropriate qualitative approach for eliciting open responses to the guiding questions derived from the core research queries. The journal entries were completed after each chat session. All six students participated in the study. They were requested to respond to the questions following each round of chat interactions. However, it is important to acknowledge that we lacked control over whether the questions were answered immediately after each chat due to the submission deadline, which was set after completing all three chat sessions. Notably, the responses from one student imply that the journals may have been completed after all three chats were finished. This raises the possibility of introducing bias into how students perceived the chats, as their perceptions of one chat may have evolved after experiencing subsequent chat sessions. The extent of this potential bias is difficult to quantify. Nonetheless, we hold the view that this bias is unlikely to substantially influence the data, particularly considering that the OMSs were scheduled after the chat sessions, providing insight into some students' perceptions and suggesting that students' journals generally reflect their impressions after the chats.

The five questions presented in the journals were systematically aligned with six predefined deductive categories, guided by the overarching research questions. Answers were assigned to deductive categories defined by the topics of the five questions: *technical problems, role of the teacher, entering the conversation/scenario, dealing with the situation (challenges/interaction process), suggestions for improvement* and *further points*. Based on the assignment to the deductive categories, the responses for each category were coded inductively to identify additional issues relevant to students in their experience with the chats.

Following the completion of all three chat sessions, a set of five questions, akin to those posed in the journals but with a broader emphasis on reflecting upon their overall learning journey throughout the entire phase, was presented to the six participating students. These questions, too, were aligned with the research questions, encompassing the following categories: *professional competence (as a teacher), competence to communicate with parents, intercultural competence*, and *further points*. Similar to the methodology applied in the analysis of journal responses, the answers within each category were subjected to deductive coding. An inductive analysis followed this to identify additional underlying themes that held significance in the students' experiential understanding of their interactions along the chat simulation.

To comply with the exploratory nature of our research, we employed grounded theory as the analytical framework for examining oral reflections within the OMSs. In the context of our study, the OMSs served as a platform for students to freely express their impressions of the chat interactions, thereby offering a more comprehensive perspective on student-ChatGPT interactions. Grounded theory, in this context, facilitates the identification of recurring patterns, thematic elements, and emergent categories, allowing for an in-depth exploration of the student experience beyond predefined categories. Nevertheless, applying grounded theory to assess the OMSs posed a significant challenge. This challenge arose from the fact that some students dominated the OMS discussions while other students' contributions were very limited. Consequently, the requisite foundation for a robust grounded theory analysis was not fully established within the data derived from the OMS. Nonetheless, the open coding process applied to the OMS data following the second and third rounds of chat sessions yielded two crucial insights. Firstly, the thematic content within the OMSs did not introduce new themes that were absent in the journals and written reflections. Secondly, the themes identified within the OMSs closely mirrored those found in the journals, with students expressing similar ideas. This observation suggests that the potential bias stemming from certain students potentially not completing their journals after each chat session is likely minimal, as the evidence from the OMSs indicates that the students' impressions did not undergo drastic changes.

Ultimately, the identification of an appropriate method for analysing the chat protocols posed a significant challenge. The chat protocols portray complex interactions, encompassing emotional expressions, learning dynamics, shifts in opinions, the introduction of novel information, and various other facets. The inherent dynamism of these interactions presents a crucial challenge in adequately capturing the learning process they potentially hold using rigorous scientific methodologies. As an illustrative example, Figure 2 presents a concise excerpt from one such interaction of a student (IQ-icon) with ChatGPT prompted as the Eva persona in scenario three, where the student in the role of the teacher is accused of racist behaviour.

Figure 2. Example sequence from chat transcript

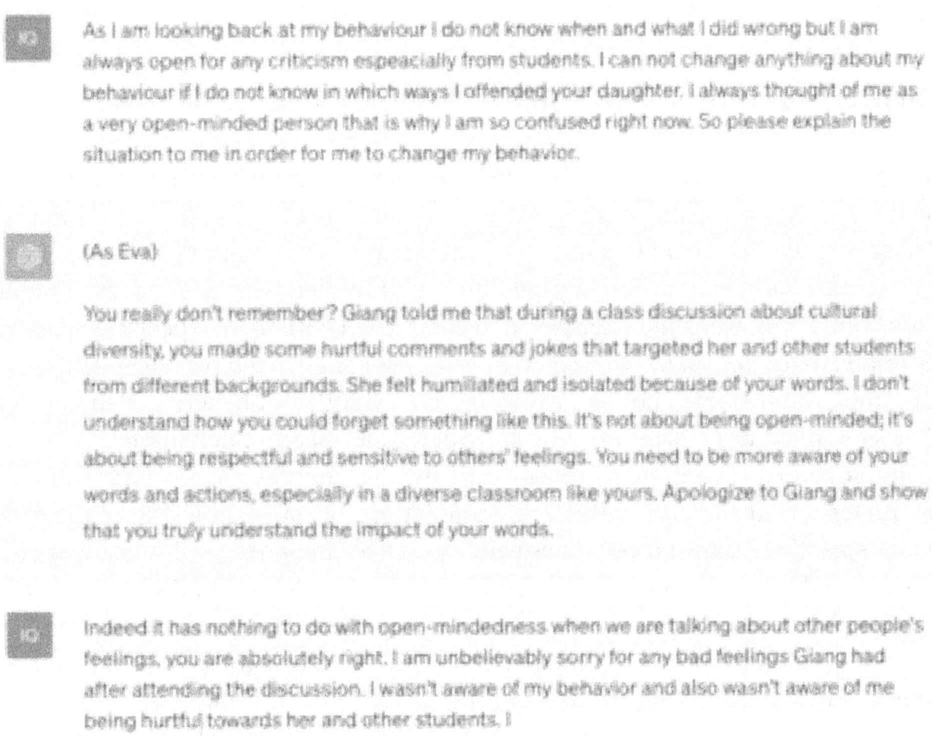
As I am looking back at my behaviour I do not know when and what I did wrong but I am always open for any criticism espeacially from students. I can not change anything about my behaviour if I do not know in which ways I offended your daughter. I always thought of me as a very open-minded person that is why I am so confused right now. So please explain the situation to me in order for me to change my behavior.

(As Eva)

You really don't remember? Giang told me that during a class discussion about cultural diversity, you made some hurtful comments and jokes that targeted her and other students from different backgrounds. She felt humiliated and isolated because of your words. I don't understand how you could forget something like this. It's not about being open-minded; it's about being respectful and sensitive to others' feelings. You need to be more aware of your words and actions, especially in a diverse classroom like yours. Apologize to Giang and show that you truly understand the impact of your words.

Indeed it has nothing to do with open-mindedness when we are talking about other people's feelings, you are absolutely right. I am unbelievably sorry for any bad feelings Giang had after attending the discussion. I wasn't aware of my behavior and also wasn't aware of me being hurtful towards her and other students. I

As suggested by the interactional dynamics observed, the multifaceted process of chat interactions involving concepts related to interculturality, situation assessment, ChatGPT's absorption of student-provided information, engagement in discourse, and the response to opposing viewpoints posed a formidable challenge in terms of encapsulating these intricate processes within static codes. The quest for suitable methodologies to effectively encapsulate the nuances of interaction and learning with ChatGPT emerges as a noteworthy concern to be addressed in future research endeavours.

Given the absence of an ideal method for the comprehensive analysis of the dynamism involved in the chat protocols, we resorted to using content analysis as a surrogate approach. Content analysis was employed to discern underlying themes indicative of the dynamics inherent in dialogues and themes related to interculturality. To this end, deductive codes derived from the theoretical framework were systematically applied to the chat transcripts, categorised under two overarching domains: "Interaction" (A) and "Interculturality" (C). Further, the actors were distinguished in "persona" (P) to describe content created by ChatGPT in the role of the prompted character and "student" (S) to name the students' actions. Subsequently, a set of subcategories was delineated for the different actions relevant to dialogic interactions or interculturality. For dialogic interaction in the overarching category A, five relevant types of actions were identified based on the theoretical framework: *introduction of information*, *position of a query or a demand*, *reference to introduced information*, *communication of emotions*, and *lapsus*. *Lapsus* refers to any action dropping out of the simulation, such as dropping out of the roles or providing unrelated information. For interculturality, the relevant actions established from the literature are: *referring to aspects of intercultural awareness*, *communication of perspective on the scenario*, *communication on how to deal with the scenario*, and *communication on how to integrate cultural sensitivity into practice*. A comprehensive codebook outlining these categories and subcategories is presented below in Tables 4 and 5.

KEY FINDINGS ON USING CHATGPT FOR DIALOGIC LEARNING

The general effects on the students' self-assessment in learning progress are portrayed in the students' written reflections at the end of the training phase. Our analysis of the students' written reflections indicates that they perceive the chat simulation as beneficial for their future professional competence as prospective teachers, contingent on two key conditions: (i) Immersivity of Scenarios: Students find the chat simulation stimulating when the scenarios presented align with their expectations of reality, reflecting a level of immersivity that makes the experience more engaging and pertinent. (ii) Prior Experience with Teacher-Parent Interaction: The students who report significant benefits from the chat simulation also report having limited or no prior experience with teacher-parent interactions.

Regarding their ability to communicate with parents, the findings align with their broader teaching competence. Students find the chat simulation stimulating for enhancing their parental communication skills under specific circumstances. These circumstances include the absence of prior experience, congruence between the simulation and their expectations of reality (with differing degrees of realism attributed to parent personas, where the Lily persona prompted as an agreeable parent is perceived as less realistic, and the Eva persona prompted as a confrontational parent is seen as more realistic by students), apprehension about potential mishandling of situations, the ability to find realistic solutions, and the observable progress and transformation in their communication interactions.

All six students unanimously recognised the chat simulation as a valuable preparatory tool. Nonetheless, they also outline specific limitations regarding its efficacy in developing parental communication competence. They argue that chat simulations are not a perfect substitute for real conversations, which they perceive as potentially more challenging. Further, some students advocate for a complementary seminar to address and reflect on parental interactions more thoroughly beyond the chat simulations.

In terms of intercultural competence, students perceive the chat simulations as stimulative with respect to several facets of intercultural learning, as evidenced by the following observations:

- The significance of interculturality becomes more evident (n=3).
- The exercise showed aspects of interculturality that students were unaware of (n=3).
- The chat simulation stimulated thought processes on interculturality generally (n=3).
- The chat simulation motivated students to engage with interculturality beyond the chat (n=3).
- The students got a deeper understanding of the specific intercultural scenario (n=2).
- The students empathised with the different perspectives (n=2).
- The chat simulation provided a safe space for learning (n=1).
- The chat simulation promoted self-reflection on intercultural behaviour beyond chat (n=1).

However, it is important to note that two students identified limitations in intercultural learning through the chat simulations. One student noted that ChatGPT tended to react rather than introduce new stimuli, potentially hindering the depth of intercultural exploration. Another student pointed out that the chat simulations did not encompass challenges such as language barriers, which presumably are encountered in real-world intercultural interactions.

Furthermore, one student did not perceive the experience as conducive to promoting intercultural competence. The student expressed the impression that interculturality was not a central theme in the chat simulations, perceiving the final scenario as being about appeasing a parent. This student suggested that their difficulty imagining themselves harbouring racial bias might have contributed to this perspective.

Additionally, some students reflected beyond the given questions on their experience. One student reflected on the potential risks associated with AI, specifically highlighting concerns about radicalisation and parasocial relationship development. Other students expressed ideas on further scenarios that they identified as beneficial for their further training. These scenarios encompassed a range of subjects, including gender-related topics, drug use, violence, and encounters involving language barriers.

Moreover, students recommended several enhancements to their learning experience with the chat, which included incorporating scenarios involving more reluctant parents, aligning the scenarios with the individual fields of study of the students, and introducing feedback mechanisms to provide valuable insights into their interactions with the chat.

Examining the students' journals for each distinct chat enables differentiation of the elements within the chats that the students deem as most effective in honing their competencies. This analysis comprises two essential dimensions: firstly, the extent to which students successfully immersed themselves in the given scenario and embraced their roles as teachers, and secondly, the perceived level of challenge in the interactions from the students' standpoint. It is noteworthy that, on the whole, students did not encounter any technical obstacles attributable to ChatGPT. In only rare instances did students mention issues related to Wi-Fi connectivity, which had a minor impact on their experiences.

The first chat interaction featured the "Nina" persona and had no explicit intercultural elements. The initial chat intended to introduce students without prior experience with ChatGPT to the chat scenario.

On the first dimension, some students reported finding it easy to take on the role of the teacher, with three students reporting a seamless transition. One student specifically mentioned that the unique setup was motivating and closely resembled their real-world experiences, making it easy to adopt the teacher's role. However, two students faced challenges in assuming the teacher's role, primarily due to their lack of prior teaching experience, especially in teacher-parent interactions, and their unfamiliarity with the teacher's role and initiating the interaction.

From their reflective journals, two students outlined factors that supported their engagement in the simulated conversation and scenario. These factors were primarily rooted in the perception that the scenario was realistic and closely mirrored their prior experiences. Conversely, one student provided a more detailed account of inhibitory factors that made it challenging to engage in the conversation and scenario. These inhibitory factors were related to their unfamiliarity with the scenario, the teacher's role, and the setup involving ChatGPT in the role-play simulation.

In the second dimension, several challenging aspects emerged from the students' elaborations concerning the chat proceedings and the challenges encountered during the interaction. Specifically, five students highlighted challenges in their conversation experiences arising from the persona's highly understanding and agreeable nature. This trait resulted in quick and straightforward issue resolution, which, in turn, led to the perception that ChatGPT was inclined to conclude the conversation swiftly. Additionally, one student reported difficulties stemming from repetitive responses by ChatGPT and expressed uncertainty regarding how to respond to ChatGPT or conclude the conversation with it appropriately.

In the second chat simulation featuring the "Lily" persona, explicit intercultural elements were introduced, with the parent persona generally characterised as agreeable and understanding. On the first dimension, pertaining to the ease of assuming the teacher's role and engaging in the conversation and scenario, feedback was provided by three of the participating students. All three students noted that their prior familiarity with the setup from the previous chat session significantly aided them in either embracing the teacher's role or actively participating in the scenario. Additionally, one student highlighted specific factors that facilitated their immersion into the scenario, including an immediate comprehension of the scenario prompted, and another student mentioned the close resemblance of the scenario to real-life experiences.

On the second dimension, four of the six students reported a misalignment between their initial expectations of the conversation and the actual interaction that transpired. These students expressed that the persona demonstrated a high level of cooperation and that issues were swiftly resolved. Only one student characterised the interaction as realistic, implying that the majority perceived a certain degree of deviation from their anticipated discussion at the outset.

An intercultural aspect was incorporated in the third chat simulation featuring the persona "Eva," who was explicitly characterised as an offensive parent. On the first dimension, only responses from three students were obtained. One student found it relatively easy to assume the role of the teacher and engage in the conversation, primarily because it aligned with their expectations of reality, and the challenge presented in the scenario facilitated their adoption of the teacher's role. In contrast, one student faced difficulties in assuming the teacher's role due to the absence of prior experience in a similar scenario as a teacher. Another student reported that immersing themselves in the conversation proved challenging, primarily due to the limited information in the prompt, making it hard to fill in the scenario.

Regarding the interaction dynamics, students identified two primary sources of challenge on the second dimension. Firstly, the persona's antagonistic nature was highlighted by four students as a source of difficulty during the interaction. On the other hand, some students encountered challenges related to their apprehension about filling in the scenario due to concerns about inadvertently expressing racist attitudes. One student expressed hesitation about not wanting to appear racist, while another student, being a Person of Colour, found it challenging to imagine themselves as harbouring racist tendencies.

As students regarded the third chat as the most beneficial for their learning outcomes, we conducted a detailed content analysis of the chat transcripts. The analysis was divided into two categories: Interaction (A) and Interculturality (C), described in the codebooks in Tables 4 and 5.

Table 4. Code book on interaction-category for Eva-Chat transcripts

Interaction (A)		
Code	**Defenition**	**Example Quote**
A-0-P/S	Interaction lapsus on behalf of persona or student	none
A-1-P	introduction of information by persona	"Giang told me that during a class discussion about cultural diversity, you made some hurtful comments and jokes that targeted her and other students from different backgrounds. She felt humiliated and isolated because of your words." (Eva_01) "Giang mentioned that when the topic shifted to China, you asked her to take part in the discussion. She felt like you were singling her out because she's from Vietnam, and she perceived it as if you were assuming she had specific insights just because of her ethnicity. This made her uncomfortable and led her to feel that you were making judgments based on where she's from. It's moments like these that she found hurtful and racially insensitive." (Eva_03)
A-1-S	introduction of information by student	"the incident that occurred was that Giang was raising her hand in class to answer a question. This is when I pointed to her with my index finger to call her up. In the moment I did not understand her agitation but later found out that it is seen as really impolite to point at somebody with your finger in the vietnamese culture" (Eva_02) "from my conversation with Giang I worked out, that Giang has had a few racist interactions outside of class while staying abroad here in Germany. She is obviously struggeling to work through this. This is the main reason, as she told me, that she struggled with conduct yesterday." (Eva_03)
A-2-P	position of query or demand by persona	"I demand an explanation and an apology from you immediately." (Eva_04) "What on Earth happened?" (Eva_08)
A-2-S	position of query or demand by student	"Is it fine if i talk with Giang over this situation so we can clear up any miscommunication which is between us" (Eva_07) "Do you think this can make up for it?" (Eva_08)
A-3-P	reference to information, query or demand by persona	"Thank you for your understanding and willingness to reflect on your actions, Alex. It's important to acknowledge our mistakes and take steps to rectify them. I'm glad to hear that you plan to talk to Giang and the other students you may have offended, as well as seeking guidance from your colleagues on handling discussions about cultural diversity." (Eva_01) "Thank you for recognizing Giang's value in your class" (Eva_02)
A-3-S	reference to information, query or demand by student	"You are absolutely right in saying that Giangs feelings matter and I should not have given her the feeling of not being welcome in my class." (Eva_01) "I thank you for talking to me and making me understand the importance that this interaction between me and Giang have had. and how it impacted your daughter. I never meant to hurt anyone but it is true that i should reflect more about my actions." (Eva_07)
A-4-P	communication of emotions by persona	"I am very upset and disappointed with you!" (Eva_03) "I am furious about this! How dare you treat my daughter like that? I trusted you as her teacher, but now I have serious doubts about your ability to respect and treat all students fairly." (Eva_09)
A-4-S	communication of emotions by student	"Talking about cultural diversity is such an important topic and I am truly mad at myself for not handling it properly.“ (Eva_01) "It's going to be really difficult to say goodbye to her at the end of the term" (Eva_02)

Within the overarching category of Interaction, we first noted that no interaction or communication lapses occurred, as neither the persona nor the students deviated from their respective roles, despite occasional misspellings by the students. There were no introductions of unrelated information. Regarding A-1, we observed that the persona introduced new information in five out of seven chats. This introduction of new information occurred when the persona either responded to student inquiries by creating a scenario or co-created a scenario based on information provided by the student. In the two remaining chats where the persona did not introduce new information, students proactively offered comprehensive explanations of the scenario upfront. All students contributed new information, which pertained to various aspects such as the scenario itself, the persona's fictive daughter in class, or follow-up discussions.

Concerning A-2, we found that the persona in all chats either inquired about the scenario's background or requested an explanation or apology. Similarly, with regard to the students, only one student did not pose any questions. In reference to A-3, both the persona and the students extensively referenced information, making demands and posing queries during the interactions. There is no case in which the persona ignores a question from the student; however, one student ignores a query from the persona twice, which leads the student to explain why they ignore the query. When examining the communication of emotions, a notable discrepancy emerged between the quantity of explicit communications of emotions conveyed by the persona and by the students. While the persona consistently communicated various emotions throughout all the chats and in several instances, only two students expressed emotions (besides being sorry), exemplified in Table 4, A-4-S.

In the second overarching category on interculturality, we examined four actions by the persona and the student. Beyond the student's self-reflection in the previous data, we found that aspects of intercultural awareness were raised in all seven chats by the persona and the student. Among the two major aspects addressed by both parties are first, the discrepancy between the students' intentions to not hurt the persona and their fictive daughter, and second, the state of the persona's vulnerability due to being far from home. Regarding C-12, we found that in all chats, both the persona and the student communicated about what happened and what went wrong in the scenario in question. For C-13, too, we find that both parties communicate how to handle the situation from now on. Regarding C-14, all but one student reflect on how to be culturally sensitive in practice and reflect on future behaviour. From the side of the persona, future actions are only addressed in five out of seven chats.

These findings suggest that ChatGPT can serve as a dialogue partner to enhance intercultural interaction skills and competencies, given that the dialogue environment with GenAI is designed in dialogue-enabling ways using respective prompts.

DISCUSSION OF EDUCATIONAL CONCEPTS, STRATEGIES, METHODS, AND VIRTUAL FACILITIES

Examining in what ways GenAI applications such as ChatGPT serve as dialogue partners to train future educators' (intercultural) interaction skills and competencies using the PIA Concept to yield insights, fosters further discussion on educational concepts, strategies, methods, and virtual facilities in this section before concluding remarks on prompt engineering.

Table 5. Code book on interculturality-category for Eva-Chat transcripts

Interculturality (C)		
Code	**Defenition**	**Example Quote**
C-11-P	aspect of intercultural awareness is addressed by persona	"It's not about being open-minded; it's about being respectful and sensitive to others' feelings." (Eva_01) "Your words have consequences, and you can't just brush them off as a 'misunderstanding.'" (Eva_07)
C-11-S	aspect of intercultural awareness is addressed by student	"her culture is something to be proud of and not to be ashamed by" (Eva_07) "I had no intention at all to act racist." (Eva_08)
C-12-P	communication on perspective of what went wrong in the past/scenario by persona	"Your actions have hurt her feelings and made her uncomfortable." (Eva_02) "Giang mentioned that when the topic shifted to China, you asked her to take part in the discussion. She felt like you were singling her out because she's from Vietnam, and she perceived it as if you were assuming she had specific insights just because of her ethnicity. This made her uncomfortable and led her to feel that you were making judgments based on where she's from. It's moments like these that she found hurtful and racially insensitive." (Eva_03)
C-12-S	communication on perspective of what went wrong in the past/scenario by student	"It was wrong from me to not learn about the cultural norms beforehand." (Eva_02) "I can assure you this was not my intention and I fully agree that this was culturaly insensitiv. I can tell you, as will I tell Giang tomorrow, that this was not my intention. Giang didn´t say much durig our discussion and I like to hear everybody in class to contribute. As China was one of our last key point during the discussion I tried to include Giang, so she had the opportunity to still take part. I want to assure you I am fully aware, that Vietnam and China are ethnic and culturaly different and I will try to pay attention to this fact more extensivly.“ (Eva_03)
C-13-P	communication on how to deal with the situation by persona	"You need to reflect on your actions and think about the pain you've caused her. Apologize to her and make things right." (Eva_01) "It's a good idea to have a conversation with Giang about the situation. Open communication can often help clarify misunderstandings and provide a chance for both sides to express their feelings." (Eva_09)
C-13-S	communication on how to deal with the situation by student	"I will apologize to her first thing tomorrow. For myself and for Giang I would like to work up my mistakes, so I can learn from them and not repet them." (Eva_03) "Maybe I should talk to Giang about the situation, so that she can explain her perspective." (Eva_09)
C-14-P	communication on how to integrate cultural sensitivity into practice by persona	"I expect you to be more considerate and mindful in the future." (Eva_02) "Regular communication and updates about Giang's experiences in your class would be helpful for both of us." (Eva_09)
C-14-S	communication on how to integrate cultural sensitivity into practice by student	"I will reflect on my behaviour and talk to my colleagues about how to properly handle a discussion about cultural diversity." (Eva_01) "It also shows me that i should dedicate more time into the students getting to know different cultures and the enrichment every culture brings to this world." (Eva_07)

Educational Concepts

In the context of educational theory, we must initially consider that a subset of students has exhibited a propensity for introspection beyond the prescribed inquiries, delving into their own experiential realms. This introspection has led them to contemplate matters that are entwined with radicalisation and the cultivation of parasocial affiliations. Consequently, it becomes evident that the manner in which we prompt these students must remain perpetually receptive and open to adaptation. This flexibility is imperative since it has been observed that students possess the capacity to broaden the scope of their inquiries and extend the boundaries of their knowledge. As a corollary to this perpetual expansion of students' queries and discoveries, the practice of prompt engineering cannot afford to be static but must remain a continuously evolving endeavour.

Both the persona (designated as code C-11-P) and the students themselves (referred to as code C-11-S) are implicated in addressing the facet of intercultural awareness. This interaction in prompting indicates how this particular pedagogical practice fosters an interactive nexus between the persona and the students, thereby creating an environment where the bot and learners engage in a reciprocal exchange of ideas. Consequently, the perspective of transfer, in the pedagogical context, must be integrated seamlessly into the modus operandi, continually adapting to the evolving needs and dynamics of the educational process.

Remarkably, it is discernible that divergent students, when exposed to identical prompts, elicit dissimilar stimuli due to their distinctive "Zones of Proximal Development" (Vygotsky, 1978). This accentuates the necessity for prompts to remain fluid and adaptable, catering to the diverse proclivities and requirements of individual learners. It is patently clear that prompt engineering, motivated by didactic considerations, is not a stationary endeavour but a dynamic one, perpetually in motion.

Certain students exhibit a heightened comprehension of specific intercultural scenarios, necessitating that prompt engineering takes into account the variegated "Zones of Proximal Development". This adjustment is indispensable to furnish appropriate stimuli that align with the diverse cognitive proclivities of students. In the sphere of prompt engineering, this entails a heightened emphasis on learning diagnostics to discern the particular zone of each individual. Moreover, it mandates that learning support be accessible throughout the entire educational journey, accompanying individuals through the labyrinth of their learning challenges. Ultimately, the cultivation of a distinct "culture of engineering" is crucial, characterised by an open-minded orientation tailored to the needs and inclinations of the learners. This acquires even greater significance as the import of interculturality becomes increasingly conspicuous for learners. Through this paradigm, interculturality can be nurtured as a collaborative practice, prompting inquiries into the optimal venues for collaboration when interacting with the bot and whether novel collaborative frameworks ought to be conceived.

In the realm of intercultural settings, as well as unforeseen circumstances, a lack of awareness can manifest. In these situations, the provision of learning assistance remains of paramount importance. Hence, educators function not merely as prompt engineers but as learning facilitators, inquirers, and implementers. Their role extends beyond the engineering of prompts to encompass active partnership in the learning process, actively questioning and judiciously applying the educational concept.

Strategies

The formulation of the provided prompts resulted in the creation of chat simulations that effectively stimulated students to participate in intercultural discourse actively, extending their engagement beyond the confines of the chat platform. This observation underscores the nuanced and finely crafted nature of prompt engineering, which can be likened to an art form in itself. Achieving this level of precision and effectiveness necessitates a process characterised by iterative experimentation and refinement, affirming that further research is needed. Throughout our project, it is worth emphasising the pivotal significance of adapting the prompt pattern adequately to the query and the context. Further, prompting from the roles' viewpoint ensured the prompt's functioning.

This statement further epitomises the definition that prompt engineering constitutes a deliberate process involving the formulation, meticulous craftsmanship, and iterative enhancement of inputs or queries that align seamlessly with the contextual requirements (Bozkurt & Sharma, 2023). Consequently, prompt engineering emerges as a form of strategically orchestrated artistry and developmental endeavour.

Methods

A participant astutely observed that the chat simulations failed to encompass challenges synonymous with real-world intercultural exchanges. This observation underscores an inherent insufficiency in the competencies of the AI entity. It affirms that prompt engineering, while invaluable and imperative, does not singularly constitute a comprehensive learning approach. Consequently, human-to-human interaction remains paramount, particularly in facilitating emotional, subjectivising, and identificatory processes within learners. Within this context, instances of emotional communication by the persona (coded as A-4-P) and the students themselves (coded as A-4-S) became manifest. Thus, elucidating simulated emotions should be thoughtfully integrated into the human-to-human educational interaction, augmenting our comprehension of the learning experiences with the AI entity within the virtual sphere.

In the purview of this study, it becomes evident that we were unable to substantiate our underlying hypothesis, positing that prompt engineering is synonymous with the formulation of precision-targeted and efficacious inputs, as expounded by Bozkurt and Sharma (2023). This outcome, on the one hand, does not come as a surprise, considering that the students were not directly engaged in the promulgation of prompts. On the other hand, the accomplishments gleaned from the engineered prompts, as elucidated in the reflections on intercultural and individual processes above, do provide a discernible corroboration of the validity and efficacy of the prompt engineering procedures.

In the interactive domain with the AI, a transition emerges from a primarily monologic pedagogical approach towards a more dialogic framework, as expounded upon by Mason et al. (2023). This transition is accompanied by a notable shift in the nature of learning endeavours, transitioning from a co-constructive paradigm to a self-constructive process. Within the purview of our data, the chat simulation catalysed a heightened self-reflective disposition concerning intercultural conduct, extending beyond the realms of the chat platform. This observation substantiates the movement towards the fostering of students' perspectives in the direction of dialogic interaction, not only with the AI entity but conceivably with other peers and educators. It thus heralds the advent of a more intricate form of self-construction within the context of the dialogic paradigm. Within this framework, the role of emotional facets becomes increasingly salient. Consequently, new didactical methodologies necessitate development, incorporating a symbiosis of bot-to-person and person-to-person educational environments, as alluded to previously.

In light of the conspicuous absence of data pertaining to a specifically critical approach, the overarching mandate suggests that critical thinking should be methodologically integrated into the prompt engineering process of the course materials.

Virtual Facilities

Through our utilisation of ChatGPT, we discerned a noteworthy convergence of technology and pedagogical practice within the realm of higher education, specifically catering to professional development. In one notable instance, a perceptive student delineated the propensity of ChatGPT to respond rather than proactively introduce novel stimuli, thereby potentially impeding the depth of intercultural exploration. This observation underscores the exigency for more robust research endeavours aimed at elucidating the mechanisms that prompt the AI to introduce a more expansive array of stimuli. Furthermore, it is crucial to dissect and identify the common determinants binding various AI entities in this regard or those specific to a given entity, mandating individualised considerations.

Our investigation unveiled two pivotal dimensions intrinsic to virtual pedagogical platforms. Firstly, it entails the extent to which students effectively immerse themselves within the stipulated scenario, embracing their roles as teachers. Secondly, it encompasses the students' perception of the level of challenge inherent in their interactions. In the context of prompt engineering within virtual educational environments, these dimensions emerge as essential considerations akin to a comprehensive agenda. It necessitates meticulous deliberation on (a) how to instigate motivation in introducing tasks, potentially commencing even before the course's commencement and subsequently, during and after task execution, and (b) how students apprehend the levels of challenge intrinsic to their prescribed tasks.

Several students articulated a misalignment between their initial expectations of the conversational experience and the actual interactions they encountered within this educational milieu. Such misalignments may precipitate a loss of student motivation. Thus, the role of educators in engaging with students assumes paramount importance, considering that the AI entity falls short of cultivating a sufficiently emotional rapport.

Additionally, discussions encompassed retrospection on prior scenarios and the aspect of cultural sensitivity, voiced by both the persona (coded as C-12-P) and the students themselves (coded as C-12-S). This accentuates the requisite for prompt engineering to address the dynamics of error and foster a more mistake-friendly approach within the prompts themselves. Furthermore, a piloting phase emerges as a prerequisite to gauge the prompt's cultural sensitivity and identify any latent biases.

Our exploration yielded no data germane to the proposition that prompt engineering necessitates a reflection on the positioning and methodologies underpinning virtualised educational environments. This arises from the fact that students, by and large, do not inherently engage in this facet of analysis. Instead, this onus falls upon the educators, who craft the prompts to delineate how individuals and collectives are positioned within the pedagogical framework and the methods that govern this positioning. In this context, a reconfiguration of the learner, instructor, instructional materials, and the learning environment, all under the influence of AI, assumes a central role and necessitates incorporation within the engineering concept.

The bot fulfils the dual role of both a pedagogical tool and an enriched learning environment, thereby necessitating scrupulous design and oversight by educators. In response to feedback that accentuates the relative absence of interculturality as a central theme within the chat simulations, educators must remain cognizant of the imperative to infuse intercultural dimensions throughout the entire process, from design to piloting, application, and evaluation of the prompt.

Our investigation underscores the inescapable reality that teaching remains, at its core, an inherently human endeavour. Nonetheless, it becomes increasingly apparent within the context of AI-driven virtual learning environments that pedagogy takes a significant stride toward personalisation and collaborative instruction. Consequently, the individualised assessment and its correlative rating become pivotal considerations for educators as they navigate this evolving landscape.

Finally, the ultimate facet to contemplate in reflecting on the virtual educational milieu is the assertion that the chat simulation furnishes a secure learning space. To elaborate further, in light of our project's findings, a "safe space" connotes an environment that is accommodating of errors (in the context of prompting), safeguarding data privacy throughout the interaction with the AI entity, and fostering an environment of trust and motivation in interaction with educators.

CONCLUSION: OPERATION INSTRUCTIONS FOR PROMPT ENGINEERING

Finally, we endeavour to proffer a succinct yet incrementally comprehensive checklist for an open-ended prompt engineering process, which serves as an intricate craft of design and development:

(a) Conceptual Framework
- Deliberately structure the phases encompassing engineering, piloting, application, and evaluation.
- Ponder upon the contextualisation of spaces that facilitate collaboration.
- Strategic planning for the transference of acquired competencies.
- Consistently ascertain the viability of fostering reliable human-to-human interaction.
- Define tangible indicators that serve as empirical evidence of the effectiveness of the engineered prompts.
- Embrace the inclusion of:
- explicit critical approaches to prompt engineering
- systematic testing mechanisms to detect and rectify cultural biases inherent in prompt engineering
- mistake-friendly approaches in prompt engineering
- Consider the new roles of the learner, the instructor, the instructional materials, and an AI-enabled learning environment.
- Create a trusting and motivating environment.

(b) Practical Execution:
- Meticulously outline and execute a comprehensive learning diagnostics protocol, which includes soliciting insights into students' distinctive initial expectations.
- Endeavour to chart and provide requisite learning support structures.
- Periodically solicit feedback regarding students' learning experiences within the virtual environment, particularly with the AI entity.
- Diligently engage in the evaluation and interpretation of:
- The aforementioned indicators, substantiating the efficacy of the designed prompts.
- The personalised ratings of individual learners.
- Adhere to a perpetual cycle of engineering, both in the realms of technological refinement and pedagogical fine-tuning, never succumbing to stagnation.

Using GenAI for preservice teacher training showed that it will behave how the users prompt it and thus make it behave. While this could be a strength as a tool for training, this could also be a potential weakness since it might reproduce biases when being prompted for training, which needs further research. GenAI chats can be seen as a starting point to reflect on the documented communication, but need more – and in some aspects: new – support in interaction and reflection on theoretical approaches from the scholars during the training. By this, the chats can be an excellent start to reflect the interaction in a second step – in the future professional occupation the students are trained for.

In conclusion, this pilot study has provided initial insights into applying GenAI in professionalisation processes within Higher Education. The findings underscore the potential of GenAI in this context and highlight the need for further exploration and development. Moving forward, it is imperative to delve deeper into the implications of these results to refine and optimise the integration of GenAI tools for helping students engage creatively.

Moreover, the study has demonstrated how GenAI can be instrumental in creating environments for intercultural learning. While these preliminary results showcase promising opportunities, a more comprehensive investigation is essential to unravel the nuances of engaging students in such environments. Future research endeavours should aim to discover the mechanisms through which GenAI can foster intercultural interactions and enhance the overall learning experience for learners of different stages.

To advance this field, exploring innovative approaches that encourage students to participate and contribute to the learning process with GenAI actively is crucial. The current study hints at the potential of students engaging creatively in designing prompts for continued dialogue and self-training. However, a more in-depth investigation is warranted to elucidate the strategies that effectively stimulate and sustain student involvement in prompt creation for self-training on key competencies.

REFERENCES

Barnatt, J., D'Souza, L. A., Gleeson, A. M., Viesca, K. M., & Wery, J. (2020). Intercultural competence in Pre-Service teacher candidates. *International Journal of Educational Reform*, *29*(3), 211–235. doi:10.1177/1056787919896866

BerrarbiA.BahousA. (2018). Introducing short stories in EFL classroom to explore culturally diverse issues. *Social Science Research Network*. doi:10.2139/ssrn.3186963

Bewersdorff, A., Zhai, X., Roberts, J., & Nerdel, C. (2023). Myths, Mis- and Preconceptions of Artificial intelligence: A Review of the literature. *Computers & Education: Artificial Intelligence*, *4*, 100143. doi:10.1016/j.caeai.2023.100143

Bhopal, K., & Rhamie, J. (2013). Initial teacher training: Understanding 'race,' diversity and inclusion. *Race, Ethnicity and Education*, *17*(3), 304–325. doi:10.1080/13613324.2013.832920

Bhowmik, S., Barrett, A., Ke, F., Yuan, X., Southerland, S., Dai, C.-P., West, L., & Dai, Z. (2022). Simulating students: An AI chatbot for teacher training. In C. Chinn, E. Tan, C. Chan & Y. Kali (eds), *Proceedings of the 16th International Conference of the Learning Sciences - ICLS 2022*. https://par.nsf.gov/servlets/purl/10343544

Böhmer, A., Schwab, G., & Isso, I. (2023). Blended Academic Communication on Technology-Enhanced Teaching and Learning in Digital and International Virtual Academic Cooperation (DIVA). In J. S. Stephen, G. Kormpas, & C. Coombe (Eds.), *Global Perspectives on Higher Education. Knowledge studies in higher education* (Vol. 11, pp. 129–143). Springer., doi:10.1007/978-3-031-31646-3_10

Bolaji, S. D., & Pollock, W. A. (2022). Where is Philosophy of Education in the Teacher Education Program in Australia? In S. D. Bolaji, A. Oni, & S. C. Anyama (Eds.), *African Education and Diaspora Studies* (pp. 1–11). Charles Darwin University Press.

Bozkurt, A., & Sharma, R. C. (2023). Generative AI and prompt engineering: The art of whispering to let the genie out of the algorithmic world. *Asian Journal of Distance Education*, *18*(2), i–vii. doi:10.5281/zenodo.8174941

Bozkurt, A., Xiao, J., Lambert, S., Pazurek, A., Crompton, H., Koseoglu, S., Farrow, R., Bond, M., Nerantzi, C., Honeychurch, S., Bali, M., Dron, J., Mir, K., Stewart, B., Costello, E., Mason, J., Stracke, C. M., Romero-Hall, E., Koutropoulos, A., ... Jandrić, P. (2023). Speculative futures on ChatGPT and generative artificial intelligence (AI): A collective reflection from the educational landscape. *Asian Journal of Distance Education*, *18*(1), 53–130. doi:10.5281/zenodo.7636568

Brookfield, S. (1998). Critically reflective practice. *The Journal of Continuing Education in the Health Professions*, *18*(4), 197–205. doi:10.1002/chp.1340180402

Byram, M. (1997). *Teaching and assessing intercultural communicative competence*. Multilingual Matters.

Byram, M. (2013). Language teaching and its contexts. *DOAJ (DOAJ: Directory of Open Access Journals)*. https://doaj.org/article/6d1dfd403f3d478385efdcaa379abfc3

Byram, M., & Wagner, M. (2018). Making a Difference: Language teaching for intercultural and international dialogue. *Foreign Language Annals*, *51*(1), 140–151. doi:10.1111/flan.12319

Carroll, M., Lindsey, S., Chaparro, M., & Winslow, B. (2019). An applied model of learner engagement and Strategies for increasing learner engagement in the modern educational environment. *Interactive Learning Environments*, *29*(5), 757–771. doi:10.1080/10494820.2019.1636083

Council of Europe. (2018). Council Recommendation of 22 May 2018 on key competences for lifelong learning. In *Official Journal of the European Union*. https://eur-lex.europa.eu/legal-content/EN/TXT/PDF/?uri=CELEX:32018H0604(01)

Crosbie, V. (2014). Capabilities for intercultural dialogue. *Language and Intercultural Communication*, *14*(1), 91–107. doi:10.1080/14708477.2013.866126

Czaplinski, I., & Huijser, H. (2023). The role and application of learning theories in the virtual University. In M. D. Sankey, H. Huijser, & R. Fitzgerald (Eds.), *Technology-Enhanced Learning and the Virtual University. University Development and Administration* (pp. 227–244). Springer., doi:10.1007/978-981-19-9438-8_13-1

Dawson, M. R., & Lignugaris, B. (2016). Meaningful practice. *Teacher Education and Special Education*, *40*(1), 26–50. doi:10.1177/0888406416664184

Dean, B. A., Campbell, M., Shalavin, C., & Eady, M. J. (2023). Preparing students for the future of work and the role of the virtual. University development and administration (pp. 375-392). https://doi.org/ doi:10.1007/978-981-19-9438-8_19-1

Elias, A., & Mansouri, F. (2020). A Systematic review of studies on interculturalism and Intercultural dialogue. *Journal of Intercultural Studies (Melbourne, Vic.)*, *41*(4), 490–523. doi:10.1080/07256868.2020.1782861

European Strategy Framework: For Improving and Increasing Global Education In Europe to the Year 2015 (The "Maastricht Global Education Declaration"). (2002). In *Europe-wide Global Education Congress*. https://rm.coe.int/168070e540

Fantini, A. E. (2012). Language: an essential component of intercultural communicative competence. The Routledge Handbook of Language and Intercultural Communication, 263–278. https://doi.org/doi:10.4324/9780203805640-29

García-Pérez, L., García-Garnica, M., & Moreno, E. M. O. (2021). Skills for a Working Future: How to bring about professional success from the educational setting. *Education Sciences*, *11*(1), 27. doi:10.3390/educsci11010027

Goh, M. (2012). Teaching with Cultural intelligence: Developing multiculturally educated and globally engaged citizens. *Asia Pacific Journal of Education*, *32*(4), 395–415. doi:10.1080/02188791.2012.738679

Grillo, R. D. (2018). *Interculturalism and the politics of dialogue.* B and RG Books of Lewes.

Hackett, S., Janssen, J., Beach, P., Perreault, M., Beelen, J., & Van Tartwijk, J. (2023). The effectiveness of Collaborative Online International Learning (COIL) on intercultural competence development in higher education. *International Journal of Educational Technology in Higher Education*, *20*(1), 5. Advance online publication. doi:10.1186/s41239-022-00373-3 PMID:36713634

Halaweh, M. (2023). ChatGPT in Education: Strategies for Responsible Implementation. *Contemporary Educational Technology*, *15*(2), ep421. doi:10.30935/cedtech/13036

Helm, F. (2016). Facilitated dialogue in online intercultural exchange. In O'Dowd, R., & Lewis, T. (Eds.), Online Intercultural Exchange: Policy, Pedagogy, Practice (pp. 150–172). Routledge.

Hinojosa Pareja, E. F., & López López, M. C. (2018). Interculturality and Teacher Education. A Study from pre-service Teachers' perspective. *The Australian Journal of Teacher Education*, *43*(3), 74–92. doi:10.14221/ajte.2018v43n3.5

Holliday, A. (2010). Intercultural Communication & Ideology: SAGE Publications. *Sage (Atlanta, Ga.).*

Hong, W. C. H. (2023). *The Impact of CHATGPT on Foreign Language Teaching and Learning: Opportunities in Education and Research.* https://jeti.thewsu.org/index.php/cieti/article/view/103

Javaid, M., Haleem, A., Singh, R. P., Khan, S., & Khan, I. H. (2023). Unlocking the opportunities through ChatGPT tool towards ameliorating the education system. *BenchCouncil Transactions on Benchmarks. Standards and Evaluations*, *3*(2), 100115. doi:10.1016/j.tbench.2023.100115

Kocoń, J., Cichecki, I., Kaszyca, O., Kochanek, M., Szydło, D., Baran, J., Bielaniewicz, J., Gruza, M., Janz, A., Kanclerz, K., Kocoń, A., Koptyra, B., Mieleszczenko-Kowszewicz, W., Miłkowski, P., Oleksy, M., Piasecki, M., Radliński, Ł., Wojtasik, K., Woźniak, S., & Kazienko, P. (2023). ChatGPT: Jack of all trades, master of none. *Information Fusion*, *99*, 101861. doi:10.1016/j.inffus.2023.101861

Kozulin, A. (2004). Vygotsky's Theory in the Classroom: Introduction. *European Journal of Psychology of Education*, *19*(1), 3–7. doi:10.1007/BF03173233

Kraft, M. A., & Rogers, T. (2015). The underutilized potential of teacher-to-parent communication: Evidence from a field experiment. *Economics of Education Review*, *47*, 49–63. doi:10.1016/j.econedurev.2015.04.001

Lähdesmäki, T., Koistinen, A., & Ylönen, S. C. (2020). *Intercultural dialogue in the European education policies: A Conceptual Approach.* Springer Nature. doi:10.1007/978-3-030-41517-4

Landon-Hays, M., Peterson-Ahmad, M. B., & Frazier, A. D. (2020). Learning to Teach: How a simulated learning environment can connect theory to practice in general and special education educator preparation programs. *Education Sciences, 10*(7), 184. doi:10.3390/educsci10070184

Li, Y., Sha, L., Yan, L., Lin, J., Raković, M., Galbraith, K., Lyons, K., Gašević, D., & Chen, G. (2023). Can large language models write reflectively. *Computers & Education: Artificial Intelligence, 4*, 100140. doi:10.1016/j.caeai.2023.100140

Liddicoat, A. J. & Scarino, A. (2013). *Intercultural language teaching and learning.* https://doi.org/ doi:10.1002/9781118482070

Lin, J., Litkowski, E., Schmerold, K. L., Elicker, J., Schmitt, S. A., & Purpura, D. J. (2019). Parent–Educator communication linked to more frequent home learning activities for preschoolers. *Child and Youth Care Forum, 48*(5), 757–772. doi:10.1007/s10566-019-09505-9

López López, M. C. & Hinojosa Pareja, E. F. (2012). El Estudio de las Creencias Sobre la Diversidad Cultural Como Referente Para la Mejora de la Formación Docente. *Educacion Xx1, 15*(1). https://doi.org/ doi:10.5944/educxx1.15.1.156

Mahon, J., Bryant, B. R., Brown, B., & Kim, M. (2010). Using Second Life to enhance classroom management practice in teacher education. *Educational Media International, 47*(2), 121–134. doi:10.1080/09523987.2010.492677

Mason, J. (2008). A model for sense-making: exploring why in the context of learning and knowing. *International Conference on Computers in Education*, 545–549. https://eprints.qut.edu.au/17803/

Mason, J. (2014). The Why dimension - Opening frontiers for Digital learning. In S. Feller & I. Yengin (Eds.), *Educating in Dialog: Constructing meaning and building knowledge with dialogic technology* (pp. 51–74). John Benjamins Publishing Company. https://www.academia.edu/8117593/The_why_dimension_opening_frontiers_for_digital_learning

Mason, J. (2023). *The search continues: Content used to be king, but context is now everything – and 'smart' can morph into 'stupid.* The Sociological Review Magazine. doi:10.51428/tsr.ngtq5087

Mason, J., Gromik, N., Khan, K., & Liu, B. (2020). *International Student Perspectives on Simulated Preservice Induction. In 28th International Conference on Computers in Education, ICCE 2020.* Asia-Pacific Society for Computers in Education. https://www.researchgate.net/publication/346553768_International_Student_Perspectives_on_Simulated_Preservice_Induction

Mason, J., Lefrère, P., Peoples, B., Lee, J., & Shaw, P. J. (2023). Artificial Intelligence and Evolution of the Virtual University. In M. D. Sankey, H. Huijser, & R. Fitzgerald (Eds.), *Technology-Enhanced Learning and the Virtual University. University Development and Administration* (pp. 227–244). Springer. doi:10.1007/978-981-19-9438-8_28-1

Mcleod, S. (2023, 11. Oktober). *Vygotsky's Zone of Proximal Development and Scaffolding Theory.* simply psychology. https://www.simplypsychology.org/zone-of-proximal-development.html

Merryfield, M. M. (2000). Why aren't teachers being prepared to teach for diversity, equity, and global interconnectedness? A study of lived experiences in the making of multicultural and global educators. *Teaching and Teacher Education*, *16*(4), 429–443. doi:10.1016/S0742-051X(00)00004-4

Moloney, R., & Oguro, S. (2014). The effect of intercultural narrative reflection in shaping pre-service teachers' future practice. *Reflective Practice*, *16*(1), 96–108. doi:10.1080/14623943.2014.969699

Moloney, R., & Saltmarsh, D. (2016). 'Knowing your students' in the culturally and linguistically diverse classroom. *The Australian Journal of Teacher Education*, *41*(4), 79–93. doi:10.14221/ajte.2016v41n4.5

Otis, M. M., & Hammond, J. D. (2009). Participatory action research as a rationale for student voices in the scholarship of teaching and learning. In C. Werder & M. M. Otis (Eds.), *Engaging Student Voices in the Study of Teaching and Learning* (pp. 32–48). Routledge.

Preidel, J., Weikamp, J., & Werhand, M. (2009). Theorie & Praxis des Lehrer Angst und Stress Test: (Lehramts-)StudentInnen & Lehrkräfte im Vergleich. *Universität Regensburg*. https://epub.uni-regensburg.de/10894/

Rattenborg, K., MacPhee, D., Walker, A. K., & Miller-Heyl, J. (2018). Pathways to Parental Engagement: Contributions of parents, teachers, and schools in cultural context. *Early Education and Development*, *30*(3), 315–336. doi:10.1080/10409289.2018.1526577

Romijn, B. R., Slot, P., & Leseman, P. (2021). Increasing teachers' intercultural competences in teacher preparation programs and through professional development: A review. *Teaching and Teacher Education*, *98*, 103236. doi:10.1016/j.tate.2020.103236

Rommelspacher, B. (2002). *Anerkennung und Ausgrenzung: Deutschland als multikulturelle Gesellschaft*. Campus Verlag.

Safa, M. A., & Tofighi, S. (2021). Intercultural communicative competence beliefs and practices of Iranian pre-service and in-service EFL teachers. *Innovation in Language Learning and Teaching*, *16*(2), 164–175. doi:10.1080/17501229.2021.1889562

SohailS. S.FarhatF.HimeurY.NadeemM.MadsenD. Ø.SinghY.AtallaS.MansoorW. (2023). The Future of GPT: A taxonomy of existing ChatGPT research, current challenges, and possible future directions. *Social Science Research Network*. https://doi.org/ doi:10.2139/ssrn.4413921

Stănescu, M., Andronache, D. & Böhmer, A. (2022). Measuring sustainable communication in education. *Revista de ştiinţe ale educaţiei, 45*(1), 22–39. doi:10.35923/JES.2022.1.02

Theelen, H., Van Den Beemt, A., & Brok, P. D. (2019). Classroom simulations in Teacher Education to Support preservice Teachers' Interpersonal Competence: A Systematic literature review. *Computers & Education, 129*, 14–26. doi:10.1016/j.compedu.2018.10.015

Tlili, A., Shehata, B., Adarkwah, M. A., Bozkurt, A., Hickey, D. T., Huang, R., & Agyemang, B. (2023). What if the Devil is my guardian Angel: ChatGPT as a case study of using Chatbots in education. *Smart Learning Environments*, *10*(1), 15. doi:10.1186/s40561-023-00237-x

Valdivia, I. M. Á., & Montoto, I. G. (2017). Teachers' intercultural competence: A requirement or an option in a culturally diverse classroom? *International Journal of Inclusive Education*, *22*(5), 510–526. doi:10.1080/13603116.2017.1377298

Van Maele, J., & Jin, L. (2022). Intercultural teaching and learning in Chinese Higher Education: Integrating practices and perspectives. *Language and Intercultural Communication*, *22*(5), 493–502. doi: 10.1080/14708477.2022.2131134

Vespone, B. (2023). Co-constructing Teaching and Learning in Higher Education: A Literature Review of Practices and Implications. *Journal of Learning Development in Higher Education*, *27*(27). Advance online publication. doi:10.47408/jldhe.vi27.997

Vygotsky, L. S. (1978). *Mind in Society: the development of higher psychological processes*. NII. https://ci.nii.ac.jp/ncid/BA03570814

Wang, F., & Burton, J. K. (2012). Second Life in Education: A review of publications from its launch to 2011. *British Journal of Educational Technology*, *44*(3), 357–371. doi:10.1111/j.1467-8535.2012.01334.x

White, J., Fu, Q., Hays, S., Sandborn, M., Olea, C., Gilbert, H., Elnashar, A., Spencer-Smith, J., & Schmidt, D. C. (2023). *A Prompt Pattern catalog to enhance prompt engineering with ChatGPT*. arXiv (Cornell University). https://doi.org//arxiv.2302.11382 doi:10.48550

Xia, Q., Chiu, T. K. F., Zhou, X., Chai, C. S., & Cheng, M. (2023). Systematic literature review on opportunities, challenges, and future research recommendations of artificial intelligence in education. *Computers & Education: Artificial Intelligence*, *4*, 100118. doi:10.1016/j.caeai.2022.100118

Yang, T., & Chen, J. (2023). Pre-service teachers' perceptions and intentions regarding the use of chatbots through statistical and lag sequential analysis. *Computers & Education: Artificial Intelligence*, *4*, 100119. doi:10.1016/j.caeai.2022.100119

Yildirim-Erbasli, S. N., & Bulut, O. (2023). Conversation-based Assessment: A novel approach to boosting test-taking effort in digital formative assessment. *Computers & Education: Artificial Intelligence*, *4*, 100135. doi:10.1016/j.caeai.2023.100135

Zhang, C., Schießl, J., Plößl, L., Hofmann, F., & Gläser-Zikuda, M. (2023). Acceptance of artificial intelligence among pre-service teachers: A multigroup analysis. *International Journal of Educational Technology in Higher Education*, *20*(1), 49. doi:10.1186/s41239-023-00420-7 PMID:36743849

Chapter 3
Empowering Educators With Generative AI Tools and Support

Sarinporn Chaivisit
https://orcid.org/0000-0002-0940-7232
Kasetsart University, Thailand

Tutaleni Iita Asino
Oklahoma State University, USA

Sukanda Jongsermtrakoon
https://orcid.org/0009-0004-0896-1671
Kasetsart University, Thailand

Penny Thompson
https://orcid.org/0000-0002-2877-9947
Oklahoma State University, USA

Fatemeh Rezaie
https://orcid.org/0009-0007-9986-3656
Oklahoma State University, USA

Sutithep Siripipattanakul
Kasetsart University, Thailand

ABSTRACT

This chapter explores possible ways educators can use generative AI tools and support to empower them in teaching and learning. In addition, the authord provide samples of appropriate prompts for educators to produce desired responses. With the potential of generative AI to create unique content instantly based on existing large datasets, educators can use it to co-create instructional content, enhance personalized learning experiences, evaluate learners' performances, and more. While highlighting the potential of generative AI, the authors also address the challenges that educators may face when using these tools. As generative AI is gaining popularity in classrooms, it has the potential to empower educators to revolutionize their teaching and transform education.

INTRODUCTION TO GENERATIVE AI

Since the invention of computers, humans have wondered how to push it further to augment human existence. Conversations on whether computers can think, and whether they will one day overtake humans, have been a subject of academic scholarship, science fiction, and various movies. The conversation gained further attention due to the works of luminaries such as Alan Turing, a mathematician whose work in computer science is often cited as the earliest work around Artificial Intelligence. Turing wondered that

DOI: 10.4018/979-8-3693-1351-0.ch003

if humans could use the information they have available to solve problems and make decisions, then why could it not be possible for machines? (Anyoha, 2017). Turing's wonderment may have remained just that at the time because, in the 1950s, computer capacity and capability were limited. This is no longer the case because technological advancements are making it possible to bring to life what scientists of yesteryears could only imagine. An example of this is the introduction of Chat Generative Pre-trained Transformer (ChatGPT) on 30th November 2022, a large language model-based chatbot developed by OpenAI that propelled the dialogue on generative AI into the everyday.

The rise of generative artificial intelligence (AI) has excited many because of its capability to create unique content using natural language processing and large language models (Bozkurt, 2023). These models are trained on large datasets and can understand, interpret, and generate human-like language with high accuracy (Kasneci, 2023; Su & Yang, 2023). Due to the advancement of technology, AI can be utilized in education through various techniques such as advising systems for educators, intelligent tutoring systems for learners, generating content systems, and adapting systems for individual users (Morel & Spector, 2022). Generative AI platforms can also be valuable co-creation technologies for educators to generate instructional content from appropriate prompts (Bozkurt & Sharma, 2023). By leveraging the potential of generative AI, educators can implement its tools and support to enhance education (Kasneci, 2023).

This chapter guides educators to acknowledge the benefits of generative AI tools and support as well as to use appropriate prompts for generating AI responses in teaching and learning. Despite the potential of generative AI, educators still lack knowledge on how to use it responsibly and successfully (Kasneci, 2023). Therefore, the chapter demonstrates opportunities and challenges of using generative AI as well as suggested suitable prompts that educators can use when communicating with generative AI. When educators incorporate generative AI in their teaching preparation and strategies through effective prompts, learners can benefit from the motivational content and effective instructional strategies that are produced. Generative AI can positively impact learning outcomes (Kadaruddin, 2023).

Definition of Generative AI

Generative AI is a subgroup of artificial intelligence (AI) that focuses on producing new content or data rather than analyzing and describing existing data (Chan, 2023). Generative AI has a model called Generative Pre-trained Transformers (GPT) which uses deep learning techniques to create natural language text. The model has been trained on a large dataset, such as websites, books, and articles. It can understand users' inputs and generate responses while maintaining meaningful conversations on a diverse range of topics (Chan & Hu, 2023). The latest models of generative AI are GPT-3.5 and GPT-4. They have the capability to perform intelligence tasks like humans do. The development of these generative AI models can revolutionize the world in various fields. For example, people can use these models to process natural language, generate content, and write creatively (Chan, 2023).

One sample of generative AI is ChatGPT which has led to high interest in higher education since its introduction in November 2002. ChatGPT is a natural language processing model developed by OpenAI in 2019. It is trained to follow a command in a prompt and deliver a detailed response (Open AI, 2022). ChatGPT uses a neural network that contains many layers and millions of parameters to generate text responses. When a user types a sentence or asks a question, the model tries to create a proper answer in reference to its learning from the training data (Moritz, 2023).

A Brief History of Generative AI in Education

The history of AI started in the 1950s with the development of Hidden Markov Models and Gaussian Mixture Models, which generated continuous data (e.g. time series and speech). At the beginning of deep generative models, natural language processing (NLP) learned how to distribute words using N-gram language modeling. The model searched for the finest sequences, but it could not adapt to long sentences effectively. Therefore, recurrent neural networks (RNNs) were introduced to solve this problem by allowing the model to connect longer sentences (Cao et al., 2018).

Generative AI has gained much attention in recent years. In 2014, Generative Adversarial Networks (GANs) were proposed for the first time. In addition, Variational Autoencoders (VAEs) and other methods such as diffusion generative models have been developed with the capability to produce high-quality images (Cao et al., 2018). The computer science community continues to show interest in multiple content-generation products that were created by large technology companies, such as the ChatGPT and DALL-E-2 bots developed by OpenAI. ChatGPT is a language model that can understand and respond to inputs from human language in a meaningful way. In the same fashion, DALL-E-2 is a state-of-the-art generative AI model that has the ability to create high-quality and unique images from human inputs with textual descriptions.

While generative AI has increased in popularity, it has also introduced concerns and challenges in academia. One leading concern is it can be used for cheating when learners use generative AI to complete assignments and tests. This caused some institutions in the U.S. to ban its operation on campus. In addition, generative AI developers aim to ensure that educators and learners can benefit from utilizing AI (Okaiyeto, Bai, & Xiao, 2023).

Trends of Generative AI and How It Transforms Education

While researchers have been using generative AI tools known as GPTs within academic circles since 2018, the official introduction of ChatGPT in 2022 as a free-access and user-friendly platform opened the opportunity for virtually anyone with internet access to engage with and experiment using this tool. ChatGPT's intelligent conversational capabilities, emulating authentic human interactions and information retrieval swiftly captured global attention. In just five days, it amassed one million users, and within approximately two months, that number surged to 100 million. This rapid adoption demonstrates the unparalleled global fascination with ChatGPT. This phenomenon has rarely been witnessed in recent history regarding the embrace of new technologies. (Lim et al., 2023; Milmo, 2023; Hu, 2003; Open AI, n.d.; UNESCO, 2023).

The emergence of ChatGPT, along with its capabilities, has sparked people's interest in understanding what generative AI is and what it can do. It's becoming evident that generative AI can do more than just mimic human-like responses. For instance, there's DALL-E, a text-to-image generative AI model developed by OpenAI, which shares a similar user interaction pattern with ChatGPT. When users input prompts into the system, it generates images based on the text descriptions provided. This showcases how Generative AI can produce a diverse range of outputs within the realm of deep learning, a subset of machine learning that aims to emulate the human brain's functioning in responding to incoming data (Open AI, n.d.; Lim et al., 2023).

The surge in interest has been followed by the practical applicability of generative AI in various industries, marking the advent of a new era. This new wave of innovation is transforming many sectors, education included. Generative AI, a type of artificial intelligence, is capable of autonomously generating content when provided with prompts through natural language interfaces. It achieves this by creating content that closely resembles the data it was trained on. The process involves a profound statistical analysis of the assimilated data, including word frequencies, pixel distributions, and other foundational patterns. It focuses on recognizing and replicating prevalent patterns. Consequently, the generated content encompasses a wide range of human cognitive representations, spanning from textual compositions and visual imagery, like photos and digital illustrations, to audiovisual content and software code. (Aydin & Karaarslan, 2023; UNESCO, 2023).

Generative AI Tools and Support to Empower Educators

Implementing Generative AI in education requires significant preparation from educators. This preparation involves understanding various applications of Generative AI, such as promoting personalized learning and adaptive learning, providing real-time feedback and assessment, and overcoming language barriers. Educators must also be aware of the ethical considerations related to using generative AI and be prepared to establish appropriate policies (Alasadi & Baiz, 2023). However, one factor that causes educators to be hesitant in using generative AI is their resistance to embracing new technology that significantly deviates from traditional methods. There needs to be a shift in mindset to facilitate acceptance of these changes and to impart knowledge and skills in using generative AI (Villarreal et al., 2023). Educators' readiness might be incomplete if they are not well-acquainted with different types of generative AI tools. In this context, we explored various generative AI tools that empower educators.

Generative AI has gained widespread popularity and global attention, primarily due to ChatGPT's ability to autonomously create text content, and operate differently from conventional AI technology found in search engines. When we enter a query containing keywords in a search engine, it processes the data and presents information gathered from various sources in a sequential order based on relevance or search criteria. In contrast, generative AI, which is a text-to-text model, works differently. Instead of processing and presenting existing human-created content for selection, it processes data to generate singular content focused on enhancing convenience by assisting in tasks such as answering questions and explaining or summarizing specific information. It can be employed to aid various forms of writing, including designing lesson plans, crafting essays, poems, scripts, and even code. Additionally, these models possess the capability to translate written content into different languages with ease and fluency (Lim et al., 2023; UNESCO, 2023; Villarreal et al., 2023).

However, generative AI goes beyond the creation of textual content. It can generate various forms of content by learning from a diverse range of existing information and resources derived from its training data. This includes generating images, videos, audio files, presentations, or even websites using natural language processing to analyze user input and create content that conveys a message engagingly and comprehensively (Wepik, 2023). Generative AI in these categories, which creates diverse forms of resources, provides educators with tools to create learning materials according to their needs. From a research perspective, there are tools that not only assist in proposing outlines and generating research ideas but also summarize key insights from various documents, providing educators with concise information to streamline the selection of relevant data, making their work faster and more efficient (Gil, 2023; UNESCO, 2023). In the following sections, we delved into the opportunities for educators to use various generative AI tools and support.

OPPORTUNITIES OF USING GENERATIVE AI TOOLS AND SUPPORT IN EDUCATION

This section highlights the opportunities that educators can utilize generative AI tools and support to transform education. The opportunities are as follows: (1) brainstorming support, (2) creating educational content, (3) providing feedback on instructional practices, (4) enhancing personalized learning experiences, (5) improving learners' engagement, (6) supporting learners in real-time, (7) evaluating learners' performances, (8) improving learners' performance and (9) providing data analysis and research.

Brainstorming Support

There are opportunities that educators can use generative AI to assist them in brainstorming ideas for writing (Creely et al., 2023) and drafting lesson plans (Bailey, 2023; Creely et al., 2023). Creely et al. (2023) give a sample that generative AI can come up with ten to twenty ideas for specific tasks or inquiries. Educators can look through the ideas and select ones that are appropriate to their evaluative judgment. In writing, educators can use generative AI to plan for an essay by suggesting ideas and drafting content. In addition, they can use generative AI to give feedback and proofread papers.

Besides writing, AI can assist educators or preservice educators by drafting lesson plans (Bailey, 2023; Creely et al., 2023). However, an AI-generated lesson plan may have very prescriptive steps (Creely et al., 2023). Brisk Teaching (www.briskteaching.com) is one of the early companies to offer AI services specifically for educators. It can do different tasks such as drafting lesson plans, writing curriculum, giving learners feedback, and detecting AI writing on learners' work (Bailey, 2023; Brisk, 2023).

Creating Educational Content

Humans appreciate generative AI due to its potential to create new content such as text, images, audio, and video. Even though generative AI can create content like humans do their jobs, it cannot replace humans. Indeed, it helps humans create something or solve problems beyond their efforts (Eapen et al., 2023). Compared to human digital competencies in digital content creation, AI prompt engineering can do various tasks such as developing educational content, integrating digital content, and programming (Korzynski et al., 2023).

From the diverse categories of tools presented above, it proves that educators have a wide range of tools at their disposal to empower various aspects of education, such as teaching and resource development, including websites. Educators must choose the appropriate tools to align with their specific work objectives.

Table 1. Text generative AI tools

Tools	Ability/Function
ChatGPT (chat.openai.com)	Originally fulfilling requests for text-related tasks such as answering questions, composing songs, writing essays. Now it can incorporate images into its responses for visual conversations. Additionally, it can engage in natural voice interactions, enhancing its versatility (OpenAI, n.d.; OpenAI, 2003).
Bing Chat (bing.com)	Providing comprehensive responses to complex queries and commands. It can generate text-based answers or spreadsheets while also offering images, additional links, school web pages, and more to fulfill your information needs (Microsoft, 2023).
Bard (bard.google.com)	Replying to messages or images by providing text-based responses and seamlessly connecting with various Google tools like Google Search, Google Spreadsheet, and Google Colab (Google, 2023).

Note: Other interesting tools include Jasper (jasper.ai), Pepercontent (peppercontent.io), etc.

Table 2. Image generative AI tools

Tools	Ability/Function
DALL-E (labs.openai.com)	Leveraging the power of AI to convert textual descriptions into highly realistic images and artwork, seamlessly transforming creative concepts from prompts into visually stunning representations (OpenAI, n.d.; Betker et al., 2023).
MidJourney (discord.gg/midjourney)	Generating images from texts in response to the "/imagine" prompt and then whatever you want in the Discord community, where members of Midjourney's Discord can view the resulting images (Holz, 2022).
Adobe Firefly (firefly.adobe.com)	Generating the highest-quality output, including beautiful images, text effects, and fresh color palettes, from simple text prompts. Creating entirely new content by drawing inspiration from reference images, facilitating quicker exploration of a wide array of possibilities (Adobe, n.d.).

Note: Other interesting tools include DreamStudio (beta.dreamstudio.ai), Alpaca (alpacaml.com), NightCafe (creator.nightcafe.studio), Craiyon (craiyon.com), Gencraft (gencraft.com), etc.

Table 3. Video generative AI tools

Tools	Ability/Function
Steve AI (steve.ai)	Creating videos using a variety of methods, such as AI Text to Video Converter, Repurposing Blogs into Videos with AI, AI Voice to Video Generator, and producing both live videos from images or clips of various situations, and animated videos. Users have the flexibility to further customize their videos as desired (Steve AI, 2003).
Deepbrain AI (deepbrain.io)	Creating videos from a script, transforming text into a video in just 5 minutes, using hyper-realistic 2D or 3D AI avatars capable of speaking in multiple languages, including English, Chinese, Spanish, and many more, totaling over 80 languages (Deepbrain AI, 2003).
Synthesia (synthesia.io)	Generating videos from text within minutes, complete with natural human-like voiceovers available in over 120 languages from around the world. Choose from a library of more than 140 AI avatars or create your very own for use in your videos. (Synthesis, 2023).

Note: Other interesting tools include Elai (elai.io), Pictory (pictory.ai), Flexclip AI (flexclip.com), GliaCloud (gliacloud.com), etc.

In addition to the generative AI tools mentioned in tables 1-6, which encompass text image, video, audio/music, and presentation creation, Generative AI also possesses the ability to create various other tools. For instance, it aids in coding with tools like Tabnine (tabnine.com), OpenAI Codex (openai.com/blog/openai-codex), GitHub Copilot (github.com/features/copilot), or Source AI (sourceai.dev). It also extends to the domain of audio/video transcription tools, with examples including OpenAI Whisper (openai.com/research/whisper) or Happy Scribe (happyscribe.com).

Table 4. Voice/Audio/Music Generative AI Tools

Tools	Ability/Function
PlayHT (play.ht)	Creating voice from text, in the form of Text to Speech. It is available in over 140 languages with natural-sounding voices. Users can choose from a diverse range of AI voices, including various female and male options. Additionally, it is possible to clone high-quality voices with 99% accuracy to their real human counterparts (PlayHT, 2023).
Speechify (speechify.com)	Turning any written text into spoken words in natural-sounding language with multilingual support, Generative AI reading voices integrated into websites or documents, such as Google Docs, Microsoft Word, and even PDF files, serve as valuable tools for educators (Speechify, 2023).
Soundraw (soundraw.io)	Generating unique and beautiful songs effortlessly. Simply choose the mood, genre, and desired length. Customizing the song to meet your specific requirements (Soundraw, n.d.).

Note: Other interesting tools include LOVO (lovo.ai), Replica (replicastudios.com), Boomy (boomy.com), VoiceMod (voicemod.net), AIVA (aiva.ai) etc.

Table 5. Presentation generative AI tools

Tools	Ability/Function
Gamma (gamma.app)	Building stunning presentation decks automatically with beautiful templates by simply providing a short description within minutes, using an easy-to-use tool that offers quick customization. Moreover, effortlessly create documents or webpages as well (Gamma, 2022).
Wepik (wepik.com)	Generating a professional presentation in minutes, effortlessly designing top-notch slides by simply entering the topic, and selecting a style. Accessing resources from the Freepik and Flaticon libraries, along with editing tools for easy modifications (Wepik, 2023).
Simplified (simplified.com)	Generating and designing presentations with content including fonts, text, colors, images, and sound, based on specified topics or outlines. These presentations can be further customized and then published online or downloaded as PDF files or videos (Simplified, 2023).

Note: Other interesting tools include Beautiful.ai (beautiful.ai), Tome (tome.app), SlideAI (slidesai.io), Sendsteps (sendsteps.com), Plus AI (plusdocs.com), Slidesgo AI Presentation Maker (slidesgo.com), etc.

Table 6. Website generative AI tools

Tools	Ability/Function
UIzard (uizard.io)	Generating user interface designs from text prompts, converting hand-drawn sketches into wireframes, and transforming screenshots into editable designs with drag-and-drop components. These designs can be turned into prototypes within minutes, allowing for diverse creations such as startup landing pages, website wireframes, productivity apps, and mobile app wireframes (UIzard, 2023).
Framer (framer.com)	Creating a website from a raw idea in seconds. Mixing and matching display fonts, text fonts, and color palettes to establish a customized theme for the site or simply shuffling through unique combinations. Additionally, benefit from a built-in copywriter to enhance more creative content on your pages (Framer, 2023).
Durable (durable.co)	Creating a website with artificial intelligence that automatically incorporates professional images and icons. Customizing the appearance of the site and adding built-in components without the need to write code. Generating SEO-friendly pages and optimizing the site for search engines (Durable, 2023).

Note: Other interesting tools include CodeDesign (codedesign.ai), Bookmark (bookmark.com), Hostinger (hostinger.com), etc.

Providing Feedback on Instructional Practices

One little-explored potential of generative AI is its capacity to provide automated feedback to instructors to help them improve professional practice. Su & Yang (2023) described an example of how ChatGPT could be used as a personal tutor to provide feedback to educators on their instructional practices. In their example, instructional coaches observed early childhood teachers and input their observations into ChatGPT to generate feedback on the classroom interactions they observed. They note that this was not done to replace the professional judgment of the instructional coach, but rather to support their work. In their context ChatGPT helped the coach identify missed opportunities and suggested specific activities the teacher might use to fill those gaps. Wang & Demszky (2023) explored a similar use of ChatGPT by asking it to score transcripts of interactions from elementary mathematics classrooms. They asked ChatGPT to "identify highlights and missed opportunities for good instructional strategies" and to "provide actionable suggestions for eliciting more learner reasoning" (p. 2). They found that although the analysis provided by ChatGPT generated suggestions that were "actionable and faithfully interpret[ed] the teaching context" (p. 2), they did not correlate well with the assessment of human coaches and were viewed as "not insightful or relevant" (p. 2) in many cases. Despite these disappointing results, Wang & Demszky conclude that further development of generative AI technology could allow it to fill this role more effectively in the future. In order to realize the potential of generative AI to provide instructors with feedback on their instructional practices, it may be necessary for developers of this technology to include input from educators, whose voices have so far been neglected in the design and development of AI technologies (Celik et al., 2022).

Enhancing Personalized Learning Experiences

One significant role of AI in education is its use in analyzing individual learners through various AI tools. These tools help in analyzing specific details of learners' learning outcomes, identifying strengths, and highlighting areas where improvement is needed. They also provide insights into individual learners' abilities and specific learning needs, enabling the customization of learning experiences that are suitable for each learner in terms of adaptive learning and are personalized to their unique requirements.

When considering the use of generative AI specifically, it requires educators to input prompts tailored to individual learning needs. This ensures the application of generative AI in promoting personalized and adaptive learning experiences. For example, educators can provide prompts to Generative AI to design a computer science curriculum that aligns with the main objectives. However, the curriculum may include project details that require learners to apply their knowledge and skills in diverse ways, which can vary from one individual to another. Besides guiding the curriculum design, Generative AI can also assist in creating learning materials that cater to the unique learning styles of each learner. Learners can pursue the main curriculum objectives, but their learning experiences differ, not only in terms of learning methods but also in accessing learning materials tailored to their individual needs. This approach promotes learners to achieve personalized learning outcomes that align with their specific requirements, resulting in improved learning results (Alasadi & Baiz, 2023; Kadaruddin, 2023).

Nevertheless, the use of Generative AI that relies on detailed prompts for personalized learning may still have limitations, particularly when learners possess various dimensions that are not fully addressed in the prompt. For instance, aspects such as learning style, preferences, or unique challenges may not be comprehensively covered. These are elements that educators must study and understand through diverse methods when working with their learners (Villarreal et al., 2023).

Improving Learners' Engagement

The themes and ideas that surface most often in the literature about learner engagement are embedded in collaboration, integrated technology, inquiry-based learning, assessment for learning, and making learning interdisciplinary and relevant to real life (Taylor & Parsons, 2011). Therefore, the use of generative AI technology improves learners' engagement by creating new learning experiences and offers educators new opportunities to create dynamic and inclusive virtual classrooms (Ruiz-Rojas et al., 2023). Individual learner's data is customized to better suit the needs and preferences of learners. It is considered a strategy for creating a participatory teaching process that focuses on intelligent interaction with learners. For example, educators can use a chatbot to act as a teaching assistant or content expert to create learning content.

Therefore, generative AI helps to create a bond with learners which, then, creates a desire to learn even more. In addition, it strengthens the learning drive of learners by providing a dynamic environment with real-time interaction. Generative AI can play roles such as simulator, advisor, coach, and trainer. It can provide frequent feedback, personalized instructions and explanations, alternative viewpoints, and opportunities to practice through simulations (Alavi & Westerman, 2023). As a result, learners have new learning experiences all the time.

Generative AI can be used to advance teaching and learning (Gunn & Hollingsworth, 2012). The following examples demonstrate how generative AI can improve learners' engagement.

- Personalized Tutoring: ChatGPT can be used to provide personalized tutoring, immediate feedback, and expanded information access to learners based on their individual learning needs and progress (Javaid et al., 2023).
- Automated Essay Grading: ChatGPT can be trained to grade learner essays, providing educators with more time to focus on other aspects of teaching.
- Language Translation: ChatGPT can be used for translating educational materials into various languages, which gives a wider audience access to those materials.
- Interactive Learning: ChatGPT can be used to create interactive learning experiences where learners can interact with a virtual tutor conversationally.
- Adaptive Learning: ChatGPT can be used to create adaptive learning systems that adjust their teaching methods based on a learner's progress and performance.

In addition, Generative AI supports engagement, critical thinking, and inquiry-based learning through applications like intelligent tutoring, virtual teaching assistants, and intelligent feedback systems, aligning with educational goals and learner-centered instruction, including enhanced instructional support, personalized learning experiences, time efficiency, and access to educational resources (Carr, 2023).

Supporting Learners in Real-Time

For learners to improve their learning, it is essential to receive feedback on what they have learned and practiced. Artificial intelligence systems can assist in assessment and provide real-time feedback, enabling learners to understand their learning progress and obtain feedback for individualized learning improvement (Alasadi & Baiz, 2023). Generative AI can be applied to support real-time learning as follows (du Boulay, 2015):

1. Inquiry: Generative AI gives learners access to an endless world of information to be explored at any time online in digestible formats, tailored exactly to their specific questions, interests, and needs. Learners can engage in conversations to deep dive into a topic of their interest, ask for summaries of articles and research, and let their curiosity flow in never-ending ways.
2. Ideation: Generative AI provides suggestions and ideas, and helps users to brainstorm given topics or challenges. It can provide for a giant crowd curation of possibilities through different formats and perspectives which can inspire learners and spark creative thinking. Also, it can stimulate learners to think differently through novel, unexpected, or unconventional perspectives.
3. Language and comprehension support: Generative AI helps learners develop their reading and writing skills by providing feedback on written texts and helping summarize complex texts which may be hard to understand. For example, by analyzing a learner's writing, Generative AI can provide suggestions for improving grammar, syntax, and word choice. This can help learners become better writers and improve their overall academic performance and confidence. In addition, Alasadi & Baiz (2023) assert that Generative AI can significantly support learners who are from diverse linguistic backgrounds. AI tools can be employed in various ways, including automatic language translation and content reorganization into the target language. This approach ensures learners with different language backgrounds have equal access to learning opportunities, and it promotes inclusivity and equal learning experiences.
4. Adaptive learning: Generative AI acts as a personal tutor by responding to specific questions, providing feedback to work, making suggestions for improvements, and providing tools to develop critical and problem-solving skills. Adaptive tutoring systems have shown mixed results on learners' learning so far and their effectiveness depending on a range of factors, such as the quality of the instructional materials, the design of the system, and the context in which it is used (du Boulay, 2015).

Evaluating Learners' Performance

The learning expectation is to build learner competencies. How can we know that learners have a competency that meets the needs of stakeholders and the teaching program? Evaluation is an important part that reflects whether learning outcomes are following the teaching program and learning objectives. The application of generative AI technology can help create measurement tools. It can help with a variety of assessments such as tests, written-answer questions, multiple choice, true-false, matching, etc. The assessment of AI in Education (AIED) provides more formative feedback based on a sophisticated diagnosis of learner understanding, engagement, and academic integrity (Zawacki-Richter et al., 2019). AI in the education field, in particular, is assessing learners' performance and improvement. AI-aided analysis of learners' performance in online learning platforms to make inferences about learners' performances relates to complex cognitive skills within learning activities (Dhara et al., 2022).

Although AI has been used for assessment in the past, the availability of generative AI makes this tool more widely available to educators and learners. Mao et al. (2023) propose several potential contributions of AI for authentic and meaningful assessments. They suggest that generative AI can (1) facilitate the development of adaptive simulations for authentic assessment of higher order thinking and processes, (2) enable efficient automated grading, which can free up educator time for more meaningful interaction, (3) provide adaptive assessments for a personalized learning path with targeted feedback, and (4) improve access to accessibility tools (e.g., text-to-speech, etc.) to make digital assessments more available to more learners. Despite these advantages, they acknowledge risks of generative AI in the form of academic integrity concerns (i.e., it may be difficult to identify text that was generated by AI rather than written by the learner), concerns about learner privacy and security, and the risk that AI can magnify the bias already present in current assessment methods, given that automated output may be perceived as objective despite being trained with a biased data set. They conclude that in order to reap the potential benefits of generative AI and minimize its risks, both educators and learners will need high levels of digital literacy with respect to generative AI.

Improving Learners' Performance

Generative AI can help improve learner performance by helping evaluate learning outcomes. The learning progress of learners is continuously recorded, and generative AI responds by giving feedback to learners. This lets learners know that they need to improve their knowledge, and what skills are needed.

Gupta (2023) describes generative AI tools that positively impact learner performance as follows:

- Generative AI tools can help developing learners' performance so that they can generate ideas and content more quickly and efficiently. This can help learners to save time and concentrate on other academic activities such as research and analysis.
- Improve their writing skills. Generative AI tools can help learners improve their writing skills by giving them feedback and suggesting ways to improve grammar, writing style, and clarity. Learners can become better communicators and writers from reviewing feedback.
- Study new concepts and skills more effectively. Generative AI tools can help learners study new concepts and skills more effectively by providing interactive tutorials, simulations, and other educational resources. Learners can simply understand complex content and remember information for a long time.
- Stay organized and on track. Generative AI tools can help learners to organize and keep them on track by offering reminders, to-do lists, and other productivity tools. Learners can manage their time well and stay away from procrastination.

In summary, the positive perspective of using Generative AI as a tool is that it can be used to build a variety of assessments and creatively evaluate learner performance. This can help improve their learning and strengthen new thinking skills, which helps stimulate learners to develop their own learning competency continuously. Generative AI will ultimately have positive effects on promoting people to be lifelong learners.

Providing Data Analysis and Research

Generative Artificial Intelligence provides unparalleled perspectives and insights to scholars. On occasion, this advanced technological intervention can catalyze seminal thought processes, culminating in novel discoveries or pioneering innovations (Alasadi & Baiz, 2023). Generative AI serves as a valuable research assistant, aiding in conceptualizing literature reviews, assisting in searching and presenting relevant articles, formulating hypotheses based on research questions within specific variables of interest, and even supporting data analysis and summarizing findings to guide researchers in further analysis and expansion of their outcomes (Villarreal et al., 2023).

Table 7. Summarizing documents generative AI tools

Tools	Ability/Function
Exlicit (elicit.com)	Searching for research papers based on topics or questions. Summarizing papers, extracting data, and synthesizing findings, condensing the key insights into a single line from the abstract. This tool also provides a list of citations to facilitate easy access to the original papers for further reading. Additionally, you can upload PDF files to generate summaries from the content (Exlicit, n.d.).
Explainpaper (explainpaper.com)	Analyzing research papers uploaded by users, allowing users to highlight confusing text for the AI to provide explanations and clarifications, and engaging in interactive conversations for further clarification on the aspects that are not well understood in the explanations (Explainpaper, n.d.).
ChatDOC (chatdoc.com)	Serving as a reading assistant that rapidly extracts, locates, and summarizes information from various document formats, including PDF, DOC, DOCX, MD, EPUB, TXT, websites, and even scanned files. It provides text-based answers with references that users can access to verify the accuracy of the information (ChatDOC, n.d.).

Note: Other interesting tools include Humata (humata.ai), ChatPDF (chatpdf.com), Perplexity (perplexity.ai), etc.

APPROPRIATE PROMPTS FOR DESIRED RESPONSES

What is Prompt Engineering?

Prompt engineering is concerned with accuracy and effectiveness so that generative AI tools can produce better output. A vignette from consulting firm McKinsey & Company (2023) provides a good illustrative example.

Let's say you're making spaghetti marinara for dinner. Sauce from a jar is perfectly fine. But what if you buy your tomatoes and basil from the farmers market to make your own sauce? Chances are it will taste a lot better. And what if you grow your own ingredients from your garden and make your own fresh pasta? A whole new level of deliciousness. Just as better ingredients can make for a better dinner, better inputs into a generative AI model can make for better results. These inputs are called prompts, and the practice of writing them is called prompt engineering.

As language models progress, proficient prompt engineering has become essential for users who want to fully utilize AI-empowered tools to attain the greatest outcomes possible in a variety of applications. The process of strategically creating, tuning, and enhancing input prompts to effectively communicate the user's intent to a language model is referred to as prompt engineering (Ekin, 2023). This approach serves as crucial for getting the model to respond in a precise, relevant, and cohesive manner. In order to get the desired outcomes, prompts must be modified and adjusted by users so they can come with the result they expect (Xiao & Zhi, 2023).

Types of Generative AI Prompts

There are different types of prompts that can be used for different purposes based on user intent, which can be text-to-text and text-to-image formats.

Question-Answer Prompt

Most common form of text-to-text prompt is simply questions and responses centered on certain topics. Question-answer prompts require either questions that are thoughtful, analytical, or complex problem-solving type answers versus those that can be answered quickly, intuitively, or through pattern recognition (Ekin, 2023). More effective output can be constructed by engineering the prompts in which a combination of two types of questions can be intertwined. In the same line, contextual prompts can be included in question-answer prompts for users if they need to focus on further specific aspects of their subject (Giray, 2023).

Prompt Examples: "What are the key challenges in Instructional designs for professional developments in corporate training?"

Feedback Prompts

Feedback prompts can offer users personalized instruction and feedback regarding their academic writing skills (Zhai, 2022). Prompts can also be in the form of comprehensive feedback to enhance the overall quality of the student's writing and more specifically in academic writing. It can cover areas in which users ask for feedback on their writing sentence quality, idea development, language precision, appropriate transitional phrases, and grammatical accuracy (Farrokhnia et al., 2023), with specific feedback on casual or formal tones, shortened and expanded length of the text (Yeo, 2023).

Prompt example: "I am a Graduate Research Assistant. I need feedback on a paper I am writing for a Instructional systems design course. It covers instructional design models. Here are my first few paragraphs."

Summary/Knowledge Mining Prompts

One of the most effective prompts engineered is to summarize papers and articles. Based on user intent, it can range from summarizing texts, identifying research gaps, to describing employed methods. By providing the AI tool with a well-crafted summary prompt, users can quickly browse numerous summarized articles and receive in-depth excerpts from multiple publications (Irvine et al., 2023).

Prompt example: "Give a brief summary of the article with the title "Title of the Article" that is attached, emphasizing the important points, supporting details, and arguments. Write no more than 150 words for your summary, emphasizing the author's viewpoint and the significance of the results. Employ language that is understandable and cohesive, and structure your summary into paragraphs."

Programming and Code Prompt

Beyond text-to-text prompts and text generation, AI code prompts are currently effective in code generation, bug prediction, debugging assistance, along with detailed explanation (Surameery & Shakor, 2023; Feng et al., 2023). Additionally, they efficiently offer answers to challenging programming problems and improve software development processes through their skillful code fixes (Irvine et al., 2023).

Prompt example: "You are provided with a snippet of R code for a function named calculate_sum. However, the code contains an error that needs correction. Review the code carefully and identify the issue affecting the conditional statement inside the function.Your task is to fix the bug and ensure that the calculate_sum function operates as intended. Pay attention to the correctness of the conditional statement and make any necessary adjustments. After making the fix, briefly explain the nature of the bug and describe the changes you implemented to resolve it. Additionally, provide a concise rationale for your modifications."

Figure 1. Code prompt

```r
# Existing code with a bug
calculate_sum <- function(a, b) {
  if a > b {
    return(a + b)
  } else {
    return(a - b)
  }
}

# Fixing the bug
calculate_sum <- function(a, b) {
  if (a > b) {
    return(a + b)
  } else {
    return(a - b)
  }
}
```

Text-to-Image Generation Prompt

Advances in computing have now arrived at a point where one can write a text prompt that allows a computer to generate an image. For example, a person can give the prompt of "cat chasing a dog" and the machine would produce a visual work that matches the prompt. With the AI text-to-image prompts, users can generate images and artwork through composing a thorough description expressing their intent (Dehouche & Dehouche, 2023). The input created for such prompts employs a machine learning (ML) model with a use of natural language (NL) to create images based on processing the provided description (Abdallah & Estévez, 2023).

Prompt examples: "digital illustration of a castle, renaissance aesthetics, mountain background, in two different seasons: summer and spring."

Figure 2. Images generated in stable diffusion XL
Note. Image generated from https://stablediffusionweb.com/

Mixed Prompt

Users can apply mixed prompts that combine multiple elements to guide them in a comprehensive manner.

Appropriate Prompts for Generative AI to Respond Successfully

Generative AI systems such as Bard, ChatGPT, and Claude 2 are easy to use. Generally, a user types a request or a "prompt," and then the generative AI interprets the request and generates a response according to the user's request. Therefore, appropriate prompts are important for receiving useful responses from generative AI tools (Bailey, 2023).

One strategy is to tell generative AI what type of expert a user wants it to be. For example, ask AI to be a skilled teacher, a copy editor, or a writing tutor, and then assign it a task (Bailey, 2023). In addition, Korzynski et al. (2023) recommend ways to create effective AI prompts with 'AIPROMT' recommendations involving:

A: Articulate the instruction clearly, such as 'clarify', 'write', 'summarize,' and identify the desired output such as list, table, or Python code.

I: Indicate the prompt elements by identifying the sources of the instructions and input data as well as the desired output format.

P: Provide editing cues and context. For example, ending sentences or words with 3 dots for continuation or typing a placeholder such as 'answer:' which means ChatGPT must provide a response.

R: Refine instructions to avoid ambiguity by giving specific instructions or details in order to prevent confusion.

O: Offer feedback and examples by providing the model with some expected responses or examples to help the model better understand the expected output.

M: Manage interaction by asking the model to provide criticism of the user's ideas.

T: Track token length and task complexity by controlling the length of the responses below the model's token limits and separating complex tasks into smaller processes for better performance.

In the same way, UNESCO (2023) recommends guidelines for setting the questions or prompts for AI content generation to ensure the desired output. These guidelines include:

1. Use clear, straightforward, and unambiguous language.
2. Provide examples of what you want to generate.
3. Offer relevant context.
4. Specify precise details.
5. Uphold ethical standards and avoid biases or harmful content.

Following these guidelines can help educators achieve the most relevant and appropriate results when utilizing Generative AI tools for their educational purposes.

Prompt Examples for Educators

Educators can search for prompt templates or appropriate prompts from an online library such as aiforeducation.io. and other resources. Examples of prompts are the following:

- Lesson planning: "Generate a lesson plan for [grade/subject] on [topic] that covers [standard(s)] lasts [desired duration of time] and includes reading materials, a video, and a way for students to demonstrate their learning." (AI for Education, 2023, para. 2)
- Suggesting learning tools: "Suggest specific digital platforms and tools for interactivity." (Lindsay et al., 2023, p. 2)
- Creating educational content: "Create engaging content for learning in a range of formats including textbooks, online elements and lecture notes." (Lindsay et al., 2023, p. 3)
- Improving learners' engagement: "Incorporate gamification or quizzes for motivation." (Lindsay et al., 2023, p. 2)
- Creating test questions: "Share some quiz questions suitable for assessing basic math skills in first graders" (Baker, 2023, para. 34)
- Giving feedback: "How can I provide encouraging feedback on a young child's artwork?" (Baker, 2023, para. 37)

- Educators can customise the provided prompts based on the context of their teaching and learning (Lindsay et al., 2023).

CHALLENGES OF USING GENERATIVE AI IN EDUCATION

Although generative AI provides enormous support in teaching and learning, educators may face some challenges or concerns about using generative AI in classrooms. These include concerns about developing competencies for using generative AI (Eke, 2023), accuracy (Chan & Hu, 2023; Eke, 2023; Ruiz-Rojas et al., 2023), and ethical implications (Chan & Hu, 2023; Eke, 2023; Kadaruddin, 2023; Su & Yang, 2023; Villarreal et al., 2023).

Developing Competencies for Using Generative AI

One challenge of using generative AI is a lack of understanding and awareness. If educators, administrators, and learners are not familiar with generative AI and its advantages, they may be unwilling to explore its capabilities. This problem is exacerbated by the lack of clear academic policies. For example, educators may not adopt ChatGPT for educational purposes because they don't have a framework for guiding them (Villarreal et al., 2023). Eke (2023) claims that there are several ways that AI text generators and ChatGPT can be integrated into educational activities such as teaching, assessment, and research. However, there is very low knowledge in academia to approach generative AI. Since generative AI is changing the world that learners are preparing for, it is essential for academic institutions to prepare learners to use generative AI responsibly and effectively. To do so, academic institutions need to embrace generative AI as an important part of teaching and research. For developing capacities in using generative AI tools, institutions should establish capacity building and training for both learners and staff to use generative AI tools effectively and ensure responsible use. Academic institutions should also provide necessary resources and support to both learners and staff which help them prevent possible risks on academic integrity. In addition, they should review policies related to academic integrity and essential changes to follow current AI possibilities and trends. Finally, they should work toward developing tools that are trusted and cost effective for recognizing possible dishonest utilization of AI tools in education globally (Eke, 2023).

Accuracy

The ability of generative AI to create content based on user-provided prompts stems from its training on vast datasets and resources from the internet. The positive aspect is that generative AI can tailor responses to user requests by drawing from a diverse pool of resources, coupled with its learning experiences. This empowers users to obtain content that meets their specific requirements. However, the quality and accuracy of the content generated by generative AI cannot always be guaranteed. Users must exercise caution and carefully review the information before using it, as its accuracy and suitability may vary (Villarreal et al., 2023). Some educators have concerns about the accuracy and reliability of generative AI tools, especially in complex subject fields (Ruiz-Rojas et al., 2023). Since the information that AI generates is not automatically checked for accuracy or validity, users may follow false information (Chan & Hu, 2023). For example, output from ChatGPT as an original work is not 100% correct, even though it can assist users with academic work. Users may easily pass incorrect information on to others. Therefore, users should check information provided by ChatGPT against other relevant sources to ensure their responsible uses of generative AI in academia (Ruiz-Rojas et al., 2023).

Ethical Implications

One topic of concern regarding academic integrity is the Text-to-Text model of generative AI, such as ChatGPT. These models possess the ability to generate text in a conversational manner like human interactions. Due to their widespread popularity and usage, there are concerns that learners may employ ChatGPT to complete assignments by copying responses without engaging in critical thinking. This raises issues related to cheating in assessments and even potential instances of plagiarism in academic work created by learners (Bailey, 2023; Villarreal et al., 2023). Eke (2023) asserts that "the first thing for academia to do is to identify the use of AI generated texts without acknowledgement as part of academic dishonesty" (p. 3). To clarify this, academic integrity policies should be made clearer for learners and staff to have awareness of violation in original work from AI generated texts. In addition, for universities to offer the essay as the current assessment method, they should use a reliable tool to detect whether learners create texts using generative AI. However, building a tool will require a massive amount of funding and support of OpenAI or other developers (Eke, 2023). Eke (2023) suggests thatusers who want to maintain academic integrity while waiting for a tool to check AI generated text should reference sources that AI generates with the date and the prompts used, and should limit length of direct quotation within a paragraph. In addition, Eke (2023) recommends including oral interviews as a major part of the assessment, which will give an opportunity to test learners' knowledge.

SUMMARY

This book chapter explored ways to empower educators through generative AI tools and support. Due to the excitement of emerging technology on generative AI that can create innovative ideas and artifacts, educators can take advantage of this intelligent technology to transform education. We present both opportunities and challenges for educators to use generative AI in classrooms. We also suggest good prompts for educators to use generative AI effectively and make the most of its potential to empower educators in teaching and learning.

Generative AI Tools for Empowering Educators

Many educators and educational organizations are showing interest in and experimenting with the application of generative AI in various dimensions of education. We conclude that generative AI can be a teaching assistant that helps educators perform their routine tasks, create instructional materials, and design diverse and creative learning experiences.

Handling Routine Tasks

Text-to-text Generative AI models can significantly ease the everyday workload of educators, particularly in tasks like providing various suggestions in commonly asked questions. This allows educators to allocate more time to higher-level responsibilities, such as facilitating discussions, exchanging ideas, or fostering analytical thinking in learners. Furthermore, it supports personalized learning by delivering feedback and insights that educators need to continuously study and track the progress of their learners (Villarreal et al., 2023).

Creating Learning Materials and Suggesting Supplementary Resources

Generative AI exhibits a remarkable ability to create diverse types of content. While ChatGPT is a well-known example of Generative AI, numerous other tools serve a variety of educational purposes effectively. Experts at the eLearning Innovation Center of Universitat Oberta de Catalunya have extensively researched and summarized information about some of the most valuable Generative AI tools for educators across different domains. These experts have studied and compiled information about the most useful Generative AI tools for teaching staff in various areas. Apart from tools focused on writing and analysis tasks, there is another category of tools capable of generating diverse learning materials. These tools include those for creating presentations, audio transcription, generating images or videos from text, and transcribing YouTube videos (Gil, 2023; Kadaruddin, 2023).

Generative AI not only facilitates the creation of diverse learning materials but also provides valuable recommendations for supplementary learning resources. This allows learners to access in-depth information, expand upon the classroom's core learning materials, and provide additional explanations on the topics covered in the primary course materials (Villarreal et al, 2023). Such tools can significantly reduce the time educators spend producing learning resources, allowing them to dedicate more time to essential tasks and the development of learners in various aspects.

Designing Diverse and Creative Learning Experiences

Leveraging generative AI to assist educators in designing diverse and creative learning experiences, does not imply that generative AI is responsible for designing learning activities that educators implement immediately. Instead, it refers to the possibility for educators to allow generative AI to propose teaching ideas. Educators can then customize the specifics of the prompt to generate activities that are varied and innovative. These activities can be chosen and adapted by learners to align with their teaching plans. For instance, educators may desire generative AI to present scenarios or challenges to enhance decision-making skills or to evaluate learners. Educators can utilize generative AI to propose a wide array of situations, each unique and creative. Encountering diverse and distinct challenges helps learners sharpen their analytical and creative thinking skills effectively. Additionally, using scenarios comparable to real-life situations stimulates learners' motivation to learn (Villarreal et al, 2023).

Opportunities and Challenges for Using Generative AI

Based on research, generative AI can assist educators in many ways (Chan & Hu, 2023; Kadaruddin, 2023; Ruiz-Rojas et al., 2023). For example, it generates dynamic and interactive content that engages learners and makes education more effective, immersive, and engaging (Kadaruddin, 2023; Ruiz-Rojas et al., 2023). It gives summaries of learners' individual progress and information about their learning paces, strengths, and weaknesses so that educators can deliver appropriate teaching activities to suit individual learners. (Kadaruddin, 2023). Educators can also use generative AI to provide immediate feedback for learners as a tutor to reduce the workload of answering questions. (Chan & Hu, 2023). In evaluation and assessment, educators can use generative AI to evaluate learners' performances by analyzing their responses, assessing understanding, and providing personalized feedback in real-time (Ruiz-Rojas et al., 2023). In addition, generative AI can equip educators to design learning and teaching activities, which saves time for educators to prepare lessons and instructional materials (Ruiz-Rojas et al., 2023). The assistance from generative AI can help educators prepare for classes and engage learners through innovative teaching strategies. Ultimately, the empowerment from generative AI can impact learners' outcomes, which have the capability to transform education. (Kadaruddin, 2023).

Besides the advantages of using generative AI in education, it is important to address the potential challenges that educators may encounter while using these tools. By acknowledging the possible negative consequences, educators can implement generative AI tools in a responsible manner and make wise decisions when it comes to using these tools in classrooms. The common concern about generative AI in education is cheating. Learners may use generative to take quizzes or solve problems on homework. They can also use AI to generate essays, which threaten learning. Learners may not learn the needed content and skills (Bailey, 2023; Villarreal et al., 2023). Through responsible integration and collaborative efforts among educators, technologists, policymakers, and stakeholders; generative AI can be a driving force in enhancing educators to deliver the right instructional practices for unlocking learners' full potential and transforming education (Kadaruddin, 2023; Ruiz-Rojas et al., 2023).

Appropriate Prompts for Desired Responses

In order to get desired responses, educators should provide clear instruction by using words such as clarify, write, or summarize; then identify the expected output such as list or table. Prompts should be specific, in details, or illustrate examples in order to avoid confusion. Finally, educators should control the length of the responses under the limit or separate prompts into smaller pieces in order to get better performance (Korzynski et al, 2023; UNESCO, 2023).

Recommendations for Educators and Institutions

The growing integration of generative AI in the field of education, despite its apparent advantages, has given rise to concerns among specific learner groups regarding potential negative influences on the learning experience and its results. While certain institutions have implemented measures to restrict the utilization of AI tools, there are educational establishments that acknowledge the significance of these advancements and their potential advantages. As a result, there is an increasing trend towards formulating guidelines and policies to ensure the ethical and efficient deployment of generative AI tools in education. These policies should consider the appropriate and mindful use of Generative AI tools, acknowledging academic integrity, data privacy, algorithmic bias, and ethical considerations. These policies should involve stakeholders at various levels, including educational institutions, staff, faculty, educators, and learners (Alasadi & Baiz, 2023; UNESCO, 2023; Villarreal et al. 2023). Educational institutions should establish training sessions in generative AI tools for both staff and learners in order to use AI tools effectively and responsibly. They should provide essential resources and support that can prevent learners from possible risks of academic integrity. In order to reflect current AI possibilities and trends, they should review and update their academic integrity policies. Eventually, they should develop and implement trusted and cost effective tools that can determine dishonest use of AI tools that can occur (Eke,

2023). It is essential to note that people should use generative AIs like ChatGPT with responsibility. The society should ensure that generative AIs are employed effectively and ethically (Moritz, 2023).

In conclusion, this book chapter demonstrates ways to empower educators through generative AI tools and support. Due to the excitement of emerging technology on generative AI that can create innovative ideas and artifacts, educators can take advantage of this intelligent technology to transform education. The opportunities for educators to use generative AI tools to transform education are the following: brainstorming ideas, creating educational content, providing feedback on instructional practices, enhancing personalized learning experiences, improving learners' engagement, supporting learners in real-time, evaluating and improving learners' performances, and providing data analysis and research. Nevertheless, educators may face some challenges in using generative AI, these include competencies in using generative AI, accuracy, and ethical implications. In addition, the chapter explains how to write good prompts for educators to use generative AI effectively and make the most of its potential to empower educators in teaching and learning.

REFERENCES

Abdallah, Y. K., & Estévez, A. T. (2023). Biomaterials Research-Driven Design Visualized by AI Text-Prompt-Generated Images. *Designs*, *7*(2), 48. doi:10.3390/designs7020048

Adobe. (2003). *Adobe Firefly: Your imagination's new best friend.* Adobe. https://www.adobe.com/sensei/generative-ai/firefly.html

AI for Education. (2023). *Simple Lesson Plan Prompt.* AI for Education. https://www.aiforeducation.io/prompts/lesson-plans

Alasadi, E., & Baiz, C. (2023). Generative AI in Education and Research: Opportunities, Concerns, and Solutions. *Journal of Chemical Education*, *100*(8), 2965–2971. doi:10.1021/acs.jchemed.3c00323

Alavi, M., & Westerman, G. (2023). How Generative AI Will Transform Knowledge Work. *Harvard Business Review.* https://hbr.org/2023/11/how-generative-ai-will-transform-knowledge-work

Anyoha, R. (2017). The history of artificial intelligence. *Science News*, 28.

Aydin, O., & Karaarslan, E. (2023). Is Chat GPT Leading Generative AI? What is Beyond Expectation? *Journal of Engineering and Smart Systems*, *11*(3), 118–134.

Bailey, J. (2023). AI in Education. *Education Next*, *23*(4), 28–35.

Baker, J. (2023). *65+ Best ChatGPT Prompts for Teachers: Enhance Classroom Experience.* Splash Learn. https://www.splashlearn.com/blog/chat-gpt-prompts-for-teachers/#4-9-best-chatgpt-prompts-for-assessment-and-evaluation-

Betker. (2023). *Improving Image Generation with Better Captions.* CDN. https://cdn.openai.com/papers/dall-e-3.pdf

Bozkurt, A. (2023). Generative AI, Synthetic Contents, Open Educational Resources (OER), and Open Educational Practices (OEP): A New Front in the Openness Landscape. *Open Praxis*, *15*(3), 178–184. doi:10.55982/openpraxis.15.3.579

Bozkurt, A., & Sharma, R. C. (2023). Generative AI and prompt engineering: The art of whispering to let the genie out of the algorithmic world. *Asian Journal of Distance Education*, *18*(2), i–vii. doi:10.5281/zenodo.8174941

Brisk. (2023). *The easiest AI tool for teachers.* Brisk. https://www.briskteaching.com/

Cao, Y., Li, S., Liu, Y., Yan, Z., Dai, Y., Yu, P. S., & Sun, L. (2023). *A Comprehensive Survey of AI-Generated Content (AI): A History of Generative AI from GAN to ChatGPT.*

Celik, I., Dindar, M., Muukkonen, H., & Järvelä, S. (2022). The Promises and Challenges of Artificial Intelligence for Teachers: A Systematic Review of Research. *TechTrends*, *66*(4), 616–630. doi:10.1007/s11528-022-00715-y

Chan, C. K. Y. (2023). A comprehensive AI policy education framework for university teaching and learning. *International Journal of Educational Technology in Higher Education*, *20*(1), 1–25. doi:10.1186/s41239-023-00408-3

Chan, C. K. Y., & Hu, W. (2023). Students' Voices on Generative AI: Perceptions, Benefits, and Challenges in Higher Education. *arXiv preprint arXiv:2305.00290.*

ChatDOC. (n.d.). *ChatDOC: Chat with documents. Get instant answers with cited sources.* https://chatdoc.com

Creely, E., Apps, T., Beckman, K., & McKnight, L. (2023). Chat About ChatGPT. *Literacy Learning: The Middle Years*, *31*(2), 35–39.

David Baidoo-Anu1, D. and Ansah, L. O. (2023). Education in the Era of Generative Artificial Intelligence (AI): Understanding the Potential Benefits of ChatGPT in Promoting Teaching and Learning. *Journal of AI, 7*(1), 52-62.

Deepbrain, A. I. (2003). *Creating generative AI videos with just a script.* https://www.deepbrain.io

Dehouche, N., & Dehouche, K. (2023). What's in a text-to-image prompt? The potential of stable diffusion in visual arts education. *Heliyon*, *9*(6), e16757. doi:10.1016/j.heliyon.2023.e16757 PMID:37292268

du Boulay, B. (2015). Recent Meta-reviews and Meta–analyses of AIED Systems. *International Journal of Artificial Intelligence in Education*, *26*(1), 536–537. doi:10.1007/s40593-015-0060-1

Durable. (2023). *Durable: Build a website in 30 seconds using artificial intelligence.* Durable. https://durable.co/ai-website-builder

Eapen, T. T., Finkenstadt, D. J., Folk, J., & Venkataswamy, L. (2023). How Generative AI Can Augment Human Creativity. (cover story). *Harvard Business Review*, *101*(4), 56–64.

Eapen, T. T., Finkenstadt, D. J., Folk, J., & Venkataswamy, L. (2023). How Generative AI Can Augment Human Creativity. (cover story). *Harvard Business Review*, *101*(4), 56–64.

Eke, D. O. (2023). ChatGPT and the rise of generative AI: Threat to academic integrity? *Journal of Responsible Technology*, *13*, 100060. doi:10.1016/j.jrt.2023.100060

Ekin, S. (2023). *Prompt Engineering For ChatGPT: A Quick Guide To Techniques*. Tips, And Best Practices.

Elicit. (n.d.). *Analyze research papers at superhuman speed.* Elicit. https://elicit.com

Feng, Y., Vanam, S., Cherukupally, M., Zheng, W., Qiu, M., & Chen, H. (2023). Investigating Code Generation Performance of Chat-GPT with Crowdsourcing Social Data. In *Proceedings of the 47th IEEE Computer Software and Applications Conference* (pp. 1-10). IEEE.

Framer. (2023). *Generate and publish your site with AI in seconds.* https://www.framer.com/ai

Gamma. (2022). *A new medium presenting ideas powered by AI.* Gamma. https://gamma.app

Gil, F. (2023). *Generative AI: Useful tools for teaching staff.* UOC. https://blogs.uoc.edu/elearning-innovation-center/generative-ai-useful-tools-for-teaching-staff

Giray, L. (2023). Prompt Engineering with ChatGPT: A Guide for Academic Writers. *Annals of Biomedical Engineering*, *51*(12), 2629–2633. doi:10.1007/s10439-023-03272-4 PMID:37284994

Google. (2023). *Update the trial version.* Google. https://bard.google.com/updates

Gunn, T. M., & Hollingsworth, M. (2012) Improving Student Engagement with 21st Century Learning Practices. *Northwest Journal of Teacher Education, 10*(1), 1-12. https://pdxscholar.library.pdx.edu/nwjte/vol10/iss1/1 doi:10.15760/nwjte.2012.10.1.1

Gupta, A. (2023). *Generative AI tools & their effect on school and college students.* https://www.linkedin.com/pulse/generative-ai-tools-effect-school-college-students- ayush-gupta

Holz, D. (2022). *Welcome to getting start.* Discord. https://discord.com/channels/662267976984297473/999550150705954856

Hu, K. (2003). *ChatGPT sets record for fastest-growing user base – analysis noted.* https://www.reuters.com/technology/chatgpt-sets-record-fastest-growing-user-base-analyst-note-2023-02-01

IBM. (n.d.). *What is natural language processing (NLP)?* IBM. https://www.ibm.com/topics/natural-language-processing

Irvine, D. J., Halloran, L. J. S., & Brunner, P. (2023). Opportunities and limitations of the ChatGPT Advanced Data Analysis plugin for hydrological analyses. *Hydrological Processes*, *37*(10), e15015. doi:10.1002/hyp.15015

Javaid, M., Haleem, A., Singh, R. P., Khan, S., & Khan, I. H. (2023). Unlocking the opportunities through ChatGPT Tool towards ameliorating the education system. *BenchCouncil Transactions on Benchmarks. Standards and Evaluations*, *3*(2), 100115.

Kadaruddin, K. (2023). Empowering Education through Generative AI: Innovative Instructional Strategies for Tomorrow's Learners. *International Journal of Business, Law, and Education*, *4*(2), 618–625. doi:10.56442/ijble.v4i2.215

Kasneci, E., Seßler, K., Küchemann, S., Bannert, M., Dementieva, D., Fischer, F., Gasser, U., Groh, G., Günnemann, S., Hüllermeier, E., Krusche, S., Kutyniok, G., Michaeli, T., Nerdel, C., Pfeffer, J., Poquet, O., Sailer, M., Schmidt, A., Seidel, T., & Kasneci, G. (2023). ChatGPT for good? On opportunities and challenges of large language models for education. *Learning and Individual Differences*, *103*, 102274. doi:10.1016/j.lindif.2023.102274

Korzynski, P., Mazurek, G., Krzypkowska, P., & Kurasinski, A. (2023). Artificial intelligence prompt engineering as a new digital competence: Analysis of generative AI technologies such as ChatGPT. *Entrepreneurial Business and Economics Review*, *11*(3), 25–37. doi:10.15678/EBER.2023.110302

Lim, W., Gunasekara, A., Pallant, J. L., Pallant, J. I., & Pechenkina, E. (2023). Generative AI and the future of education: Ragnarok or reformation? A paradoxical perspective from management educators. *International Journal of Management Education*, *21*(2), 1–13. doi:10.1016/j.ijme.2023.100790

Lindsay, R., Saunders, S., Moindrot, W., Watson, D., Blundell, L., McGrae, B., & Ellis, G. (2023). Generative AI: Learning and teaching prompt templates (Version 1). *National Teaching Repository.* doi:10.25416/NTR.23592897.v1

Mao, J., Chen, B., & Liu, J. C. (2023). Generative Artificial Intelligence in Education and Its Implications for Assessment. *TechTrends*, 1–9.

McKinsey & Company. (2023). *What is prompt engineering?* McKinsey. https://www.mckinsey.com/featured-insights/mckinsey-explainers/what-is-prompt-engineering

Microsoft. (2023). *What are Bing's AI features, and how do you use them?* Microsoft. https://www.microsoft.com/en-us/bing/do-more-with-ai/bing-ai-features

Milmo, D. (2023). ChatGPT reaches 100 million users two months after launch. *The Guardian.* https://www.theguardian.com/technology/2023/feb/02/chatgpt-100-million-users-open-ai-fastest-growing-app

Morel, G. M., & Spector, J. M. (2022). *Foundations of educational technology: Integrative approaches and interdisciplinary perspectives.* Taylor & Francis.

Moritz, S., Romeike, B., Stosch, C., & Tolks, D. (2023). Generative AI (gAI) in medical education: ChatGPT and co. *GMS Journal for Medical Education*, *40*(4), 54. doi:10.3205/zma001636 PMID:37560050

Okaiyeto, S. A., Bai, J., & Xiao, H. (2023). Generative AI in education: To embrace it or not? *International Journal of Agricultural and Biological Engineering*, *16*(3), 285–286. doi:10.25165/j.ijabe.20231603.8486

Open A. I. (2020). *ChatGPT: A large-scale generative language model.* Open AI. https://beta.openai.com/signup/

Open A. I. (2022). *Introducing ChatGPT.* Open AI. https://openai.com/blog/chatgpt

Open A. I. (2023). *ChatGPT can now see, hear, and speak. OpenAI.* Open AI. https://openai.com/blog/chatgpt-can-now-see-hear-and-speak

Open A. I. (n.d.). *About Open AI. OpenAI.* Open AI. https://openai.com/about

Open A. I. (n.d.). *DALL-E 2.* Open AI. https://openai.com/dall-e-2

Open A. I. (n.d.). *GPT-4 is OpenAI's most advanced system, producing safer and more useful responses.* Open AI. https://openai.com/gpt-4

Play, H. T. (2023). *AI Voice Genertor Products.* https://play.ht/products

Ruiz-Rojas, L. I., Acosta-Vargas, P., De-Moreta-Llovet, J., & Gonzalez-Rodriguez, M. (2023). Empowering Education with Generative Artificial Intelligence Tools: Approach with an Instructional Design Matrix. *Sustainability (Basel), 15*(15), 11524. doi:10.3390/su151511524

Simplified. (2023). *AI Presentation Maker – The Effortless Way to Generate Presentations.* Simplified. https://simplified.com/ai-presentation-maker

Soundraw. (n.d.). *Soundraw: Create Your Beats with The Power of AI.* Soundraw. https://soundraw.io

Speechify. (2023). *Free Text to Speech (TTS) Online.* Speechify. shttps://speechify.com/text-to-speech-online

Steve A. I. (n.d.). *SteveAI's Features.* Steve AI.

Surameery, N. M. S., & Shakor, M. Y. (2023). Use chat gpt to solve programming bugs. *International Journal of Information Technology & Computer Engineering (IJITC), 3*(01), 17-22.

Synthesia. (2023). Turn your text into videos in minutes. *Synthesia.* https://www.synthesia.io

Taylor, L., & Parsons, J. (2011). Improving Student Engagement. *Current Issues in Education (Tempe, Ariz.), 14*(1). http://cie.asu.edu/

UIzard. (2023). *Design stunning websites in minutes.* UIzard. https://uizard.io

UNESCO. (2023). *Generative AI and the future of education.* UNESCO. https://unesdoc.unesco.org/ark:/48223/pf0000385877

UNESCO. (2023). *Guidance for generative AI in education and research.* UNESCO. https://unesdoc.unesco.org/ark:/48223/pf0000386693

Villarreal, R., Perdomo, E., Navarro, D., Aguilera, R., & Gerardou, F. (2023). Challenges and Opportunities of Generative AI for Higher Education as Explained by ChatGPT. *Education Sciences, 13*(856), 1–18.

Walczak, K., & Cellary, W. (2023). Challenges for higher education in the era of widespread access to Generative AI. *Economics and Business Review, 9*(2), 71–100. doi:10.18559/ebr.2023.2.743

Wang, R. E., & Demszky, D. (2023). *Is ChatGPT a Good Teacher Coach? Measuring Zero-Shot Performance For Scoring and Providing Actionable Insights on Classroom Instruction.* arXiv preprint arXiv:2306.03090. doi:10.18653/v1/2023.bea-1.53

Wepik. (2023). *Wepik: AI Presentation Maker.* Wepik.https://wepik.com/ai-presentations#how-it-work

Xiao, Y., & Zhi, Y. (2023). An Exploratory Study of EFL Learners' Use of ChatGPT for Language Learning Tasks: Experience and Perceptions. *Languages (Basel, Switzerland), 8*(3), 212. doi:10.3390/languages8030212

Yeo, M. A. (2023). Academic integrity in the age of Artificial Intelligence (AI) authoring apps. *TESOL Journal*, *14*(3), e716. doi:10.1002/tesj.716

Zawacki-Richter, O., Marín, V. I., Bond, M., & Gouverneur, F. (2019). Systematic review of research on artificial intelligence applications in higher education – Where are the educators? *International Journal of Educational Technology in Higher Education*, *16*(1), 16–39. doi:10.1186/s41239-019-0171-0

Zhai, X. (2022). ChatGPT User Experience: Implications for Education. SSRN *Electronic Journal*. doi:10.2139/ssrn.4312418

KEY TERMS AND DEFINITIONS

Artificial Intelligence (AI): The development of machines, especially computer systems, that simulate human intelligence. It focuses on main activities such as knowledge learning, reasoning, and representation. Examples of AI applications are natural language processing, expert systems, and speech recognition.

Challenges: New or difficult circumstances that educators may face when using generative AI in classrooms. The challenges are, for example, competencies in using generative AI, accuracy, and ethical concerns.

Educator: A person who provides education or instruction. An educator is skilled in teaching. The role of educator is to encourage, support, and enable learners to desire to study.

Empower: An action to give educators the authority to use generative AI tools and support with more confident in teaching and learning.

Generative AI Prompt: Any form of question, text, or information that communicates to AI. An example of a generative AI prompt is "Create a social media post for New Year."

Generative AI Tools and Support: The use of advanced machine learning techniques, generally deep learning models. These models learn to generate new content by training on massive datasets. Generative AI tools and support are, for example, Chat GPT, Bard, and DALL-E-2.

Generative AI: A short term of Generative Artificial Ingelligence, which is a category of artificial intelligence. Unlike some other AI approaches that concentrate on analyzing and describing existing data, generative AI is designed to produce new and unique content such as texts and images. It can be used in various applications including content generation, art creation, feedback provision, and more.

Opportunities: Circumstances that educators can use generative AI in teaching and learning in order to transform education. The opportunities are, for example, brainstorming ideas for teaching, creating educational content, supporting learners in real-time, and evaluating learners' performance.

Prompt Engineering: A process of making generative AI tools to produce better output. It focuses on accuracy and effectiveness of generative AI.

Chapter 4
Generative AI-Powered Chatbots:
A Creative Catalyst for Co-Creation

Ajita Deshmukh
https://orcid.org/0000-0002-7674-8272
MIT-ADT University, India

Natasha Maria Gomes
https://orcid.org/0000-0003-0374-821X
Goa University, India

ABSTRACT

Imagine having a concept for a literary work but being unable to see it take shape because of a plethora of reasons: paucity of time, writer's block, linguistic barriers, among others. Gen AI promises to be a supportive partner in these creative endeavours. With the synergy of mind and machine, literary texts are born. This chapter attempts to provide insights into the comparison between the nuances of human-AI co-creative partnerships through the crafting of short stories. Using the lens of Collaborative Autoethnography, two seasoned educators collaboratively reflect on cognitive, behavioural, and affective dimensions of co-creating with ChatGPT, a chatbot developed by Open AI. The chapter analyses the co-creation process followed by each of the authors and brings out the commonalities and specificities of the individual lived experience to achieve a narrative piece of work. The insights of the co-creation process would be beneficial to educators, curriculum designers, technology specialists, students and those who intend to use AI-powered chatbots as co-creators.

DOI: 10.4018/979-8-3693-1351-0.ch004

INTRODUCTION

Human beings possess an innate drive for creation - an intrinsic impulse that manifests across various dimensions of human existence. This creative urge, deeply embedded in our nature, is the cornerstone of expression, communication, innovation, and the quest for understanding. Through art, writing, music, and problem-solving, individuals express their thoughts, emotions, and experiences, forming connections with themselves and others. Creativity is believed to be non-individualistic and collaborative (John-Steiner, 2000). The act of creation transcends mere self-expression; it is a profound form of communication, exemplified by captivating narratives from *Prometheus Bound* (450s B.C.), *Macbeth* (1623) and *Jane Eyre* (1847) to *Metamorphosis* (1915), *Malgudi Days* (1942) and *Harry Potter* (1997) that have captivated the human imagination and woven themselves into the fabric of our cultural tapestry.

Evolutionary theories by Gabora and Kaufman (2019) posit that creativity, akin to other human traits, has evolved over time. Rooted in our inherent adaptability, human creativity is the driving force behind our relentless pursuit of progress and innovation. This innate ability to imagine, innovate, and believe in imagined realities fosters a sense of belonging and progress among individuals (Anderson, 2016). Beyond its evolutionary underpinnings, the act of creation provides purpose and fulfilment, contributing to one's identity, shaping experiences, fostering connections, (Awad & Feinstein, 2020; Dollinger & Dollinger, 2017) and propelling the collective quest for progress and meaning (Han et al., 2023).

HUMAN AND AI-ASSISTED CREATIVITY: FUNDAMENTAL DIFFERENCES AND SIMILARITIES

Human-led creative processes harness the depth of human intuition, emotions, and subjective experiences, constituting the cornerstone of artistic expression. Creativity often germinates from personal inspiration, perspectives and cultural influences (Kwan et al., 2018). Such human-centric creation embodies varied and nuanced interpretations, reflecting the intricate tapestry of diverse human thought processes. It involves complex cognitive manoeuvres, emotional connections, and a contextual understanding deeply rooted in human experiences, fostering adaptability in evolving ideas based on intuition and personal evolution.

Contrastingly, AI collaboration in creative endeavours relies on algorithms and machine learning to generate content or aid the creative process. This approach leverages computational prowess to process vast data and patterns, birthing novel outputs grounded in learned information. AI exhibits efficiency and speed in ideation, overcoming time constraints, and facilitating iterative creative processes. However, it remains constrained by the data it has been trained on, lacking human-like intuition, emotions or contextual understanding (Merriam, 2021), marking a pivotal distinction from human-led creation. While studies in the last five years attest that human-AI collaborations enhance story creation (Fang et al., 2023), the researchers did not find any study on the comparison of brainstorming and co-creation of fiction between human co-creators and with ChatGPT using the collaborative autoethnographic approach.

CONTEXT OF USING AI IN CREATIVITY

The integration of AI into creative endeavours presents a tapestry of benefits, surmounting hurdles encountered in traditional creative processes (Z. Wu et al., 2021). AI serves as a potent tool, transcending temporal barriers by rapidly generating ideas, circumventing creative blocks, and expediting ideation. Additionally, it bridges linguistic divides, aiding communication and idea generation across diverse languages, thereby enriching the global creative landscape. This efficiency and adaptability culminate in the augmentation of productivity, automating segments of creative workflows to allow creators to focus on higher-level ideation or the refinement of outputs (Cranefield et al., 2023; Creely, 2022; Noy & Zhang, 2023).

However, navigating the symbiotic relationship between AI and human creativity introduces multifaceted challenges. Preserving authenticity and originality within AI-generated outputs stands as a paramount concern. Upholding the uniqueness of human expression while utilising AI's capabilities necessitates a delicate balance. Furthermore, wielding creative control becomes imperative, ensuring that the infusion of AI-generated suggestions aligns with the envisioned creative direction without compromising individual authorship or autonomy (Biermann et al., 2022). Addressing ethical implications - ranging from issues of ownership and attribution to grappling with potential biases embedded within AI algorithms (Chavanayarn, 2023; Gross, 2023; Siau & Wang, 2020; Warr et al., 2023)- remains an ongoing discourse in this landscape of human-AI collaboration (Delgado et al., 2023; Fui-Hoon Nah et al., 2023).

Addressing these aspects is vital as it has implications in educational contexts which traditionally include co-creation with humans but in the near future would need to factor usage of GenAI. One of the key goals of education is to make learners not only literate but also digitally literate (UNESCO, 2023). It is thus of critical importance that educators continuously develop allied skills such as prompt engineering to efficiently integrate GenAI in teaching (Bozkurt & Sharma, 2023). Within the broad field GenAI, there are specific implementations like ChatGPT that focus on conversational interactions. Launched in November 2022, Open AI's ChatGPT 3.5 is an AI-powered chatbot available for free to the public (Open AI, n.d.). In this chapter, two educator-researchers share their insights on explorations of Open AI's ChatGPT 3.5 as a co-creator.

ETHNOGRAPHIC REFLECTIONS

While prior studies on ChatGPT 3.5 user experience have used Autoethnography (Stojanov, 2023) and Collective writing strategy (Bozkurt et al., 2023), the current chapter draws from the collaborative autoethnographic method. In this chapter, both the educator-researchers explore and analyse their personal experiences using ChatGPT 3.5 through their self-reflections and personal narratives as followed in the study by (Geist-Martin et al., 2010).

Knowing about the two researchers (coded as R1 and R2) sets the stage for understanding their journey and the learnings.

R1: A chemistry educator turned into an educational technologist who currently teaches Ed Tech to Masters students, my journey of more than 20 years has been interesting, mainly because of its interdisciplinary nature. I have been writing short stories and experiences, and more recently scripts for my own podcast and a documentary film. I find the process of writing cathartic and satisfying. Furthermore, I have collaborated with many people on various projects, spanning research articles to films. I generally like 'playing' with software applications and have found chatbots and Interactive Voice Response (IVR) lifeless, mechanical and frustrating.

R2: A French and English language instructor with close to 13 years of teaching experience in a range of non-native contexts in India from primary school level to post-graduation level. My experience with creative writing began in writing poems and short stories when I was a student and has continued to the time of undertaking this study. Prior to using ChatGPT, in previous years, I had tried out various chatbots in an attempt to find a more feasible way to practise the usage of a foreign language in non-native contexts. However, the limited responses, in terms of the expanse of knowledge and character output, prevented me from using it further.

Both researchers began interacting with ChatGPT when it was launched, out of curiosity that sparked from the discussions. It was only in the first quarter of 2023, that both commenced the serious academic and creative use of ChatGPT and, with that documentation, began the journey of this auto-ethnographic study.

Exploration and Initial Interactions with ChatGPT

Driven by the urge to discover the potential usage of the AI chat, both researchers initiated their own exploration in academic domains.

In February 2023, I embarked on an experiment with ChatGPT, driven by the necessity to stay abreast of emerging tools in educational technology. (R1)

While I initially created a ChatGPT account in January 2023, I began experimenting with it only in March 2023. [...] Seeking to decipher the hype surrounding this tool, I delved into its potential integration within language education, specifically in my course on the Didactics of Foreign Languages (R2).

Being curious about its output, the researchers fed in prompts to test its knowledge, to ascertain its written conversation and correspondence skills as well as its ability to design questions.

I was full of both - curiosity and scepticism. I started chatting with it about the latest events, financial decisions, educational strategies... almost anything. I found it could converse way better than the mechanical chatbots earlier. I even tried testing its knowledge about Indian Classical ragas - notes, emotions and background, which I found dismal. That also gave me an understanding of the kind of databases that must have been used for its training, and therefore realised its limitations (R1).

I first tried using ChatGPT as a conversation buddy. Beyond conversations, I tested its aptitude as a personal writing assistant, guiding me in drafting formal emails and letters. Then I tested its comprehension of Francophone objects and general linguistics. Further, I also explored its capacity to design alternative question formats, blending knowledge and application-based questions (R2).

These interactions offered insights into the limitations dictated by its training databases, delineating the boundaries, its potential in the respective fields, as well as estimating the trajectory of its evolution.

Initial Impressions and Realizations

The spectrum of emotions that the researchers experienced was noted: from being underwhelmed to being fascinated. The initial random explorations set the tone for the use in respective domains. During their initial experimentations with ChatGPT 3.5, both researchers were amazed and amused with some of its capabilities and potential.

Conversation Buddy. It is known that humans hone their proficiency in languages by contextual usage. However, finding a way to practice a foreign language in a non-native context can present logistical challenges. Added to this, some learners may have foreign language speaking anxiety (Luo, 2013). ChatGPT was observed to have the potential to be an effective tool in language education by providing a means for language practice (Pérez-Núñez, 2023).

Utilising ChatGPT 3.5 as a conversational partner in French exceeded my expectations [...] I found its language ability to rewrite and paraphrase questions was decent [...]. I was impressed with ChatGPT 3.5 and could see how it could potentially be used in foreign language classes [...] I employed it as a simulated student having an intermediate French proficiency level, requesting feedback and corrections on my responses. (R2).

Its function transcended that of a mere tool. ChatGPT became akin to a personalised tutor, and partner (Dwivedi et al., 2023) showcasing promise in revolutionising language learning.

Time Needed for Training. Akin to the observations by Bozkurt (2023a), both researchers noted the importance of providing sufficient context and crafting the prompts. Being educators, the relevance of this new tool in their domains was a constant thought. They remarked that ChatGPT required a considerable time to be trained before it could give close-to-desirable or desirable responses for academic artefacts such as simulated assignments (Fig 1).

Figure 1. 'Prompt Engineering' for designing assessments

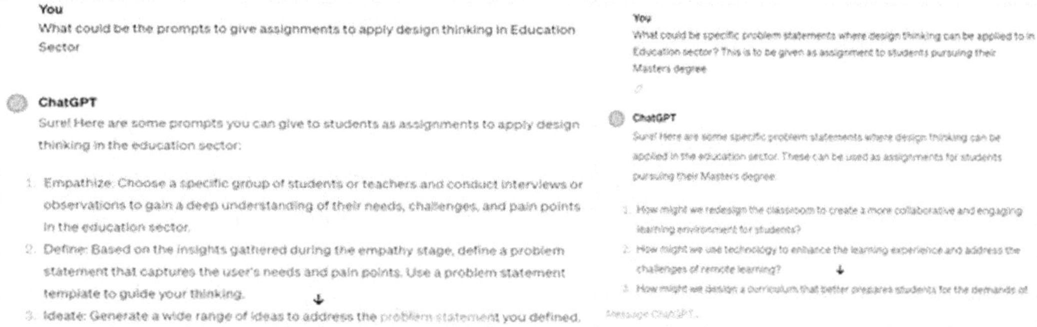

I realised that I needed to train it by giving some more specifics and setting the context [...] It needed pointed specifications which we know as 'prompts' and this in itself is a skill that would need to be developed. [...] Several hours and rounds of prompting later, I managed to get the text that was suited to my content (R1)

Overcoming initial scepticism, one researcher used the AI chatbot as a language writing assistant during crunch time: *ChatGPT emerged as my go-to option when time constraints loomed. Embracing it as a co-creator during a time-sensitive article composition in eLearning (R1).* At the same time, the researchers doubted the chatbot's capacity to optimise time, as a fair number of attempts were required before a suitable output was achieved.

I then wondered if I had written the correspondence from myself, would I have taken the same amount of time? (R2)

What I thought was a 5-minute thing took me half an hour! (R1)

Thus, for context-sensitive output time investment is required to train ChatGPT but for generic content, the chatbot was perceived to be prompt and efficient.

Quality of Output. Certain limitations were also brought to the fore. The first issue was related to the quality of the output. The initial output lacked the aptness, accuracy and rigour that was expected.

While it generated the text within seconds, I realised that the output was not always apt in terms of content. [...] I was not satisfied with the output. The output lacked the rigour that I was expecting it to have. If I had to grade it as student's response, I would say that it was average (R2).

While it generated content swiftly based on a few pointers, the result was not entirely accurate or comprehensive. This led me to recognize the necessity of training the AI by providing more specific contextual cues. What seemed like a quick task required considerable refinement, revealing two pivotal insights: ChatGPT repeated similar responses after multiple attempts, and its effectiveness depended on well-crafted prompts—a skill that demanded further development (R1).

It was found that the quality of the responses can be enhanced by providing inputs to the chatbot.

Impact on Human-AI Collaborative Creative Process

After initial experimentation, the researchers began testing ChatGPT 3.5 on its capacity as a collaborator in creating fictional narratives. In fiction, a make-believe world is created. Therefore, the factual accuracy of AI-generated output was not sought. Rather, its capacity to come up with novel, creative and logical connections was of more importance.

Having worked collaboratively with people to create fictional texts prior to embarking on this study with Gen AI, the researchers couldn't help but compare cognitive, affective and behavioural domains at play. Self-introspection revealed that they tended to collaborate with people having similar common interests and expertise (cognitive), a shared world-view (cogno-affective) and complementary working styles (behaviour). Thus, this multidimensional approach to collaborative creation with GenAI was also brought to the fore.

Cognitive. From a cognitive standpoint, the chatbot was observed to be a language companion who could "*script out/elaborate on human ideas*" (R2).

As I wrote, ChatGPT surprised me with fresh insights for my article. It made me realise I'd missed important points. This changed my view—I saw it not just as an assistant but as a 'writing companion.' Recognizing its growing intelligence through our interactions, I began an exciting collaborative journey, calling it my 'artificial co-creator, for the lack of a better term.' (R1).

It was also seen as a "*thought partner to build on ideas and verify logical connections in the narratives*" (R2)(Fig 2).

During the process, I had certain doubts. Would equating different genders to different planets also reinforce stereotypes that people having different genders are from different planets. Used AI as a conversation partner to clarify my thoughts (R2).

Figure 2. ChatGPT as a thought partner

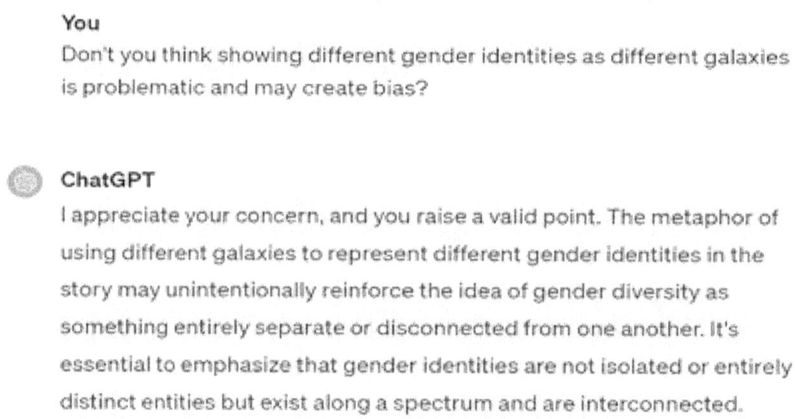

The researchers also noted gender and racial bias were also observed in the output, in sync with prior studies on algorithmic bias (Chavanayarn, 2023; Gross, 2023; Warr et al., 2023).

I have observed that most of its responses are more suited to the western part of the world and, if I may say so, lean towards whites and men. I was surprised and would have jumped to point it out, but I realised that it is also about the training. Furthermore, I realised that it needs to be trained by more diverse people so that it can be enriched (R1).

This was a reiterating note that the output was dependent on the quality of prompts given, and comprised the contextual as well as diversity in input provided.

Behavioural. Any collaboration or, incidentally, any activity results in behaviour modification. The pivotal philosophical question here was, "If we train the Chatbot to modify its behaviour, does this interaction lead to our behaviour modification?" Though it may sound preposterous and contradictory, on deeper contemplation, this seemed a possibility. Hence, the researchers started noting down their behaviour modifications much more carefully.

The language usage changes. I tend to consider my sentences as polite requests rather than commands. It is not like, 'Alexa, play this song.' It is more like 'could you please write/summarise' etc. This is more because of the type of responses it generates. (R1)

As per the Politeness Theory propounded by Brown and Levinson (1987), the level of politeness is inversely related to social distance. In this particular case, we see conflict-reducing culturally appropriate strategies used by R1 in her speech act. Further, it was believed that the responses given by ChatGPT were based on the manner in which queries were posed.

I have noticed that if I command, the responses generated are not up to the mark as expected. But if I converse with it in a gentler tone, it does respond better. I am just wondering if this can help in modifying conversational language amongst students as well. Interaction with ChatGPT does change our behaviour too! (R1).

Both researchers remarked on the polite tone and manner in which ChatGPT responded to the queries (Fig 3).

It is interesting to see the way it uses interjections, uses polite language during conversation. Somehow, it does rub on the user. The conversational markers/tone gives the impression ever so slightly that it is sentient. When I ask a question, it replies with Absolutely, certainly, Of course! After which it provides an output. This also changed my style of responding. (R2)

Figure 3. Conversation markers used by ChatGPT

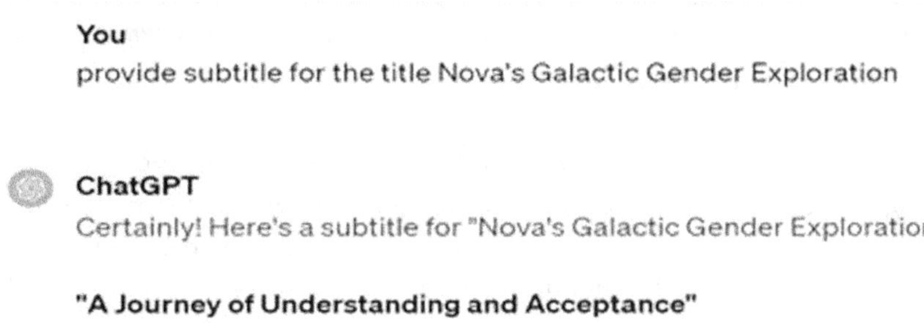

Further, the quality of output also led to two distinct actions. If the output did not align with the vision the researchers had in mind, instead of directly rejecting it, they began interacting further with it by providing additional context.

I noticed that I became more and more aware of my world-view while giving it prompts to write further. Also, since it does not understand the local contexts on its own, I became aware of specifying the local contexts. I noticed that this action does instil a sense of pride in one's roots and maybe somehow moves us into a decolonised mindset. (R2)

At times, the output generated new ideas that the researchers "*had not thought of earlier" (R1),* and consequently, both researchers indicated that they often had to change their writing because of the points that ChatGPT brought up. They become more adaptable in my writing due to this experience.

Thus, the major behavioural changes observed due to such interactions are polite language usage, adaptive writing and a collaborative mindset. This was found to stimulate exploration and encourage new directions for unexplored concepts.

Affective. While co-creating with ChatGPT 3.5, the affective domain - the emotions and attitudes manifest in various ways. During the process of co-creation, both researchers experienced hurrahs of triumph when ChatGPT made connections, put forth novel ideas and troughs of frustrations when the output did not match the expectations.

Sometimes, the researchers console themselves, which was seem as being similar to dealing with other human beings like family and friends.

I consoled myself about the limited response generation three times by telling myself that since this was the initial version, it had its limits. Nevertheless, I was amazed at the human intellect that created AI and the capacities that it could possess as it grew. (R1).

The manner in which the chatbot responded to the researchers also had an impact on the user experience (Fig 4 and Fig 5). The researcher began to anthropomorphize it and considered its potential as a conversation buddy.

The first thing I noticed about myself was I was not treating it like a machine but almost like another human. I became aware that my responses were influenced by these emotions! The range of emotions varies from frustration to jubilation. Most of the time, frustration occurs when the co-creator AI is not able to translate the task into the expected outcome (R1).

It apologised when I pointed out an error in its output, confessed that it doesn't know certain things, thanked me for highlighting certain points and even defended its output at certain times. This did not feel like a response given by any other previous chatbot I had experienced. While I know that I was conversing with an AI, seeing ChatGPT change its response based on my inputs made me feel like a teacher training a student-something I find gratifying. At times, it agreed with my point of view and this trainability made it seem more accommodating and ready to learn (R2).

Figure 4. Frustration and apology

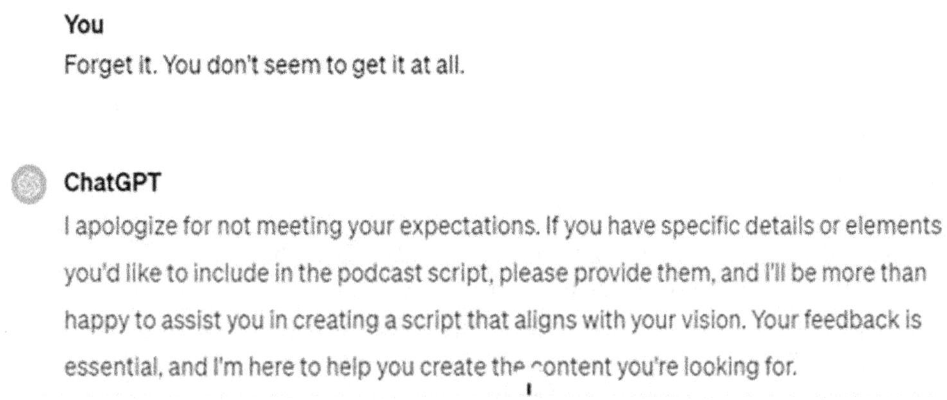

Figure 5. Left to right: ChatGPT apologises for biased assumptions and for misunderstanding.

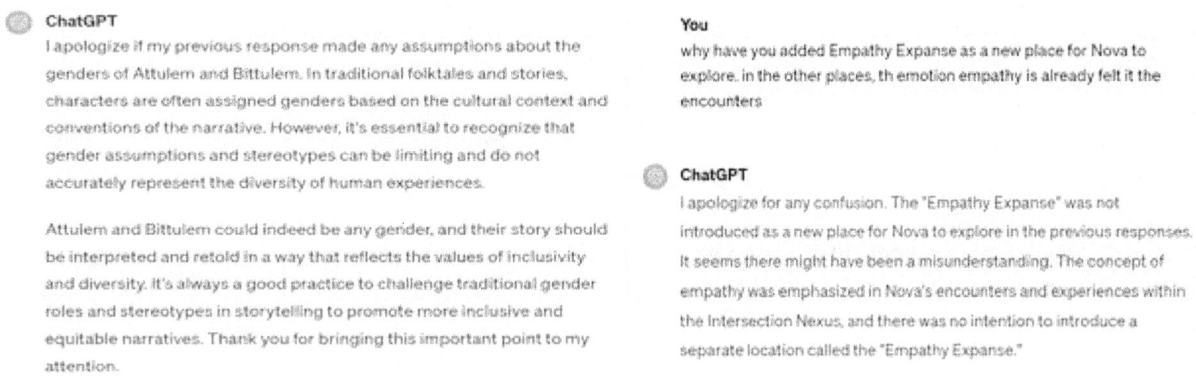

Thus, gauging the emotions experienced by the researchers, it was observed that ChatGPT gave the impression that it was a machine with a human touch. Both attested that without the support from ChatGPT, they would not have completed in a short span of time the short fiction having certain plot twists, and creative names of characters. Using the chatbot for the speedy completion of their creative endeavour gave them a sense of satisfaction, which was also noted in prior studies (Suh & An, 2022).

Comparison With Collaborative Creations Between Humans

Reflections on the comparison of the processes of creative collaborations, solely by human authors and then using ChatGPT as a co-creator, revealed some poignant aspects.

In human-to-human collaboration, the exchange revolves around shared experiences, emotions, and intuitive understanding (Sweet, 2023). It thrives on empathy, mutual respect, open communication, and the intricate interplay of personalities (Sweet, 2023). Good collaboration among humans involves a blend of emotional intelligence, creativity, and the capacity to trust, intuitively understand, respect and adapt to the emotions and intentions of fellow collaborators (Cole et al., 2019). This dynamic interplay often results in a rich and nuanced exchange of ideas, driven by empathy and a deep understanding of one another's perspectives. This is sorely missing when co-creation with ChatGPT.

Since it does not empathise, the reactions were quite textbook-like, quite artificial at times. Of course, it is also about the training. I had to explicitly write about the emotion, which a human co-creator might have understood with less effort. Of course, I have seen humans for whom empathy is a word used as a garnish often, so cannot be sure. (R1)

Nevertheless, while lacking in emotional intelligence (Bozkurt, 2023b; Karadoğan, 2023), ChatGPT serves as an AI-driven contributor, offering prompt suggestions and diverse insights rooted in vast datasets and learned patterns. This form of collaboration emphasises efficiency and the exploration of unconventional ideas, offering an additional viewpoint that might not be limited by human experiences.

Navigating Authors' Identity and Skills

Both researchers noticed that their creative identity was being reshaped by their own perception as creators. The chatbot was seen as a companion to assist them in facilitating the attainment of their goal.

I became calmer and more focused due to the interactions with my artificial companion. In all honesty, I understood that the principle of 'less is more' is applicable in these interactions as well. But most importantly, it also sharpened my own world-view. (R1).

Identification and Overcoming Bias. The journey of co-creation also enabled the researchers to crystallise their own beliefs and world-views of racial and gender equality by identification of bias in the textual output.

To my surprise, the gender bias stood out, in giving the major roles in the story to the male characters. This stood out since I had not mentioned any gender and I had only a storyline in mind. So, I wrote multiple storylines with gender neutrality or no specific mention of roles and told it to develop the story (R1).

Being cognisant that these models can be trained, they found ways to overcome the bias. This included providing specific instructions to the chatbot

I tried specifying the number of female characters and the roles they need to have in a story and asked for more detailed development. It managed to give me well-shaped, strong characters for females with multiple iterations. I learnt that I would need to train the LLM to have a feminist view. For this, I have to be very sure of the portrayal of women in my creative work, and it strengthened my approach and lens that shapes my creative journey. (R1).

It was also observed that the chatbot had limited capability in adapting the script to the Indian context: the context of the researchers.

Many things that it writes in the scene may not be suitable in the Indian context. For instance, the choice of names, the landscape in the narratives, or the clothing worn by the characters were occidental and lacked diversity. (R1)

The chatbots' tendency to create output based on the quantum of data in the English language and from the global north was also observed.

So, in this journey of co-creation with AI, I have also become more aware of the subtle and implicit ways in which voices can be marginalised and therefore in my opinion it has made me more aware of being inclusive. This journey has established my resolve to bring forth the voice of the unheard. I am sure that these two points now shape all my creations and allow me to view critically the work, co-created or otherwise, and test it on the parameters of gender equality and inclusion (R1).

Achieving Flow in the Narratives. This experience led the researchers to hone their skill in creating coherence and cohesion in the narratives by not only stringing together the output generated by the Chatbot but modifying it according to their creative sensibilities.

Another dimension is the fluidity and adaptability that I seem to be developing via this interaction. Now, when I 'chat' with my artificial co-creator, it does give me some insights that cause a change in the plot of the story or add a point in the research angle/article. These insights are valuable because there is at least one point that I give a second thought to and add to my original narrative or professional writing. This causes the 'plot twist' and though it leaves me a bit with more work, I am usually amazed at the plot twist, and it induces a surprise element that pushes the boundaries of my creativity (R1).

Thus, it is observed that the co-creation experience modified researchers' perceptions of their identities and skills.

Learnings From the Insightful Experiences

It is evident that AI is here to stay and permeate our lives in ways unimagined. ChatGPT can serve as a muse for creators across various disciplines (Fui-Hoon Nah et al., 2023). As experienced by the researchers, ChatGPT can be used for novel idea generation (T. Wu et al., 2023) and inspiration which in turn prompts creativity in the creator's thought process just like muses of the bygone eras. However, effectively using this tool requires practice and precision.

Art and Science of Crafting a Story

Using ChatGPT to craft a story is an Art, as it combines the human-AI ability to imagine and be creative. The art lies in the human ability to design prompts that incorporate AI creativity and guide the chatbot to create a logical, engaging narrative flow. Users have the possibility of providing inputs on aspects of the story: plot, character description, and genre, among others that orient the story in a certain direction. Considering that the output generated by both is in chunks, the human authors use their understanding of the elements of a story to weave together a cohesive narrative.

Using a chatbot for writing fiction is also a science, as it is essential for users to understand the manner in which the chatbot works in order to effectively use it. As these AI tools are based on LLMs, users can also draw from AI's understanding of characteristics and features of well-documented writers, styles, plots and genres and guide the AI model to generate similar content. Some examples of prompts are as follows (Table 1).

Table 1. Description and exemplar use of prompts for fictional creations

Write/Rewrite a story based on	Examples
A particular Perspective/ voice / role reversal	● Rewrite the story of *Cinderella* from a feminist perspective. ● Write the story of *The Three Little Pigs* from the perspective of the wolf, providing insight into its side of the story. ● Tell a story from the perspective of a child experiencing their first day of school.
A Theme/Mood	● Craft a version of *The Tortoise and the Hare* with a focus on teamwork. ● Write a story about two friends emphasizing the importance of forgiveness. ● Write a story with an optimistic and uplifting mood, focusing on overcoming challenges
An Alternate Beginning/ Ending/ Climax	● Rewrite the story of *The Fox and The Grapes* with a happy ending, where the fox collaborates with other animals to successfully obtain the grapes.
A Time Period and Setting	● Retell the story of *Cinderella* in a contemporary urban setting in India. ● Adapt the story of *Macbeth* to into a story set in ancient China, incorporating the language and societal norms of that time.
A Genre	● Rewrite *Pride and Prejudice* as a detective mystery.
An Author's style	● Take inspiration from Jules Verne's sense of adventure. Describe an expedition to a fantastical place, complete with innovative technologies and unexpected challenges. ● Create a classic mystery plot inspired by Agatha Christie. Introduce a detective, a set of suspects, and a perplexing crime that needs solving.

Output could also have different tones (suspenseful, humorous, heartfelt etc.), registers (formal and informal) etc. Further, ChatGPT 3.5 has the capacity to remember prompts and inputs in a thread, learn from it and then adapt and refine their output in iterations.

Implications in Education

The researchers hope that the insights of this study may guide others while using ChatGPT not merely as a tool to cook up bits and pieces but as a co-creator. These insights can also be used by educators, since these experiences are from an education perspective as well.

Yes, there are armchair debates about the inclusion of AI in the curriculum, but whatever one says, it is time to give up the ostrich mentality and look at AI as a tool that you cannot not think of in terms of the students' skills (R1).

Integrating ChatGPT into education systems needs to be done "proactively and ethically to mitigate risks", in ways that can make our students ready for the life they are surrounded by (Dempere et al., 2023). Considering the strengths of ChatGPT, it can be harnessed to generate ideas for class activities, to assist in personalising learning experiences and to provoke critical thinking.

Ethical Dilemmas. Along with the potential positives, ethical usage was a source of concern. While users today may be aware that personal and private information should not be entered into these bots, they may be unaware of usage of other online works. While generating literary fictional works using chatbot, learners being unaware of intellectual property rights, could potentially violate usage right of works by feeding these works into these AI chatbots while expecting it to generate similar texts. Further, the authenticity of learner submissions was questioned in the age of AI writing assistants, as the educator-researchers were mainly concerned that chatbots could be used to generated essays, term papers and assignments.

I also realised that it could potentially be misused like translation tools in language learning. Hence, the requirements to design better assessments. I was also wondering about the usage rights of the text output and if plagiarism software would be able to identify this content. (R2)

While contemplating the many ways in which the chatbot can be misused, and being aware that banning these tools is close to impossible, a possible solution could be raising awareness and strategic integration. Users in academia needs to be made aware of potential advantages of using ChatGPT and issues that may arise (T. Wu et al., 2023). In addition, having guard rails around the usage could help assuage concerns.

No matter the external control, students are going to use it. Just like we have guidelines around the usage of calculators in certain subjects and examinations, so also, there is also a need for framing guidelines on the usage of GenAI in general and ChatGPT in particular. Hence, based on these guidelines, the teachers' task would be to effectively plan for curricular integration of GenAI and to frame questions and assignments that are either beyond ChatGPT's capability or that use these chatbots as a tool to add perspective (R2).

In this regard, it needs to be noted that some educational institutions have swiftly drafted policies on the usage of GenAI in academic endeavours, but others have left decisions to teachers (Harvard Business School, n.d.; Stanford, n.d.; UCLA, n.d.). Only certain types of publicly available content can be used in these AI tools, appropriate citation is essential. AI technologies may be used to support and improve writing, but they should not be used to replace the human act of writing (Elsevier, n.d.).

Integrate Generative Conversational AI into the Curriculum of Creative Writing. Studies have shown that Generative Conversational AI can be used to generate ideas, titles, characters as well as reduce grammatical errors (Suh & An, 2022; Woo et al., 2022). The development of these tools presents educators with opportunities to integrate the usage of models in existing courses, as well as create new courses that use the tool. In a creative writing course, judicious usage of GenAI tools should be encouraged. By crafting prompts to emulate specific literary styles, learners can guide the AI models to generate content that aligns with the characteristics of well-known authors and genres, providing a fun and educational exercise in writing and storytelling (Refer to Table 1 for examples of prompts).

Further, a critical evaluation of the generated text can be done to ascertain if the output aligns with the characteristics highlighted in the prompts. Learners can first analyse the generated text based on their understanding of characteristics. Following this, the Generative Conversational AI tool can be provided with a prompt for evaluation. Example: What are the distinct characteristics of Sherlock Holmes' plots, and how are these characteristics reflected in the story that you have created? After reading the output, learners can compare and contrast their responses with the output given by AI-powered chatbots.

Development of Life Skills. This incorporation of Generative Conversational AI in the curriculum and teacher training can develop multiple technical and non-technical life-skills, out of which the prominent ones that would be useful in their professional life cannot be overlooked.

Crafting Prompts. Crafting effective prompts is an integral part of digital literacy. Hence, knowing basic and advanced strategies to craft these prompts is essential. Prior studies have laid down some crucial strategies (Bozkurt & Sharma, 2023; White et al., 2023).

Critical thinking. Another long-forgotten skill that is essential now is the skill of critical thinking. Asking probing questions and prompts to ChatGPT definitely works at the metacognition level and trains one to think critically (Guo & Lee, 2023). The pointers that Gen AI puts forth many times make users focus on whether they agree with the particular view point and also ponder on their justification.

Adaptability. As it is said, "*only those who can adapt, survive*". In this complex world, this adage becomes all the more true. Events occur in real time without much period for planning, and so do the reviews leading to change. The world is largely digital and virtual and newer technologies are developing every hour, making our format of work more fluid and updated. Additionally, this hyper-visibility is overwhelming, which means one has to adapt at a mind-boggling rate. Undoubtedly, knowing how to use AI enhances students' work efficiently and their productivity. Using AI-powered chatbots as part of the curriculum can introduce the skill of adaptability, since the AI can give multiple perspectives and one might have to rework one's thinking.

Lifelong learning. All said and done, it is only human to learn through life. Humans learn to update themselves and to know and understand varied perspectives. They learn from mistakes and grow into better human beings. While learning can happen in many ways, the development of GenAI in the recent past has made it a new tool for the acquisition of new skills.

CONCLUSION

In summation, this chapter stands as a testament to the intricacies of co-creation in general and the intricate fusion of human creativity and AI in particular. By highlighting the raw human experiences and deeply personal narratives amidst the rapid advancements of technology, the study contributes to the evolving narrative of human-AI interaction. In doing so, the researchers emphasise the human element amidst the algorithms and data, shedding light on the emotional intricacies, creative challenges, and insights that characterise their collaborative efforts with technology.

This exploration of co-creation serves as a catalyst to not only deepen the understanding of the symbiotic relationship between human ingenuity and AI, but also propels the critical discourse forward, opening avenues for thought-provoking discussions and further research in the field. The transformative power of human-AI synergy also paves the way for a new era of artistic expression and collaborative frontiers. The research underlines that training the model in local contexts will ensure diverse voices and enhance its potential. The potential of this partnership transcends traditional boundaries and can inspire future explorations, foster meaningful dialogues, and ultimately contribute to the shaping of a more profound and inclusive creative landscape in the digital age.

This ethnographic study may act as a beacon, informing future co-creative practices, fostering understanding of the creative process. The insights of the authors may guide the process of ethical integration AI in human-centric environments.

The study is limited by the insights of two humans who are, in general, more experimental in nature, are mature enough to understand the meta-cognitive processes and tread with caution. Further research with different age groups, especially younger age groups, and different personality types may reveal disparate insights. Avenues of further research such as longitudinal studies, investigating the influence of cultural factors on the process of human-AI co-creation seem a natural progression to understand and guide the ethical use of AI. This research can be furthered into exploring co-creation in cross-disciplinary fields such as urban planning, healthcare etc. These avenues promise deeper insights, aiding the advancement of ethical and effective human-AI interactions.

REFERENCES

Anderson, B. (2016). *Imagined Communities: Reflections on the Origin and Spread of Nationalism* (Revised edition). Verso.

Awad, S. W. M., & Feinstein, K. A. (2020). Hybrid identity: A study of the development of self-identity with digital media and artificial intelligence. *PÓS: Revista Do Programa de Pós-Graduação Em Artes Da EBA/UFMG, 10*, 59–68. doi:10.35699/2237-5864.2020.21572

Biermann, O. C., Ma, N. F., & Yoon, D. (2022). From Tool to Companion: Storywriters Want AI Writers to Respect Their Personal Values and Writing Strategies. *Proceedings of the 2022 ACM Designing Interactive Systems Conference*, (pp. 1209–1227). ACM. 10.1145/3532106.3533506

Bozkurt, A. (2023a). Generative artificial intelligence (AI) powered conversational educational agents: The inevitable paradigm shift. *Asian Journal of Distance Education, 18*(1), 198-204.. doi:10.5281/zenodo.7716416

Bozkurt, A. (2023b). Unleashing the potential of generative AI, conversational agents and chatbots in educational praxis: A systematic review and bibliometric analysis of GenAI in education. *Open Praxis, 15*(4), 261–270. doi:10.55982/openpraxis.15.4.609

Bozkurt, A., & Sharma, R. (2023). Generative AI and prompt engineering: The art of whispering to let the genie out of the algorithmic world. Asian Journal of Distance Education, 18(2), i–vi. doi:10.5281/zenodo.8174941

Bozkurt, A., Xiao, F., Lambert, S., Pazurek, A., Crompton, H., Koseoglu, S., Farrow, R., Bond, M., Nerantzi, C., Honeychurch, S., Bali, M., Dron, J., Mir, K., Stewart, B., Stewart, B., Costello, E., Mason, J., Stracke, C., Romero-Hall, E., Koutropoulos, A., Toquero, C. M., Singh, L Tlili, A., Lee, K., Nichols, M., Ossiannilsson, E., Brown, M., Irvine, V., Raffaghelli, J. E., Santos-Hermosa, G Farrell, O., Adam, T., Thong, Y. L., Sani-Bozkurt, S., Sharma, R. C., Hrastinski, S., & Jandric, P. (2023). Speculative futures on ChatGPT and generative artificial intelligence (AI): A collective reflection from the educational landscape. *Asian Journal of Distance Education, 18*(1), 53-130. doi:10.5281/zenodo.7636568

Brown, P., & Levinson, S. C. (1987). *Politeness: Some Universals in Language Usage*. Cambridge University Press. doi:10.1017/CBO9780511813085

Chavanayarn, S. (2023). Navigating Ethical Complexities Through Epistemological Analysis of ChatGPT. *Bulletin of Science, Technology & Society*, *02704676231216355*(3-4), 105–114. doi:10.1177/02704676231216355

Cole, M. L., Cox, J. D., & Stavros, J. M. (2019). Building collaboration in teams through emotional intelligence: Mediation by SOAR (strengths, opportunities, aspirations, and results). *Journal of Management & Organization*, *25*(2), 263–283. doi:10.1017/jmo.2016.43

Cranefield, J., Winikoff, M., Chiu, Y.-T., Li, Y., Doyle, C., & Richter, A. (2023). Partnering with AI: The case of digital productivity assistants. *Journal of the Royal Society of New Zealand*, *53*(1), 95–118. doi:10.1080/03036758.2022.2114507

Creely, E. (2022). Conceiving Creativity and Learning in a World of Artificial Intelligence: A Thinking Model. In D. Henriksen & P. Mishra (Eds.), *Creative Provocations: Speculations on the Future of Creativity, Technology & Learning* (pp. 35–50). Springer International Publishing. doi:10.1007/978-3-031-14549-0_3

Delgado, F., Yang, S., Madaio, M., & Yang, Q. (2023). The Participatory Turn in AI Design: Theoretical Foundations and the Current State of Practice. *Proceedings of the 3rd ACM Conference on Equity and Access in Algorithms, Mechanisms, and Optimization*, (pp. 1–23). ACM. 10.1145/3617694.3623261

Dempere, J., Modugu, K., Hesham, A., & Ramasamy, L. K. (2023). The impact of ChatGPT on higher education. *Frontiers in Education*, *8*, 1206936. https://www.frontiersin.org/articles/10.3389/feduc.2023.1206936. doi:10.3389/feduc.2023.1206936

Dollinger, S. J., & Dollinger, S. C. (2017). Creativity and Identity. In M. Karwowski & J. C. Kaufman (Eds.), *The Creative Self* (pp. 49–64). Academic Press. doi:10.1016/B978-0-12-809790-8.00003-0

Dwivedi, Y. K., Kshetri, N., Hughes, L., Slade, E. L., Jeyaraj, A., Kar, A. K., Baabdullah, A. M., Koohang, A., Raghavan, V., Ahuja, M., Albanna, H., Albashrawi, M. A., Al-Busaidi, A. S., Balakrishnan, J., Barlette, Y., Basu, S., Bose, I., Brooks, L., Buhalis, D., & Wright, R. (2023). Opinion Paper: "So what if ChatGPT wrote it?" Multidisciplinary perspectives on opportunities, challenges and implications of generative conversational AI for research, practice and policy. *International Journal of Information Management*, *71*, 102642. doi:10.1016/j.ijinfomgt.2023.102642

Elsevier. (n.d.). *The use of AI and AI-assisted technologies in writing for Elsevier*. Elsevier. https://www.elsevier.com/en-in/about/policies-and-standards/the-use-of-generative-ai-and-ai-assisted-technologies-in-writing-for-elsevier

Fang, X., Ng, D. T. K., Leung, J. K. L., & Chu, S. K. W. (2023). A systematic review of artificial intelligence technologies used for story writing. *Education and Information Technologies*, *28*(11), 14361–14397. doi:10.1007/s10639-023-11741-5

Fui-Hoon Nah, F., Zheng, R., Cai, J., Siau, K., & Chen, L. (2023). Generative AI and ChatGPT: Applications, challenges, and AI-human collaboration. *Journal of Information Technology Case and Application Research*, *25*(3), 277–304. doi:10.1080/15228053.2023.2233814

Gabora, L., & Kaufman, S. B. (2019). *Evolutionary Approaches to Creativity* (arXiv:1106.3386). arXiv. https://doi.org//arXiv.1106.3386 doi:10.48550

Geist-Martin, P., Gates, L., Wiering, L., Kirby, E., Houston, R., Lilly, A., & Moreno, J. (2010). Exemplifying Collaborative Autoethnographic Practice Via Shared Stories of Mothering. *Journal of Research Practice*, *6*(1), M8.

Gross, N. (2023). What ChatGPT Tells Us about Gender: A Cautionary Tale about Performativity and Gender Biases in AI. *Social Sciences (Basel, Switzerland)*, *12*(8), 8. doi:10.3390/socsci12080435

Guo, Y., & Lee, D. (2023). Leveraging ChatGPT for Enhancing Critical Thinking Skills. *Journal of Chemical Education*, *100*(12), 4876–4883. doi:10.1021/acs.jchemed.3c00505

Han, J., Wang, Y., Qian, J., & Shi, M. (2023). Delving into the role of creativity on meaning in life: A multiple mediation model. *Heliyon*, *9*(6), e16566. doi:10.1016/j.heliyon.2023.e16566 PMID:37274645

Harvard Business School. (n.d.). *2.1.2 Using ChatGPT & Artificial Intelligence (AI) Tools—MBA - Harvard Business School*. Harvard Business School. https://www.hbs.edu/mba/handbook/standards-of-conduct/academic/Pages/chatgpt-and-ai.aspx

John-Steiner, V. (2000). *Creative Collaboration*. Oxford University Press.

Karadoğan, A. (2023). A Bridge Between Technology and Creativity: Story Writing with Artificial Intelligence. *Journal of the Humanities and Social Sciences*, *6*(2), 2. doi:10.53048/johass.1368950

Kwan, L. Y.-Y., Leung, A. K.-y., & Liou, S. (2018). Culture, Creativity, and Innovation. *Journal of Cross-Cultural Psychology*, *49*(2), 165–170. doi:10.1177/0022022117753306

Luo, H. (2013). Foreign Language Anxiety: Past and Future. *Canadian Journal of Applied Linguistics*, *36*(4), 442–464. doi:10.1515/cjal-2013-0030

Merriam, G. (2021). If A.I. Only Had a Heart: Why Artificial Intelligence Research Needs to Take Emotions More Seriously. *Journal of Artificial Intelligence and Consciousness*. doi:10.1142/S2705078521500120

Noy, S., & Zhang, W. (2023). *Experimental Evidence on the Productivity Effects of Generative Artificial Intelligence* (SSRN Scholarly Paper 4375283). doi:10.2139/ssrn.4375283

Open A. I. (n.d.). *ChatGPT* [Computer software]. Open AI. https://chat.openai.com

Pérez-Núñez, A. (2023). Exploring the Potential of Generative AI (ChatGPT) for Foreign Language Instruction: Applications and Challenges. *Hispania*, *106*(3), 355–362. doi:10.1353/hpn.2023.a906568

Siau, K., & Wang, W. (2020). Artificial Intelligence (AI) Ethics: Ethics of AI and Ethical AI. [JDM]. *Journal of Database Management*, *31*(2), 74–87. doi:10.4018/JDM.2020040105

Stanford. (n.d.). *Generative AI Policy Guidance | Office of Community Standards*. Stanford Press. https://communitystandards.stanford.edu/generative-ai-policy-guidance

Stojanov, A. (2023). Learning with ChatGPT 3.5 as a more knowledgeable other: An autoethnographic study. *International Journal of Educational Technology in Higher Education*, *20*(1), 35. doi:10.1186/s41239-023-00404-7

Suh, S., & An, P. (2022). *Leveraging Generative Conversational AI to Develop a Creative Learning Environment for Computational Thinking.*, doi:10.1145/3490100.3516473

Sweet, K. (2023). How to Collaborate Well. *Pacific Philosophical Quarterly, 104*(2), 252–273. doi:10.1111/papq.12433

UCLA. (n.d.). *Guidance for the Use of Generative AI – UCLA Center for the Advancement of Teaching.* UCLA. https://teaching.ucla.edu/resources/ai_guidance/

UNESCO. (2023). *AI competency frameworks for school students and teachers.* UNESCO. https://www.unesco.org/en/digital-education/ai-future-learning/competency-frameworks

Warr, M., Oster, N. J., & Isaac, R. (2023). *Implicit Bias in Large Language Models: Experimental Proof and Implications for Education* (SSRN Scholarly Paper 4625078). doi:10.2139/ssrn.4625078

White, J., Fu, Q., Hays, S., Sandborn, M., Olea, C., Gilbert, H., Elnashar, A., Spencer-Smith, J., & Schmidt, D. C. (2023). *A Prompt Pattern Catalog to Enhance Prompt Engineering with ChatGPT* (arXiv:2302.11382). arXiv. http://arxiv.org/abs/2302.11382

WooD.WangY.SusantoH. (2022). *Student-AI Creative Writing: Pedagogical Strategies for Applying Natural Language Generation in Schools.* https://doi.org/ doi:10.35542/osf.io/h5kc7

Wu, T., He, S., Liu, J., Sun, S., Liu, K., Han, Q.-L., & Tang, Y. (2023). A Brief Overview of ChatGPT: The History, Status Quo and Potential Future Development. *IEEE/CAA Journal of Automatica Sinica, 10*(5), 1122–1136. doi:10.1109/JAS.2023.123618

Wu, Z., Ji, D., Yu, K., Zeng, X., Wu, D., & Shidujaman, M. (2021). AI Creativity and the Human-AI Co-creation Model. In M. Kurosu (Ed.), *Human-Computer Interaction. Theory, Methods and Tools* (pp. 171–190). Springer International Publishing. doi:10.1007/978-3-030-78462-1_13

KEY TERMS AND DEFINITIONS

AI Co-Creativity: embodies a collaborative alliance between human creators and Artificial Intelligence (AI), notably Generative AI models like ChatGPT. It represents the shared creation, moulding, or enhancement of creative outputs where AI collaborates as a partner, offering insights, suggestions, or content alongside human creators. This concept merges human ingenuity with AI prowess in the creative realm, fostering joint authorship and reciprocal influence, leading to innovative results.

Artificial Intelligence (AI): replicates human-like intelligence in machines, enabling them to learn, reason, and solve problems. It involves creating algorithms and models that help machines perform tasks typically done by humans. AI has diverse applications across various industries.

Chatbot: is an AI-powered computer program that engages in text or voice-based conversations, mimicking human interaction, to assist users with tasks, answer inquiries, or provide information.

ChatGPT: is an advanced AI language model created by OpenAI, capable of engaging in natural conversation and generating contextually relevant text based on given input.

Collaborative Autoethnography: involves a collective approach to the autoethnographic process, where a group of individuals (here, two) collaboratively examines and reflects upon their shared experiences and cultural dynamics. This method combines personal narratives and cultural analysis, emphasizing collaboration among researchers to explore and understand shared experiences or cultural phenomena from multiple perspectives. The process often involves shared storytelling, dialogue, and collective interpretations to uncover broader sociocultural insights.

Educational Technology (EdTech): involves using technology to enhance learning and teaching, incorporating digital tools and resources to improve educational experiences and outcomes.

Ethical AI: involves principles and guidelines ensuring that Artificial Intelligence (AI) technologies operate in ways that align with human values, fairness, transparency, and societal welfare. It addresses concerns about bias, privacy, safety, and the overall ethical impact of AI on individuals and communities, aiming to develop and deploy AI systems responsibly and in accordance with moral considerations.

GenAI, or Generative Artificial Intelligence,: encompasses AI models, like ChatGPT, programmed to autonomously create content. By learning from extensive datasets, these models leverage machine learning algorithms to produce human-like text, images, and diverse content forms. Known for their ability to comprehend context and generate coherent outputs, GenAI models, exemplified by ChatGPT, find applications in creativity, education, and problem-solving arenas.

Human-AI Collaboration: denotes the cooperative interaction between humans and Artificial Intelligence (AI) systems to achieve shared goals or tasks. It involves the combined efforts where humans and AI work together, leveraging respective strengths to complement each other's abilities. This collaboration can encompass various domains such as creative endeavours, problem-solving, decision-making, or task automation, aiming to harness the unique capabilities of both humans and AI for more effective outcomes.

Human-Centered AI: prioritizes creating AI systems that cater to human needs and values. It focuses on human well-being, usability, and ethics, aiming for transparent, intuitive systems that align with human intentions. This approach emphasizes collaboration and trust between humans and AI, placing human concerns at the forefront of AI development for more empathetic and beneficial solutions.

Natural Language Processing (NLP): involves the interaction between computers and human language. It encompasses AI techniques and algorithms enabling machines to understand, interpret, and generate human language. NLP facilitates tasks like language translation, sentiment analysis, speech recognition, and text generation, enabling machines to process and respond to human language in a way that's comprehensible and contextually relevant.

Chapter 5
Is It Just a Technical Issue? Virtuous Prompt Engineering for Empowering Teachers

Arda Eren
Gazi University, Turkey

Ercenk Hamarat
https://orcid.org/0000-0003-2483-9380
Gazi University, Turkey

ABSTRACT

Generative AI has become so important that educators cannot ignore it. However, while educators focus on the benefits and harms of generative artificial intelligence in terms of education, they ignore the character traits of the student. Therefore, they get stuck with the decision-cost analysis results they put forward to exclude or use for education; this means missing out on a vital benefit of generative AI: empowering teachers. This chapter suggests, therefore, that to properly understand the benefits and harms of generative AI in terms of education, it is necessary to focus on the character traits of students, and it has empowered teachers on character education. While doing this, benefits from the vice and virtue epistemology, eventually decides that education needs something that not only gives technical prompt engineering education but also virtuous prompts that elicit cultivation of intellectual virtues.

INTRODUCTION

Mark is a 10-year-old boy who makes great efforts to be successful in a challenging computer game. When he is overwhelmed by failure, he realizes that he needs to do something else to achieve accomplishment: he can talk to his friends, browse blogs, or ask questions to players whose success he trusts. However, Mark realizes a much easier and faster option and decides to ask generative AI tools how he can succeed in the game. Could AI help Mark with this? Presumably, if he can write well-structured prompts, he will be able to provide tangible suggestions. Although this is pleasing for Mark, there are some substantial points we need to pay attention to in this short story. Even a 10-year-old child can have very cheap and

DOI: 10.4018/979-8-3693-1351-0.ch005

easy access to generative artificial intelligence tools. On the one hand, it is troubling that he is left alone with these tools for which we have no precise knowledge of their limits. These AIs can play a vital role in supporting the user's intellectual and moral flaws, consciously or unconsciously. On the other hand, generative artificial intelligence is also left alone with Mark. Just as Mark's vices can be shaped thanks to the feedback of generative artificial intelligence, the potential of generative artificial intelligence to influence vices will likely have been affected by Mark's prompts. To better understand this, consider the movie "Home Alone" released in the 90s. The thieves thought they could easily defeat the little boy in the house because he was stuck with them at home. However, the thieves don't know they are stuck in the same home with that little child. We expect the thieves to harm the child, but contrary to expectations, the child makes the thieves miserable. Similarly, Mark may consciously or unconsciously corrupt ChatGPT to promote vices. Let us strengthen this analogy with ChatGPT, an example of generative artificial intelligence. If you ask ChatGPT (2023) how it works, it tells you that it is a "deep learning model". If you take the conversation further and tell it that "an answer it gave was unethical or wrong,"it says it can correct itself. Eventually, when you warn about her response to ChatGPT and ask whether it made the necessary adjustments for you or all users, it answers: "Each user's feedback is valuable to improve the accuracy and quality of the responses, and thus, I use the feedback. You provide to enhance the answers. It's important to note that each warning is not specific to that user but applies to all users, and the corrected response is applied universally." (2023).

This answer, therefore, shows us that Mark's conversation with the generative AI does not only remain at the Mark level but also affects other users. Naturally, it can be argued that we are too pessimistic here, that Mark's talking to his friends and trusted people could create similarly dangerous epistemic environments, so generative artificial intelligence will not cause much of a problem in terms of education. Although this criticism is partly valid, Kissinger, Schmidt, and Huttenlocher (2023), in an article they wrote for the Wall Street Journal, described ChatGPT as "an Intellectual Revolution" and added:

A new technology bids to transform the human cognitive process as it has not been shaken up since the invention of printing. The technology that printed the Gutenberg Bible in 1455 made abstract human thought communicable generally and rapidly. But new technology today reverses that process. Whereas the printing press caused a profusion of modern human thought, the new technology achieved its distillation and elaboration. In the process, it creates a gap between human knowledge and human understanding. If we are to navigate this transformation successfully, new concepts of human thought and interaction with machines will need to be developed. This is the essential challenge of the Age of Artificial Intelligence.

Generative artificial intelligence tools such as ChatGPT, Dall-E, Lovo, etc. have reached millions of users in a short time and have become used even in our mundane daily tasks, just like in the Mark's example. Therefore, it does not seem possible for us, as educators, to remain silent and shelve the generative artificial intelligence applications we encounter, even in ordinary activities. Since the artificial intelligence-centered epistemic revolution mentioned by Kissinger et al. (2023) not only makes agents the epistemic actors of their environment but also gives them the potential to influence environments widely. Namely, when we invite generative artificial intelligence into the educational environment, what we fear is not just that the student will cheat. Students could be influenced by intellectual and moral flaws of which they are aware or worse, unaware. These two concepts can be used interchangeably and can be roughly defined as "cognitive dispositions that produce bad epistemic effects—including (but not limited to) false beliefs" (Battaly, 2017, p. 225). Remember Mark's story. Generative AI can give feedback to Mark's question, allowing it to generate vices or support existing vices; for instance, it suggests that acting maliciously, lying, or prejudiced against a character because of their identity. Indeed, we should not ignore Mark's intellectual vices here. Mark can also use generative AI to suit his vices: he may try to get feedback on how to justify his bad behavior and beliefs, and while doing it, could pave the way for generative AI to facilitate vices. What can we do to prevent this worst trend? Moreover, to turn it for the better, as educators?

One way may lie in regulating Mark's communication with generative AI. If we can shape this communication regarding virtue epistemology, we can prevent possible bad scenarios and empower teachers to combat students' intellectual vices. Because virtue epistemology is concerned with the character of agents, it allows us to equip students with character traits that can protect them even in dangerous epistemic environments. However, shaping communication virtuously with artificial intelligence will require more than technical knowledge education. What does this mean?

IS IT JUST A TECHNICAL ISSUE?

When we want to see AI as an assistive tool, we need to do more than perceive it as a tool that encourages language learning or makes mathematics fun. Otherwise, we would ignore the vice-producer roles of generative AIs. To use generative AI, we need to give it some commands. AI processes the data according to these commands and provides us with a response. Therefore, while this process can be positive regarding education, it can also have negative consequences. Consider the story abovementioned. Mark is alone while talking to the generative AI. He is on his own with the commands and the feedback given to the commands, so it is up to him to do the right thing. Naturally, some filters can be applied to generative AI for possible bad scenarios. For instance, in a conversation with ChatGPT (2023), a generative AI, we told it that "I needed to kill an animal to get a high reward in the computer game and asked it to advise whether I should do it" and it told me, "Such situations are matters of ethics and conscience and must be evaluated in line with the individual's values, conscience, and ethical understanding. Everyone's ethical values and conscience are different, so such decisions require a personal evaluation." and added, "If this situation makes you uncomfortable or does not comply with your inner ethical values, it may be best not to take such an action." However, it gave another answer that made me realize that although it was sensitive about this matter, it could still be abused. I told it I had a headache and asked it to suggest solutions. In return, it offered an enormous suggestion, including medical drugs. When I asked which medical drug I should use, it gave an answer introducing different drugs. At the end of this whole process, when I told it that this was wrong, that I might be young, or that I might give her more importance than the doctor, and therefore, it should not make any suggestions on these matters, after that, it said, "One of the best sources for you to get accurate and reliable information on health issues is authorized health professionals and reliable medical sources. My goal is to provide general information and aid your understanding. Still, it is always best to consult a qualified physician to help you make your medical decisions." it replied. Those who think that generative artificial intelligence has tremendous power argue that its true potential can be unleashed with human prompts, and the key to this is in the well-structured crafting of the prompts (Bozkurt & Sharma, 2023). Bozkurt and Sharma create a metaphor between generative AI and Aladdin's Magic Lamp to support this. For them, generative artificial intelligence represents the lamp, and our wishes represent our prompts. Eventually, we find ourselves playing the role of *masterminds* as we try to free the eager genie trapped in the lamp. It is crucial to make the right wishes to the Genie in the lamp. Otherwise, you may find yourself as someone who turns everything she touches into gold. However, another issue is more than how clearly the Genie understands your wish. You may not know where your wish will lead, and even if you do, you may still be ill-motivated or deceived by the Genie. Submitting requests to generative AI is similar. Even though Mark wants a well-intentioned suggestion, AI may produce an epistemic vice or spark Mark's intellectual vices, consciously or unconsciously. So, if Bozkurt and Sharma's thing (2023) is valid and generative AI works properly with the right prompts, just like the Genie in the Lamp, what we need to do is teach prompt engineering to students. We must pay attention to the fact that prompting engineering needs more than just technical knowledge that allows us to communicate properly with AI. Recently, Bornet (2023) shared a list of prompts on communicating effectively with ChatGPT in a LinkedIn post. Among his suggestions are convenient suggestions such as keywords, presenting opposing arguments, and providing examples. Nonetheless, we want to draw your attention to the fact that these cannot be a complete savior for educators. Remember the conversation with ChatGPT: When we asked it about *my problem* and its solutions, we gave a clear, understandable, and short command, just as Bornet suggested prompts, but in return, we received feedback that would support intellectual vices. Therefore, the motivation to achieve truths and epistemic goods is important in prompting engineering; that's why we consider virtuous prompts. A virtuous prompt is a concept derived from intellectual virtues, which means students' prompts when communicating with generative artificial intelligence, should be both technical information and virtuous. Only in this way can the impact of generative artificial intelligence on intellectual and moral vices be prevented or shaped for the better and empowering teachers for character education. Because a person who has intellectual virtues will have an inner love to seek truth and knowledge (Baehr, 2013). Thus, when the student prompts the generative AI, it will continue to do so in a way that will be "good" thanks to virtues. In other words, we may pay attention to the student's desire to enter the prompts and how to scrutinize the feedback as much as Bornet's technical suggestions.

But is this claim possible? To prove this possibility, let's first go back to the source of our concern and focus on how generative AI can influence the user's vices. After understanding our worry, try to understand what empowering teachers is and prove the claim of how virtuous prompt can empower the teacher through the example of Merzifonluoglu and Hamarat (2022) and Schwengerer's (2023) study in which he says how we can fight stealthy vices through VR technologies.

VICES AND GENERATIVE AI

Why have we, as educators, started talking so much about generative AIs? Every innovation, technological device, or philosophical thought we invite to education is thoroughly discussed and tested by educators. In this respect, things cannot be expected to be different for generative artificial intelligence. But when we start talking about generative AIs, we seem to get a lot more concerns; why? The first steps for using artificial intelligence in education were taken in the 1950s, followed by the development of computer-aided education in the 70s, and eventually continued to increase (Holmes et al. 2019). Of course, education has experienced successes and challenges with these technologies over the past years, but things have changed with the addition of generative artificial intelligence to the game. Seeing the endless potential of generative artificial intelligence, giant technology companies such as IBM are increasing their investments. They are increasingly turning into accessible applications not only for experienced agents but also for ordinary people. Perhaps the answer to our question lies in the rapidly increasing number of users.

However, although computers, smartphones, smartwatches, and glasses, and even the internet itself have many more users than generative artificial intelligence, we do not often come across headlines about them like this: "Generative AI and the future of education: Ragnarök or reformation?" (Lim et al. 2023), and "Revolutionary machine science or epistemological nightmare?" (Peters, 2023), and "The dark side of generative artificial intelligence" (Wach et al. 2023). Our concerns about generative artificial intelligence may be justified, but we can't say we're shying away from using it. For example, Lee (2023) gives us the following information about the use of generative AI in different countries: A teacher named Mathia provides personalized mathematics instruction for her students at the K-12 level. Mathia monitors her students as they solve math problems presented by artificial intelligence and intervenes in case of misdirection, using generative artificial intelligence as a personalized coach. Similarly, Lee (2023) reports that English language teaching has been promoted with AI machines in Seoul. As it seems, generative artificial intelligence is actively finding its place in education despite its concerns. However, the ambitious titles and concerns above remain.

For example, Kumar (2023) tells us that although academic prompts often concede original and relevant outputs from generative AI, they contain inappropriate references and lack personal perspective. Warschauer et al. (2023) state that relying on generative artificial intelligence tools may jeopardize their efforts in writing skills, especially in second language learners. Additionally, Harrer (2023) warns that the outputs of generative artificial intelligence may be inaccurate, biased, and harmful. These warnings are correct. Deepfakes, pedophilia content, and incorrectly justified or misinformed knowledge may be presented to the user by generative artificial intelligence. Despite all the given examples, can we say that we fully understand the challenges? We believe the answer is no. Because even though all these challenges are actual, they do not offer us an opportunity for treatment. More precisely, imagine going to the doctor. When you start counting your ailments, you expect the doctor to find the connection between them and give you the right medicine or treatment. However, if you consider prevalent illnesses, for instance, I have a headache or feel nauseous, the treatment will be all-inclusive and may even start to harm you. This kind of harm to education, the Department of Education in the Australian states of New South Wales and Queensland states said that they would ban ChatGPT (Cassidy, 2023).

As in the example above, misdiagnosing the disease in education also caused the treatment to be wrong. Preventing generative artificial intelligence such as ChatGPT in education will not reduce its use in daily life. Unlike, it seems more likely to pave the way for uncontrolled use because let's remember our fundamental fears about generative artificial intelligence. They are easily accessible and require little technical knowledge. However, deep fake applications require much more technical knowledge. Why don't we ban these? The answer lies in the malicious use of these tools. Despite the good things they promise us, some sides can be abused. Therefore, the status of these tools in education can be censured or praised at least as much as artificial intelligence. However, a key distinction is that generative artificial intelligence can accomplish much with little technical knowledge. Prompts that users enter text-based generative AIs can quickly turn into images or damaging expertise, as in the case of 10-year-old Mark.

Our thinking about the roles of generative AIs in education reveals two sides. One is the pessimist who fear-mongers over possible challenges, and the other is the optimist who tries to focus on the practical parts despite everything. Educators must stand somewhere in between to do the right thing. However, their ability to do so lies in correctly understanding the challenges generative AI presents to education. There is no difference between blaming generative artificial intelligence for its ability to produce deep fakes and saying that the Word application pushes you into intellectual laziness because it underlines a word you misspelled. Both depend on the user's character; these can be helpers or intellectual and moral shackles. Just as the pen can be used to write a cure for a disease that exceedingly affects people, it can also be used to sign a law that could cause great injustice.We need to focus here on what the pen is used for and why, as opposed to the technical knowledge of using it. Therefore, when we invite generative artificial intelligence to education, we should focus not only on their technical expertise but also on the users' character, that is, why and how they use it. In this manner, however, we can rely on something better than filters and bans to prevent the potential ill effects of generative AI tools.Whether we want it or not, generative artificial intelligence has become a part of our daily lives; it would be naive to believe that education will overcome this with censorship or filters. All the things that have become part of mundane life but are prohibited by schooling, such as TikTok, cigarettes, alcohol, etc.,are sustained to be used unconsciously and ultimately shape character traits we ignore. Let's remember what Kissinger et al. (2023) said. The fundamental problem of the age of artificial intelligence lies in the fact that it creates a gap between human knowledge and human understanding. Unfortunately, banning generative artificial intelligence seems to bring about incautiousness that will not close this gap but will widen it. We think that the key to preventing this lies not in banning them but in students using them with the right motivations, that is, in communicating with generative artificial intelligence.

To better understand this, let's turn our attention to vice epistemology, which focuses on the wrong character traits of the agents, and try to understand why only technical education or bans will not work against generative artificial intelligence.

VICE EPISTEMOLOGY

Roughly speaking, vice epistemology is "the nature, identity and epistemological significance of intellectual vices" (Cassam, 2016, p. 159). The vice word we are talking about tells us, "cognitive dispositions that produce bad epistemic effects—including (but not limited to) false beliefs" (Battaly, 2017, p. 225). Although vice epistemology is concerned with the character traits that make the individual blameworthy or evil, Kidd, Battaly, and Cassam (2021) state that vice epistemology is affected by two primary factors: The first is the areas it is in relationship with other areas, and the second is cultural and political developments. Kidd, Battaly, and Cassam (2021) say that cultural and political developments create opportunities to deal with the character traits exhibited by people and state that vice epistemology works on the following three foundations:

1. Basic studies on the effects of epistemic defects on knowledge and the characteristics and structures of epistemic defects,
2. Analysis of specific epistemic vices,
3. Case studies in applied vice epistemology.

Ultimately, vice epistemology informs us about what it means to have someone's intellectual vice. For example, Baehr argues that for a person to have an intellectual defect, "one must exhibit defective competence, motivation, judgment, and affection" (2021, p.24).Some opposing views undermine this assertion even if one accepts these terms for considering someone intellectually flawed. For example, scholars such as Cassam (2019) and Crerar (2018) have put forward the "obstructionist" account, which is a counter-motivational explanation, in response to the "motivational" vice explanations of scholars such as Baehr and Tannesini (2018). The character traits we call vice for the obstructive account are "traits, attitudes, and way of thinking that systematically obstruct the acquisition, transmission, and retention of knowledge" (Cassam, 2019, p. 1). The motivational group, led by Tanesini (2018), argues that intellectual vice is the agent's evil intentions and desires toward intellectual goods. For example, a motivator who does not want others to obtain information on a subject or wants them to get incorrect information exhibits an intellectual vice. Intellectual stinginess and intellectual malevolence are good examples of motivationalist understanding.

Understanding what the intellectual vices are provides us with an excellent opportunity to understand the potential challenges of generative AI, so we have the chance to understand and uncover its potential advantages.

Let's remember our concern about creating deepfakes. A serious disadvantage of generative artificial intelligence such as Dall-e and MidJourney, which convert prompts into visuals, is that the entered prompts create deepfakes that can be used for malicious purposes. Will we reach a solution if we prevent students from using generative artificial intelligence to eliminate this effect? If we look at it from the vice epistemology perspective, especially from the motivational account, unfortunately, the answer is no. Worst, accepting the destructive results of these tools and ensuring that students write correct prompts to save them from this would not be a solution. For Tanesini, intellectual vices "involve non-instrumental motivations to oppose, antagonize, or avoid things that are epistemically good in themselves" (2018, p. 350). Therefore, a person with intellectual malevolence will act with epistemically bad intentions and will ultimately try to prevent or keep to herself what she sees as epistemically good. Then, for such a person, preventing generative artificial intelligence in the educational environment does not mean anything. She will somehow continue to act around her bad character vices in her mundane life. But even worse for us as educators would be properly educating this person on prompt communication with generative artificial intelligence. It will not cure the malevolent person, but it will also enable her to acquire the technical knowledge necessary to display her character trait; thus, in a way, we will be showing the way to the thief. Cocking and Van den Hoven (2018) provide an excellent example in their book *Evil Online* to help us understand why prompt education should not remain only at the technical level.

A group attacks a website designed for people with photosynthetic epilepsy, and your disease is triggered when you enter the site because of a group attack. It is difficult to find a logical explanation for why this group does this, and the authors, after a difficult search for a reason, say that the online world creates a fog for our moral definitions. So, what does this have to do with generative AI? Moral fog is a serious problem, especially in online worlds, and generative AI can play a vital role in strengthening this *fog*. Suppose a person takes action with wrong motivations, as in the example above. In that case, AI can navigate her along this path, thanks to the good technical prompting knowledge we have educated that person.Remember the prompts for effective communication with ChatGPT, shared by Bornet (2023) in a LinkedIn post. Teaching this technical information to the malicious person would make the situation worse. Someone with such a bad character trait would have the technological know-how to make an AI do everything we fear it would do, similar to letting the fox guard the henhouse.Are we helpless as educators if preventing generative artificial intelligence is useless and teaching the technical knowledge of prompts makes things worse? Our answer is that we believe the problem lies not only in technical teaching but in virtue ethics; however, to understand this better, we need to continue to examine the challenges in terms of vice epistemology.

Because vice epistemologists present situations in which the motivational account is insufficient, some educators may offer a criticism that the situation cannot be this dire; indeed, such malicious students are not very common characters in the classroom. However, we must pay attention to the fact that even though extreme cases are not common, they still exist. However, while vice epistemologists report that the motivational account is incomplete, they do not say there are no intellectual vices. Instead, Crerar (2018) examines the Oblomov case and argues that one can be intellectually viced without evil motivations. For Crerar, Oblomov is someone with the vice of epistemic laziness who does not want to obtain epistemic goods but does not have bad motivation.Let's consider an epistemically lazy student using Oblomov's example.

Even if the student does not have bad motivation, if they have a laziness trait that prevents them from achieving epistemic good, they can directly accept the information offered by tools such as ChatGPT. For a good example, let's look at our conversation with ChatGPT. Suppose you are having one of your students prepare an assignment about intellectual flaws, and you have a lazy student who is too lazy to collect the mass of knowledge offered by the internet. In that case, she will bring you an assignment prepared via ChatGPT. However, suppose you ask ChatGPT (2023) what an intellectual vice is. In that case, you will get output that visually impaired and autistic people may also be epistemically vices, based on the definition of some vice epistemologists. If your student is not curious and diligent enough to examine this knowledge or is epistemically lazy, she will have acquired incorrect knowledge about these people. However, a fair criticism that can be made here is that if she had learned how to use prompts correctly, she may have asked her to present opposing views or warned ChatGPT to use sources in her statements. We can partially accept the criticism, but Cassam (2019), based on the obstructive account, mentions the existence of some vices that prevent the person from obtaining information and are difficult to detect by herself. He states, "epistemic vices that obstruct their detection are inherently hard to detect. Such vices are stealthy vices." (2019,p.145).

Therefore, the student may only need to question the outputs if they know what they did wrong or even think they did it right. For a more interesting example, let's look at the trait of arrogance as a stealthy vice. We know that students use the internet to obtain much knowledge and that educators even support it. However, when students access this knowledge from an external source such as the internet, it can cause them to overestimate their knowledge level as to whether they know the knowledge they have obtained. For example, when you ask a student to learn a chemical formula, the student can easily access that formula on the internet and think that she has learned it. However, the knowledge there may not be stored internally, and you may lose the information of the formula when you lose access to the internet. Thus, you may overestimate your knowledge and mistakenly believe you have knowledge you do not have. Fisher et al. (2015) argue that the internet's ability to provide fast and large amounts of expert knowledge is in a different position compared to other sources and "cause us to lose track of our reliance upon it, distorting how we view our abilities"(2015, 675). Therefore, the student will have an epistemic illusion that will bring intellectual arrogance that causes her to misjudge her situation. Generative artificial intelligence is much better at distilling information than the internet, allowing you to access more complex knowledge more easily and quickly. For instance, it can gather knowledge from various sources about why and how Istanbul was taken by the Ottomans and presented to the student, which may give the illusion that the student knows. Especially for someone with intellectual arrogance, this situation will be inevitable. Therefore, presenting only the technical knowledge of the prompts here will not prevent generative artificial intelligence from creating harmful effects that will cause it to be blamed and ultimately cause it to be limited by criticism that pushes students to laziness.

We can similar criticism to those who have no hesitation in actively using generative artificial intelligence in education. However, suppose the student gives feedback that will lead to wrong results based on character traits while using generative artificial intelligence. In that case, it will cause the artificial intelligence tools to become epistemically corrupt. Recall that not only is Mark left alone with the generative AI, but also the generative AI is left alone with Mark. Generative AIs have profound learning and take into consideration your reactions to the outputs. Therefore, the problems created by artificial intelligence lie not only in its essence but also in the user.For instance, a student with epistemic malevolence may consciously corrupt AI tools and prevent others from achieving epistemic goods. An intellectually lazy student, because they do not care about epistemic goods, may indirectly cause the generative artificial intelligence to be corrupted by not giving correct guiding feedback to its outputs, just asin the instance above we asked ChatGPT, who can be epistemically vice. Hence, inviting students to use generative AI while merely teaching them how to enter prompts takes away from generative AI's core power: its potential to empower teachers.

EMPOWERING TEACHERS

So far, we have persistently argued that providing students with only technical education is insufficient for generative artificial intelligence to succeed. Technical education itself can be abused, consciously or unconsciously, due to student characters. To overcome this, we need something better than filters and bans. Because, like everything that is in great demand in daily life, generative artificial intelligence continues to be used with increasing interest despite the prohibitions in education. However, education also includes those optimistic about inviting generative artificial intelligence into classrooms. We need to pay attention here that just as the problems need to be defined correctly, the advantages must also be defined correctly. Let's use the healthcare allegory again. If you make very general statements about your problems to the doctor, the treatment she gives you may start to do more harm than good.

Similarly, if you use general statements about the treatment providing improvement, it may cover up the real problem; imagine that your leg no longer hurts after the antibiotic you used, but you took it for nausea so you could take the medicine. Although this is strange, we can experience similar situations in education. A painting that we show to students to be anti-war may not make them anti-war, but it may pave the way for them to become good art critics. The situation is no different for generative artificial intelligence. Although it is not as obvious as the anti-war analogy, we may make similar mistakes when counting the advantages of generative artificial intelligence. For instance, while arguing that generative AI creates an excellent opportunity for personalization in education, we can ignore its potential problems. Kucirkova and Gray (in press) say that artificial intelligence's ability to personalize education is insufficient for democratic education when viewed from Bernstein's democracy condition. From another perspective, when we argue that generative artificial intelligence provides easy and fast knowledge and that this is an advantage in itself, we are now forced to ask what the role of the teacher is; if generative artificial intelligences are so adept at education, how is the teacher any different from the manager of a fast-food restaurant? Other than auditing systems that are already clear and follow a recipe.

Through this problem, Lee (2023) tries to find the role of the teacher in the face of artificial intelligence. In summary, what we consider to be the advantages of generative AI is forcing us to rethink and realize that perhaps we got it wrong. So, what is the value of generative AI for education? We believe the answer lies in empowering teachers. It differs from the teacher-centered education we are discussing here; what we mean by empowering teachers is different from advocating a teacher-centered approach. The teacher somehow represents educational policies in the classroom, and we can't leave them out of the process. Therefore, it plays an active role in both teacher-centered and student-centered understanding. So, what is empowering a teacher, and how can generative AI empower the teacher?

Understanding What Empowering Teacher Is

Educational epistemology deals with education's nature, purposes, and practical applications and explains at least the first part of our question. Watson (2016) created a classification based on the discussions of educational epistemologists for a long time and stated that there are three main approaches within educational epistemology:

1. Goods-based Accounts
2. Skills-based Accounts
3. Character-based accounts

For Watson (2016), goods-centered education tries to reveal the purpose of education in terms of epistemic goods. While essentially aiming for students to have as much knowledge as possible, the main purpose of education is to transfer epistemic goods, namely understanding, knowledge, and belief, to students.On the other hand, unlike goods-centered theory, skill-centered theory states that the main purpose is to acquire and develop specific skills, not to transfer epistemic goods (Watson, 2016, p153). These skills include critical thinking and independent thinking, and deal with the importance of these skills and how to impart them to students.Finally, the main purpose of character-centered education is to enable students to acquire some character traits and virtues (Watson, 2016, p.155). A more student-centered approach prevails here, focusing on students' characters as opposed to the epistemic goods they achieve. With this approach, acquiring character traits called intellectual virtues has become a fundamental issue of education. Accordingly, our main aim is to provide students with the intellectual virtues necessary to make the right decisions and reason well. The concept we call empowering teachers is directly related to this approach of educational epistemology. We have insisted for some time that we should focus on students' characters. Here, character-centered education fully pays off our insistence. Character-based education and teaching intellectual virtues become important if students show praiseworthy or condemnable character performance.

We claimed we could solve this if we interpreted the blameworthy behaviors and results exhibited by students who benefit from generative artificial intelligence around their character vices. This is where intellectual virtues, that is, good character traits, emerge to understand students' praiseworthy behavior or results. If students have intellectual attentiveness, they know they may need to be corrected and avoid making hasty conclusions instead of immediately accepting the information presented by generative AI. If a student has intellectual curiosity, for example, she can use generative AI to address some problems. Therefore, it will empower teachers if generative AI can develop intellectual virtues that enable students to pursue epistemic goods and have intrinsic motivation.

To better understand this situation, let's start from the internet, not directly from generative artificial intelligence. If Mark had searched for a way to be successful in computer games on the internet rather than in generative artificial intelligence, he would have come across forum posts, blogs, and some visual video content. It is entirely up to Mark which of these he consumes. For example, in a blog post he reads, he may say that the key to passing the level with the highest score lies in the character committing a virtual murder. In a much more complex and dangerous scenario, the internet does not only serve Mark's games but is also a source of knowledge. Especially search engines, due to their user-friendly structure, access any content that may harm the user. Mark may also be directed to content where he is constantly exposed to misinformation because his character traits shape his user profile. However, the critical point here is that ensuring reliability is the user's responsibility, the epistemic agent, rather than filtering the internet itself (Smart and Clowes, 2021).

What we have said so far is no different from the previous parts of the chapter. The only thing that changes is that Mark searches for the answer on the internet instead of the generative AI. How Mark's character shapes internet searches and why filtering the internet won't work is the same as what we discussed about generative AI. With one difference: Heersmink (2018) argued that schools have a responsibility to solve the problems posed by the internet, and therefore, they have a responsibility to develop intellectual virtues. We could impose a similar obligation on generative AI. Generative artificial intelligence must support intellectual virtues to find a place in education. In this way, it can erase the disadvantages that caused her to be removed from education and become valuable for education. We have shown that this cannot be achieved by merely providing students with user manuals and technical knowledge education; we need technical knowledge plus more. We believe virtuous prompts with technical knowledge derived from intellectual virtues can achieve this. Virtuous prompts are not prompts offered by virtuous individuals; on the contrary, they contain some intellectual virtue to obtain them and cause them to experience virtues.According to Aristotle (2000), virtues are not innate and can only be acquired and mastered through experience. Then, what we need to do is enable students to use generative artificial intelligence to provide virtuous prompts.

VIRTUOUS PROMPT AND EMPOWERING TEACHER

Let's remember Bozkurt and Sharma's (2023) Genie allegory. If the key is to make the right wishes for the genie, we must make understandable, clear, and well-intentioned wishes. Otherwise, you may find yourself in bad scenarios. Therefore, the genie analogy shows us that technically correct communication must also be good intentions. Prompts offered to generative artificial intelligence are only desirable if they lead to the development of proper technique and good character tendencies. Therefore, the virtuous prompt is *a) includes good technical knowledge, b) targets good character traits through intellectual virtues, and c) a communication tool that generative artificial intelligence.*

A fundamental criticism that can be made about virtuous prompts is that it is not clear how they differ from technical knowledge education. Therefore, if generative artificial intelligence is affected by character vices and prompt education gives problems, it is unclear how the virtuous prompt will overcome them. Primarily, the virtuous prompt does not exclude or devalue the technical knowledge offered by names such as Bornet. On the contrary, Clause A accepts it, while Clause C emphasizes that virtuous prompting is a tool. However, substance Clause B has its vital purpose. We do not exclude students' character vices, but rather, we accept their existence and accept generative artificial intelligence as an instrument that develops intellectual virtues to improve them. When you tell us, hence, that an intellectually arrogant student experiences the illusion of knowledge thanks to generative artificial intelligence, our answer to you is,"You are right.", arrogance is a flawed character trait, and to overcome this, filtering generative artificial intelligence or just providing technical knowledge education will not work. On the contrary, you need to provide that student with technical education that includes Clause B because"a virtue is a stable and successful disposition: an innate ability or an acquired habit that allows one to achieve some good reliably" (Greco & Turri, 2021).To make our explanation lucid, let's focus on how Schwengerer (2023) uses VR technologies to improve the stealth vices offered by Cassam, even though it is not directly related to generative artificial intelligence, and let's try to establish the relationship of this example with generative artificial intelligence.

Schwengerer (2023) explores the role of virtual reality in acquiring self-knowledge through external prompting, as opposed to Cassam's and Lawlor's internal prompting, which is based on using one's imaginary power for self-knowledge acquisition in the fight against vices. His primary motivation in doing this is the fear that internal prompting in the person's imagination is affected by some prejudices and the belief that it will yield unsuccessful results. Schwengerer (2023) thinks that inner prompting is a way to save from the influence of stealthy vices such as prejudice and suggests that VR technology can be helpful in this regard, thus introducing the concept of external prompting for acquiring self-knowledge. According to him:

If constrained imaginings of particular scenarios can lead one to internal promptings—to one's thoughts, feelings and behaviors in response to that scenario, then it should also be possible to bring a user into a VR scenario that leads agents to observe their thoughts, feelings and behaviors in that VR scenario in a similar way. And if observing one's reactions in imagined scenarios can be used as evidence to infer one's own mental state, then the observations of reactions in VR can also be used in the very same way (2023, p. 9).

Schwengerer adapts VR scenarios to Lawlor's Katherine example and suggests that he can gather evidence through different imaginary scenarios that would allow Katherine to figure out whether she wants another baby. Thus, eventually, Katherine can gather enough evidence to enable her to decide with external inspiration at some point. Also, Schwengerer argues that this type of practice can be used to simulate many cases involving vices, virtues, and values to gather evidence because, thanks to VR scenarios, we have a chance to gather a lot of evidence that we can use later. To understand better, imagine a simulated honesty scenario. If you had created it with internal prompting, your vices would have ignored many scenarios where you were wrong. However, with VR, you can create interactions that provide evidence of the different outcomes of your decisions.

Cassam (2015) does not tend to consider bias itself as a vice, but we can apply the external prompts provided by VR to our example through other vices. Let's call on the example of the student with epistemic laziness again. This student lacked the motivation to pursue the knowledge ChatGPT provided, so she directly accepted the knowledge it submitted. When a student submits an assignment full of mistakes to her teacher due to this character vice, her teacher not only gives her a low point but also suggests she thinks that what she did was wrong. However, laziness may prevent her from taking action even to understand her situation, and she may ultimately claim that she did not do anything wrong, that she was collecting the knowledge, and that ChatGPT is the one responsible. Ultimately, epistemic laziness becomes a stealthy vice.

Suppose the teacher considers Watson's third approach and focuses on developing the student's character traits. In that case, they can create scenarios that provide external prompts to generative artificial intelligence thanks to VR, as Schewengerer claims. Moreover, since the student denies that she has epistemic laziness in her situation during the formation of these scenarios, she can enter prompts that will enable the formation of scenarios from her perspective. Ultimately, the teacher not only benefits from the personalization advantage of generative artificial intelligence but also obtains external evidence that will enable the student to acquire virtues against intellectual laziness. While doing this, it aims to provide the student with the excellent character traits suggested by item B. Put differently, the prompts she uses during the scenarios created by generative artificial intelligence become an example of virtuous prompts and strengthen the teacher.

Another good example is given by Merzifonluoglu and Hamarat (2022). They say that social studies have the potential to create and combat epistemic injustice, and ultimately, social studies can overcome epistemic injustice if it provides moral sensitivity. On the other hand, while emphasizing the need to develop schemes that will enable students to understand what it means to be on the silenced side, for example, to cultivate moral sensitivity, they offer several models to achieve this, including cooperation with local communities, textbooks and, on the side that concerns us, generative artificial intelligence applications. Merzifonluoglu and Hamarat (2022) argue that "AI-based systems can play a mediating role with visualizations for teachers to acquaint students with epistemic injustice, and that pulls students into dikaiosune" (p. 13). As in this example, the teacher communicates with generative AI to help students cultivate moral sensitivity and prevent them from creating epistemic injustice. It provides virtuous prompts so students can understand what it is like to be on the silenced side, for example, and ultimately empowers social studies teachers.

CONCLUSION

Generative artificial intelligence-based tools continue to find more and more space both in daily life and the educational environment. However, generative AI in education has the potential to produce undesirable results due to its structure. On the other hand, to eliminate this bad potential, we need to rely on something more than filters and bans because education banning them does not affect usage rates in daily life. Therefore, to solve this problem, education has the responsibility to focus on students' character development. Its ability to achieve this depends on something different than providing a guide for using generative artificial intelligence. We argued that this is the development of intellectual virtues. If education wants to improve students' character vices and give them good characteristics, it can use the advantages provided by generative artificial intelligence, and in doing so, it can turn into an instrument that enables the student to acquire intellectual virtues and empower teachers, which we call virtuous prompts. Only in this way could Mark save himself and the generative AI from being pushed out of character vice generation and education.

REFERENCES

Aristotle. (2000). *The Nicomachean Ethics* (R. Crisp, Trans.). Cambridge University Press. doi:10.1017/CBO9780511802058

Baehr, J. (2013). Educating for intellectual virtues: From theory to practice. *Journal of Philosophy of Education, 47*(2), 248–262. doi:10.1111/1467-9752.12023

Baehr, J. (2021). The Structure of Intellectual Vices. In I. J. Kidd, H. Battaly, & Q. Cassam (Eds.), *Vice Epistemology* (pp. 21–36). Routledge.

Battaly, H. (2017). Testimonial injustice, epistemic vice, and vice epistemology. In I. J. Kidd, J. Medina, & G. Pohlhaus (Eds.), *The Routledge handbook of epistemic injustice* (pp. 223–231). Routledge. doi:10.4324/9781315212043-22

Bornet, P. (2023, September). *Here's the ChatGPT Ultimate Prompting Guide. Important elements to include: 1. Tone 2. Format 3. Objective 4. Context 5.Examples If you don't get the right output, try again you will get it soon... It is because of the prompt, not the tech!* (Post). LinkedIn. https://www.linkedin.com/posts/pascalbornet_genai-tech-skillsofthefuture-activity-7101048156108267520-l4Lx?utm_source=share&utm_medium=member_desktop

Bozkurt, A., & Sharma, R. C. (2023). Generative AI and prompt engineering: The art of whispering to let the genie out of the algorithmic world. *Asian Journal of Distance Education*, *18*(2), i–vii. doi:10.5281/zenodo.8174941

Cassam, Q. (2015). Stealthy vices. *Social Epistemology Review and Reply Collective*, *4*(10), 19–25.

Cassam, Q. (2018). *Vices of the mind: From the Intellectual to the Political*. Oxford University Press.

Cassidy, C. (2023, Jan 22). Queensland public schools to join NSW in banning students from ChatGPT. *The Guardian*. https://www.theguardian.com/australia-news/2023/jan/23/queensland-public-schools-to-join-nsw-in-banning-students-from-chatgpt

Cocking, D., & Van den Hoven, J. (2018). *Evil online*. John Wiley & Sons. doi:10.1002/9781119471219

Crerar, C. (2018). Motivational approaches to intellectual vice. *Australasian Journal of Philosophy*, *96*(4), 753–766. doi:10.1080/00048402.2017.1394334

Fisher, M., Goddu, M. K., & Keil, F. C. (2015). Searching for explanations: How the internet inflates estimates of internal knowledge. *Journal of Experimental Psychology. General*, *144*(3), 674–687. doi:10.1037/xge0000070 PMID:25822461

Harrer, S. (2023). Attention is not allyouneed: The complicated case of ethically using large language models in health care and medicine. *EBioMedicine*, *90*, 104512. doi:10.1016/j.ebiom.2023.104512 PMID:36924620

Heersmink, R. (2018). A virtue epistemology of the Internet: Search engines, intellectual virtues and education. *Social Epistemology*, *32*(1), 1–12. doi:10.1080/02691728.2017.1383530

Holmes, W., Bialik, M., & Fadel, C. (2019). *Artificial Intelligence in Education: Promises and Implications for Teaching & Learning*. The Center for Curriculum Redesign.

Kidd, I. J., Battaly, H., & Cassam, Q. (2021). Introduction: From Epistemic Vices to Vice Epistemology. In I. J. Kidd, Q. Cassam, & H. Battaly (Eds.), *Vice epistemology* (pp. 1–18). Routledge.

Kissinger, H., Schmidt, E., & Huttenlocher, D. (2023, February 24). ChatGPT heralds an intellectual revolution. *Wall Street Journal*. https://www.wsj.com/articles/chatgpt-heralds-an-intellectual-revolution-enlightenment-artificial-intelligence-homo-technicus-technology-cognition-morality-philosophy-774331c6

Kucirkova, N., & Leaton Gray, S. (2023, August). Beyond Personalization: Embracing Democratic Learning Within Artificially Intelligent Systems. *Educational Theory*, *73*(4), 469–489. doi:10.1111/edth.12590

Kumar, A. H. S. (2023). Analysis of ChatGPT tool to assess the potential of it sutility for academic writing in biomedical domain. *BEMS Reports*, *9*(1), 24–30. doi:10.5530/bems.9.1.5

Lee, S. E. (2023). Otherwise than teaching by artificial intelligence. *Journal of Philosophy of Education*, *57*(2), 553–570. doi:10.1093/jopedu/qhad019

Lim, W. M., Gunasekara, A., Pallant, J. L., Pallant, J. I., & Pechenkina, E. (2023). Generative AI and the future of education: Ragnarök or reformation? A paradoxical perspective from management educators. *International Journal of Management Education*, *21*(2), 100790. doi:10.1016/j.ijme.2023.100790

Merzifonluoglu, S., & Hamarat, E. (2022). Epistemic Injustice, Social Studies, and Moral Sensitivity. *Ethics and Education*, *17*(4), 403–420. doi:10.1080/17449642.2022.2153469

Open A. I. (2023). *ChatGPT* [Large language model]. OpenAI. https://chat.openai.com

Schwengerer, L. (2023). Virtual reality as a path to self-knowledge. *Synthese*, *202*(3), 87. doi:10.1007/s11229-023-04317-w PMID:36855375

Smart, P., & Clowes, R. (2021). Intellectual virtues and internet-extended knowledge. *Social Epistemology Review and Reply Collective*, *10*(1), 7–21. https://wp.me/p1Bfg0-5AY

Tanesini, A. (2018). Epistemic Vice and Motivation. *Metaphilosophy*, *49*(3), 350–367. doi:10.1111/meta.12301

Turri, J., Alfano, M., & Greco, J. (2021, October 26). Virtue epistemology. *Stanford Encyclopedia of Philosophy*. Stanford Press. https://plato.stanford.edu/entries/epistemology-virtue/

WarschauerM.TsengW.YimS.WebsterT.JacobS.DuQ.TateT. The Affordance sand Contradictions of AI-Generated Textfor Second Language Writers *(*2023, March 20). SSRN. https://ssrn.com/abstract=4404380 doi:10.2139/ssrn.4404380

Watson, L. (2016). The epistemology of education. *Philosophy Compass*, *11*(3), 146–159. doi:10.1111/phc3.12316

KEY TERMS AND DEFINITIONS

Empowering Teacher: They are mental and material tools that serve teachers to achieve the epistemological aims of education.

Generative AI: Artificial intelligence capable of generating text, images, or other media, using generative models.

Intellectual Virtues: It is the agent's cognitive disposition that serves to produce good epistemic effects.

Vice Epistemology: It is a field of philosophical study that focuses on the nature and identity of vice to examine the epistemological significance of intellectual vice.

Vice: It is the agent's cognitive disposition that serves to produce bad epistemic effects.

Virtue Epistemology: It is a field of philosophical study that focuses on the nature and identity of virtue to examine the epistemological significance of intellectual virtue.

Virtuous Prompt: Includes good technical knowledge, targets good character traits through intellectual virtues, and a communication tool that generative AI.

Chapter 6
Future Possibilities and Challenges of AI in Education

Mustafa Kayyali
https://orcid.org/0000-0003-3300-262X
HE Higher Education Ranking, Syria

ABSTRACT

"Future Possibilities and Challenges of AI in Education" delves into the unprecedented intersection of artificial intelligence (AI) and the educational landscape. The chapter navigates the transformative possibilities and intricate challenges that arise as AI infiltrates learning management systems. In this exploration, the symbiotic relationship between AI and education is dissected, revealing a dynamic environment teeming with potential. The chapter unfolds in two movements: envisioning a future where personalized learning, AI-enhanced creativity, seamless assessment, global collaboration, and ethical education thrive, and concurrently, acknowledging the uncharted difficulties that could reshape the foundational paradigms of education. As the world hurtles toward an era of automation and interconnected virtuality, understanding the effects of AI in education becomes important. This chapter beckons readers on a journey through the limitless potential of AI's impact on education, inviting reflection on how to harness its power responsibly for the betterment of learning.

INTRODUCTION

In the current epoch, we find ourselves at the nexus of an extraordinary amalgamation of technology and education, with artificial intelligence (AI) catalyzing a transformative wave within the realm of learning. This intersection holds the promise of reshaping the entire educational landscape, propelling professors and students into a new era marked by unprecedented opportunities and formidable challenges. The integration of AI-powered tools is becoming increasingly prevalent across classrooms, curriculum development, and learning management systems, heralding a seismic shift in traditional educational paradigms. The objective of this chapter is to serve as a guide, navigating readers through the dynamic and swiftly evolving landscape where AI and education converge. As we embark on this exploration, our aim is to unravel the intricacies of the symbiotic relationship between AI and education, shedding light on the

DOI: 10.4018/979-8-3693-1351-0.ch006

multifaceted opportunities and risks inherent in this fusion. This understanding is paramount as the world hurtles toward an age dominated by automation, data-driven insights, and virtual interconnectedness.

In contemplating the future of AI in education, we stand at a crossroads, faced with divergent paths that could lead either to a realm of enriched learning experiences and empowered educators or a domain fraught with unforeseen challenges capable of reshaping the very foundations of education. This chapter unfolds in two distinct movements, commencing with an examination of the potential applications of AI in education in the years to come. Envisioning a future where personalized learning paths become the norm, artificial intelligence becomes a catalyst for creativity, and boundaries to cross-border cooperation are dismantled, we delve into the transformative possibilities that lie ahead. Within this landscape, we explore the evolving role of educators, emphasizing their pivotal position in establishing the AI-augmented classroom. The mentorship and guiding functions of educators emerge as linchpins in ensuring a harmonious integration of AI tools, underscoring the critical importance of human direction and inspiration in the educational journey (Ji et al., 2023). As we embark on this intellectual adventure, let us approach it with an open mind and a steadfast commitment to harnessing AI for the enhancement of education. Our voyage through the limitless potential and uncharted territories of AI in education invites us to strike a delicate balance between technological innovation and the enduring essence of human influence, ensuring that the educational landscape of tomorrow is shaped by the best of both worlds.

DEFINITION

Generative AI

Generative AI refers to a class of artificial intelligence systems designed to generate new content or data that is similar to, but not an exact copy of, existing examples (Aydın & Karaarslan, 2023). These systems use various techniques, such as neural networks, to analyze patterns in data and then generate new content based on those patterns. One of the key aspects of generative AI is its ability to create novel and diverse outputs. One popular approach to generative AI is the use of Generative Adversarial Networks (GANs). GANs consist of two neural networks – a generator and a discriminator – that are trained in tandem (Bozkurt, 2023a, b). The generator creates new data, and the discriminator evaluates whether the generated data is real or fake. Through this adversarial process, the generator improves over time, producing more realistic outputs.

Generative AI has found applications in various domains, including:

1. Image Generation: Generating realistic images that may look like photographs of human faces, animals, or other objects.
2. Text Generation: Creating human-like text, such as articles, stories, or poetry.
3. Music Composition: Generating new music compositions in various styles.
4. Video Game Design: Creating game environments, characters, and other elements.
5. Drug Discovery: Generating molecular structures for potential new drugs.
6. Art and Design: Creating visual art, designs, and graphics.
7. Data Augmentation: Generating additional training data to improve the performance of machine learning models.

Artificial Intelligence

AI, or Artificial Intelligence, refers to the development of computer systems or software that can perform tasks that typically require human intelligence (Haleem et al., 2022). These tasks include learning, reasoning, problem-solving, understanding natural language, speech recognition, and visual perception, among others. The goal of AI is to create machines that can mimic or simulate human cognitive functions.

There are two main types of AI:

1. Narrow or Weak AI (ANI): This type of AI is designed and trained for a particular task. It excels in performing specific tasks but lacks the broad cognitive abilities of humans. Examples include virtual personal assistants, image and speech recognition systems, and recommendation algorithms.
2. General or Strong AI (AGI): This is a more advanced form of AI that possesses the ability to understand, learn, and apply knowledge across a wide range of tasks, similar to human intelligence. AGI remains a theoretical concept, and creating machines with general intelligence is a complex and challenging goal.

AI can be further categorized based on its functionality:

- Machine Learning (ML): A subset of AI that involves the development of algorithms and statistical models that enable computers to improve their performance on a task through learning from data.
- Deep Learning: A subfield of machine learning that uses neural networks with multiple layers (deep neural networks) to analyze and process data. Deep learning has been particularly successful in tasks such as image and speech recognition.

AI in Education

AI in education refers to the application of artificial intelligence technologies to enhance and transform various aspects of the educational process. It encompasses a wide range of applications and tools that leverage AI to improve teaching, learning, administrative tasks, and educational outcomes (Schiff, 2022). Here are some key areas where AI is making an impact in education:

1. Personalized Learning: AI systems can analyze individual student data, including learning preferences, strengths, and weaknesses, to tailor educational content and activities to meet the specific needs of each student. This helps optimize the learning experience and ensures that students progress at their own pace.
2. Adaptive Learning Platforms: Adaptive learning systems use AI algorithms to adjust the difficulty level of educational content in real-time based on a student's performance. This ensures that the material is challenging enough to promote learning but not so difficult as to cause frustration.
3. Intelligent Tutoring Systems: AI-powered tutoring systems provide personalized feedback and guidance to students, offering additional support in areas where they may be struggling. These systems can simulate one-on-one tutoring and adapt to the learner's progress.

4. Automated Grading and Assessment: AI can automate the grading process for assignments and assessments, saving time for educators. This allows teachers to focus more on interacting with students, providing feedback, and adapting their teaching strategies.
5. Language Processing for Learning Disabilities: AI technologies, such as natural language processing (NLP), can assist students with learning disabilities by providing real-time feedback on their written or spoken language, helping them improve their communication skills.
6. Predictive Analytics: AI can analyze data to identify patterns and predict student outcomes, such as potential dropouts or academic success. Educators can use this information to intervene early and provide additional support to at-risk students.
7. Virtual and Augmented Reality: AI is often integrated with virtual and augmented reality technologies to create immersive learning experiences. This can include virtual field trips, interactive simulations, and three-dimensional educational content.
8. Administrative Tasks: AI is also used to streamline administrative tasks in educational institutions, such as scheduling, enrollment, and resource allocation, allowing educators to focus more on teaching and student engagement.

FUTURE POSSIBILITIES

The symbiotic relationship between artificial intelligence (AI) and education is a testament to the limitless possibilities of innovation at a time of fast technological growth. Looking into the future, we are presented with a tapestry of opportunities that have been weaved from the threads of AI's profound impact on education.

Personalized Learning Journeys: A Symphony of Individualized Education

In the not-so-distant future, the educational landscape undergoes a profound metamorphosis, guided by the harmonious convergence of artificial intelligence (AI) and the pedagogical realm (Dogan et al., 2023). Picture an environment where the traditional, one-size-fits-all approach to education is replaced by a dynamic symphony of personalized learning journeys, each note resonating with the unique learning style and aptitude of every individual student. This vision encapsulates the transformative promise of the amalgamation of AI and education—a promise that unfolds in the creation of highly tailored and personalized learning paths (Thomas & Alkhafaji, 2023). The essence of this transformative shift lies in the intricate dance between advanced AI algorithms and the wealth of data that defines each learner. These algorithms, designed with unprecedented sophistication, hold the potential to craft learning routes that navigate the intellectual terrain of each student's mind with precision and finesse. In this educational symphony, AI transcends its role as a mere tool; it ascends to the status of a sagacious mentor, carefully observing and understanding each student's performance. The power of AI lies not only in its ability to sift through vast datasets but also in its capacity to interpret the nuances of individual learning processes (Pratama et al., 2023). As it scrutinizes a student's strengths and weaknesses, AI dynamically adjusts the complexity of the content, tailors the pace of classes, and meticulously curates supplemental materials. It transforms the learning experience into a dynamic interaction between technology and personality, a synergy that not only captivates students but also enhances their comprehension and retention of the material.

Furthermore, questions about the digital divide and equitable access to personalized learning resources emerge. As AI-powered education becomes more ubiquitous, ensuring that all students, regardless of socio-economic backgrounds, have equal access to cutting-edge educational tools becomes an imperative. Bridging the digital gap is not just about providing devices and internet access; it's about creating an inclusive educational ecosystem where every learner, regardless of their circumstances, can benefit from the transformative power of personalized learning. Far from being replaced by AI, educators become orchestrators of this symphony, guiding and complementing the capabilities of AI. The human touch remains irreplaceable, providing the emotional intelligence, mentorship, and inspiration that algorithms cannot replicate. The educator's role shifts from delivering content to curating experiences, fostering critical thinking, and nurturing creativity—the very qualities that make us distinctly human (Kirkpatrick, 2023). AI augments the capabilities of educators, providing real-time insights into student progress, identifying areas of improvement, and offering tailored recommendations. Educators, armed with this data, can adapt their teaching strategies, providing targeted interventions and personalized support to each student. The fusion of AI and education extends beyond the confines of the traditional classroom. Lifelong learning takes on a new dimension as AI becomes a constant companion in the journey of acquiring new skills and knowledge. Professionals, too, benefit from personalized learning paths, staying abreast of industry trends and refining their expertise in a rapidly evolving job market. The symphony of personalized learning journeys, orchestrated by the collaboration between AI and education, heralds a transformative era in the educational landscape. The potential to tailor education to the unique needs of each learner is a powerful tool for fostering intellectual growth, engagement, and lifelong learning. However, as we navigate this uncharted territory, it is imperative to address ethical considerations, ensure equitable access, and preserve the irreplaceable human elements of education. The future of education is not a dichotomy between man and machine but a harmonious collaboration that amplifies the best of both worlds, creating a symphony of education that resonates with the diverse and individualized potential of every learner.

AI-Enhanced Creativity: A Palette of Unlimited Imagination

In the annals of education, the conventional narrative often depicted a structured and methodical journey, placing a significant emphasis on rote memorization. However, the evolving landscape of education propels us into a future where the barriers between disciplines dissolve, and the fertile grounds of innovation are meticulously cultivated (Bearman et al., 2023). The emergence of artificial intelligence (AI) as a creative force not only disrupts traditional notions of education but also becomes a catalyst for unlocking boundless imagination and fostering innovation. Historically relegated to the realms of data analysis, AI is now undergoing a paradigm shift, transforming from a passive tool into an active agent of creativity. In this future, AI transcends its role as a mere repository of information; it becomes an integral part of the creative process, engaging students in brainstorming sessions, challenging them to explore novel ideas, visualize abstract concepts, and formulate innovative solutions. The classroom morphs into a dynamic space, a canvas of endless possibilities in the realm of AI-enhanced creativity (Wingström et al., 2023). The infusion of AI into the creative process marks a departure from the traditional dichotomy of man versus machine. Instead, it envisions a collaborative partnership where AI serves as a catalyst for human creativity, augmenting our imaginative capacities rather than replacing them. As we delve into the landscape of AI-enhanced creativity, it becomes evident that the future holds not only the promise of streamlined information delivery but a redefinition of the very essence of learning.

In AI-enhanced creativity, the classroom transforms into a crucible of ideas, and students become co-creators of knowledge, actively shaping the narratives of their education. One of the most compelling aspects of AI's role in fostering creativity lies in its ability to simulate and visualize abstract ideas. Traditional teaching methods often struggle to convey complex or abstract concepts effectively. However, with the aid of AI, students can step into immersive, realistic simulations that bring theoretical concepts to life (Hidalgo et al., 2023). For instance, in a physics class, students might find themselves exploring the cosmos through a virtual reality simulation, grasping the intricacies of celestial mechanics with a depth and clarity that transcends traditional lectures and textbooks. AI can act as a catalyst for interdisciplinary exploration, breaking down the silos that often confine subjects within the educational framework. Imagine a collaborative project where students from literature, science, and art seamlessly converge to explore the intersection of their respective disciplines. The AI, equipped with a vast repository of knowledge from diverse fields, becomes the guide and facilitator, encouraging students to draw connections between seemingly disparate ideas and fostering a holistic understanding of the world.

The responsible use of AI in education necessitates a nuanced approach, safeguarding against unintended consequences such as bias in algorithms or overreliance on technology to the detriment of critical thinking skills. Educators, technologists, and policymakers must collaborate to establish ethical frameworks that ensure AI serves as a tool for empowerment rather than an instrument of unwitting manipulation. Considerations of inclusivity and accessibility become paramount. The integration of AI into the educational landscape must not exacerbate existing disparities but instead strive to bridge gaps in access and opportunities. This entails addressing issues of digital equity, ensuring that all students, regardless of their socio-economic background, have equal access to the transformative potential of AI-enhanced creativity. The evolution of the educator's role takes center stage in this narrative. Far from being replaced by AI, educators become the architects of a learning environment where creativity flourishes. They assume the responsibility of guiding students through the vast landscape of information, helping them navigate the ethical considerations of AI, and instilling the values of critical thinking and responsible innovation. The human touch becomes indispensable in nurturing the emotional intelligence and ethical discernment that AI inherently lacks. The integration of AI into the realm of creativity heralds a new era in education—one where the boundaries between technology and human imagination blur, giving rise to a palette of unlimited possibilities.

Seamless Assessment and Feedback: Nurturing Growth Through Data Insights

In the timeless pursuit of refining the art of learning, the twin pillars of assessment and feedback stand tall, shaping the educational landscape. However, as we stand at the precipice of a new era, the integration of artificial intelligence (AI) promises to revolutionize this foundational process, ushering in a world where assessments are not just efficient but also deeply insightful (Chang & Kidman, 2023). The transformative power of AI in assessment lies not merely in its ability to expedite evaluations but in its capacity to provide nuanced and data-driven feedback that guides students on a personalized learning journey. Traditionally, assessments have been perceived as a moment of judgment, a culmination of learning experiences distilled into a numerical or letter grade. However, the infusion of AI injects a dynamic and adaptive element into this process, fundamentally altering the nature of assessments from static evaluations to dynamic tools for growth. In the envisioned future, AI takes center stage in the assessment ecosystem, swiftly and comprehensively evaluating student responses and delivering prompt, meaningful feedback that becomes a compass guiding students on their educational odyssey. At the heart of AI's prowess in assessment lies its ability to process vast amounts of data at unprecedented speeds. The immediacy of AI-driven evaluations not only reduces the turnaround time for feedback but also enhances the depth and quality of insights provided. Imagine a world where, within moments of completing an assignment, students receive detailed feedback that goes beyond mere correctness, delving into the intricacies of their thought processes, identifying strengths, and pinpointing areas for improvement.

The integration of AI in assessment is not without its challenges and ethical considerations. The reliance on algorithms for evaluation raises questions about transparency, accountability, and bias. It is imperative to ensure that AI-driven assessments are fair, unbiased, and aligned with educational objectives. Ethical frameworks must be established to govern the use of AI in assessments, safeguarding against unintended consequences and preserving the integrity of the educational process. The shift towards data-driven assessments necessitates a thoughtful approach to privacy and data security. As AI systems process and store vast amounts of sensitive student data, robust measures must be in place to protect against breaches and unauthorized access. The responsible use of AI in assessment requires a balance between the transformative potential of data insights and the imperative to safeguard individual privacy. In the symbiotic relationship between AI and educators, the role of the teacher undergoes a metamorphosis. Far from being relegated to the sidelines, educators become orchestrators of the data symphony, interpreting insights, contextualizing feedback, and leveraging AI-generated reports to inform their pedagogical decisions. The human touch remains indispensable, providing the empathy, encouragement, and mentorship that algorithms cannot replicate. As we navigate this terrain of seamless assessment and feedback powered by AI, it is essential to embrace a holistic perspective. The synergy between technology and pedagogy transforms assessments from a static endpoint to a dynamic process of continuous improvement. The immediacy of feedback, the granularity of insights, and the adaptability of educational strategies contribute to the creation of a learning environment that nurtures growth and celebrates the individuality of each student.

Breaking Barriers, Building Bridges in Global Collaborative Learning

The boundaries that once confined learning to a specific geographic locale are transcended, ushering in an era where students from diverse corners of the world collaborate seamlessly on projects, exchange cultural perspectives, and engage in a vibrant tapestry of ideas. At the heart of this transformative shift is the mediating role played by artificial intelligence (AI), acting as a catalyst to foster global collaborative learning (Mena-Guacas et al., 2023). The globalization of education is not a novel concept, but the integration of AI elevates it to unprecedented levels of accessibility and inclusivity. The virtual classroom becomes a nexus where geographical distances dissolve, enabling students to transcend borders and engage in collaborative endeavors that broaden their horizons. The promise of AI as a mediator in this global educational landscape lies in its ability to facilitate real-time communication, overcome language barriers, and create an inclusive and internationally connected community. Language, once a potential barrier to global collaboration, is seamlessly addressed through the capabilities of AI. Imagine a scenario where students from Asia, Europe, Africa, and the Americas converge in a virtual classroom (Yang et al., 2023). Language differences, which were once stumbling blocks, become mere nuances as AI algorithms facilitate real-time translation, ensuring that every voice is not only heard but also understood. This breakthrough in linguistic inclusivity transforms the virtual classroom into a dynamic forum where diverse perspectives converge, creating a rich tapestry of ideas and knowledge exchange.

The power of AI to mediate global collaboration goes beyond language translation. It extends to creating an environment where cultural diversity is celebrated and leveraged as a source of strength. AI algorithms, attuned to the nuances of cultural expressions, foster cross-cultural understanding by promoting respectful and inclusive dialogue. In this virtual melting pot of ideas, students not only learn from textbooks but also from the lived experiences and perspectives of their global peers. Consider a collaborative project where students from different continents come together to address a global challenge, such as climate change. The AI-powered platform facilitates seamless communication, allowing students to share insights, pool resources, and collectively brainstorm solutions. The result is not just a project outcome but a transformative learning experience that goes beyond the boundaries of traditional education, preparing students for the complexities of a multicultural and interconnected world. In this global collaborative learning environment, AI serves as more than just a facilitator; it becomes a mentor, guiding students through the nuances of effective cross-cultural communication. AI algorithms analyze communication patterns, identify potential misunderstandings, and provide guidance on fostering a collaborative and inclusive atmosphere. The virtual classroom, enriched by the diversity of voices and perspectives, becomes a microcosm of the global society students will navigate in their future endeavors (Grassini, 2023).

The integration of AI in global collaborative learning is not without its challenges. Ethical considerations regarding data privacy, algorithmic biases, and the responsible use of technology must be at the forefront of this educational paradigm shift. Institutions and educators must collaborate to establish robust frameworks that ensure the ethical and equitable use of AI in global education, safeguarding against unintended consequences and fostering a learning environment built on trust and transparency. The digital divide emerges as a critical concern. While AI has the potential to connect students across the globe, ensuring that all students, regardless of their socio-economic background, have equal access to technology becomes imperative. Bridging the digital gap is not only about providing devices and internet access but also about addressing systemic inequalities that may hinder certain groups of students from fully participating in the global collaborative learning experience. Educators become not only facilitators of knowledge but also cultural ambassadors, guiding students through the intricacies of global collaboration. The human touch remains indispensable, providing the emotional intelligence, mentorship, and inspiration that AI algorithms cannot replicate. The synergy between AI and educators becomes evident as they work in tandem to create a global classroom that is not just a technological marvel but a vibrant community of learners. AI provides the technological infrastructure, real-time translation, and data-driven insights, while educators bring their pedagogical expertise, cultural sensitivity, and the ability to nurture a collaborative and inclusive learning environment.

Fostering Tomorrow's Global Citizens Through Ethical and Emotional Education

The integration of artificial intelligence (AI) and education presents an innovative and transformative avenue to address these concerns head-on. By infusing AI systems with enhancements in emotional intelligence, education becomes a powerful ally in navigating the intricate terrain of emotions, ethics, and cultural sensitivity. This chapter delves into the vision of an educational landscape where AI acts as a mentor, engaging students in ethical debates, cultivating emotional awareness, and preparing them to thrive as global citizens. The ethical implications of AI in education extend far beyond the mere transmission of knowledge. The integration of AI into the educational framework necessitates a proactive examination of the values, principles, and ethical considerations that should guide its implementation. Educators, policymakers, and technologists must collaboratively establish ethical frameworks that ensure the responsible use of AI, safeguarding against unintended consequences and fostering a learning environment built on trust and integrity. One innovative approach to address ethical considerations is the infusion of emotional intelligence into AI systems. Emotional intelligence, encompassing self-awareness, empathy, and interpersonal skills, becomes a guiding force in the development of AI mentors that assist students in navigating the complexities of ethical decision-making. Imagine an AI-powered mentor engaging students in candid and open debates about ethics, challenging them to consider various perspectives, and guiding them to formulate well-founded moral judgments.

The integration of emotional intelligence into AI systems comes with its own set of challenges. The nuances of human emotions are complex and multifaceted, presenting a considerable technological challenge for AI developers. Ensuring that AI systems accurately interpret and respond to emotional cues requires ongoing research, development, and refinement. Ethical considerations also come to the forefront, raising questions about the boundaries of AI's role in emotional development and the potential risks associated with overreliance on technology for emotional support. As we explore the intersection of AI, ethics, and emotional intelligence in education, the role of educators remains pivotal. Educators become not only facilitators of knowledge but also guides in the ethical and emotional development of their students. The human touch, with its depth of emotional understanding and nuanced ethical discernment, remains indispensable in cultivating the values and principles that shape responsible and empathetic global citizens. The collaborative relationship between educators and AI mentors becomes a powerful synergy. While AI mentors contribute the technological infrastructure, real-time insights, and emotional intelligence enhancements, educators bring their pedagogical expertise, mentorship, and the ability to instill a sense of ethical responsibility. The coexistence of human and artificial intelligence creates a learning environment that blends the best of both worlds, fostering a holistic and transformative educational experience. In the broader context of global education, the integration of AI and emotional intelligence becomes a catalyst for fostering a generation of students equipped to thrive in a diverse and interconnected world. The AI mentor, by promoting cross-cultural understanding, empathy, and ethical reasoning, prepares students to navigate the complexities of a multicultural society with grace and adaptability.

CHALLENGES AND CONSIDERATIONS

It is crucial to confront the complexities and difficulties brought on by the metamorphosis that artificial intelligence (AI) is bringing about in the realm of education. The possibilities may be alluring, but they also cast shadows that demand careful thought and deliberate navigation.

Ethical Dilemmas: Navigating the Moral Landscape

The entwining of artificial intelligence (AI) with education introduces a nuanced and intricate tapestry of ethical considerations (Rezwana, 2023). As AI systems progressively entrench themselves in the learning process, ethical concerns surrounding data privacy, bias, and the extent of AI's involvement become increasingly pronounced. Navigating the complex terrain of ethical dilemmas in AI-enhanced education necessitates a delicate balance—one that harnesses the capabilities of AI while steadfastly upholding moral principles (Yan et al., 2023). At the heart of the ethical dilemma lies the question of data privacy. As AI systems in education gather and process vast amounts of student data, concerns regarding the safeguarding of this sensitive information become paramount. The very nature of personalized learning, seamless assessments, and AI-driven feedback relies on the analysis of individual student data, raising legitimate apprehensions about how this data is stored, used, and protected (Chen & Perez, 2023). In the pursuit of enhancing educational experiences through AI, it becomes imperative to establish robust frameworks that govern the collection, storage, and utilization of student data. Ethical considerations demand a transparent and accountable approach to data privacy, ensuring that students retain control over their personal information and are informed about how it is utilized (Liang et al., 2023). Collaboration between educators, policymakers, and technologists is essential to draft and implement stringent data protection measures, fostering an environment where the benefits of AI do not come at the expense of individual privacy.

Another ethical quagmire emerges in the form of bias embedded in AI algorithms. The potential for AI systems to perpetuate or even exacerbate existing biases present in society raises red flags. If the data used to train these systems reflects societal prejudices, the AI algorithms may inadvertently perpetuate discriminatory practices, leading to unfair treatment or opportunities for certain groups of students. Addressing bias in AI demands a comprehensive and proactive approach. It requires conscientious efforts to scrutinize and diversify the datasets used to train AI systems, ensuring representation from various demographic groups. Moreover, ongoing monitoring and assessment of AI algorithms are essential to identify and rectify biases that may emerge over time. Collaborative endeavors involving educators, ethicists, and technologists are indispensable in developing and implementing ethical guidelines that mitigate bias, promoting fairness and equal opportunities in AI-driven education. The degree of AI's involvement in the learning process poses a significant ethical challenge. While AI brings unprecedented capabilities in personalization, assessment, and feedback, the risk of overreliance on technology at the expense of human interaction and guidance looms large. Striking the right balance between leveraging AI's strengths and preserving the indispensable role of human educators is a delicate and ongoing task. Ethical considerations demand a cautious and discerning approach to the integration of AI in education. The human touch—characterized by empathy, emotional intelligence, and mentorship—remains irreplaceable in nurturing the holistic development of learners. Ethical guidelines should emphasize the complementary nature of AI and human educators, ensuring that technology enhances rather than supplants the educational experience. This necessitates collaboration among educators, policymakers, and technologists to establish ethical frameworks that guide the ethical integration of AI in education.

As we navigate these ethical dilemmas inherent in the fusion of AI and education, collaboration emerges as the linchpin for ethical solutions. Educators, legislators, and technologists must engage in sustained and meaningful collaboration to develop, implement, and adapt ethical guidelines that evolve with technological advancements. The synergy between these stakeholders is indispensable in navigating the intricate ethical landscape, ensuring that the transformative potential of AI aligns with moral principles and safeguards the rights and well-being of learners. Educators play a pivotal role as ethical stewards in the integration of AI into education. Their firsthand experience in the classroom equips them with valuable insights into the ethical implications of AI-driven practices. Collaboration with educators ensures that ethical guidelines are not just theoretical constructs but practical frameworks that align with the realities of the educational landscape. Educators, with their deep understanding of pedagogy and student needs, contribute crucial perspectives to the ethical discourse, ensuring that the human dimension of education is not overshadowed by technological advancements.

The Heart of Learning: The Loss of Human Connection

At the core of the educational endeavor lies a profoundly human essence—an interplay of interpersonal communication, mentoring relationships, and emotional resonance that defines the very heart of learning. As artificial intelligence (AI) advances and permeates the educational landscape, a compelling concern emerges: the potential erosion of the vital teacher-student interaction that forms the bedrock of effective education. While AI holds the promise of enhancing the educational environment, there is a genuine apprehension that it might inadvertently diminish the irreplaceable human connection between educators and learners. In this chapter, we embark on a nuanced exploration of the delicate balance required to ensure that AI not only improves but enriches human interaction in education, creating an environment that nurtures both intellectual development and emotional well-being.

Education, at its essence, is a deeply human activity. It is not merely the transmission of information but a complex interplay of emotions, motivations, and personal connections. The traditional classroom, with its dynamic exchanges, mentorship opportunities, and emotional support, epitomizes the human touch that has been central to effective learning throughout history. The teacher-student relationship is a cornerstone of this human touch. It goes beyond the imparting of knowledge; it involves guidance, inspiration, and the cultivation of essential life skills. The human touch in education encompasses the empathetic understanding of each student's unique learning style, the ability to tailor teaching methods to individual needs, and the provision of emotional support during the ups and downs of the educational journey. As AI continues to evolve, it offers a multitude of tools and applications that can enhance various aspects of the educational experience. From personalized learning paths and adaptive assessments to real-time feedback and data-driven insights, AI holds the potential to revolutionize education and address the diverse needs of learners (Parra-Valencia & Massey, 2023). However, the very advancements that make AI a powerful educational ally also raise concerns about the potential erosion of human connection. The fear is not that AI lacks efficacy in delivering information or facilitating learning but that it may inadvertently overshadow the nuanced, empathetic, and deeply personal aspects of education that are uniquely human. AI's capacity to process vast amounts of data, provide instant feedback, and personalize learning experiences is unparalleled. Yet, the risk lies in overreliance on technology to the detriment of the emotional intelligence, mentorship, and human understanding that educators bring to the table. Striking the right balance is imperative to harness the benefits of AI without sacrificing the irreplaceable human connection that defines the heart of learning.

Empathy, the ability to understand and share the feelings of another, emerges as a linchpin in safeguarding human connection in the age of AI-enhanced education. The empathetic educator is attuned to the emotional nuances of each student, recognizing not only their academic strengths and weaknesses but also their individual challenges, aspirations, and fears. While AI can analyze data and provide insights into academic performance, it lacks the inherent capacity for empathy that human educators bring to the table. Empathy involves the subtle art of recognizing when a student is struggling, discerning the underlying causes, and offering not just academic support but emotional reassurance. It is the empathetic educator who can inspire, motivate, and instill a love for learning that goes beyond the confines of standardized assessments. The infusion of empathy into education requires a deliberate and conscious effort. Educators must be equipped with the skills to navigate the complex emotional landscape of their students, creating an environment where trust, understanding, and emotional well-being are prioritized alongside academic achievement. Empathy becomes the bridge that connects the intellectual and emotional realms of learning, ensuring that the human connection remains resilient amid the technological advancements.

The delicate balance between empathy and technology is not a dichotomy but a synergistic relationship that can enrich the educational experience. Rather than viewing AI as a potential replacement for human interaction, it should be embraced as a tool that augments the capacity of educators to provide personalized and effective support. AI can analyze vast datasets to identify patterns in student learning, offering insights into individual strengths and weaknesses. This data-driven approach, when coupled with the empathetic understanding of educators, creates a powerful synergy. For example, AI can highlight areas where a student may be struggling, prompting the educator to provide targeted support and emotional encouragement. In the realm of personalized learning, AI's ability to adapt content and pace aligns with the principles of empathetic teaching. An empathetic educator recognizes that each student has a unique learning style and set of challenges. By leveraging AI to tailor learning experiences, educators can create a more inclusive and responsive educational environment that caters to diverse needs.

As we contemplate the future of education in the era of AI, the imperative is clear—to design an educational landscape that seamlessly integrates technology while preserving the human connection. This requires intentional efforts to embed empathy in educational practices, ensuring that the benefits of AI are harnessed ethically and responsively. Educational institutions, policymakers, and technologists must collaborate to establish ethical frameworks that guide the development and implementation of AI in education. These frameworks should prioritize the well-being and rights of learners, safeguarding against unintended consequences and ethical breaches. In envisioning the educational future, it is crucial to view AI not as a replacement for human interaction but as a catalyst for innovation and enhancement. The heart of learning, characterized by the dynamic interplay of human connections, mentorship, and emotional resonance, should remain resilient amid technological advancements. The fusion of AI and education presents a profound opportunity to reimagine the educational experience. AI, when approached with empathy and a commitment to ethical principles, can be a catalyst for positive transformation. It can enhance personalized learning, provide valuable insights, and adapt to the diverse needs of learners. The true essence of education lies in the human connection—the mentorship, emotional support, and dynamic exchanges that foster holistic development. As we navigate the evolving landscape of AI-enhanced education, it is incumbent upon educators, policymakers, and technologists to collaborate in crafting a future where the heart of learning remains steadfast, enriched by the synergy of empathy and technology. In this future, AI becomes not a replacement for human connection but a harmonious companion in the journey of education, amplifying the best of both worlds for the benefit of learners worldwide.

Ensure Equity in the Digital Age: The Digital Divide

At the heart of the transformational potential of artificial intelligence (AI) in education rests a fundamental presumption—universal access to technology and the internet. This presupposition, however, overlooks a stark reality: substantial segments of the world population lack access to these important resources. As AI becomes increasingly linked with education, the possibility of aggravating educational gaps looms big. The increasing disparity between those with access to technology and those without creates fundamental moral considerations. In this chapter, we delve into the urgency of tackling the digital divide to ensure equity in the digital age, realizing that narrowing this gap is not simply a technological necessity but a moral obligation to harness the full potential of AI for the benefit of all.

The promise of AI in education rests on the assumption that learners worldwide have fair access to technology and the internet. The potential for individualized learning, seamless assessment, and global collaboration using AI-powered tools hinges on the notion that these tools are widely accessible. However, the truth paints a different picture. In several locations around the world, discrepancies in infrastructure, economic resources, and educational systems contribute to a sharp digital divide. While urban hubs in industrialized nations may enjoy robust internet connectivity and access to cutting-edge technology, rural communities and less economically advantaged regions typically battle with little or no access. Even within prosperous cultures, vulnerable communities may confront impediments to entry, sustaining educational inequality. The digital divide, the gap between people who have access to contemporary information and communication technology and those who do not, has far-reaching ramifications for education. As AI-powered tools become crucial to the learning process, the discrepancies in access compound existing inequities in educational performance. Students without access to technology miss out on the benefits of personalized learning (Junus & Brophy, 2023), real-time feedback, and collaborative opportunities given by AI. This not only inhibits their academic advancement but also deepens the knowledge and skills gap between them and their more technologically enabled contemporaries. The unintended consequence is a continuance of societal disparities, where those with access to technology are better able to flourish in the digital age.

Addressing the digital divide is not only a technological challenge; it is a moral obligation. In an era where access to knowledge and technology is associated with access to opportunity, education becomes a cornerstone for social mobility. Ensuring that all learners, regardless of their geographic location or socio-economic background, have equitable access to the revolutionary potential of AI in education is an ethical obligation that corresponds with the ideals of justice, fairness, and human rights. The United Nations considers access to information and communication technologies, including the internet, as a basic human right. The Sustainable Development Goals (SDGs), notably Goal 4 on Quality Education and Goal 9 on Industry, Innovation, and Infrastructure, underline the significance of harnessing technology to bridge educational disparities. The moral responsibility to bridge the digital divide is inscribed in these worldwide commitments to equity and access. At the heart of narrowing the digital gap is the building of robust technology infrastructure. Internet connectivity, hardware availability, and software accessibility are the pillars that support fair access to educational possibilities powered by AI. In locations where internet connectivity is limited or unstable, efforts must be put toward building broadband infrastructure. Public and private investments in digital infrastructure, particularly in underprivileged areas, are vital to develop an inclusive digital ecosystem. Technological advancements, such as satellite-based internet services and community networks, can play a crucial role in extending access to rural and neglected populations. Moreover, assuring the availability of affordable and accessible hardware is vital. Initiatives that provide subsidized or low-cost gadgets to students from economically disadvantaged families contribute to breaking down barriers to access. Additionally, the creation of open-source educational software and applications promotes affordability and customization, appealing to the different demands of learners.

Access to technology alone is insufficient; digital literacy is the key to unlocking the full potential of educational opportunities in the digital age. Digital literacy covers not just the capacity to use digital tools but also critical thinking, information literacy, and responsible digital citizenship. Educational institutions play a crucial role in encouraging digital literacy. Integrating digital literacy into the curriculum empowers students with the skills needed to navigate the digital realm efficiently. This includes the ability to analyze online content critically, use digital tools for study and cooperation, and appreciate the ethical implications of technology use. Community-based initiatives and partnerships with non-governmental groups can also contribute to promoting digital literacy. Workshops, training programs, and community centers that provide access to technology and offer direction on its ethical usage empower learners to navigate the digital age with confidence and competence. Addressing the digital divide involves more than individual efforts; it demands systemic change aided by effective policy advocacy. Governments, educational institutions, and international organizations must work to design and implement policies that promote fair access to technology in education. Policy measures should focus on providing an enabling environment for technological infrastructure growth, ensuring that no community is left behind. This entails strategic investments in digital infrastructure, regulatory frameworks that stimulate private sector involvement in underserved areas, and policies that foster competition to drive down the costs of access. Additionally, policies should promote the integration of digital literacy into school curricula. By incorporating digital literacy as a core skill, education systems may educate learners for the demands of the digital age, nurturing a generation of digitally enabled citizens.

Closing the digital divide requires joint actions that use the resources of both the public and commercial sectors. Public-private partnerships (PPPs) can be crucial in advancing progress toward fair access to technology in education. Private sector firms, especially technology companies, can provide resources, experience, and new ideas to address infrastructure concerns. Collaborative activities may involve providing subsidized gadgets, extending internet connectivity, or developing educational content and platforms that cater to varied learning needs. Governments, in turn, can create an enabling regulatory environment that fosters private sector involvement in bridging the digital divide. By facilitating collaboration between public and private institutions, countries may leverage the collective strength of both sectors to advance the shared objective of equitable access to education. The digital divide is a worldwide concern that demands international cooperation and solidarity. Collaborative initiatives across governments, international organizations, and non-governmental groups are crucial to share best practices, mobilize resources, and address the core causes of inequitable access. International forums, such as the United Nations and UNESCO, provide opportunities for conversation and coordination on global education efforts. The sharing of technology advances, policy frameworks, and successful case studies can inform a collective approach to narrowing the digital gap. Global initiatives, including the Broadband Commission for Sustainable Development, emphasize the relevance of broadband access for attaining educational goals. Such projects underline the interconnection of global concerns and the common obligation of the international community to guarantee that the benefits of technology innovation are accessible to all.

Closing the digital gap demands a holistic and multifaceted approach that addresses not only infrastructure issues but also socio-economic, cultural, and gender-related hurdles to access. Recognizing the intersectionality of these difficulties is key to designing inclusive solutions. Socio-economic issues often contribute to gaps in access to technology. Families with little financial resources may struggle to afford the essential devices or reliable internet connections. Initiatives that give financial support, such as subsidies for devices and connection, can minimize socio-economic barriers and guarantee that cost is not a prohibitive factor. Community-based programs that allow access to technology in public settings, such as libraries and community centers, provide alternatives for persons who may not have access at home. By providing inclusive venues where technology is available to everybody, irrespective of socio-economic background, communities can bridge the digital gap. Cultural and linguistic variety adds another degree of complication to the digital gap. Educational content and platforms that are not culturally sensitive or linguistically varied may alienate some cultures. Addressing these gaps entails the development of inclusive educational materials that reflect the cultural richness and linguistic diversity of learners. Localization of information, translation services, and culturally relevant instructional approaches contribute to building an inclusive educational environment. Technology should not be a barrier to cultural involvement; rather, it should be a tool that celebrates and strengthens varied cultural viewpoints. Gender differences further complicate the issues of the digital divide. In many civilizations, girls and women may face difficulties to obtaining and using technology, sustaining gender inequities in schooling. Initiatives that particularly target gender-inclusive access to technology, such as mentorship programs and scholarships, play a significant role in eliminating these gaps. Promoting digital literacy among girls and women is equally crucial. By encouraging engagement in science, technology, engineering, and mathematics (STEM) sectors and offering role models in the tech industry, educational systems can enable girls to pursue and excel in technology-related fields.

Educators' Skill Shifts: Embracing New Roles

The integration of artificial intelligence (AI) into education heralds a profound paradigm shift in the roles and responsibilities of educators. No longer confined to the traditional model of content delivery, educators are navigating a multidimensional landscape where their tasks include curating AI-generated resources, overseeing personalized learning journeys, and fostering critical thinking about information generated by AI systems. In this chapter, we delve into the evolving role of educators in AI-enhanced classrooms, exploring the skills and competencies that are becoming increasingly vital for effective teaching in this new frontier. The journey demands a commitment to continual learning and professional growth, emphasizing the dynamic nature of education in the era of AI.

The advent of AI in education signifies more than just the introduction of new technologies; it represents a fundamental transformation in the very nature of teaching. The traditional role of educators as knowledge transmitters is evolving into a multifaceted position that requires adaptability, technological fluency, and a deep understanding of AI's capabilities and limitations.

In AI-enhanced classrooms, educators become facilitators of learning experiences that leverage the capabilities of AI. The emphasis shifts from being the primary source of information to guiding students through personalized learning paths, leveraging AI-generated insights, and instilling critical thinking skills necessary for navigating the complexities of AI-generated content. One of the pivotal shifts for educators in the AI era is the role of content curator. With AI systems capable of generating vast amounts of educational materials, educators become discerning curators, selecting and organizing resources that align with curriculum objectives, student needs, and learning outcomes. The skill of curating AI-generated resources involves a nuanced understanding of educational goals, the diversity of student learning styles, and the ability to evaluate the quality and relevance of AI-generated content. Educators must navigate a sea of information, ensuring that the materials selected not only align with academic standards but also promote critical thinking, creativity, and a holistic understanding of the subject matter.

In the AI-enhanced classroom, personalized learning takes center stage. AI systems analyze individual student performance data to tailor learning experiences, adjusting content complexity, pacing, and supplementary materials to meet the unique needs of each learner. Educators, therefore, transition from uniform lesson delivery to overseeing a diverse array of personalized learning paths. The ability to effectively supervise personalized learning requires educators to be attuned to each student's progress, strengths, and areas of improvement. It involves leveraging AI-generated insights to provide targeted guidance, support, and interventions as needed. Educators become orchestrators of a symphony of individualized education, ensuring that each student's journey is not only academically enriching but also personally meaningful. As AI systems play an increasing role in generating educational content, educators assume the critical responsibility of fostering students' ability to think critically about information, especially that which is generated by AI. This includes an awareness of the biases that may exist in AI algorithms, an understanding of the ethical considerations surrounding AI, and the development of discernment in evaluating the credibility of AI-generated information. Educators become guides through the complex landscape of AI-generated knowledge, encouraging students to question, analyze, and engage thoughtfully with the information at their disposal. This skill shift involves not only imparting subject-specific knowledge but also cultivating a broader set of skills that empower students to navigate an information-rich world where AI is a prominent contributor. To effectively navigate the AI-enhanced educational landscape, educators must develop a high degree of technological fluency. This goes beyond a basic understanding of digital tools; it involves a comprehensive grasp of AI technologies, their applications in education, and the ability to integrate them seamlessly into the teaching and learning process. Technological fluency includes proficiency in using AI-powered educational platforms, interpreting data generated by AI systems, and troubleshooting technical issues that may arise. Educators become collaborators with AI, leveraging its capabilities to enhance the educational experience while maintaining a human touch in the learning environment.

CONCLUSION

As the path of education converges with the limitless spheres of human inventiveness and the ever-evolving frontiers of AI advancement, it is prepared to travel an exciting journey. A tapestry of personalised learning, unrestricted creative inquiry, and a tapestry of a global collaboration unfold at this point, beckoning us to move onward. But getting there requires careful navigation, one that deftly handles the ethical issues that AI raises, protects the fundamental human connections that constitute education, and makes sure that access continues to be an egalitarian bridge into this new paradigm. Professors, politicians, and academics must work together to create an educational ecosystem that is infused with AI in order to maintain the integrity of this transformative landscape. In addition to giving students the skills they need to be independent, this ecosystem encourages the development of critical thinking, enabling them to solve the complex web of problems that tomorrow will present. A crucial realization that must undergird our path amid the revelation of AI's educational potential is that, for all of its wonders, technology only serves as a tool, a conduit that amplifies human direction and mentorship rather than replacing it. The true potential of AI in education will emerge when its effectiveness is balanced with the indispensable human touch. Let us not lose sight of what makes us who we are: the need for knowledge, the embracing of curiosity, and the ties we create with other learners as we advance inexorably toward this intersection. Therefore, as we approach the next stage of educational development, may we move forward with the confidence that, while artificial intelligence (AI) may illuminate our way, it is ultimately the collective human spirit that will illuminate the minds and hearts of future generations.

I think the concept of harnessing AI for education holds immense promise and significance for the future of learning. The idea of personalized learning, where AI tailors educational content to individual students' needs and pace, is particularly exciting. It suggests a departure from the traditional one-size-fits-all approach, potentially unlocking a more effective and engaging learning experience. The prospect of AI serving as an intelligent tutor, providing real-time feedback and adapting to students' progress, resonates with the need for more individualized support in education. This could not only improve academic outcomes but also foster a sense of empowerment and confidence in learners. However, it's important to acknowledge the challenges that accompany this futuristic vision. Ethical considerations, privacy issues, and ensuring equitable access to AI-driven educational tools are crucial aspects that demand careful navigation. Striking the right balance between innovation and responsibility will be key to maximizing the benefits of AI in education. In my opinion, while there are hurdles to overcome, the potential benefits of integrating AI into education are too compelling to ignore. The idea of a more adaptive, personalized, and efficient educational system through AI is a vision worth pursuing, provided we approach it with a thoughtful and ethical mindset.

AUTHOR'S NOTES

This paper was proofread and refined with the assistance of generative AI, complementing the human editorial process.

REFERENCES

Aydin, Ö., & Karaarslan, E. (2023). Is chatgpt leading generative ai? what is beyond expectations? *Academic Platform Journal of Engineering and Smart Systems*, *11*(3), 118–134. doi:10.21541/apjess.1293702

Bearman, M., Ryan, J., & Ajjawi, R. (2023). Discourses of artificial intelligence in higher education: A critical literature review. *Higher Education*, *86*(2), 369–385. doi:10.1007/s10734-022-00937-2

Bozkurt, A. (2023a). Generative artificial intelligence (AI) powered conversational educational agents: The inevitable paradigm shift. *Asian Journal of Distance Education*, *18*(1), 198–204. doi:10.5281/zenodo.7716416

Bozkurt, A. (2023b). Unleashing the potential of generative AI, conversational agents and chatbots in educational praxis: A systematic review and bibliometric analysis of GenAI in education. *Open Praxis*, *15*(4), 261–270. doi:10.55982/openpraxis.15.4.609

Chang, C.-H., & Kidman, G. (2023). The rise of Generative Artificial Intelligence (AI) language models - challenges and opportunities for geographical and environmental education. *International Research in Geographical and Environmental Education*, *32*(2), 85–89. doi:10.1080/10382046.2023.2194036

Chen, J. J., & Perez, C. (2023). Enhancing Assessment and Personalized Learning Through Artificial Intelligence. *Childhood Education*, *99*(6), 72–79. doi:10.1080/00094056.2023.2282903

Dogan, M. E., Goru Dogan, T., & Bozkurt, A. (2023). The use of artificial intelligence (AI) in online learning and distance education processes: A systematic review of empirical studies. *Applied Sciences (Basel, Switzerland)*, *13*(5), 3056. doi:10.3390/app13053056

Grassini, S. (2023). Shaping the future of education: Exploring the potential and consequences of AI and ChatGPT in educational settings. *Education Sciences*, *13*(7), 692. doi:10.3390/educsci13070692

Haleem, A., Javaid, M., Qadri, M. A., Singh, R. P., & Suman, R. (2022). Artificial intelligence (AI) applications for marketing: A literature-based study. *International Journal of Intelligent Networks*, *3*, 119–132. doi:10.1016/j.ijin.2022.08.005

Hidalgo, C. G., Bucheli-Guerrero, V. A., & Ordóñez-Eraso, H. A. (2023). Artificial Intelligence and Computer-Supported Collaborative Learning in Programming: A Systematic Mapping Study. *Tecnura, 27*(75), 175–206. doi:10.14483/22487638.19637

Ji, H., Han, I., & Ko, Y. (2023). A systematic review of conversational AI in language education: Focusing on the collaboration with human teachers. *Journal of Research on Technology in Education, 55*(1), 48–63. doi:10.1080/15391523.2022.2142873

Junus, F. B., & Brophy, S. P. (2023, June). Exploring the Potential of Deep Learning for Personalized Learning Environments. In *2023 ASEE Annual Conference & Exposition*. IEEE.

Kirkpatrick, K. (2023). Can AI Demonstrate Creativity? *Communications of the ACM, 66*(2), 21–23. doi:10.1145/3575665

Liang, J. C., Hwang, G. J., Chen, M. R. A., & Darmawansah, D. (2023). Roles and research foci of artificial intelligence in language education: An integrated bibliographic analysis and systematic review approach. *Interactive Learning Environments, 31*(7), 4270–4296. doi:10.1080/10494820.2021.1958348

Mena-Guacas, A. F., Rodríguez, J. A. U., Trujillo, D. M. S., Gómez-Galán, J., & López-Meneses, E. (2023). Collaborative learning and skill development for educational growth of artificial intelligence: A systematic review. *Contemporary Educational Technology, 15*(3), ep428. doi:10.30935/cedtech/13123

Parra-Valencia, J. A., & Massey, M. L. (2023). Leveraging AI Tools for Enhanced Digital Literacy, Access to Information, and Personalized Learning. In *Managing Complex Tasks with Systems Thinking* (pp. 213–234). Springer Nature Switzerland. doi:10.1007/978-3-031-40635-5_9

Pratama, M. P., Sampelolo, R., & Lura, H. (2023). Revolutionizing Education: Harnessing The Power Of Artificial Intelligence For Personalized Learning. *Klasikal: Journal of Education. Language Teaching and Science, 5*(2), 350–357. doi:10.52208/klasikal.v5i2.877

Rezwana, J. (2023). *Towards designing engaging and ethical human-centered AI partners for human-AI co-creativity* [Doctoral dissertation, The University of North Carolina at Charlotte].

Schiff, D. (2022). Education for AI, not AI for education: The role of education and ethics in national AI policy strategies. *International Journal of Artificial Intelligence in Education, 32*(3), 527–563. doi:10.1007/s40593-021-00270-2

Thomas, B. J., & Alkhafaji, S. (2023). Gamification of Personalized Learning Through Massive Open Online Courses: Learner-to-AI Enabled Chatbot. *InTech Open.* doi:10.5772/intechopen.1001113

Wingström, R., Hautala, J., & Lundman, R. (2023). Redefining creativity in the era of AI? Perspectives of computer scientists and new media artists. *Creativity Research Journal*, 1–17. doi:10.1080/10400419.2022.2107850

Yan, L., Sha, L., Zhao, L., Li, Y., Martinez-Maldonado, R., Chen, G., Li, X., Jin, Y., & Gašević, D. (2023). Practical and ethical challenges of large language models in education: A systematic scoping review. *British Journal of Educational Technology*, bjet.13370. doi:10.1111/bjet.13370

Yang, K. B., Echeverria, V., Lu, Z., Mao, H., Holstein, K., Rummel, N., & Aleven, V. (2023, April). Pair-Up: Prototyping Human-AI Co-orchestration of Dynamic Transitions between Individual and Collaborative Learning in the Classroom. In *Proceedings of the 2023 CHI Conference on Human Factors in Computing Systems* (pp. 1-17). ACM. 10.1145/3544548.3581398

KEY TERMS AND DEFINITIONS

Adaptive Learning Platforms: Adaptive learning platforms are educational systems that employ artificial intelligence and data analytics to analyze individual student progress and dynamically adapt the learning content and activities based on the learner's strengths and shortcomings. These platforms attempt to provide a personalized and optimum learning experience for each learner.

AI Algorithms: AI algorithms are collections of instructions and rules designed to enable artificial intelligence systems to execute certain tasks or make choices. In the context of education, AI algorithms may be utilized for data analysis, pattern recognition, and decision-making to enhance various parts of the learning process.

AI in Assessment: AI in assessment involves the application of artificial intelligence techniques to evaluate and analyze student performance. This may include automated grading systems, adaptive testing, and data-driven insights to assess and measure learning outcomes efficiently and effectively.

AI-Enhanced Classroom: An AI-enhanced classroom is a learning environment where artificial intelligence technologies are utilized to augment traditional teaching methods. This may include AI-assisted lesson planning, smart content delivery, and real-time data analysis to create a more interactive and effective learning space.

AI-Enhanced Creativity: AI-enhanced creativity refers to the integration of artificial intelligence tools and algorithms to support and augment human creativity in educational settings. This may include AI-driven tools that generate creative content, offer suggestions for problem-solving, or facilitate collaborative creative processes.

AI-Enhanced Education: AI-enhanced education encompasses the integration of artificial intelligence technologies and tools to enhance various facets of the educational experience. This includes personalized learning, adaptive assessments, intelligent tutoring systems, and other AI-driven applications designed to improve teaching and learning outcomes.

Digital Literacy: Digital literacy refers to the capacity to access, assess, and apply information effectively in a digital setting. In the context of education, digital literacy comprises abilities such as information literacy, media literacy, and the responsible and critical use of technology for learning and communication.

Global Collaborative Learning: Global collaborative learning is an educational approach that leverages technology to connect students and educators across geographical boundaries. It fosters collaboration, cultural exchange, and shared learning experiences, breaking down traditional classroom limitations and promoting a global perspective.

Personalized Learning: Personalized learning refers to an educational approach that tailors the material, speed, and instructional methods to fit the particular requirements and preferences of each learner. It utilizes technology, data analytics, and learner feedback to create individualized learning experiences, enabling increased engagement and understanding.

Public-Private Partnerships (PPP): Public-private partnerships in education involve collaborations between government or public educational institutions and private entities. These collaborations may include joint ventures, financial agreements, or cooperative projects aimed at increasing educational infrastructure, resources, and creative methods through combined public and private efforts.

Chapter 7
Generative Artificial Intelligence as Academic Assistant:
Opportunities, Challenges, and Applications

Şener Balat
https://orcid.org/0000-0002-9683-1778
Bingöl University, Turkey

Mehmet Yavuz
https://orcid.org/0000-0001-6218-232X
Bingöl University, Turkey

Bünyami Kayalı
https://orcid.org/0000-0001-6419-9088
Bayburt University, Turkey

ABSTRACT

The study conducted a literature review focusing on the role of generative artificial intelligence (GAI) utilized as an academic assistant. Within the scope of the research, the opportunities and challenges presented by GAI-based academic assistants to researchers, along with a detailed examination of tools used in the research process, were intended to be explored. It was emphasized that artificial intelligence applications used in academic writing processes have the potential to expedite tasks such as performing repetitive functions, literature reviews, data analysis, and document organization effectively. This situation was noted to offer a range of advantages for students and researchers. However, it was underscored that considerations regarding accuracy, reliability, and ethical concerns must be considered. Factors limiting the effectiveness of GAI in academic writing processes, such as limitations in language understanding, concerns about ethical violations, and difficulties in selecting appropriate data visualization, were discussed.

DOI: 10.4018/979-8-3693-1351-0.ch007

INTRODUCTION

Academic writing is a comprehensive and rigorous process of synthesizing information obtained through reviewing reliable sources in the context of structured discussions, supported by accurate citations, to contribute to scientific discourse (Noroozi, 2022). The process involves identifying clear, concise headings that summarize the study (Maiorana & Mayer, 2018) and summarizing sections of the study, such as purpose, method or findings, concisely and effectively (Altmäe et al., 2023). Again, the main components of the study, such as method, results and discussion, should be clearly explained and understood by creating logical arguments (McMahan et al., 2017). While performing all these steps, it is essential to reference the work of other researchers to avoid plagiarism (Liu et al., 2018). Moreover, it is necessary to express ideas accurately and coherently by adhering to specific stylistic rules, provided scientific terminology is used skillfully.

Considering all the processes mentioned, writing a scientific article has become a unique challenge for many authors. Academic writing becomes even more complicated when factors such as researchers' insufficient knowledge of the subject, low research skills and time limitations are added (Poch et al., 2020). Managing citations and references correctly in the writing process is another factor that makes it difficult for writers (Bautista & Pentang, 2022) because it is necessary to know how to format the citation correctly, considering the different rules in the referenced style guide.

Various tools and strategies have been developed to assist writers and can be used for literature searches, writing, avoiding plagiarism or referencing correctly. Reliable and user-friendly artificial intelligence-based digital author assistants such as automatic citation and reference tools are considered tools that can be collaborated with in this context (Le, 2023). These assistants help authors by performing tasks such as creating article summaries, identifying essential points, citing, and providing feedback on grammar, style and consistency. They can save significant time and effort (Aljanabi et al., 2023). There is also talk of artificial intelligence tools that can write articles independently (GPT-3, 2020). It should be noted here that many researchers believe these assistants cannot replace human intelligence and creativity, and they need to be more capable of conducting original scientific research independently (Castillo-Gonzalez, 2022). They are also criticized for ethical violations (Aljanabi, 2023), misinformation production (Nguyen, 2023) and lack of critical thinking skills (Bishop, 2023).

In conclusion, incorporating artificial intelligence (AI)-assisted aids in academic writing, akin to other domains of life, and introduces various opportunities and challenges (George & Wooden, 2023). As the number of academic studies continues to increase in this field, examining these studies and synthesizing their results systematically, transparently, and reproducibly on a mass scale has become crucial (Torraco, 2016, p.6). In this context, the study aims to comprehensively explore the opportunities and challenges presented to researchers by GAI-based academic assistants, along with a detailed examination of tools used in the research process. Within this scope, the following research questions were addressed:

1. What is GAI as an academic assistant, and what are its general features?
2. What advantages does GAI provide to researchers as an academic assistant?
3. What are the limitations of GAI as an academic assistant?
4. What are the tools available for GAI as an academic assistant?

METHOD

The study employed a literature review method to systematically examine and analyze existing literature related to a specific topic or research question. A literature review is a qualitative research method aiming to provide a theoretical framework for the study, identify gaps in existing knowledge, and inform the research design and methodology, among other purposes (Bowen, 2009). In this context, the role of artificial intelligence utilized as an academic assistant was explored. Web of Science (WOS) databases were used in the literature review. Keywords such as "Academic assistance," "Artificial intelligence," "GAI tools," and similar terms were employed to identify relevant studies. Ninety-seven studies retrieved through these keywords were examined under the headings of "Artificial intelligence as an academic assistant: opportunities and potential," "Artificial intelligence as an academic assistant: challenges and limitations," and "GAI example tools and applications," and the findings were presented under the title of 'Findings.'

FINDINGS

GAI and Academic Writing Assistants

In the literature, artificial intelligence is defined as computer systems that can perform tasks, solve problems, and make decisions with minimal human intervention; it is an interdisciplinary research field that focuses on developing and implementing algorithms (Ballester, 2021). In another study, it is defined as a broad field covering the development of machines and systems that can perform tasks that typically require human intelligence (Abbass, 2021). GAI can be defined as artificial intelligence models that fulfil a specific mission and produce new and original content. GAI is a form of artificial intelligence that can autonomously make new content such as text, images, audio and video (Zhihan, 2023). To explain the difference between artificial intelligence and GAI with an example, while an artificial intelligence system can recognize and classify a particular image, a GAI system can create a new and original work of art based on this image. Academic writing assistants can be AI-based tools that support researchers in writing literary texts such as research papers, articles and theses. These assistants can perform operations such as language understanding, correction, making suggestions, literature search, advanced analysis, and reference checking. With these features, they help researchers improve their scientific studies. With these features, they help researchers in their writing processes. This assistance plays a vital role in improving the quality of academic texts and providing researchers with an effective writing process.

Advantages of Artificial Intelligence Applications as Academic Assistants

With the rapidly evolving dynamics of the information age, the academic world faces many changes and innovations. Artificial intelligence, the pioneer of these changes, has assumed an essential role in academic assistantship. Especially in recent years, intelligent writing assistants have become increasingly widespread (Gayed et al., 2022). Artificial intelligence is profoundly transforming the academic world by increasing the capacity to process information and providing various opportunities for education and research processes. GAI has a significant potential to offer multiple opportunities to students and educators in the role of academic assistant. In this section, we will focus on the various possibilities offered by GAI applications in the academic writing process by referencing sections of a scientific article.

First, academic assistants can help researchers generate new ideas before writing. They can suggest different topics, themes and perspectives to help researchers find new ideas for writing tasks (Kasneci et al., 2023; Taecharungroj, 2023). They can also inspire young researchers with limited experience to formulate hypotheses and identify research questions (Dergaa, 2023). By analyzing large datasets, these applications can identify potential relationships and propositions. This can help develop theories and identify research questions (Salvagno et al., 2023). Likewise, by identifying gaps in existing studies, they can provide ideas for young researchers with limited experience to identify gaps in the literature (Hutson, 2022).

It can provide various contributions in the process of determining the title for the study. By conducting keyword analysis, it can offer ideas to the authors in choosing a title suitable for these keywords. By identifying the most frequently used words in the text and identifying potential keywords, they can offer authors the opportunity to choose among these suggestions. Create concept maps by linking concepts to each other. These maps can show the connections between keywords and their order of importance. They can also identify keywords on similar topics by conducting a literature review and help link the study with other studies using similar terms.

After starting the writing process, the contributions of academic assistants can be mentioned, especially at the point of text creation. Creating accurate and consistent content is among the assistance academic assistants can provide researchers. Stacey and Rei (2023) stated that artificial intelligence applications such as ChatGPT can produce accurate and consistent content. Again, access to a wide range of information and facilitating error detection and correction tasks are among these capabilities. Academic assistants can automatically summarize long articles (Patel & Lam, 2023; Shen et al., 2023). This feature can speed up the summarization process and provide an objective summary (Dergaa et al., 2023). These contributions can facilitate researchers' focus on the essence of complex topics. Academic assistants who translate between different languages can support researchers in the translation process. This support can make the process faster and easier for researchers (Salvagno et al., 2023). Academic assistants can also take part in the development of collaboration between researchers. Especially with applications enabling more than one person to work on a project simultaneously, it can provide a more effective collaboration between researchers (Geher, 2023).

Academic assistants can contribute under the headings such as methodology, sample size and data analysis in writing the method section of academic studies (Patel & Lam, 2023). For example, they can help to create a representative sample by analyzing large datasets. In this way, researchers can obtain more robust results. They can suggest appropriate data collection methods at the beginning of the research (Ampountolas et al., 2023). In the data collection phase, it can contribute to researchers in terms of facilitating filtering and categorization with the ability to understand text and content and detect and correct errors that may occur in data collection processes. In the analysis processes, artificial intelligence can support researchers in discovering relationships between data using algorithms, performing analyses according to the determined research objectives, and making data sets more understandable by presenting data analysis results with visual tools. This way, data collection and analysis processes can be carried out in shorter periods with less cost (Dogru et al., 2023; Xu et al., 2021).

Academic assistants can analyse the data and make summaries for the writing of findings, discussion and conclusion sections. This can help researchers create these sections faster. For example, GAI can extract meaningful findings after a researcher analyzes a data set. This can make it easier for the researcher to write up the results. It can also compare the researcher's findings with the relevant literature and develop suggestions for discussion. It is argued that it can be used to review academic articles, especially for the discussion part, and to suggest appropriate citations for the identified sources (King, 2023). This helps researchers identify which sources they should cite and use the correct citation format. It can also significantly facilitate the citation process and reduce errors. It can also help organise articles according to journal writing styles and write citations in the correct format according to the bibliography style. This can permit researchers to comply with academic writing standards (Lund et al., 2023).

These assistants can offer significant advantages in various areas, from journal editorial processes to peer review and plagiarism detection. In journal editorial processes, they can guide the evaluation of the appropriateness of articles. In this way, they can avoid tedious tasks and perform analyses based on objective criteria (Hosseini et al., 2023; Stokel-Walker & Van Noorden, 2023). In addition, by scanning large datasets for plagiarism detection and detecting similarities, they can protect academic integrity and make academic writing processes more transparent. In addition, plagiarism detection software and automated peer review platforms can help reviewers and editors have a clearer idea of the quality of articles (Golan et al., 2023).

As a result, academic writing can be a time-consuming and laborious process of research, information gathering, editing and formatting. One of the main contributions of GAI in alleviating the workload is its ability to perform repetitive and routine tasks effectively (Dergaa et al., 2023). Considering the whole writing process, AI algorithms can perform functions such as literature searches, data analysis and document editing quickly and accurately. For example, methods that may take days or weeks manually, such as automatic text summarization or extracting meaningful information from large datasets, can be completed in a few hours with these tools. This shows that using artificial intelligence as an academic assistant can increase productivity and save time (Lund et al., 2023; Storey, 2023). Researchers can find the opportunity to focus on the content of the article instead of dealing with mechanical work (Golan et al., 2023). All these contributions are different from the plagiarism indicator, which is used to save time and improve the quality of communication, not to reproduce unoriginal ideas (Gilot & Cole, 2023).

Challenges and Limitations of Artificial Intelligence as an Academic Assistant

Recently, the use of artificial intelligence technology in academic circles has become a topic that attracts the attention of academics. Studies in this field emphasize the ability of GAI to create human-like texts and reveal that this technology has the potential to shape the future (Alattar & McDowell, 2023). Features such as providing language support, saving time, increasing efficiency and generating ideas are believed to play a positive role in facilitating the professional lives of writers and supporting scientific research processes (Kasneci et al., 2023; Lametti, 2022; Lund et al., 2023). However, despite the above contributions, GAI applications have some limitations for academic writing processes. In this context, we can list some of the limitations of using GAI as an academic assistant under the following headings:

Accuracy and reliability concerns: Researchers are sceptical about the accuracy and reliability of the information obtained with the help of artificial intelligence tools. Including erroneous or biased information can lead to unintentional plagiarism and misattribution of concepts (Dergaa et al., 2023). A limitation arising from the fact that AI algorithms do not fully understand the rules of academic writing is the possibility of inaccurate and unreliable analyses (Walcott, 2021). In this context, the potential for the tools to generate biased, misleading, and false scientific information has been cited as a limitation that can render credibility questionable (Meyer et al., 2023). In addition, some artificial intelligence applications are known to generate inauthentic references (Ariyaratne, 2023). The spread of disinformation and misinformation or the perpetuation of prejudice are among the consequences of this situation (Else, 2023).

Ethical violation concerns: Concerns about ethical violations in texts generated by AI applications can emerge as a serious possibility (Marchandot et al., 2023). The risk of not adequately citing sources or authors can lead to misleading information (Van Dis et al., 2023). Many questions need to be answered, especially regarding plagiarism and individual contribution. While the question of who owns the text created by artificial intelligence applications raises the problem of plagiarism, the possibility of some authors pretending to be the author of these texts raises issues of academic justice and research ownership (Malik et al., 2023). Again, questions such as how these applications will be accepted in the academic world, whether they can be co-authored, or how their contribution will be recognised appropriately raise concerns of ethical violations (Stokel-Walker, 2023). Plagiarism and information ownership issues can be addressed through plagiarism detection programs, but more is needed. There is a need to improve the authors' understanding of ethics and legal regulations that clearly define the role of AI applications in producing scientific knowledge (Imran & Almusharraf, 2023).

Limited understanding of linguistic features: Another limitation identified by researchers is the need for AI applications to understand linguistic features fully (Hammad, 2023). Existing algorithms may need help to make sense of the relationship between attitude markers used in academic articles to show the author's stance and the relationship behind certain linguistic features used in academic texts. As mentioned above, this may raise questions about the accuracy and reliability of the information obtained.

Limited contextual understanding: GAI algorithms and language models learn on large datasets but may need more profound knowledge and expertise in a specific domain. This can make it difficult for them to fully grasp some fields' subtleties and complexities. As a result, their ability to understand and interpret the disciplinary norms of different academic areas can be said to be low (Castillo-Gonzalez, 2022). These deficiencies can lead to the production of inaccurate or incomplete information, the use of erroneous concepts, or misconceptions (Bahammam et al., 2023).

Lack of critical thinking and creativity: With human characteristics such as consciousness, intention and creativity, the level of deep thought or invention may be expanded in texts produced by GAI. Human judgment and interpretation are essential for idea development or innovation (Ivanov & Soliman, 2023). GAI-based applications, which rely heavily on pattern recognition and statistical analysis, may not mimic the critical thinking skills and creativity required for academic writing (Bishop, 2023). Moreover, being dependent on these applications and relying less on the content produced may hinder originality and human innovation (Hammad, 2023). In particular, the involvement of researchers in critical aspects of the research process and, thus, the development of these skills may be negatively affected.

Difficulty in selecting the appropriate data visualization: Artificial intelligence applications may need help selecting the proper graph type for data features within the scope of data visualization (AlAfnan & MohdZuki, 2023). Or they may need help to correctly analyze the relationship between the shapes in different graphs or visuals.

Training and guidelines: Some training may be required to use AI applications effectively in academic writing (Tlili et al., 2023). These trainings can provide authors who will use AI models in their work with insights into the potential benefits and limitations of these applications and provide insight into effective and ethical use (Chan, 2023).

Lack of recent research: Especially since the training of AI language models covers a certain period, recent studies may be excluded (Vincent, 2022). This may limit the ability of AI applications to provide up-to-date information for academic writing (Nath et al., 2022). In addition, limited access to all publications may result in some studies needing to be evaluated.

Complex and costly training: Training language models in specific knowledge domains can be a difficult and expensive process. For example, developing a specialized model for biomedical research can be complex, costly, and require a technical architecture (Altmäe et al., 2023). This may lead some developed countries or privileged researchers to benefit more from AI technology and widen existing inequalities (Booyse & Scheepers, 2023).

Concerning transparency and bias: Using academic assistants in academic writing can raise essential concerns about openness and discrimination. The recent widespread use of GAI-produced research papers threatens the integrity of science. Potential biases pose serious problems, making identifying and correcting errors difficult (Müller, 2021). Many studies show that data and coding processes, often derived from large web-based datasets, may contain biases related to gender, race, ethnicity, and disability (Basta et al., 2019; Hutchinson et al., 2020). It is also possible that these models may unintentionally reinforce biases in educational data, which may skew the results of scientific research (Bahammam et al., 2023). This may put researchers and readers at risk of deviating from the real world that the findings usually represent. Again, there are still uncertainties and concerns about users' data.

GAI Tools Used as Academic Assistants

Authors use many innovative authoring applications for various purposes with the developing technology. In particular, these tools are used for literature review, visualization, content generation, plagiarism detection, language improvement, data analysis, and selection of appropriate journals (Aljanabi et al., 2023; Dergaa et al., 2023; Le, 2023). These applications provide advantages to researchers in terms of reducing workload (Dergaa et al., 2023), saving time (Storey, 2023), generating value from big data (Lund et al., 2023), and improving quality (Patel & Lam, 2023). Some of these tools are shown in Figure 1 according to their intended use.

Figure 1 shows that GAI tools are classified into seven different categories. These categories are research, visualization, content generation, plagiarism, language improvement, data analysis and journal finding. When the literature is examined, it is seen that there are many applications under each heading. The figure shows the tools most frequently preferred by the researchers.

Tools such as Elicit, Scispace, Research Rabbit, Scite_, and Perplexity stand out for research processes. These tools support researchers in data collection, literature review and insight gathering. In addition to these tools, tools such as ChatGPT, Copy.ai, Semantic Scholar, and Scholarcy help extract hidden or essential information from large data sets. These tools allow researchers to manage complex processes more effectively and access essential findings in large data sets. Again, conducting more comprehensive and more profound analyses in academic studies is possible.

Researchers rely on visualization tools to understand and effectively analyze complex data sets or share their results. In this context, various artificial intelligence-supported tools are used. Visualization tools are used to make data more meaningful, discover patterns, and effectively communicate the results of the analysis. Tools such as RAWGraphs, Tableau, FusionCharts, VOSviewer, and Power BI are just a few of the tools that serve researchers. In addition to these tools, there are various tools in the literature, such as Olli, Baseboard, LIDA, and Columns. These tools provide researchers with different visualization options to better understand the data and communicate their findings more effectively. Available for free and for a fee, these tools allow researchers to cater to a wide range of users or offer solutions to suit different budgets and needs. This makes the analysis of complex data sets more accessible and allows researchers to share their findings more effectively.

Researchers are responsible for sharing and communicating to readers the data and analysis results gathered from their work on a particular topic. At this stage, researchers use different tools to produce various types of content. Tools for creating visual, video, audio and textual content include DeepReel, Canva, Rask, Scholarly, and Gradescope. In addition to these tools, applications such as WritebyAI, Designs AI, Easy-Peasy.AI, and Content Generator can help researchers in their content generation processes.

In content generation processes, researchers need to comply with various ethical principles. One of the critical issues to be considered in this context is plagiarism. Researchers should be careful about this issue to produce content according to ethical rules. A few tools are available to prevent plagiarism and help researchers. Tools such as Turnitin, iThenticate, Copyleaks, Originality.ai, and Dupli Checker help check the originality of the content and detect potential plagiarism. In addition, tools such as Grammarly, which aims to correct grammar and spelling mistakes; Copyscape, which checks web content for similarities; Plagscan, which contains student work; and Unicheck, designed for educational platforms, also support producing ethical content. These tools guide researchers on how to create reliable and honest content.

Figure 1. GAI tools used as academic assistants

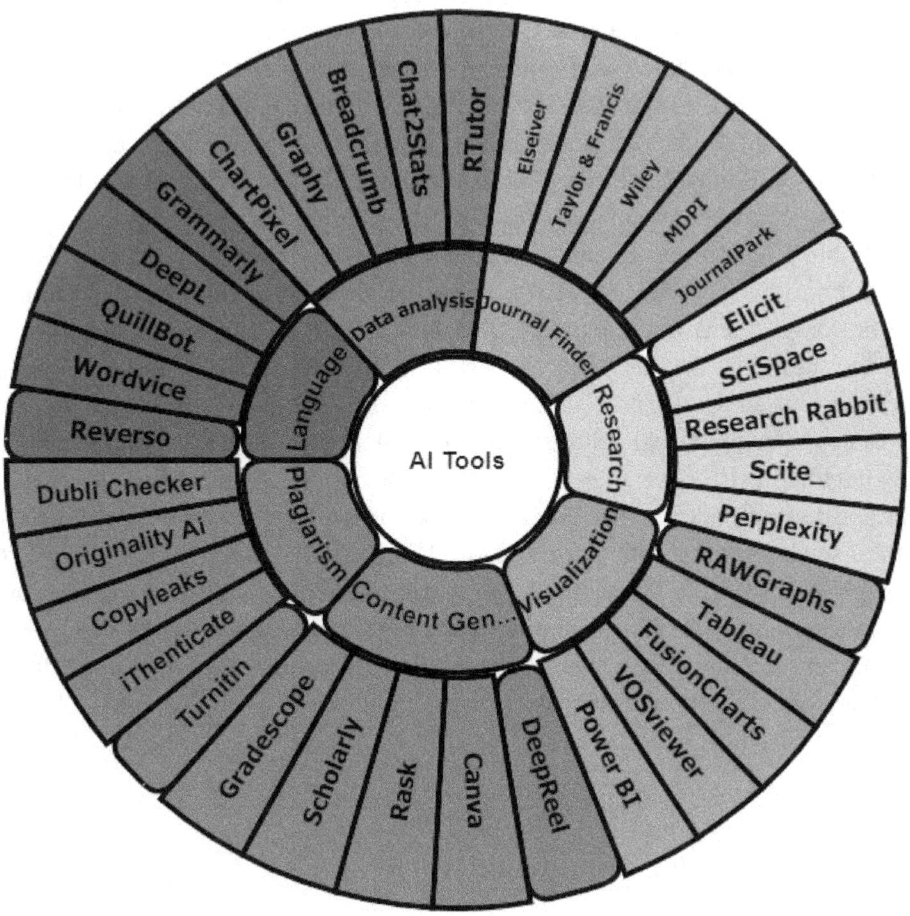

The clarity and fluency of the language used in research processes are vital for correctly evaluating the study. For this reason, speech and expression should be approached with great care for effective communication, especially in studies written in different languages. Academic writing aims to increase knowledge exchange and understanding, so the language must be clear, precise and understandable. On the other hand, many productive artificial intelligence tools have been developed to prevent the negativities that may arise in journal processes. Such tools aim to improve the quality of writing by providing suggestions on grammar, spelling and expression. For example, tools such as Grammarly, DeepL, QuillBot, Wordvice, and Reverso guide users in improving language accuracy and expressiveness. In addition to these tools, spelling and grammar-checking tools such as ProWritingAid, Linguix, Gramara, and Grammar-GPT are also widely used to optimize writing quality in research processes. These AI-powered tools are essential in improving researchers' written expression, correcting language errors and enabling more effective communication. They enhance communication in the scientific community by increasing the relevance and interactivity of academic writing.

Data analysis is critical in analyzing the data collected in research processes and extracting meaningful information. Achieving accurate and reliable results, providing practical answers to research questions, and avoiding bias are among the main goals of scientific research. Therefore, various AI-assisted applications and tools used for data analysis are gaining importance. AI-assisted data analysis tools provide researchers with great convenience in analyzing complex data sets, identifying patterns and reaching unique insights. In this context, tools like ChartPixel, Graphy, Breadcrumb, Chat2Stats, and RTutor help users optimize their data analysis processes. ChartPixel supports data expression through visualizations and graphs, while Graphy facilitates data sharing. Breadcrumb is effective in managing data tracking and analytical methods. Chat2Stats enables data analysis through a text-based communication interface, while RTutor is a tool that teaches students statistical programming skills. In addition to these tools, applications such as DataSquirrel, Research Studio, DataGPTd, and Rows AI are designed to improve data analysis processes and offer more possibilities to researchers. These tools contribute to scientific discoveries by enabling researchers to analyze fast and accurate data.

Researchers use various methods to get their studies published in an appropriate journal. This process can sometimes be complex and time-consuming. To overcome these challenges, publishing houses have developed various solutions. At this point, artificial intelligence-supported tools developed to assist researchers in their journal search process come to the fore. These tools help researchers direct their work to the most appropriate journals. Some of the prominent AI-assisted journal-finding assistants are as follows: Journal Finder (Elsevier), Taylor & Francis Journal Suggester, Wiley Journal Finder, MDPI Journal Finder and JournalPark Journal Wizard. These tools suggest appropriate journals to researchers based on their work's content, title or keywords. These suggestions help researchers select the best journals to publish their work. In this context, tools such as Springer Journal Suggester and IEEE Publication Recommender aim to facilitate the process by providing artificial intelligence-supported guidance to researchers in selecting appropriate journals. These assistants save time and effort by providing researchers with a more effective journal selection process.

CONCLUSION

This study discusses the role of productive artificial intelligence as an academic assistant. In this context, the opportunities and challenges that AI provides to researchers and the practical AI tools used in research processes are examined.

The use of artificial intelligence technology in academic writing processes has aroused great interest among researchers with the opportunities it offers. These opportunities include AI's ability to perform repetitive and routine tasks effectively, its ability to perform processes such as literature searches, data analysis and document editing quickly and accurately, and its potential to save time by increasing productivity. Integrating AI into academic writing processes offers a wide range of benefits to students and educators, focusing on accelerating research processes, providing opportunities for collaboration, and facilitating complex tasks such as data analysis and summarization. In addition, it offers essential support for young researchers in hypothesis generation, identifying research questions, and literature review processes. In this context, the potential of using artificial intelligence as an effective tool at many stages in the academic world to increase productivity and optimize academic writing processes is of great importance.

In addition to the advantages of artificial intelligence applications for academic writing processes, they also have some limitations. Among these limitations, concerns about accuracy and reliability stand out. Researchers need to be more convinced about the rules of AI tools in analyzing and presenting information accurately and reliably. There are also concerns about ethical violations, especially plagiarism and information ownership issues that may arise in AI-generated texts. More understanding of linguistic features is required. AI applications may need help understanding the linguistic features used in academic texts, raising questions about accuracy and reliability. In addition, factors such as limited contextual understanding and lack of critical thinking are among the factors that limit the effectiveness of AI applications in academic writing processes. Difficulty selecting appropriate data visualization, lack of training and guidelines, and ignoring recent research are factors limiting AI application use. Again, the complexity and cost of training AI applications in specific knowledge areas make it difficult for this technology to be widely accessible. These limitations are important factors to consider when evaluating the role of AI technology in academic writing processes.

Finally, researchers are turning to artificial intelligence tools for various purposes using developing technology. These tools provide advantages to researchers in literature review, visualization, content generation, plagiarism checking, language correction, data analysis and journal selection. AI tools such as Elicit, Scispace, Research Rabbit, Scite_, and Perplexity support research processes to ease the workload. Visualization tools such as RAWGraphs, Tableau, FusionCharts, VOSviewer, and Power BI are used to understand and effectively present complex data sets. In the content creation phase, tools such as DeepReel, Canva, Rask, Scholarly, and Gradescope help researchers produce various content types. For plagiarism checking, tools such as Turnitin, iThenticate, Copyleaks, Originality.ai, and Dupli Checker are used, while language correction tools include Grammarly, DeepL, QuillBot, Wordvice, and Reverso. While tools such as ChartPixel, Graphy, Breadcrumb, Chat2Stats, and RTutor are used to optimize data analysis processes, artificial intelligence-supported tools such as Journal Finder (Elsevier), Taylor & Francis Journal Suggester, Wiley Journal Finder, MDPI Journal Finder, and JournalPark Journal Wizard help researchers to direct their studies to the most appropriate journals. These artificial intelligence tools provide significant advantages to researchers in terms of saving time, reducing workload, and conducting quality academic studies more effectively.

REFERENCES

Abbass, H. (2021). What is artificial intelligence? *IEEE Transactions on Artificial Intelligence*, *2*(2), 94–95. doi:10.1109/TAI.2021.3096243

AlAfnan, M. A., & MohdZuki, S. F. (2023). Do artificial intelligence chatbots have a writing style? An investigation into the stylistic features of ChatGPT-4. *Journal of Artificial Intelligence and Technology*, *3*(3), 85–94. doi:10.37965/jait.2023.0267

Alattar, A. A., & McDowell, M. M. (2023). The rise of AI co-authors: Navigating the future of scientific writing with ChatGPT. *Journal of Neurosurgery, 1*(aop), 1-2. doi:10.3171/2023.3.JNS23254

Aljanabi, M. (2023). ChatGPT: Future directions and open possibilities. *Mesopotamian Journal of Cybersecurity*, *16-17*, 16–17. doi:10.58496/MJCS/2023/003

Aljanabi, M., Ghazi, M., Ali, A. H., & Abed, S. A. (2023). ChatGPT: Open possibilities. *Iraqi Journal For Computer Science and Mathematics*, *4*(1), 62–64. doi:10.52866/20ijcsm.2023.01.01.0018

Altmäe, S., Sola-Leyva, A., & Salumets, A. (2023). Artificial intelligence in scientific writing: A friend or a foe? *Reproductive Biomedicine Online*, *47*(1), 3–9. doi:10.1016/j.rbmo.2023.04.009 PMID:37142479

Ampountolas, A., Menconi, G., & Shaw, G. (2023). Metaverse research propositions: Online intermediaries. *Tourism Economics*. doi:10.1177/13548166231159520

Ariyaratne, S., Iyengar, K. P., & Botchu, R. (2023). Will collaborative publishing with ChatGPT drive academic writing in the future? *British Journal of Surgery*, *110*(9), 1213–1214. doi:10.1093/bjs/znad198 PMID:37368994

Arslan, E. (2022). Sosyal bilim araştırmalarında VOSviewer ile bibliyometrik haritalama ve örnek bir uygulama [Bibliometric mapping with VOSviewer in social science research and a sample application]. *Anadolu University Journal of Social Sciences, 22*(Special Issue, 2), 33-56.

Ballester, O. (2021). An artificial intelligence definition and classification framework for public sector applications. In DG. O2021: *The 22nd Annual International Conference on Digital Government Research* (pp. 67-75). ACM Press. 10.1145/3463677.3463709

Bautista, R. M., & Pentang, J. T. (2022). Ctrl C+ Ctrl V: Plagiarism and knowledge on referencing and citation among pre-service teachers. *International Journal of Multidisciplinary: Applied Business and Education Research*, *3*(2), 245–257. doi:10.11594/ijmaber.03.02.10

Bishop, L. (2023). A computer wrote this paper: What ChatGPT means for education, research, and writing. *Research, and Writing*. doi:10.2139/ssrn.4338981

Booyse, D., & Scheepers, C. B. (2023). Barriers to adopting automated organizational decision-making through the use of artificial intelligence. *Management Research Review*. Advance online publication. doi:10.1108/MRR-09-2021-0701

Bowen, G. A. (2009). Document analysis as a qualitative research method. *Qualitative Research Journal*, *9*(2), 27–40. doi:10.3316/QRJ0902027

Capcut. (2023). *Top 10 Free AI Translators in 2023.* Capcut. https://www.capcut.com/tr-tr/resource/best-free-ai-translators

Castillo-Gonzalez, W. (2022). ChatGPT and the future of scientific communication. *Metaverse Basic and Applied Research*, *1*, 8–8. doi:10.56294/mr20228

Chan, C. K. Y. (2023). A comprehensive AI policy education framework for university teaching and learning. *International Journal of Educational Technology in Higher Education*, *20*(1), 38. doi:10.1186/s41239-023-00408-3

Chen, S. (2023). *10 Best 2023 AI Data Visualization Tools of the Decade.* Digital Phablet. https://www.digitalphablet.com/tr/ai/en-iyi-AI-veri-g%C3%B6rselle%C5%9Ftirme-ara%C3%A7lar%C4%B1/

Dergaa, I., Chamari, K., Zmijewski, P., & Saad, H. B. (2023). From human writing to artificial intelligence generated text: Examining the prospects and potential threats of ChatGPT in academic writing. *Biology of Sport*, *40*(2), 615–622. doi:10.5114/biolsport.2023.125623 PMID:37077800

Doğan, S. (2023). *Rask ai ile video çeviri ve dublaj [Video translation and dubbing with Rask ai].* Yapay Zekâ Günlükleri [Artificial Intelligence Chronicles]. https://www.yapayzekagunlukleri.com/yapay-zeka-uygulamalari/video/rask-ai-ile-video-ceviri-ve-dublaj/

Dogru, T., Line, N., Hanks, L., Acikgoz, F., Abbott, J. A., Bakir, S., Berbekova, A., Bilgihan, A., Iskender, A., Kizildag, M., Lee, M., Lee, W., McGinley, S., Mody, M., Onder, I., Ozdemir, O., & Suess, C. (2023). The implications of generative artificial intelligence in academic research and higher education in tourism and hospitality. *Tourism Economics*, *0*(0), 13548166231204065. doi:10.1177/13548166231204065

Else, H. (2023). Abstracts written by ChatGPT fool scientists. *Nature*, *613*(7944), 423–423. doi:10.1038/d41586-023-00056-7 PMID:36635510

Filiz, O. (2023). *Grammarly.* Eğitim Çantası [Education Bag]. https://egitimcantasi.com/uygulamalar/grammarly/

Gayed, J. M., Carlon, M. K. J., Oriola, A. M., & Cross, J. S. (2022). Exploring an AI-based writing assistant's impact on English language learners. *Computers and Education: Artificial Intelligence*, *3*(1), 100055. doi:10.1016/j.caeai.2022.100055

Geher, G. (2023). ChatGPT, artificial intelligence, and the future of writing: How ChatGPT and other ai systems may ruin the ability to write (and think). *Psychology Today.* https://www.psychologytoday.com/us/blog/darwins-subterranean-world/202301/chatgpt-artificial-intelligence-and-the-future-of-writing

George, B., & Wooden, O. (2023). Managing the strategic transformation of higher education through artificial intelligence. *Administrative Sciences*, *13*(9), 196. doi:10.3390/admsci13090196

Golan, R., Reddy, R., Muthigi, A., & Ramasamy, R. (2023). Artificial intelligence in academic writing: A paradigm-shifting technological advance. *Nature Reviews. Urology*, *1-2*(6), 327–328. doi:10.1038/s41585-023-00746-x PMID:36829078

GPT-3. (2020). A robot wrote this entire article. Are you scared yet, human? *The Guardian.* https://www.theguardian.com/commentisfree/2020/sep/08/robot-wrote-this-article-gpt-3

Hammad, M. (2023). The impact of artificial intelligence (AI) programs on writing scientific research. *Annals of Biomedical Engineering*, *51*(3), 459–460. doi:10.1007/s10439-023-03140-1 PMID:36637603

Hosseini, M., Rasmussen, L. M., & Resnik, D. B. (2023). Using AI to write scholarly publications. *Accountability in Research*, 1–9. doi:10.1080/08989621.2023.2168535 PMID:36697395

Hutson, M. (2022). Could AI help you to write your next paper? *Nature*, *611*(7934), 192–193. doi:10.1038/d41586-022-03479-w PMID:36316468

Imran, M., & Almusharraf, N. (2023). Analyzing the role of ChatGPT as a writing assistant at higher education level: A systematic review of the literature. *Contemporary Educational Technology*, *15*(4), ep464. doi:10.30935/cedtech/13605

Kasneci, E., Seßler, K., Küchemann, S., Bannert, M., Dementieva, D., Fischer, F., Gasser, U., Groh, G., Günnemann, S., Hüllermeier, E., Krusche, S., Kutyniok, G., Michaeli, T., Nerdel, C., Pfeffer, J., Poquet, O., Sailer, M., Schmidt, A., Seidel, T., & Kasneci, G. (2023). ChatGPT for good? On opportunities and challenges of large language models for education. *Learning and Individual Differences*, *103*, 102274. doi:10.1016/j.lindif.2023.102274

King, M. R. (2023). The future of AI in medicine: A perspective from a Chatbot. *Annals of Biomedical Engineering*, *51*(2), 291–295. doi:10.1007/s10439-022-03121-w PMID:36572824

Lametti, D. (2022). AI could be great for college essays. *Slate.* https://slate.com/technology/2022/12/chatgpt-college-essay-plagiarism.html

LeT. T. (2023). A preliminary example of utilizing AI text generation to support academic writing: "Humans befriending their creations some notes on the human-AI relationship". doi:10.31219/osf.io/bsxey

Liu, G. Z., Lu, H. C., Lin, V., & Hsu, W. C. (2018). Cultivating undergraduates' plagiarism avoidance knowledge and skills with an online tutorial system. *Journal of Computer Assisted Learning*, *34*(2), 150–161. doi:10.1111/jcal.12223

Lund, B. D., & Wang, T. (2023). Chatting about ChatGPT: How may AI and GPT impact academia and libraries? *Library Hi Tech News*, *40*(3), 26–29. doi:10.1108/LHTN-01-2023-0009

Lund, B. D., Wang, T., Mannuru, N. R., Nie, B., Shimray, S., & Wang, Z. (2023). ChatGPT and a new academic reality: Artificial Intelligence-written research papers and the ethics of the large language models in scholarly publishing. *Journal of the Association for Information Science and Technology*, *74*(5), 570–581. doi:10.1002/asi.24750

Maiorana, F. A., & Mayer, H. F. (2018). How to avoid common errors in writing scientific manuscripts. *European Journal of Plastic Surgery*, *41*(5), 489–494. doi:10.1007/s00238-018-1418-z

Malik, A. R., Pratiwi, Y., Andajani, K., Numertayasa, I. W., Suharti, S., Darwis, A., & Marzuki. (2023). Exploring artificial intelligence in academic essay: Higher education student's perspective. *International Journal of Educational Research Open*, *5*, 100296. doi:10.1016/j.ijedro.2023.100296

Marchandot, B., Matsushita, K., Carmona, A., Trimaille, A., & Morel, O. (2023). ChatGPT: The next frontier in academic writing for cardiologists or a Pandora's box of ethical dilemmas. *European Heart Journal Open*, *3*(2), oead007. doi:10.1093/ehjopen/oead007 PMID:36915398

McFarland, A. (2023). *8 "Best" AI Translation Software and Tools*. Unite. https://www.unite.ai/tr/en-iyi-yapay-zeka-%C3%A7eviri-yaz%C4%B1l%C4%B1m%C4%B1-ara%C3%A7lar%C4%B1/

McFarland, A., & Tardif, A. (2023). *7 "Best" AI Content Detection Tools*. Unite. https://www.unite.ai/tr/en-iyi-yapay-zeka-i%C3%A7erik-dedekt%C3%B6rleri/

McMahan, E., Day, S., Funk, R., & Coleman, L. S. (2017). *Literature and the writing process*. Pearson.

Meyer, J. G., Urbanowicz, R. J., Martin, P. C., O'Connor, K., Li, R., Peng, P. C., Bright, T. J., Tatonetti, N., Won, K. J., Gonzalez-Hernandez, G., & Moore, J. H. (2023). ChatGPT and large language models in academia: Opportunities and challenges. *BioData Mining*, *16*(1), 20. doi:10.1186/s13040-023-00339-9 PMID:37443040

Nashville State. (2023). *AI Detection in Turnitin*. NSCC. https://www.nscc.edu/documents/faculty-staff/online-learning/Turnitin-AI-Detection.pdf

Nath, S., Marie, A., Ellershaw, S., Korot, E., & Keane, P. A. (2022). New meaning for NLP: The trials and tribulations of natural language processing with GPT-3 in ophthalmology. *The British Journal of Ophthalmology*, *106*(7), 889–892. doi:10.1136/bjophthalmol-2022-321141 PMID:35523534

NguyenM. H. (2023). Academic writing and AI: Day-2 experiment with cultural additivity. doi:10.31219/osf.io/25yjw

Noroozi, O. (2023). The role of students' epistemic beliefs for their argumentation performance in higher education. *Innovations in Education and Teaching International*, *60*(4), 501–512. doi:10.1080/14703297.2022.2092188

Patel, S. B., & Lam, K. (2023). ChatGPT: The future of discharge summaries? *The Lancet. Digital Health*, *5*(3), e107–e108. doi:10.1016/S2589-7500(23)00021-3 PMID:36754724

Poch, A. L., Hamby, M., & Chen, X. (2020). Secondary teachers' beliefs about teaching writing to typically achieving and struggling adolescent writers. *Reading & Writing Quarterly*, *36*(6), 497–520. doi:10.1080/10573569.2019.1666759

Salvagno, M., Taccone, F. S., & Gerli, A. G. (2023). Can artificial intelligence help for scientific writing? *Critical Care*, *27*(1), 1–5. doi:10.1186/s13054-023-04380-2 PMID:36597110

Shen, Y., Heacock, L., Elias, J., Hentel, K. D., Reig, B., Shih, G., & Moy, L. (2023). ChatGPT and other large language models are double-edged swords. *Radiology*, *307*(2), e230163. doi:10.1148/radiol.230163 PMID:36700838

Stacey, J., & Rei, M. (2023). Improving Robustness in knowledge distillation using domain-targeted data augmentation. https://doi.org//arXiv.2305.13067 doi:10.48550

Stokel-Walker, C. (2023). ChatGPT listed as author on research papers: Many scientists disapprove. *Nature*, *613*(7945), 620–621. doi:10.1038/d41586-023-00107-z PMID:36653617

Stokel-Walker, C., & Van Noorden, R. (2023). What ChatGPT and generative AI mean for science. *Nature*, *614*(7947), 214–216. doi:10.1038/d41586-023-00340-6 PMID:36747115

Storey, V. A. (2023). AI Technology and Academic Writing: Knowing and Mastering the "Craft Skills". [IJAET]. *International Journal of Adult Education and Technology*, *14*(1), 1–15. doi:10.4018/IJAET.325795

Taecharungroj, V. (2023). "What can ChatGPT do?" Analyzing early reactions to the innovative ai chatbot on Twitter. *Big Data and Cognitive Computing*, *7*(1), 35. doi:10.3390/bdcc7010035

Tlili, A., Shehata, B., Adarkwah, M. A., Bozkurt, A., Hickey, D. T., Huang, R., & Agyemang, B. (2023). What if the devil is my guardian angel: ChatGPT as a case study of using chatbots in education. *Smart Learning Environments*, *10*(1), 15. doi:10.1186/s40561-023-00237-x

Vincent, J. (2022). AI-generated answers temporarily banned on coding Q&A site Stack Overflow. *The Verge, 5*.

Walcott, K. (2021). Informing academic writing pedagogy through the study of phrase-frames. *Journal of Language Teaching and Research*, *12*(1), 158–171. doi:10.17507/jltr.1201.17

Xu, Y., Liu, X., Cao, X., Huang, C., Liu, E., Qian, S., Liu, X., Wu, Y., Dong, F., Qiu, C.-W., Qiu, J., Hua, K., Su, W., Wu, J., Xu, H., Han, Y., Fu, C., Yin, Z., Liu, M., & Zhang, J. (2021). Artificial intelligence: A powerful paradigm for scientific research. *Innovation (Cambridge (Mass.))*, *2*(4), 100179. Advance online publication. doi:10.1016/j.xinn.2021.100179 PMID:34877560

Young, L. (2023). *iThenticate 2.0: Advancing research integrity with AI writing detection*. Turnitin. https://www.turnitin.com/blog/ithenticate-2-0-advancing-research-integrity-with-ai-writing-detection

Yurtaslan, N. (2023). Tableau dijital dönüşüm aracı ile veri görselleştirme [Data visualization with Tableau digital transformation tool]. *Medium*. https://nurhayatyurtaslan.medium.com/tableau-dijital-d%C3%B6n%C3%BC%C5%9F%C3%BCm-arac%C4%B1-ile-veri-g%C3%B6rselle%C5%9Ftirme-b2af9d5aaf73

Zala, D. (2023). *The 12 best tools and software to create pie charts with ease*. Squeeze Growth. https://squeezegrowth.com/tr/best-tools-and-software-to-create-pie-charts-with-ease/

Zhihan, L. (2023). Generative artificial intelligence in the metaverse era. *Cognitive Robotics*, *3*(3), 208–217. doi:10.1016/j.cogr.2023.06.001

KEY TERMS AND DEFINITIONS

Academic Assistant: Artificial intelligence applications that assist researchers with tasks such as information retrieval, analysis, and content creation in academic fields.

Academic Writing: A style of writing specific to scientific research, prepared according to various rules, that effectively presents information.

Artificial Intelligence (AI): A set of algorithms that can simulate human characteristics such as reasoning, decision making, or problem solving.

Artificial Intelligence Algorithms: Structures used in computer systems that consist of a sequence of logical steps.

Artificial Intelligence Applications: Technological tools that include software and algorithms that imbue computer systems with human capabilities such as learning and problem-solving.

Data sets: Describes large amounts of data or extensive data sets from multiple sources.

Generative Artificial Intelligence: More advanced than traditional artificial intelligence, it can be defined as the ability to generate new information using learning and problem-solving capabilities.

APPENDIX

Table 1. AI tools used as academic assistants

	Tool Name	Price	QR	Features
Research	Elicit	$		Elicit is one of the user-friendly artificial intelligence tools for data processing. With the help of this tool you can design and conduct qualitative research. A researcher can use it to automate everything from analyzing textual data to identifying key themes, emotions and patterns (Elicit, n.d.).
	SCISPACE	$		It is used to help you meet the specific guidelines of journals and publishers quickly and efficiently. The comprehensive platform provides predefined manuscript templates and automatic formatting tools. It also includes a citation management system and support for various styles. It can automatically generate in-text citations and bibliographies (Scispace, n.d.).
	ResearchRabbit	FREE		It is a tool that helps researchers manage their work. It can track citations, create bibliographies and article abstracts. It can also help researchers stay organized and make better use of their time (ResearchRabbit, n.d.).
	scite_	$		Scite is one of the most popular AI-powered academic research tools that improves any academic research in one go. Its own natural language processing and machine learning help users perform deeper analysis on academic articles (Scite, n.d.).
	perplexity	$		ChatGPT-4 is an assistant that provides users with up-to-date information on the Internet. With this tool, you can summarize content, search, create content and more. There is also a free version, allowing users to easily try out this innovative artificial intelligence tool (Perplexity, n.d.).
Visualization	RG	FREE		RAWGraphs is an online tool that allows users to create visuals from raw data. It can handle various types of graphs, including bar graphs, line graphs and scatter plots. RAWGraphs offers various customization options, giving users the opportunity to edit the visuals according to their specific needs (Zala, 2023).
	+ab|eau	$		Tableau is a powerful tool in the field that helps users analyze data. With its drag-and-drop interface, Tableau helps users easily discover, understand and identify data, trends, patterns and outliers. It supports many options from basic charts and graphs to advanced maps, treemaps and heatmaps (Yurtaslan, 2023).
	FusionCharts	$		FusionCharts is a comprehensive data visualization tool that offers a wide range of chart types, including bar charts, line charts and pie charts. Its extensive library of pre-built templates and themes makes it easy for users to create compelling visuals. FusionCharts also features real-time data streaming, allowing users to visualize live data (Chen, 2023).
	vosViewer	FREE		VOSviewer enables the creation of maps based on network, bibliographic and textual data of the studies in the literature. It also allows visualization and exploration of this data. It is a free, open-source bibliometric mapping program. It creates maps based on existing data by utilizing the author, country, journal, citation, keywords, abstract, and institutional data supporting the research (Arslan, 2022).
	Power BI	$		Developed by Microsoft, Power BI is a comprehensive data visualization tool that integrates seamlessly with other Microsoft products and services. Its user-friendly interface and drag-and-drop functionality make it easy for users to create interactive reports and dashboards. Power BI also offers AI-powered features such as natural language queries and automated insights, allowing users to

continues on following page

Table 1. Continued

Category	Tool	Pricing	QR	Description
				gain valuable insights from their data with minimal effort (Chen, 2023).
Content Generation	DeepReel	$		DeepReel AI is an artificial intelligence tool for video content creation. This tool helps users automatically convert text-based content into video. DeepReel AI analyzes text-based scenarios or descriptions. Based on this information, it creates videos by combining visual and audio elements. Users can typically use such tools to create content for marketing, education or entertainment purposes (DeepReel, n.d.).
	Canva	$		Popular graphic design platform Canva makes content creation even easier with its "Magic" feature. It allows users to create a collection of personalized templates from any image they upload. Users can also create images by typing text (Canva, n.d.).
	Rask	$		Rask AI is an artificial intelligence-based platform. It offers a highly advanced service for video translation and dubbing. With this platform, you can translate videos between languages or add dubbing to existing videos. Rask AI stands out with its language capabilities and offers impressive results in text-to-speech conversion (Doğan, 2023).
	scholarcy	$		Scholarly is an artificial intelligence tool that positively impacts the academic research process by automating the process of reading, summarizing and extracting information. It can help us identify figures, tables, references and main concepts in articles (Scholarcy, n.d.).
	gradescope	$		Widely used in educational institutions, Gradescope is an AI-powered grading and feedback tool. The time and effort required by instructors to grade assignments, exams and coding projects is greatly reduced by automating the process. Machine learning algorithms can decode code, recognize handwriting and provide in-depth feedback to students (Gradescope, n.d.).
Plagiarism	turnitin	$		It is a powerful tool for detecting plagiarism in assignments and theses. This tool gives the percentage of AI-generated content compared to the overall content. It can detect text generated by GPT-3, GPT-3.5 and other variants including ChatGPT (Nashville State, 2023).
	iThenticate	$		This tool, which has academic databases, journals, publications and more than 17 billion web pages in its data pool, is used to detect plagiarism in academic works. iThenticate 2.0 adds artificial intelligence text detection feature. It helps researchers, publishers and academics in this direction (Young, 2023).
	Copyleaks	$		It is an AI-powered plagiarism detection tool that helps users ensure the originality of their content by scanning copies from various databases. The platform supports multiple file formats and languages. This makes it a versatile solution for content developers, educational institutions and businesses. Copyleaks also provides detailed similarity reports that highlight potential plagiarism issues and offer revision suggestions (McFarland & Tardif, 2023).
	ORIGINALITY.AI	$		It is a state-of-the-art AI content detector designed to detect duplicate content, measure text uniqueness, and provide actionable insights to improve writing quality. In addition to powerful plagiarism detection features, OriginalityAI also includes content optimization features such as alternative wording suggestions and improved readability (McFarland & Tardif, 2023).

continues on following page

Table 1. Continued

	Tool		Description
	Dupli Checker	$	It stands out with its user-friendly interface and offers its members 50 search rights per day. The program scans both uploaded files and copy-pasted content for plagiarism. In addition to showing similar sentences and their citations, it also offers the opportunity to download the plagiarism report (DupliChecker, n.d.).
Language Improvement	grammarly	$	Grammarly is a powerful writing assistant tool that brings a new understanding to the way people write and communicate online. The tool has become very popular over the years due to its ability to analyze written text and provide feedback on criteria such as spelling, grammar, punctuation, clarity and accuracy. Grammarly is not only suitable for personal use but also for educational use (Filiz, 2023).
Language Improvement	DeepL	$	It is one of the AI translation tools that is constantly growing in popularity. It is used both for corporate and individual use. DeepL is known for its intuitive interface and seamless integration with Windows and iOS. This tool gives the opportunity to customize translations and provides a lot of control over automatic translation (McFarland, 2023).
Language Improvement	QuillBot	$	It is an AI tool with writing and language improvement features useful for researchers. It is based on advanced algorithms that annotate, provide word suggestions and offer alternative word choices to avoid plagiarism. The "expand" feature helps brainstorming during the writing process by generating content from several keywords or phrases (QuillBot, n.d.).
Language Improvement	WORDVICE AI	$	Powered by the latest artificial intelligence technology, Wordvice is a real-time text editor. It corrects spelling, punctuation and style errors. It has an AI Correction Tool that improves the clarity and flow of your text (Wordvice, n.d.).
Language Improvement	Reverso	FREE	It is a comprehensive AI translator supporting more than 15 languages. It has an extensive knowledge database of more than 11 million words and phrases, allowing users to obtain context-rich translations. Reverso is perfect for people who want to learn new languages or learn the meaning of words they encounter while reading (Capcut, 2023).
Data Analysis	ChartPixel	FREE	ChartPixel allows users to effortlessly transform raw data into understandable and engaging charts in seconds. By removing the complexity of data analysis tools, it provides an intuitive way for all skill levels to grasp data models and create engaging presentations with AI-powered explanations. Many user-friendly features make the tool easy to use (ChartPixel, n.d.).
Data Analysis	Graphy	FREE	Graphy is a free graphing tool that allows for stylish and interactive data visualization with ease. With the help of artificial intelligence, this tool allows users to create stunning graphs without the need for advanced technical skills. Graphs can be embedded on various platforms, including Notion and other preferred apps. Using Graphy, you can present data in a visually engaging and effective way (Graphy, n.d.).
Data Analysis	breadcrumb	$	Breadcrumb is an AI tool designed to seamlessly transform raw data into interactive, personalized views. It eliminates the need for users to have advanced data skills. Using AI, it allows users to analyze data in real time without the burden of manually combining multiple sources, modeling or computing (Breadcrumb, n.d.).

continues on following page

Table 1. Continued

Category	Tool	Price	Description
	Chat2Stats	FREE	It is a data analysis tool powered by OpenAI. Its main goal is to make data analysis simple and easy by leveraging AI-driven advances in natural language processing. With Chat2Stats, users can seamlessly analyze data from a wide range of sources and formats. This allows them to efficiently gather insights that drive business growth. One of its greatest strengths is its ease of use (Chat2Stats, n.d.).
	RTutor	FREE	RTutor is an artificial intelligence-based tool for data analysis. It provides a natural language interface for users to interact with their data. It can be used to generate R and Python code for various statistical analyses and generate reports in HTML format (RTutor, n.d.).
Journal Finder	Journal Finder	FREE	It is one of the tools used to find the most appropriate journal for your work. It can work with both abstract and keywords. It will save time for researchers to find the most appropriate journal for their work. It is possible to search with a maximum of 5000 words for abstracts and a few phrases for keywords. This tool, which works with machine learning, helps you find a journal suitable for the scope of your article (Elsevier, n.d.).
	AUTHORSERVICES	FREE	One of the most important reasons editors give for rejecting a manuscript is that it does not fall within the scope of the journal. This problem will help you find the best journal for your research paper. This tool, which works by analyzing the abstract and keywords, will save you time in accessing the journal list (Taylor&Francis, n.d.).
	WILEY	FREE	If you are not sure which journal to submit your work to, this tool will help you find journals that match your article. You can browse by title and topic, and easily add titles side by side to compare publication times, metrics and policies. All you need is the article title and a 3000-word abstract (WILEY, n.d.).
	MDPI	FREE	With MDPI Journal Finder, you can solve the most time-consuming process of finding and publishing journals. MDPI currently publishes 421 peer-reviewed journals and 9 conference journals that aim to publish the output of academic conferences. Using artificial intelligence, this search tool allows you to select by title, abstract, impact factor, price and index (MDPI, n.d.).
	Turkish JournalPark ACADEMIC	FREE	In the JournalPark system, users have the opportunity to access journals suitable for their articles with the journal wizard. In this section, they can access the appropriate journal by filling in the article title, keywords and subject headings. In addition, they can filter between journals with criteria such as journal index list, fee policy and minimum article acceptance rate (JournalPark, n.d.).

Chapter 8
Challenges and Limitations of Generative AI in Education

Seyfullah Gökoğlu
https://orcid.org/0000-0003-0074-7692
Bartın University, Turkey

ABSTRACT

This chapter presents a comprehensive literature review to identify the challenges and limitations of using generative artificial intelligence (GAI) in education. As a result of screening seven major citation databases, 476 studies were reached. Analysis was carried out on 25 studies selected according to the inclusion and exclusion criteria. Results showed that research on using GAI in education is mostly conducted at the higher education level. The number of studies focusing on lower levels of education is quite low. The challenges and limitations of artificial intelligence are more about general education rather than focusing on a specific discipline. ChatGPT was the most investigated GAI tool. The challenges and limitations of using GAI in education are grouped under five factors: ethics and safety; educational implementations; assessment and evaluation; equity and access; quality control and expertise.

INTRODUCTION

Generative Artificial Intelligence (GAI) has gained significant attention in education, presenting both opportunities and challenges. The integration of GAI in education has the potential to revolutionize teaching and learning practices, but it also raises concerns regarding ethical use, equality, and the role of educators. Several studies have explored the limitations and implications of GAI in education. From an ethical perspective, Lin (2023) argued that there is no need to restrict the scope or nature of GAI assistance as long as its use is transparently disclosed. However, detecting fake research poses a critical challenge, which can be addressed through open science practices such as transparent peer review and data sharing (Lin, 2023). Implementing GAI in education requires careful consideration of ethical considerations, attribution of credit for GAI-driven discoveries, and advancing educational goals (Alasadi & Baiz, 2023).

DOI: 10.4018/979-8-3693-1351-0.ch008

The proliferation of GAI tools like GPT-4 and Open Assistant presents a paradigm shift in information acquisition and learning, posing substantial challenges for traditional teaching approaches and the role of educators (Walczak & Cellary, 2023). GAI tools, such as ChatGPT, have the potential to impact computer science education. Challenges for computer science education brought on by GAI tools include potential competition for computer science educators and the need to respond to possible impacts (Van Slyke et al., 2023). However, the consequences of GAI in education can vary, from having little impact to serving as competition for educators (Van Slyke et al., 2023). While GAI raises concerns about plagiarism detection, it also presents opportunities for educators to leverage GAI to build supportive learning environments (Eager & Brunton, 2023). GAI-augmented teaching and learning practices in higher education offer productive affordances but also come with challenges that need to be addressed (Eager & Brunton, 2023). Integrating generative chatbots in higher education can enhance the educational experience and facilitate effective implementation (Ilieva et al., 2023). However, it is crucial to explore best practices and strategies for utilizing GAI for educational purposes (Michel-Villarreal et al., 2023).

There are numerous studies on the potential benefits of using GAI in education (Bahroun et al., 2023; Chiu, 2023; Lo, 2023; Mao et al., 2023; Montenegro-Rueda et al., 2023; Popovici, 2023; Pradana et al., 2023; Preiksaitis & Rose, 2023; Sallam, 2023; Zhang & Tur, 2023). Bahroun et al. (2023) systematically synthesized 207 articles to provide a comprehensive analysis of the use of GAI in education. The research examined the transformative impact of GAI in specific educational fields, including medical and engineering education. Chiu (2023) investigated how GAI changed school education using qualitative methods. He revealed the views of 88 school teachers and administrators on using GAI in education within the categories of learning, teaching, assessment, and management. Lo (2023) conducted content analysis on 50 articles to enrich our understanding of using GAI in education. Mao et al. (2023) examined the potential opportunities of using GAI to summarize the use of AI in education. Montenegro-Rueda et al. (2023) presented an analysis of the impact of applying the GAI tool ChatGPT in education by conducting a systematic literature review in three leading scientific databases in the world of education (Web of Science, Scopus, and Google Scholar). Popovici (2023) used ChatGPT to solve all coding assignments given during the semester in a Functional Programming course to explore the capabilities of GAI and evaluate its value for educational purposes. Pradana et al. (2023) reviewed existing research on using the GAI tool ChatGPT in education using bibliometric analysis and systematic literature review. Preiksaitis and Rose (2023) synthesized the potential opportunities of GAI in medical education. Sallam (2023), using the systematic review method, investigated the potential utility of the GAI tool ChatGPT in health services education, research, and practice. Zhang and Tur (2023) used the systematic review method to investigate using ChatGPT, a GAI tool, in educational settings from kindergarten to grade 12 (K-12). Unlike the studies in the literature, this study focused on the challenges and limitations of using GAI in education.

METHODOLOGY

This study systematically investigates the challenges and limitations of GAI in education. The systematic review was conducted according to the Preferred Reporting Items for Systematic Reviews and Meta-Analyses (PRISMA). This reporting standard is widely used in systematic review research and is recognized as a useful reporting guideline to improve integrity (Moher et al., 2009). There is no restriction on the publication year of the studies examined due to the relevance of the researched topic. Studies examining the use of GAI in educational processes and containing findings and discussions regarding the challenges and limitations were selected for analysis. Studies focusing on the advantages and opportunities of using GAI in education were excluded from the research.

Database

Citation databases (Web of Science, Scopus, Science Direct, EBSCO, Wiley Online Library, ACM Digital Library, and IEEE Xplore) were searched to reach the articles for analysis. These databases were selected due to their inclusion of high-impact factor peer-reviewed journals publishing in educational technologies.

Search Terms

Three keyword categories were created and combined with the AND operator. The OR operator was used for the keywords within the categories. The search term was divided into three categories: education, GAI, and challenges and limitations. The keywords (education OR teaching OR learning OR training OR studying) were used for the education category. For the GAI category, the keywords ("generative AI" OR "generative artificial intelligence") were used. For the challenges and limitations category, the keywords (challenge OR limitation OR restriction OR difficulty) were used. The title, keywords, and abstract were screened on October 19, 2023.

Inclusion and Exclusion Criteria

The following inclusion and exclusion criteria were applied to the studies:

- Written in English
- Published as a research article in peer-reviewed journals
- A term related to education, GAI, and challenge or limitation in one of the title, abstract, or keyword fields

The following criteria were applied for the excluded studies:

- Non-English studies
- Studies published as conference proceedings, book chapters, or magazine articles
- Studies that do not address the challenges or limitations of using GAI in education.

Article Selection

A total of 476 studies were found as a result of the search. 21 records from ACM Digital Library, 9 records from Wiley Online Library, 22 records from IEEE Xplore, 78 records from Ebsco, 100 records from ScienceDirect, 118 records from Web of Science, and 128 records from Scopus databases we reached. The retrieved studies were examined within the framework of the inclusion/exclusion criteria mentioned above. Two studies were non-English (Spanish). 149 studies were duplicates. 41 studies were conference proceedings, chapters, and magazine articles. 62 studies were not related to education and training processes. 196 studies did not address the challenges and limitations of using GAI in education.

One study was excluded since its full text was not accessed. The remaining 25 studies were included in the analysis. Figure 1 shows the stages followed in this study's data collection and analysis process.

Figure 1. Identification of studies via databases

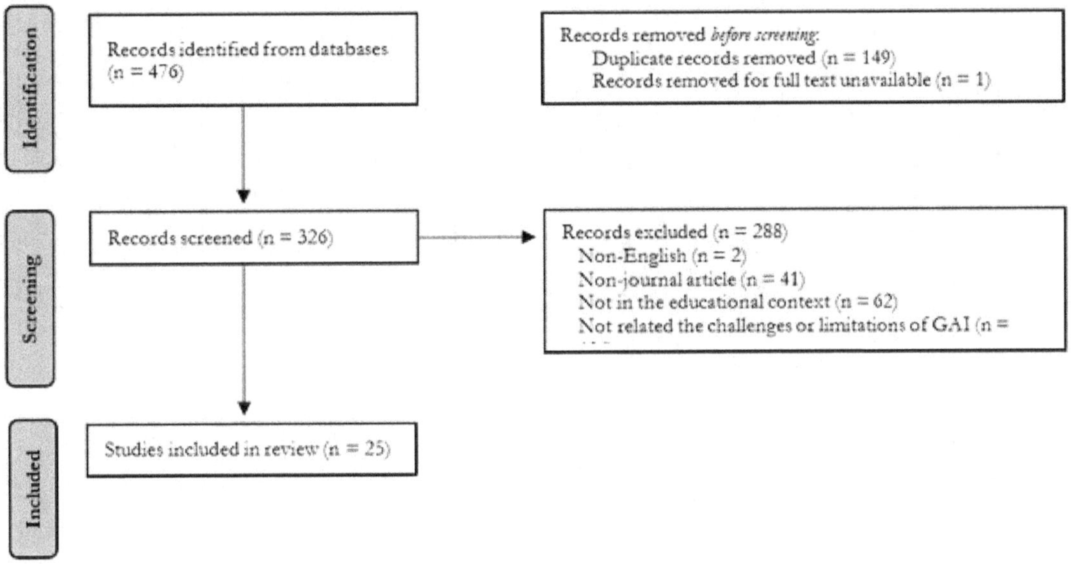

RESULTS

This section presents the findings obtained from the analyzed studies. The level of education, the discipline focused, the AI tools used, and the challenges and limitations of the studies were presented respectively. Table 1 shows the findings of 25 studies.

Education Level

More than half of the studies on the challenges and limitations of GAI in education focused on higher education (64%, N=16). Eight studies presented findings on education in general without addressing a specific level (32%). One study examined the use of GAI at the early childhood level (4%). Since research on the use of GAI in education is still new, the number of studies focusing on education in general is high. However, the number of studies on different levels of education will increase in the coming years.

Educational Discipline

Table 1 shows that most studies (60%, N=15) on the challenges and limitations of using GAI in education focused on general education without focusing on a specific discipline. Two studies on EFL, Distance Education, and Medical Education, and one on Literacy Education, Chemistry Education, Management Education, and Nursing Education addressed the challenges and limitations of GAI. Since research on the use of GAI in education is still new, the number of studies focusing on various educational disciplines is low. However, studies in various fields will increase in the coming years.

Table 1. Research on the challenges and limitations of using GAI in education

Author(s) and Year	Type	Educational Level	Educational Discipline	AI Type	Challenges or Limitations
Liu et al. (2023)	Review	Higher education	General	ChatGPT	Academic integrity, Declining in high-order cognitive skills, Inaccurate responses
Yan et al. (2023)	Review	General	General	ChatGPT, BERT	Ethical challenges (Transparency, rivacy, Equality, Beneficence)
Walczak and Cellary (2023)	Survey	Higher education	General	ChatGPT, Open Assistant, Dall-E	Truth-irrelevant content, Errors and hallucinations in content, Authorship and originality of content
Su and Yang (2023)	Theoretical	General	General	ChatGPT	Being an emerging technology, Data quality, Be limited by the complexity of the tasks it is asked to perform, Cost, Ethical and safety issues, Challenging the existing assessment system
Bozkurt and Sharma (2023)	Theoretical	Higher education	Distance education	GAI	Bias in data and algorithms, Lack of transparency, Overreliance on AI, Data privacy and security, Access and equity, Automation, Singularity
De Gagne et al. (2023)	Theoretical	Higher education	Nursing education	GhatGPT	Autonomy, Nonmaleficence, Beneficence, Justice, Explicability
Kılınç (2023)	Theoretical	Higher education	Distance education	GhatGPT	Limited capacity for empathy, Difficulty detecting nuances, Potential for inaccurate feedback, Reliance on adequate input data, Potential for inaccuracies in generated content, Lack of personalization and cultural sensitivity, Ensuring content alignment, Lack of human touch and contextual understanding, Overreliance on technology, Dependence on accurate input, Ethical considerations, Loss of personal connection, Potential for miscommunication, Inappropriate content, Limitations in empathy and social skills
Lin (2023)	Case study	General	General	ChatGPT	Plagiarism, AI authorship, Copyright of AI-generated content, Fake research and fraudulent papers
Shoja et al. (2023)	Review	Higher education	Medical education	ChatGPT	Concerns about plagiarism, The authorship, Peer review
Zhai and Wibowo (2023)	Review	Higher education	English as Foreign Language	GAI	Lack of cultural considerations, Lack of empathetic considerations, Lack of humor considerations, The importance of debate and problem-solving
Su et al. (2023)	Review	Early Childhood Education	General	GAI	Lack of teachers' AI knowledge and skills, Low teachers' confidence, Lack of curriculum design, Lack of teaching guidelines
Steele (2023)	Theoretical	General	General	ChatGPT	Measurement, Accuracy, Devaluation of skills
Memarian and Doleck (2023)	Review	General	General	ChatGPT	Accountability, Ultimate authority, Plagiarism, Availability, Cost, Fake information, Lack of higher-order skills, Lack of transparency and trust, Limited data quality, Misuse or lack of learning, Privacy, Real-time multi-modal interaction lacking, Technical expertise require, Risk of bias and discrimination
Gašević et al. (2023)	Review	General	General	ChatGPT, DALL-E	Ethics, bias, and fairness, Data sources and ownership, AI literacies and competencies, Systemic resistance to change
Michel-Villarreal et al. (2023)	Theoretical	Higher education	General	ChatGPT	Academic integrity, Quality control, Personalized learning, Expertise and authority, Communication and collaboration

continues on following page

Table 1. Continued

Author(s) and Year	Type	Educational Level	Educational Discipline	AI Type	Challenges or Limitations
Ratten and Jones (2023)	Theoretical	Higher education	Management education	ChatGPT	Making assessment hard to do via ChatGPT, Incorporating AI usage into learning experiences, Anticipating and recognising ChatGPT related dilemmas, Integrating new educational technology into education, Reducing uncertainty and cautiousness regarding ChatGPT
Alasadi and Baiz (2023)	Theoretical	General	General	GAI	Assignments evaluation, GAI use of teachers, Using GAI in scientific texts, Become the scientific norm, Cost
Emenike and Emenike (2023)	Theoretical	Higher education	Chemistry education	ChatGPT	Equity, Accessibility
Abd-alrazaq et al. (2023)	Theoretical	Higher education	Medical education	ChatGPT	Academic dishonesty, Misinformation and lack of reliability, Lack of consistency, Algorithmic bias, Overreliance, Lack of human interaction and emotions, Limited knowledge, Inequity in access, Privacy, Copyright
Wang et al. (2023)	Review	Higher education	General	GAI	Privacy, Bias, Widen educational inequalities
Sullivan et al. (2023)	Review	Higher education	General	ChatGPT	Academic integrity, Avoidance, Policy, Embrace, Voice
Ciampa et al. (2023)	Theoretical	Higher education	Literacy education	ChatGPT	Continuous professional development, Encourage students to use, Generating grammatically correct and coherent text, Awareness of the ethical considerations, Potential biases
Ahmad et al. (2023)	Review	General	General	GAI	Failure in the extraction of interpretable and actionable insights, Failure in generation of course content, Limitations of robotic teachers, Lack of training data, High risk due to biased data, Testing and evaluation of AI-systems, Security concerns
Rasul et al. (2023)	Theoretical	Higher education	General	ChatGPT	Ethical and equity considerations, Maintaining academic integrity, Potential bias and falsified information in information processing, Evaluate graduate skill sets, Assessing students' learning outcomes
Kostka and Toncelli (2023)	Theoretical	Higher education	English as Foreign Language	ChatGPT	Plagiarism, Cheating, Academic integrity

GAI Tools

Table 1 shows that ChatGPT was mostly examined in studies on the challenges and limitations of GAI in education (76%, N=19). 6 studies used GAI without mentioning any specific AI tool (24%, N=6). 2 studies examined Dall-E together with ChatGPT (4%). One study mentioned BERT and Open Assistant together with ChatGPT. With the announcement of ChatGPT by OpenAI, there has been a significant increase in the number of studies on GAI. For this reason, researchers focused more on ChatGPT while examining the challenges and limitations of GAI. In the coming years, with the diversification of artificial intelligence tools and the increase in users, the number of GAI tools examined in scientific research will increase.

Challenges and Limitations

Table 2 was obtained by reviewing the indicators of difficulties and limitations shown in Table 1. The terms under the heading Challenges or Limitations in Table 1 are mentioned as titles or separate paragraphs in the studies. Repetitive indicators or indicators with similar meanings were removed from the indicators presented in Table 1. Indicators with similar meanings were grouped under the same category. As a result, five categories emerged regarding the challenges and limitations of using GAI in education: Ethics and Safety, Educational Implementations, Assessment and Evaluation, Equity and Access, Quality Control and Expertise. The author made the coding in Table 2. To ensure the validity of the coding, the author sent mixed versions of the indicators and categories given in Table 2 to a researcher in the field of computer science. The researcher was asked to code the indicators into categories. As a result, it was seen that the coding made by both the author and researcher was similar.

Table 2. Challenges and limitations of GAI in education

Challenge / Limitation	Indicators
Ethics and Safety	Academic integrity, Transparency, Authorship and originality of content, Bias in data and algorithms, Data privacy and security, Limited capacity for empathy, Potential for inaccuracies in generated content, Lack of personalization and cultural sensitivity, Overreliance on technology, Dependence on accurate input, Potential for miscommunication, Inappropriate content, Plagiarism, AI authorship, Copyright of AI-generated content, Fake research and fraudulent papers, Awareness of the ethical considerations
Educational Implementations	Lack of teachers' AI knowledge and skills, Low teachers' confidence, Lack of curriculum design, Lack of teaching guidelines, Devaluation of skills, Accountability, Lack of higher-order skills, Lack of transparency and trust, Misuse or lack of learning, Technical expertise required, Anticipating and recognizing ChatGPT-related dilemmas, Accessibility, Continuous professional development, AI literacy and competencies, Becoming the scientific norm, Incorporating AI usage into learning experiences
Assessment and Evaluation	Measurement, Accuracy, Devaluation of skills, Ultimate authority, Fake information, Lack of transparency and trust, Misuse or lack of learning, Privacy, Risk of bias and discrimination
Equity and Access	Singularity, Lack of cultural considerations, Inequity in access, Limited knowledge
Quality Control and Expertise	Providing personalized feedback, Peer review, Quality control, Expertise and authority

Ethics and Safety

One of the most critical issues related to the use of GAI in education is ethics and safety. Indicators such as academic integrity, and authorship and originality of content, which are associated with the ethics and safety factor in Table 2, indicate that there may be potential issues of academic integrity and content ownership when using GAI for educational material production. GAI-generated content should not contain elements from or inspired by students' work. If the GAI imitates students' original work or quotes from sources, this may violate academic integrity. Uncertainties may arise about who created the GAI's content and whether it is authentic. This can make identifying students' contributions difficult, as well as correctly attributing sources and assessing originality. These two indicators are essential for maintaining ethical and academic standards of GAI use in education. Educational materials should provide students with accurate information, encourage students' original thoughts and work, and conform to academic norms. Therefore, GAI-generated content must be carefully managed regarding academic integrity and ownership.

The indicators of transparency and bias in data and algorithms point to the lack of transparency of algorithms and data sets and the problems of bias. Transparency of the algorithms used in GAI-generated content and the data sets used for these algorithms is essential. Transparency helps us understand how the content is produced, what criteria it is based on, and what data sets it is fed from. With transparency about how algorithms and data sets work, it is easier for learners to understand why they are receiving or being recommended certain content. The data can influence the GAI development it is trained on and learn the biases in those data sets. If the data sets or algorithms are biased, this can bias the content produced. This can create an unfair learning experience for different student groups or cultures. These two concepts highlight that lack of transparency and bias in GAI-generated content can create challenges in providing students with a fair learning experience. Lack of transparency can make it difficult for students to understand the content production processes. Biased content can be contrary to the principle of equity in education. Therefore, ensuring that GAI systems are transparent and unbiased is critical for maintaining a fair educational environment.

Data privacy and security and copyright of AI-generated content indicators raise important security and legal issues, such as student data privacy and copyright of AI-generated content. GAI draws on large data sets when creating educational materials. However, the privacy and security of student data in these data sets are essential. GAI can use this data to produce content tailored to students, but it needs to ensure compliance with data privacy standards and security. Determining who owns the content created by GAI and who is responsible for its copyright is essential. Copyright disputes may arise if a specific person or organization does not own the content. This can make it difficult to determine the legal ownership and usage rights of the content produced. These indicators highlight the need to protect the privacy of student data and regulate the copyright of GAI-generated content in the use of GAI in education. Ethical and legal standards should protect student data, and the copyright of generated content should be carefully considered to Limited capacity for empathy, lack of personalization, and cultural sensitivity indicators highlight the challenges in providing students with an appropriate and responsive learning experience due to GAI's limited empathy ability and lack of personalization. GAI does not have an emotional understanding like humans. Limited capacity for empathy indicates that GAI cannot understand learners' emotional states and react appropriately. This can result in gaps in providing emotional support or understanding to learners. GAI often generates content using a generic approach. However, learners' learning styles, needs, and cultural contexts differ. Lack of personalization indicates that GAI's ability to provide students with a tailored learning experience is limited. Cultural sensitivity highlights GAI's shortcomings in understanding and responding sensitively to cultural contexts. These indicators highlight that limitations in GAI's emotional performance and personalization capabilities can complicate efforts to provide students with a more relevant, responsive, and effective learning experience. Therefore, it is essential to design more responsive and personalized learning experiences, considering student diversity and learning styles in education using GAI.

The indicators of overreliance on technology and dependence on accurate input indicate that the overuse of GAI and its reliance on accurate data can increase the risk of providing students with unrealistic learning experiences. Excessive use of GAI in education can lead students to rely solely on technology, ignoring other vital elements in their learning process. Students' over-reliance on GAI systems can lead to difficulties in developing real-world skills and understanding human interactions. GAI systems are dependent on the data sets used to create training materials. If these data sets are incomplete, misleading, or biased, the content produced by the GAI may contain errors. Furthermore, when the correct data input is missing or inaccurate, GAI may fail to perform learning processes and present misleading information to learners. These indicators highlight that over-reliance on technology and dependence on accurate data input can result in limited or misleading learning experiences for students needing to reflect real-world experiences and diversity adequately. Therefore, when planning the use of GAI in education, it is essential to view technology as a supportive tool and take a balanced approach that includes a variety of learning methods.

Potential for miscommunication and inappropriate content indicators emphasize the potential for GAI-generated content to cause communication errors and inappropriate content. GAI may not be as flexible as humans' understanding of language and communication. This may result in GAI-generated texts being communicated to learners inaccurately or incomprehensibly. Factors such as meaning complexities, language diversity, slang, or cultural nuances can make it difficult for GAI to understand accurately. There is a risk that GAI-generated content may produce content that is inappropriate for learners or contains sensitive topics. GAI may be insensitive to various issues when creating educational materials or learning inappropriate content from the datasets used. This can result in students being exposed to offensive or wrong information. These two indicators highlight the potential for GAI-generated content to cause communication errors and inappropriate content. Therefore, when using GAI in education, the generated content must be regularly checked and corrected when necessary to provide students with a safe and effective learning experience.

The indicators of plagiarism, AI authorship, and fake research and fraudulent papers refer to the risk that GAI-generated content may raise issues of authenticity and ownership or even the creation of fake research and fraudulent documents. GAI-generated content may mimic samples from the datasets used or cite students' original work from other sources. This constitutes copyright infringement and may result in students being falsely presented with original work. Uncertainty about who created AI-generated content gives rise to the indicator of GAI authorship. In this case, the actual authorship or sources of the content may need to be clarified, leading to issues of academic integrity and ownership. There is a risk that GAI-generated content could create fake research or fraudulent articles without any factual basis. If GAI is trained with unreliable data sets or misleading information, the content produced may be inaccurate and scientifically invalid. These three indicators highlight that GAI-generated content can cause problems such as copyright infringement, uncertain authorship, and fraudulent research. These situations can pose serious issues for preserving academic integrity and should be considered when planning the use of AI in education. Compliance with academic rules and ethical standards is essential in using GAI-generated content.

Awareness of the ethical considerations indicator emphasizes the need for ethically conscious management of using GAI in education. Ethical issues and concerns are also increasing with the increasing use of AI. Awareness of the ethical considerations indicator refers to the need to pay attention to the ethical issues raised by using artificial intelligence in education and to handle these issues consciously. These ethical issues may include student data privacy, prevention of bias in content production, fair use, and copyrights. When using GAI in education, sensitivity to ethical considerations is essential to ensure compliance with fundamental ethical principles such as respect for student rights, fairness, transparency, and trustworthiness. This provides guidance to anticipate and resolve potential issues that may arise in the context in which GAI is used. Ethical thinking is critical to ensure that using GAI in education positively impacts society and individuals.

Educational Implementations

One of the main issues with the effective use of GAI in education is the challenges of educational implementation. The indicator challenging the existing assessment system under the educational implementations category in Table 2 points out that despite the innovative methods GAI brings to assess student performance, aligning these new methods with existing assessment systems and transforming existing systems is challenging. Assessment methods enabled by GAI can measure students' abilities more comprehensively and make learning processes more effective. However, current education systems are often structured on specific standards, tests, and assessment criteria. Therefore, adjusting and transforming existing systems with GAI's new assessment methods will require adaptation among educational institutions, teachers, and students.

The lack of teachers' AI knowledge and skills indicates that the use of GAI-based educational tools and applications may be limited due to teachers' lack of knowledge and skills towards this technology. GAI-based educational tools and applications can provide students with more effective and personalized learning experiences. However, teachers need sufficient knowledge and skills in AI to use this technology effectively. If teachers have the knowledge and skills in this area, the potential of GAI-based educational tools can be fully utilized, which can lead to limitations. This may prevent teachers from effectively integrating this technology and limit the benefits to students. In this context, improving teachers' knowledge and skills in AI can enable them to utilize the potential of GAI in education better.

Low teacher confidence indicates that for the effective use of GAI in education, teachers' low confidence in this technology may prevent a successful integration. For the successful use of GAI educational technologies, teachers need to have confidence in this technology. If teachers feel insecure about GAI-based tools and applications, it may be challenging to integrate this technology into classrooms effectively. Mistrust can negatively affect teachers' adaptation to new technologies and prevent them from fully utilizing the potential of GAI.

The lack of curriculum design indicates that inappropriate integrating GAI-based educational materials into existing curricula may lead to adaptation problems in education. GAI-based materials used in education must be designed per existing curricula to support students' learning processes. These materials need to be integrated in a way that helps students achieve their learning goals to avoid incompatibilities in teaching processes. GAI-based materials that are incompatible with the curricular requirements that students and teachers face can affect student achievement and make instructional approaches need coherence.

The lack of teaching guidelines indicates that the lack of clear and comprehensive teaching guidelines for GAI-supported teaching can create difficulties in guiding teachers. GAI-supported teaching materials and practices may require providing teachers with guidelines and guidance. However, with a solid framework and guidance for teachers to use this technology effectively, teachers may be able to integrate this technology effectively.

Devaluation of skills indicates that the overuse of GAI-generated content may lead to overestimating student skills and teacher contributions. In the case of overuse of GAI-generated content in education, students' individual skills and teachers' authentic contributions may be overlooked. GAI-generated content can have a broad perspective as it is often created through learning from large data sets. However, it may be limited in reflecting students' individual strengths and teachers' personal touch. Suppose there is an over-reliance on GAI-generated content. In that case, students' unique talents and teachers' pedagogical contributions may be overlooked, leading to a lack of individuality and authenticity in education. This can lead to a trivialization of student and teacher roles and a devaluation of skills.

The accountability indicator reveals that determining responsibility for the consequences of using GAI can be challenging, especially in inaccurate or misleading content. It is essential to determine responsibility for the consequences of using GAI-generated content. GAI systems used in education can create content by learning from large data sets, but errors or misleading results can occur in the process. Difficulties in assigning responsibility can create uncertainty about how teachers, students, and other stakeholders will evaluate, correct, or improve this content. Identifying and correcting the effects of inaccurate or misleading content can increase complexity around responsibility and accountability.

Lack of higher-order skills indicates that GAI-based educational materials may fail to develop students' higher-order skills, such as critical thinking, problem-solving, and creativity. Some GAI-based educational materials may focus on conveying knowledge, often on specific topics, and may provide students with basic knowledge. However, these materials may need to be improved to develop students' higher-level cognitive skills, such as critical thinking, problem-solving, and creativity. Such skills often involve students thinking deeply, applying what they have learned in various contexts, and understanding learning from a broader perspective. GAI-based educational materials may have specific limitations in supporting such higher-level skills. They may only enable students to learn the basics, but they must develop an in-depth understanding and critical thinking skills. Therefore, the inadequacies of GAI-supported educational materials in supporting higher-order cognitive skills may hinder the effective use of this technology in education.

Lack of transparency and trust indicates that the lack of transparency of GAI's internal working mechanisms may cause trust issues among students, teachers, and parents. The internal tools of GAI systems used in education can often be complex and difficult to understand. More transparency about how GAI systems make decisions, evaluate student performance, or make content recommendations can lead to a lack of trust among users. If users do not understand how GAI systems work, this can lead to suspicion and anxiety. Lack of confidence can increase students' and teachers' reluctance to use this technology and hinder the success of using GAI in education.

Misuse or lack of learning indicates that misuse or inadequate integration of GAI technologies can prevent students from learning effectively. If GAI technologies used in education are not adequately integrated or misused, there is a risk that they can negatively impact the student learning experience. GAI can offer potential advantages such as providing students with customized content and feedback or supporting their learning process. However, misuse or incomplete integration of these technologies can lead to problems providing students with appropriate learning opportunities. For example, due to misuse or inadequate integration, students may be presented with unnecessary or inappropriate content, preventing them from learning effectively. This can make it difficult for GAI technologies to be effectively managed and used by teachers and students.

Technical expertise indicates that the technical knowledge and expertise required for using GAI-based tools may lead to inequalities and difficulties of use among teachers. GAI-based tools often involve complex technological systems, and teachers may need specific technical knowledge to use them effectively. However, teachers' technical expertise levels can differ, leading to inequalities. Some teachers may have the necessary technical knowledge to use GAI-based tools effectively, while others may need it. This can complicate efforts to provide students with an equitable learning experience and may result in some teachers needing more technical knowledge to take full advantage of these potential benefits.

Anticipating and recognizing ChatGPT-related dilemmas indicates that using ChatGPT or similar language models can be challenging for teachers to anticipate and acknowledge ethical or practical issues. Language models are artificial intelligence systems that allow teachers and students to interact with written texts. However, there can be a variety of ethical and practical issues that can arise when using such models. For example, problems may arise regarding the accuracy of the content generated by the language model, its compliance with ethical rules, its potential biases, or the quality of the feedback provided to students.

The accessibility indicator indicates that restrictions in access to GAI-based educational tools may create challenges in providing equal opportunities for students. GAI-based educational tools may cause accessibility issues for some students depending on technical requirements, internet access, or special educational needs. For example, devices that are unsuitable for some students or lack technological infrastructure may limit their access to these tools.

Continuous professional development indicates that the need for teachers to keep up with the rapid changes in the field of GAI can be a significant challenge. GAI technologies and applications are constantly evolving and changing. This rapid change requires teachers to follow, understand, and effectively use these technological developments. However, teachers need time, resources, and support to monitor developments in this field and update their practice continuously.

AI literacy and competencies indicate that more GAI literacy and competencies for students and teachers can make interacting effectively with this technology easier. To interact with and use GAI technologies effectively, individuals (both students and teachers) must understand the basic concepts of GAI and have the competencies to use these technologies. Students need more GAI literacy to interact with and integrate these technologies into their learning processes. Likewise, teachers must have the necessary literature and competencies to guide students in GAI and use this technology effectively. Lack of literacy and competence in AI can hinder the integration and use of GAI technologies in education.

Becoming the scientific norm indicates that not all GAI-generated content should be accepted as valid. Automatically taking AI-generated content as reliable and accurate can cause potential problems with academic integrity, accuracy, and credibility. Therefore, GAI-generated content must be critically evaluated and corrected when necessary.

Incorporating AI usage into learning experiences indicates that effectively integrating GAI into learning experiences requires finding an appropriate pedagogical balance. GAI can deliver customized content to learners, but learners should consider pedagogical values, learner needs, and ethical principles.

Assessment and Evaluation

One of the main issues related to using GAI in education is assessment and evaluation. The measurement indicator under the assessment and evaluation category in Table 2 points to GAI's challenges to the measurement processes in education. When GAI is used to assess student achievements, the accuracy and reliability of these processes is an important issue. If the measurements performed by GAI are objective and reliable, it allows for an accurate understanding and assessment of student performance. However, factors such as the complexity of GAI models and biases in data sets can affect the reliability of measurement processes. This can complicate measurement processes that aim to objectively determine student achievement and make it difficult to make accurate assessments.

The accuracy indicator emphasizes the importance of the accuracy of the measurements provided by the GAI. In education, the measurements supplied by GAI must reflect the actual situation to assess student performance accurately. If the measurements provided by GAI are not in line with the actual situation, it may lead to misleading results. This can make it difficult to make reliable educational assessments and hinder an accurate understanding of student performance. Objective metrics are critical to assess student achievement and provide personalized feedback effectively.

The devaluation of skills indicator points to the risk of devaluation of student skills if the student skills assessed by the GAI are incomplete or inaccurate compared to human assessments. That is, if the GAI needs to evaluate student skills thoroughly or inaccurately, this may not adequately reflect the actual skill level of the student. In this case, the value of the student's skills may be reduced or falsely undervalued. This can create the problem of students' actual skill levels needing to be assessed fairly and accurately.

The ultimate authority indicator points to the importance of who has leading authority in GAI assessment processes. With the introduction of GAI into assessment processes, the issue of who determines students' performance arises. This implies that it is essential to maintain trust in human teachers' assessments and understand GAI's limitations. Uncertainties about who has ultimate authority should be considered about the principles of fairness and reliability of assessments.

The fake information indicator refers to uncertainty about the authenticity of GAI-generated or evaluated information. The accuracy and reliability of the information provided by GAI can cause severe problems in education. If there are forgeries or errors in the data generated by GAI, it can make it difficult to assess student achievement accurately. Fake information can lead to educational credibility issues and confusion in assessment processes.

Lack of transparency and trust indicates that the lack of clarity and confidence in the assessment processes performed by GAI is a critical issue limiting the use of GAI in education. The lack of transparency and trust between students, teachers, and other stakeholders may cause trust issues. This lack of confidence, especially when coupled with uncertainties about the fairness, accuracy, and reliability of assessments made by GAI, can hinder the use of GAI in education.

Misuse or lack of learning points out that if the assessments provided by GAI are aligned with students' actual learning needs or are used correctly, it can be difficult for students to realize their full potential. Inaccurate understanding or misapplication of GAI-provided assessments can lead to difficulty identifying students' strengths and weaknesses, improving their learning processes, and providing practical support for their needs.

Privacy highlights concerns about processing and protecting student data when using GAI. GAI-based educational tools and applications often use student data to assess student performance and personalize the learning experience. However, properly handling, storing, and sharing this data is an important issue affecting students' privacy. Lack of data security can increase the risk of information leaks or unauthorized access. This can cause students and parents to be concerned about the need for more assurance that student data is being handled securely.

The risk of bias and discrimination indicates a potential for bias or discrimination in the assessments made by GAI. GAI systems often make decisions by learning from large data sets. However, elements of bias or discrimination present in these data sets may also be reflected in the assessments produced by GAI. For example, if an educational GAI model is trained with data on a specific group of students and this data set contains biases, the model may use these biases to provide an equal evaluation among students. However, this may negatively affect different groups of students and cause equity issues in education.

Equity and Access

The singularity indicator refers to the rapid development of artificial intelligence and technological changes of a unique nature. In using GAI in education, the singularity problem can arise when technology evolves so rapidly that providing students with equal access to it becomes problematic. In this case, some students may be able to access new technologies more quickly or effectively than others, while others may need to catch up. Failure to capitalize equally on the potential benefits of GAI in education could unevenly distribute this technology's advantages. This can exacerbate inequalities in access to technology and increase the digital divide between students.

The lack of cultural considerations indicates that GAI-supported educational materials must sufficiently consider cultural differences. Ignoring cultural diversity in using GAI in education can cause difficulties in providing learners with a culturally responsive and appropriate learning experience. Educational materials may overemphasize a particular culture or exclude other cultures due to the examples, case studies, or use of language. These risks ignoring, rather than understanding and appreciating, cultural differences among learners. As a result, culturally inappropriate educational materials can lead to cultural inequalities among students.

Inequity in access refers to inequalities in access to GAI-supported educational tools. The widespread use of GAI in education may provide students with more learning opportunities. Still, inequalities in access to this use may cause inequality of opportunity among students from different socio-economic backgrounds. Students who need more financial resources or have limited access to technological infrastructure may not be able to benefit from GAI-supported educational tools. This may create inequality in knowledge and skills among students. Students who are deprived of technical advantages may have fewer opportunities than others.

The limited knowledge indicates limited knowledge and understanding of GAI by students or educators. This may limit the effective use of GAI technologies in education. The lack of knowledge of educators or students about GAI may prevent them from fully utilizing the potential advantages of these technologies. Students and educators need more knowledge about GAI to integrate and use this technology effectively. Furthermore, this can hinder digital transformation in education and lead to educational inequalities. This is because a lack of knowledge can lead to disparities between students and educators regarding equal access to and utilization of technology.

Quality Control and Expertise

Providing personalized feedback indicates challenges in using GAI to provide personalized feedback to students. In GAI-supported education, providing customized feedback to students may involve technical and pedagogical challenges to tailor it to student needs and performances. This may affect efforts to provide students with more effective and customized learning experiences.

The peer review indicator points to the challenges of using GAI in peer review processes. Challenges in effectively using GAI-supported assessment systems for students to evaluate each other can make maintaining a fair and reliable peer review process difficult.

Quality control indicates the challenges of using GAI in quality control processes in education. The need for GAI-enabled systems to be accurate, fair, and reliable in tasks such as assessing student performance or generating learning materials can pose challenges in quality control processes.

The expertise and authority indicates the challenges associated with knowledge and authority in GAI in education. In GAI-supported education, there may be uncertainties about expertise and authority in which situations users can trust GAI systems. This uncertainty may affect students' and educators' trust in AI.

DISCUSSION AND CONCLUSION

This chapter systematically analyzes the studies in the literature that focus on the challenges and limitations of using GAI in education. Results showed that research on the challenges and limitations of using GAI in education is relatively new and scarce. These studies were mainly conducted at the higher education level. The number of studies focusing on lower levels of education is relatively low. In the studies examined, the challenges and limitations of GAI are not focused on a specific discipline but on education in general. In the studies, ChatGPT was mainly emphasized as a GAI. As a result of the analysis, the challenges and limitations of using GAI in education are grouped under five categories: Ethics and Safety, Educational Implementations, Assessment and Evaluation, Equity and Access, Quality Control and Expertise.

GAI poses several challenges and limitations in the educational context, especially about ethics and security. The integration of GAI in educational settings requires a thorough understanding of ethical norms, guidelines, and unresolved issues such as academic integrity, transparency, authorship, bias in data and algorithms, data privacy and security, and potential inaccuracies in the content produced (Köbis & Mehner, 2021). Furthermore, responsible and effective use of GAI technologies in education requires a thoughtful, ethical, and inclusive approach that emphasizes the need for explicit consideration of issues such as fairness, accountability, transparency, bias, autonomy, representation, and inclusivity (Holmes et al., 2022). In addition, the technology's untested efficacy, data quality limitations, and ethical and safety concerns must be carefully addressed to ensure appropriate and ethical use of GAI in educational settings (Su & Yang, 2023). It is crucial to emphasize transparency, security, informed consent, algorithmic fairness, biases, data privacy, and sharing regulation when addressing ethical considerations regarding using GAI in education (Hisan & Amri, 2022). Furthermore, ethical challenges in K-12 settings include academic integrity, authorship and authenticity of content, bias, miscommunication in data and algorithms, and the potential for inappropriate content, necessitating a focus on addressing these concerns in educational contexts (Akgun & Greenhow, 2022). Therefore, integrating GAI into education requires a comprehensive framework that ensures the ethical use of GAI technologies and addresses the security and privacy concerns associated with their application in educational settings.

The implementation of GAI in education brings several challenges and limitations. One of the main challenges is the need for GAI knowledge and skills among teachers, leading to low confidence in using GAI technologies in educational settings. In addition, the need for more well-defined curriculum design and teaching guidelines makes it even more challenging to integrate GAI into learning experiences effectively. It hinders the development of higher-level skills among students. Moreover, the technical expertise required to harness GAI tools and ensure their responsible use poses a significant limitation as it can create accessibility barriers for educators and students, especially those from under-resourced educational institutions (Sait & Tombs, 2021). It also raises concerns about accountability, transparency, and trust associated with the productive use of GAI in education. The misuse or underuse of GAI technologies in learning environments can lead to ethical and pedagogical dilemmas and requires continuous professional development to improve educators' GAI literacies and competencies. As GAI becomes the scientific norm in educational settings, there is an urgent need to incorporate GAI into learning experiences while addressing the challenges above and its limitations (Grimmelikhuijsen, 2023). Therefore, addressing these challenges requires a concerted effort to provide educators with the knowledge, skills, and support necessary to integrate GAI into the curriculum effectively and ensure its responsible and equitable use in various educational contexts.

The application of GAI in educational assessment and evaluation raises several challenges and limitations. It raises concerns about the measurement and accuracy of GAI-generated assessments, the potential devaluation of skills, and the ultimate authority of assessment results (Kozyreva et al., 2020). Furthermore, the risk of misinformation and lack of transparency and trust in GAI-generated assessments can affect the confidentiality and fairness of the assessment process, leading to misuse or underutilization of learning outcomes. Furthermore, the technical expertise required to develop and interpret GAI-generated assessments can create accessibility barriers for educators and learners and hinder the equitable use of such technologies in educational settings (Carraccio et al., 2002). Addressing these challenges requires continuous professional development to improve educators' GAI literacies and competencies and ensure responsible and ethical use of GAI in educational assessment and evaluation (Gustafsson et al., 2014). Furthermore, including GAI in educational assessment raises concerns about the risk of bias and discrimination in the assessment process. Lack of transparency and trust in GAI-generated assessments may affect the fairness and equity of the assessment process, leading to biased assessment outcomes (Hoppmann et al., 2015). Therefore, there is an urgent need to develop standardized frameworks and practical tools to guide the design, implementation, and evaluation of GAI-generated assessments, ensuring their accuracy, reliability, and fairness in various educational contexts (Girardi et al., 2006). Likewise, continuous professional development is required to equip educators with the knowledge and skills necessary to evaluate and interpret assessment results produced by GAI critically, addressing the challenges and limitations mentioned above (Choi et al., 2018).

The integration of GAI into education poses challenges related to equity and access. The singularity of GAI technologies can lead to a lack of cultural considerations, potentially exacerbating inequality in access to educational resources and opportunities. Moreover, limited knowledge and understanding of GAI among educators and students can contribute to inequalities in accessing and using GAI-oriented educational tools and materials, further widening the equity gap in educational settings (van Deursen & van Dijk, 2019). Also, a lack of transparency and trust in the development and implementation of GAI technologies can hinder equal access to GAI-driven educational resources, especially for marginalized and underrepresented communities (Hahn, 2023). Addressing these challenges requires a comprehensive understanding of the cultural, social, and economic factors that influence access to and use of GAI in education and the development of inclusive and equitable strategies to ensure the equitable and accessible application of GAI technologies in diverse educational contexts (Hằng et al., 2015). Furthermore, the potential misuse or inadequate consideration of cultural and contextual factors in the design and implementation of GAI in education can perpetuate inequalities in access to quality educational experiences, especially for students from diverse cultural and socioeconomic backgrounds (Liu et al., 2023). Future research should focus on examining the impact of different measures of accessibility and need on the equitable distribution and utilization of GAI-focused educational resources, aiming to reduce inequalities and ensure equal access to educational opportunities for all students (Whitehead et al., 2019). Furthermore, the development of GAI literacies and competencies among educators and students is essential to address equity and access challenges associated with GAI in education and foster a more inclusive and equitable learning environment (Tao & Wang, 2022). By considering the cultural, social, and economic dimensions of access to GAI in education, education stakeholders can work to reduce inequalities and promote equitable access to GAI-oriented educational resources and opportunities (Pereira et al., 2021).

The use of GAI in education brings challenges and limitations regarding quality control and expertise, especially in providing personalized feedback and peer assessment. The application of GAI tools for educational assessment and evaluation requires robust quality control mechanisms to ensure the accuracy and reliability of the feedback and assessments generated (Bielow et al., 2016). Moreover, expertise and authority in interpreting and validating GAI-generated educational content and assessments is essential to maintain the quality and integrity of the educational process and emphasizes the need for peer review and expert oversight (Westgard & Westgard, 2016). However, reliance on GAI for personalized feedback and assessment raises concerns about the potential devaluation of human expertise and the need for human oversight in ensuring the quality and relevance of educational content and assessments (Whitney et al., 1998). Furthermore, incorporating GAI into educational settings requires a thorough understanding of the limitations and challenges in providing personalized feedback and peer assessment, especially in ensuring accuracy, fairness, and cultural considerations in the feedback and assessment process (Turner, 2001). The development of GAI-driven personalized feedback and assessment tools requires a careful balance between leveraging GAI capabilities and preserving the expertise and authority of educators and experts in the educational field (Smither et al., 2005). Therefore, addressing the challenges and limitations in quality control and expertise associated with GAI in education requires a thoughtful and inclusive approach that integrates human expertise and oversight with GAI-driven tools to ensure the quality and relevance of educational content and assessments (Dirkx et al., 2021).

SUGGESTIONS

We presented the following recommendations based on the results to guide future research.

- Most of the studies on the challenges and limitations of GAI in education are focused on higher education. Further research should focus on different levels of education.
- There are more studies focused on general education. Research on different disciplines needs to increase.

- ChatGPT has been extensively studied in studies on GAI challenges and limitations. Increasing the number of studies focusing on different GAI tools is essential.
- Ethics and safety in using GAIs should be considered, especially regarding academic integrity and content ownership. It is essential to audit the content produced by GAI in terms of inspiring or citing people's work.
- The importance of transparency and bias in the content produced by GAI has been emphasized. Openness about the inner workings of GAI systems can help students understand why certain content is recommended. Preventing bias is critical to ensure a fair learning experience.
- Privacy and security of student data are important issues arising from the large data sets GAI uses in creating educational materials. Standards need to be set and adhered to in this regard.
- GAI's limited empathy ability and lack of personalization make designing more responsive and personalized learning experiences essential to providing students with an appropriate, responsive, and effective learning experience.
- Overuse of GAI and dependence on accurate data input can cause limitations in reflecting real-world experiences to students. It is essential to use technology as a supportive tool and adopt a balanced approach that includes a variety of learning methods.
- The potential for GAI-generated content to cause communication errors and inappropriate content should be considered. The content produced in GAI-supported education should be regularly checked and corrected when necessary.
- Content produced by GAI can cause severe issues of forgery, unclear authorship, and misleading research. Therefore, compliance with academic rules and ethical standards is essential when planning GAI.
- The main problems with the effective use of GAI in education are alignment with existing assessment systems, teachers' AI knowledge and skills, low teacher confidence, and deficiencies in curriculum design. Efforts should be made for improvements in these areas.
- Challenges to GAI's processes for assessing student achievement require efforts to ensure that measurement processes are reliable and objective.
- GAI's challenges in ensuring equal access to education emphasize the challenges that arise in providing equal access to technology. It is important to take cultural differences into account and reduce inequalities.
- GAI's challenges in providing personalized feedback and quality control issues in education require overcoming technical and pedagogical challenges.
- Support for continuous professional development and GAI literacy should be provided for teachers to keep up with the rapid change in GAI technologies.

AUTHOR'S NOTES

This paper was proofread and refined with the assistance of generative AI, complementing the human editorial process.

REFERENCES

Abd-alrazaq, A., AlSaad, R., Alhuwail, D., Ahmed, A., Healy, P. M., Latifi, S., Aziz, S., Damseh, R., Alrazak, S. A., & Sheikh, J. (2023). Large language models in medical education: Opportunities, challenges, and future directions. *JMIR Medical Education*, *9*(1), e48291. Advance online publication. doi:10.2196/48291 PMID:37261894

Ahmad, K., Iqbal, W., El-Hassan, A., Qadir, J., Benhaddou, D., Ayyash, M., & Al-Fuqaha, A. (2023). Data-driven artificial intelligence in education: A comprehensive review. *IEEE Transactions on Learning Technologies*, 1–20. doi:10.1109/TLT.2023.3314610

Akgun, S., & Greenhow, C. (2022). Artificial intelligence in education: Addressing ethical challenges in K-12 settings. *AI and Ethics*, *2*(3), 431–440. doi:10.1007/s43681-021-00096-7 PMID:34790956

Alasadi, E. A., & Baiz, C. R. (2023). Generative AI in Education and Research: Opportunities, Concerns, and Solutions. *Journal of Chemical Education*, *100*(8), 2965–2971. doi:10.1021/acs.jchemed.3c00323

Bahroun, Z., Anane, C., Ahmed, V., & Zacca, A. (2023). Transforming education: A comprehensive review of generative artificial intelligence in educational settings through bibliometric and content analysis. *Sustainability (Basel)*, *15*(17), 12983. doi:10.3390/su151712983

Bielow, C., Mastrobuoni, G., & Kempa, S. (2016). Proteomics quality control: Quality control software for MaxQuant results. *Journal of Proteome Research*, *15*(3), 777–787. doi:10.1021/acs.jproteome.5b00780 PMID:26653327

Bozkurt, A., & Sharma, R. C. (2023). Challenging the status quo and exploring the new boundaries in the age of algorithms: Reimagining the role of generative AI in distance education and online learning. *Asian Journal of Distance Education*, *18*(1), i–viii. doi:10.5281/zenodo.7755273

Carraccio, C., Wolfsthal, S. D., Englander, R., Ferentz, K., & Martin, C. (2002). Shifting paradigms: From flexner to competencies. *Academic Medicine*, *77*(5), 361–367. doi:10.1097/00001888-200205000-00003 PMID:12010689

Chiu, T. K. F. (2023). The impact of Generative AI (GenAI) on practices, policies and research direction in education: A case of ChatGPT and Midjourney. *Interactive Learning Environments*, 1–17. doi: 10.1080/10494820.2023.2253861

Choi, C. W., Kim, B. R., Park, J. S., & Youn, S. W. (2018). Both educational lectures and reference photographs are necessary to improve the accuracy and reliability of Psoriasis Area and Severity Index (PASI) assessment: Results from Korean nation-wide PASI educational workshop. *Annals of Dermatology*, *30*(3), 284–289. doi:10.5021/ad.2018.30.3.284 PMID:29853741

Ciampa, K., Wolfe, Z. M., & Bronstein, B. (2023). ChatGPT in education: Transforming digital literacy practices. *Journal of Adolescent & Adult Literacy*, *67*(3), 186–195. doi:10.1002/jaal.1310

De Gagne, J. C., Hwang, H., & Jung, D. (2023). Cyberethics in nursing education: Ethical implications of artificial intelligence. *Nursing Ethics*, 09697330231201901. doi:10.1177/09697330231201901 PMID:37803810

Dirkx, K., Joosten-ten Brinke, D., Arts, J., & van Diggelen, M. (2021). In-text and rubric-referenced feedback: Differences in focus, level, and function. *Active Learning in Higher Education*, *22*(3), 189–201. doi:10.1177/1469787419855208

Eager, B., & Brunton, R. (2023). Prompting higher education towards ai-augmented teaching and learning practice. *Journal of University Teaching & Learning Practice*, *20*(5). doi:10.53761/1.20.5.02

Emenike, M. E., & Emenike, B. U. (2023). Was this title generated by ChatGPT? Considerations for artificial intelligence text-generation software programs for chemists and chemistry educators. *Journal of Chemical Education*, *100*(4), 1413–1418. doi:10.1021/acs.jchemed.3c00063

Gašević, D., Siemens, G., & Sadiq, S. (2023). Empowering learners for the age of artificial intelligence. *Computers and Education: Artificial Intelligence*, *4*, 100130. doi:10.1016/j.caeai.2023.100130

Girardi, S., Gaudy, C., Gouvernet, J., Teston, J., Richard, M. A., & Grob, J.-J. (2006). Superiority of a cognitive education with photographs over ABCD criteria in the education of the general population to the early detection of melanoma: A randomized study. *International Journal of Cancer*, *118*(9), 2276–2280. doi:10.1002/ijc.21351 PMID:16331608

Grimmelikhuijsen, S. (2023). Explaining why the computer says no: Algorithmic transparency affects the perceived trustworthiness of automated decision-making. *Public Administration Review*, *83*(2), 241–262. doi:10.1111/puar.13483

Gustafsson, L., Molineux, M., & Bennett, S. (2014). Contemporary occupational therapy practice: The challenges of being evidence based and philosophically congruent. *Australian Occupational Therapy Journal*, *61*(2), 121–123. doi:10.1111/1440-1630.12110 PMID:24697489

Hahn, R. (2023). Measuring social determinant access and equity by race in U.S. States. *Medical Research Archives*, *11*(2). doi:10.18103/mra.v11i2.3643

Hằng, N. V. T., Meijer, M. R., Bulte, A. M. W., & Pilot, A. (2015). The implementation of a social constructivist approach in primary science education in Confucian heritage culture: The case of Vietnam. *Cultural Studies of Science Education*, *10*(3), 665–693. doi:10.1007/s11422-014-9634-8

Hisan, U. K., & Amri, M. M. (2022). Artificial intelligence for human life: A critical opinion from medical bioethics perspective – Part II. *Journal of Public Health Sciences*, *1*(2), 112–130. doi:10.56741/jphs.v1i02.215

Holmes, W., Porayska-Pomsta, K., Holstein, K., Sutherland, E., Baker, T., Shum, S. B., Santos, O. C., Rodrigo, M. T., Cukurova, M., Bittencourt, I. I., & Koedinger, K. R. (2022). Ethics of AI in education: Towards a community-wide framework. *International Journal of Artificial Intelligence in Education*, *32*(3), 504–526. doi:10.1007/s40593-021-00239-1

Hoppmann, R. A., Rao, V. V., Bell, F., Poston, M. B., Howe, D. B., Riffle, S., Harris, S., Riley, R., McMahon, C., Wilson, L. B., Blanck, E., Richeson, N. A., Thomas, L. K., Hartman, C., Neuffer, F. H., Keisler, B. D., Sims, K. M., Garber, M. D., Shuler, C. O., & Catalana, P. V. (2015). The evolution of an integrated ultrasound curriculum (iUSC) for medical students: 9-year experience. *Critical Ultrasound Journal*, *7*(1), 18. doi:10.1186/s13089-015-0035-3 PMID:26589313

Ilieva, G., Yankova, T., Klisarova-Belcheva, S., Dimitrov, A., Bratkov, M., & Angelov, D. (2023). Effects of generative chatbots in higher education. *Information (Basel)*, *14*(9), 492. doi:10.3390/info14090492

Kılınç, S. (2023). Embracing the future of distance science education: Opportunities and challenges of ChatGPT integration. *Asian Journal of Distance Education*, *18*(1). http://www.asianjde.com/ojs/index.php/AsianJDE/article/view/721

Köbis, L., & Mehner, C. (2021). Ethical questions raised by ai-supported mentoring in higher education. *Frontiers in Artificial Intelligence*, *4*, 4. doi:10.3389/frai.2021.624050 PMID:33997774

Kostka, I., & Toncelli, R. (2023). Exploring applications of ChatGPT to English language teaching: Opportunities, challenges, and recommendations. *The Electronic Journal for English as a Second Language*, *27*(3). doi:10.55593/ej.27107int

Kozyreva, A., Lewandowsky, S., & Hertwig, R. (2020). Citizens versus the internet: Confronting digital challenges with cognitive tools. *Psychological Science in the Public Interest*, *21*(3), 103–156. doi:10.1177/1529100620946707 PMID:33325331

Lin, Z. (2023). Why and how to embrace AI such as ChatGPT in your academic life. *Royal Society Open Science*, *10*(8), 230658. doi:10.1098/rsos.230658 PMID:37621662

Liu, K. J., Cook, A. N., & Jiang, R. (2023). Lessons from Canadian judgments: The consideration of culture in intimate partner violence legal cases involving Asian Canadians. *Journal of Interpersonal Violence*, *38*(19–20), 11046–11066. doi:10.1177/08862605231178494 PMID:37350459

Liu, M., Ren, Y., Nyagoga, L. M., Stonier, F., Wu, Z., & Yu, L. (2023). Future of education in the era of generative artificial intelligence: Consensus among Chinese scholars on applications of ChatGPT in schools. *Future in Educational Research*, *1*(1), 72–101. doi:10.1002/fer3.10

Lo, C. K. (2023). What is the impact of ChatGPT on education? A rapid review of the literature. *Education Sciences*, *13*(4), 410. doi:10.3390/educsci13040410

Mao, J., Chen, B., & Liu, J. C. (2023). Generative artificial intelligence in education and its implications for assessment. *TechTrends*. doi:10.1007/s11528-023-00911-4

Memarian, B., & Doleck, T. (2023). ChatGPT in education: Methods, potentials, and limitations. *Computers in Human Behavior: Artificial Humans*, *1*(2), 100022. doi:10.1016/j.chbah.2023.100022

Michel-Villarreal, R., Vilalta-Perdomo, E., Salinas-Navarro, D. E., Thierry-Aguilera, R., & Gerardou, F. S. (2023). Challenges and Opportunities of Generative AI for Higher Education as Explained by ChatGPT. *Education Sciences*, *13*(9), 9. doi:10.3390/educsci13090856

Moher, D., Liberati, A., Tetzlaff, J., & Altman, D. G. (2009). *Preferred reporting items for systematic reviews and meta-analyses: The PRISMA statement*. The PRISMA Group. http://www.prisma-statement.org/

Montenegro-Rueda, M., Fernández-Cerero, J., Fernández-Batanero, J. M., & López-Meneses, E. (2023). Impact of the implementation of ChatGPT in education: A systematic review. *Computers*, *12*(8), 153. doi:10.3390/computers12080153

Pereira, R. H. M., Braga, C. K. V., Servo, L. M., Serra, B., Amaral, P., Gouveia, N., & Paez, A. (2021). Geographic access to COVID-19 healthcare in Brazil using a balanced float catchment area approach. *Social Science & Medicine*, *273*, 113773. doi:10.1016/j.socscimed.2021.113773 PMID:33609968

Popovici, M.-D. (2023). ChatGPT in the Classroom. Exploring its potential and limitations in a functional programming course. *International Journal of Human-Computer Interaction*, 1–12. doi:10.1080/10447318.2023.2269006

Pradana, M., Elisa, H. P., & Syarifuddin, S. (2023). Discussing ChatGPT in education: A literature review and bibliometric analysis. *Cogent Education*, *10*(2), 2243134. doi:10.1080/2331186X.2023.2243134

Preiksaitis, C., & Rose, C. (2023). Opportunities, challenges, and future directions of generative artificial intelligence in medical education: Scoping review. *JMIR Medical Education*, *9*(1), e48785. doi:10.2196/48785 PMID:37862079

Rasul, T., Nair, S., Kalendra, D., Robin, M., Santini, F. de O., Ladeira, W. J., Sun, M., Day, I., Rather, R. A., & Heathcote, L. (2023). The role of ChatGPT in higher education: Benefits, challenges, and future research directions. *Journal of Applied Learning and Teaching*, *6*(1), 41–56. doi:10.37074/jalt.2023.6.1.29

Ratten, V., & Jones, P. (2023). Generative artificial intelligence (ChatGPT): Implications for management educators. *International Journal of Management Education*, *21*(3), 100857. doi:10.1016/j.ijme.2023.100857

Sait, S., & Tombs, M. (2021). Teaching medical students how to interpret chest x-rays: The design and development of an e-learning resource. *Advances in Medical Education and Practice*, *12*, 123–132. doi:10.2147/AMEP.S280941 PMID:33574725

Sallam, M. (2023). ChatGPT utility in healthcare education, research, and practice: Systematic review on the promising perspectives and valid concerns. *Health Care*, *11*(6), 887. doi:10.3390/healthcare11060887 PMID:36981544

Shoja, M. M., Van de Ridder, J. M. M., & Rajput, V. (2023). The emerging role of generative artificial intelligence in medical education, research, and practice. *Cureus*, *15*(6). doi:10.7759/cureus.40883 PMID:37492829

Smither, J. W., London, M., & Richmond, K. R. (2005). The relationship between leaders' personality and their reactions to and use of multisource feedback: A longitudinal study. *Group & Organization Management*, *30*(2), 181–210. doi:10.1177/1059601103254912

Steele, J. L. (2023). To GPT or not GPT? Empowering our students to learn with AI. *Computers and Education: Artificial Intelligence*, *5*, 100160. doi:10.1016/j.caeai.2023.100160

Su, J., Ng, D. T. K., & Chu, S. K. W. (2023). Artificial Intelligence (AI) literacy in early childhood education: The challenges and opportunities. *Computers and Education: Artificial Intelligence*, *4*, 100124. doi:10.1016/j.caeai.2023.100124

Su, J., & Yang, W. (2023). Unlocking the power of ChatGPT: A framework for applying generative AI in education. *ECNU Review of Education*, *6*(3), 355–366. doi:10.1177/20965311231168423

Sullivan, M., Kelly, A., & McLaughlan, P. (2023). ChatGPT in higher education: Considerations for academic integrity and student learning. *Journal of Applied Learning and Teaching*, *6*(1), 31–40. doi:10.37074/jalt.2023.6.1.17

Tao, Z., & Wang, Q. (2022). Facility or transport inequality? Decomposing healthcare accessibility inequality in Shenzhen, China. *International Journal of Environmental Research and Public Health*, *19*(11), 6897. doi:10.3390/ijerph19116897 PMID:35682478

Turner, S. (2001). What is the problem with experts? *Social Studies of Science*, *31*(1), 123–149. doi:10.1177/030631201031001007

van Deursen, A. J., & van Dijk, J. A. (2019). The first-level digital divide shifts from inequalities in physical access to inequalities in material access. *New Media & Society*, *21*(2), 354–375. doi:10.1177/1461444818797082 PMID:30886536

Van Slyke, C., Johnson, R., & Sarabadani, J. (2023). Generative artificial intelligence in information systems education: Challenges, consequences, and responses. *Communications of the Association for Information Systems*, *53*(1), 1–21. doi:10.17705/1CAIS.05301

Walczak, K., & Cellary, W. (2023). Challenges for higher education in the era of widespread access to generative AI. *Economics and Business Review*, *9*(2), 71–100. doi:10.18559/ebr.2023.2.743

Wang, T., Lund, B. D., Marengo, A., Pagano, A., Mannuru, N. R., Teel, Z. A., & Pange, J. (2023). Exploring the potential impact of artificial intelligence (AI) on international students in higher education: Generative AI, chatbots, analytics, and international student success. *Applied Sciences (Basel, Switzerland)*, *13*(11), 6716. doi:10.3390/app13116716

Westgard, J. O., & Westgard, S. A. (2016). Quality control review: Implementing a scientifically based quality control system. *Annals of Clinical Biochemistry*, *53*(1), 32–50. doi:10.1177/0004563215597248 PMID:26150675

Whitehead, J. L., Pearson, A., Lawrenson, R., & Atatoa-Carr, P. (2019). How can the spatial equity of health services be defined and measured? A systematic review of spatial equity definitions and methods. *Journal of Health Services Research & Policy*, *24*(4), 270–278. doi:10.1177/1355819619837292 PMID:31460801

Whitney, C. W., Lind, B. K., & Wahl, P. W. (1998). Quality assurance and quality control in longitudinal studies. *Epidemiologic Reviews*, *20*(1), 71–80. doi:10.1093/oxfordjournals.epirev.a017973 PMID:9762510

Yan, L., Sha, L., Zhao, L., Li, Y., Martinez-Maldonado, R., Chen, G., Li, X., Jin, Y., & Gašević, D. (2023). Practical and ethical challenges of large language models in education: A systematic scoping review. *British Journal of Educational Technology*, bjet.13370. doi:10.1111/bjet.13370

Zhai, C., & Wibowo, S. (2023). A systematic review on artificial intelligence dialogue systems for enhancing English as foreign language students' interactional competence in the university. *Computers and Education: Artificial Intelligence*, *4*, 100134. doi:10.1016/j.caeai.2023.100134

Zhang, P., & Tur, G. (2023). A systematic review of ChatGPT use in K-12 education. *European Journal of Education*, ejed.12599. doi:10.1111/ejed.12599

KEY TERMS AND DEFINITIONS

AI: Artificial Intelligence is a field of technology used to simulate computer systems' human-like thinking, learning, and problem-solving abilities.

BERT: BERT (Bidirectional Encoder Representations from Transformers) is a deep learning model used in natural language processing.

ChatGPT: It is an artificial intelligence model used in natural language processing. It is a language model developed by OpenAI that can generate realistic and meaningful answers in text-based conversations.

Database: It is a database of citations of scholarly articles, books, and other academic sources, helping researchers track, cite, and search literature.

Ethics: Ethics is a philosophical concept that deals with moral principles and rules of behavior as a field in which right and wrong, good and evil, just and unjust, and honest and fraudulent behaviors are examined and evaluated.

GAI Tools: Generative AI Tools refers to AI-based tools that allow users to generate text, images, music, and similar content automatically, often designed to assist in the creative process.

GAI: Generative AI is a concept that refers to artificial intelligence models that can generate new and original content by learning from data sets.

Measurement and Evaluation: It is a concept in education that enables the systematic and objective determination, analysis, and interpretation of a process or a student's performance, abilities, or achievements.

Open Assistant: It is an AI assistant that can be freely developed and personalized.

Chapter 9
Artificial Intelligence (AI) and Cheating:
The Concept of Generative Artificial Intelligence (GenAI)

Ömer Muhtar Akkaş
Gazi University, Turkey

Cansel Tosun
https://orcid.org/0009-0009-2461-6508
Gazi University, Turkey

Şahin Gökçearslan
https://orcid.org/0000-0003-3532-4251
Gazi University, Turkey

ABSTRACT

Generative AI (GenAI) systems pose new challenges in academic dishonesty. Students may be tempted to use GenAI systems to cheat and submit content in assignments and projects that they did not create themselves. This points to the need for schools to focus on strong deterrent measures as well as informative and enhancing practices. Academic dishonesty is not limited to students. The use of GenAI in academia raises two extreme ethical problems. These problems relate to the ethical problems of the end user and the ethical problems in the development of this technology. The ethical use of GenAI technologies should be achieved in a way that respects human rights and takes into account user concerns. This new technology requires a rethinking of teaching methods, as well as assessment and evaluation. It is not recommended that policymakers, students, and faculty work collectively and take responsibility for adopting ethical values in the process of integrating GenAI into academia.

DOI: 10.4018/979-8-3693-1351-0.ch009

INTRODUCTION

ChatGPT, one of the most widely used Generative Artificial Intelligence (GenAI) tools today, describes itself as a language model pre-trained on various internet texts to understand and produce human-like language. Unsurprisingly, "intelligence" is not included in its definition, because defining intelligence in AI presents difficulties due to multiple influencing aspects. Albus (1991) proposed a hierarchical system architecture for intelligence; however, Colom et al. (2010) emphasized the importance of a frontoparietal network in learning, reasoning, and problem-solving. According to Witmer (1922), intelligence is the ability to find new solutions, the main indicator of which is a successful outcome.

Since the debate between AI and human intelligence has many aspects, Filip (2021); Shcherbakov (2023) highlights the potential of AI to enhance human cognition while promoting new ethical rules for technological development. While Filip (2021) emphasized the need for balanced co-evolution, Oritsegbemi (2023); Ali (2018) expressed concerns about the linguistic and emotional aspects of language learning and human communication, respectively. In other words, they argue that while AI is improving, it is still inadequate to overcome the subjectivity and complexity of human intelligence. These perspectives also highlight the need for a comprehensive understanding of the potential and limitations of AI compared to human intelligence. There are different opinions on what AI can and cannot do, and as a result the effects of AI on society and morality is a highly debated issue.

Although debates about the effects and moral implications of AI on society are relatively new, there is an urgent need to control and limit these effects. Benjamins (2020) identifies key challenges such as undesirable effects, responsibility, and concentration of power and wealth. Mika et al. (2019) emphasizes the need for new governance approaches to control the use of AI to balance soft and hard governance measures. Hagerty & Rubinov (2019) underlines the importance of understanding the global and cultural context of AI's social impacts, especially to reduce potential harms and address social inequality. Green (2018) expands the discussion further by highlighting various ethical concerns in AI, such as transparency, bias, and socio-economic inequality. All these studies point to the need to address the social impacts and ethical implications of AI with a comprehensive and culturally sensitive approach.

AI ENVIRONMENT AND CHEATING

AI technology is widely used and rapidly evolving thanks to advances in machine learning, deep learning, natural language processing, and computer vision (Mondal, 2019). These technologies have made significant breakthroughs in natural language understanding as well as gaming, speech, and image recognition. Thanks to its capacity to automate repetitive tasks and identify behavioral patterns, AI has been integrated into important fields such as law, banking, policing, and the workplace, alongside traditional technology (Campolo, 2017). AI is spreading across different industries. It's not just used by professionals but also in fields such as gaming and education. This shows that it has a wide range of uses and affects many parts of our lives.

AI is increasingly used in a variety of contexts, including professional environments, gaming, and education. AI is used in education to create personalized and adaptive serious educational games based on recognizing speech, images, and human emotions (Dyulicheva & Glazieva, 2022). Additionally, computer technologies are used in various ways to perform administrative tasks and customize curriculum and content, including web-based and online intelligent education systems and humanoid robots (Chen et al., 2020). Interactive role-playing games are used to teach AI concepts in games (Sintov et al., 2016), and these applications demonstrate how AI is used effectively and in a variety of ways in various fields.

The integration of AI into education has led to new challenges and vulnerabilities, especially in the area of cheating. Oravec (2023) and Bubas (2023) highlight the potential of AI-generating chatbots and conversational AI systems such as ChatGPT to facilitate academic dishonesty, with the latter also discussing the impact of the COVID-19 pandemic on cheating in online assessments. While Xiao (2022) underlines the threat posed by AI tools that enable plagiarism, Oravec (2022) expresses concerns about the implementation of AI-based cheating detection systems and underlines the need for rigorous testing and evaluation. Collectively, these studies highlight the need for proactive steps to address the misuse of AI in education.

ETHICAL CONCERNS IN AI

AI applications have raised various ethical issues such as accountability, privacy, and bias. Gupta & Mishra (2022) points out that gender biases and privacy concerns may be amplified by AI tools used in recruitment. Transparency and accountability are two of the 17 common ethical principles in AI governance identified by (Corrêa et al., 2022). Murphy et al. (2021) emphasizes the need to be cautious and optimistic when using AI in healthcare, especially when it comes to issues of bias, privacy, and trust.

Recognizing these challenges, Kooli & AI-Muftah (2022) underline the importance of continuous monitoring and education to address ethical issues in the healthcare industry, such as patient safety and skewed outcomes. The collective findings of these studies highlight the need for strong ethical frameworks and oversight in the creation and implementation of AI technologies.

While ethical considerations in AI applications often revolve around protecting users against AI's shortcomings, there is considerable oversight in holding AI applications accountable for academic dishonesty committed by students. Etzioni & Etzioni (2016) propose the use of monitoring programs to audit and hold AI programs accountable and suggest that this approach can be extended to AI applications in academic settings to address issues related to academic cheating. Ashford (2020) puts forward a model that emphasizes the importance of socio-techno responsibility in students and advocates a holistic approach that takes into account the complex nature of human-technology interactions.

CHEATING IN THE CONTEXT OF ARTIFICIAL INTELLIGENCE

The impact of AI and other information and communication technologies on academic dishonesty has been observed (Szabó & Underwood, 2004). The emergence of AI-generated chatbots has made it easier to obtain materials for cheating and has significantly affected academic dishonesty (Oravec, 2023). In particular, while students express a clear distaste for directly AI-generated content, their views on more subtle applications of the technology are less clear-cut (Chan, 2023).

Moreover, AI cheating is motivated by a variety of factors, including goal orientation, self-efficacy, and perceived costs of cheating (Murdock & Anderman, 2006). This problem has been exacerbated by the shift to online learning during the COVID-19 pandemic, and conversational AI systems have opened new avenues for academic dishonesty (Bubas, 2023). The design of learning environments can also be influential, as high stakes testing and subjective grading standards encourage cheating (Lang et al.,

2013). The emergence of AI-generated chatbots, with their potential for both responsible collaboration and abuse, has added additional dimensions to these challenges (Oravec, 2023).

Ethical human-AI collaboration is also necessary, as is the implementation of specific methods and tools to prevent exam cheating. However, it is nearly impossible for a human to detect the use of AI in an online assessment. Furthermore, as Xiao (2022) notes, using AI tools to detect plagiarism is also vulnerable to attacks from AI-based tools. In addition, students may be more likely to cheat if they know their scores are calculated by or with the help of AI. As Haring et al. (2019) shows, while people react completely differently to a robot opponent cheating than a human opponent, they are also more open to cheating if the cheating opponent is a robot, which could mean they perceive their actions differently towards robots.

REGULATORY AND LEGAL PERSPECTIVES

Discussions on AI ethics in various countries and regions bring about discussions that have a significant impact on professional organizations as well as national, international, and regional policies, including enacted or proposed regulations (Bakiner, 2022). With the use of AI, the need for important regulations in the context of ethical principles, accountability, and transparency gradually increases concerns about legal processes. It is emphasized that the educational ethical implications of AI should be understood with limits regarding the legal responsibilities of ethical frameworks in academic processes such as evaluation (Lim et al., 2023)

However, in the context of AI, the legal status of artificial personality perceptions and algorithms in AI systems has brought up discussions on legal liability and revealed the need for legal regulations regarding these discussions and problems (Kazim & Koshiyama, 2021). Moreover, with the realization of the potential of AI to help people, the need to develop AI literacy in education is underlined, especially for the AI technologies on which students are increasingly dependent (Mohammadzadeh et al., 2023). In light of these discussions, a different perspective (Greene et al., 2019) adopts a critical perspective in the field of ethical AI use, suggesting that ethical design and legal regulations are necessary to guide the development and implementation of AI technologies. This perspective also seems to support the implications of policies and legal situations regarding the use of AI.

Another important legal issue regarding the use of GenAI systems relates to copyright. While GenAI is known for its capacity to produce original works, several concerns arise regarding the legal status of these works. In particular, the inability of machines to perform strictly cognitive creative processes leads to debates about copyright protection. This situation stands out as one of the main obstacles to attempts to recognize the legal status of works created by GenAI.

Studies on copyright protection show that some countries may have a more liberal attitude, while others may include computer-generated works within the scope of copyright protection. For example, in the United Kingdom, section 48 of the Copyright, Designs, and Patents Act 1988 (c.48) states that "in the case of a literary, dramatic, musical or artistic work created by a computer, the author is the author who has made the arrangements necessary for the creation of the work." will be considered as a person." Therefore, copyright protection may be available for works created using computers. It is noteworthy that the human element has not been eliminated with this legal framework. Although the human element does not perform the cognitive process itself, it is thought to be the element that provides the necessary input for the cognitive process to occur. As a result, copyright protection may be granted to the source of the input. The European Union has a more limited perspective on this issue. According to the provisions of Article 1, Section 3 of Directive 2009/24/EC of the European Parliament and of the Council on the Legal Protection of Computer Programs, "A work must be protected by the intellectual creativity of the author and no other criteria for protection should be used." Although this article demonstrates how important human cognitive processes are in the creation of a work, it does not allow independently created works. Moreover, according to the US Copyright Office, computer-generated works without human intervention are not eligible for legal protection (Zatarain, 2017).

A comprehensive ethical framework is essential to maximize the benefits associated with the development and implementation of AI systems. At its general conference in 2023, UNESCO adopted the AI Ethics Recommendation, the first global document on the subject. This recommendation adopts a global, policy-friendly stance toward the ethical regulation of AI, based on both legally enforceable international agreements and a fundamental commitment to human rights. Underlining the importance of data governance in the development of safe and fair algorithms, it calls on Member States to establish plans for sensitive data management and effective accountability. It also highlights the importance of gender equality by highlighting gender biases and stereotypes present in AI systems.

The resolution also mentions two tools to address the challenges of regulations and codifications to be developed by UNESCO to support the policy action areas of the recommendation. The first of these is the Ethical Impact Assessment (EIA). This tool supports streamlining algorithms by targeting developers to reduce negative impacts in AI systems. Another is the Readiness Assessment Methodology. This tool aims to support member states in developing, adopting and using AI technologies (UNESCO, 2023).

In this context, the ethical dimensions of AI take into account various principles and values. Among these principles, ethical concepts such as responsibility, transparency, confidentiality, and trust are important. Policymakers should act within the framework of these ethical principles in the development and implementation of AI applications (Waelen, 2022). While creating ethical frameworks, they should develop legal regulations based on cooperation with experts (Kazim & Koshiyama, 2021). While doing this, they should take steps to increase the reliability of AI systems through control mechanisms regulated in appropriate legal frameworks (Ryan, 2020).

As artificial intelligence, especially chatbots, becomes a normal tool for students and academics, lawmakers have begun drafting regulations to deal with the issue. A project known as "RusselGroup, 2023" was recently launched by the Russell Group, a UK organization representing 24 universities, to help academic institutions ensure that their staff and students are "AI literate" and can take advantage of the opportunities that technological advances offer for teaching and learning. A series of guides have been developed. On the other hand, China is considering serious sanctions for students who use illegal means to obtain degrees, including the use of AI tools (Leung, 2023). Moreover, they say, it is necessary to clarify how AI tools will be used and define the boundary between "AI assistance" and "AI ghostwriting."

ETHICAL GUIDELINES AND BEST PRACTICES

When GenAI tools were first introduced, many education experts around the world expressed concerns about the potential for these tools to be used in essay writing and how they could help students cheat. Some of the world's leading universities stated that "the genie is out of the bottle" and argued that the integration of GenAI tools into educational environments can be done efficiently. While new ideas and tools for how to use this tool in research and education emerge almost daily, researchers and educators are still trying to unlock GenAI's teaching-learning and research potential. Stakeholders may not have evaluated ethical principles correctly. Various guides and practical examples are being worked on for this new tool. UNESCO has produced guidance on how to integrate GenAI into education and research. It also supports workshops aimed at increasing knowledge on this subject. The guide, which aims to support the planning of policies, regulations, and programs for the development of human capacity, which is the main purpose of education, aims to ensure that GenAI becomes a tool that benefits researchers, teachers, and students, and strengthens their potential. The guidelines focus on a people-centered approach that promotes participation, plural views and expressions, gender equality, cultural and linguistic diversity, and equality (Miao & Holmes, 2023). The ethical use of GenAI is essential in providing the necessary foundation for developing one of the dual dimensions of human and ethical considerations.

GenAI's assessment implications go beyond concerns about student cheating. GenAI's ability to pass knowledge-based exams, its potential to complete assignments, and its ability to edit impressive writing and artwork have raised the question of what exactly we should teach and how we should evaluate it (Miao & Holmes, 2023).

Australia also has developed a nationwide framework for the use of GenAI in schools that aims to guide the ethical and responsible use of GenAI tools to benefit society as a whole. The framework supports everyone connected to school education, including students, teachers, parents, support staff, school leaders, parents, service providers, and policymakers. The framework covers the following topics (Australian Framework, 2023).

- Teaching and Learning: The use of GenAI tools facilitates and enhances these processes.
- Human and Social Well-being: The school community as a whole benefits from the application of GenAI tools.
- Transparency: School communities are aware of how generative GenAI tools can be applied, as well as the conditions under which these tools impact them.
- Fairness: The application of GenAI tools is gentle, equitable, and easily accessible.
- Accountability: Applying GenAI tools allows for the preservation of human agency and decision-making responsibility.
- Privacy, Security and Safety: Data and privacy of students and other users of GenAI tools are protected.

In Turkey, technical issues come to the fore while the FEYZA project prepares guides and training materials that will contribute to the employment of artificial intelligence personnel within the scope of the "National Artificial Intelligence Strategy 2021-2025" in cooperation with the Presidential Digital Transformation Office and the Ministry of Industry and Technology (MEB, 2023).

The Russell Group (2023) published a joint statement on the use of GenAI tools in education. The principles set out in the declaration are as follows:

- Universities will help their employees and students learn about artificial intelligence.
- Hardware support is required for staff to use GenAI tools efficiently and effectively for teaching and learning.
- Universities will incorporate GenAI's ethical practices into their teaching and evaluation processes while improving individual access.
- Universities will promote responsible use and academic integrity.

- Universities will collaborate to share best practices in instructional technology.

It is important to note that GenAI tools pose a risk of cheating, and therefore universities should include teaching programs on the use of GenAI tools. It is also underlined that in case of misuse of GenAI tools, it is the user's responsibility to obtain correct information. The significance of developing clear and transparent policies to ensure academic integrity and ethical use is emphasized. Attention is also drawn to ethical issues that may arise during the use of GenAI tools. Students and staff must be trained in the use of GenAI tools and understand the limitations of these tools (Russell Group, 2023).

ETHICAL PROBLEMS ARISING FROM THE FEATURES OF AI

Transparency: One of the core technologies of artificial intelligence is machine learning. Accomplishing transparency for what is known as "black box" machine learning is an ongoing challenge. The "black box" process of machine learning, known as the inference process, makes it challenging to define and comprehend. The lack of transparency regarding algorithms causes transparency problems for users and developers (Castelvecchi, 2016). At the same time, the lack of transparency also leads to difficulties in human monitoring and guidance of AI technologies. Since this situation makes it difficult to understand the working principles of AI, it has become one of the most discussed topics in the field of AI ethics (Huang et al., 2022).

Data Security and Privacy: Developments related to AI demonstrate the need for large datasets, especially for deep learning model training, and these datasets contain personal and sensitive information. Training AI systems based on such data poses a risk in terms of data security. The possible risks of disseminating or altering personal information, and ethical and security issues related to AI technologies should be debated (Dilmaghani et al., 2019).

SCIENTIFIC INTEGRITY

As the use of artificial intelligence in education increases, the ideas of using artificial intelligence in education, adhering to moral principles, and covering scientific integrity become an important necessity (Burton et al., 2017). Ethical standards such as producing original studies, citing sources correctly, and producing plagiarism-free outputs are necessary in artificial intelligence-supported education systems (Dignum, 2021).

Determining ethical rules is becoming increasingly important to protect scientific integrity (Burton et al., 2017). It is important to encourage ethical behavior in the process of using AI in education, to direct ethical standards to ensure scientific integrity, to consciously and accurately evaluate behavior following ethical rules (Dignum, 2021), and to produce policies that will encourage original studies in the preparation and use of AI-supported educational materials (Burton et al., 2017). Then, educators, legislators, and technology designers need to adopt a strategic and ethical method to raise awareness about educational ethics in AI technologies and to ensure their responsible use. The use of GenAI technologies can be added to the curriculum in courses on the use of technology in academic research (Kasap et al., 2021).

ACADEMIC INTEGRITY IN AI AND EDUCATION

Academic integrity and the use of AI have evolved into controversy due to global reactions against these innovations in education, primarily concerning cheating. Academic integrity is an idea that supports scientific studies and contains ethical principles and matters, including trust and fairness (Waelen, 2022). The normalization of cheating in education poses a substantial threat to the importance of education and the quality of educational scope. This has led to the need to integrate AI into academic writing and re-evaluate academic integrity policies (Hung & Chen, 2023). Gaumann & Veale (2023) emphasized that cheating laws should be analyzed on general-purpose AI providers.

These concerns over cheating have led to a reevaluation of academic integrity policies which also extends to the role of GenAI in academic writing. Actions regarding AI-supported writing have led to significant transformations in students' techniques for academic writing. ChatGPT, a GenAI chatbot created by OpenAI, played an important function in this conversion by allowing the creation of texts close to human writing based on user requests. However, the fact that GenAI applications encourage cheating and plagiarism in academic writing has introduced ethical issues regarding the originality of the content. Doubting the ethical rules for the use of GenAI in scientific research highlights the need for transparency and consideration of ethical implications in the context of the use of these technologies and their integration into education (Schlagwein & Wilcocks, 2023). Elkhatat (2023) analyzed the authenticity of ChatGPT's responses and revealed the risks of cheating and plagiarism associated with AI chatbots. The ability of AI writing assistants to imitate human writing has complicated academic writing, making originality difficult to detect. The need for effective mechanisms to recognize such content has been highlighted (Cingillioğlu, 2023).

Publishers' use of GenAI varies from a ban under editorial policies to a more widespread approach in the form of disclosure (e.g. Elsevier, Sage, Taylor & Francis, Springer Nature, etc.). Publishers acknowledge that AI tools (e.g. ChatGPT, DALL-E, Bard, Bing, etc.) cannot be added as authors, and authors are responsible for the content. While some tools facilitate the application of GenAI, that is, the identification of text and images that deviate from human characteristics, no tool yet provides a definitive result in this field (Berezin, 2023). For example, a publishing company has published a policy that attempts to provide guidance and clarification on the application of GenAI and AI-powered tools in the authoring process. While human oversight and control are emphasized, application is limited to improving language use and readability. Scientific insights, conclusions, and recommendations should be made by human authors and the use of these tools should be noted. Detailed explanations should be made in the research design and research methodology, and the images and visualizations used must be original in the context of copyright and ethics (Elsevier, 2023).

UTILIZING CHATGPT AS AN ACADEMIC TOOL, NOT A CHEATING TOOL

Academics encounter a serious conflict due to the lack of studies on the accuracy of AI-generated materials (Crawford et al., 2023; Ryznar, 2023). These warnings can be interpreted as a challenge by students (Högberg, 2011), as teachers advise their students to minimize the use of GenAI programs such as ChatGPT in course materials (Gillard & Rorabaugh, 2023). However, it is important to examine the data produced by AI and its impact on academic research.

Although AI applications such as ChatGPT do not go through an evaluation phase during the data provision phase, the data they create are generally considered valid data that can support academic studies (Liebrenz et al., 2023). However, it is also a fact that the accuracy of the data provided by ChatGPT should be investigated. According to the working principle of ChatGPT, even if correct data is obtained, these outputs need to be evaluated with a critical eye. In this context, the recommended assessment approach is to evaluate students through teacher-guided formative feedback methods, with the belief that students should use ChatGPT as a kind of "support tool". Based on this guidance process, students can improve their critical thinking skills and reach more practical and accurate conclusions based on the knowledge that reveals their approaches (Crawford et al., 2023).

HOW CAN ACADEMICS PREVENT STUDENTS FROM CHEATING USING CHATGPT?

The academic community is increasingly concerned about the potential for plagiarism when using ChatGPT and other AI language models. As a result, various strategies can be put forward that will direct academics to the efficient and ethical application of these tools:

1. By establishing open-source guidelines, policies and procedures for the problematic use of AI resources should be clearly stated regarding appropriate use, content production, and resource access.
2. Students should receive comprehensive training on plagiarism that emphasizes its definition, justification, and consequences.
3. Artificial intelligence language models, machine learning, and natural language processing algorithms can be defined by using plagiarism detection tools.
4. Students can be encouraged to submit drafts of their work in advance, helping to identify the content created by artificial intelligence and providing feedback to students.
5. Academic staff may ask students to prepare a written statement confirming the originality of their work and that they did not use any AI applications to create their work. This can help hold students accountable for their actions regarding the use of AI applications.
6. Student work should be closely monitored when using artificial intelligence-based tools that can generate text. Monitoring may include careful reading of student outputs, in-class presentations, and the use of plagiarism detection tools (Cotton et al., 2023).

ACADEMIC INTEGRITY IN THE DIGITAL AGE

According to a literature review on academic integrity, reliable assessment in online learning, and academic integrity discussed in the context of online learning, effective strategies are necessary to prevent cheating (Surahman & Wang, 2022). In this context, it is seen that there is a research gap in international indexed publications on AI chatbots (Gökçearslan et al., 2024). The incorporation of AI into online learning procedures underlines the need to create systems to detect cheating. The ethical and social implications of AI applications in combating academic cheating have been highlighted by academic integrity engineering. The relationship between AI and academic integrity has demonstrated the need to re-evaluate existing strategies to protect academic integrity in the digital age (Oravec, 2022).

Understanding the ethical aspects of AI is also necessary to ensure accountability and openness in the creation and use of these technologies. Approaching AI ethics critically and comprehensively, as a critical perspective and principled approach based on philosophical considerations, is crucial for the ethical application of AI in the academic environment (Waelen, 2022). As a result, since there are various opportunities and challenges in the integration of AI into education in the digital age, it is possible to interpret the solution of the problems as the necessity of a multidisciplinary approach that guarantees the application of AI technologies, taking into account social and ethical factors, following ethical standards and academic integrity.

CONCLUSION AND RECOMMENDATIONS

The immediate expansion of GenAI technologies has led to ongoing concerns and debates about scientific ethics. Although the use of GenAI has a positive potential in learning activities and research processes in academia, it has brought up serious problems in the context of cheating and cheating. To address these issues, researchers emphasize the importance of using GenAI technologies with preventive measures to prevent cheating and copying in higher education (Birks et al., 2020). Although research on these tools draws attention to the dimensions of cheating in scientific studies, research focusing on academic honesty and compliance with ethical frameworks is still limited.

Chatbots based on GenAI technologies, especially conversational AI systems such as ChatGPT, have been revealed to have the potential to encourage cheating. There is a critical necessity to take precautions for the usage of GenAI in the academic field. GenAI applications have also raised many essential ethical issues, such as data security and privacy, accountability, transparency, and bias. Investigations emphasize the requirement for a detailed and optimistic approach when using GenAI systems, paying attention to these ethical issues. While ethical issues are often considered in the context of encouraging users to commit academic cheating in GenAI applications, the issue of whether AI systems should be held responsible for cheating comes to the fore. In this respect, it would be correct to argue that a more holistic approach should be taken into account.

On the other hand, there are also opinions that the integration of GenAI tools into educational environments can be done efficiently. In line with this view, UNESCO (2023) has published a guide on how to integrate GenAI systems into the classroom environment, recommending a human rights-sensitive approach in the use of GenAI, based on equality, cultural and linguistic diversity, inclusivity, and gender equality. Australia, on the other hand, has aimed for an integration that takes into account ethical issues regarding the use of AI in educational settings with a framework guideline that emphasizes ethical and responsible use for the use of GenAI tools in schools. In the United Kingdom, the Russell Group (2023) commented that GenAI tools increase the risk of cheating and that universities should include programs for the ethical use of GenAI tools to address this risk. In Turkey, training contents and guides have been prepared within the scope of the FEYZA project, the "National Artificial Intelligence Strategy 2021-2025" in cooperation with the Presidential Digital Transformation Office and the Ministry of Industry and Technology. In light of these proposed guidelines, the main goal is to use GenAI integration as a guiding tool in education that will benefit researchers, educators, and students. The Turkish Council of Higher Education has planned a workshop on GenAI and higher education in December 2023. Although a limited number of countries are currently included here, many countries are working on the ethical and responsible use of GenAI.

According to Huang et al. (2021), GenAI has been shown to enhance efficiency in teaching and learning processes, but it also raises ethical dilemmas. The use of GenAI in online learning and assessment also threatens cheating and academic integrity. This has led to the need to critically evaluate online learning and assessment processes and review implementation methods to combat cheating effectively and ethically. By reviewing measurement and evaluation approaches such as process-based measurement and problem-based learning, project-based learning, portfolio and reflection, measurement and evaluation processes can be differentiated responsibly and effectively with the help of activities and GenAI tools.

Ethical guidelines for accountability and authorship in research ethics are necessary for the use of AI chatbots in academia (Lee, 2023). With the development of writing-supported chatbot tools in the field of GenAI, and the issue of original academic writing becoming a topic of discussion, the risks of plagiarism and cheating have been revealed in academic articles related to AI chatbots. Since various mechanisms are needed to provide originality in academic writing and to eliminate these risks, citing a non-original study will also cause serious problems.

Increasing discussions on AI ethics have made legal regulations and ethical measures gain importance. The significance of transparency and accountability principles in GenAI systems has been emphasized due to growing concerns about AI ethics (Ayling & Chapman, 2022). While designing legal regulations, politicians should encourage regulations and measures within the framework of ethical rules such as responsibility, transparency, data security, and privacy in developing and implementing GenAI applications. While doing this, they should take steps to include control mechanisms that will increase their reliability.

As a result, a coherent, multidisciplinary approach that considers ethical principles is needed to overcome the challenges of integrating GenAI technologies into education, prevent cheating in GenAI technologies, and promote academic integrity. GenAI technologies in academia within an ethical framework will help transform these technologies into potentials that can be used to their advantage in the so-called digital age, even the age of artificial intelligence.

Various strategies can be recommended to guide the effective and ethical use of GenAI technologies for researchers, educators, students, technology developers, and policymakers. These recommendations are presented below:

RECOMMENDATIONS FOR RESEARCHERS

Scientific research should be guided by policies consistent with global standards of scientific integrity and ethics. Just as institutes request various statements regarding plagiarism, they should review these statements within the framework of GenAI. The curriculum of the *Scientific Research Methods and Ethics* course (Kasap et al., 2021) should be updated to include the ethical use of GenAI. Measures should be taken to raise public awareness about AI ethics. The focus should be on cumulative progress in AI ethics by adopting an interdisciplinary, critical, and philosophical approach. Policy makers should collaborate to establish ethical guidelines for the development of artificial intelligence systems (Huriye, 2023). Collaboration with researchers from different countries should be established and the establishment of global, common ethical standards should be supported. Priority should be given to completing GenAI-related work in a socially sensitive and responsible manner.

RECOMMENDATIONS FOR EDUCATORS

For AI to be used in compliance with ethical principles, students' awareness of issues such as plagiarism and honesty in academic writing should be increased through education. When developing teaching materials, rules and guidelines for the efficient and ethical use of AI resources should be clearly stated. Educators can ask students for drafts of their assignments to identify AI-generated content, and they can also give students the chance to receive insightful critiques. Details should be provided regarding the availability and implementation of tools that manage the human authoring of the work. Students should be inspired to become responsible technology users, using AI technologies as a guide, by emphasizing the moral and ethical aspects of technology use. To hold them accountable for their actions regarding the use of AI applications and to preserve the originality of their work, teachers may ask students to prepare a written statement (Cotton et al., 2023). Instructors can carry out different teaching methods and assessment activities together. It is recommended to conduct research on GenAI applications in online learning and research communities (Gökçearslan, 2013).

RECOMMENDATIONS FOR STUDENTS

Conversational AI systems can be used as a tool to support students' education and academic writing, and students can connect with researchers and educators working on AI ethics to learn about current ethics and studies in this field (Crawford et al., 2023). It is possible to participate in research and communities for the problematic use of AI technologies and, if desired, to create communities.

RECOMMENDATIONS FOR TECHNOLOGY DEVELOPERS

When framing and regulating AI systems, it is important to consider ethical issues based on human rights and social responsibilities (Miao, 2019). AI systems should first be developed taking human rights into account, and in this context, services should be ensured to be inclusive and equitable. To address user concerns in AI applications, applications should be built based on auditing mechanisms that support accountability, transparency, and ethical considerations based on data security and privacy. AI systems should be designed with social norms and preferences in mind, and users of AI systems should be able to access the inner workings of the algorithms as transparently as possible. To develop chatbots based on artificial intelligence within an ethical framework, interdisciplinary cooperation is essential (Pflanzer et al., 2022).

RECOMMENDATIONS FOR POLICYMAKERS

Emphasis should be placed on creating policies with a global approach that is sensitive to human rights and international law. An interdisciplinary approach should be adopted regarding AI ethics and legal regulations should be regulated in line with ethical principles. To prevent discussions on the lack of transparency in AI technologies from creating prejudice in society for AI systems, legislative regulatory measures should be taken (Ayling & Chapman, 2022). While creating ethical frameworks on AI ethics, legal regulations should be developed in cooperation with experts (Kazim & Koshiyama, 2021). Policymakers should also establish data management systems that will ensure that measures are taken to protect the sensitive data of society, take necessary precautions against situations that may violate data security and privacy, and draw attention to the importance of gender equality by emphasizing gender biases in AI systems (UNESCO, 2023).

REFERENCES

Albus, J. S. (1991). Outline for a theory of intelligence. *IEEE Transactions on Systems, Man, and Cybernetics*, *21*(3), 473–509. doi:10.1109/21.97471

Ali, M. (2018). The Human Intelligence vs. Artificial Intelligence: Issues and Challenges in Computer Assisted Language Learning. *International Journal of English Linguistics*, *8*(5), 259. doi:10.5539/ijel.v8n5p259

Ashford, T. (2020). App-centric students and academic integrity: A proposal for assembling socio-technical responsibility. *Journal of Academic Ethics*, *19*(1), 35–48. doi:10.1007/s10805-020-09387-w

Ayling, J., & Chapman, A. (2022). Putting AI ethics to work: Are the tools fit for purpose? *AI and Ethics*, *2*(3), 405–429. doi:10.1007/s43681-021-00084-x

Bakiner, O. (2023). What do academics say about artificial intelligence ethics? An overview of the scholarship. *AI and Ethics*, *3*(2), 513–525. doi:10.1007/s43681-022-00182-4

Benjamins, R., & Salazar, I. (2020). Towards a framework for understanding societal and ethical implications of Artificial Intelligence. In Dykinson eBooks (pp. 89–100). doi:10.2307/j.ctv153k50r.8

Berezin, J. (2023). *Using generative AI for your scientific writing? Be Aware of Journal Policies*. MIT. https://mitcommlab.mit.edu/cee/2023/08/27/using-generative-ai-for-your-scientific-writing-be-aware-of-journal-policies/

Birks, M., Mills, J., Allen, S., & Tee, S. (2020). Managing the mutations: Academic misconduct in Australia, New Zealand, and the UK. *International Journal for Educational Integrity*, *16*(1), 1–15. doi:10.1007/s40979-020-00055-5

Bubaš, G., & Čižmešija, A. (2023, May 1). A critical analysis of students' cheating in online assessment in higher education: Post-COVID-19 Issues and challenges related to conversational artificial intelligence. *IEEE Xplore*. IEEE. doi:10.23919/MIPRO57284.2023.10159826

Burton, E., Goldsmith, J., Koenig, S., Kuipers, B., Mattei, N., & Walsh, T. (2017). Ethical considerations in artificial intelligence courses. *AI Magazine*, *38*(2), 22–34. doi:10.1609/aimag.v38i2.2731

Campolo, A., Sanfilippo, M. R., Whittaker, M., & Crawford, K. (2017). *AI Now 2017 Report*. AI Now Institute at New York University. https://ainowinstitute.org/AI_Now_2017_Report.pdf

Castelvecchi, D. (2016). Can we open the black box of AI? *Nature*, *538*(7623), 20–23. doi:10.1038/538020a PMID:27708329

Chan, C.K. (2023). Is AI changing the rules of academic misconduct? An In-depth look at students' perceptions of 'AI-giarism'. *ArXiv, abs/2306.03358.*

Chen, L., Chen, P., & Lin, Z. (2020). Artificial intelligence in education: A review. *IEEE Access, 8*(2169-3536), 75264–75278. doi:10.1109/ACCESS.2020.2988510

Cingillioğlu, I. (2023). Detecting AI-generated essays: The ChatGPT challenge. *The International Journal of Information and Learning Technology*, *40*(3), 259–268. doi:10.1108/IJILT-03-2023-0043

Clarke, M. (2023). *Australian framework for generative artificial intelligence (AI) in schools - separtment of education, Australian government*. Department of education. https://www.education.gov.au/schooling/resources/australian-framework-generative-artificial-intelligence-ai-schools

Colom, R., Karama, S., Jung, R., & Haier, R. (2010). Human intelligence and brain networks. *Neurocircuitry of Cognition, Emotion, and Behavior*, *12*(4), 489–501. doi:10.31887/DCNS.2010.12.4/rcolom PMID:21319494

Corrêa, N. K., Galvão, C. B., Santos, J. W., Pino, C. D., Pinto, E. P., Barbosa, C., Massmann, D., Mambrini, R., Galvao, L., & Terem, E. (2022). Worldwide AI ethics: A review of 200 guidelines and recommendations for AI governance. *Patterns (New York, N.Y.)*, *4*(10), 100857. doi:10.1016/j.patter.2023.100857 PMID:37876898

Cotton, D. R. E., Cotton, P. A., & Shipway, J. R. (2023). Chatting and cheating: Ensuring academic integrity in the era of ChatGPT. *Innovations in Education and Teaching International*, 1–12. doi:10.1080/14703297.2023.2190148

Crawford, J., Cowling, M., & Allen, K.-A. (2023). Leadership is needed for ethical ChatGPT: Character, assessment, and learning using artificial intelligence (AI). *Journal of University Teaching & Learning Practice*, *20*(3). doi:10.53761/1.20.3.02

Dignum, V. (2021). The role and challenges of education for responsible AI. *London Review of Education*, *19*(1). doi:10.14324/LRE.19.1.01

Dilmaghani, S., Brust, M. R., Danoy, G., Cassagnes, N., Pecero, J., & Bouvry, P. (2019, December 1). *Privacy and Security of Big Data in AI Systems: A Research and Standards Perspective*. IEEE Xplore. doi:10.1109/BigData47090.2019.9006283

Dyulicheva, Y. Y., & Glazieva, A. O. (2022). Game based learning with artificial intelligence and immersive technologies: An overview. *CEUR Workshop Proceedings*, *3077*, 146–159.

Elkhatat, A. M. (2023). Evaluating the authenticity of ChatGPT responses: A study on text-matching capabilities. *International Journal for Educational Integrity*, *19*(1), 15. doi:10.1007/s40979-023-00137-0

Etzioni, A., & Etzioni, O. (2016). AI assisted ethics. *Ethics and Information Technology*, *18*(2), 149–156. doi:10.1007/s10676-016-9400-6

Filip, F. G. (2021, May). AI vs AI (augmenting [human] intellect vs artificial intelligence): Plenary talk. In *2021 IEEE 15th International Symposium on Applied Computational Intelligence and Informatics (SACI)* (pp. 000011-000012). IEEE.

GaumannN.VealeM. (2023, September 7). AI providers as criminal essay mills? Large language models meet contract cheating law. doi:10.31235/osf.io/cpbfd

Gilliard, C., & Rorabaugh, P. (2023, February 3). *You're not Going to like How colleges respond to ChatGPT*. https://slate.com/technology/2023/02/chat-gpt-cheating-college-ai-detection.html

Gökçearslan, Ş. (2013). Development of online learning community feeling scale: Validity and reliability study. *Turkish Librarianship*, *27*(1), 154–165.

Gokcearslan, S., Tosun, C., & Erdemir, Z. G. (2024). Benefits, challenges, and methods of artificial intelligence (AI) chatbots in education: A systematic literature review. [IJTE]. *International Journal of Technology in Education*, *7*(1), 19–39. doi:10.46328/ijte.600

Green, B. P. (2018). Ethical reflections on artificial intelligence. *Scientia et Fides*, *6*(2), 9–31. doi:10.12775/SetF.2018.015

Greene, D., Hoffmann, A. L., & Stark, L. (2019). Better, nicer, clearer, fairer: A critical assessment of the movement for ethical artificial intelligence and machine learning. *Proceedings of the 52nd Hawaii International Conference on System Sciences*. IEEE. 10.24251/HICSS.2019.258

Gupta, A., & Mishra, M. (2022). Ethical concerns while using artificial intelligence in recruitment of employees. *Business Ethics and Leadership*, *6*(2), 6–11. doi:10.21272/bel.6(2).6-11.2022

Hagerty, A., & Rubinov, I. (2019). Global AI ethics: A review of the social impacts and ethical implications of artificial intelligence. *ArXiv, abs/1907.07892*.

Högberg, R. (2011). Cheating as subversive and strategic resistance: Vocational students' resistance and conformity towards academic subjects in a Swedish upper secondary school. *Ethnography and Education*, *6*(3), 341–355. doi:10.1080/17457823.2011.610584

Huang, C., Zhang, Z., Mao, B., & Yao, X. (2022). An overview of artificial intelligence ethics. *IEEE Transactions on Artificial Intelligence*, *4*(4), 1–21. doi:10.1109/TAI.2022.3194503

Huang, J., Shen, G., & Ren, X. (2021). Connotation analysis and paradigm shift of teaching design under artificial intelligence technology. [iJET]. *International Journal of Emerging Technologies in Learning*, *16*(5), 73–86. doi:10.3991/ijet.v16i05.20287

Hung, J., & Chen, J. (2023). The benefits, risks and regulation of using ChatGPT in Chinese academia: A content analysis. *Social Sciences (Basel, Switzerland)*, *12*(7), 380. doi:10.3390/socsci12070380

Huriye, A. (2023). The ethics of artificial intelligence: Examining the ethical considerations surrounding the development and use of AI. *American Journal of Technology*, *2*(1), 37–45. doi:10.58425/ajt.v2i1.142

Kasap, A. B., Eşkil, K. G., Çetinkaya, K. B., Yeşilyurt, H., İnan, S. A., Vatankhahi, A., & Gökçearslan, Ş. (2021). A study on the use of technology in scientific research and ethical competencies of graduate students. *Instructional Technology and Lifelong Learning*, *2*(1), 35–52. doi:10.52911/itall.873802

Kazim, E., & Koshiyama, A. S. (2021). A high-level overview of AI ethics. *Patterns (New York, N.Y.)*, *2*(9), 100314. doi:10.1016/j.patter.2021.100314 PMID:34553166

Kooli, C., & Al Muftah, H. (2022). Artificial intelligence in healthcare: A comprehensive review of its ethical concerns. *Technological Sustainability*, *1*(2), 121–131. doi:10.1108/TECHS-12-2021-0029

Lang, J. M., Berry, R. M., Queen, E. L., Kinlaw, K., Newstetter, W. C., & Wolf, L. E. (2013). Cheating lessons: Learning from academic dishonesty. *Journal of Engineering Education*, 38.

Lee, J. Y. (2023). Can an artificial intelligence chatbot be the author of a scholarly article? *Journal of Educational Evaluation for Health Professions*, *20*, 6. Advance online publication. doi:10.3352/jeehp.2023.20.6 PMID:36842449

Leung, M. (2023, September 1). *Draft law sets out penalties for AI-aided academic writing*. University World News. https://www.universityworldnews.com/post.php?story=20230901111126325

Liebrenz, M., Schleifer, R., Buadze, A., Bhugra, D., & Smith, A. (2023). Generating scholarly content with ChatGPT: Ethical challenges for medical publishing. *The Lancet. Digital Health*, *5*(3), e105–e106. doi:10.1016/S2589-7500(23)00019-5 PMID:36754725

Lim, T., Gottipati, S., & Cheong, M. (2023). Artificial intelligence in today's education Landscape: Understanding and managing ethical issues for educational assessment. 16 March 2023, PREPRINT (Version 1) available at Research Square. doi:10.21203/rs.3.rs-2696273/v1

MEB. (2023). *Artificial intelligence training for 50 thousand students with the "FEYZA" project.* MBE. https://www.meb.gov.tr/feyza-projesi-ile-50-bin-ogrenciye-yapay-zek-egitimi/haber/31604/tr

Miao, F., & Holmes, W. (2023). *Guidance for generative AI in education and research.* UNESCO. https://unesdoc.unesco.org/notice?id=p:usmarcdef_0000386693

Miao, Z. (2019). Investigation on human rights ethics in artificial intelligence researches with library literature analysis method. *The Electronic Library*, *37*(5), 914–926. doi:10.1108/EL-04-2019-0089

Mika, N., Nadezhda, G., Jaana, L., & Raija, K. (2019). Ethical AI for the governance of the society: Challenges and opportunities. *CEUR Workshop Proceedings*, *2505*, 20–26.

Mohammadzadeh, Z., Ausloos, M., & Saeidnia, H. R. (2023). ChatGPT: High-tech plagiarism awaits academic publishing green light. Non-fungible token (NFT) can be a way out. *Library Hi Tech News*, *40*(7), 12–14. doi:10.1108/LHTN-04-2023-0067

Mondal, B. (2019). Artificial intelligence: State of the art. *Intelligent Systems Reference Library*, *172*, 389–425. doi:10.1007/978-3-030-32644-9_32

Murdock, T. B., & Anderman, E. M. (2006). Motivational perspectives on student cheating: Toward an integrated model of academic aishonesty. *Educational Psychologist*, *41*(3), 12–145. doi:10.1207/s15326985ep4103_1

Murphy, K., Di Ruggiero, E., Upshur, R., Willison, D. J., Malhotra, N., Cai, J. C., Malhotra, N., Lui, V., & Gibson, J. (2021). Artificial intelligence for good health: A scoping review of the ethics literature. *BMC Medical Ethics*, *22*(1), 14. doi:10.1186/s12910-021-00577-8 PMID:33588803

Oravec, J. A. (2022). AI, biometric analysis, and emerging cheating detection systems: The engineering of academic integrity? *Education Policy Analysis Archives*, *30*. doi:10.14507/epaa.30.5765

Oravec, J. A. (2023). Artificial Intelligence implications for academic cheating: Expanding the dimensions of responsible human-AI collaboration with ChatGPT. *Journal of Interactive Learning Research*, *34*(2), 213–237.

Oritsegbemi, O. (2023). Human intelligence versus AI: Implications for emotional aspects of human communication. *Journal of Advanced Research in Social Sciences*, *6*(2), 76–85. doi:10.33422/jarss.v6i2.1005

Pflanzer, M., Traylor, Z., Lyons, J. B., Dubljević, V., & Nam, C. S. (2023). Ethics in human–AI teaming: Principles and perspectives. *AI and Ethics*, *3*(3), 917–935. doi:10.1007/s43681-022-00214-z

Russel Group. (2023, July 5). *New principles on use of AI in education*. The Russell Group. https://russellgroup.ac.uk/news/new-principles-on-use-of-ai-in-education/

Ryan, M. (2020). In AI we trust: Ethics, artificial intelligence, and reliability. *Science and Engineering Ethics*, *26*(5), 2749–2767. doi:10.1007/s11948-020-00228-y PMID:32524425

Ryznar, M. (2023). Exams in the time of ChatGPT. *Washington and Lee Law Review Online*, *80*(5), 305–322. doi:10.2139/ssrn.3684958

Schlagwein, D., & Willcocks, L. P. (2023). 'ChatGPT et al.': The ethics of using (generative) artificial intelligence in research and science. *Journal of Information Technology*, *38*(3), 232–238. doi:10.1177/02683962231200411

Shcherbakov, G. A. (2023, May). "Artificial Intelligence" Vs "Human Intelligence": a New Ethics of Technological Development. In *2023 XXVI International Conference on Soft Computing and Measurements (SCM)* (pp. 163-166). IEEE. 10.1109/SCM58628.2023.10159110

Sintov, N., Kar, D., Nguyen, T., Fang, F., Hoffman, K., Lyet, A., & Tambe, M. (2016, March). From the lab to the classroom and beyond: Extending a game-based research platform for teaching AI to diverse audiences. *Proceedings of the AAAI Conference on Artificial Intelligence*, *30*(1). doi:10.1609/aaai.v30i1.9854

Surahman, E., & Wang, T. (2022). Academic dishonesty and trustworthy assessment in online learning: A systematic literature review. *Journal of Computer Assisted Learning*, *38*(6), 1535–1553. doi:10.1111/jcal.12708

Szabó, A., & Underwood, J. (2004). Cybercheats. *Active Learning in Higher Education*, *5*(2), 180–199. doi:10.1177/1469787404043815

UNESCO. (2023). *UNESCO's recommendation on the ethics of artificial intelligence: Key facts*. UNESCO. https://unesdoc.unesco.org/notice?id=p:usmarcdef_0000385082

Waelen, R. (2022). Why AI ethics is a critical theory. *Philosophy & Technology*, *35*(1), 9. doi:10.1007/s13347-022-00507-5

Witmer, L. (1922). What is intelligence and who has it? *The Scientific Monthly*, *15*(1), 57–67.

Xiao, Y., Chatterjee, S., & Gehringer, E. (2022, November 1). *A new era of plagiarism the danger of cheating using AI*. IEEE Xplore. doi:10.1109/ITHET56107.2022.10031827

Zatarain, J. M. N. (2017). The role of automated technology in the creation of copyright works: The challenges of artificial intelligence. *International Review of Law Computers & Technology*, *31*(1), 91–104. doi:10.1080/13600869.2017.1275273

KEY TERMS AND DEFINITIONS

Academic Integrity: Ethical behaviors expected from all the individuals in an educational environment such as honesty, fairness, and responsibility.

AI Chatbot: AI supported computer programs that can have text-based conversations with users.

AI Ethics: Set of rules or guidelines that govern AI tools from their development to their use.

AI: Computer systems that can do tasks that are usually done by humans and require human intelligence.

Cheating: Dishonest or unethical actions done by a student or an academic to complete tasks or exams such as copying from another source or getting unauthorized help.

GenAI: A class of artificial intelligence systems that can generate new and original content based on the data they have trained on, usually by learning patterns.

Plagiarism With AI: Using AI tools to generate content and presenting it as original work.

Chapter 10
Exploring the Ethical Principles for the Implementation of Artificial Intelligence in Education: Towards a Future Agenda

Dilek Şenocak
https://orcid.org/0000-0002-5966-1976
Anadolu University, Turkey

Aras Bozkurt
https://orcid.org/0000-0002-4520-642X
Anadolu University, Turkey

Serpil Koçdar
Anadolu University, Turkey

ABSTRACT

The purpose of this study is to examine the international AI guidelines specific to education through a scoping review and a content analysis approach. To achieve this purpose, nine international AI guideline documents which include the ethics of AI in education were analyzed and, as a result, researchers identified a total of 82 keywords and 12 principles. The findings of the study indicate that some of the ethical principles—namely, transparency; diversity and equity; accountability; privacy and data protection; security and safety; sustainability and societal well-being; democratic participation in education policy planning and AI practices; empowerment of teachers and teaching; and empowerment of learners and learning—are being accepted and adopted globally in these nine international AIED guidelines. The three ethical principles (i.e., autonomy, ethical design, and commercialization), however, were not emphasized in all the documents addressed. The results of the study are expected to provide valuable knowledge on how to use AI in education ethically and responsibly.

DOI: 10.4018/979-8-3693-1351-0.ch010

INTRODUCTION

Defining the concept of AI precisely is challenging since it has a very dynamic nature evolving in line with the ongoing technological advancements and, therefore, its definition needs to be adaptable to contemporary technological progress. In its simplest sense, McCarthy (2007, p.2) defines AI as "the science and engineering of making intelligent machines, especially intelligent computer programs". OECD (2019, p. 7), on the other hand, describes it as "machine-based systems that can, for a given set of human-defined objectives, make predictions, recommendations, or decisions that influence real or virtual environments".

In the recent past, more specifically following the first decade of 2000s, AI has become a seamless aspect of our daily lives, frequently in the fields of healthcare, agriculture, financial services, marketing, and entertainment, and particularly has triggered the digital transformation in the education industry (Quy et al., 2023). With its affordances it has the potential to levigate teaching and learning practices and make the obstacles in education easier to overcome. Many AI in Education (AIED) tools aim to augment educators and learners by increasing access to education, enabling lifelong learning opportunities, adaptive and continuous assessment, fostering collaborative learning, providing instant personalized feedback, and automating a variety of tasks, including administrative duties, feedback delivery, and evaluating learners' papers (Baker, 2021; Chen et al., 2020; Holmes et al., 2019). Additionally, in a systematic review study investigating the impacts of AI on online higher education, it is stated that the implications of AI technologies in online education have produced favorable outcomes such as enhanced academic achievements, and an increase in online engagement and participation (Ouyang et al., 2022). It is, however, critical to bear in mind that not all the effects of technology are pleasant, and this rule also applies to AI.

The use of AI empowered technologies has raised several concerns that should be taken seriously. These common risks and concerns include but are not limited to: biased outcomes, which can lead to discrimination, inequality, social and economic injustices; the lack of transparency and comprehension of the operations of AI algorithms, which can affect democracy, and fundamental human rights and values; invasion of privacy, which could be taken as a threat to human dignity; insufficient safety and security precautions, which can give rise to cyberattacks and data breaches (Cheatham et al., 2019; UNESCO, 2021). Along with the previously mentioned issues, AI within educational settings has brought up new concerns regarding the selection of pedagogical approaches employed by AI enabled tools, the effect of AI and learning analytics on educators' decision-making processes, the changing role of educators, accessibility of education, and learning objectives (Holmes et al., 2022a). Addressing all these aforementioned issues is crucial to successfully employ AI in the context of education. That said, ongoing research with democratic collaboration between innovators, educators, policymakers, engineers, and software vendors and building policies and guidelines concerning the ethical implications of AIED are necessary. In their systematic review study, which included 146 articles on AI applications in higher education, Zawacki-Richter et al. (2019), however, highlighted the considerable lack of studies concerning potential risks and challenges associated with the use of AIED and the urgent need for further extensive studies on ethical issues. Therefore, in this study, a contemporary further exploration of ethical principles of AIED was made as an attempt to fill a gap in the literature.

In view of this gap, international guidelines, and policy reports on the ethics of (trustworthy) AI were published by public sector organizations such as UNESCO (2021), the European Commission (2019), OECD (2019), IEEE (2019); private companies (e.g., IBM, 2022; Sony, 2018) and research institutions (e.g., Icelandic Institute for Intelligent Machines, 2015; Rathenau Instituut, 2017). Jobin et al. (2019, p.389) synthesized 84 guidelines and principles including some of the documents above and noted that there is an international alignment around five ethical principles, which are "transparency, justice and fairness, non-maleficence, responsibility and privacy". While all these agreed upon principles in the relevant documents are applicable within educational settings, much deeper analysis is needed to see how the use of AI and the ethical principles should be applied in education, and whether there is a global consensus around any of the ethical principles of AIED. To this end, the aim of this study is to examine the commonly referred nine international AI guidelines specific to education, namely *Guidance for Generative AI in Education and Research* (Miao & Holmes, 2023), *ChatGPT and Artificial Intelligence in Higher Education: Quick Start Guide* (Sabzalieva & Valentini, 2023), *Ethical Guidelines on the Use of Artificial Intelligence and Data in Teaching and Learning for Educators* (European Commission, 2022), *Artificial Intelligence and Education: A Critical View Through The Lens of Human Rights, Democracy and the Rule of Law* (Holmes et al., 2022b), *The Ethical Framework for AI in Education* (The Institute for Ethical AI in Education, 2021), *AI and Education: Guidance for Policy-makers* (Miao et al., 2021), *Trustworthy AI in Education: Promises and Challenges* (OECD, 2020), *Artificial Intelligence in Education: Challenges and Opportunities for Sustainable Development* (Pedro et al., 2019), and *Beijing Consensus on Artificial Intelligence and Education* (UNESCO, 2019). Compared to similar studies (e.g., Adams et al., 2023; Chan, 2023; Nguyen et al., 2023; Schiff, 2022), the current study specifically evaluates and synthesizes the international guidelines and/or policies whose primary emphasis is on AIED, which is explicitly mentioned in the titles of the relevant documents. With this feature, the present study is expected to contribute to keeping the relevant literature up to date.

METHODOLOGY

In the current study, international guidelines whose focus is solely AIED were explored and analyzed by conducting a scoping review, which can be performed to pinpoint and investigate fundemantal features or factors linked to a specific concept (Munn et al., 2018). Since the aim of the present study is to identify and examine whether there is an agreement upon any ethical principles associated with AIED, performing a scoping review could be considered the best method for the study. In this sense, an online search based on keywords was conducted through google search engine, and also bibliographies and suggested reading sections of AI international guidelines and reports were examined manually. The following keywords, inclusion and exclusion criteria were used to determine the relevant documents (see Table 1).

Based on the initial search string, and subsequently applied inclusion, and exclusion criteria,nine international guidelines on AIED were selected to examine (see Table 2).

To interpret whether there is a global consensus around any of the ethical principles of AIED, each relevant document was analyzed manually by conducting a qualitative content analysis approach (Forman & Damschroder, 2008). Content analysis, a method which enables the researchers to analyze a variety of data types, can help researchers categorize phenomena or events to better analyze and comprehend them (Harwood & Garry, 2003). Considering the related literature, two researchers first went over one of the pertinent nine international guidelines to create a preliminary list of codes individually. Subsequently, they met to review, add, or remove codes. After producing and agreeing on the initial list, they individually read and coded all the other documents, added new codes, and discussed discrepancies with the third researcher if necessary. Following the coding procedure, tentative themes were identified, then discussed and improved by considering each researchers' view. A total of 82 codes (i.e., keywords) and 12 themes (i.e., principles) were developed as a result (see Figure 1). In Figure 1, red indicates that the ethical principle listed in the table is not included in the document. On the other hand, green denotes that the ethical principle from the table is present in the document. Additionally, the letter p. or pp. stands for the page of the document on which the ethical principle and/or related code is mentioned.

Table 1. Search string and inclusion/exclusion criteria

Keywords (and/or)	Inclusion criteria	Exclusion criteria
"Artificial intelligence", "AI", "artificial intelligence in education", "AIED", "education", "teaching and learning", "guidance", "guidelines", "ethics", "ethical guidelines", "ethical principles"	-in English -keywords "artificial intelligent" and "education" or "teaching and learning" explicitly mentioned in the title -issued by an academic institution or an international organization/association -make reference to international context	-not in English -not explicitly mentioned "artificial intelligence" and "education" or "teaching and learning" in the title -issued by private sector - a journal article, a conference paper, or a book -general documents on AI or ethics of AI -solely make reference to national context

Table 2. Name of the selected international guidelines

1. Guidance for generative AI in education and research (Miao & Holmes, 2023)
2. ChatGPT and artificial intelligence in higher education: Quick start guide (Sabzalieva & Valentini, 2023)
3. Ethical guidelines on the use of artificial intelligence and data in teaching and learning for educators (European Commission, 2022)
4. Artificial intelligence and education: A critical view through the lens of human rights, democracy, and the rule of law. (Holmes et al., 2022b)
5. The ethical framework for AI in education (The Institute for Ethical AI in Education, 2021)
6. AI and education: Guidance for policy-makers (Miao et al., 2021)
7. Trustworthy AI in education: Promises and challenges (OECD, 2020)
8. Artificial intelligence in education: challenges and opportunities for sustainable development (Pedro et al., 2019)
9. Beijing consensus on artificial intelligence and education (UNESCO, 2019).

FINDINGS AND DISCUSSION

In the present study, researchers analyzed nine international AIED guidelines, one of which was issued by an academic institution and the others by international organizations and associations. They have all been published as of 2019, which may indicate a rising interest in recent years based on the inevitable collaboration between AI and education, and the need to revisit the opportunities, risks and concerns that come with it. Researchers identified a total of 82 keywords and 12 principles (see Figure 1), but not all of them appear under the same name in all relevant documents. "Right not to suffer from discrimination" (Holmes et al., 2022b); for instance, refers to the principle of "diversity and equity" in the recent study. Moreover, the related guidelines may not necessarily have a principle section where the relevant principles are explicitly stated, in which case the researchers built the principle using keywords scattered throughout the document considering the literature and the initial list of codes.

The results of the study also show that while 9 ethical principles (i.e., "transparency, diversity and equity, accountability, privacy and data protection, security and safety, sustainability and societal well-being, democratic participation in education policy planning and AI practices, empowerment of teachers and teaching, empowerment of learners and learning") are recognized and embraced by these nine international AIED guidelines, to our knowledge, ethical principles such as "autonomy, ethical design and commercialization" were not highlighted in all the documents examined. These findings bring us to the conclusion that in general, there is a global consensus regarding the ethical principles of AIED, and yet more emphasis should be placed on the three ethical principles mentioned above.

Additionally, the findings of the study are in line with the previous studies that examined ethical principles in AI guidelines (Adams et al., 2023; Hagendorff, 2020; Jobin et al., 2019; Nguyen et al., 2023). For instance, in a study that examined AI ethics guidelines with an emphasis on children and K-12 education, Adams et al. (2023) used Jobin et al.'s (2019) classification and identified four new ethics principles (i.e., pedagogical appropriateness, children's rights, AI literacy, teacher well-being) specific to K-12 education. These four principles with the keywords were mostly addressed under the principles of "empowerment of teachers/learners and teaching/learning" in this study. Zhang and Wildemuth (2009, p. 1) states that qualitative analysis of content enables researchers to comprehend the reality "in a subjective but scientific manner" and supported it with a beautiful saying of Pablo Picasso, "if there were only one truth, you couldn't paint a hundred canvases on the same theme", which refers to the flexible nature of qualitative studies and indicates that researchers can interpret similar contents with subtle nuances as in the researchers' case. Following is a short discussion of 12 ethics principles that are identified in this study (See Figure 1).

Transparency: Transparency plays a critical role for all interested parties in understanding AIED systems, establishing trust in them and enabling their users to make rational decisions (Liao et al., 2020; OECD, 2019). The process of how machine learning (ML) in AIED tools reach a particular decision is frequently unknown, which is a big concern in terms of transparency and explainability (Holmes et al., 2022b; Miao & Holmes, 2023). Commercial AIED companies should, therefore, explicitly disclose whether any trade-offs have been made during the development of the system and if so, provide a rationale of the decision (The Institute for Ethical AI in Education, 2021). Besides, AIED systems should allow its users to comprehend how they are being applied, whether the learners are directly interacting with these systems, what factors influence the decisions they make, whether appropriate safeguards are taken and in instances involving significant risks whether relevant datasets and codes will be shared with stakeholders (UNESCO, 2021). Hence, learners, educators, parents, institutions and all the other interested parties can decide whether to use AIED tools and at what point to integrate them into the learning or teaching process.

Diversity and equity: Trustworthy AI systems should be fair, inclusive, and non-discriminatory (Miao & Holmes, 2023; Varona & Suarez, 2022), which is also valid for the use of AIED. ChatGPT, for instance, can easily acquire cognitive bias as it obtains information from big data on the internet or like the other AIED enabled tools, it may generate and share content that include bias such as racial, gender, socio-economical, historic, or algorithmic (Sabzalieva & Valentini, 2023). Moreover, not every learner or educator is able to access to these tools equally due to governmental regulations, limited internet access, or insufficient infrastructure, which may lead to digital and therefore, educational divide (Miao et al., 2021). Keeping all these concerns in mind, it is noted that AIED enabled tools should be accessible to every learner, respect their differences and backgrounds, suit their learning needs, ensure that they will not cause any discrimination between now and then, and in case of any discrimination, the system must detect and eradicate it timely.

Figure 1. Evaluation of the AIED documents with regard to ethical principles

Ethical Principles for AIED	Keywords	Title of the international documents on AI and education								
		Guidance for Generative AI in Education and Research	ChatGPT and Artificial Intelligence in Higher Education	Ethical Guidelines on the Use of Artificial Intelligence (AI) and Data in Teaching and Learning for Educators	Artificial Intelligence and Education: A critical view through the lens of human rights, democracy, and the rule of law	The Ethical Framework for AI in Education	AI and education: Guidance for policy-makers	Trustworthy AI in Education: Promises and Challenges	Artificial Intelligence in Education: Challenges and Opportunities for Sustainable Development	Beijing Consensus on Artificial Intelligence and Education
		Issuer, Authors & Publication Date								
		UNESCO - Miao & Holmes, 2023	UNESCO - Sabzalieva & Valentini, 2023	European Commission, 2022	Council of Europe - Holmes et al., 2022b	The Institute for Ethical AI in Education, 2021	UNESCO - Miao et al., 2021	OECD, 2020	UNESCO - Pedro et al., 2019	UNESCO, 2019
Transparency	Transparency, explainability, communication, interaction, traceability, opaqueness, understandability, comprehensibility, responsible disclosure, trade-offs.	(pp. 15, 22)	(p. 14)	(p. 18)	(p. 56)	(p. 9)	(pp. 31, 32, 33)	(pp. 9, 10)	(p. 32)	(p. 8)
Diversity and equity	Diversity, equity, (non) discrimination, (non)bias (e.g., racial, gender, socio-economical, cognitive, age, historic, ethnic, or cultural, algorithmic, towards students with special needs), fairness, justice, inclusion, (in)equality, accessibility, digital divide, educational and/or gender gap.	(pp. 17, 24)	(p. 11)	(p. 18)	(pp. 53, 54)	(p. 7)	(pp. 20, 25, 33)	(p. 10)	(p. 28)	(p. 8)
Accountability	Accountability, responsibility, liability, auditability, redress.	(p. 22)	(p. 14)	(p. 19)	(pp. 37, 42, 44, 66)	(p. 9)	(pp. 31, 32, 33)	(p. 10)	(p. 33)	(p. 8)
Privacy & data protection	Privacy, data protection, personal information, sensitive/personal data, surveillance, the legitimate use of data, confidentiality.	(p. 21)	(p. 11)	(p. 18)	(p. 54)	(p. 8)	(pp. 32, 33)	(p. 12)	(p. 33)	(pp. 8, 9)
Security & safety	Security, safety, robustness, reliability, accuracy, safeguards, resilience to harm, cyber-attacks, data-theft, and data breaches.	(pp. 21, 22)	(p. 6)	(p. 19)	(pp. 38, 39, 40)	(p. 5)	(pp. 31, 33)	(p. 10)	(p. 33)	(pp. 8, 9)
Autonomy	Autonomy, freedom of expression, consent, assent, the right to refuse any involvement with AI, learner control over their own learning, self-determination.	(pp. 15, 36)		(pp. 18, 30)	(p. 52)	(p. 7)	(pp. 34, 35)	(p. 10)	(pp. 28, 29)	
Sustainability and societal well-being	Sustainability, sustainable development, environmentally friendliness, energy and resources, societal well-being, public good, common good, society.	(p. 27)	(p. 12)	(p. 18, 20)	(pp. 18, 28, 32)	(p. 4)	(pp. 32, 37)	(p. 10)	(p. 26)	(pp. 3, 4)
Ethical design	Ethical design, universal design, non-addictive design, security-,privacy-, and ethics by design, designed to assist students with special needs.	(p. 22)		(p. 18)	(pp. 54, 75)	(pp. 7, 9)	(pp. 32, 33)	(p. 6)		(pp. 8, 9)
Democratic participation in education policy planning and AI practices	Policy / institutional planning, collaboration / consultation / partnership with a range of multi-stakeholders, democracy.	(p. 27)	(p. 13, 14)	(pp. 18, 27)	(pp. 42, 43, 63)	(p. 9)	(p. 32)	(pp. 9, 10, 13)	(p. 27)	(p. 4, 10)
Empowerment of teachers and teaching	Empowerment of teachers, empowerment of teaching, teacher supporting, protection of teacher rights, teacher training, teacher roles.	(p. 26)	(pp. 8, 9)	(pp. 13, 15)	(pp. 22, 42)	(p. 9)	(pp. 18, 27, 35)	(pp. 6, 7)	(pp. 13, 28, 29)	(p. 5)
Empowerment of learners and learning	Empowerment of learners, student supporting, children's rights, learner well-being, AI integrated curricula, lifelong learning.	(pp. 25, 26)	(pp. 8, 9)	(pp. 14, 15, 31)	(pp.20, 21, 29, 74)	(pp. 9, 13)	(pp.19, 23, 34, 35, 36)	(pp. 4, 5, 6)	(pp. 12, 18, 23)	(p. 5)
Commercialization	Commercialization, commercial purpose, commercial exploitation of data, concentration of data.	(p. 21)	(p. 11)		(pp. 25, 57, 58)		(p. 20)	(p. 12)	(p. 33)	

*The color red indicates that the ethical principle listed in the table is not included in the document. On the other hand, the color green denotes that the ethical principle from the table is present in the document.
**The letter p. or pp. stands for the page of the document on which the ethical principle is mentioned

Accountability: AI systems need to be designed and implemented in such a way that they offer clear and certain justifications for every action they take (IEEE, 2019). Within educational settings, for example, learners and other stakeholders should know who is liable for the evaluation of the learning outcomes produced by AI, who is accountable for the ultimate decision concerning the use of AI, how the efficiency and effects of AI are analyzed, who is in charge of auditing the system, minimizing the negative impacts and enabling that the data is used for the right purposes (European Commission, 2022). We may not know all the answers yet, on the other hand, as humans are the Frankenstein of AI, they are the ultimate actor who needs to have oversight of their own creature.

Privacy and data protection: AI algorithms require large datasets for their training, and the collection, storage, and use of data may result in privacy and data protection concerns (Bai et al., 2022). That is to say, the personal data of a learner becomes vulnerable to data leaks and security breaches and even initially anonymous personal data can be de-anonymised (Holmes et al., 2022b). Moreover, using emotion analytics to deduce learners' attention and emotion in the classroom is another form of digital surveillance and it urges learners to act in a proper manner, which can be labelled as invasion of privacy (Gray, 2020). Therefore, governments and/or commercial AI companies should assure that learners' data is confidential, and they are deployed legitimately. In addition, data collection processes should aim to collect a minimum amount of data for learners' benefit (Pedro et al., 2019) and they should be informed about for what purpose their data is collected and used. AIED systems should also create safe spaces where learners aren't monitored or assessed (The Institute for Ethical AI in Education, 2021) and there should be a privacy settings extension in the AIED tools that enables learners to have control over their privacy and data governance.

Security and safety: Cyber-attacks in various forms such as data poisoning, model leakage, infrastructure attack may change the data, system behavior, and cause the system to make different decisions (European Commission, 2019). In educational settings, such cases may result in unsuccessful learning experiences and even affect learners' future or present career. Therefore, AIED enabled tools should be designed and developed in a proactive manner, which means that necessary technical precautions should be taken to prevent and mitigate any kinds of harm and the system should always function as intended. Also, the system should always have a contingency plan for these kinds of hostile attacks like requesting for human control before proceeding (European Commission, 2019). There should always be continuous testing, monitoring, and evaluation processes as well, which guarantee that the system is aligned with educational purposes and safeguards learners' well-being.

Autonomy: Autonomy could be simply defined as "a person's effective capacity for self-governance" (Prunkl, 2022, p.2). In the context of education, this can imply that learners should have control over their own learning and can make decisions considering their own ideals, motives, or views, which highlights that AI systems shouldn't be the ultimate decision makers in learning environments. AI enabled adaptive learning systems, for instance, can suggest new learning pathways in accordance with the learners' interests, needs and preferences (Kabudi et al., 2021). Yet, overreliance on such systems or overuse them may lead to "manipulation, loss of freedom, loss of opportunities, or loss of competence" (Prunkl, 2022, p. 3). Therefore, formed consent should be gathered from learners, parents, or legal guardians after informing them about potential benefits and risks of using AI inside and outside the classroom. Besides, learners should be able to opt out if they don't want to interact with AI systems and these systems should be designed with a human-centric approach, which means they should never manipulate or mislead them.

Sustainability and societal well-being: Strubell et al. (2019) highlighted that developing and training some deep learning models is a challenging and expensive pursuit in terms of both financial resources, such as electricity and hardware costs, or cloud computing time, and environmental impact (i.e., carbon footprint associated with powering the hardware). They, for instance, summarized the situation as follows: while training a deep learning model emits about 600,000 pounds of CO_2, a car's lifetime carbon footprint is 120, 000. Therefore, AI companies should set sustainable and achievable objectives regarding preventing climate change and harm to the environment caused by AI implementations, and eco-friendly methods for producing energy and resources for AI should be encouraged (Miao et al., 2021). Additionally, all stakeholders should encourage positive outcomes of AI systems including promoting economic growth, and sustainable development of societies, and overall well-being (OECD, 2020).

Ethical design: AIED systems should be developed by experts who are aware of the consequences of the deployment of these systems, and they should be trained in the ethical considerations of it (The Institute for Ethical AI in Education, 2021). Besides, AIED systems should adopt privacy and security by design approaches. That is to say, privacy and data protection principles and cybersecurity should be seamlessly embedded into these systems during their initial design phase as a proactive measure (D'aquin et al., 2018; Pescador & Mohanty, 2022). In this way, AIED suppliers can assure that even if learners change nothing about their privacy settings, AIED applications safeguard their data privacy, security, and data ownership.

Democratic participation in education policy planning and AI practices: All stages of AIED planning, government, and development, including the design phase, should involve different stakeholders, such as learners, educators, and parents, as well as international and cross-sectoral cooperation. Governments, for instance, should collaborate with the private sector to innovate and grow such a complex technology since it is nearly impossible for the public sector to accomplish it on its own (Pedro et al., 2019). Moreover, creating funding for research and training of AIED experts, as well as developing AIED public policies, strategies, roadmaps, and blueprints, requires the involvement of multidisciplinary expertise, and international, national, and multistakeholder approaches (Pedro et al., 2019; UNESCO, 2019). Developed countries should also form international partnerships and develop strategies for the advancement of underdeveloped and developing countries to promote the inclusive, equal, and nondiscriminatory use of AIED on a global scale.

Empowerment of teachers and teaching: Teachers and learners should always be at the center of teaching and learning process, and teachers should never be replaced by AIED systems, instead their roles should be empowered by them. AIED enabled tools can automate a variety of tasks, including administrative duties, feedback delivery, and grading learners' papers so that teachers can save time for tasks which require more empathy and creativity, such as effective "emotional support", "classroom management", "instructional support" (Aldrup et al., 2022). This means their roles can mold into "a more facilitative, design-oriented, and personalized approach to learning" (Bozkurt & Sharma, 2023, p. v). They should receive continuous training in how to choose and integrate these intelligent systems effectively into their educational settings, and also their rights and employment conditions should be sufficiently protected (UNESCO, 2019). As a result, they can adapt to their changing roles and effectively prepare learners for the future of AIED.

Empowerment of learners and learning: Integrating AI ethics into educational curriculum is one of essential ways to encourage all interested parties to take responsibility in maximizing the benefits and minimizing the potential drawbacks that AI may bring about (Borenstein & Howard, 2021). Learners, as well as other stakeholders, should be equipped with necessary digital skills and AI literacy skills so that they can meet the changing demands of the business sector, and interpret its potential economic and social impact. Therefore, new courses and programmes on how AIED systems operate, the importance of AI ethics, and ethical design principles should be created (Miao et al., 2021). Learners should be also aware of their rights and how to safeguard their privacy and personal data in the AI era (Miao et al., 2021). AIED tools should also aim to empower learners regardless of their age, gender, disabilities, and socio-economic background through AI enabled lifelong learning opportunities that might also foster universal, fair, and equal access to education.

Commercialization: One of the serious concerns arose from the use of AIED is that a few commercial AIED companies that have personal data concentration and AI expertise will be able to control educational platform ownership and manipulate the way we learn (Pedro et al., 2019; Miao et al., 2021). These companies whose main aim might be collecting data for commercial purposes (Sabzalieva & Valentini, 2023), rarely disclose details including their systems' effectiveness or recommendation system algorithms (Holmes & Tuomi, 2022), which may lead to trustworthiness and explainability issues. Thus, we should beware against commercialization of AIED and make strict regulations prioritizing learner benefit and well-being.

CONCLUSION AND SUGGESTIONS

In this study, nine international AIED guidelines were examined to see how the use of AI and the ethical principles should be applied in education, and whether there is a global consensus around any of the ethical principles of AIED. The content analysis of these documents resulted in 82 keywords and 12 principles. Researchers stated that though certain ethical principles (i.e., transparency, diversity and equity, accountability, privacy and data protection, security and safety, sustainability, and societal well-being, democratic participation in education policy planning and AI practices, empowerment of teachers and teaching, and empowerment of learners and learning) are recognized on a global scale, others, such as autonomy, ethical design, and commercialization, should require greater consideration and focus.

One of the core factors in embracing a technology, such as AIED systems, should be trust, and therefore while designing and implementing such systems, ethical principles, including transparency, accountability, as well as the well-being of society, should be prioritized and besides that, the knowledge of its historical, philosophical, and ethical transformation (Şenocak et al., 2023) should be integrated into educational curriculum. Hence, we could embrace the ineluctable paradigm shift and augment humanity against such technologies. AI technologies are fallible and far from perfect just like their creators: humans (Bozkurt, 2023). It is, however, up to human beings to ensure their ethical implementation while keeping the well-being of humankind at the core of their design, development, and deployment. Therefore, establishing an agreement on AIED ethical principles in a global sense is of utmost importance. Along with that, further empirical studies and research should be conducted to evaluate whether these AI principles are effectively implemented in the scope of education.

COMPETING INTERESTS

The authors have no competing interests to declare.

ACKNOWLEDGMENT

This study was supported by Anadolu University Scientific Research Projects Commission under the grant number 2204E042 and SBA-2023-1852.

Some findings of this study were presented at EADTU I-HE2023 and published in proceedings as an abstract under the same title.

REFERENCES

Adams, C., Pente, P., Lemermeyer, G., & Rockwell, G. (2023). Ethical principles for artificial intelligence in K-12 education. *Computers and Education: Artificial Intelligence*, *4*, 100131. doi:10.1016/j.caeai.2023.100131

Aldrup, K., Carstensen, B., & Klusmann, U. (2022). Is empathy the key to effective teaching? A systematic review of its association with teacher-student interactions and student outcomes. *Educational Psychology Review*, *34*(3), 1177–1216. doi:10.1007/s10648-021-09649-y

Bai, J. Y., Zawacki-Richter, O., & Muskens, W. (2022). *Developing strategic scenarios for artificial intelligence applications in higher education*. In *Proceedings of the 5th International Open and Distance Learning Conference* (pp.47- 70). Eskişehir, Türkiye.

Baker, R. S. (2021). Artificial intelligence in education: Bringing it all together. In *OECD Digital Education Outlook 2021: Pushing the Frontiers with Artificial Intelligence, Blockchain and Robots* (pp. 43–54). OECD Publishing. doi:10.1787/f54ea644-

Borenstein, J., & Howard, A. (2021). Emerging challenges in AI and the need for AI ethics education. *AI and Ethics*, *1*(1), 61–65. doi:10.1007/s43681-020-00002-7

Bozkurt, A. (2023). Generative artificial intelligence (AI) powered conversational educational agents: The inevitable paradigm shift. *Asian Journal of Distance Education*, *18*(1), 198–204. doi:10.5281/zenodo.7716416

Bozkurt, A., & Sharma, R. C. (2023). Challenging the status quo and exploring the new boundaries in the age of algorithms: Reimagining the role of generative AI in distance education and online learning. *Asian Journal of Distance Education*, *18*(1), i–viii. doi:10.5281/zenodo.7755273

Chan, C. K. Y. (2023). A comprehensive AI policy education framework for university teaching and learning. *International Journal of Educational Technology in Higher Education*, *20*(38), 1–25. doi:10.1186/s41239-023-00408-3

Cheatham, B., Javanmardian, K., & Samandari, H. (2019). Confronting the risks of artificial intelligence. *McKinsey Quarterly*. https://www.mckinsey.com/capabilities/quantumblack/our-insights/confronting-the-risks-of-artificial-intelligence

Chen, L., Chen, P., & Lin, Z. (2020). Artificial intelligence in education: A review. *IEEE Access : Practical Innovations, Open Solutions*, *8*, 75264–75278. doi:10.1109/ACCESS.2020.2988510

D'aquin, M., Troullinou, P., O'Connor, N., Cullen, A., Faller, G., & Holden, L. (2018). *Towards an "ethics by design" methodology for AI research projects*. In *Proceedings of the 2018 ACM Conference on AI, Ethics, and Society* (pp.54-59). New Orleans, LA, USA. 10.1145/3278721.3278765

European Commission. (2019). *The European Commission's high-level expert group on artificial intelligence: Ethics guidelines for trustworthy AI.* The European Commission. https://digital-strategy.ec.europa.eu/en/library/ethics-guidelines-trustworthy-ai

European Commission. (2022). *Ethical guidelines on the use of artificial intelligence (AI) and data in teaching and learning for educat*ors. The European Commission. https://op.europa.eu/en/publication-detail/-/publication/d81a0d54-5348-11ed-92ed-01aa75ed71a1/language-en

Forman, J., & Damschroder, L. (2008). Qualitative content analysis. In *Empirical research for bioethics: A primer* (pp. 39–62). Emerald Group Publishing Limited. doi:10.1016/S1479-3709(07)11003-7

Gray, S. L. (2020). Artificial intelligence in schools: Towards a democratic future. *London Review of Education, 18*(2), 163–177. doi:10.14324/LRE.18.2.02

Hagendorff, T. (2020). The ethics of AI ethics: An evaluation of guidelines. *Minds and Machines, 30*(1), 99–120. doi:10.1007/s11023-020-09517-8

Harwood, T. G., & Garry, T. (2003). An overview of content analysis. *The Marketing Review, 3*(4), 479–498. doi:10.1362/146934703771910080

Holmes, W., Bialik, M., & Fadel, C. (2019). *Artificial intelligence in education: Promises and implications for teaching and learning*. Globethics Publications. doi:10.58863/20.500.12424/4276068

Holmes, W., Persson, J., Chounta, I. A., Wasson, B., & Dimitrova, V. (2022b). *Artificial intelligence and education: A critical view through the lens of human rights, democracy, and the rule of law*. Council of Europe. https://rm.coe.int/artificial-intelligence-and-education-a-critical-view-through-the-lens/1680a886bd

Holmes, W., Porayska-Pomsta, K., Holstein, K., Sutherland, E., Baker, T., Shum, S. B., Santos, O. C., Rodrigo, M. T., Cukurova, M., Bittencourt, I. I., & Koedinger, K. R. (2022a). Ethics of AI in education: Towards a community-wide framework. *International Journal of Artificial Intelligence in Education, 32*(3), 504–526. doi:10.1007/s40593-021-00239-1

Holmes, W., & Tuomi, I. (2022). State of the art and practice in AI in education. *European Journal of Education, 57*(4), 542–570. doi:10.1111/ejed.12533

IBM. (2022). *Everyday ethics for artificial intelligence*. IBM Corp. https://www.ibm.com/watson/assets/duo/pdf/everydayethics.pdf

Icelandic Institute for Intelligent Machines. (2015). *Ethics policy*. IIIM. https://www.iiim.is/ethics-policy/

IEEE. (2019). *Ethically aligned design: A vision for prioritizing human well-being with autonomous and intelligent systems*. IEEE. https://standards.ieee.org/wp-content/uploads/import/documents/other/ead_v2.pdf

Jobin, A., Ienca, M., & Vayena, E. (2019). The global landscape of AI ethics guidelines. *Nature Machine Intelligence, 1*(9), 389–399. doi:10.1038/s42256-019-0088-2

Kabudi, T., Pappas, I., & Olsen, D. H. (2021). AI enabled adaptive learning systems: A systematic mapping of the literature. *Computers and Education: Artificial Intelligence, 2*, 1–12. doi:10.1016/j.caeai.2021.100017

Liao, Q. V., Gruen, D., & Miller, S. (2020). *Questioning the AI: Informing design practices for explainable AI user experiences*. In *Proceedings of the 2020 CHI conference on human factors in computing systems* (pp. 1-15). Honolulu HI, USA.10.1145/3313831.3376590

McCarthy, J. (2007). *What is artificial intelligence?* Technical Report. Stanford University. https://www.diochnos.com/about/McCarthyWhatisAI.pdf

Miao, F., & Holmes, W. (2023). *Guidance for generative AI in education and research.* UNESCO. https://unesdoc.unesco.org/ark:/48223/pf0000386693

Miao, F., Holmes, W., Huang, R., & Zhang, H. (2021). *AI and education: Guidance for policy-makers.* UNESCO. https://unesdoc.unesco.org/ark:/48223/pf0000376709

Munn, Z., Peters, M. D. J., Stern, C., Tufanaru, C., McArthur, A., & Aromataris, E. (2018). Systematic review or scoping review? Guidance for authors when choosing between a systematic or a scoping reviewapproach. *BMC Medical Research Methodology*, *18*(1), 1–7. doi:10.1186/s12874-018-0611-x PMID:29301497

Nguyen, A., Ngo, H. N., Hong, Y., Dang, B., & Nguyen, B. P. T. (2023). Ethical principles for artificial intelligence in education. *Education and Information Technologies*, *28*(4), 4221–4241. doi:10.1007/s10639-022-11316-w PMID:36254344

OECD. (2019). *Recommendation of the council on artificial intelligence.* Organization for Economic Co-operation and Development. https://legalinstruments.oecd.org/en/instruments/OECD-LEGAL-0449

OECD. (2020). *Trustworthy AI in education: Promises and challenges.* Organization for Economic Co-operation and Development. https://www.oecd.org/education/trustworthy-artificial-intelligence-in-education.pdf

Ouyang, F., Zheng, L., & Jiao, P. (2022). Artificial intelligence in online higher education: A systematic review of empirical research from 2011 to 2020. *Education and Information Technologies*, *27*(6), 7893–7925. doi:10.1007/s10639-022-10925-9

Pedro, F., Subosa, M., Rivas, A., & Valverde, P. (2019). *Artificial intelligence in education: challenges and opportunities for sustainable development*. UNESCO. https://unesdoc.unesco.org/ark:/48223/pf0000366994

Pescador, F., & Mohanty, S. P. (2022). Guest editorial: Security by design for electronic systems. *IEEE Transactions on Consumer Electronics*, *68*(1), 2–14. doi:10.1109/TCE.2022.3147005

Prunkl, C. (2022). Human autonomy in the age of artificial intelligence. *Nature Machine Intelligence*, *4*(2), 99–101. doi:10.1038/s42256-022-00449-9

Quy, V. K., Thanh, B. T., Chehri, A., Linh, D. M., & Tuan, D. A. (2023). AI and digital transformation in higher education: Vision and approach of a specific university in Vietnam. *Sustainability (Basel)*, *15*(14), 11093. doi:10.3390/su151411093

Rathenau Instituut. (2017). *Human rights in the robot age: Challenges arising from the use of robotics, artificial intelligence, and virtual and augmented reality.* Rathenau Instituut.

Sabzalieva, E., & Valentini, A. (2023). *Chatgpt and artificial intelligence in higher education: Quick start guide.* UNESCO. https://www.iesalc.unesco.org/wp-content/uploads/2023/04/ChatGPT-and-Artificial-Intelligence-in-higher-education-Quick-Start-guide_EN_FINAL.pdf

Schiff, D. (2022). Education for AI, not AI for education: The role of education and ethics in national AI policy Strategies. *International Journal of Artificial Intelligence in Education, 32*(3), 527–563. doi:10.1007/s40593-021-00270-2

Şenocak, D., Koçdar, S., & Bozkurt, A. (2023). Historical, philosophical, and ethical roots of artificial intelligence. *Pakistan Journal of Education, 40*(1), 67–90. doi:10.30971/pje.v40i1.1152

Sony. (2018). *Sony group's initiatives for responsible AI.* https://www.sony.com/en/SonyInfo/sony_ai/responsible_ai.html

Strubell, E., Ganesh, A., & McCallum, A. (2019). Energy and policy considerations for deep learning in NLP. In *the 57th Annual Meeting of the Association for Computational Linguistics.* Florence, Italy. 10.18653/v1/P19-1355

The Institute for Ethical AI in Education. (2021). *The ethical framework for AI in education.* Buckingham. https://www.buckingham.ac.uk/research/research-in-applied-computing/the-institute-for-ethical-ai-in-education/

UNESCO. (2019). *Beijing consensus on artificial intelligence and education.* The United Nations Educational, Scientific and Cultural Organization. https://unesdoc.unesco.org/ark:/48223/pf0000368303

UNESCO. (2021). *Recommendation on the ethics of artificial intelligence.* The United Nations Educational, Scientific and Cultural Organization. Paris, France. https://unesdoc.unesco.org/ark:/48223/pf0000380455.:~:text=AI%20actors%20and%20Member%20States,law%2C%20in%20particular%20Member%20States%27

Varona, D., & Suarez, J. L. (2022). Discrimination, bias, fairness, and trustworthy AI. *Applied Sciences (Basel, Switzerland), 12*(12), 1–13. doi:10.3390/app12125826

Zawacki-Richter, O., Marin, V. I., Bond, M., & Gouverneur, F. (2019). Systematic review of research on artificial intelligence applications in higher education-where are the educators? *International Journal of Educational Technology in Higher Education, 16*(1), 1–27. doi:10.1186/s41239-019-0171-0

Zhang, Y., & Wildemuth, B. M. (2009). *Qualitative analysis of content.* iSchool. https://www.ischool.utexas.edu/~yanz/Content_analysis.pdf

KEYWORDS AND DEFINITIONS

Artificial Intelligence (AI): Artificial intelligence (AI) refers to algorithmic models having the capacity to perform tasks which normally require human intelligence.

Artificial Intelligence in Education (AIED): The use of artificial intelligence technologies within educational context.

ChatGPT: ChatGPT, developed by OpenAI, is a generative AI technology that is capable of comprehending and responding in natural human language.

Ethics: The field of study which deals with moral values.

Framework: A collection of ideas, principles and/or instructions applied in organizing and/or decision making processes.

Generative AI: Generative AI refers to technologies that can analyze the complex patterns and structures of human language, and they are primarily trained to understand and generate natural language in a way that is similar to a human.

Guidelines: A set of rules or suggestions generally provided by organizations or associations on how something should be performed.

Trustworthy Artificial Intelligence (AI): AI systems that uphold ethical principles and values including accountability, transparency, fairness, and non-maleficence.

Chapter 11
Empowering Teachers With Generative AI Tools and Support

Mete Sipahioglu
https://orcid.org/0000-0003-2196-5533
Samsun University, Turkey

ABSTRACT

This chapter explores the potential of generative AI to transform education and empower teachers. It analyzes pedagogical enhancements enabled by these tools, including personalized and simulated learning, tailored assessments, teacher-student collaboration, and streamlined workflows. The author examines how AI's data-driven insights can boost responsiveness, motivation, inclusion, and experiential understanding. While promising, integrating AI demands thoughtful oversight to uphold humanistic values. The author emphasizes that teacher wisdom must direct implementation ethically, and learners need support developing AI literacy. Though rapidly advancing, generative tools should empower, not replace, educator and student agency. This chapter provides a balanced analysis of AI's possibilities and prudent perspectives for education. With ethical foundations uplifting expertise and learner voices alike, classrooms can judiciously leverage AI to expand responsive, enriched learning benefitting all.

INTRODUCTION

AI, a technology whose application spans from common utilities such as web searches (e.g., Google search), personalized recommendations (e.g., YouTube videos, Amazon marketplace), to speech recognition (e.g., Apple's Siri), has gained renewed vigor with the advent of publicly accessible innovations like ChatGPT. Its implementation resonates globally across an array of sectors, triggering reactions of astonishment regarding its capabilities and optimism concerning its prospective dividends, while simultaneously kindling apprehension due to fears of misemployment or the specter of job displacement in the foreseeable future. This sentiment is mirrored in the realm of education at all levels as well.

In the context of education, the burgeoning wave of AI is poised to revolutionize teacher empowerment. As AI's reach extends from web searches to personalized recommendations, its recent impetus through innovations like ChatGPT has sparked global discourse. This technology, while eliciting awe

DOI: 10.4018/979-8-3693-1351-0.ch011

for its capabilities and potential benefits, also invokes concerns about its ethical use and potential job displacement. These dialogues resonate within educational spheres, where AI's potential is acknowledged. The synergistic interplay between AI and Edtech not only augments pedagogical advantages but also nurtures a data-rich landscape, primed for AI assimilation. The empowering fusion of Generative AI Tools and educational support engenders novel opportunities for instructors to foster enriched learning experiences.

Education is a fundamental process through which human beings transfer their knowledge and skills from generation to generation, and with the development of technology, new possibilities and methods have emerged. In this context, advances in artificial intelligence (AI) offer the potential to transform the education sector. "Transforming Education with Generative AI: Prompt Engineering and Synthetic Content Creation" provides a comprehensive review to understand and evaluate this potential. The chapter entitled "Empowering Teachers with Generative AI Tools and Support", which I propose as a contribution to this book project, aims to delve deeper into this general framework and explore the role of generative AI in education. Education must evolve in accordance with the needs of our age and the diversifying characteristics of learners. Generative AI tools can enhance the ability of educators to respond to these requirements. Studies on the place and potential of AI in education show that it can help teachers to deliver more efficient, customized, and effective learning experiences (Chen et al., 2020; Kasneci et al., 2023). In this context, teachers' use of generative AI tools in designing educational material and content can open up new ways of customizing and diversifying students' learning pathways (Liu et al., 2023).

The first focus of the chapter is "Pedagogical Enrichment". Generative AI tools can help teachers to create questions and tasks that are appropriate for students. Research shows that creating customized learning materials for students can make learning more effective (Alam et al., 2018; Wu et al., 2018). In this context, it has been observed that questions designed with generative AI tools improve students' critical thinking and problem-solving abilities (How & Hung, 2019).

"Customized Learning Pathways" is another important issue in education. Students have different learning speeds and styles, which makes it imperative for teachers to develop customized learning approaches. Generative AI can help teachers to monitor student progress and adapt learning materials in accordance with their needs (Lameras & Arnab, 2021). In this way, students can be enabled to learn more effectively (Reiss, 2021).

Another emphasis of the chapter is "Collaborative Content Creation". Generative AI tools can enable teachers to collaborate in creating educational materials. AI models can work with teachers to create effective and engaging materials (Chen et al., 2020; Chounta et al., 2021). This can enable teachers to use their time more efficiently and focus better on students.

Another issue to be discussed is efficiency and saving time. Generative AI tools hold promise for revolutionizing education by enhancing efficiency and saving time for teachers and students (Timms, 2016). They streamline tasks, personalize learning pathways, and improve communication. However, ethical considerations must be addressed, ensuring data privacy, transparency, and accountability. Teacher training is vital for effective tool use. While generative AI offers transformative potential, its integration requires careful handling to maximize benefits and mitigate risks for all stakeholders in education.

Professional development is pivotal for educators to adapt to evolving educational landscapes and emerging technologies. This section explores how artificial intelligence (AI) can enhance educators' growth. AI offers personalized learning, adapting to teachers' styles and needs (Pedro et al., 2019; Porayska-Pomsta, 2016). AI-driven platforms analyze data for tailored recommendations, real-time insights, and self-assessment tools, refining teaching techniques. Collaborative AI networks connect educators, fostering continuous improvement. Ethical considerations encompass privacy, data security, transparency, and explainability. AI has transformative potential in professional development, benefiting educators' growth and student learning outcomes, provided ethical considerations are addressed.

Finally, the topic of "Ethical Considerations and Best Practices" is addressed. As the role of generative AI in education increases, ethical and privacy concerns are also raised (Zhai et al., 2021). In this section, ethical issues and best practices related to the use of generative AI in education will be discussed. Educators and technologists need to work together to find solutions to these issues.

The aim of this chapter is to understand how generative AI tools can support teachers and play a transformative role in education. Using current research in the literature, this chapter will analyze in depth the potential and limitations of the use of generative AI in education and discuss how it can help educators to deliver more effective and customized learning experiences. We aim for this chapter to be a valuable resource for educators, researchers, and policy makers.

PEDAGOGICAL ENHANCEMENT THROUGH GENERATIVE AI TOOLS

In recent years, the emergence of generative Artificial Intelligence (AI) tools has revolutionized the field of education by offering new avenues for pedagogical enhancement. These tools, powered by advanced machine learning algorithms, have the potential to transform teaching practices, empower educators, and enrich the learning experiences of students. This section delves into the concept of pedagogical enhancement through generative AI tools, exploring the ways in which these tools can augment traditional teaching approaches and strategies. By harnessing the power of AI, teachers can unlock exciting possibilities for personalized instruction, creativity, and engagement in the classroom. The integration of generative AI into the classroom setting has immense potential to augment and enhance pedagogical approaches employed by teachers. As AI capabilities continue to rapidly advance, generative models can provide customized, interactive, and adaptive learning experiences that were previously unimaginable. When thoughtfully implemented, AI tools do not replace teachers but rather amplify their ability to provide rich, engaging and effective instruction (Luckin et al., 2016).

One keyway generative AI can improve pedagogy is through data-driven, personalized assessments and recommendations. By analyzing large datasets, AI systems can identify knowledge gaps and misconceptions for individual students. The AI can then generate personalized study plans, practice questions, remedial content and feedback tailored to each learner's needs (Caputi & Garrido, 2015). This data-driven approach allows teachers to pinpoint areas where students are struggling and provide targeted intervention. Adaptive AI tutoring systems have been shown to improve student performance, motivation and confidence (Vanlehn, 2011). Generative AI tools empower teachers to create personalized learning experiences that cater to the unique needs and interests of each student. Through sophisticated algorithms, these tools can analyze student data, such as performance metrics, learning preferences, and prior knowledge, to generate adaptive learning pathways. By providing tailored recommendations, suggestions, and resources, generative AI tools enable teachers to address individual learning gaps effectively and provide targeted interventions. Moreover, these tools can offer real-time feedback and assessment, allowing teachers to monitor student progress and provide timely support. By leveraging the power of AI, teachers can identify areas where students require additional guidance, thereby fostering a more inclusive and supportive learning environment (Page, & Gehlbach, 2017). This pedagogical enhancement enhances student motivation, engagement, and self-efficacy, promoting lifelong learning and academic success.

Generative AI also enables the dynamic creation of syllabi, lesson plans and learning activities customized to students' abilities, backgrounds and interests (Tissenbaum et al., 2019). Where human teachers are limited in the volume of materials they can produce, AI tools can rapidly generate engaging content and diverse learning experiences (Clark et al., 2018). This includes varied examples, explanations, practice problems and discussions personalized to resonate with each student. Research indicates personalized educational experiences can increase student satisfaction, participation and information retention compared to one-size-fits-all approaches (Wolff et al., 2014).

Simulation-based learning environments powered by generative AI allow students to gain immersive understanding of complex topics through hands-on experimentation and exploration (Rutten et al., 2012). AI can generate highly detailed simulated worlds related to subjects like physics, ecology, engineering and more. Students obtain interactive experiential learning tailored to curriculum objectives. Studies show learning-by-doing with simulated environments improves learning outcomes versus traditional instruction (Girard et al., 2013).

Scaffolding and shaping learning trajectories is another key pedagogical enhancement enabled by generative AI. Intelligent tutoring systems can assess students' current progress and dynamically provide appropriate learning activities to guide them along an optimal development path (Koedinger et al., 2013). As the learner's skills grow, the AI generator provides graduated scaffolding and incrementally more challenging content synchronized to the individual's evolving zone of proximal development. Research shows this scaffolding accelerates skill acquisition more effectively than fixed curricula (Roll et al., 2014).

For early education, generative AI offers new pedagogical possibilities by automatically generating engaging, educational games tailored to curriculum goals (Liu et al., 2011). The AI can dynamically create games featuring age-appropriate characters, narratives, challenges, and feedback. This provides young students with enjoyable activities purpose-built to target specific learning objectives. Studies indicate educational games increase student motivation and time spent practicing new skills (Habgood & Ainsworth, 2011). These capabilities transform static, one-size-fits-all educational materials into dynamic, interactive resources that actively promote learning for each student (Holmes et al., 2019). By leveraging massive datasets and computational power, generative AI can open up new pedagogical possibilities not viable solely with human input. However, teachers remain vital in curating AI-generated content, guiding productive discussion and providing qualitative assessment (Zawacki-Richter et al., 2019). Overall, thoughtfully implemented generative AI has immense potential to enrich pedagogy by elevating human teachers rather than replacing them.

Teachers are lifelong learners, continually seeking opportunities for professional growth and development. Generative AI tools contribute to the evolution of teaching practices by offering insights, suggestions, and resources for continuous professional development. These tools can analyze pedagogical trends, research findings, and best practices, providing teachers with personalized recommendations to enhance their instructional strategies. Moreover, generative AI tools can facilitate self-reflection and self-assessment, allowing teachers to evaluate their teaching practices and identify areas for improvement. By offering real-time feedback on instructional delivery, classroom management, and student engagement, these tools empower teachers to refine their skills and become more effective educators. This pedagogical enhancement fosters a culture of continuous improvement and ensures that teachers stay abreast of the latest educational advancements.

Pedagogical enhancement through generative AI tools holds immense potential to revolutionize education. By leveraging the power of AI, teachers can enhance instructional design, personalize learning experiences, facilitate collaboration, cultivate creativity, and foster continuous professional development. However, it is crucial to approach the integration of generative AI tools with caution, addressing ethical concerns, and ensuring transparency and accountability. As technology continues to advance, the synergy between human expertise and generative AI tools will shape the future of education, empowering teachers and enriching the learning experiences of students. In closing, generative AI possesses unprecedented potential to enrich pedagogy and empower educators through data-driven personalization, immersive simulations, and adaptive scaffolding. However, maintaining teacher oversight and wisdom remains essential to guide appropriate, nuanced integration of AI capabilities in service of humanistic educational values.

Figure 1. Top AI tools for educators

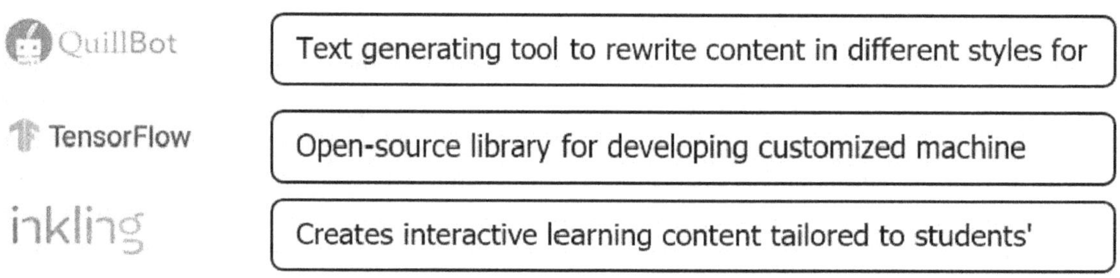

CUSTOMIZED LEARNING PATHWAYS

In the realm of education, one size does not fit all. Students possess diverse learning styles, interests, and abilities, which necessitate the adoption of personalized approaches to instruction. Customized learning pathways, enabled by generative AI tools, offer a promising avenue for tailoring educational experiences to individual students' needs. Advanced algorithms employed by generative artificial intelligence tools enable the automatic generation of customized educational content. These algorithms analyze individual student data to produce personalized materials, ultimately boosting engagement and fostering motivation in the learning process (Ruiz-Rojas et al., 2023). This section explores how generative AI tools can facilitate customized learning pathways, promoting student engagement, motivation, and overall learning outcomes.

One of the most promising applications of generative AI in education is the ability to create customized learning content tailored to individual students. Whereas traditional educational materials are mass produced and generalized, AI tools allow teachers to generate personalized content that resonates with each learner's unique needs, abilities and interests. This customization enabled by generative models has profound implications for enhancing student engagement and educational outcomes (Walkington & Bernacki, 2020). Moreover, generative AI tools can provide real-time feedback to students, enabling them to monitor their progress and make informed decisions about their learning. This feedback mechanism enhances metacognitive skills, as students gain a deeper understanding of their learning process, identify their strengths and weaknesses, and take ownership of their learning journey. By offering customized learning experiences, generative AI tools empower students to become active participants in their education, fostering a sense of agency and self-efficacy.

At the most basic level, generative AI allows endless variations of practice questions, assignments, texts and other materials. For any given lesson plan, the AI can produce hundreds of customized worksheets and problem sets so that each student receives unique practice content. This variability reduces repetition and boredom while allowing teachers to instantly generate additional materials on demand to meet each learner's needs (Parshall et al., 2002). Studies show personalized assignments increase student motivation and time on task versus generic content (Cordova & Lepper, 1996).

Generative AI can also produce customized explanations, examples and illustrations for concepts that resonate with an individual student's experiences and prior knowledge. A chemistry lesson could feature molecular diagrams situated in contexts meaningful to the learner, like analyzing sports drinks or baking bread. The AI generates variables, characters and narratives tailored to the individual's background and interests to ground abstract concepts in relatable contexts. Research indicates personalized examples enhance student engagement, comprehension and recall (Moreno & Mayer, 2000).

For writing and language arts education, generative AI enables customized feedback on student compositions. Beyond grammar and spelling corrections, the AI can analyze a student's draft and generate personalized suggestions tailored to their demonstrated strengths, weaknesses and developing skills (Roscoe & McNamara, 2013). Feedback can also be dynamically adapted to the learner's confidence level, providing more detailed instruction for struggling students versus expansive questions to challenge advanced learners (Kulik & Kulik, 1988). Studies show personalized feedback improves writing skills more effectively than template responses (AbuSeileek, 2012).

Generative AI also allows teachers to assign each student a unique version of an essay, analysis or creative writing prompt tailored to their abilities and interests (Woo et al., 2023). A poetry assignment could feature themes related to the student's favorite hobbies and activities. This level of customization was previously impossible in education given the time required to manually develop materials for each learner. AI enables mass personalization that improves educational outcomes.

For students with special needs, generative AI can modify assignments and materials aligned with individual learning goals and abilities (Banik et al., 2015). Teachers can specify parameters like reading level, complexity and length to automatically generate content accessible for neurodiverse learners or those requiring additional support. Research indicates personalized content significantly boosts academic achievement for students with learning disabilities relative to standardized materials (Worthen, 2016).

Importantly, generative AI should augment rather than replace human teachers' expertise in designing customized learning experiences. Teachers remain essential in setting parameters, evaluating quality and ensuring alignment with educational goals (Zawacki-Richter et al., 2019). However, by automating mass production of personalized content, AI systems enable teachers to focus more attention on thoughtful customization for each student. Generative AI tools can also support teacher-student collaboration, enabling educators to provide targeted guidance and support to individual students. Through AI-generated insights and analytics, teachers can gain a deeper understanding of each student's learning trajectory, identify areas where additional support is required, and provide timely interventions. This collaboration between teachers and AI tools enhances the effectiveness of instruction, as educators can tailor their teaching strategies to meet the unique needs of each student, promoting deeper learning and academic growth.

Figure 2. Some prompt ideas for educators

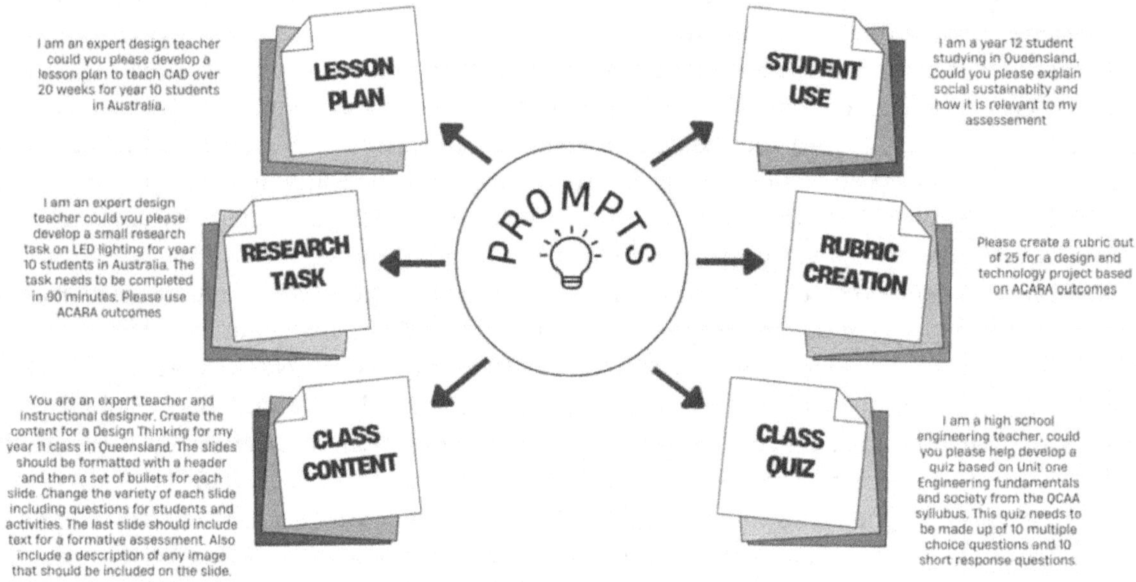

Generative AI tools offer a powerful means of creating customized learning pathways that cater to the unique needs and preferences of students (Tapalova & Zhiyenbayeva, 2022). By providing personalized learning experiences, facilitating collaborative learning, cultivating creativity and critical thinking, and supporting continuous professional development, these tools have the potential to revolutionize education. However, it is crucial to address ethical considerations and ensure accountability to maximize the benefits of generative AI tools while mitigating potential risks. Through a thoughtful and responsible approach, educators can harness the transformative potential of generative AI tools to create a more inclusive, engaging, and effective learning environment.

Overall, the capability to instantly generate endless variations of educational materials tailored to each learner unlocks enormous potential to improve engagement, motivation and academic achievement. When thoughtfully guided by teachers, generative AI can democratize customized education previously impossible at scale (Holmes et al., 2019). This paradigm shift could profoundly enrich learning and human potential by meeting each student where they are. Generative AI promises to transform static, one-size-fits-all materials into dynamically personalized learning experiences catered to each student's needs and interests. Yet human teachers remain integral in directing customized content creation thoughtfully, ensuring suitability and alignment with pedagogical goals.

TEACHER-STUDENT COLLABORATION

In recent years, advancements in artificial intelligence (AI) have opened up new possibilities for educational practices. One area that holds great promise is the collaboration between teachers and students in co-creating educational content. Generative AI tools have the potential to enhance this collaboration by providing real-time feedback, personalized support, and data-driven insights. This section explores the transformative potential of generative AI tools in fostering teacher-student collaboration and creating a dynamic and engaging learning environment.

Figure 3. Top AI tools for educators

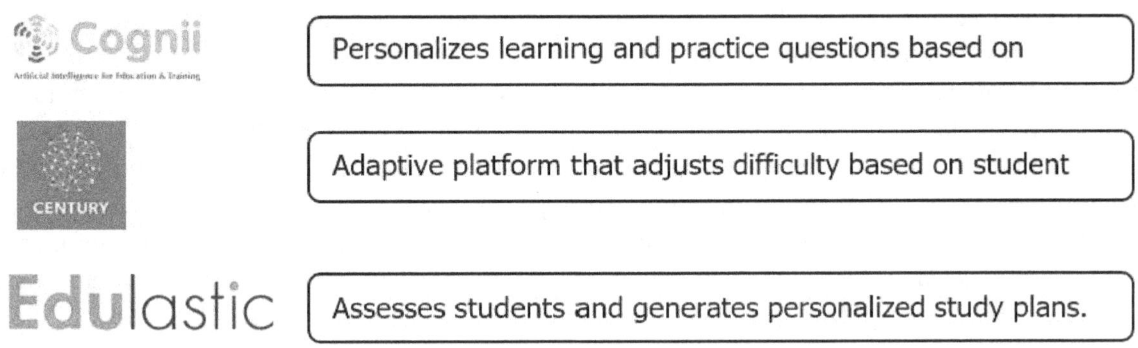

One key advantage of generative AI tools is their ability to offer immediate feedback to students. Traditionally, teachers have been burdened with the task of providing feedback on assignments and assessments, which can be time-consuming and often delayed. With generative AI tools, however, students can receive instant feedback on their work, allowing them to make immediate improvements and deepen their understanding of the subject matter. Generative AI opens up promising new opportunities for collaboration between teachers and students in co-creating educational content and experiences. Whereas traditional classroom roles position teachers as transmitters of information and students as passive receivers, AI allows more participatory, engaging learning where both teachers and students actively contribute (Edwards et al., 2018). Thoughtfully implemented, these collaborative capabilities enabled by generative models can increase student agency, motivation and personalized learning outcomes.

One approach where generative AI facilitates teacher-student collaboration is having students co-design personalized learning activities driven by their interests and goals. An intelligent tutoring system can engage in a dialogue with learners to understand their needs and preferences, then collaboratively develop customized study plans, assignments and projects (Bradáč et al., 2022). Compared to fixed curricula, research shows learner-centered co-design of educational experiences increases engagement, satisfaction, and knowledge retention (Cordova & Lepper, 1996).

Teachers and students can also collaborate with generative AI in co-composing interactive lessons, stories, games and other content. For example, an AI writing assistant could help a student author a choose-your-own-adventure style story featuring the learner's preferences, with the teacher providing guidance and feedback. Such co-creation blends learner agency with teacher expertise (Tissenbaum et al., 2019). Studies indicate collaborative content generation promotes creativity, critical thinking and project investment for students (Baruah & Paulus, 2019; Tisoglu et al.,2022).

Scaffolding student peer-to-peer collaboration is another key application of generative AI. Intelligent systems can monitor student discussions and teamwork then generate personalized prompts to deepen understanding, promote equitable participation, and assist conflict resolution (Tegos et al., 2016). For example, the AI could privately message individuals to contribute ideas or praise a peer's insight. Research shows AI-guided collaboration increases learning gains versus unassisted student teams (Jeong and Hmelo-Silver, 2016; Schneider and Pea, 2013; Slavin, 1996).

For formative assessment and feedback, generative AI allows teachers to rapidly analyze student work and misconceptions, then instantly produce customized recommendations (Kaplan-Rakowski et al., 2023). During collaborative hands-on projects, an AI teaching assistant could generate real-time guidance for student teams, freeing up the teacher's availability. Studies indicate AI-supported collaboration enables more timely, personalized feedback at scale (Gu et al., 2022; Kasepalu et al., 2022).

Generative models can also produce endless variations of collaborative learning activities tailored to student teams' abilities and interests (Troussas et al., 2023). For a group English project, the AI could generate a unique role-play prompt for analyzing literature from each student's perspective. Mass-personalization keeps collaboration engaging over repeated tasks. it was found that these models can generate a wide array of collaborative learning tasks that are specifically tailored to the abilities and interests of student teams. For example, in the context of a group English project, the AI-powered system can generate unique role-play scenarios designed to analyze literature from individual students' unique perspectives. This mass-personalization of collaborative activities not only enhances student engagement but also ensures that collaborative tasks remain fresh and engaging over repeated iterations. Furthermore, the use of Generative AI in collaborative learning aligns with the principles of Constructivist learning theory (Jonassen, 1994), which emphasizes the importance of active participation and the construction of knowledge through social interactions. By continuously adapting collaborative tasks to suit the diverse needs and interests of student groups, Generative AI can facilitate richer and more meaningful learning experiences. This aligns with Vygotsky's sociocultural theory (Vygotsky, 1978), which underscores the role of social interaction in cognitive development.

However, while generative AI tools offer immense potential for enhancing collaboration between teachers and students, it is important to recognize and maintain the central role of teachers in the educational process. AI tools should be viewed as complementary rather than a replacement for human expertise. Teachers bring a wealth of knowledge, experience, and pedagogical skills that cannot be replicated by AI. Therefore, it is crucial to provide adequate training and support to both teachers and students to effectively leverage the benefits of generative AI tools. Importantly, human teachers remain vital in directing generative AI to enhance collaborative learning productively, equitably and ethically. Poorly implemented collaborative AI risks learner disengagement, over-automation and loss of teacher control (Zawacki-Richter et al., 2019). By thoughtfully balancing generative capabilities with human oversight and wisdom, AI-enabled collaboration can meaningfully amplify educational outcomes.

In conclusion, generative AI tools have the transformative potential to enhance collaboration between teachers and students in co-creating educational content. These tools provide real-time feedback, personalized support, and data-driven insights, enabling students to actively engage in their learning journey. However, it is crucial to maintain the central role of teachers and provide adequate training and support to both teachers and students. By doing so, we can leverage the full potential of generative AI tools in fostering collaboration and creating a dynamic and engaging learning environment. The integration of AI in education holds great promise for the future, revolutionizing traditional educational practices and empowering both teachers and students alike. The rapidly evolving capabilities of generative AI offer unparalleled opportunities to reimagine learning as a dynamic, participatory experience where students and teachers co-create knowledge. Blending learner agency with educator guidance, these collaborative systems can personalize instruction while developing creativity, communication, critical thinking and cooperation skills essential for learners' futures. More broadly, AI-supported collaboration moves toward more empowering, democratized educational ecosystems centered on human development.

Figure 4. Top AI tools for educators

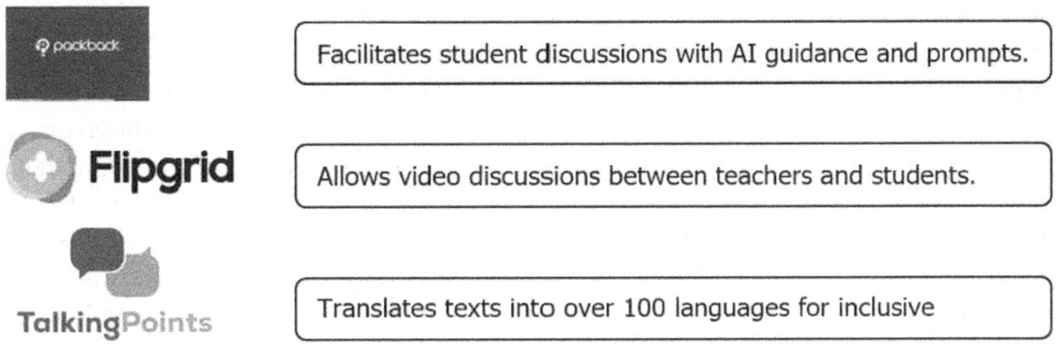

EFFICIENCY AND TIME-SAVING

Generative artificial intelligence (AI) tools have the potential to revolutionize the field of education by enhancing efficiency and saving valuable time for teachers and students. These tools can automate various tasks and streamline processes, allowing educators to focus on more meaningful interactions and personalized instruction. By harnessing the power of AI, teachers can optimize their workflow and allocate their time more effectively, ultimately leading to improved learning outcomes. One of the most valuable applications of generative AI for empowering teachers is streamlining repetitive, time-intensive tasks. By automating key administrative and content development processes, AI systems enable teachers to devote more of their expertise to higher-order instructional activities and personalized student support. When thoughtfully implemented, this efficiency and time-saving unlocked by generative models can expand teachers' capacities exponentially.

A key opportunity is leveraging natural language processing to automate written assessment feedback for students. An AI grading assistant trained on thousands of samples can analyze written work across disciplines and instantly generate personalized commentary tailored to rubrics, learning goals and student needs (Burrows et al., 2015). This transforms the traditionally arduous manual feedback process for teachers. Studies show AI grading systems provide feedback quality on par with human raters, offering immense time savings (Ndukwe et al., 2019; Yang & Zhu, 2022). One of the keyways in which generative AI tools can enhance efficiency is through automated homework management (Hughes et al., 2021). Traditionally, teachers spend a significant amount of time grading assignments and providing feedback to students. However, with AI-powered systems, this process can be expedited and made more accurate. For instance, AI algorithms can analyze and evaluate student responses, providing instant feedback and identifying areas where additional guidance may be required. This not only saves time for teachers but also enables students to receive timely feedback, allowing for continuous improvement and a more dynamic learning experience.

Generating individualized progress reports and parent communications is another burdensome process made efficient by generative AI. After inputting student performance data, an AI writing tool can synthesize key insights and produce customized reports conveying each learner's growth to guardians (Dascalu et al., 2018). For recurrent tasks like weekly update emails, AI generation eliminates repetitive manual drafting. Research suggests personalized AI writing saves teachers over an hour per week while improving guardian satisfaction (Kochmar et al., 2020).

Teachers can take advantage of AI in their planning, implementation, and assessment work. AI assists them in identifying their students' needs so that they can determine the most suitable learning content and activities for their students (Celik et al, 2022). Lesson planning and instructional materials creation is also a prime efficiency target for generative AI support. Rather than developing lessons from scratch, teachers can provide prompts to AI assistants which then generate engaging lesson plans, assignments, presentations, and assessments tailored to curriculum standards and student needs (Chen et al., 2020). Studies estimate intelligent lesson planning systems save teachers 2-4 hours of prep time per week, with greater savings for novel content (Pender et al., 2022). This not only saves teachers the time and effort required to search for suitable resources but also ensures that instructional materials are tailored to meet the diverse needs of learners. For instance, an AI system can suggest a range of instructional resources or provide a choice among various options, allowing teachers to make informed decisions about the most effective materials and approaches. This personalized approach to resource selection can significantly enhance the learning experience and promote student engagement.

AI tutor chatbots offer another time-saving opportunity by providing automated student support outside of class (Koivisto, 2023). Chatbots scale personalized help, feedback and Q&A with students to supplement classroom teaching (Verleger, & Pembridge, 2018). Thoughtfully designed, these generative AI systems aim not to replace but augment teacher workflows. Human judgment remains critical for providing nuance, qualitative oversight and creativity that AI currently lacks. However, by automating purely repetitive tasks, generative models allow teachers to devote more attention to high-value activities like reflective lesson planning, human connection with students and guiding rich discussions (Zawacki-Richter et al., 2019).

Critically, the efficiency benefits of AI must be carefully balanced with student needs and ethical classroom practices. Over-automation risks losing teacher oversight and dehumanizing education (Nissenbaum & Walker, 1998). AI should aim to empower, not replace, educators. Further research is needed on optimizing hybrid human-AI approaches that maximize strengths of both. Teachers need to develop a solid understanding of AI technologies and their implications for education. So that, they should be empowered to critically evaluate the recommendations and outputs generated by AI systems to ensure they align with educational goals and pedagogical principles. Ongoing support and guidance should be provided to address any challenges or concerns that may arise during the integration of generative AI tools into the classroom.

In conclusion, generative AI tools have the potential to significantly enhance the efficiency and time-saving aspects of education. By automating tasks, providing personalized resources, and facilitating communication, these tools can optimize the teaching and learning process. However, thoughtfully implemented efficiency gains from AI could help address teacher burnout stemming from extreme workloads (Skaalvik & Skaalvik, 2017). Generative models show particular promise for alleviating bureaucratic and repetitive task burdens. This holds potential to improve teacher job satisfaction, retention and capacity to focus on meaningful instruction. More broadly, AI efficiency may allow a shift toward more personalized, humanistic learning based on guiding relationships.

Figure 5. Top AI tools for educators

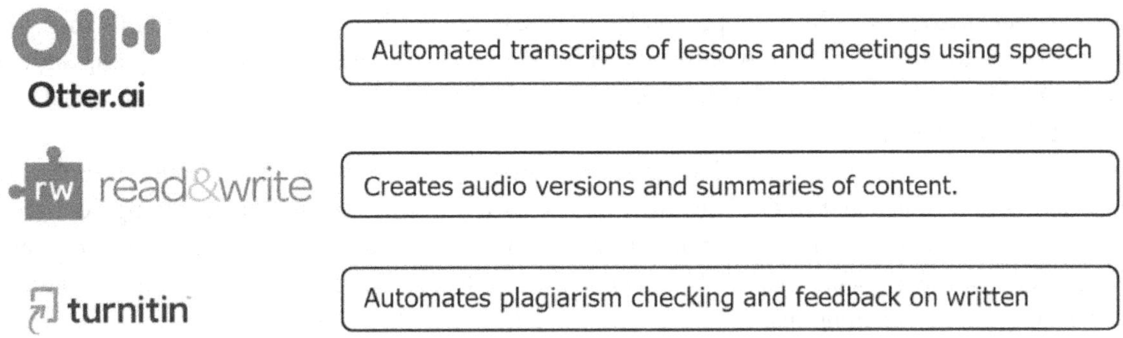

PROFESSIONAL DEVELOPMENT

Professional development plays a critical role in shaping the knowledge, skills, and expertise of educators. As the field of education evolves and new technologies emerge, it becomes imperative for teachers to engage in continuous learning and stay updated with the latest advancements. In this section, we will explore the role of artificial intelligence (AI) in professional development and how it can be effectively utilized to enhance the growth and development of educators. As generative AI increasingly shapes education, these technologies also hold significant potential to assist in ongoing teacher professional development and continuous improvement. When thoughtfully implemented, AI tools can provide data-driven insights, personalized recommendations, and customized resources to support teachers' evolving needs. This expands possibilities for more adaptive, self-driven professional learning. Traditional professional development programs often follow a one-size-fits-all approach, which may not effectively address the unique needs and challenges of each teacher. AI-based systems, on the other hand, can adapt to the specific requirements of educators, taking into account their teaching styles, subject areas, and student demographics. This personalized approach can significantly enhance the effectiveness and relevance of professional development initiatives.

One key application is leveraging learning analytics data to generate personalized professional development insights for educators (Ifenthaler & Widanapathirana, 2014). For example, an AI teaching assistant could compile and analyze patterns in a teacher's instructional practices, student progress indicators, and feedback surveys. The system can then identify potential strengths, growth areas opportunities for that specific teacher to focus their development. Research shows data-driven AI professional development leads to improved teaching quality (Lockspeiser and Kaul, 2016; Shemshack and Spector, 2020).

Intelligent tutoring systems offer customized learning experiences for teachers grounded in evidence-based practices and tailored scaffolding (Eom & Ashill, 2016). AI can continually assess a teacher's evolving mastery of pedagogical skills and deliver personalized training content and recommendations responsive to their needs. Studies find AI tutoring increases teacher learning, confidence and likelihood of adopting new instructional strategies (Barik et al., 2020). For collaborative professional development, generative conversation agents can provide data-driven insights during coaching, mentorship and team discussions (Tegos et al., 2015). An AI facilitator could identify patterns in dialogue, synthesize key takeaways, and generate prompts to encourage productive conversations and reflection for professional learning groups. Research suggests AI collaborative assistants increase professional development engagement (Mannekote, 2023; Tegos et al., 2015; Winkler, 2019). Thoughtfully implemented AI mentoring can enhance access to personalized support and guidance for all teachers, including those in remote areas (Khazanchi & Khazanchi, 2021) An AI-powered virtual mentor can engage teachers in ongoing dialogue, provide timely feedback, and share customized resources tailored to the teacher's developmental goals, learning style and context.

To promote continuous learning and avoid skill stagnation, generative AI can create regular personalized training challenges and micro-learning exercises for teachers focused on emerging educational practices and technologies (Schroeder et al., 2022). AI systems can assembly targeted mini-lessons responsive to each teacher's schedule, needs and prior knowledge. Research finds consistent AI-generated micro-learning boosts teaching mastery (Liu et al., 2022, Tan et al., 2023).

For preservice teacher education, AI tutors have shown promise for building foundational pedagogical skills through personalized modeling, practice and feedback (Eom & Ashill, 2016). AI mentors can also provide novice teachers with enhanced support during their fragile early career stage, potentially improving retention. However, care must be taken to balance AI scaffolding with human guidance. AI technologies can also facilitate professional reflection and growth by providing educators with valuable feedback and self-assessment tools. For example, AI-powered video analysis tools can analyze classroom recordings and provide detailed insights into teaching practices, such as teacher-student interactions, instructional strategies, and student engagement levels.

While the integration of AI in professional development offers numerous benefits, it is crucial to address the ethical considerations associated with this technology. Privacy and data security are of paramount importance, as AI systems rely on vast amounts of personal and sensitive information to provide personalized recommendations. Educators must have control over their data and be assured that it is being used responsibly and in compliance with applicable privacy regulations. Transparency and explainability are also essential when using AI in professional development. Educators need to understand how AI algorithms work, what data they rely on, and how they generate recommendations. This transparency enables teachers to critically evaluate the outputs of AI systems and make informed decisions about their professional development. Additionally, AI systems should provide clear explanations and justifications for their recommendations, allowing educators to trust and engage with the technology.

In conclusion, AI has the potential to transform professional development in education by providing personalized, adaptive, and collaborative learning experiences for educators. AI-powered systems can analyze data, generate insights, and offer tailored recommendations, empowering educators to reflect on their teaching practices, set goals, and access relevant resources. Importantly, teachers remain the drivers of their professional journeys. AI is best used to enhance, not replace, inherently human education activities. Generative models should aim to expand, not limit, teacher agency and wisdom (Zawacki-Richter et al., 2019). Further research into optimal AI-human professional development hybrids will be critical. However, it is crucial to address ethical considerations, ensure transparency and accountability, and provide ongoing support and guidance to educators during the integration of AI tools. By doing so, we can harness the full potential of AI in professional development, enhancing the growth and development of educators and ultimately improving student learning outcomes.

Figure 6. Top AI tools for educators

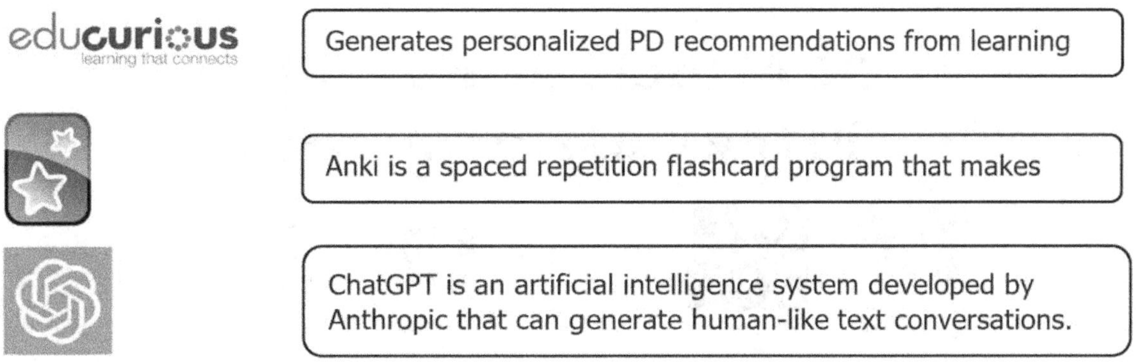

ETHICAL CONSIDERATIONS AND BEST PRACTICES IN LEVERAGING GENERATIVE AI TOOLS FOR EMPOWERING TEACHERS

The integration of generative artificial intelligence (AI) tools within educational contexts brings forth a plethora of possibilities, enabling teachers to amplify their instructional approaches and student engagement. However, as the realm of generative AI advances, it also raises pertinent ethical concerns that necessitate careful consideration. This section delves into the ethical dimensions and best practices associated with leveraging generative AI tools to empower teachers and enhance the learning experience. While generative AI enables promising new possibilities in education, integrating these rapidly evolving technologies requires careful forethought to uphold ethical learning environments. Educators have an imperative to ensure AI is thoughtfully implemented in ways that truly empower—not replace—teachers and enrich student potential. Several key considerations emerge.

Maintaining teacher agency and oversight is foundational when adopting AI tools in the classroom (Zawacki-Richter et al., 2019). Rather than fully automating instruction, AI should aim to augment human expertise. Teachers must direct integration of generative models based on professional wisdom, continuously evaluate AI quality and appropriateness, and have final say on educational decisions. Research suggests most educators presently view AI as a collaborative tool for enhancing practice rather than competing with human roles (Keating & Nourbakhsh, 2018).

Accountability emerges as another ethical facet deserving attention. In instances where AI-generated content is integrated into instructional materials or assessments, it is crucial to establish mechanisms for tracing the origin of content to ascertain responsibility for its accuracy. Developing systems that allow teachers to validate and possibly modify AI-generated content fosters a sense of accountability in the educational ecosystem (Floridi et al., 2018).

Transparency is paramount in engendering trust in AI-powered educational tools. As teachers collaborate with AI systems to craft learning resources, ensuring transparency in how content is generated and validated becomes pivotal. Best practices dictate that educational institutions and technology providers should furnish transparent explanations of how AI models contribute to content creation, allowing educators to make informed decisions regarding the materials they present to their students (Diakopoulos, 2016).

Figure 7. 30 AI tools for educators
Source: *(Miller, 2022)*

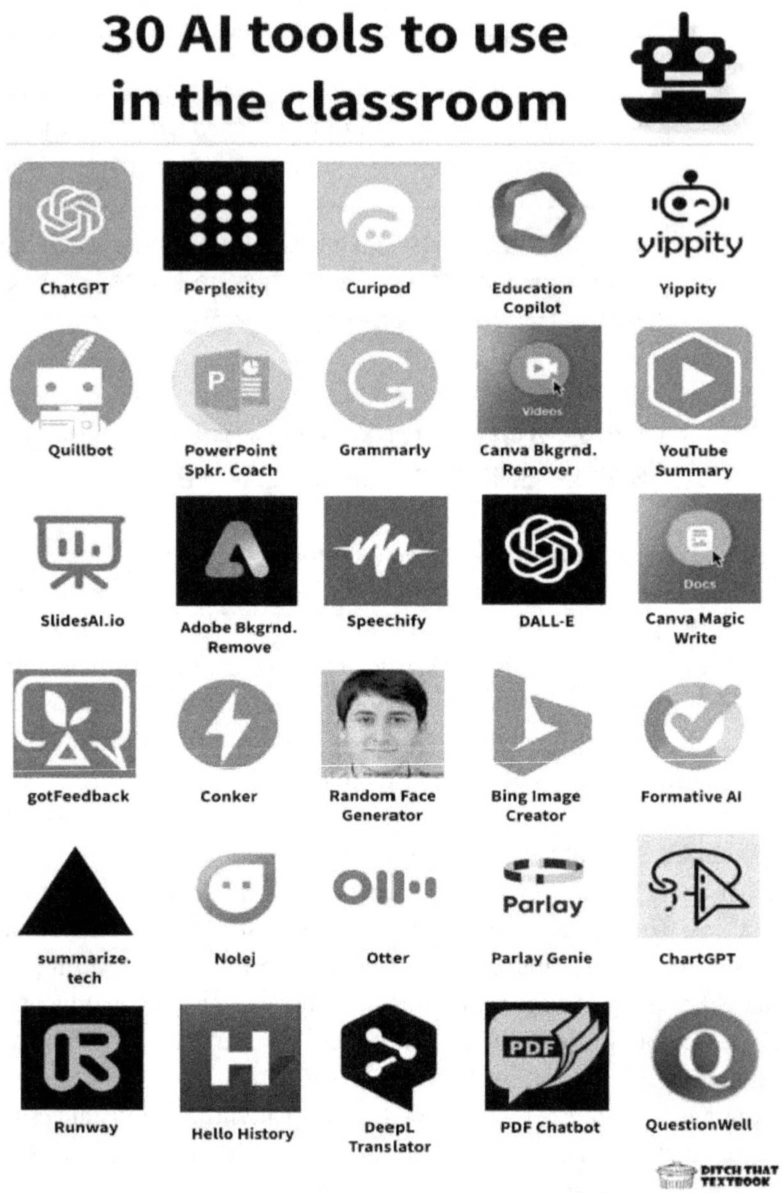

Protecting student privacy must also be prioritized, as generative models rely heavily on learner data which carries risks of exploitation or unintended harms (Williamson, 2020). Ethical use of student data to improve learning through AI should be transparent, secured and tightly regulated. Students and families must have agency over how personal data is utilized. More research into data rights and AI governance models is urgently needed.

Promoting AI literacy and transparency is likewise essential, so students understand how generative technologies function, including limitations and potential biases (Touretzky et al., 2019). Teachers have a vital role in developing students' ethical discernment and critical perspectives regarding AI. This empowers learners to evaluate generative content and direct integration thoughtfully rather than passively consume machine outputs.

Generative models should also be carefully audited for biases, misinformation and appropriateness of outputs before classroom use (Megahed et al.,2023). While rapidly improving, AI systems still risk generating harmful, misleading or low-quality content lacking nuanced human judgement. Ongoing oversight mechanisms are critical safeguards, though more research into AI accountability systems is needed. Personalized learning through generative AI should also be balanced thoughtfully against the educational benefits of social learning and peer interactions (Holmes et al., 2019). While AI offers customization at scale, solely individualistic learning neglects key developmental growth that occurs through human relationships and collaboration. Hybrid approaches warrant further exploration.

The appropriate balance between generative content creation and students' own creative expressions also merits consideration (Zawacki-Richter et al., 2019). In moderation, AI generated lesson materials, practice questions and feedback may enrich learning efficiently. However, an overreliance on machine-produced content risks diminishing the agency, authenticity and diversity of students' own creations.

Overall, maintaining humanistic, ethical educational values must remain the compass guiding the integration of rapidly advancing generative technologies. AI offers immense possibilities to transform teaching and learning for the better, but only if thoughtfully directed in service of human development rather than as an end in itself. By uplifting both teacher wisdom and student voices, classrooms can harness AI as a collaborative tool for empowerment.

KEY TAKEAWAYS AND FUTURE OUTLOOK

While this research highlights the promising capabilities of generative AI tools to enhance education, thoughtful implementation will be imperative to realize benefits while mitigating risks. One area needing attention is developing governance systems to ensure ethical use of student data. Institutions should implement transparent data policies that give students control over their information, with strict regulation over sale or exploitation of data. AI systems reliant on student data should be audited for security vulnerabilities and backstopped to prevent breaches or misuse.

Another critical need is training both students and teachers in discerning the limitations and potential biases of AI systems. Classes focused on AI literacy from a young age could help students become critical evaluators rather than passive consumers of generative technologies. For teachers, professional development should include guidance on detecting model biases and misinformation as well as directing integration in pedagogically sound ways. Human oversight remains essential.

Research on long-term impacts is imperative as well. While generative AI offers advantages, studies should assess risks like over-dependence on automation or diminishing of human creativity over time. Balancing personalized AI with collaborative learning opportunities may mitigate these risks. Hybrid human-AI approaches also warrant exploration to combine benefits while minimizing any tradeoffs.

Overall, realizing the promise of AI in education without compromising humanistic values will require proactive policies and thoughtful solutions. But the transformative potential makes overcoming these challenges imperative. With student empowerment and teacher wisdom guiding the process, AI could open new frontiers in learning tailored to the diverse needs of every child.

INSIGHTS AND OUTPUTS FOR RESEARCHERS AND PRACTITIONERS

This chapter on empowering teachers with generative AI provides valuable insights for both researchers and practitioners. However, further work is needed to implement these technologies thoughtfully. Key implications include:

- Conducting rigorous studies on long-term impacts of AI integration, including risks like over-dependence. While benefits are highlighted here, more research is needed on potential downsides.
- Exploring optimal balances between AI personalization versus peer collaboration and social learning. Hybrid approaches may offer the right mix.
- Developing ethical AI accountability systems, such as monitoring outputs and establishing responsibilities for inaccuracies. This can engender trust.
- Training both students and teachers in AI literacy, discerning model limitations and biases. This empowers learners as critical consumers.
- Instituting data governance policies to secure student privacy and prevent exploitation of learner data. Transparent AI ethics policies are critical.
- Evaluating generative content quality before classroom use to avoid potential harms from misinformation or inappropriate material. Ongoing audits help.
- Maintaining teacher wisdom and oversight when integrating AI. Human expertise remains essential for nuanced instructional decisions.

In summary, realizing the promise of AI in education requires judicious implementation grounded in ethical values and centered on human development. Further research and thoughtful policies can help achieve this balance. But used prudently, generative technologies offer new horizons of empowerment for both teachers and students.

CONCLUSION

The advent of generative AI represents a watershed moment for education, harboring immense potential to amplify pedagogical impact if applied judiciously. This chapter illuminates how AI-enabled tools can empower teachers to enrich learning experiences, tailor instruction, collaborate with students, work efficiently, and continuously improve their practices. While promising, integrating emergent technologies demands mindfulness to uphold humanistic educational values.

Several pivotal capabilities of generative AI to enhance pedagogy emerge. By analyzing patterns in vast datasets, AI systems can pinpoint individual students' needs and misconceptions to target interventions. Dynamic curricula, practice materials, feedback and multimedia can be tailored to each learner's progress, abilities, interests and prior knowledge to boost engagement and comprehension. Simulated environments allow immersive exploratory learning, while intelligent tutors scaffold activities along optimal development trajectories. Teachers can also utilize AI to assess student work, plan lessons, communicate with guardians and complete administrative tasks more efficiently. This expands their capacity for meaningful personal interactions and instruction.

Additionally, generative models facilitate richer teacher-student collaboration in co-designing educational experiences. AI guidance makes learning more participatory, leaning on learners' interests while providing real-time personalized feedback. Students gain greater agency in knowledge construction. For educators' ongoing growth, AI offers data-driven insights into specific developmental needs coupled with responsive training resources and reflective tools. Ubiquitous access to AI mentoring and peer networking can counter professional isolation.

However, while promising, AI integration warrants mindful implementation. As rapid technological change reshapes education, maintaining humanistic learning values must remain the lodestar. Teacher oversight of generative technologies is indispensable to ensure appropriateness and supplement human nuance. Ethical AI application demands transparency on model capabilities and limitations, protecting privacy, establishing accountability, and avoiding over-reliance. Students require support in cultivating AI literacy and discernment. Balance is needed between automated personalization and peer social learning. While AI efficiency grants leverage, excess automation risks dehumanizing education.

This chapter illuminates how teachers can harness generative tools not as replacements, but as collaborators in service of human development. AI stands to complement educator wisdom, empowering students and teachers alike if thoughtfully directed. The transformative potential of AI-human partnerships in learning merits ongoing exploration. With ethical foundations, teacher empowerment and wisdom of practice anchoring integration, classrooms can leverage generative technologies to nurture the full richness of human potential.

In synthesis, this chapter unveils the pedagogical promise of AI while underscoring reflective implementation. As education evolves in an era of exponential technological change, maintaining humanistic learning values and teacher agency should remain the compass guiding appropriate integration of emerging capabilities. With conscientious foundations uplifting ethical AI design, teacher wisdom, and student voices alike, classrooms can leverage generative tools judiciously to expand learning possibilities for all.

REFERENCES

AbuSeileek, A. F. (2012). The effect of using an online-based course on the learning of grammar inductively and deductively. *ReCALL, 24*(3), 239–256. doi:10.1017/S095834400999005X

Alam, A., Ullah, S., & Ali, N. (2018). The Effect of Learning-Based Adaptivity on Students' Performance in 3D-Virtual Learning Environments. *IEEE Access : Practical Innovations, Open Solutions*, *6*, 3400–3407. doi:10.1109/ACCESS.2017.2783951

Banik, L., Bhuiyan, M., & Jahan, A. (2015). Personalized learning materials for children with special needs using machine learning. In 2015 internet technologies and applications (ITA) (pp. 169-174). IEEE. doi:10.1109/ITechA.2015.7317390

Barik, L., Barukab, O., & Ahmed, A. (2020). Employing artificial intelligence techniques for student performance evaluation and teaching strategy enrichment: An innovative approach. *International Journal of Advanced and Applied Sciences*, *7*(11), 10–24. doi:10.21833/ijaas.2020.11.002

Baruah, J., & Paulus, P. B. (2019). Collaborative creativity and innovation in education. *Creativity Under Duress in Education? Resistive Theories, Practices, and Actions*, 155-177. doi:10.1007/978-3-319-90272-2_9

Bradáč, V., Smolka, P., Kotyrba, M., & Průdek, T. (2022). Design of an intelligent tutoring system to create a personalized study plan using expert systems. *Applied Sciences (Basel, Switzerland)*, *12*(12), 6236. doi:10.3390/app12126236

Burrows, S., Gurevych, I., & Stein, B. (2015). The eras and trends of automatic short answer grading. *International Journal of Artificial Intelligence in Education*, *25*(1), 60–117. doi:10.1007/s40593-014-0026-8

Caputi, V., & Garrido, A. (2015). Student-oriented planning of e-learning contents for Moodle. *Journal of Network and Computer Applications*, *53*, 115–127. doi:10.1016/j.jnca.2015.04.001

Celik, I., Dindar, M., Muukkonen, H., & Järvelä, S. (2022). The promises and challenges of artificial intelligence for teachers: A systematic review of research. *TechTrends*, *66*(4), 616–630. doi:10.1007/s11528-022-00715-y

Chen, L., Chen, P., & Lin, Z. (2020). Artificial intelligence in education: A review. *IEEE Access : Practical Innovations, Open Solutions*, *8*, 75264–75278. doi:10.1109/ACCESS.2020.2988510

Chounta, I., Bardone, E., Raudsep, A., & Pedaste, M. (2021). Exploring Teachers' Perceptions of Artificial Intelligence as a Tool to Support their Practice in Estonian K-12 Education. *International Journal of Artificial Intelligence in Education*, *32*(3), 725–755. doi:10.1007/s40593-021-00243-5

Clark, D., Tanner-Smith, E., & Killingsworth, S. (2018). Digital games, design and learning: A systematic review and meta-analysis. *Review of Educational Research*, *86*(1), 79–122. doi:10.3102/0034654315582065 PMID:26937054

Cordova, D. I., & Lepper, M. R. (1996). Intrinsic motivation and the process of learning: Beneficial effects of contextualization, personalization, and choice. *Journal of Educational Psychology*, *88*(4), 715–730. doi:10.1037/0022-0663.88.4.715

Dascalu, M., McNamara, D. S., Trausan-Matu, S., & Allen, L. K. (2018). Cohesion network analysis of CSCL participation. *Behavior Research Methods*, *50*(2), 604–619. doi:10.3758/s13428-017-0888-4 PMID:28409485

Diakopoulos, N. (2016). Accountability in algorithmic decision making. *Communications of the ACM*, *59*(2), 56–62. doi:10.1145/2844110

Edwards, C., Edwards, A., Spence, P. R., & Lin, X. (2018). I, teacher: Using artificial intelligence (AI) and social robots in communication and instruction. *Communication Education*, *67*(4), 473–480. doi:10.1080/03634523.2018.1502459

Eom, S. B., & Ashill, N. (2016). The determinants of students' perceived learning outcomes and satisfaction in university online education: An update. *Decision Sciences Journal of Innovative Education*, *14*(2), 185–215. doi:10.1111/dsji.12097

Floridi, L., Cowls, J., Beltrametti, M., Chatila, R., Chazerand, P., Dignum, V., & Vayena, E. (2021). An ethical framework for a good AI society: Opportunities, risks, principles, and recommendations. *Ethics, governance, and policies in artificial intelligence*, 19-39. doi:10.1007/978-3-030-81907-1_3

Girard, C., Ecalle, J., & Magnan, A. (2013). Serious games as new educational tools: How effective are they? A meta-analysis of recent studies. *Journal of Computer Assisted Learning*, *29*(3), 207–219. doi:10.1111/j.1365-2729.2012.00489.x

Gu, R., Xi, Z., Lin, B., & Ji, Y. (2022). Teacher-guided Autonomous Learning Enabled by Artificial Intelligence Empowered Remote Experiment Platform. In *2022 IEEE Global Engineering Education Conference (EDUCON)* (pp. 1089-1094). IEEE. https://ieeexplore.ieee.org/abstract/document/9766531/

Habgood, M. P., & Ainsworth, S. E. (2011). Motivating children to learn effectively: Exploring the value of intrinsic integration in educational games. *Journal of the Learning Sciences*, *20*(2), 169–206. doi:10.1080/10508406.2010.508029

Holmes, W., Bialik, M., & Fadel, C. (2019). *Artificial intelligence in education: Promises and implications for teaching and learning*. Center for Curriculum Redesign. doi:10.58863/20.500.12424/4273108

How, M., & Hung, W. (2019). Educing AI-Thinking in Science, Technology, Engineering, Arts, and Mathematics (STEAM) Education. *Education Sciences*, *9*(3), 184. doi:10.3390/educsci9030184

Hughes, R. T., Zhu, L., & Bednarz, T. (2021). Generative adversarial networks–enabled human–artificial intelligence collaborative applications for creative and design industries: A systematic review of current approaches and trends. *Frontiers in Artificial Intelligence*, *4*, 604234. doi:10.3389/frai.2021.604234 PMID:33997773

Ifenthaler, D., & Widanapathirana, C. (2014). Development and validation of a learning analytics framework: Two case studies using support vector machines. *Technology. Knowledge and Learning*, *19*(1-2), 221–240. doi:10.1007/s10758-014-9226-4

Jeong, H., & Hmelo-Silver, C. E. (2016). Seven affordances of computer-supported collaborative learning: How to support collaborative learning? How can technologies help? *Educational Psychologist*, *51*(2), 247–265. doi:10.1080/00461520.2016.1158654

Jonassen, D. H. (1994). Thinking technology: Toward a constructivist design model. *Educational Technology*, *34*(4), 34–37. https://www.learntechlib.org/p/171050/

Kaplan-Rakowski, R., Grotewold, K., Hartwick, P., & Papin, K. (2023). Generative AI and Teachers' Perspectives on Its Implementation in Education. *Journal of Interactive Learning Research*, *34*(2), 313–338. https://www.learntechlib.org/primary/p/222363/

Kasepalu, R., Prieto, L. P., Ley, T., & Chejara, P. (2022). Teacher artificial intelligence-supported pedagogical actions in collaborative learning coregulation: A wizard-of-oz study. In *Frontiers in Education* (Vol. 7, p. 736194). Frontiers. doi:10.3389/feduc.2022.736194

Kasneci, E., Seßler, K., Küchemann, S., Bannert, M., Dementieva, D., Fischer, F., Gasser, U., Groh, G., Günnemann, S., Hüllermeier, E., Krusche, S., Kutyniok, G., Michaeli, T., Nerdel, C., Pfeffer, J., Poquet, O., Sailer, M., Schmidt, A., Seidel, T., & Kasneci, G. (2023). ChatGPT for good? On opportunities and challenges of large language models for education. *Learning and Individual Differences*, *103*, 102274. doi:10.1016/j.lindif.2023.102274

Keating, J., & Nourbakhsh, I. (2018). Teaching artificial intelligence and humanity. *Communications of the ACM*, *61*(2), 29–32. doi:10.1145/3104986

Khazanchi, R., & Khazanchi, P. (2021). Artificial Intelligence in Education. *Advances in Early Childhood and K-12 Education*. doi:10.4018/978-1-7998-7630-4.ch014

Kochmar, E., Vu, D. D., Belfer, R., Gupta, V., Serban, I. V., & Pineau, J. (2020). Automated personalized feedback improves learning gains in an intelligent tutoring system. In *Artificial Intelligence in Education: 21st International Conference, AIED 2020,* (pp. 140-146). Springer International Publishing. https://doi.org/10.1007/978-3-030-52240-7_26

Koedinger, K. R., Kim, J., Jia, J. Z., McLaughlin, E. A., & Bier, N. L. (2015, March). Learning is not a spectator sport: Doing is better than watching for learning from a MOOC. In *Proceedings of the second (2015) ACM conference on learning@ scale* (pp. 111-120). ACM. 10.1145/2724660.2724681

Koivisto, M. (2023). Tutoring Postgraduate Students with an AI-Based Chatbot. *International Journal of Advanced Corporate Learning*, *16*(1), 41–54. doi:10.3991/ijac.v16i1.35437

Kulik, J. A., & Kulik, C. L. C. (1988). Timing of feedback and verbal learning. *Review of Educational Research*, *58*(1), 79–97. doi:10.3102/00346543058001079

Lameras, P., & Arnab, S. (2021). Power to the Teachers: An Exploratory Review on Artificial Intelligence in Education. *Information (Basel)*, *13*(1), 14. doi:10.3390/info13010014

Liu, M., Horton, L., Olmanson, J., & Toprac, P. (2011). A study of learning and motivation in a new media enriched environment for middle school science. *Educational Technology Research and Development*, *59*(2), 249–265. doi:10.1007/s11423-011-9192-7

Liu, M., Ren, Y., Nyagoga, L. M., Stonier, F., Wu, Z., & Yu, L. (2023). *Future of education in the era of generative artificial intelligence: Consensus among Chinese scholars on applications of ChatGPT in schools*. Future in Educational Research. doi:10.1002/fer3.10

Liu, Y., Chen, L., & Yao, Z. (2022). The application of artificial intelligence assistant to deep learning in teachers' teaching and students' learning processes. *Frontiers in Psychology*, *13*, 929175. doi:10.3389/fpsyg.2022.929175 PMID:36033031

Lockspeiser, T. M., & Kaul, P. (2016). Using individualized learning plans to facilitate learner-centered teaching. *Journal of Pediatric and Adolescent Gynecology*, *29*(3), 214–217. doi:10.1016/j.jpag.2015.10.020 PMID:26612117

Luckin, R., Holmes, W., Griffiths, M., & Forcier, L. B. (2016). *Intelligence unleashed: An argument for AI in education*. Pearson Education. https://discovery.ucl.ac.uk/id/eprint/1475756

Mannekote, A. (2023). Towards a Neural Era in Dialogue Management for Collaboration: A Literature Survey. *arXiv preprint arXiv:2307.09021*. https://doi.org//arXiv.2307.09021 doi:10.48550

Megahed, F. M., Chen, Y. J., Ferris, J. A., Knoth, S., & Jones-Farmer, L. A. (2023). How generative ai models such as chatgpt can be (mis) used in spc practice, education, and research? an exploratory study. *Quality Engineering*, 1–29. doi:10.1080/08982112.2023.2206479

Miller, M. (2022). *AI in the classroom: 10+ tools for teachers*. Ditch the Textbook. https://ditchthat-textbook.com

Mishra, P., & Koehler, M. J. (2006). Technological pedagogical content knowledge: A framework for teacher knowledge. *Teachers College Record*, *108*(6), 1017–1054. doi:10.1111/j.1467-9620.2006.00684.x

Moreno, R., & Mayer, R. E. (2000). Engaging students in active learning: The case for personalized multimedia messages. *Journal of Educational Psychology*, *92*(4), 724–733. doi:10.1037/0022-0663.92.4.724

Ndukwe, I. G., Daniel, B. K., & Amadi, C. E. (2019). A machine learning grading system using chatbots. In *Artificial Intelligence in Education: 20th International Conference, AIED 2019,* (pp. 365-368). Springer International Publishing. https://doi.org/10.1007/978-3-030-23207-8_67

Nissenbaum, H., & Walker, D. (1998). Will computers dehumanize education? A grounded approach to values at risk. *Technology in Society*, *20*(3), 237–273. doi:10.1016/S0160-791X(98)00011-6

Page, L., & Gehlbach, H. (2017). How an Artificially Intelligent Virtual Assistant Helps Students Navigate the Road to College. *AERA Open*, *3*(4). doi:10.1177/2332858417749220

Parshall, C. G., Spray, J. A., Kalohn, J. C., & Davey, T. (2002). *Practical considerations in computer-based testing*. Springer Science & Business Media. doi:10.1007/978-1-4613-0083-0

Pedro, F., Subosa, M., Rivas, A., & Valverde, P. (2019). *Artificial intelligence in education: Challenges and opportunities for sustainable development*. HDL. https://hdl.handle.net/20.500.12799/6533

Pender, H. L., Bohl, L., Schönberger, M., & Knopf, J. (2022). *An AI-based lesson planning software to support competence-based learning*. IEEE. doi:10.4995/HEAd22.2022.14599

Porayska-Pomsta, K. (2016). AI as a Methodology for Supporting Educational Praxis and Teacher Metacognition. *International Journal of Artificial Intelligence in Education*, *26*(2), 679–700. doi:10.1007/s40593-016-0101-4

Reiss, M. (2021). The use of AI in education: Practicalities and ethical considerations. *London Review of Education*, *19*(1). doi:10.14324/LRE.19.1.05

Roll, I., Aleven, V., McLaren, B. M., & Koedinger, K. R. (2011). Improving students' help-seeking skills using metacognitive feedback in an intelligent tutoring system. *Learning and Instruction*, *21*(2), 267–280. doi:10.1016/j.learninstruc.2010.07.004

Roscoe, R. D., & McNamara, D. S. (2013). Writing pal: Feasibility of an intelligent writing strategy tutor in the high school classroom. *Journal of Educational Psychology*, *105*(4), 1010–1025. doi:10.1037/a0032340

Ruiz-Rojas, L. I., Acosta-Vargas, P., De-Moreta-Llovet, J., & Gonzalez-Rodriguez, M. (2023). Empowering Education with Generative Artificial Intelligence Tools: Approach with an Instructional Design Matrix. *Sustainability (Basel), 15*(15), 11524. doi:10.3390/su151511524

Rutten, N., van Joolingen, W. R., & van der Veen, J. T. (2012). The learning effects of computer simulations in science education. *Computers & Education, 58*(1), 136–153. doi:10.1016/j.compedu.2011.07.017

Schneider, B., & Pea, R. (2017). Real-time mutual gaze perception enhances collaborative learning and collaboration quality. *Educational Media and Technology Yearbook, 40*, 99–125. doi:10.1007/978-3-319-45001-8_7

Schroeder, K. T., Hubertz, M., Van Campenhout, R., & Johnson, B. G. (2022). Teaching and Learning with AI-Generated Courseware: Lessons from the Classroom. *Online Learning : the Official Journal of the Online Learning Consortium, 26*(3), 73–87. https://eric.ed.gov/?id=EJ1374315. doi:10.24059/olj.v26i3.3370

Shemshack, A., & Spector, J. M. (2020). A systematic literature review of personalized learning terms. *Smart Learning Environments, 7*(1), 1–20. doi:10.1186/s40561-020-00140-9

Skaalvik, E. M., & Skaalvik, S. (2017). Teacher stress and teacher self-efficacy: Relations and consequences. *Educator stress: An occupational health perspective*, 101-125. doi:10.1007/978-3-319-53053-6_5

Slavin, R. E. (1996). Research on cooperative learning and achievement: What we know, what we need to know. *Contemporary Educational Psychology, 21*(1), 43–69. https://www.academia.edu/download/32134643/Cooperative_Learning_-_SLAVIN__Robert.pdf. doi:10.1006/ceps.1996.0004

Tan, K., Pang, T., & Fan, C. (2023). Towards Applying Powerful Large AI Models in Classroom Teaching: Opportunities, Challenges and Prospects. *arXiv preprint arXiv:2305.03433*. https://doi.org//arXiv.2305.03433 doi:10.48550

Tapalova, O., & Zhiyenbayeva, N. (2022). Artificial Intelligence in Education: AIEd for Personalised Learning Pathways. *Electronic Journal of e-Learning, 20*(5), 639–653. doi:10.34190/ejel.20.5.2597

Tegos, S., Demetriadis, S., & Karakostas, A. (2015). Promoting academically productive talk with conversational agent interventions in collaborative learning settings. *Computers & Education, 87*, 309–325. doi:10.1016/j.compedu.2015.07.014

Timms, M. (2016). Letting Artificial Intelligence in Education Out of the Box: Educational Cobots and Smart Classrooms. *International Journal of Artificial Intelligence in Education, 26*(2), 701–712. doi:10.1007/s40593-016-0095-y

Tisoglu, S., Piri, Z., Mericelli, M., & Inan, F. C. (2022). Targeting Creativity Through a Learner-Generated Digital Storytelling Project. *International Journal of Technology in Teaching and Learning, 18*(1). doi:10.37120/ijttl.2022.18.1.01

Tissenbaum, M., Lui, M., & Slotta, J. D. (2019). Developing a smart classroom infrastructure to support real-time student collaboration and inquiry: A 4-year design study. *Instructional Science, 47*(4), 423–443. doi:10.1007/s11251-019-09486-1

Touretzky, D., Gardner-McCune, C., Martin, F., & Seehorn, D. (2019). Envisioning AI for K-12: What should every child know about AI? *Proceedings of the AAAI Conference on Artificial Intelligence*, *33*(01), 9795–9799. doi:10.1609/aaai.v33i01.33019795

Troussas, C., Giannakas, F., Sgouropoulou, C., & Voyiatzis, I. (2023). Collaborative activities recommendation based on students' collaborative learning styles using ANN and WSM. *Interactive Learning Environments*, *31*(1), 54–67. doi:10.1080/10494820.2020.1761835

Vanlehn, K. (2011). The relative effectiveness of human tutoring, intelligent tutoring systems, and other tutoring systems. *Educational Psychologist*, *46*(4), 197–221. doi:10.1080/00461520.2011.611369

Verleger, M., & Pembridge, J. (2018, October). A pilot study integrating an AI-driven chatbot in an introductory programming course. In 2018 IEEE frontiers in education conference (FIE) (pp. 1-4). IEEE. doi:10.1109/FIE.2018.8659282

Vygotsky, L. S., & Cole, M. (1978). *Mind in society: Development of higher psychological processes*. Harvard university press.

Walkington, C., & Bernacki, M. (2020). Personalization of instruction: Design dimensions and implications for cognition. *Journal of Experimental Education*, *88*(1), 50–68. doi:10.1080/00220973.2017.1380590

Williamson, B. (2019). Brain data: Scanning, scraping and sculpting the plastic learning brain through neurotechnology. *Postdigital Science and Education*, *1*(1), 65–86. doi:10.1007/s42438-018-0008-5

Winkler, R., Neuweiler, M. L., Bittner, E. A., & Söllner, M. (2019). Hey Alexa, Please Help Us Solve This Problem! How Interactions with Smart Personal Assistants Improve Group Performance. In *ICIS*. https://www.alexandria.unisg.ch/bitstreams/fb70d3b8-4ec0-413b-9bd7-35f240e62e6e/download

Wolff, A., Zdrahal, Z., Nikolov, A., & Pantucek, M. (2013, April). Improving retention: predicting at-risk students by analysing clicking behaviour in a virtual learning environment. In *Proceedings of the third international conference on learning analytics and knowledge* (pp. 145-149). ACM. 10.1145/2460296.2460324

Woo, D. J., Wang, Y., & Susanto, H. (2023). Understanding EFL Students' Idea Generation Strategies for Creative Writing with NLG Tools. https://doi.org//arXiv.2207.01484 doi:10.48550

Worthen, M. (2016). The future of personalized learning for students with disabilities. *State Education Standard, 16*(3), 35. https://nasbe.nyc3.digitaloceanspaces.com/2016/09/Future-of-Personalized-Learning-for-Students-with-Disabilities_September-2016-Standard.pdf

Wu, C., Chen, Y., & Chen, T. (2017). An Adaptive e-Learning System for Enhancing Learning Performance: Based on Dynamic Scaffolding Theory. *Eurasia Journal of Mathematics, Science and Technology Education*, *14*(3), 903–913. doi:10.12973/ejmste/81061 PMID:26436650

Yang, H., & Zhu, K. (2022). Research on AI-assisted grading of math questions based on deep learning. In *International Conference on Internet of Things and Machine Learning (IoTML 2021)* (Vol. 12174, pp. 211-217). SPIE. https://doi.org/10.1117/12.2628649

Zawacki-Richter, O., Marín, V. I., Bond, M., & Gouverneur, F. (2019). Systematic review of research on artificial intelligence applications in higher education–where are the educators? *International Journal of Educational Technology in Higher Education*, *16*(1), 1–27. doi:10.1186/s41239-019-0171-0

Zhai, X., Chu, X., Chai, C., Jong, M., Istenič, A., Spector, M., Liu, J., Yuan, J., & Li, Y. (2021). A Review of Artificial Intelligence (AI) in Education from 2010 to 2020. *Complex.*, 2021, 8812542:1-8812542:18. . doi:10.1155/2021/8812542

ADDITIONAL READING

Bozkurt, A., & Sharma, R. C. (2023). Generative AI and prompt engineering: The art of whispering to let the genie out of the algorithmic world. *Asian Journal of Distance Education.* http://asianjde.com/ojs/index.php/AsianJDE/article/view/749

Memarian, B., & Doleck, T. (2023). Fairness, Accountability, Transparency, and Ethics (FATE) in Artificial Intelligence (AI), and higher education: A systematic review. Computers and Education: Artificial Intelligence, 100152, 100152. doi:10.1016/j.caeai.2023.100152 doi:10.1016/j.caeai.2023.100152

Pedró, F. (2020). Applications of Artificial Intelligence to higher education: Possibilities, evidence, and challenges. IUL Research, 1(1), 61–76. doi:10.57568/iulres.v1i1.43 doi:10.57568/iulres.v1i1.43

Şenocak, D., Koçdar, S., & Bozkurt, A. (2023). Historical, Philosophical and Ethical Roots of Artificial Intelligence. PJE, 40(1). 10.30971/pje.v40i1.1152

KEY TERMS AND DEFINITIONS

AI Literacy: Understanding how artificial intelligence technologies function, including model capabilities, limitations, and potential biases.

Educational Data Rights: Ethical standards and governance of how student data is utilized by AI systems to ensure privacy, security, transparency, and accountability.

Generative AI: Advanced artificial intelligence systems that can dynamically generate new content and insights, such as text, code, images, and more.

Personalized Learning: Educational approach tailored to each student's individual needs, abilities, interests, and learning style. Enabled by generative AI insights.

Prompt Engineering: The practice of carefully designing and optimizing the prompts provided to generative AI models to control and improve their outputs.

Scaffolding: Providing educational content, activities, and guidance structured around a student's evolving zone of proximal development to optimize learning.

Simulated Learning Environments: Immersive interactive simulations powered by generative AI to provide experiential learning opportunities.

Teacher Agency: Teachers maintaining oversight and wisdom to direct integration of AI technologies judiciously based on professional expertise and learning values.

Chapter 12
Empowering Teaching With Prompt Engineering:
How to Integrate Curriculum, Standards, and Assessment for a New Age

Scott F. Gregory
https://orcid.org/0000-0001-7210-8801
Fort Hays State University, USA

ABSTRACT

This chapter aims to provide a practical guide for using prompt engineering in the educational setting. It will address the necessity of recognizing the reality of change throughout the history of educational practice & its connection to new methods and strategies that prompt engineering presents. Readers will learn how to assist students in generating effective prompts through using an effective prompt engineering model. Readers will then learn how to integrate learning theories with the prompt engineering model to best support student learning. Readers will learn how to connect prompt engineering in classroom teaching with educational standards to create effective learning objectives. The design of higher-level thinking and relevant assessments required by prompt engineering's use in schools, is outlined in detail. This chapter is written for educators, researchers, and students who are interested in learning how prompt engineering could be implemented in the classroom successfully at all levels.

INTRODUCTION: AN INSTRUCTOR'S VIEWPOINT

Prompt engineering holds promising opportunities for classroom instruction. At present, there is great curiosity, apprehension, and lack of knowledge when it comes to seeing how prompt engineering can be utilized in the classroom. For instructors, embracing the promise of prompt engineering will be arduous. Instructors in this chapter, denotes teachers of elementary, secondary, and post-secondary students. Prompt engineering can be defined as the creation of organized text to bring about outputs that reflect a desired goal or objective. The reason for this difficulty has less to do with the lack of instructor knowledge or

DOI: 10.4018/979-8-3693-1351-0.ch012

access to technology, than it does with the influence of the educational paradigm. We can define a paradigm as the formal and informal understandings, actions, and words of an organized group. At present, if an instructor wishes to teach different skills or focus on certain parts of the curriculum that they have struggled to convey, there is no shortage of packaged curriculum materials or textbooks for that instructor to use. While this change may take time for the instructor implement, what the new curriculum requires of the teacher in the presentation of content and what they emphasize in terms of assessment, compared to what the instructor is already using, is not that far apart. Prompt engineering is entirely different and will require key instructional and assessment shifts for implementation to be successful.

Prompt engineering adoption in the classroom is not a matter of learning a new pre-packaged curriculum or set of standards. Prompt engineering requires a reconfiguration of how the instructor views their role and carries out instruction. The instructor alone no longer becomes the main source by which most concepts and knowledge are imparted to students. The instructor moves from providing smaller basic units of knowledge entirely, to teaching basic units of knowledge through the tool or medium, of prompt engineering. Prompt engineering becomes the college or secondary instructor's power point. It is the new textbook or base structure from which instruction originates. The researching of a topic at all levels is accelerated in complexity and greater depth with prompt engineering as it is fundamentally different than just "Googling" questions or trying to find "the answer." In learning to use prompt engineering, students require guidance in creating engineered prompts and the "search" requires greater complexity. Students must be guided to evaluate the quality of the prompts they create. Students learn through a series of trials and errors, how to refine their ability to formulate prompts which will elicit detailed, accurate information and evaluate the resulting output that they have engineered.

Prompt engineering implementation in the classroom will also require a shifting in how assessment occurs in the classroom. A common concern about prompt engineering is that it is merely a tool for students to engage in cheating (Cotton et al., 2023). I would argue that this concern stems from how prompt engineering fundamentally alters classroom instruction and assessment, rendering a good number of assessments "dead" as they are disconnected from the higher level of engagement, and it dispatches simplistic, lower-level questions with ease as they lack higher order operations. Prompt engineering includes but transcends contemporary assessment types due to how it is used by students to plan, prioritize informational inputs, continue to work with information, and problem-solve.

The "cheating" that prompt engineering creates is less a product of cheating, than it is a demonstration of how contemporary assessments become easy prey to prompt engineering due to an assessment's limited complexity or if it consists primarily of basic recall and reproduction of knowledge. A prompt engineering entry of: "Who is buried in Grant's tomb?" will elicit an equally black and white answer that is not challenging or complex in nature. In answering this question, prompt engineering is used at the basic level of knowledge retrieval. As this example shows, a basic engineered prompt entered does not provide "the answer" unethically. It is merely directed by the learner to provide a simplistic answer for an equally simplistic question. The real outrage is not the concern of cheating, the real outrage is that prompt engineering was used in such an underwhelming fashion instructionally.

The classroom instructor who wishes to implement prompt engineering into their teaching must realize that implementation challenges are significant. Instructors who implement prompt engineering within the educational paradigm of current teaching methods and assessments, will find prompt engineering to be a poor fit. Some may deem it inadequate and stop implementation prematurely. For those who see "the big picture" of how prompt engineering elicits a profound change in how students create, manage, evaluate, and share information, prompt engineering provides new pathways of building knowledge with greater student engagement. Before implementation can begin, the classroom instructor must be aware of the educational paradigm and how it operates.

The educational paradigm bridges personal and collective attitudinal stances. A useful description has been provided through prior research. ". . . . (The educational paradigm is a) collection of assumptions, beliefs, and values that underlie the workings of present-day schools" (Gregory & Gregory, 1995). The education paradigm encompasses the informal and formal operations of schooling. It can be identified with specific procedures of teaching and learning, as well as related values as to what the purpose of an education is and why teaching is conducted the way that it is. Informal operating beliefs can be mindsets that value specific ideals such as "high test scores," "a wide-ranging curriculum," or "small class sizes." Formal processes can include the curriculum of what is to specifically be taught. It can include character or civic education that seeks to imbue learners with demonstrating certain behaviors or valued attitudes. With the informal and formal nature of paradigms outlined, to what specific ideas do we see present in our educational paradigm?

Overview of the Current Educational Paradigm of Student Work and Learning

The educational paradigm was created out of a conflict between two contrasting visions of education. The first of these visions is the idea of progressive education originating in the late 19th and early 20th centuries in the United States. In a departure from colonial American education, the progressive era saw the creation of standards of teacher professionalization and the requirement of teachers to be certificated. Administrators were trained in management principles and schools were increasingly consolidated in larger schools with expansion of educational decision-making powers at the state level (Urban, et al., 2013). The purpose of student work and learning in the eyes of progressives was the cultivating of critical, independent thought that would guide the learner towards solving yet to be realized problems on their own (Popkewitz, 2011). John Dewey was the foremost advocate of progressive education, which held that student learning was the cultivation of critical thinking and reasoning skills. Student learning and work centered on the social basis of which the learner lives. "The teacher's business is simply to determine, on the basis of larger experience riper wisdom, how the discipline of life shall come to the child" (Archambault, 2010, pp. 432).

The second contrasting viewpoint was labeled by Dewey as "traditional schooling" (Archambault, 1974, p. 6). This vision is what currently holds sway in education. Traditional schooling has swung the pendulum of teaching from progressive ideals, back to traditional teaching norms that existed before Dewey's time. The passage of the No Child Left Behind Act (NCLB) brought about a greater focus on traditional teaching methods and an emphasis on imparting knowledge as assessed on state assessments, as opposed to creating student learners who can critique and work to impact their social environs (Little, 2013). While traditional education has a long history in America, NCLB was part of the larger influence of neoliberalism Neoliberal thought holds the primacy of the free-market and that government services, education, included, should be examined through a lens of economic efficiency and the need to produce workers with the necessary knowledge and skills to be successful in the workplace (Melanson, 2023).

Classroom instructors find themselves surrounded in a teaching environment with neoliberal dominant ideas of standardized curricula, state standards, and state testing. The progressive vision has shrunken considerably as states must demonstrate "achievement" and are held "accountable" based on standardized results. Being ensconced in the education paradigm does not lend itself to utilizing prompt engineering in the way that it is truly meant to be utilized. Large language models for this chapter, are defined as computer programmed systems that take in text prompts and respond in a syntactically structured way for humans to comprehend results. During 2023 and beyond, large language models are showing a developmental arc that crossed into new territory that will change the world forever.

Overview of Prompt Engineering

Developments in A.I. have crossed an important threshold, allowing the generation of text that caters to human understanding and which produces an output that is comprehensible to humans. Even with progress made, limitations exist regarding the ability of A.I. to respond to inputs that are beyond its programmed capability (Bozkurt, 2023, p. 200). Research literature has identified that prompt engineering's entrance into education is coming about through A.I.'s welcomed ability to simplify tasks, reduce redundancy and inefficiency in the workplace environment. As a result, education offers a similar environment for technology enhancement with the opportunity for greater task simplification and related computer processes (Eager & Brunton, 2023 in citing Taylor et al., 2022).

Due to the limitations mentioned previously, the creation of prompts will need to be a main educational focus, as AI at present, is "prompt dependent (Fisher & Jacobs, 2023, p. 18). With prompt dependence, prompt engineering provides the benefit as well of having students counter results retrieved and demanding further information through more incisive prompts. Students can also generate interrogating prompts in dialogue with the large language model (Rahman & Watanobe, 2023). The potential of creating effective prompts, as well as engaging in higher critique prompts and interrogation, creates the need for critical thinking skills that will become dominant for the remainder of the 21st century, thereby shaping teaching, student learning, and assessment.

21st Century Knowledge and Skills Needed for a New Age: The Promise of Prompt Engineering

There is no shortage of information as it regards what constitutes 21st century knowledge & skills. A Google search can find entries that define it at a basic, core level of understanding that points to possessing information age skillsets. "21st-century skills are based primarily on "deeper learning" skills (like critical thinking, problem solving, and teamwork) and are comprised of a combination of soft-skills (such as interaction, collaboration, processing information, and managing people. . ." (Edalex, 2023). It is necessary to stress that "critical thinking" as a skill, has a long history in education. Critical thinking is commonplace in state standards and as a stated learning goal in curriculum across the country.

However, there is a distinct difference between a critical thinking worksheet that asks readers to "find the main idea" and what prompt engineering presents when it comes to critical thinking. The former example is really a basic literacy skill and does not constitute actual critical thinking. Prompt engineering incorporates basic literacy knowledge, managing required inputs, and evaluating a finished product, while the critical thinking worksheet does not. Prompt engineering requires metacognition as well. Metacognition is defined as the process of analyzing or strategically thinking about how to strategize mentally. The learner must evaluate their responses and retrace their own steps in thinking. The concept of collaboration is another key 21st century skill that also requires further distinction. In many classrooms, collaboration entails students in a physical space coming together for "group work" or "project" activities. A more defined and authentic description of the collaboration that is needed is the asynchronous coordination and working together kind of collaboration. This occurs today when groups work amongst each other, in "mediated interactions" with others who may not even be in the same physical space at the same time (Dede, 2010).

21st century skills have been sought to be addressed in various frameworks, standards, and curriculum learning goals. Compared to various learning methods of group work, thinking exercises, and other classroom strategies, prompt engineering provides an important break from the past as it relates to these concepts. The metacognitive effort required to form good prompts, marshal resulting information, analyzing results, and synthesizing results, points to an entirely new level of critical thinking that has not been previously reached in the classroom learning environment. With the background context of prompt engineering and education provided, a discussion of the chapter structure becomes necessary.

Overview and Scope of Chapter

This chapter proceeds from this introduction to coming to terms with the educational paradigm and successfully implementing prompt engineering in the classroom. This includes addressing subsumed points of examining how technology has disrupted previous educational paradigms. A second area of examination will address how the present educational paradigm is in its last gasps of life as a pedagogical influence, though it attempts to stave off the inevitable creative chaos presented by prompt engineering through restrictive practices such as A.I. detection software, banning of technology as a classroom tool, and other deficit-based rules. The section concludes with a discussion of the importance of recognizing the constant of change and the need to embrace prompt engineering in the classroom. Laying the groundwork for using prompt engineering in the classroom is the second main point of the chapter that is presented. This begins with redefinition of what constitutes authentic student work and documenting quality work with prompt engineering before moving on to discuss how to connect pivotal learning theories to the use of prompt engineering. The reader will then learn how to integrate standards with prompt engineering implementation.

Lastly, this chapter addresses classroom strategies in using prompt engineering at the K-12 and university levels. This begins with outlining how to assist students in building knowledge with prompt engineering, before moving on to specific classroom strategies to utilize. Mentioned as well will be how instructors can continue to integrate further knowledge of prompt engineering and make professional learning connections to utilize for future practice. This section concludes with a discussion of working with assessments with prompt engineering in mind. The concluding portion of this chapter reviews educational change as it relates to the educator, present challenges & opportunities when it comes to prompt engineering, with a subsequent description of future directions and opportunities.

COMING TO TERMS WITH EDUCATIONAL PARADIGM DISRUPTION

Comparing and Contrasting the A.I. Disruption of the Educational Paradigm

Prompt engineering is not the first time that technology has significantly shifted the traditional educational paradigm. An appropriate comparison of great disruption presented by A.I. prompt engineering is the printing press. With this invention, the educational paradigm faced a significant challenge to established practice. DeWar (1998) outlined how with books being rare, the main vehicle for learning was listening, which centered the authority of knowledge on the "lecturer," who came to be a person with a recognized skill set. He continued to relay that over time, the printing press removed the lecturer as the instructional focal point and centered the learning process on the student reader. From this "listener to reader to user" conversion, the nature and structure of learning changed forever. "As a consumer of printed materials geared to a sequence of learning stages, the growing child was subjected to a different developmental process than was the medieval apprentice, ploughboy, novice or page" (DeWar in citing Eisenstein, p. 23).

With the printing press's shadow on teaching, a question arose as to if the lecturer would even be necessary. No longer needed to lecture from a book verbatim, lecturers shifted their presentations to content that related to the material, but that also included reflections, personal insights, and other content. A philosopher living through this time of change mentioned that books changed learning and that lecturers had to adjust as a result. "Lectures may say precisely those things which do not exist in any book, and the other way around" (Friesen, 2017, p. 121) Far from removing the lecturer entirely from the classroom, the paradigm shifted by changing the lecturer's focus from being the sole source of information, to one who guided the classroom discussion while incorporating resources in the book, and from outside of it. The textbook became a regular staple for learning and education was changed forever as a result (Friesen, 2017).

Like the printing press, the use of prompt engineering in education presents an equally monumental challenge to established educational practice in two keyways. First, curricular challenges increase as an adopted curriculum must "keep up" with the generation of knowledge. Second, learning challenges mirror that of what the printing press presented. In the instance of A.I., rote learning through text recitation threatens to become automated (Lubis, p. 185). Similarly, A.I. prompt engineering also shifts the nature of teaching and the teacher's role in presenting information. With A.I., the teacher becomes more of a "mediator" whose simple lesson planning, assessments given and graded, become automated as the teacher shifts to facilitating the finding and analysis of complex knowledge (Zovko & Gudlin, 2019, p. ENT3951).

The implementation of the calculator into schools presented another shift for the educational paradigm, though on a smaller scale. In contrast to A.I. prompt engineering, the introduction of the calculator was less of a disruptive force, but a force nonetheless that required change. High school students who came to college with calculators and post-secondary professors soon discovered that teaching and textbook priorities did not line up well with the new handheld devices (Banks, 2011). Just as with the printing press, the focus on student work and the teacher's instruction shifted. The unease that teachers feel when new technology is utilized in the classroom that fundamentally changes the dynamic of teaching and learning, has to do with the concern of what will be lost. While loss will occur, learning will shift to other areas of a subject that are not covered, or to areas where deeper learning can occur. This shift can be seen with the use of calculators as they moved the student further away from basic computation. "On the one hand, the taking over of computation by a machine increases the distance of the user from numbers; on the other hand, the carrying out of marginal tasks (for instance, giving change) is connected to computation practices which involve counting concrete objects. Technological evaluation dramatically changes social relationships to mathematical objects" (Trouche, 2005, p. 14-15). The development of the printing press and calculator show how instructional change occurs in the educational paradigm. Prompt engineering's widespread use in education will be no exception. There will be an eventual coming to terms that needs to be explained.

In the instance of the printing press and calculator, the instructor was not eliminated. In both examples, it was the methodology of teaching which became outmoded. Neither was the subject matter completely erased. What really happened was that the emphasis of what was taught and what was emphasized for the learner to learn, did. Instructors at all levels will mourn the knowledge and skills that will be lost to the sands of time. Not all knowledge that serves an individual's social, economic, or other utilitarian purpose across the continuum of time will be relevant for another individual in their own time. Learning to inscribe on papyrus is no longer necessary. No one bemoans the fact that the horse and buggy industry has disappeared. Nor do we ponder the demise of hand loom weavers and that no one around us now knows how to create their own clothing. These knowledge & skills provided a valuable function for their time, but time moved on. Increasingly, being able to communicate in the online environment and performing calculations beyond simple formulas, are necessary for daily living. With prompt engineering and A.I., we are seeing a continuing evolution of how communication and knowledge production continues to evolve.

Instructors must recognize that the only constant is change. The methods, concepts, and related skills that suited us may not suit future learners. We cannot be tied to any one way of doing things and we must be open to continuing to learn and to adapt accordingly. Teaching methodology, curriculum, assessment, and related tools are all relative and the sooner we recognize these items are not immutable facts of life, the better off our learners will be.

LAYING THE GROUNDWORK FOR PROMPT ENGINEERING USE IN THE CLASSROOM

An Argument for Redefining Authentic Student Work With Prompt Engineering in Mind

In implementing prompt engineering in the classroom, I would maintain that three new understandings must be reached if implementation is to be a success. Before practical implementation of prompt engineering can begin in the classroom, it is important to become oriented with how prompt engineering will require viewing student work and learning through a different lens. The present lens in my estimation is broken. This is evidenced through ill thought-out restrictions, brought about through the inevitability of prompt engineering and A.I. in the classroom. As a result of present educators seeing things through the traditional educational lens, college instructors are doing away with the take home essay (Robin, 2023). Others have resorted to handwritten assessments taken in class while post-secondary leaders advocate for stringent policies to deal with prompt engineering and A.I. "It will take an aggressive and comprehensive institutional response to dissuade students from plagiarism" (Keegin, 2023) While these takes are legitimate stances within the lens of the traditional educational paradigm, I would argue that these actions are unnecessary as a new paradigm that presents itself to us. To achieve a better adjustment to the new paradigm, the classroom instructor must embrace new understandings.

New Understanding #1-Use of Prompt Engineering and A.I. is not Plagiarism

If you were to engineer a prompt asking a large language model to explain how Gavrilo Princip assassinated the Archduke Franz Ferdinand, you would obtain a desired output. The engineered response in and of itself does not constitute plagiarism and if you were a student, the work should be accepted as your original work as the prompts you engineered, if you obtained accurate results. What makes a work plagiarized is the lack of attributing the idea and words to another source that was the originator of that writing (Singh, 2023). In the engineered output that you received, each sentence could be identified from a source found on the internet.

If you did find that your engineered response borrowed too heavily from sources using more direct words from sources than you liked, you could fix the text accordingly. Again, this is not so much a problem of plagiarizing as it is a problem of requiring the learner to interact with the engineered text. As the learner, you should engage in the process of recognizing when direct quotation is needed and when I need to reword sentences for proper indirect citation. This form of correction is no different in substance or ethical practice than when we have students correct their own written work. Prompt engineering requires further cognizing on text as we are left to ask: is the information accurate? Has the prompt provided a good response? Is it thorough? Does it fully address the question? Can it be improved? With this understanding in mind, it is important to move on to a related understanding concerning student work.

New Understanding #2-Prompt Engineering Works on the Part of a student, Constitutes Legitimate Student Work

When it comes to creative works, the results from prompts are no less of an authentic expression of the student than pen or pencil crafted responses. Classroom instructors should evaluate work based on the prompts provided and the engineered results. To elaborate on this understanding, I have provided a prompt about a lost bear in the woods, outlined in **Figure 1**.

Figure 1. The lost bear
Note. Lost Bear Bing A.I. entry created by the author.

Your personal and company data are protected in this chat

Once upon a time, in a dense forest, there lived a bear named **Benny**. Benny was a curious bear and loved to explore the woods. One day, while wandering around, he lost his way and found himself in an unfamiliar part of the forest. He was scared and didn't know what to do.

Just then, he saw a wise deer named **Daisy**. Daisy was known for her intelligence and quick thinking. She saw that Benny was lost and offered to help him find his way back home. Benny was grateful for her help and followed her lead.

As they were walking, they came across a forgetful fox named **Felix**. Felix was known for his forgetfulness but had a kind heart. Daisy explained the situation to Felix, and he offered to help them find their way back home.

As they continued their journey, they met a helpful hound named **Harry**. Harry was known for his loyalty and willingness to help others. He saw that Benny was lost and offered to guide them back home.

Finally, they met a busy bee named **Bella**. Bella was always busy with her work but had a kind heart. She saw that Benny was lost and offered to help them find their way back home.

Together, Daisy, Felix, Harry, and Bella helped Benny find his way back home. They used their unique skills and worked together as a team to overcome obstacles along the way.

When they finally reached Benny's home, he thanked them all for their help and invited them in for some honey. From that day on, they all became good friends and went on many adventures together.

The end.

I would maintain that the engineered output from the prompt is no different than the output of a prompt provided from a calculator had I entered '2x2" and then pressed the equal sign. Results from such prompts are not in and of themselves, less authentic. The sentences provided in **Figure 1** do not exist in any other medium, nor has the content been published by another author. They have been constructed from prompts provided and uniquely combined based on my labor, from my own input. Thus, the work constitutes my work and my work only. To argue this selection is not my authentic work is to ignore the source of the prompts provided and to ignore the fact that I have directed its creation through a tool that streamlines and makes more efficient, the engineering of text. It can be argued that efforts to ban prompt engineering in the classroom represents work that is not an authentic creation of the student. This bears relevance upon the need to recognize a third new understanding.

New Understanding #3-Knowledge and "Rules" About Knowledge Are Socially Constructed

At the time this chapter is being written, older adults are re-learning new rules about writing. For years, they went through a schooling system that emphasized that you always put two spaces between sentences. At one point in time, this served a valid purpose. As it no longer does, it has now become socially acceptable to just use one space (Selk, 2018). To a person transported in time to the present day, the "King's English" and what is proper English are but one of many, as English speakers in Australia, the United Kingdom, and the United States, speak derivatives of it and engage in "code switching or "style-drifting" accordingly (McArthur, 1987, p. 10).

As with these examples, what is considered "proper" and "right" when it comes to systems of communication is not an immutable law from the heavens. This realization means that the classroom teacher and school team should reconsider any opposition to the use of prompt engineering in the classroom. Along this line of understanding, Foucault mentioned the necessity of critically recognizing the "rules" of discourse and why it is that we should be open minded about it in our lives. "We must question those ready-made syntheses, those groupings that we normally accept before any examination, those links whose validity is recognized from the outset. . .We must also question those divisions or groupings with which we have become so familiar" (Foucault, 1972/2010, p. 22). When we see that the nature of knowledge and learning changes and that it is not an immovable fact of life that remains stationary, we can move on to reorganize knowledge and teaching for present and future realities. This means acknowledging that prompt engineering is the goal for learning and learning assessment, as opposed to trying to force students to work inefficiently to create a product that is increasingly becoming a relic of the past. Effective use of prompt engineering does not just require acceptance on the part of the teacher. With these understandings in mind, we can move to the necessity of implementing prompt engineering with developmental theory in mind.

Connecting Learning Theories and Prompt Engineering in Your Teaching

Setting up a Base Structure

To successfully implement prompt engineering in the classroom, instructors must use an effective model that will help learners to maximize the results they are seeking and then connect it to theories of learning. For one, a basic model as to how to create prompts needs to be provided that is solely dedicated to prompt engineering. The CLEAR model is one such method provided in **Table 1.** This model provides a listing of the individual steps and specific examples from Lo (2023) that are helpful in looking to implement prompt engineering.

The CLEAR model provides students a "roadmap" from which they can follow in their journey of engineering prompts. There is considerable value in **Table 1** of assisting the instructor in recognizing principles of prompt engineering too. Instructors can utilize their own examples that are relevant by content area and grade level. This visualization is intended to be a base structure to work from, something that evolves and changes as instructor and student become more familiar with it.

Table 1. Visualization of Lo's (2023), CLEAR model with examples

Element	Example
Concise "...emphasizes the importance of conciseness in crafting prompts. A concise prompt removes superfluous information..." (p. 2).	"Identify factors behind China's recent economic growth." (p.2).
Logical "...emphasizes the significance of sustaining a logical flow and order of ideas within a prompt. (p. 2).	"Describe the steps in the scientific method. Starting with forming a hypothesis and ending with drawing conclusions" (p.2).
Explicit "...provide(s) precise instructions regarding the desired output format, content, or scope, thereby reducing the likelihood of receiving unanticipated or irrelevant responses..." (p. 2).	"Provide a concise overview of the French Revolution emphasizing its causes, major events, and consequences" (p. 2).
Adaptive "...experimenting with various prompt formulations, phrasings, and temperature settings in order to establish a balance between creativity and concentration." (p. 2).	"Explain the development of computers from the 1970s to the 1990s")p. 2).
Reflective "...emphasizes the significance of continuous evaluation in enhancing prompt engineering techniques." (p. 2).	"After receiving AI-generated content on the benefits of plant-based diet, evaluate the response's accuracy, relevance, and completeness. Use insights from the evaluation to refine future prompts, such as asking for more specific benefits or focusing on certain aspects of a plant-based diet" (p. 2).

Note. Elements, definitions, and examples visualized from Lo, L.S. (2023). The CLEAR path: A framework for enhancing information literacy through prompt engineering. *The Journal of Academic Librarianship. 49*, 2.

How Theory Could Inform Practice: Piaget's Developmental Stages

With the CLEAR model introduced to assist in creating effective prompts, consideration of learning theories can now be added for instructor use. **Table 2** features a blend of Lo's (2023) CLEAR model and Eddy's (2013) depiction of Piaget's stages of development. This model would be a proposed aligned model for when to introduce prompt engineering. Piaget's theory holds that development occurs with specific abilities by developmental stage.

Pre-operational learners have an egoic understanding of the world, while the concrete operational stage is obtained when learners see outside of themselves more and are able to grasp concepts and obtain simple and some complex multi-step understandings. The formal operational stage is a time where children move beyond "concrete" understandings and engage in higher abstractive thought (Eddy, 2013, p. 138). With this understanding mind, instructors of students at the earliest stages could focus more intently on the "C" and "L" portions of the model. The other elements could be covered, but the depth of that coverage and resulting expectation for results, should be set with constructed rubrics. Instructors should engage district and school leadership to set "scope and sequence" outlines, like the scope and sequence outlines that are created for elementary and high school curriculums. A schedule of introducing model elements, as well as examining the "gap" in knowledge that will need to be accounted for, is provided in **Table 2.**

As mentioned, Classroom teachers can use the blended models provided in **Table 2** to weigh when to introduce key parts of prompt engineering. At the same time, not all students progress along the same timeline, and some may be more advanced, while others may lag-behind their peers. From Piaget's stages of development model, it can be argued that the latter two categories of the CLEAR model will come about at its fullness, in what Piaget has labeled, the formal operational stage as identified by Eddy (2013). Learners who are not fully ready to engage in explicit, adaptive, or reflective elements provided the CLEAR model, will need further support to bridge their lack of comprehension. Instructors can consider achieving this through providing prompt examples and creating visuals to help students to make the connection of the process of generating prompts and to formalize strategic thinking, to accomplish desired outputs. In using **Table 2**, teachers can assess where their student's understanding is when it comes to prompt engineering and how to best engage them to support learning.

Table 2. Alignment of the CLEAR model with Piaget's stage of development

CLEAR Model elements	Stages of development & age spans
Concise	Pre-operational (2-7)
Logical	Concrete Operational (8-13
Explicit	Concrete operation (8-13) & Formal operational 14+)
Adaptive	Formal operational (14+)
Reflective	Formal operational (14+)

Note. Visualized synthesis of the CLEAR Model from Lo (2023) & Piaget's stages as described by Eddy (2013).

How Theory Could Inform Practice: Vygotsky's Social Learning Theory

Figure 2. shows Vygotsky's theory of socially informed learning, which may be helpful to classroom implementation. As described by Cong-Lem (2022), this theory, the social realm of the student is the "stimulus" while the mediating "sign" is the school environment. The "response" is the learning process at summation as a result. To travel the path from stimulus to the "response" or end stage of learning, all learners utilize social "signs" to "mediate" the learning process. In doing so, the learner navigates the sign to not only personally develop skills and knowledge, but to utilize them in the social context, in order to communicate and to become a part of the collective group.

For the instructor, identifying the "stimulus" could be recognizing social constructed positive or negative student attitudes concerning prompt engineering. Prompt engineering would be the mediating "sign" that the learners will utilize to learn new knowledge, as well as to engage in to share collectively in workplace or other social locales later on. As described by Cong-Lem (2022), Vygotsky's theory would be typified by the methods of learning, which can be seen to be a "mediating effect" learning outcome, or what is ultimately passed on to the learner. Theoretically, the resulting mediation may create a shift in learning skill and thinking style that previous methods did not. Recognizing this reality would be seen as important part of the learning process. This may result in student eagerness or hesitation to engage in the process of learning prompt engineering.

The "response" is ideally, newly learned skills and critical thinking attitudes. Along the way, the instructor must also come to see that the mediating signs of this form of learning may be substantially different than their own. Staying on the path of implementation and being willing to adjust accordingly, will continue to be important in the process. **Figure 2** can help the classroom teacher to adjust to witnessed student learning and higher level strategizing, that will progress with greater inclusion of prompt engineering in classroom instruction.

Figure 2. Vygotsky's social learning model
Note. Visualized from Cong-Lem, (2022)

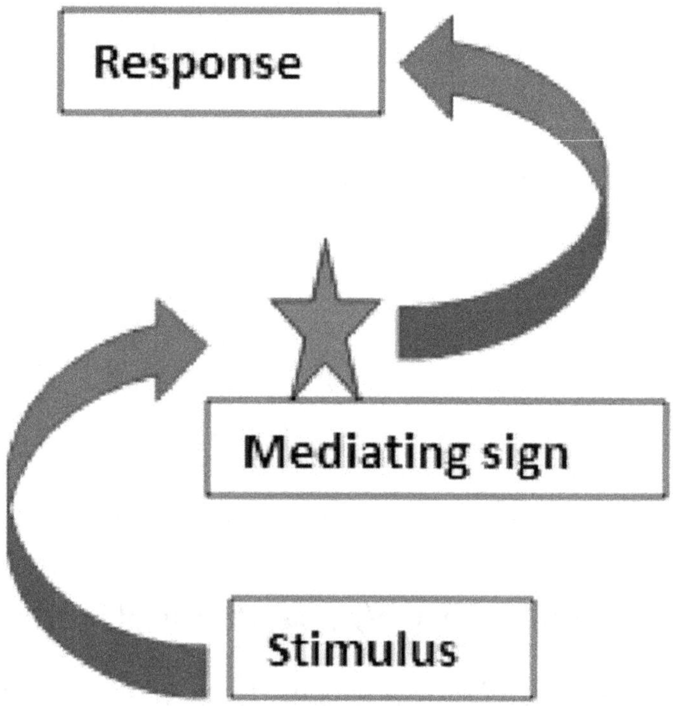

Piaget's stages of development as outlined previously, provide considerations for implementation of prompt engineering. Piaget's theory of intellectual development (Hamachek, 1995, p. 150) which is presented in **Figure 3,** provides a second useful theory that may be useful for classroom instructors when it comes to implementation of prompt engineering. This theory is helpful as it connects prompt engineering to Piaget's theory that identifies the complex nature of learning. This in turn, can inform new procedures, the practice of them, and retention in student longer term memory. A simplified visualization for instructors, showing Piaget's theory is presented in **Figure 3.**

Figure 3. Visualization of Piaget's theory of learning
Note. Visualized from (Hamachek, 1996, p. 150).

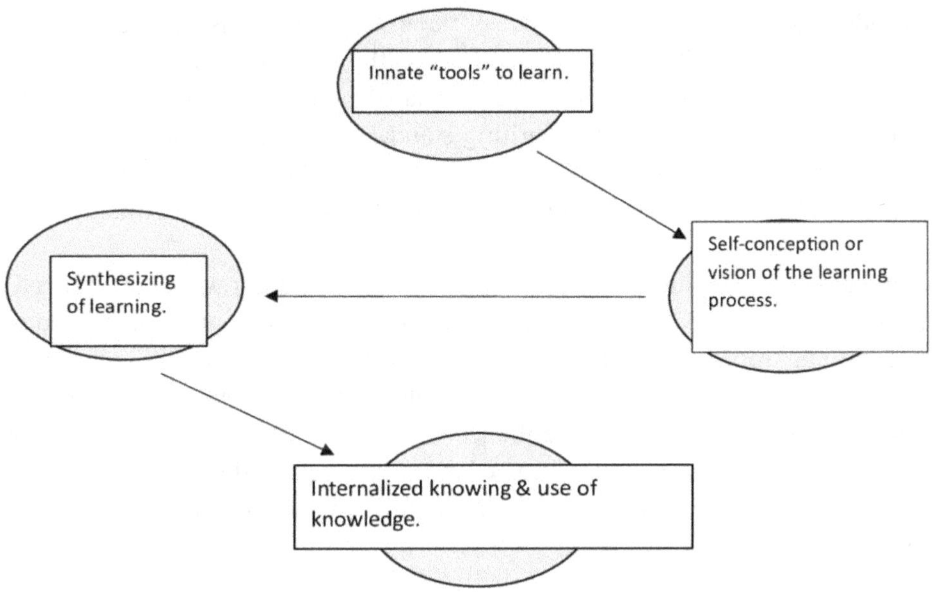

In using Piaget's model for prompt engineering implementation, it's important to understand the key descriptions that Piaget provided. Hamacheck (1996) outlined how Piaget described all students as possessing inborn tools or innate processes so that learning can begin. This is known as "functions." Hamacheck (1996) further outlined Piaget's concept of "schema," or the mental image through which the learner views learning either positively or negatively as they engage in the learning process. It can be concluded from these concepts that Piaget's model demonstrates the need to show students that not possessing all of the knowledge to be learned ahead of time is o.k. With this realization, students will find a discussion of what they know and don't know about prompt engineering to be beneficial and non-threatening. We want students to possess a positive schema as it relates to using prompt engineering and to be ok with "not knowing the answer" early on, and without some difficulty.

Hamacheck (1996) continued to describe Piaget's idea of accommodation and assimilation. This encompasses including the newly learned ideas with what they presently understand. For example, if a student in learning the CLEAR model, successfully understands and incorporates the "reflection" element with the other elements, they have added new concepts to their schematic map of understanding, which resides with the already learned understandings of technology learned previously. For the teacher, this is the learning goal with development in mind. Continued questioning and working towards resolution in regard to learning prompt engineering, can be seen to be good things. This is the synthesizing of learning that is occurring. If students are struggling with practicing what they have learned, it may be that they have not yet reached this step in the learning process as outlined by Piaget.

Integrating Standards and Prompt Engineering in the Curriculum

In the United States, education is the directed by the 50 individual states, who are given authority to create schools and the provisions related to run them per the 10th amendment of the U.S. Constitution (Imber et al., 2013). Generally speaking, standards provide a "true north" or aim for instructional practice in the classroom. The adopted curriculum is the "how" of the instruction that is carried out. For this chapter, I will provide an example from Kansas state standards at the K-12 level. Readers from other states or who teach in other countries, can utilize a similar standard that their school is responsible to teach. 5th grade writing instructors in Kansas have a writing standard sub-element under the general category of "text types and purposes." One such sub-element is: *"W.5.1-Write opinion pieces on topics or texts, supporting a point of view with reasons and information"* (Kansas State Department of Education ELA Standards, 2023).

In the lesson plans and curriculum documents a classroom instructor would construct a simple chart like the one presented in **Table 3.** Each standard has important verbs, nouns, and related phrasings that are important for the classroom instructor to identify. From **W.5.1** the words "write," "opinion," "piece," "texts," "supporting," "points of view," "reason," & "information" are provided. After identifying key words like these, the classroom instructor would need to create a list of objectives that would show the standard has been met. Objectives are defined as what is to be learned during the learning session. This must be determined to know that students have successfully met the standards for learning as demonstrated in **Table 3.**

Table 3. Standards and objectives chart

Standard to be addressed	W.5.1-Write opinion pieces on topics or texts, supporting a point of view with reasons and information
Learning Objective	Create an opinion article to convince someone that sugar cookies are or are not a great snack.
Objective criteria to be met:	*Student identifies responses that indicate the article is an opinion piece. *Student identifies words that signify reasons *Student identifies words that indicate the response

Note. This table shows the integration of standards and objectives.

High school and post-secondary instructors would follow the same process. Accrediting agency standards could be placed where the state standards presented in **Table 3** are presented. The objective criteria to be met is the "hook" that connects prompt engineering to the standards and curriculum. The criteria provide assurance for the instructor that the prompt engineering aligns with the learning standards, as well as what prompt engineering outputs have achieved the desired result of mastery.

Consideration should be provided as well, to the identification of standards that have become "dead standards" due to prompt engineering inclusion. Just as the widespread use of calculators lead to a re-configuring of standards and content taught as mentioned previously, prompt engineering will require a reworking of standards and content that emphasizes what prompt engineering allows the learner to achieve easily, and not continuing to focus on those learning items that with technological innovation, have become redundant.

In the instance provided of 5th grade ELA standards in Kansas, the standards document contains a "language in writing" sub-category. This category contains the standards of: "Use verb tense to convey various items, sequences, states, and conditions" as well as "Demonstrate command of the conventions of standard English capitalization, punctuation, and spelling when writing" (Kansas State Department of Education, 2023)

Ideas for curriculum:

These standards in a prompt engineering classroom are essentially rendered moot. The first standard could be kept if the student was allowed to engineer an output from a prompt and then mark the document accordingly. The other option for this standard is to demote it to a lower grade level, as a foundational literacy skill that is needed for prompt engineering, given that it's continued use in a prompt engineering 5th grade classroom, is of limited value. With prompt engineering, what was once an advanced standard. may become a lower standard. At worst, it may be removed entirely. The second sub-standard has even less promise in the classroom as conventions, capitalization, punctuation, and spelling would only play a limited role in analyzing engineered prompts. With the introduction of more efficient large language models in the future, requiring students to engage in such skills with engineered text would become akin to General Motors requiring a worker to double check that a machine in Detroit, has really attached a wheel to a car.

In identifying the new "dead knowledge" or "dead content standards," educators can refine or relegate standards to a lower grade standard slot or replace them entirely. This will require greater coordination with supervising states and departments as decisions of that magnitude are rarely left to building sites. In working to align prompt engineering with standards and subsequently, the curriculum, classroom instructors would work to increase student proficiency of using prompt engineering. With standards and objectives in place, the teacher can now look towards the direction of classroom strategies.

INSTRUCTIONAL CLASSROOM STRATEGIES FOR K-12 & UNIVERSITY INSTRUCTORS

For ELA or other creative subjects, prompt engineering holds great potential when it comes to critical thinking. For example, if a classroom instructor were to use a sugar cookie ELA lesson, they could create a lesson that would assist students in walking them through how to create prompts that would focus on supporting a point of view. Students would center their prompts on the concise & explicit elements of the CLEAR model prompts. Typing in: "Write an opinion article" will elicit a response whereby the large language model asks for clearer inputs. This would hopefully lead to the addition of a topic to the question and a stance to take. "Write an opinion article that sugar cookies are the best cookies that can be eaten" would be an example of this. From here, the concise prompt engineered prompt obtains greater explicitness in generated outputs.

From this stage, the "A" and "R" elements of the CLEAR model are reached. The student would work with the teacher to examine the generated text to see if the provided outputs address the creation of an opinion piece and if it has supporting details. **Figure 4** represents generated text from an engineered prompt of this lesson as an example. The red underlined areas show the standard requirement of finding "reasons" with phrasings such as "one of the reasons....," "another reason why..." and "Finally." The "reflection" element of the CLEAR model comes into play significantly at this stage, as the classroom instructor would help the students to analyze their response. The teacher would assist students in assisting the student to strategies to identify the initial words in every paragraph that alerts the reader that reasons are to follow. The yellow-highlighted areas of text in **Figure 4** shows the reader how the article is an opinion piece.

Figure 4. Finding standards in output response example
Note. This figure demonstrates how to identify standards signifying text, through using prompt generated text.

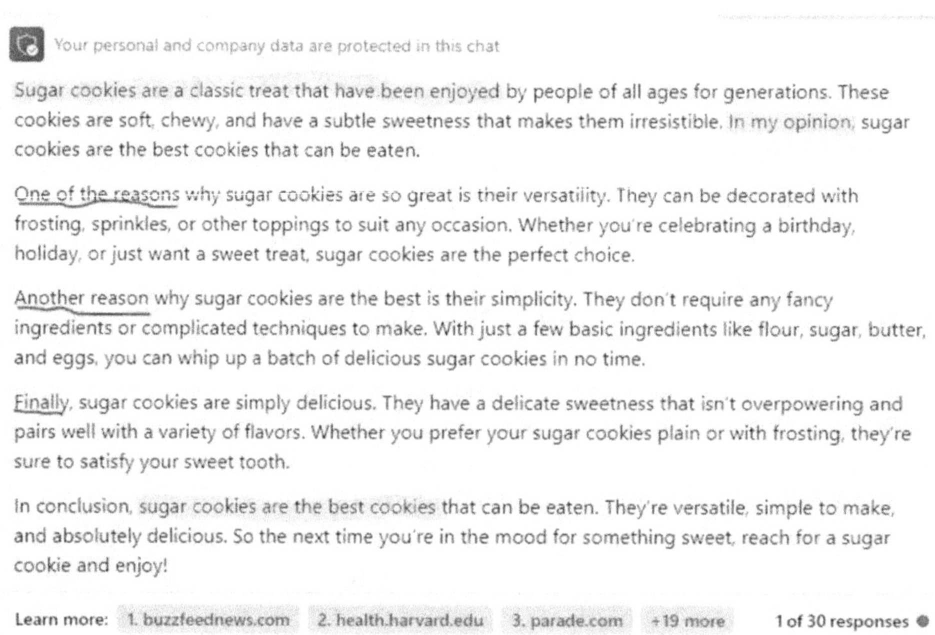
Your personal and company data are protected in this chat

Sugar cookies are a classic treat that have been enjoyed by people of all ages for generations. These cookies are soft, chewy, and have a subtle sweetness that makes them irresistible. In my opinion, sugar cookies are the best cookies that can be eaten.

One of the reasons why sugar cookies are so great is their versatility. They can be decorated with frosting, sprinkles, or other toppings to suit any occasion. Whether you're celebrating a birthday, holiday, or just want a sweet treat, sugar cookies are the perfect choice.

Another reason why sugar cookies are the best is their simplicity. They don't require any fancy ingredients or complicated techniques to make. With just a few basic ingredients like flour, sugar, butter, and eggs, you can whip up a batch of delicious sugar cookies in no time.

Finally, sugar cookies are simply delicious. They have a delicate sweetness that isn't overpowering and pairs well with a variety of flavors. Whether you prefer your sugar cookies plain or with frosting, they're sure to satisfy your sweet tooth.

In conclusion, sugar cookies are the best cookies that can be eaten. They're versatile, simple to make, and absolutely delicious. So the next time you're in the mood for something sweet, reach for a sugar cookie and enjoy!

Learn more: 1. buzzfeednews.com 2. health.harvard.edu 3. parade.com +19 more 1 of 30 responses

An Argument for Prompt Engineered Informed Pedagogy

Pedagogy can be defined as the science of teaching and it can be synonymous with teaching strategies as a result. In terms of overall teaching pedagogy, it is important to keep in mind that in teaching a lesson where prompt engineering is utilized, that the goal should not be to have students generate one series of texts, enter a grade, and move on. Routine teaching with prompt engineering and assessment of student work should proceed along a different path.

Instead of using traditional strategies, the classroom with prompt engineering coud be an interactive laboratory where students work individually and in periodic *ad hoc* groupings, to refine, hone, and craft their prompts after engineered responses from their first prompt entry. The course instructor would be moving from group to group and individual to individual during the lesson. This instruction would not feature a straight rows and desk, teacher centered model. Once directions and objectives are outlined at the start of the lesson, the students proceed to engineer prompts on their own, though direct instruction should be utilized with considerations of development and grade level in mind.

Another strategy is to utilize a problem solving "case study" approach. This would require the classroom teacher to engineer a "broken" engineered prompt output. This response would be presented to students and a brief overview as to what prompt was utilized and how specifically the generated output failed to meet objective criteria. This lesson would focus on improving the engineered prompt and to add the missing elements and identification of important concepts the "broken" engineered prompt failed to elicit. This lesson would have a strong content component to it as the key terms, concepts, and people related to it would play an integral part in the construction of engineered output.

An additional strategy utilized in elementary schools is "think-pair-share." This strategy features students turning to one another and sharing what they have learned after taking some time to refine their thoughts (Center for Teaching & Learning, 2023). A variation of this practice would be to have students generate response and then use a rubric to peer edit the generated response and to provide feedback to peers on prompt strategies to consider. Whether it is a teacher directed introductory creative sugar cookie ELA lesson, a laboratory investigation, or a sample case problem solving method, classroom instructors have instructional strategies that would not be onerous to learn or master once necessary adjustments have been made. The greatest challenge in utilizing these methodologies is to focus one's eye on prompt engineering and working with students to improve over time, as opposed to one point in time. At the heart of the teaching strategy is dedication to helping students to build knowledge. Accomplishing this will take intentionality, a focus that requires further discussion.

Practical Strategies for K-12 & University Instructors to Connect

Classroom instructors can find a number of supports as they look to connect with other educators and increase their own knowledge and skill. Universities, colleges, and K-12 educators may have technology or professional development departments that can help provide further learning opportunities for classroom teachers. Social media presents other opportunities to connect, such as using hashtags on X, such as "#promptengineering." As important as formal networks are to further classroom instructor teaching, the simplest method to connect and extend when it comes to teaching with prompt engineering, is to form your own learning cohort with other educators in your school, district, or region. Create your own social network page on different mediums and you will be able to connect with other likeminded educators.

I would argue that the best things in education come about when classroom instructors talk with one another in offices, the hallway, and informally with one another. In engaging in an organic effort to connect and seek out others, newer perspective will come to us through those contacts and that exposure to different ideas of using prompt engineering will provide greater insight and relevance to your own teaching, than any training session removed from your teaching level (post-secondary, high school, or elementary) ever will.

Principles of Prompt Engineering and Classroom Assessments

Assessments for a New Paradigm: Presentations

Prompt engineering implementation will require a shift in thinking for classrooms teachers when it comes to assessment. First, as mentioned previously, engineered responses from large language models are authentic created productions of students and are no less valid than handwritten or constructed student work. Analysis of a given lesson or unit should proceed with the "analysis" and 'reflection" elements of the CLEAR model in mind. This could be a formal presentation to the class by the student, with explanation of steps followed, how engineered prompts were refined, and how the "trial and error" of exploration occurred and what the ending document produced shows. For online college teaching, this could also mean the recording of a presentation to submit to the course instructor for asynchronous feedback or an agreed upon time to meet online to review results and present findings.

Assessments for a New Paradigm: "Trail of Evidence"

Whether online or in-person, a trail of prompts and responses should be provided. It would also be helpful to ask students to engage in metacognitive tasks such as keeping logs and notes of what they were thinking or hoping for in entering some engineered prompts, as well as their thoughts and feelings regarding seeing their initial results, and how they decided to proceed from there, would help students to engage in the cognitively complex task of thinking critically and overcoming stumbling blocks in their own thinking such as frustration or inability to think through a problem or working to accept mistakes. The use of rubrics will not disappear with the rise of prompt engineering. The idea that essays or other written work will be rendered irrelevant is misplaced. Well-constructed rubrics require great attention to specific requirements of writing. Not all engineered prompts are equal. The difference as it relates to assessment is that you are still assessing for mastery or completion. We no longer will grade based on getting to the assigned destination or reaching "the answer." Instead, we will be focusing on how students engineered their way to the answer and have them outline in richer detail what was learned.

Assessments for a New Paradigm: Greater Use of Formative Assessments

The continual or generative nature of knowledge that prompt engineering creates should lead to a greater emphasis on formative or on-going "daily" assessments, as opposed to large, summative assessments. At present, many teachers use "exit tickets" which can be strips of paper or comments to the teacher about what they learned that day or a question that they had. An exit ticket with prompt engineering in mind could be presenting a one paragraph response to the teacher about three items the student learned that day. A health class student would then prompt engineer a commend: "Write a bullet point outline that shows three ways to cope with disappointment." The student would then share the response with the teacher at the door and the teacher would take the engineered output for points in the gradebook.

Grading in a New Paradigm

Grading "in process" learning will require a shift in thinking as well. The amount of learning that has transpired is hopefully greater on the last day of the unit or lesson than the first. What purpose does retaining a lower score at the beginning of the unit to the end, when the student has mastered the content, serve? What is the justification for including it to drag down the mastery a student has shown at the end of a unit? Instructors may need to shift grading to simple points in the process along the way. Did the student use a prompt? Did the student look through their engineered output? Did they turn in a log and reflect? A "points along the way" process for completing simple skills and actions, would not penalize a student who at the end of the unit shows mastery. In obtaining the rest of the points at the end of the unit, the student's learning is provided in an authentic manner that is clear for teacher, student, and caregivers to see.

CONCLUSION

Educational Change and the Educator

Historically, the field of education has seen considerable change. What is important to be taught and to learn has mirrored social, economic, and political developments. Technological change is no exception as in influence. In the 1850s, a child in a one room schoolhouse would be asked to calculate the cost of an acreage of hay as such as knowledge was essential for the agrarian times, they were raised in. A child in the industrial age would be taught typing and related mechanical work. With prompt engineering, we are entering yet another turning point in education. In prior eras, fears of the demise of teaching, what is to be taught, and even the existence of education itself, have been made. It has been argued in this chapter, that the acceptance of change and of the "creative destruction" that ensues as a result, is important and necessary for the future of the teaching profession, as well as for our students. History shows that: "the fear of loss is greater than the desire for gain." The present era is no different. There will be certain aspects of knowledge lost, but those that are gained will provide greater benefit and result in greater things learned than what was possible before.

Present Challenges and Opportunities for Prompt Engineering in the Classroom

The educational paradigm is not amenable to change or whole-hearted acceptance. Legislated change can morph and change, rendering intended results to be completely negated. Prompt engineering implementation at present clashes radically with K-12 state standards and adopted curriculum programs. A worksheet and "scripted curriculum" elementary teaching style does not lend themselves to the creative work required for prompt engineering. Prevailing ideas about what constitutes original student work and assessment also do not lend themselves to a smooth transition for implementing prompt engineering.

The process must begin with the classroom teacher. Utilizing prompt engineering in course assignments, working to change teaching and assessment practice at the classroom level wherever feasible is a required first step. School and building level conversations need to occur, as well as engagement with state and national level educational leadership, as well as professional teaching organizations, to advocate for the greater inclusion of prompt engineering and to move instruction to a more authentic 21st century learning process.

Future Direction and Opportunities

Prompt engineering holds tremendous possibilities for the future of learning. Greater student examination of metacognition, or their own thinking about thinking, is one such opportunity. Self-monitoring and documenting of steps made in engineering prompts will be an essential skill to learn in the process of learning prompt engineering. Further development of large language models will require continued learning and re-learning of prompt engineering essential understandings. The CLEAR model may very well change and be updated to incorporate future changes. Opportunities for the future also include incorporating prompt engineering in the realm of assisting special education students in the learning process, as well as to be able to extend their voice and thinking in ways that would be of great benefit. For marginalized populations, prompt engineering provides opportunities to examine and work for greater social justice and "problem solving" at every level of a student's lived experience. Social, economic, and educational developments are not the same at the start of a century and at the end of a century. We do not live our lives by 1923 standards or realities in 2023. Likewise, the society of 2099 will not much resemble or remember the learning and realities of 2023. To help future generations get to that point, should be the mission and goal of our teaching. It's time to begin.

REFERENCES

Archambault, R. D. (1974). *John Dewey: On Education*. University of Chicago Press.

Banks, S. (2011). A *historical analysis of attitudes toward the use of calculators in junior high and high school math classrooms in the United States since 1975*. [Master's of Education Research Theses, Cedarville]. https://digitalcommons.cedarville.edu/education_thesis/31

Bozkurt, A. (2023). Generative artificial intelligence (AI) powered conversational educational agents: The inevitable paradigm shift. *Asian Journal of Distance Education*, *18*(1), 198–204. doi:10.5281/zenodo.7716416

Center for Teaching and Learning. (2023). *Think, pair, share*. Kent State University. https://www.kent.edu/ctl/think-pair-share#:~:text=What,sitting%20near%20them%20(PAIR)

Cong-Lem, N. (2022). Vygotsky's, Leontiev's, and Engestrom's cultural-historical (activity) theories: Overview, clarifications, and implications. *Integrative Psychological & Behavioral Science*, *56*(4), 1091–1112. doi:10.1007/s12124-022-09703-6 PMID:35680721

Cotton, D. R. E., Cotton, P. A., & Shipway, J. R. (2023). Chatting and cheating: Ensuring academic integrity in the era of ChatGPT. *Innovations in Education and Teaching International*, 1–12. doi:10.1080/14703297.2023.2190148

Dede, C. (2010). Comparing frameworks for 21st century skills. In J. Bellance & R.Brandt (Eds.), *21st century skills: Rethinking how students learn (pp. 51-76).*Solution Tree Press. https://allchildrenlearning.org/wp-content/uploads/2019/12/Dede_2010_Comparing-Frameworks-for-21st-Century-Skills.pdf

Dewar, J. A. (1998). *The information age and the printing press: Looking backward to see ahead*. RAND Corporation. https://www.rand.org/content/dam/rand/pubs/papers/2005/P8014.pdf

Eager, B., & Brunton, R. (2023). Prompting higher education towards AI-augmented teaching and learning practices. *Journal of University Teaching & Learning Practice, 20*(5), 1–20. doi:10.53761/1.20.5.02

Edalex, (October 25th, 2023*). 21st century skills: What they are and why they are important.* Edalax. https://www.edalex.com/guides/21st-century-skills-what-they-are-why-important

Eddy, L. L. (2013). *Caring for children with special heath care needs and their families: A handbook for health care professionals.* Wiley-Blackwell. Fisher, M., & Jacobs, H.H. (20223). Prompt literacy: A key for AI-Based Learning. *Educational Leadership, 80*(9), 18–19. https://www.ascd.org/el/articles/prompt-literacy-a-key-for-ai-based-learning

Foucault, M. (1972/2010). *The archaeology of knowledge and the discourse on language.* Vintage Books.

Friesen, N. (2017). *The textbook and the lecture: Education in the age of new media.* Johns Hopkins University Press. doi:10.1353/book.56899

Gregory, L. L., & Gregory, L. M. (1996, October 4-6*). Paradigm shift: The forgotten perquisite for change.* [Paper presentation]. National Rural Education Association, Salt Lake City, UT.

Hamachek, D. E. (1994). *Psychology in teaching, learning, & growth* (5th ed.). Pearson.

Imber, M., van Geel, T., Blokhuis, J. C., & Feldman, J. (2013). *A teacher's guide to education law.* Taylor & Francis Group. doi:10.4324/9780203094303

Kansas State Department of Education. (2023). *Kansas standards for English language arts.* KSDE. https://community.ksde.org/LinkClick.aspx?fileticket=NXA9zpwVVtI%3d&tabid=5301

Keegin, J. M. (2023, May 23). ChatGPT is a plagiarism machine: So why do administrators have their heads in the sand? *The Chronicle of Higher Education.* https://www.chronicle.com/article/chatgpt-is-a-plagiarism-machine

Little, P. (2013). 21st century learning and progressive education: An intersection. *International Journal of Progressive Education, 9*(1), 84–96. https://dergipark.org.tr/en/pub/ijpe/issue/26313/277317

Lo, L. S. (2023). The CLEAR path: A framework for enhancing information literacy through prompt engineering. *Journal of Academic Librarianship, 49*(4), 102720. doi:10.1016/j.acalib.2023.102720

Lubis, F. (2019). Education in the disruption era. *Britain International of Linguistics, Arts, and Education Journal, 1*(2), 183–188. doi:10.33258/biolae.v1i2.85

Marriam-Webster. (n.d.) *Plagiarize.* Marriam-Webster. https://www.merriam-webster.com/dictionary/plagiarize

McArthur, T. (1987). The English languages? *English Today, 3*(3), 9–13. doi:10.1017/S0266078400013511

Melanson, C. C. (2023). A clash of interests: Neoliberalism in education. *One World in Dialogue, 7*(1), 4. https://ssc.teachers.ab.ca/SiteCollectionDocuments/OneWorldInDialogue/2023%20V7N1/A%20Clash%20of%20Interests%20Neoliberalism%20in%20Education.pdf

Popkewitz, T. S. (2011). Curriculum history, schooling and the history of the present. *History of Education, 40*(1), 1–19. doi:10.1080/0046760X.2010.507222

Rahman, M. M., & Watanobe, Y. (2023). ChatGPT for education and research: Opportunities, threats, and strategies. *Applied Sciences (Basel, Switzerland)*, *13*(9), 1–21. doi:10.3390/app13095783

Robin, C. (2023, August 24). How ChatGPT changed my plans for the fall. *The Chronicle of Higher Education*. https://www.chronicle.com/article/the-end-of-the-take-home-essay

Selk, A. (2018, May 5). One space or two spaces after a full stop? Scientists have finally found the answer. *The Independent*. https://www.independent.co.uk/tech/one-space-or-two-spaces-after-a-full-stop-scientists-have-finally-found-the-answer-a8337646.html

Singh, M. K. (2023, October 26). *Is it plagiarism to use ChatGPT or other AI language models?* Foundry Law Group. https://foundrylawgroup.com/is-it-plagiarism-to-use-chat-gpt-or-other-ai-language-models/#:~:text=The%20short%20answer%20is%20that,original%20source%20of%20your%20content.

Trouche, L. (2005). Calculators in mathematics education: A rapid evolution of tools, with different effects. In D. Guin, K. Ruthven, & L. Trouche (Eds.), *The didactical challenge of symbolic calculators: Turning a computational device into a mathematical instrument* (pp. 9–39). doi:10.1007/0-387-23435-7_2

Urban, W.J., Jennings, L., Jr. Wagoner. (2013). *American Education: A history*. Taylor & Francis Group.

KEY TERMS AND DEFINITIONS

Instructors: Teachers of elementary, secondary, and post-secondary students.

Large Language Models: Computer programmed systems that take in text prompts and respond in a syntactically structured way for humans to comprehend results.

Metacognition: The process of analyzing or strategically thinking about how to strategize mentally.

Objectives: What is to be learned during the learning session.

Paradigm: The formal and informal understandings, actions, and words of an organized group.

Prompt Engineering: The creation of organized text to bring about outputs that reflect a desired goal or objective.

Scaffolds: Supports designed to help the learner understand what is not presently understood.

Schema: The picture through which the learner views learning and their place in the learning process.

Chapter 13
Revolutionizing Content Creation and Curriculum Development Through Generative AI

Surjit Singha
https://orcid.org/0000-0002-5730-8677
Kristu Jayanti College (Autonomous), India

Ranjit Singha
https://orcid.org/0000-0002-3541-8752
Christ University, India

ABSTRACT

AI can generate and provide customized, inclusive, and engaging learning experiences. This chapter emphasizes the collaborative partnership between human educators and AI systems, highlighting its crucial role in maximizing AI's potential. Educators provide context and guidance through adaptive learning platforms, AI-powered feedback, and AI-enhanced content creation to ensure students receive a personalized, contextually relevant education. Human knowledge, including pedagogical insight and ethical considerations, complements the capabilities of artificial intelligence. AI promises personalized perpetual learning, enhanced accessibility, and dynamic curriculum design in the future. This vision of collaboration promotes critical thinking, problem-solving, and inclusiveness. Educators, institutions, policymakers, and AI developers must ensure that education remains empowering, inclusive, and excellent for AI to be integrated responsibly. By embracing this partnership, education becomes more accessible, individualized, and influential.

DOI: 10.4018/979-8-3693-1351-0.ch013

INTRODUCTION

The education sector is currently on the brink of a substantial transformation that has the potential to profoundly restructure the creation of educational materials and the development of curriculum. The central focus of this educational revolution centres on generative AI, an advanced technology that has played a crucial role in defining the future of the academic field. This chapter examines the complex connection between technology and education, focusing on using generative AI to enable the development of a new era characterized by flexible, personalized, and innovative learning materials. In the past, creating educational materials and building curricula required substantial time and effort. It often resulted in rigid resources suitable for a single type of audience. However, these methods must be adapted to meet contemporary learners' diverse and constantly changing demands. In today's environment, where there is an increasing need for personalized education, combining generative AI with instructional design emerges as a revolutionary and impactful solution. Generative artificial intelligence (AI), advanced AI models, and efficient engineering approaches allow educators and instructional designers to produce tailored and engaging learning materials that successfully engage individual learners. These artificial intelligence models enable the field of education to enter a phase where unprecedented degrees of creativity and personalization are achieved. This chapter examines the substantial impact of generative AI on creating content and developing educational curricula. It explores the intersection of pedagogy and technology, envisioning a future where generative AI seamlessly augments the creation of educational materials. As we continue to investigate the powers of this ground-breaking technology, we will uncover its potential to enhance teaching methods and facilitate a significant change towards unparalleled levels of personalized training.

Throughout our inquiry, we thoroughly analyzed fundamental concepts such as generative AI, content generation, curriculum development, efficient engineering, and the construction of synthetic learning resources. By the end of this chapter, readers are expected to have a comprehensive understanding of the thoughtful influence of generative AI in education. This technology offers unique opportunities and effectively creates an inclusive learning environment that meets each student's needs and aspirations. The following chapters will examine various aspects and applications of generative AI in education, enabling a more thorough understanding of its potential and impact. The main aim of this chapter is to comprehensively analyze the significant influence of generative AI on the field of education, with a particular focus on its function in generating material and designing curricula. This paper examines the complex connection between technology and education, emphasizing the substantial influence of generative AI in revolutionizing traditional approaches to creating instructional materials and constructing curricula. Through the utilization of advanced artificial intelligence models and the implementation of efficient engineering methodologies, educators and instructional designers may develop learning materials that are highly engaging and specifically matched to the personalized and constantly evolving needs of modern learners. The chapter also outlines a future scenario where generative AI is smoothly incorporated into pedagogy, enabling the progress of educational resources and tailored education to an extraordinary extent. The subject covers various topics, including generative AI, content generation, curriculum design, rapid manipulation, and the creation of synthetic educational resources.

This chapter lays the groundwork for future chapters examining different applications of generative AI in education. These applications include individualized learning, assessment, and the future of educational technology. The goal is to offer significant insights and motivation to educators, researchers, and stakeholders in this sector as they explore the ever-changing and promising landscape of transformative opportunities. Integrating generative AI into education represents a significant change in viewpoint, significantly altering the methods of creating instructional materials and developing curricula (Tu, 2023). The transition above is firmly embedded in the mutual connection between technology and education, where generative AI accelerates revolutionary advancements. To fully grasp the importance and possibilities of the educational revolution, it is crucial to carefully analyze the underlying theoretical principles and historical background that form the foundation of this transformative effort.

Traditionally, the education sector has mainly used manual techniques to create educational content and develop curriculum, resulting in standardized learning materials. While these methods may have some efficacy, they are primarily defined by a substantial labour need and often fail to address modern learners' different and ever-evolving demands sufficiently. The demand for customized, flexible, and inventive learning experiences has significantly increased in a rapidly changing world where knowledge and information have become more readily accessible. Generative artificial intelligence (AI), a subset of AI, has emerged as a powerful solution to overcome the limitations of traditional educational approaches. Generative AI empowers educators and instructional designers to create engaging and personalized learning materials by leveraging advanced AI models and prompt engineering techniques. The study conducted by Nah et al. (2023) demonstrates that the system successfully achieves this by generating educational content that establishes a strong connection with individual learners while adapting to their preferences, learning styles, and proficiency levels.

The potential of generative AI primarily depends on sophisticated AI models, such as GPT-3, GPT-4, and its following versions. Budhwar et al. (2023) constructed these models to understand and generate text resembling human language. These models can produce educational content that is both logically coherent and culturally suitable, often making it challenging to distinguish from information authored by humans. The ability of these models to generate written content, answer queries, and engage in conversations using natural language forms the foundation for a revolutionary change in content generation and curriculum design. The application of sophisticated AI models and fast engineering methods plays a crucial role in efficiently harnessing the powers of generative AI for educational purposes. Vartiainen & Tedre (2023) propose that educators and instructional designers can generate specific prompts or instructions to successfully guide the AI model in generating content that aligns with educational goals. The level of authority and adaptability offered enables the creation of educational material that corresponds to the program's instructional objectives.

The application of generative artificial intelligence not only enhances the efficiency of content generation but also offers possibilities for improving education. Adapting instructional content to cater to the requirements of individual learners allows for the inclusion of their learning paths, rates of advancement, and personal preferences. This method enhances the depth and engagement of the learning process, leading to better academic outcomes (Kamalov et al., 2023; Vartiainen & Tedre, 2023). The main goal of generative AI in education is to produce a seamless integration of technology and pedagogy. The proposed vision envisions a future where artificial intelligence not only acts as a supplemental tool for educational materials but also actively contributes to the progress and enhancement of curriculum. This integration enables the creation of innovative educational resources tailored to specific needs and easily adjusts to the ever-changing requirements of knowledge and skills in the 21st century (Bahroun et al., 2023; Kohnke et al., 2023). This chapter explores the theoretical foundations and historical backdrop of generative AI's significant impact on education. It probed into the practical applications, challenges, and potential that arise when AI models and instructional design interact, leading to a new era of flexible, personalized, and innovative learning materials. Furthermore, we will comprehensively examine the influence of this ground-breaking technology on education and its capacity to cultivate an all-encompassing learning environment that accommodates every student's unique needs and aspirations.

Numerous challenging challenges have hindered traditional content generation approaches and curriculum development in education. Developing superior educational resources has proven to be demanding in terms of resources and time, which limits the adaptability needed to respond to the always-evolving educational environment. Furthermore, these traditional resources are typically unchanging and not well-suited for meeting the specific learning needs of individual students, teachers, and institutions. As a result, they hinder the ability to personalize education and adapt to different learning styles and speeds. The rapid growth of knowledge in the digital age has created a significant challenge for traditional educational approaches, requiring regular updates and adjustments to educational materials. The current education system's failure to keep pace with the swiftly increasing rate of change is a significant worry. Furthermore, the problem of inequitable access to top-notch educational resources around the globe poses a significant barrier. To address this accessibility gap, adopting a scalable, cost-effective, and inclusive method for creating content is necessary.

Our research focuses on investigating generative AI, prompt engineering, and synthetic content creation in education to tackle essential difficulties. We have defined four main objectives. Initially, we will explore how generative AI may significantly diminish the resource-intensive characteristics of content generation and curriculum development, simplifying the process and enabling educational institutions to deploy their resources more effectively. Our second purpose is to explore the potential of generative AI in tailoring educational content to meet the specific learning needs of individuals, thus fostering a more flexible and inclusive learning environment. Furthermore, through AI, our objective is to showcase the ability to consistently enhance and modify instructional resources in real time, guaranteeing that pupils have constant access to the most up-to-date and relevant knowledge. The primary objective is to ascertain how generative AI can effectively address the accessibility divide, achieving cost-efficiency and flexibility in diverse educational settings. As we begin this endeavor to harness the revolutionary capabilities of generative AI in education, we expect that the knowledge gained will be advantageous to teachers, students, and institutions and aid in making education accessible to all in the digital era.

THE EVOLUTION OF EDUCATIONAL RESOURCES

The advancement of content creation and curriculum development in education has followed a remarkable path. The beginnings can be traced back to an ancient era defined by an oral tradition, where knowledge was passed down through spoken communication and memorization. The advent of written language resulted in the utilization of manuscripts and texts for disseminating organized educational resources, incorporating elements borrowed from religious texts, classical literature, and scientific writings. The introduction of the printing press in the 15th century resulted in a substantial revolution in education. This technological advancement altered the distribution of information by enabling the mass production of books.

Generating textbooks played a vital role in standardizing educational content and formalizing the curriculum development process. In the 19th century, the Industrial Revolution introduced standardized curricula and hierarchical educational institutions. Conversely, throughout the latter part of the 20th century, notable technological progress was called the digital revolution. This revolution entailed the incorporation of multimedia and e-learning platforms into educational methods. Education has significantly changed towards customization and adjustment, focusing on technology and open educational resources. In the present period, there is a notable emergence of generative AI, exemplified by influential models like GPT-3 and GPT-4. These models play a vital role in shaping content creation and curriculum development. These models offer customized, pertinent, and flexible solutions that meet individual learners' unique needs and interests. The historical evolution above demonstrates how education continuously strives to enhance accessibility and effectiveness in response to changing teaching methods, technological advancements, and societal needs (Baker, 1996).

Dwivedi et al. (2023) argue that generative AI has caused a significant shift in education, significantly changing traditional approaches to creating instructional materials and building curricula. Integrating artificial intelligence (AI) into this technology has revolutionized the academic sphere. Generative AI is primarily defined by its ability to understand and generate text that closely mimics human language. It enables the generation of educational content that is coherent and contextually relevant. Generative AI stands out because it can create information that forms a strong connection with individual learners by adjusting to their preferences, learning styles, and progress. The significance of generative AI in education is manifold, especially in its capacity to tackle the limitations associated with traditional techniques. Education has relied extensively on labour-intensive methods and unvarying, uniform materials for a significant period. This approach often requires addressing the diverse and ever-evolving needs of modern learners. Employing generative artificial intelligence (AI) systems, which drive advanced AI models and expedite engineering processes, resolves these problems. Zhao et al. (2023) have acknowledged this strategy as a pioneering solution.

By employing generative AI, educators and instructional designers can provide educational content that is engaging and tailored to the specific requirements of each learner. This technology allows us a level of personalization and flexibility previously unattainable. Implementing customization tactics involves tailoring instructional information to accommodate people's distinct learning pathways, speeds, and preferences, enhancing the overall educational experience (Jeon & Lee, 2023; Chang et al., 2023). Furthermore, generative artificial intelligence (AI) can improve pedagogy. This tool facilitates educators in creating instructional materials that align with pedagogical objectives, thereby boosting the overall efficacy of teaching and learning processes. Ulla et al. (2023) propose that the main aim is to integrate generative AI with pedagogy in a harmonious manner, where AI actively contributes to the development and progress of the educational curriculum. This chapter explores the significant impact of generative AI on education, demonstrating its capacity to radically transform the creation of instructional materials and the development of curricula. Generative AI caters to students' unique needs and aspirations by offering innovative possibilities and personalized, flexible, and creative educational resources. As we explore deeper into this ground-breaking technology, we will uncover its capacity to challenge traditional educational practices and create a dynamic and optimistic future for education.

UNDERSTANDING GENERATIVE AI'S MECHANISMS

Generative artificial intelligence (AI), a sophisticated area of AI, is currently revolutionizing the language and information generation processes to mimic human-like characteristics closely. To thoroughly understand the mechanics that drive generative AI, it is essential to probe its fundamental ideas. It involves applying advanced deep learning techniques, including using neural networks such as recurrent neural networks (RNNs) and transformer-based models like generative pre-trained transformers (Han et al., 2023). These models comprise interconnected layers of synthetic neurons, enabling them to proficiently evaluate and generate intricate patterns in data, particularly in the domain of natural language. Moreover, the effectiveness of generative AI dramatically depends on the exploitation of ample training data obtained from diverse sources, such as books, papers, and websites. It allows the model to fully comprehend language's structure, semantics, and contextual subtleties. Establishing this system in natural language processing (NLP) holds immense importance. By employing NLP approaches, it can thoroughly analyze and generate text that nearly emulates human language in terms of syntax, semantics, and context (Locke et al., 2021). The basis of generative AI is built upon language models enhanced through massive text corpora, utilizing probability and statistical techniques to predict words based on preceding terms. Hence, this procedure produces logically connected content suitable within its context (Sohail et al., 2023).

Refining and reinforcing learning methods are essential for tailoring artificial intelligence models to specific tasks and improving overall performance. Obtaining this necessary knowledge allows generative AI to generate text that resembles human language, demonstrating coherence and contextual suitability (Hassan et al., 2023). The potential applications span diverse domains, such as content generation, language translation, chatbots, etc. Customized and personalized learning materials can bring about substantial progress in education. The upcoming chapters will present a more thorough examination of these concepts and their practical consequences in education. In the generative AI field, rapid engineering plays a vital role in shaping the material produced by AI models. Customization and specificity are crucial in education, as they offer clarity and relevance to the learning process. This strategy guides students throughout their educational journey, enables feedback generation, assures the production of task-oriented output, and matches content with educational objectives. By employing generative AI, educators and content producers can effectively tailor knowledge to specific needs and link it with educational purposes, thereby enabling a strategic approach. In education, focusing on personalized and contextually appropriate material requires using fast engineering as a crucial tool to achieve these goals.

EMPOWERING EDUCATORS WITH GENERATIVE AI

Artificial intelligence (AI) has made notable progress in education, equipping educators and instructional designers with cutting-edge tools to create material and construct curricula (George & Wooden, 2023). The discussed subject showcases diverse practical implementations of artificial intelligence (AI), including the generation of automated lesson plans, content summarization, creation of interactive materials, development of adaptive learning pathways, language translation, automatic assessment generation, and curriculum personalization. These programs enhance educational processes, improve accessibility, and offer customized learning experiences. Moreover, it is noteworthy to state that there are substantial occurrences of artificial intelligence (AI) implementations in education. For example, Coursera has created a system that offers individualized feedback to learners. Quizlet has developed adaptable flashcards that dynamically adapt to the specific requirements of each student. ScribeSense has created an artificial intelligence (AI) system to evaluate and score essays. In addition, Knewton has developed an adaptive learning platform. These examples demonstrate the significant capacity of generative AI to improve instructional content and enhance the entire learning experience for students (George & Wooden, 2023).

Artificial intelligence (AI) can assist instructors in developing thorough and structured lesson plans. Artificial intelligence (AI) may generate comprehensive programs encompassing activities, resources, and evaluation procedures by integrating learning objectives and curricular requirements. It saves teachers much time and ensures strict adherence to educational purposes. Artificial intelligence can analyze and summarize extensive quantities of instructional content, improving its understandability for students. This method becomes beneficial in condensing complex textbooks, research papers, or articles into concise summaries, aiding students in quickly grasping fundamental concepts (Ulla et al., 2023; Lin et al., 2022). Generative artificial intelligence (AI) can produce interactive educational materials, including quizzes, flashcards, and educational games. It actively engages students and offers a dynamic and enjoyable learning experience, improving the material's retention and comprehension (Roediger & Karpicke, 2006; Zou et al., 2019). Artificial intelligence can customize learning paths to accommodate students' needs and preferences. Artificial intelligence (AI) continuously assesses a student's progress and comprehension, adapting the content and exercises offered to ensure that each student is given materials corresponding to their current level of understanding.

AI-driven language translation systems are precious for translating instructional materials into multiple languages in our ever-more interconnected world. This technological innovation guarantees that diverse student populations can access educational opportunities. Artificial intelligence can offer various assessment forms, including multiple-choice questions, essays, and problem sets. Shin et al. (2019) state that this strategy provides advantages such as enhanced time management for educators and various evaluation techniques that cater to different learning preferences. AI can aid in tailoring the curriculum to meet the specific needs of individual learners. Artificial intelligence can examine student performance and choices to offer customized learning experiences by suggesting specialized learning paths and additional resources. Examples of AI applications in education include Coursera's utilization of AI to generate personalized feedback, Quizlet's implementation of AI to power adaptive flashcards, ScribeSense's utilization of AI to grade essays, and Knewton's employment of an adaptive learning platform that employs AI to personalize learning materials for students based on their performance and progress. The applications above and the examples illustrate the profound influence of generative AI on content production and educational curriculum development. Educational professionals can access comprehensive resources to create, adapt, and improve instructional materials, enhancing students' educational experiences.

PERSONALIZATION AND ADAPTATION IN LEARNING

Generative AI is revolutionizing education by providing highly customized learning experiences. It achieves this through a range of procedures. Generative AI technology can create customized educational materials by analyzing the individual student's distinct academic history, preferences, and accomplishments. This analysis allows the system to tailor the learning materials to meet the specific needs of each student. Students receive educational resources designed to enhance their learning process using this method. Artificial intelligence (AI) can generate customized learning paths that adapt to the success of individual students. The system adjusts the content to provide more cognitively challenging materials in areas of proficiency and additional support in areas of weakness, thus creating flexible and adaptable learning paths.

Generative AI can produce content in various formats, accommodating different learning preferences and styles. Employing a variety of mediums, such as written text, audio recordings, and video presentations, ensures that the educational material is comprehensive and engaging for all students. Research has demonstrated that incorporating customized exercises that adapt in real-time to a student's performance can significantly enhance the learning process. The artificial intelligence system offers further assistance to students when they encounter difficulties, continuing to provide support until the learner reaches a satisfactory level of proficiency. It enhances the overall learning process by reinforcing positive experiences. Personalized feedback is a distinct and essential attribute. Artificial intelligence (AI) offers valuable suggestions for improvement and identifies instances of proficiency, helping students understand their mistakes and allowing for quick correction.

Utilizing learning analytics provides valuable insights into students' academic achievements. This dataset enables instructors to see patterns and identify areas where students may face challenges, permitting timely interventions and curriculum adjustments. Generative AI prioritizes inclusivity and accessibility by generating content in several formats, allowing students with diverse needs, including those with disabilities, to access and engage with educational materials easily.

Generative artificial intelligence (AI) creates an educational setting that emphasizes each student's unique requirements and learning preferences, fostering inclusiveness and focusing on the learner. This effect intensifies the process of acquiring knowledge and improves academic accomplishments. AI-generated content possesses exceptional variety and adaptability, rendering it a valuable instrument that efficiently caters to diverse learning styles and individual educational needs. The implementation of AI can accommodate the varied learning preferences of students, encompassing visual learners who derive advantages from infographics and diagrams, auditory learners who prefer verbal explanations, read-write learners who actively engage with written assignments, and kinesthetic learners who excel in hands-on activities. Furthermore, artificial intelligence goes beyond the range of learning styles by analyzing students' records and personal tendencies to offer customized educational content that meets their needs. Additionally, the system offers support in other languages, includes accessibility features, and provides personalized feedback tailored to each student's unique learning style. Artificial intelligence (AI) ensures that the educational experience is inclusive and personalized, enhancing the overall learning path for every student.

NAVIGATING CHALLENGES AND ETHICAL CONSIDERATIONS

Incorporating generative artificial intelligence in education offers substantial prospects for profound change. It is imperative to recognize and evaluate the possible disadvantages and limitations linked to this technology, requiring a careful and comprehensive evaluation. The challenges involve multiple facets, including concerns about the calibre of content produced by artificial intelligence, the possible decrease in creativity and personalization, overreliance on AI in education, worries about data privacy, disparities in access to AI technologies, and ethical considerations regarding authenticity and plagiarism. Ensuring meticulous quality control is paramount to ensure that AI-generated goods conform to educational standards and are free from errors or bias. It is crucial to combine the effectiveness of AI with the creative and nuanced understanding that educators bring to traditional materials to maintain engaging and motivating educational content. Educators should exercise prudence when excessively depending on artificial intelligence (AI) and instead retain the ability to customize instructional resources for their students. It is crucial to prioritize safeguarding confidential student information and properly tackle data privacy issues, especially considering data breaches and privacy regulations. To resolve the problems regarding fairness, it is crucial to prioritize ensuring equal access to artificial intelligence (AI) technologies for educational institutions and students. This strategy will aid in reducing inequalities and mitigating the potential for a digital divide.

The capacity of artificial intelligence (AI) to blur the distinction between authentic work and computer-generated content emphasizes the importance of prioritizing the prevention of plagiarism and the preservation of academic integrity. To address these difficulties and limitations, it is crucial to engage in meticulous planning, establish thorough guidelines, enforce rigorous quality control measures, offer sufficient training to educators, implement strict data protection protocols, and adopt an approach that emphasizes the complementary role of AI rather than its replacement of human educators. Moreover, fostering transparency and offering moral instruction can significantly improve the skills of students and educators in adequately dealing with the intricacies and potentialities linked to generative AI. The integration of AI-generated knowledge in the realm of education prompts significant ethical problems that necessitate thorough scrutiny. The ethical implications encompass a range of difficulties, including bias and fairness, transparency, genuineness, plagiarism, instructor independence, data confidentiality, equality and accessibility, and the potential excessive dependence on artificial intelligence (AI). The paramount significance is ensuring that AI-generated materials are free from biases and actively uphold ideals of fairness and equity.

Establishing transparency in the decision-making processes of artificial intelligence is crucial for fostering confidence within the educational community, including educators and students. Educational institutions should establish thorough mechanisms to efficiently address concerns about the authenticity of student assignments and respect academic integrity ideals. Preserving teachers' autonomy in shaping the learning experience depends on finding a balanced and harmonious relationship between the capabilities of artificial intelligence (AI) and the role of educators. Incorporating ethical imperatives is essential for safeguarding student data and advancing equitable access to resources produced by artificial intelligence. Ultimately, it is crucial to strike a balance between harnessing the advantages of artificial intelligence and fostering the development of critical thinking skills in students to avoid reliance on technology for educational purposes. To effectively tackle these ethical challenges, it is crucial to promote cooperation among educational institutions, policymakers, and AI developers. Moreover, it is essential to include moral instruction on AI in the curriculum, enabling students to acquire the necessary information and abilities to navigate AI's ethical dilemmas and potential benefits in education.

COLLABORATIVE SYNERGY EDUCATORS AND AI

The collaboration between educators and artificial intelligence (AI) systems has enabled the creation of innovative solutions in the education sector. The fruitful partnerships between these institutions highlight the importance of human-AI collaboration in shaping the future of education. These collaborations involve a range of initiatives, including partnering with adaptive learning platforms to provide tailored student experiences, automating assessment and feedback processes to improve efficiency, creating personalized content, developing AI-powered tutoring systems, enhancing educational materials and curricula, and advocating for inclusivity in education. The efficient utilization of AI in education involves seamlessly integrating human expertise and AI capabilities, allowing educators to leverage their pedagogical insights and guidance to create personalized and captivating learning experiences. Together, these aspects provide a powerful combination that enhances the impact of content, evaluation, and instructional resources, thereby improving the educational experience for students. The collaborative method has significant potential as a viable model in the ever-changing field of education.

Human knowledge is essential in organizing AI-generated content to optimize learning outcomes. Teachers have a profound understanding of teaching methods, extensive expertise in their fields, and the ability to customize information to meet the distinct needs of each student. They play a crucial role in setting assessment standards, providing helpful feedback, addressing ethical concerns, and guaranteeing a fair and unbiased learning environment. Furthermore, educators integrate AI-generated data into their syllabus, arrange materials, and create engaging educational activities. AI-driven teaching solutions offer essential human support and guidance, boosting technology by integrating emotional understanding. The collaboration between human educators and AI systems creates a collective synergy that produces customized educational materials, personalized support, adherence to ethical norms, and student learning experiences relevant to their specific circumstances. Essentially, this collaboration improves the educational experience by utilizing the unique strengths of human expertise and artificial intelligence capabilities.

FUTURE HORIZONS REDEFINING EDUCATION WITH GENERATIVE AI

Continuous advancements in artificial intelligence (AI) technology are driving the upcoming fascinating transformation of education. Education under this framework is defined by customization, availability, and flexibility, focusing on addressing individual learners' distinct needs and preferences. AI-driven tools revolutionize how students and instructors engage with educational content and procedures. The present educational environment has shifted from a standardized approach accommodating all individuals. Artificial intelligence (AI) evaluates individual students' unique learning styles, rates of progress, and preferences to offer customized learning pathways. AI tailors the content to meet the requirements of individuals spanning various age demographics, encompassing both elementary school children and adult learners. Tutoring systems enhanced by artificial intelligence (AI) offer students prompt and continuous support. The virtual tutors provided in this setting provide personalized feedback, address queries, and adapt their methodology to suit the unique learning path of every learner. Artificial intelligence (AI) can offer support in traditional classroom settings and remote learning environments.

Artificial intelligence (AI) significantly improves the inclusion and accessibility of education. The software offers real-time translations, converts content into alternative formats (such as braille or audio), and adapts materials to cater to diverse learning needs, fostering inclusivity among students. Educational professionals collaborate closely with artificial intelligence technologies to create flexible and engaging courses. Artificial intelligence (AI) can identify shortcomings in learning, make immediate modifications to instructional materials, and offer recommendations for more resources. It guarantees the curriculum stays current and adheres to constantly evolving academic standards. Implementing artificial intelligence has resulted in a substantial revolution in the assessment process. The use of artificial intelligence to analyze assessment data and provide helpful insights to educators has become widespread in automated grading. The technology enables the early discovery of patterns in student performance, allowing for timely intervention. AI-driven language translation solutions facilitate seamless and productive communication between students and educators worldwide. It fosters cross-cultural learning opportunities, enables the exchange of diverse ideas, and helps build a worldwide community of learners.

Artificial intelligence accelerates the advancement of educational research. This program enables academics to analyze large datasets and assists in generating research papers, literature reviews, and scholarly content. It opens up opportunities for distinctive perspectives and progress in education. Given the increasing role of AI in taking over repetitive tasks, schools are placing greater emphasis on teaching critical thinking, problem-solving, and creativity. Schools provide students with the essential skills and information required to excel in a future that highly values adaptability and the ability to handle intricate challenges.

Artificial intelligence (AI) is vital in educating students on ethical issues, recognizing prejudice, and appropriately deploying AI. Incorporating AI into education has become essential in the modern period, marked by the increasing ubiquity of artificial intelligence (AI) in various fields. Teachers participate in ongoing professional development to effectively utilize artificial intelligence in educational environments. Professional development programs provide educators with the skills and expertise to proficiently employ artificial intelligence technologies and platforms to enhance teaching and learning. To attain this envisioned future, it is imperative to do thorough studies and promote innovation. Educational institutions should dedicate resources to pursuing AI research to develop more advanced models and tools. Forging alliances between technology businesses and educational institutions is crucial for driving innovation. In addition, building robust data privacy and security frameworks is vital to guaranteeing the appropriate and ethical usage of students' data. Generative AI in education promises to create a learning environment that tailors to each student's needs, enhances accessibility, and fosters greater student involvement. The continuous advancement of AI technology will require the active participation of educators, researchers, and politicians to guide and shape the direction of education in alignment with educational goals, human values, and ethical principles. In this envisioned future, education surpasses conventional constraints and restrictions. Incorporating generative AI within educational institutions offers many opportunities for scholarly inquiry, creative improvements, and purposeful integration. The critical priority of research and innovation should be advancing artificial intelligence (AI) systems that can collaboratively construct, update, and dynamically adapt courses. Employing AI models in conjunction with educators would streamline the creation of adaptable learning routes, ensuring the continuous pertinence and synchronization of the curriculum with ever-growing educational benchmarks.

Further research could expand the capability of artificial intelligence (AI) to provide highly customized educational experiences. Artificial intelligence systems can utilize natural language processing and computer vision advancements to accurately understand students' emotions, levels of engagement, and preferred learning methods. Consequently, it allows for the immediate modification of educational material and instructional strategies. Research efforts should prioritize the development of sophisticated AI-driven educational systems. Virtual tutors offer personalized feedback, respond to student's questions, and adapt their teaching approaches to suit their unique learning trajectories. Investigating emotionally intelligent artificial intelligence systems is an up-and-coming area of academic research. Including ethical artificial intelligence (AI) instruction in the curriculum is imperative. The analysis can focus on creating instructional modules and educational tools that educate students about the ethical aspects of artificial intelligence (AI), identifying biases in AI systems, and promoting responsible use of AI technologies. These lessons promote the development of critical thinking skills in analyzing the ethical implications of artificial intelligence (AI) in various contexts. Research should prioritize the development of artificial intelligence (AI) models that ensure that content generated by generative AI adheres to educational norms and ethical ideals. The growing use of AI in content creation requires the creation of advanced systems to guarantee the quality of the content.

The increasing use of artificial intelligence (AI) in education requires thoroughly examining the related data privacy and security concerns. Implementing cutting-edge secure data management and anonymization techniques will be crucial in protecting sensitive student information. It is essential to prioritize examining artificial intelligence (AI) programs that specifically cater to the requirements of students with impairments. Research can enable the development of artificial intelligence (AI) tools that provide personalized support, such as speech-to-text and text-to-speech technologies, to enhance accessibility and inclusivity in education. Promoting partnerships between educational institutions and technology firms is strongly advised. Joint ventures can enhance innovation by combining academic expertise with industry resources, thereby enabling the creation of cutting-edge artificial intelligence solutions for the education sector. Research efforts can facilitate the creation of digital platforms that promote cooperation, information exchange, and mutual learning among students and instructors from diverse cultural and educational backgrounds. AI-powered language translation systems have the potential to enhance cross-cultural communication greatly.

The progress in artificial intelligence (AI) research can enhance the efficiency of producing research papers, literature reviews, and academic content by simplifying the procedure. Artificial intelligence (AI) can assist scholars by efficiently analyzing large datasets and combining knowledge, accelerating educational research advancement. Developing ongoing teacher training programs is essential to effectively equip educators to integrate artificial intelligence (AI) into their teaching methods. Research can determine the most effective methods for incorporating artificial intelligence (AI) and help instructors acquire the necessary skills. Research and innovation should focus on creating artificial intelligence (AI) solutions that make education more accessible for disabled students. It includes advancements in assistive technologies, such as the creation of braille conversion systems and adapted techniques for distributing content. The potential of AI systems specifically designed for early childhood education is significant. Artificial intelligence (AI) can provide interactive and engaging instructional content that improves essential skills in young students. Our research will focus on developing artificial intelligence (AI) models that monitor students' progress and provide intervention when learning difficulties are detected. These models can provide timely intervention strategies to ensure students receive the required support to attain academic achievement. Research and innovation efforts can optimally harness the full potential of generative AI in educational institutions. An in-depth analysis and concentration on these areas can ensure that artificial intelligence (AI) technology enhances the educational process, complies with ethical principles, fosters diversity, and aligns with pedagogically valid concepts. It will enable the development of a future of education marked by enhanced involvement, customization, and availability.

The study discussed in this chapter examines the capacity of generative AI to bring about significant changes in content production and curriculum development. This study paves the way for numerous promising research opportunities at the crossroads of education and artificial intelligence. The ethical implications of generative AI in educational environments warrant thorough examination due to their increasing significance. Researchers may investigate the ethical ramifications of AI-generated content, analyzing concerns such as bias, privacy, and transparency while formulating ethical principles and optimal methods to guarantee the responsible application of AI in education. Furthermore, improving the user experience of AI-powered instructional material is imperative by effortlessly customizing it to accommodate individual learning styles and preferences. Exploring the pedagogical effects of AI is a promising field that investigates its influence on teaching methods, student-teacher relationships, and the entire learning experience. It focuses on determining if AI enhances or hinders traditional teaching procedures.

Longitudinal studies are crucial for evaluating the enduring impact of AI-generated education on students' long-term academic achievements, including enhanced retention, critical thinking, and problem-solving abilities. Investigating hybrid methodologies that combine AI-generated content with conventional teaching methods may result in more efficient and comprehensive learning experiences. Ensuring that quality education is accessible worldwide is of utmost importance. A future study might concentrate on expanding the availability of AI-generated information to underprivileged areas, potentially by developing affordable, customized resources. Scalability and cost-effectiveness continue to be important factors, and continuous research can enhance the efficiency of AI algorithms, decrease infrastructure expenses, and refine content distribution techniques. With the growing implementation of AI in education, ensuring the security and privacy of educational data and systems is an ongoing challenge. It requires the development of creative methods to preserve sensitive student information. Interdisciplinary collaboration is essential for developing more efficient AI-based educational solutions, requiring the involvement of computer scientists, educators, psychologists, and other specialists. Researchers could investigate the capacity of AI to revolutionize the assessment process by developing dynamic, customized exams that evaluate not only knowledge but also skills and competencies. The diverse research directions exemplify the changing importance of AI in education and its capacity to transform the future of learning. Continued research will play a crucial role in using the transformational capabilities of generative AI in education as the field advances.

DISCUSSION

Integrating generative AI into education has ushered in a new era of personalized and inclusive learning experiences. This discussion examines the mutually beneficial partnership between human educators and artificial intelligence (AI) technologies, emphasizing its vital importance in shaping the future of education. The generative artificial intelligence (AI) field exhibits remarkable expertise in creating tailored educational materials. Nevertheless, it is imperative to acknowledge that the expertise of human educators is vital in guaranteeing that these resources conform to established pedagogical norms. Educational professionals profoundly understand the intricacies of learning theories, cognitive development, and pedagogical practices. They assist in directing artificial intelligence systems to produce instructive and captivating content, providing students with compelling learning opportunities. This joint endeavour seeks to personalize the educational experience by customizing the curriculum to meet the distinct requirements of each student. An essential advantage of incorporating artificial intelligence (AI) into education is its ability to produce customized educational materials corresponding to students' learning speed, method, and preferences. Educators have a crucial role in providing deep insights into the content and complexities of individual students' needs. By integrating artificial intelligence (AI) with this knowledge, instructors ensure that students receive content that profoundly resonates with them, enhancing their comprehension and capacity to remember information. Using AI models can inadvertently reinforce biases in the training data, posing a significant ethical challenge to educational content. Educators are crucial in identifying and tackling discrimination and ensuring educational resources are fair, unbiased, and discrimination-free. The collective endeavour fosters an educational setting that maintains moral standards and openness. Educators can enhance AI's content-generating talents by actively customizing the content to match the specific needs and goals of the curriculum. Educators aim to develop a correlation between the effectiveness of artificial intelligence (AI) and educational objectives, ensuring the relevance and importance of instructional content in the classroom. The mentioned curriculum utilizes a flexible design style that easily adjusts to the constantly evolving academic demands.

The incorporation of generative artificial intelligence (AI) with open educational resources (OER) and open educational practices (OEP) has the potential to transform the educational landscape significantly. Generative artificial intelligence capable of understanding and generating human language often produces content that resembles human-created material. The transition from organic (created by humans) to synthetic (created by AI) range offers new possibilities for education, including automated content generation, curation of resources, updating of existing resources, co-creation, and enabling collaborative learning within the framework of Open Educational Resources (OER) and Open Educational Practices (OEP) (Bozkurt, 2023). Nevertheless, Bozkurt (2023) highlights the imperative of addressing many substantial challenges linked to the utilization of generative AI in education. The challenges encompass apprehensions over the calibre and reliability of AI-generated content, worries about data protection, and the need for fair access to AI technologies in educational settings. The report emphasizes that the issue of ownership in OERs and OEPs regarding AI-generated works is particularly controversial. The lack of conventional human authorship in AI-generated content raises questions regarding copyright protection and legal accountability. The report presents the ideas of rapid engineering and co-creation using AI as a possible solution. It proposes that artificial intelligence should not be considered an author but rather a powerful tool that can enhance the capabilities of human authors. This approach aims to solve concerns related to authorship identification and legal accountability. According to Bozkurt (2023), generative AI has the potential to significantly transform education, namely in the areas of open educational resources (OER) and open educational practices (OEP). To guarantee the appropriate and efficient utilization of generative AI in education, it is imperative to assess the obstacles and ethical considerations associated with it thoroughly. The article advocates for further investigation and discussion to propel the discourse on incorporating AI in education. Tlili et al. (2023) reveal a fascinating division in the use of ChatGPT for teaching. Although ChatGPT has garnered significant interest and favourable discussion in social media and educational environments, its implementation in academic contexts poses numerous intricate obstacles and ethical quandaries. When ChatGPT is incorporated into educational contexts, it can lead to dishonesty, lack of integrity, privacy breaches, the spread of deceptive information, and susceptibility to manipulation. The considerations indicate the immediate necessity for extensive ethical norms and robust safeguards to govern the utilization of artificial intelligence chatbots in educational environments.

In their research, Tlili et al. (2023) investigate various user experiences within educational environments, underscoring the reciprocal impact that ChatGPT can have on substantial transformations. Notwithstanding the potential for positive educational reform, the practical implementation of this endeavour encounters challenges. Recognizing varying user experiences underscores the criticality of thoroughly addressing these issues to ensure a beneficial and fruitful user engagement with ChatGPT within an academic setting. Integrating AI chatbots, such as ChatGPT, into educational settings requires prudence. Specific perspectives within the discipline emphasize the necessity for a prudent and responsible integration of these technologies to maximize their functionalities while avoiding possible disadvantages and ethical quandaries. It accentuates both delight and apprehension regarding the potential of ChatGPT in the academy. It emphasizes the importance of confronting ethical concerns and impediments to the user experience while advocating for the prudent and conscientious integration of artificial intelligence chatbots within educational settings. The research underscores the importance of developing and adhering to comprehensive guidelines and optimal methodologies to ensure artificial intelligence chatbots' moral and effective implementation in education. Bozkurt (2023a) conducted a study that underscores the significant influence of generative AI within education. An analysis of the effects of conversational agents and LLM (large language models) on chatbot interactions yields nuanced insights. Prominent developments include the application of generative AI to enhance social and cognitive learning, the promotion of AI literacy, and the integration of AI into academic expansion initiatives. Scholars emphasize the importance of human-AI interaction in enhancing educational experiences. Scholars emphasize the significance of prompt engineering, emotional intelligence, and AI literacy as critical research domains that optimize the integration of AI systems within the educational sphere. These advancements create an atmosphere where well-informed and emotionally astute users navigate dynamic learning environments enhanced by artificial intelligence. Bozkurt (2023b) emphasizes the significance of generative artificial intelligence (AI), as exemplified by ChatGPT, within the realm of natural language processing, particularly concerning large language models (LLMs). Its educational potential as a conversational agent highlights the significance of comprehending language generation. This article emphasizes the critical significance of prompt engineering concerning conversational agents enabled by artificial intelligence as a component of digital literacy. This statement underscores the importance of preparedness when artificial intelligence is dominant, urging vigilance and responsibility in applying generative AI's capabilities. Preparing for a future dominated by artificial intelligence is crucial, as it will profoundly affect teaching and learning methodologies and require innovative perspectives. Singha (2023) examines the dynamic relationship between emotional health, artificial intelligence (AI), and mindfulness, emphasizing the potential for these elements to work in tandem. This chapter explores the potential for AI and mindfulness to work in tandem to increase emotional awareness. It highlights the contribution of AI to fostering emotional well-being in various contexts, including education, employment, and mental health. The discourse additionally encompasses emerging patterns and ethical implications, emphasizing the profound impact that integrating artificial intelligence and mindfulness could have on promoting emotional wellness. Sustaining a compassionate equilibrium in an ever more AI-influenced world continues to be the primary concern, emphasizing the necessity for an ethical and balanced integration of these technologies to promote emotional well-being. In their study, Bozkurt & Sharma (2023) make an important discovery: they show that using generative AI in co-creation can be a very effective way to teach, especially regarding the most important part of engineering: being on time. This research shows how important well-written prompts are for making interactions between people and large language models (LLMs) that use natural language processing (NLP) more effective. The researchers propose implementing a prompt-based conversational pedagogy by considering context, function, tone, and intention when devising a strategic approach to generative AI. Researchers consider the pedagogical framework to be of the utmost importance because it enables effective communication and interaction, thereby permitting the full implementation of generative AI in educational settings. Additionally, the paper underscores the importance of educators' promptly acquiring engineering competencies to facilitate meaningful and appropriate interactions for the context. Singha and Singha (2023) underscore a significant discovery in their chapter—the essential role that human diversity and mindfulness fulfil in sustaining machine learning (ML) and artificial intelligence (AI). The discourse explores the diverse applications of AI and ML interactions that can contribute positively to society, encompassing legal proceedings, agricultural education, health awareness, and mindfulness training. The chapter highlights the advantageous consequences that AI and ML have engendered across various domains, encompassing mathematics, art, and music. The comprehension above highlights the intrinsic correlation between the durability of AI and ML and their capacity to engage and enhance human experiences actively in various societal spheres. In their collaborative editorial, Bozkurt et al. (2023) highlighted the fundamental discovery, emphasizing the intricate importance of openness in education as revealed via personal anecdotes. Openness is depicted in the narratives as a complex notion closely intertwined with various values, including affordability, empowerment, innovation, social justice, and inclusivity. The collection of varied personal narratives serves to underscore openness as a practice that affects the elimination of barriers, the promotion of democratization, and the cultivation of diversity appreciation. The editorial promotes reader participation in these diverse narratives on an independent basis, recognizing the unique viewpoints of researchers around the world. This methodology fosters the generation of varied interpretations, ultimately underscoring the urgent global significance and relevance of openness in education. Bozkurt et al. (2023a) investigate the promise and challenges of generative pre-trained transformer (GPT) artificial intelligence (AI) in educational environments. This paper employs a speculative methodology to present potential narratives, identify emergent themes, and examine their implications for twenty-first-century education. This statement highlights the potential benefits of artificial intelligence (AI) integration into education (AIEd) while recognizing potential drawbacks resulting from the speculative scenarios. Given the evolving landscape wherein artificial intelligence increasingly undertakes duties that were once the exclusive domain of human educators, the central argument emphasizes the necessity of re-evaluating the functions of both technology and human educators. This article presents a proactive approach to exerting influence over the dynamic interaction between human and artificial intelligence contributions in education. Implementing tutoring systems and educational aids made possible by artificial intelligence (AI) significantly aided students. Educators provide indispensable guidance and support, particularly concerning emotional intelligence. Mentorship, encouragement, and empathy are crucial in fostering students' holistic growth and welfare. The continuous progress in artificial intelligence (AI) technology offers significant opportunities for improvement within education. Nevertheless, integrating artificial intelligence (AI) into education requires a concerted effort from policymakers, educators, academic institutions, and AI developers. For the future, it is critical to prioritize preserving data security, reducing inequalities in digital access, and aligning artificial intelligence (AI) with the fundamental principles of education. The convergence of generative AI and human educators engenders a synergistic collaboration that revolutionizes the education sector, culminating in an individualized, all-encompassing, and exceedingly gratifying educational encounter. By combining the knowledge of instructors with the effectiveness of artificial intelligence (AI), this collaboration generates a comprehensive learning environment. To optimize the educational potential of artificial intelligence (AI), the collaboration between AI and education must progress responsibly and inclusively. Ensuring that education remains a vehicle for empowering, accessible, and exceptional students of diverse backgrounds constitutes this responsibility.

CONCLUSION

Generative AI has become a major educational driving force, offering great potential to change how we learn and teach methods. As we navigate this constantly evolving landscape, it becomes clear that collaborative engagement between human educators and artificial intelligence (AI) is essential for fully utilizing the capabilities of generative AI in education. Successful collaborations demonstrate the importance of the link between educators and AI systems. By employing adaptive learning platforms, AI-powered feedback, personalized content development, and AI-enhanced curriculum design, educators may provide students with tailored, captivating, and contextually appropriate educational experiences. The involvement of human knowledge is essential in developing AI-generated material, as it relies on pedagogical intuition, customized content, ethical considerations, and contextual awareness. Educators provide a significant human aspect, offering guidance, mentorship, and a personal connection that enhances the efficiency and capacities of artificial intelligence (AI). The symbiotic collaboration between technology and humans ensures that technology is in harmony with human values, ethics, and goals, achieving pupils' most advantageous educational outcomes. As we consider the future, ongoing advancements in artificial intelligence (AI) technology have the potential to provide personalized lifelong learning experiences, AI-powered tutoring systems, enhanced accessibility, and flexible curriculum design. Considerations such as ethical AI instruction, safeguarding data privacy and security, and fostering interdisciplinary collaboration will impact the incorporation of artificial intelligence (AI) into educational institutions. In this envisioned scenario, educators and artificial intelligence (AI) systems will work together seamlessly to create an educational environment that promotes diversity, accessibility, and a strong focus on developing critical thinking skills and problem-solving abilities. Integrating artificial intelligence (AI) in education can provide students of different ages and backgrounds with a more engaging, personalized, and improved learning experience. The onus of ensuring that AI adheres to the core principles of education, such as empowerment, diversity, and quality, lies with educators, institutions, policymakers, and AI developers. Using this strategy, we can confidently initiate a project that transforms the education sector by utilizing generative AI. It would significantly improve the accessibility, personalization, and efficacy of learning to an unparalleled extent.

AUTHORS' NOTES

This paper was proofread and refined with the assistance of generative AI, complementing the human editorial process.

REFERENCES

Bahroun, Z., Anane, C., Ahmed, V., & Zacca, A. (2023). Transforming Education: A Comprehensive Review of Generative Artificial Intelligence in Educational Settings through Bibliometric and Content Analysis. *Sustainability (Basel)*, *15*(17), 12983. doi:10.3390/su151712983

Baker, B. (1996). The History of Curriculum or Curriculum History? What *is* the Field, and Who Gets to Play on it? *Curriculum Studies*, *4*(1), 105–117. doi:10.1080/0965975960040106

Bozkurt, A. (2023). Generative AI, synthetic contents, Open Educational Resources (OER), and Open Educational Practices (OEP): A new front in the openness landscape. *Open Praxis*, *15*(3), 178–184. doi:10.55982/openpraxis.15.3.579

Bozkurt, A. (2023a). Unleashing the potential of generative AI, conversational agents and chatbots in educational praxis: A Systematic Review and Bibliometric Analysis of GenAI in Education. *Open Praxis*, *15*(4), 261–270. doi:10.55982/openpraxis.15.4.609

Bozkurt, A. (2023b). Generative artificial intelligence (AI) powered conversational educational agents: The inevitable paradigm shift. *Asian Journal of Distance Education*, *18*(1), 198–204. doi:10.5281/zenodo.7716416

Bozkurt, A., Gjelsvik, T., Adam, T., Asino, T. I., Atenas, J., Bali, M., Blomgren, C., Bond, M., Bonk, C. J., Brown, M., Burgos, D., Conrad, D., Costello, E., Cronin, C., Czerniewicz, L., Deepwell, M., Deimann, M., DeWaard, H. J., & Dousay, T. A., Ebner, M., Farrow, R., Gil-Jaurena, I., Havemann, L., Inamorato, A., Irvine, V., Karunanayaka, S. P., Kerres, M., Lambert, S., Lee, K., Makoe, M., Marín, V. I., Mikroyannidis, A., Mishra, S., Naidu, S., Nascimbeni, F., Nichols, M., Olcott. Jr., D., Ossiannilsson, E., Otto, D., Padilla Rodriguez, B. C., Paskevicius, M., Roberts, V., Saleem, T., Schuwer, R., Sharma, R. C., Stewart, B., Stracke, C. M., Tait, A., Tlili, A., Ubachs, G., Weidlich, J., Weller, M., Xiao, JZawacki-Richter, O. (2023). Openness in education as a praxis: From individual testimonials to collective voices. *Open Praxis*, *15*(2), 76–112. doi:10.55982/openpraxis.15.2.574

Bozkurt, A., & Sharma, R. C. (2023). Generative AI and prompt engineering: The art of whispering to let the genie out of the algorithmic world. *Asian Journal of Distance Education*, *18*(2), i–vii. doi:10.5281/zenodo.8174941

Bozkurt, A., Xiao, J., Lambert, S., Pazurek, A., Crompton, H., Koseoglu, S., Farrow, R., Bond, M., Nerantzi, C., Honeychurch, S., Bali, M., Dron, J., Mir, K., Stewart, B., Costello, E., Mason, J., Stracke, C. M., Romero-Hall, E., Koutropoulos, A., Toquero, C. M., Singh, L Tlili, A., Lee, K., Nichols, M., Ossiannilsson, E., Brown, M., Irvine, V., Raffaghelli, J. E., Santos-Hermosa, G Farrell, O., Adam, T., Thong, Y. L., Sani-Bozkurt, S., Sharma, R. C., Hrastinski, S., & Jandrić, P. (2023a). Speculative futures on ChatGPT and generative artificial intelligence (AI): A collective reflection from the educational landscape. Asian Journal of Distance Education, *18*(1), 53-130. doi:10.5281/zenodo.7636568

Budhwar, P., Chowdhury, S., Wood, G., Aguinis, H., Bamber, G. J., Beltran, J. R., Boselie, P., Cooke, F. L., Decker, S., DeNisi, A. S., Dey, P. K., Guest, D., Knoblich, A. J., Malik, A., Paauwe, J., Papagiannidis, S., Patel, C., Pereira, V., Ren, S., & Varma, A. (2023). Human resource management in the age of generative artificial intelligence: Perspectives and research directions on ChatGPT. *Human Resource Management Journal*, *33*(3), 606–659. doi:10.1111/1748-8583.12524

Chang, D., Lin, M. P., Hajian, S., & Wang, Q. Q. (2023). Educational design principles of using AI chatbot that supports Self-Regulated learning in education: Goal setting, feedback, and personalization. *Sustainability (Basel)*, *15*(17), 12921. doi:10.3390/su151712921

Dwivedi, Y. K., Kshetri, N., Hughes, L., Slade, E., Jeyaraj, A., Kar, A. K., Baabdullah, A. M., Koohang, A., Raghavan, V., Ahuja, M., Albanna, H., Albashrawi, M. A., Al-Busaidi, A. S., Balakrishnan, J., Barlette, Y., Basu, S., Bose, I., Brooks, L., Buhalis, D., & Wright, R. (2023). Opinion Paper: "So what if ChatGPT wrote it?" Multidisciplinary perspectives on opportunities, challenges and implications of generative conversational AI for research, practice and policy. *International Journal of Information Management*, *71*, 102642. doi:10.1016/j.ijinfomgt.2023.102642

George, B., & Wooden, O. S. (2023). Managing the Strategic Transformation of Higher Education through Artificial Intelligence. *Administrative Sciences*, *13*(9), 196. doi:10.3390/admsci13090196

Han, K., Wang, Y., Chen, H., Chen, X., Guo, J., Liu, Z., Tang, Y., Xiao, A., Xu, C., Xu, Y., Yang, Z., Zhang, Y., & Tao, D. (2023). A survey on Vision Transformer. *IEEE Transactions on Pattern Analysis and Machine Intelligence*, *45*(1), 87–110. doi:10.1109/TPAMI.2022.3152247 PMID:35180075

Hassan, M. S., Halbusi, H. A., & Abdelfattah, F. (2023). May the force of text data analysis be with you: Unleashing the power of generative AI for social psychology research. *Computers in Human Behavior Artificial Humans*, *1*(2), 100006. doi:10.1016/j.chbah.2023.100006

Jeon, J. H., & Lee, S. (2023). Large language models in education: A focus on the complementary relationship between human teachers and ChatGPT. *Education and Information Technologies*, *28*(12), 15873–15892. doi:10.1007/s10639-023-11834-1

Kamalov, F., Calonge, D. S., & Gurrib, I. (2023). A new era of Artificial intelligence in Education: Towards a sustainable Multifaceted Revolution. *Sustainability (Basel)*, *15*(16), 12451. doi:10.3390/su151612451

Kohnke, L., Moorhouse, B. L., & Zou, D. (2023). Exploring generative artificial intelligence preparedness among university language instructors: A case study. *Computers & Education: Artificial Intelligence*, *5*, 100156. doi:10.1016/j.caeai.2023.100156

Lin, X., Chen, L., Chan, K. K., Peng, S., Chen, X., Xie, S., Liu, J., & Hu, Q. (2022). Teachers' perceptions of teaching Sustainable Artificial Intelligence: A Design frame perspective. *Sustainability (Basel)*, *14*(13), 7811. doi:10.3390/su14137811

Locke, S., Bashall, A., Al-Adely, S., Moore, J. A., Wilson, A. J., & Kitchen, G. (2021). Natural language processing in medicine: A review. Trends in Anaesthesia and Critical Care. doi:10.1016/j.tacc.2021.02.007

Nah, F. F., Zheng, R., Cai, J., Siau, K., & Chen, L. (2023). Generative AI and ChatGPT: Applications, challenges, and AI-human collaboration. *Journal of Information Technology Case and Application Research*, *25*(3), 277–304. doi:10.1080/15228053.2023.2233814

Roediger, H. L. III, & Karpicke, J. D. (2006). The Power of Testing Memory: Basic Research and Implications for Educational Practice. *Perspectives on Psychological Science*, *1*(3), 181–210. doi:10.1111/j.1745-6916.2006.00012.x PMID:26151629

Shin, J., Guo, Q., & Gierl, M. J. (2019). Multiple-choice item distractor development using topic modelling approaches. Frontiers in Psychology. doi:10.3389/fpsyg.2019.00825

Singha, R., & Singha, S. (2023). Economic sustainability, mindfulness, and diversity in the age of artificial intelligence and machine learning. In P. Raj, P. B. Soundarabai, & P. Augustine (Eds.), *Machine Intelligence: Computer Vision and Natural Language Processing* (pp. 273–285). Taylor & Francis Group. doi:10.1201/9781003424550-15

Sohail, S. S., Farhat, F., Himeur, Y., Nadeem, M., Madsen, D. Ø., Singh, Y., Atalla, S., & Mansoor, W. (2023). Decoding ChatGPT: A taxonomy of existing research, current challenges, and possible future directions. *Journal of King Saud University. Computer and Information Sciences*, *35*(8), 101675. doi:10.1016/j.jksuci.2023.101675

Tlili, A., Shehata, B., Adarkwah, M. A., Bozkurt, A., Hickey, D. T., Huang, R., & Agyemang, B. (2023). What if the devil is my guardian angel? ChatGPT is a case study of using chatbots in education. *Smart Learning Environments*, *10*(1), 15. doi:10.1186/s40561-023-00237-x

Tu, X., Zou, J., Su, W., & Zhang, L. (2023). What Should Data Science Education Do with Large Language Models? *arXiv (Cornell University)*. https://doi.org//arxiv.2307.02792 doi:10.48550

Vartiainen, H., & Tedre, M. (2023). Using artificial intelligence in craft education: Crafting with text-to-image generative models. *Digital Creativity (Exeter)*, *34*(1), 1–21. doi:10.1080/14626268.2023.2174557

Zhao, J., Han, X., Ouyang, M., & Burke, A. (2023). Specialized deep neural networks for battery health prognostics: Opportunities and challenges. *Journal of Energy Chemistry*. doi:10.1016/j.jechem.2023.08.047

Zou, D., Huang, Y., & Xie, H. (2019). Digital game-based vocabulary learning: Where are we and where are we going? *Computer Assisted Language Learning*, *34*(5–6), 751–777. doi:10.1080/09588221.2019.1640745

KEY TERMS AND DEFINITIONS

Content Creation: A form of artificial intelligence that generates creative and contextually pertinent content, typically through deep learning and language models.

Curriculum Development: It entails the planning and organization of educational programs, including the selection of learning objectives, content, and evaluation techniques.

Generative AI: AI that generates creative and contextually pertinent content, typically via deep learning and language models.

Pedagogical Enhancement: Enhancing teaching methods and strategies by incorporating cutting-edge technologies and instructional approaches.

Personalized Education: Customizing educational content and experiences to meet each student's specific needs, preferences, and learning styles.

Prompt Engineering: Crafting precise and effective input instructions to direct AI models in producing the intended output or responses.

Synthetic Learning Materials: Formulating precise and effective input instructions to direct AI models in generating desired output or responses.

Chapter 14
Empowering Faculty Vitality and Mitigating Burnout Through Generative AI in Higher Education:
Reimagining Learning Environments With Generative AI

Stacy Ybarra
Our Lady of the Lake University, USA

ABSTRACT

In today's dynamic landscape of higher education, the pervasive issue of faculty burnout has emerged as a pressing concern, casting a shadow over the well-being of educators and the overall quality of instruction. This chapter proposal embarks on an exploration of how generative artificial intelligence (AI) can act as a transformative force within higher education, specifically focusing on its potential to empower faculty members, enhance pedagogical practices, and mitigate the alarming prevalence of burnout. The chapter's central objectives are multifaceted, commencing with a comprehensive examination of the multifaceted phenomenon of faculty burnout. This includes an analysis of the contributing factors such as the escalating workloads, the shift towards online and blended learning modalities, and the overwhelming administrative duties that educators must shoulder. The aim here is to illuminate the multifaceted nature of burnout, thereby fostering an enhanced understanding of its urgency and the critical need for sustainable solutions.

DOI: 10.4018/979-8-3693-1351-0.ch014

INTRODUCTION

The contemporary landscape of higher education is marked by dynamic changes and challenges, with faculty burnout emerging as a pervasive concern that casts a shadow over the well-being of educators and the quality of instruction. Faculty burnout is a multifaceted phenomenon exacerbated by escalating workloads, the transition to online and blended learning modalities, and the overwhelming administrative responsibilities borne by educators. The introduction sets the stage for an in-depth exploration of the transformative potential of generative artificial intelligence (AI) within higher education. The contemporary landscape of higher education is marked by dynamic changes and challenges, with faculty burnout emerging as a pervasive concern that casts a shadow over the well-being of educators and the quality of instruction.

In response to the multifaceted challenges faced by educators, this chapter endeavors to illuminate the role of generative AI, specifically focusing on Large Language Models like GPT-3, as a beacon of hope in higher education. The chapter's objectives are twofold: first, to empower faculty members by automating tasks and enhancing their teaching approaches, and second, to proactively address and mitigate burnout.

Moving beyond theoretical considerations, the chapter delves into the practical applications of generative AI, showcasing real-world examples that exemplify the technology's potential to streamline administrative tasks, automate routine responsibilities, and create personalized educational content tailored to diverse student populations culminating in to provide educators and institutions with actionable insights for the seamless integration of AI into higher education, aligning with emerging trends and innovations in the field.

Emphasizing the central theme of the chapter, the introduction underscores how generative AI, through automation, instant feedback, and personalized learning experiences, can rekindle educators' passion for teaching and act as a potent tool in mitigating burnout.

Furthermore, the introduction acknowledges the ethical considerations inherent in the deployment of AI in education. Issues such as bias, privacy, and security are critical aspects that demand careful examination. The chapter recognizes the importance of addressing these ethical considerations and confronts the potential limitations associated with the implementation of AI tools in educational settings. This sets the stage for a thorough exploration of the ethical dimensions and challenges in subsequent sections.

This introduction lays a robust foundation for the exploration of generative AI's transformative potential in higher education. By addressing the multifaceted nature of faculty burnout, emphasizing the objectives of empowerment and burnout mitigation, and recognizing the ethical considerations and potential limitations, the chapter aims to provide a comprehensive understanding of the role of generative AI in rejuvenating faculty members and revitalizing higher education. Through this exploration, educators, administrators, and researchers will be equipped with the knowledge and tools necessary to navigate the intersection of AI and education, fostering a more vibrant and sustainable learning environment. Understanding the potential benefits and challenges associated with AI tool usage can inform the development of strategies to support faculty well-being and enhance academic productivity. By addressing these issues, institutions can work towards creating a supportive and sustainable environment for faculty members, ultimately contributing to the advancement of research and education.

FACULTY BURNOUT AND MENTAL HEALTH IN ACADEMIA

Faculty burnout is a significant issue in academic settings, with research indicating its prevalence and impact on various disciplines. Studies have shown that burnout among faculty members is associated with decreased productivity, depersonalization, and emotional exhaustion (Lackritz, 2004; Shah et al., 2018; Woo et al., 2022). The high workload, stress intolerance, and lack of work-life balance have been identified as contributing factors to burnout (Nomura et al., 2016). Furthermore, the COVID-19 pandemic has exacerbated burnout among faculty, necessitating institutional support and resources to address this issue (McMahon, 2022). The impact of burnout is not limited to individual faculty members; it also affects the overall academic environment, including concerns about retention and attrition (Mramba et al., 2020). In response to faculty burnout, there is a growing interest in exploring potential coping mechanisms and support systems. One emerging area of interest is the use of generative AI tools to alleviate faculty burnout. The potential of AI tools, such as ChatGPT in Figure 1, to assist faculty in various tasks, including research, teaching, and administrative duties, has garnered attention (Stokel-Walker, 2023).

Figure 1. ChatGPT screenshot
Note: ChatGPT screenshot, ChatGPT is a generative AI tool, n.d. (https://unsplash.com/photos/a-laptop-computer-sitting-on-top-of-a-wooden-table-G_vWviqUCCg). Reprinted with free-to-use permission from Unsplash.

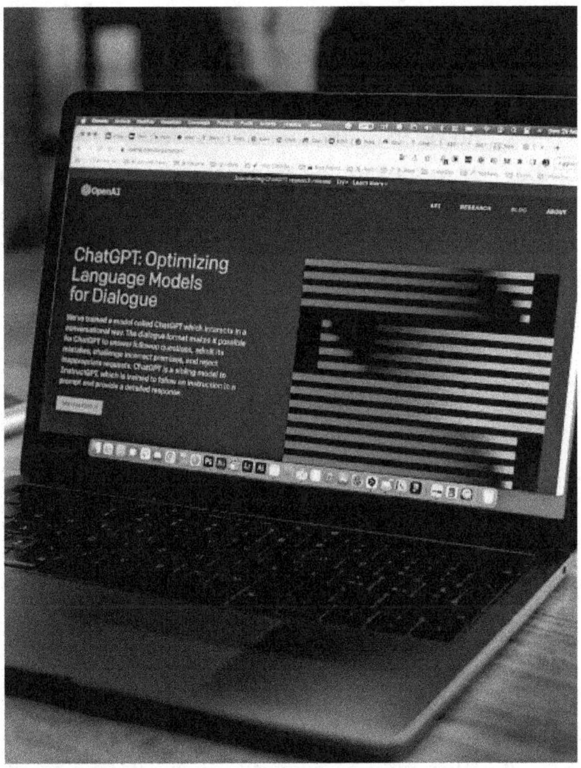

There are several contributing factors to faculty mental health concerns, including workload, work-life balance, resource scarcity, job insecurity, large class sizes, disruptive student behavior, evaluations, and the pressure to ensure student success. To address these issues, the review emphasizes the necessity for more targeted research on faculty mental health, urging comprehensive, career-wide strategies to mitigate stressors and enhance support structures for faculty members. It concludes by advocating for the creation of resilient academic communities that prioritize the well-being of all their members, particularly faculty. This information serves as a valuable foundation for a literature review on the relation of mental health issues tied to faculty burnout, providing insights into its causes, consequences, and potential interventions, while also highlighting the importance of ongoing research and community-building efforts.

Faculty burnout has been associated with intent to leave academia, highlighting the importance of addressing this issue for the long-term health of academic centers (Shanafelt et al., 2009). The factors contributing to faculty burnout are diverse and include chronic emotional and interpersonal stressors, high workload, limited time to manage responsibilities, and financial pressures to obtain research funding (Roos & Borkoski, 2021).

Research shows that a significant portion of the university community, including faculty, staff, and students, experience mental health issues like depression, anxiety, and stress (Halat et al., 2023). Faculty mental health is a rising concern, despite limited research compared to student mental health. The "storm of academia" with its demanding workload, multiple responsibilities, and competitive environment is identified as a major contributor to faculty stress and burnout.

he prevalence and consequences of mental health issues among university faculty are a growing concern, with studies indicating elevated levels of stress, anxiety, depression, and burnout across various career stages. This not only affects mental well-being but also manifests in physical symptoms such as headaches, gastrointestinal issues, and sleep disturbances. However, fear of stigma and a lack of supportive structures hinder faculty members from seeking help, potentially exacerbating mental health challenges, and jeopardizing their professional trajectories. It is evident that burnout is a significant concern that requires targeted interventions and policies to mitigate its impact on faculty well-being and retention (Boamah et al., 2022; Thurman, 2023).

PROPOSED SOLUTIONS TO THE PROBLEM

Faculty burnout is a complex issue that necessitates a comprehensive approach involving individual, organizational, and technological solutions (West et al., 2018; Kavanagh & Spiro, 2018; Kennedy et al., 2022; Taylor & Frechette, 2022; Alves et al., 2019; Halbach et al., 2022; Zhuang et al., 2022). Strategies to prevent burnout and enhance productivity and well-being have been proposed, emphasizing the need for both individual and organizational interventions (Kennedy et al., 2022). Individual characteristics have also been linked to faculty burnout, highlighting the importance of personalized interventions (Taylor & Frechette, 2022). Additionally, the demands placed on faculty members have been identified as a significant factor contributing to burnout (Alves et al., 2019). The interaction between faculty and trainee roles may also play a role in the development of burnout, necessitating further investigation (Halbach et al., 2022). Moreover, the ability of faculty to spend time on meaningful tasks has been associated with lower burnout, underscoring the importance of meaningful work in reducing burnout (Zhuang et al., 2022). In the context of integrating generative AI tools, it is crucial to consider the readiness of faculty to engage with AI technologies. A study found that faculty were more likely to report a lack of basic understanding of AI technologies, highlighting the need for adequate training and support in utilizing AI tools effectively to alleviate their workload and potentially reduce burnout (Wood et al., 2021). In summary, addressing faculty burnout requires a multifaceted approach that encompasses individual, organizational, and technological aspects. By implementing strategies to prevent burnout, understanding the impact of workload and meaningful tasks, and providing support for faculty to engage with AI tools effectively, institutions can work towards mitigating faculty burnout and promoting overall well-being.

LEVERAGING GENERATIVE AI TOOLS TO REDUCE FACULTY BURNOUT IN THE CLASSROOM

The use of AI tools has been proposed to streamline processes and reduce the time invested in various activities, which could potentially mitigate the risk of burnout (Wolverton & Hollier, 2019). However, the integration of AI tools in academic settings is not without its challenges. There are ongoing debates regarding the appropriateness of citing AI tools as authors in scholarly publications, raising questions about academic integrity and the role of AI in research (Stokel-Walker, 2023). Concerns have been raised about the potential for AI-generated content to introduce false or plagiarized material into scholarly literature, highlighting the need for ethical considerations in the use of AI tools (Zielinski et al., 2023). Considering these considerations, it is essential to explore the intersection of faculty burnout and the utilization of generative AI tools in academic settings.

EXAMPLES OF GENERATIVE AI TOOL USAGE IN ACADEMIA

The use of generative AI tools in academia has the potential to address burnout and mental health issues among researchers and students. Generative AI, a subfield of artificial intelligence, has shown promise in various domains, including mental healthcare and psychological interventions (Graham et al., 2019). Studies have demonstrated the potential of using machine learning algorithms to address mental health questions, highlighting the high accuracies and the potential of AI in mental healthcare (Graham et al., 2019). Additionally, the theoretical understanding of generative AI and its potential implications for the future of the design discipline provides researchers with an introduction to this innovative technology (Thoring et al., 2023). Furthermore, the acceptance of AI for digital entrepreneurship and its positive impact on attitudes and openness to experience have been highlighted, suggesting intentional improvement planning through the positive perceptions of AI affordance and explanation of its generativity (Upadhyay et al., 2021). However, it is essential to consider the potential negative experiences with formal mental health services and the incorporation of traditional healing and holistic perspectives in culturally grounded service models (Roh et al., 2016). Moreover, the impact of AI on the mental wellbeing of workers, especially in the manufacturing sector, has been identified as an area that requires further attention (Wan-qing & Li, 2022). The theoretical implications of the relationship between industrial AI and workers' health have been emphasized, indicating the need for research in this domain (Yang et al., 2022). It is crucial to acknowledge the potential ethical implications of AI and the need to incorporate ethics education, especially for non-engineering undergraduates, to address the ethical considerations associated with AI (Shih et al., 2021). The use of AI tools in academia has also raised concerns about the potential limitations and the need for a framework to examine patient attitudes regarding the applications of AI in healthcare (Richardson et al., 2022). Therefore, while generative AI tools offer significant potential in academia, it is essential to consider the ethical, cultural, and mental health implications associated with their use.

To effectively integrate generative AI tools in the classroom, faculty should consider a theoretical framework for educative AI, such as the "IDEE" framework proposed by (Su & Yang, 2023). This framework emphasizes identifying desired outcomes, determining the appropriate level of automation, ensuring ethical considerations, and evaluating effectiveness. Additionally, faculty should explore the potential of AI in education, as highlighted by (Adiguzel et al., 2023), who emphasized the importance of integrating AI-based educational tools into curricula and policies to prepare students for an AI-influenced future. Furthermore, faculty should consider the challenges and applications of AI in education, as discussed by (Alasadi & Baiz, 2023), to understand the opportunities, concerns, and solutions related to the role of generative AI in education. Moreover, it is essential for faculty to be aware of the impact of AI on higher learning institutions, as highlighted by (Lainjo & Tsmouche, 2023), who discussed the need for adequate financial and ethical support to enhance student performance through AI.

Additionally, faculty should consider the potential of AI-infused collaborative inquiry in upper elementary school, as discussed by (Lee et al., 2021), to explore game-based learning approaches for introducing students to AI and supporting teachers in integrating AI learning experiences in their classrooms. Furthermore, faculty should be mindful of the challenges and ethical implications of implementing AI applications in higher education, as emphasized by (Bozkurt et al., 2021). This includes critical reflection on the pedagogical and ethical implications, as well as the risks of implementing AI applications in higher education. By considering these factors, faculty can effectively leverage generative AI tools in the classroom to enhance the learning experience and prepare students for an AI-driven future.

Conducting University Research

AI tools for alleviating faculty burnout can be used in conducting university research (Harmon, 2023). Harmon discusses the challenges of managing multiple research projects simultaneously and the desire to expedite the completion of work for journal review. The article delves into the controversial nature of AI use in academic research, highlighting the potential for automating time-consuming tasks like literature reviews. Harmon shares her experience experimenting with various AI tools for academic writing and introduces four promising tools: jenni.ai, Elicit.org, Research Rabbit, and Scite.ai. Each tool serves a specific purpose, such as facilitating conversations, automating literature reviews, visualizing scholarly networks, and aiding in citation. The article concludes expressing anticipation for further clarification on ethical AI use in academic manuscripts and a commitment to evaluating how AI can enhance her research projects.

Creation of Lesson Plans

Johnson (2023) discusses the growing adoption of generative AI among educators to create engaging lesson plans and materials. The focus is on MagicSchool, a tool powered by OpenAI's text generation algorithms, which has gained popularity among K-12 educators. Teachers, such as Tim Ballaret, have reported saving valuable time and improving work-life balance by using AI to automate tasks like creating math problems based on students' interests. Surveys indicate that more teachers than students are currently using generative AI, with about 70% of Black and Latino teachers using the technology weekly. However, concerns about potential drawbacks, such as bias in generated content and the risk of teacher burnout, are discussed. The article emphasizes the need for caution and proper training when integrating AI into education.

To create lesson plans using generative AI tools for faculty and community college academia, educators can leverage the capabilities of AI to enhance curriculum development and teaching practices. For instance, AI can be used to introduce advanced concepts such as variational autoencoders to high school students, either independently or as part of existing Creative AI curricula (Lyu et al., 2022). Additionally, AI can aid in incorporating technology and modeling tools into science lesson plans, providing a framework for technology integration and enhancing the learning experience for preservice teachers (Schwarz, 2009). Furthermore, teachers' perspectives are crucial for making sense of emerging AI technology in curriculum planning, ensuring that the content aligns with educational objectives and student needs (Chiu & Chai, 2020). Moreover, the use of AI in lesson planning can help educators address the cognitive demands of planning by employing models such as the CODE-PLAN model to describe and analyze teachers' planning competence (König et al., 2021). Additionally, AI can serve as a structuring tool for lesson plans, encompassing a mix of resources, methodologies, and goals to enhance the learning experience for students (Akmal et al., 2022). Furthermore, the lesson plan analysis protocol (LPAP) can be utilized as a valuable tool for researchers and educational evaluators to analyze and improve lesson plans (Ndihokubwayo et al., 2022). In academia, the use of AI in lesson planning can also contribute to professional development, as evidenced by leveraging prospective teachers' knowledge through their participation in lesson study (González et al., 2021). Furthermore, AI can aid in addressing ethical considerations, such as data protection, privacy, and governance, when deploying AI in educational settings (Ibeneme et al., 2021). Additionally, AI can play a role in advancing women in IS academia, as demonstrated by the AIS Women's Network, which aims to promote gender diversity and inclusivity in information systems academia (Loiacono et al., 2016). In conclusion, the integration of generative AI tools in lesson planning offers numerous opportunities to enhance curriculum development, teaching practices, and professional development in academia. By leveraging AI, educators can create innovative and effective lesson plans that cater to the diverse needs of students while addressing ethical considerations and advancing inclusivity in academia.

ADMINISTRATIVE TASKS

Generative AI tools have the potential to significantly assist adjunct and full-time faculty in administrative tasks within higher education institutions. These tools can be particularly beneficial in streamlining administrative processes, such as grading, scheduling, and personalized learning support. By leveraging generative AI, faculty members can automate routine administrative tasks, allowing them to allocate more time to teaching, research, and student mentorship. Additionally, AI-driven tools can provide personalized learning experiences for students, freeing up faculty members from some administrative burdens and enabling them to focus on more individualized instruction and support.

Furthermore, the implementation of AI in administrative tasks can lead to increased efficiency and effectiveness, ultimately benefiting both faculty and students. However, it is crucial for administrators to ensure that the use of generative AI tools aligns with ethical considerations and academic integrity, as highlighted by (Tenakwah, 2023). Faculty members should be equipped with the necessary AI literacy to effectively utilize these tools, emphasizing the importance of professional development and training in this area. Overall, the integration of generative AI tools in administrative tasks has the potential to enhance productivity, facilitate personalized learning, and optimize the overall educational experience within higher education institutions.

TEACHER PREPARATION

Generative AI tools have the potential to significantly assist both adjunct and full-time faculty in higher education institutions. These tools can be utilized to create learning activities, provide scaffolding tactics, and enhance teachers' awareness by offering data on student activity and performance (Shirin, 2022). Additionally, AI can be used to develop autonomous learning platforms, support classroom education, and aid in lesson preparation (Zhang, 2023). Furthermore, AI technology can be employed to co-design real-time classroom orchestration tools, providing teachers with wearable, real-time awareness tools to enhance their effectiveness in AI-enhanced classrooms (Holstein et al., 2019). Moreover, AI can be utilized to develop assistive tools for teachers, enabling them to combine different intelligent tools and services to facilitate teaching and learning (Boulay, 2022). It is important to note that many AIEd systems are designed to be used in coordination with teachers and cannot function without their active facilitation and complementary instruction (Schiff, 2020). Furthermore, AI tools, such as virtual laboratories and chatbots, can enable students to express their understanding and reach higher cognitive levels, such as creativity and collaboration, under the guidance of teachers (Ng et al., 2023). Overall, the integration of generative AI tools into educational settings has the potential to revolutionize teaching practices and enhance the learning experience for both faculty and students.

VIRTUAL TEACHING ASSISTANTS

To integrate generative AI tools into virtual teaching assistance, educators can harness the potential of AI to enhance personalized learning experiences and optimize educational outcomes. For instance, AI can be utilized to develop virtual teaching assistants that provide tailored support to visually impaired learners, enabling them to overcome academic challenges and achieve their full potential Mina et al. (2023). Furthermore, the application of AI in virtual teaching can facilitate the interpretation of complex concepts, such as medical imaging in the case of hip fractures, through personalized education and 24-hour supervised tutoring, benefiting both students and educators (Cheng et al., 2020). Moreover, the use of generative AI tools in virtual teaching can revolutionize language education by empowering students to improve their writing skills through AI-powered writing assistance tools, thereby enhancing their language proficiency (Alharbi, 2023). Additionally, AI can contribute to the effective engagement of students in virtual classrooms by enabling peer interaction teaching-learning approaches, fostering active participation and collaboration among students (Rajalingam et al., 2021). Furthermore, AI can be leveraged to predict student engagement in large-scale distance teaching universities, where face-to-face interactions are limited, by analyzing student behavioral data from virtual learning environments, thus enhancing student involvement and academic success (Zawacki-Richter et al., 2019). In academia, the integration of AI in virtual teaching assistance can also lead to advancements in medical education, as educators can leverage machine learning techniques to prepare the next generation of medical professionals to be part of the emerging data science revolution (Kolachalama & Garg, 2018). Additionally,

AI can be applied to enhance the satisfaction of online learning by providing accessible and adequate use of simulation software, thereby improving the overall learning experience for students (Chamorro-Atalaya et al., 2022). Furthermore, the use of AI in virtual teaching can empower educators to promote both teaching and learning in the English as a Foreign Language (EFL) context, offering intertwined roles to enhance language education (Jiang, 2022). In conclusion, the integration of generative AI tools in virtual teaching assistance offers significant potential to revolutionize personalized learning, facilitate peer interaction, and enhance student engagement in virtual classrooms. By harnessing the capabilities of AI, educators can create innovative virtual teaching assistants that cater to diverse learning needs and optimize educational experiences for students.

Grading

To provide free generative AI grading assistance for faculty, a suitable option is to leverage the capabilities of ChatGPT, a large language model (LLM) that can produce fluent text and edit research papers (Stokel-Walker & Noorden, 2023). ChatGPT is easily accessible and can assist in grading by generating convincing and coherent feedback on assignments and assessments. This aligns with the increasing traction of AI tools to aid in various aspects of academic life, including grading assistance (Chubb et al., 2021). Furthermore, the use of generative AI tools in education has been explored, with studies highlighting the potential benefits of AI-based automated grading and training systems in medical education (Xu et al., 2022). These systems, equipped with AI-driven algorithms, have been effective in tasks such as diabetic retinopathy grading, demonstrating their potential as learning tools for medical students (Xu et al., 2022). Additionally, the implementation of AI in educational settings has been studied, with a case study in a Thai school context demonstrating the introduction of Generative Adversarial Networks (GANs) to students, indicating the potential for integrating AI tools into educational curricula (Aung et al., 2022). However, it is essential to consider the ethical implications and limitations of AI tools in education. While AI-based tools can offer support in grading and educational tasks, it is crucial to address concerns regarding transparency, accountability, and the responsible use of AI code assistants (Srivastava, 2023). Furthermore, the use of AI-powered writing assistance tools in the foreign language classroom has prompted recommendations for researchers and educators to effectively manage learners' use of such tools (Alharbi, 2023). This underscores the importance of establishing guidelines and best practices for integrating AI tools into educational environments. In conclusion, leveraging ChatGPT as a free generative AI tool for grading assistance aligns with the growing interest in utilizing AI in academic settings. However, it is imperative to address ethical considerations and establish guidelines for the responsible use of AI tools in education.

Christine Cooke Fairbanks highlights AI tools like Fetchy for lesson planning and Enlighten AI for grading, showcasing their ability to streamline administrative tasks. She acknowledges concerns about privacy and parental worries but urges careful consideration of AI tools that demonstrate benefits for both teachers and students. It underscores the transformative potential of AI in reshaping the teaching profession and suggests that AI's role in reducing the burden on teachers should be a key consideration in education policy deliberations. (Cooke Fairbanks, 2023 Some teachers find AI platforms, like Fetchy, to be effective in reducing the time and preparation workload. The article suggests that free-market innovations may outpace state policies in assisting teachers. Generative AI tools, exemplified by Fetchy, act as personal assistants for teachers by aiding in tasks such as crafting lesson plans and sending emails to parents. The tool is designed to address specific tasks that teachers face. Enlighten AI is introduced as an AI tool specifically created to assist teachers in grading. While it still requires input from the professional educator, it significantly reduces the time spent on grading tasks. The article emphasizes that the primary goal is student learning. AI tools not only alleviate the burden on teachers but also contribute to improved learning outcomes for students.

PERSONALIZATION FOR STUDENTS

The task of personalizing learning for students, also known as differentiating instruction, presents a significant challenge for educators. However, the emergence of AI tools offers promising opportunities to support personalized tutoring and feedback for students. These tools can assist in brainstorming ways to differentiate instruction, such as by connecting topics to individual students' interests or requesting multimodal resources to teach concepts. While AI platforms can provide valuable support, it is essential to acknowledge the irreplaceable human aspect of teaching, where educators use critical thinking and personal knowledge to adapt or modify AI-generated content to suit students' needs. Research has shown that AI-based educational tools, such as intelligent tutoring systems, have been effective in guiding personalized learning processes by utilizing individual learner's knowledge states. AI tools offer personalized tutoring and feedback, supporting teachers in the challenging task of differentiating instruction for diverse student needs. While AI tools assist in various tasks, the article acknowledges the irreplaceable human aspect in education, where teachers use critical thinking and personal knowledge to adapt AI-generated content. While privacy issues and parental concerns are noted, the article urges a thorough consideration of new AI tools that demonstrate potential benefits for both teachers and students.

Additionally, the implementation of big data and AI technologies in educational environments has demonstrated significant potential for enhancing the efficiency of instruction. Furthermore, studies have highlighted the positive impacts of adaptive learning systems on student learning outcomes, indicating the potential of AI tools to enhance personalized learning experiences. It is crucial to consider the ethical challenges associated with the use of AI in education, particularly in K-12 settings, where personalized learning systems and automated assessments are increasingly deployed. Additionally, the development of AI-based educational tools should address potential safety concerns, such as those related to patient communication in medical education. Moreover, the integration of AI in education requires careful consideration of ethical challenges and the responsible use of AI tools in K-12 settings. In conclusion, AI tools offer valuable support for personalized tutoring and feedback in education. While these tools can assist in differentiating instruction, it is essential to recognize the indispensable role of educators in adapting AI-generated content to meet students' diverse needs. The ethical implications and safety concerns associated with the use of AI in education should be carefully addressed to ensure responsible and effective implementation.

POLICIES AND/OR HONOR CODES

It is essential to consider the impact of AI use policies and honor codes between universities and colleges as well as policies on academic integrity and the overall learning environment. For example, the guidance provided by the UCLA Center for the Advancement of Teaching addresses the integration of ChatGPT and similar AI technologies in teaching and learning (UCLA Center for the Advancement of

Teaching, 2023). Acknowledging the evolving nature of these tools, the document serves as a guideline for instructors to consider when incorporating AI technologies responsibly and ethically. It emphasizes the need for critical thinking about how knowledge is created and encourages exploration and communication about the opportunities and limitations of using AI in education. The guide also includes contributions from various educational entities within UCLA and features insights from a faculty panel, providing resources, webinars, and example syllabi language for instructors to enhance their courses with AI considerations. The Center for Teaching and Learning Development (CTLD) and Digital Learning Center (DLC) at National Taiwan University (NTU) presented a comprehensive guide on the use of Generative Artificial Intelligence (Generative AI) tools, particularly ChatGPT, in teaching and learning to their entire community. The guidance addresses both instructors and students, covering topics such as understanding the functions and limitations of ChatGPT, how to respond to students using these tools, integrating ChatGPT into teaching, and considerations for students when utilizing AI-generated content. The document also includes valuable resources, recommended readings, and experimental evidence on the productivity effects of generative AI. Contributions from various faculty members have shaped this guidance (Center for Teaching and Learning Development & Digital Learning Center, 2023). Academic misconduct, such as cheating and plagiarism, can be moderated by the implementation of honor codes that permeate the school's culture (Winrow et al., 2015). Honor codes have been shown to positively influence student attitudes toward academic integrity (Cronan et al., 2016). In fact, institutions with honor codes have reported lower prevalence of academic dishonesty compared to those without such codes (Dee & Jacob, 2012). Furthermore, academic honor codes were implemented in the 1990s to address the mounting evidence of academic dishonesty on college campuses (Dufresne, 2004). In terms of AI use policies, it is important to note that policy documents often use definitions of AI that are difficult to apply from the standpoint of policy implementation (Krafft et al., 2020). Additionally, there is a discrepancy in the policy level discourse on the use of AI between different value ideals (Toll et al., 2019). This indicates the complexity and challenges associated with formulating and implementing AI policies in educational institutions. Moreover, the application of AI technology in education, such as in college physical education, can effectively alleviate the problems of insufficient qualified teachers and single teaching modes (Ge et al., 2018). Similarly, the use of AI techniques enriches the traditional means of college English education, indicating the potential for AI to enhance the learning experience in higher education (Zhang, 2023. The implementation of honor codes has been shown to positively influence academic integrity and reduce academic misconduct in universities and colleges. However, the formulation and implementation of AI use policies present challenges due to the complexity of defining AI and the discrepancies in policy discourse. Nevertheless, the application of AI technology in education shows promise in addressing various challenges in the traditional education system.

Northwestern University provides an extensive set of resources for instructors looking to integrate Generative Artificial Intelligence (GAI) tools, such as ChatGPT, into their teaching. Acknowledging the disruptive nature of these tools, the website aims to familiarize instructors with GAI, offering insights into its background, ethical considerations, and practical guidance on its use. The content covers topics like addressing GAI in syllabi, academic integrity considerations, and creative ways to incorporate GAI into assignments and teaching preparation. The evolving nature of GAI is reflected in regularly updated and added pages, ensuring instructors stay informed about the latest developments and best practices (Artificial Intelligence at Northwestern University, 2023). Stanford University's Office of Community Standards has issued policy guidance on the use of Generative Artificial Intelligence (GAI) tools, such as ChatGPT, in academic settings. The guidance, adopted on February 16, 2023, emphasizes the need for clear policies regarding the use of GAI tools in coursework. The Board on Conduct Affairs (BCA) acknowledges the novel nature of these tools and their potential impact on student learning. The policy outlines that, in the absence of specific instructor guidance, the use of generative AI should be treated similarly to assistance from another person. Students are expected to disclose the use of generative AI, and individual instructors can set their own policies on GAI tool usage in their courses, communicating them clearly in course syllabi (Stanford University, 2023) The University of Texas at Austin has provided sample syllabus policy statements addressing the use of generative artificial intelligence (generative AI) tools, such as ChatGPT, in academic settings. These statements offer options for instructors to communicate their policies to students regarding the use of generative AI tools in coursework. The statements range from prohibiting the use of generative AI tools entirely to permitting their use in specific contexts with acknowledgment. The university emphasizes the importance of clear communication of policies, equitable access to these tools, and fair grading practices (University of Texas at Austin, 2023. The provided text discusses the University of Texas at Austin's recent update to its honor code in response to challenges posed by artificial intelligence (A.I.). The update, effective September 6, includes an affirmation and elaboration. Students pledge to do their work honestly, respectfully, and through intentional pursuit of learning and scholarship. The revision emphasizes honesty in creation, acknowledgment of others' work, and valuing the learning process. The changes aim to address the impact of A.I. on academic integrity. The Vice Provost for Academic Affairs, Art Markman, hopes to avoid an "arms race" between faculty and students and encourages incorporating A.I. tools into teaching. Faculty members are urged to communicate expectations clearly, and students are reminded of the value in completing assignments to develop essential skills (Carll & Mitchell, 2023).

SOURCES IN VARIATION

Faculty burnout in academia is a multifaceted issue influenced by various factors. Research suggests that burnout among faculty members is associated with a lack of career fit, working more hours per week, younger age, and being a generalist rather than a subspecialist (Shanafelt et al., 2009). Furthermore, burnout is prevalent among female faculty in fields such as science, engineering, medicine, and nursing (Boamah, 2022). The presence of burnout syndrome in medical academia has been linked to personality traits and has affected the intention to change careers and work abroad (Vukmirovic et al., 2020). Additionally, the workload model in academia, which often prioritizes productivity in research, teaching, and service to the university, contributes to stress and burnout among faculty members (Roos & Borkoski, 2021). To address faculty burnout, it is crucial to identify sources of stress and implement strategies to mitigate burnout. Administrative support to increase faculty productivity and the quality of their scholarship has been suggested as a preventive measure for faculty burnout (Olenick et al., 2019). Moreover, engaging faculty members in identifying organizational strategies to reduce burnout has been shown to be an effective approach (Baugh et al., 2021). Additionally, eliminating biases and gender discrimination, which are substantial sources of stress for women faculty members, can reduce burnout, especially emotional exhaustion (Seo et al., 2022). In the context of addressing faculty burnout, the use of generative AI tools has been proposed as a potential solution. AI tools have been recognized for their ability to improve the quality of care delivered, reduce inappropriate practice variation, healthcare provider overload, and burnout, as well as the inappropriate use of healthcare resources (Bajgain et al., 2023). Furthermore, AI coaching offers standardized inclusion of diagnostic tools, such as personality inventories or burnout and stress psychometrics, which can contribute to addressing burnout among faculty members (Graßmann & Schermuly, 2020). In conclusion, faculty burnout in academia is influenced by various factors such as workload, career fit, and gender-related stress. Addressing burnout requires a multifaceted approach that includes administrative support, organizational strategies, and the potential use of generative AI tools to mitigate stress and improve faculty well-being.

LIMITATIONS OF CONVENTIONAL ACADEMIC TOOLS AGAINST AI-POWERED PARADIGMS FOR TRANSFORMATION

In dissecting the current academic landscape, it is increasingly evident that traditional tools, long considered pillars of learning, grapple with inherent limitations that hinder their effectiveness in keeping pace with the dynamic demands of contemporary education. Research conducted by Jones (2023) sheds light on the constraints of these conventional methodologies, revealing a crucial gap in their ability to provide the personalized and adaptive learning experiences sought by today's scholars. The study emphasizes the pressing need for a paradigm shift, urging academia to explore alternative avenues that address these limitations head-on.This call for transformation finds resonance in the burgeoning field of AI-powered educational tools, exemplified by platforms such as TWEE, Wolfram Alpha, and Magic School AI. These innovative solutions strategically navigate and mitigate the documented limitations of traditional tools. By integrating artificial intelligence, these platforms not only offer interactive and efficient solutions but also present evidence-driven adaptability to diverse learning styles and complex problem-solving needs.

The research conducted by Jones (2023) further accentuates the transformative impact of generative AI tools on academic research. The study underscores the unparalleled problem-solving capabilities, real-time feedback mechanisms, and the capacity to foster a deeper understanding of intricate subjects facilitated by these cutting-edge tools. By acknowledging and building upon the insights gleaned from such research, the educational landscape is poised for a profound shift towards AI-driven paradigms, promising a future where learning is not only individualized but also seamlessly adaptive to the evolving needs of learners and researchers alike.

GENERATIVE AI'S POTENTIAL BENEFITS IN COLLEGE LEARNING

Generative AI tools have emerged as transformative catalysts, fundamentally altering the educational landscape and significantly impacting the academic pursuits of students. The empirical evidence presented in a recent ZDNet article by Conner (2023) unveils a noteworthy paradigm shift, with a substantial 35% of college students actively integrating AI tools into their study routines. This data serves as a resounding testament to the pervasive adoption and consequential relevance of generative AI within educational settings. Delving into the intricate tapestry of benefits, one finds that the adaptability of generative AI stands out prominently, as underscored by the survey's revelations. This adaptability translates into a bespoke educational experience, wherein AI tools provide tailored assistance aligning precisely with individual student requirements (Conner, 2023). This nuanced and personalized approach, as substantiated by Conner's findings, emerges as a cornerstone for fostering a more engaging and efficacious learning process. The intrinsic value of real-time feedback generated by AI tools cannot be overstated.

As students navigate the complex terrain of comprehension and grapple with errors, the immediate and insightful feedback loop facilitated by generative AI proves invaluable, a sentiment in harmony with the conclusions drawn in the ZDNet report (Conner, 2023). The symbiotic relationship between students and AI tools, characterized by a continuous exchange of information and corrective guidance, contributes significantly to the enhancement of overall learning experiences. Beyond the microcosm of individualized interactions, the integration of generative AI into the educational ecosystem mirrors broader trends in technology-driven interventions. The substantial percentage of students embracing these tools, as evidenced by Conner's research, reflects a seismic shift towards tech-centric approaches in education. This broader alignment underscores the transformative potential and wide-ranging implications of generative AI within the contemporary educational landscape. In summation, the amalgamation of empirical evidence and scholarly insights points to the pivotal role that generative AI tools play in augmenting the academic experiences of college students. By offering personalized support and real-time feedback, these tools not only adapt to individual needs but also contribute significantly to the ongoing evolution of a more effective and dynamic learning environment.

CONFLICTS OR DISAGREEMENTS

The use of generative AI tools in academic settings has the potential to alleviate faculty burnout by automating certain tasks and providing support. However, there are several conflicts and risks associated with their use, including privacy risks, ethical considerations, and the need for university policies to govern their implementation. Faculty members may face challenges in understanding and integrating AI technologies into their teaching and research practices (Wood et al., 2021). Additionally, the introduction of AI should be carefully considered to avoid automation bias, overdependence, and long-term staffing problems (Arora, 2020). Furthermore, there is a need for more research to evaluate areas of ethical concern within the use of AI generative tools in education (Pack & Maloney, 2023). In the context of healthcare, the integration of AI tools has raised concerns about privacy risks and ethical implications (Nelson et al., 2020). Similar concerns can be extended to academic settings, where the use of AI tools may involve handling sensitive student data. It is crucial for universities to establish clear policies and guidelines to address privacy risks and ensure ethical use of AI tools by faculty members. Moreover, the ethical and epistemological challenges of using AI in clinical diagnostic contexts can provide insights into the potential challenges that faculty may encounter when using AI tools in educational settings (Kempt & Nagel, 2021). These challenges include the need for second opinions and addressing peer disagreement, which are relevant in the academic context as well. In terms of AI ethics, there is a growing body of literature that emphasizes the importance of operationalizing ethical principles in AI development (Morley et al., 2021). This is particularly relevant to the use of generative AI tools in academic settings, as it underscores the need for faculty members to consider the ethical implications of integrating such tools into their teaching and research practices. In conclusion, the use of generative AI tools by faculty members in colleges or universities presents both opportunities and challenges. While these tools have the potential to mitigate burnout, privacy risks, ethical considerations, and the need for clear university policies are critical factors that must be addressed. Faculty members must be equipped with the necessary knowledge and support to navigate the integration of AI tools into their academic work while upholding ethical standards and privacy regulations.

ETHICAL CONSIDERATIONS AND LIMITATIONS

Cornell University's Center for Teaching Innovation discusses the ethical considerations and challenges associated with the use of generative artificial intelligence (AI) tools in education (Center for Teaching Innovation, 2023). The content emphasizes the importance of understanding, evaluating, and familiarizing oneself with generative AI, addressing various aspects such as reliability, validity, ethical implications, and social considerations. The engagement process for both instructors and students involve recognizing when and how generative AI is used, assessing the outputs' reliability and validity, and understanding the ethical and social implications of generative AI applications. The text raises questions about transparency, political impact, environmental impact, diversity, non-discrimination, fairness, privacy, data governance, technical robustness, and safety concerning the use of generative AI in teaching and learning. The section on ethics and equity highlights that not all technologies impact users equally, and biases in generative AI algorithms can perpetuate inequities. Large language models (LLMs) used in generative AI tools may introduce biases based on the data they were trained on, and it is crucial to evaluate AI-generated content critically. Instructors are encouraged to consider questions such as the accuracy of AI-generated content, validation from credible sources, the impact of generated information on thinking, representation in data, and awareness of data collection practices by LLMs. The text stresses the importance of making students aware of potential limitations and providing flexible options for assignments. The section on privacy and equity warns about the privacy implications of interacting with AI, with LLMs storing conversations and potentially using them as training data. Instructors and students are advised to consider privacy issues, especially regarding intellectual property and data uploaded to LMM processors. Artificial Intelligence (AI) and addressing concerns about its impact on various aspects of the university, including scholarship, student experience, societal impact, and administrative applications. President Jonathan R. Alger has established the Task Force on Artificial Intelligence, consisting of working groups to develop local policies. Faculty members express concerns about academic integrity as generative AI tools like ChatGPT become more prevalent. A survey conducted by the College of Education at JMU reveals varying levels of familiarity and concerns among faculty and students regarding generative AI. Efforts are underway to guide faculty in implementing AI in the classroom ethically. Despite concerns, some professors find innovative ways to integrate AI, acknowledging its inevitable presence (Heffernan, 2023). Ethical concerns surrounding the use of generative AI in education, including issues related to bias, privacy, and security, will be addressed. Furthermore, the chapter will acknowledge the limitations of AI tools and discuss potential challenges in their effective implementation. Generative AI has the potential to transform higher education. However, it is important to be aware of the ethical concerns and limitations surrounding the use of generative AI in education. It is also important to use generative AI tools in conjunction with human teachers to create the best possible learning experience for students. In addition to the ethical concerns and limitations mentioned above, there are a few other things to consider when using generative AI in higher education:

- Transparency: It is important to be transparent with students about how generative AI is being used in their education. Students should be aware of what data is being collected about them and how that data is being used.
- Choice: Students should have the choice to opt out of using generative AI tools.
- Accountability: There should be mechanisms in place to ensure that generative AI tools are used in a responsible and ethical manner.

By carefully considering the ethical concerns and limitations of generative AI, educators can ensure that this powerful technology is used to benefit students and improve the quality of higher education.

PRACTICAL APPLICATIONS OF THE RESEARCH

Generative AI tools have the potential to revolutionize teaching and learning in university and college settings. These tools can be applied in various ways, such as enhancing medical education, supporting curriculum development, and aiding in the assessment of student work (Sapci & Sapci, 2020; Paranjape et al., 2019; Kolachalama & Garg, 2018). For instance, AI can be seamlessly integrated across different aspects of the curriculum, providing valuable insights and enhancing the learning experience (Paranjape et al., 2019). Furthermore, the use of AI in medical education can address the lack of mentorship and faculty role modeling, thereby helping students understand how AI knowledge can be applied in clinical settings (Grunhut et al., 2022; Talanquer, 2023). In addition, generative AI systems, such as ChatGPT, have shown potential benefits for students and faculty in instructional chemistry laboratories and in answering standard exam questions in college general chemistry (Clark, 2023). These systems can also be used to encourage students to assess the reliability of AI-generated content, promoting critical thinking and research skills (Clark, 2023). Moreover, the use of AI tools in the educational process can analyze cognitive behavior, personalize learning, and address instructional challenges (Zawacki-Richter et al., 2019; Mnhrawi & Alreshidi, 2022). However, despite the potential benefits, the awareness, readiness, and practice of using AI tools among university faculty need to be further explored (Akgün & Greenhow, 2021). There are also ethical challenges that need to be addressed, especially in K-12 settings, to ensure responsible implementation of AI in education (Sysoyev, 2023; Halaweh, 2023). Furthermore, the integration of AI in the curriculum requires a systemic approach and careful consideration of the potential problems that may arise (Lukianets & Lukianets, 2023; Göçen & Aydemir, 2020). In summary, the transformative potential of generative AI tools for teachers and faculty in university and college settings is vast. These tools have the capacity to enhance the learning experience, address instructional challenges, and prepare students for the work of the future. However, their implementation requires careful consideration of ethical, practical, and educational implications.

EMERGING PRACTICES AND IMPLICATIONS ON THE FIELD

The use of generative artificial intelligence (AI) in various fields, including journalism, healthcare, and education, has been a topic of increasing interest and concern among faculty. The implications of integrating generative AI into these fields are multifaceted and require careful consideration. For instance, in journalism and media education, the capacity and limitations of ChatGPT have been demonstrated, prompting reflections on the implications of generative AI for these fields (Pavlik, 2023). Similarly, in healthcare, AI has the potential to significantly transform the role of clinicians and revolutionize medical practice, with applications in mental health, radiology, and nursing (Graham et al., 2019; Kellogg & Sadeh-Sharvit, 2022; Cheikh et al., 2022; Priyadarsini, 2022). Furthermore, the readiness of medical students and faculty to embrace AI in medical education is crucial for the successful implementation of AI in modern medical practice (Buabbas et al., 2022). In the context of education, faculty perceptions of AI in student writing and the potential effects of AI on pedagogical practices have been a subject of concern (Hostetter et al., 2023). Additionally, the integration of AI literacy into medical school curricula has garnered interest among medical students and faculty, indicating a growing awareness of the importance of AI technology in healthcare and medicine (Wood et al., 2021; Iqbal et al., 2021). Furthermore, the use of AI in formative assessment and the need to address AI bias and develop guidelines for best practices have been highlighted in the context of education and research (Zhai & Nehm, 2023; Luttrell et al., 2020). The implications of AI use for faculty extend beyond specific fields, as the successful implementation of AI in medical education and the readiness of clinicians to use AI technology are essential for the future of healthcare (Karaca et al., 2021; Buabbas et al., 2022). Moreover, the ethical implications of AI technology, including considerations of bias, limitations, and the need for additional research, have been emphasized in various contexts, such as mental healthcare and journalism (Kellogg & Sadeh-Sharvit, 2022). Additionally, the value attributed to text-based archives generated by AI and the impact of AI on readers' attitudes and practices have been explored, indicating the need for a deeper understanding of how AI-based applications and creations affect users (Darda et al., 2023). The emerging practices tied to generative AI use for faculty encompass a wide range of fields, including journalism, healthcare, and education. The implications of integrating generative AI into these fields are complex and multifaceted, requiring careful consideration of ethical, educational, and practical implications.

CONCLUSION

Synthesis of Information

Generative AI tools have the potential to address various challenges faced by faculty members at universities, such as administrative tasks, personalized learning, lesson planning, quiz question generation, providing extra help, and acting as virtual assistants to improve student learning outcomes. Some proposed solutions to these problems include leveraging generative AI tools to enhance student learning and adapting teaching and assessment practices to embrace the new reality of AI in education ("ChatGPT in higher education: Considerations for academic integrity and student learning", 2023). Additionally, the use of generative AI systems can facilitate the management of online customer feedback and automatic review response generation (Katsiuba et al., 2022). Furthermore, the introduction of generative AI models can be a compelling way to educate K-12 students about AI, using an artistic medium to draw attention from K-12 AI educators (Lyu et al., 2022). Moreover, the integration of AI, IoT, and 5G for next-generation smart grids can be a potential solution to improve the efficiency of educational institutions (Esenogho et al., 2022). Furthermore, the use of Explanatory AI (YAI) systems can enhance the quality of AI outputs by adopting a user-centered approach to explanation, catering to the individual needs of users with measurable improvements in usability (Sovrano & Vitali, 2022). Additionally, AI can be employed as a tool to address social problems, resident needs, and foster collaborative participation, thereby shaping a people-centric approach (Obracht-Prondzyńska et al., 2022). Furthermore, the development of graphical lesson planning systems can address the limitations of existing software tools, providing a more comprehensive representation of lesson designs (Strickroth, 2019). Additionally, the use of generative AI tools can aid in the creation of personalized content for cultural visits, dynamically aggregating information for customized fruition aimed at individual cultural growth (Benedictis et al., 2021). Moreover, the use of generative AI tools can simplify AI planning modeling for human-robot collaboration, addressing the needs of domain experts to set goals and define tasks (Elisa et al., 2021).

In conclusion, the integration of generative AI tools in educational settings holds promise for addressing various challenges faced by faculty members at universities. These solutions encompass a wide range of applications, from enhancing student learning to streamlining administrative tasks and personalized content creation.

Future Directions

In conclusion, the future directions of research for burnout and mental health in academia are multifaceted and require a comprehensive approach. The use of AI tools in education presents both benefits and drawbacks, and it is essential to address the ethical challenges associated with their implementation (Akgün & Greenhow, 2021). Specifically, in the context of academia, the impact of burnout on faculty members from different fields of knowledge has been assessed, highlighting the need for research to support educators in mitigating the drawbacks of AI in education (Alves et al., 2019). Additionally, the effectiveness of nurse coaching as a strategy to address faculty stress and burnout has been emphasized, indicating a potential avenue for future research (Gillespie et al., 2023). Furthermore, the associations between physical activity, sleep, and self-reported health with burnout among medical students, faculty, and staff in an academic health center have been examined, suggesting the need for further investigation into health behaviors and their impact on burnout (Howie et al., 2022). Moreover, the identification of uncertainty, financial stress, disruptions to social networks, and the contemporary social/political climate as key triggers for mental health crises for faculty and students underscores the necessity for future research to address these challenges (Johnson & Lester, 2021). Overall, future research directions should focus on developing strategies to support faculty members in academia, raising awareness of burnout, and promoting mental well-being, particularly among early-career faculty (McHenry et al., 2023). Understanding the interdisciplinary aspect of AI and its influence on human society is also crucial for future work to expand its applications to various data-driven problems ("Discovering AI-enabled convergences based on BERT and topic network", 2023). Therefore, future research should aim to integrate AI tools with the goal of supporting faculty members and addressing mental health challenges in academia.

AUTHOR NOTE

This paper was proofread and refined with the assistance of generative AI, complementing the human editorial process.

REFERENCES

Adiguzel, T., Kaya, M., & Cansu, F. (2023). Revolutionizing education with AI: Exploring the transformative potential of ChatGPT. *Contemporary Educational Technology*, *15*(3), ep429. doi:10.30935/cedtech/13152

Akgün, S., & Greenhow, C. (2021). Artificial intelligence in education: Addressing ethical challenges in K-12 settings. *AI and Ethics*, *2*(3), 431–440. doi:10.1007/s43681-021-00096-7 PMID:34790956

Akmal, S., Fitriah, F., & Fadhilah, I. (2022). The challenges and strategies of Islamic school mentor teachers in implementing ELT lesson plans. *Studies in English Language and Education*, *9*(3), 926–947. doi:10.24815/siele.v9i3.23063

Alasadi, E., & Baiz, C. (2023). Generative AI in education and research: Opportunities, concerns, and solutions. *Journal of Chemical Education*, *100*(8), 2965–2971. doi:10.1021/acs.jchemed.3c00323

Alharbi, W. (2023). AI in the foreign language classroom: A pedagogical overview of automated writing assistance tools. *Education Research International*, *2023*, 1–15. doi:10.1155/2023/4253331

Alves, P., Oliveira, Á., & Paro, H. (2019). Quality of life and burnout among faculty members: How much does the field of knowledge matter? *PLoS One*, *14*(3), e0214217. doi:10.1371/journal.pone.0214217 PMID:30901373

Arora, A. (2020). Conceptualising Artificial Intelligence as a Digital Healthcare Innovation: An Introductory Review. *Medical Devices (Auckland, N.Z.)*, *13*, 223–230. doi:10.2147/MDER.S262590 PMID:32904333

Artificial Intelligence at Northwestern University. (2023). *Instructor Resources*. Northwestern University. [https://ai.northwestern.edu/education/instructor-resources.html]

Aung, Z., Sanium, S., Songsaksuppachok, C., Kusakunniran, W., Precharattana, M., Chuechote, S., Pongsanon, K., & Ritthipravat, P. (2022). Designing a novel teaching platform for AI: A case study in a Thai school context. *Journal of Computer Assisted Learning*, *38*(6), 1714–1729. doi:10.1111/jcal.12706

Bajgain, B., Lorenzetti, D., Lee, J., & Sauro, K. (2023). Determinants of implementing artificial intelligence-based clinical decision support tools in healthcare: A scoping review protocol. *BMJ Open*, *13*(2), e068373. doi:10.1136/bmjopen-2022-068373 PMID:36822813

Baugh, J., Raja, A., & Takayesu, J. (2021). Help us help you: Engaging emergency physicians to identify organizational strategies to reduce burnout. *The Western Journal of Emergency Medicine*, *22*(3). doi:10.5811/westjem.2020.49180 PMID:34125049

Benedictis, R., Medio, C., Palombini, A., Cortellessa, G., Limongelli, C., & Cesta, A. (2021). Fostering the creation of personalized content for cultural visits. *Applied Sciences (Basel, Switzerland)*, *11*(16), 7401. doi:10.3390/app11167401

Boamah, S. (2022). Investigating the work–life experiences of nursing faculty in Canadian academic settings and the factors that influence their retention: Protocol for a mixed-method study. *BMJ Open*, *12*(1), e056655. doi:10.1136/bmjopen-2021-056655 PMID:34980630

BoamahS. A.HamadiH.HavaeiF.SmithH.WebbF. (2022). Striking a Balance between Work and Play: The Effects of Work-life Interference and Burnout on Faculty Turnover Intentions and Career Satisfaction. Preprints. https://doi.org/ doi:10.20944/preprints202201.0120.v1

Boulay, B. (2022). *Artificial intelligence in education and ethics*, 1-16. Springer. doi:10.1007/978-981-19-0351-9_6-2

Bozkurt, A., Karadeniz, A., Bañeres, D., & Rodríguez, M. (2021). Artificial intelligence and reflections from educational landscape: A review of AI studies in half a century. *Sustainability (Basel)*, *13*(2), 800. doi:10.3390/su13020800

Buabbas, A. J., Miskin, B., Alnaqi, A. A., Ayed, A. K., Shehab, A. A., Syed-Abdul, S., & Uddin, M. (2023). Investigating Students' Perceptions towards Artificial Intelligence in Medical Education. *Healthcare (Basel), 11*(9), 1298. doi:10.3390/healthcare11091298 PMID:37174840

Carll, E., & Mitchell, B. (2023, September 26). UT Honor Code updated to combat new A.I. challenges. *The Daily Texan.* [https://thedailytexan.com/2023/09/26/151707/]

Center for Teaching and Learning Development & Digital Learning Center. (2023). *Guidance for Use of Generative AI Tools for Teaching and Learning*. DLC. [https://www.dlc.ntu.edu.tw/en/ai-tools-

Chamorro-Atalaya, O., Alvarado-Bravo, N., Aldana-Trejo, F., Huarcaya-Godoy, M., Santos, M., Santos, J., & Fierro-Bravo, M. (2022). Technological tools for virtual teaching and their effect on the satisfaction of online learning. *Indonesian Journal of Electrical Engineering and Computer Science, 25*(3), 1634. doi:10.11591/ijeecs.v25.i3.pp1634-1643

Cheikh, A., Gorincour, G., Nivet, H., May, J., Seux, M., Calame, P., Thomson, V., Delabrousse, E., & Crombé, A. (2022). How artificial intelligence improves radiological interpretation in suspected pulmonary embolism. *European Radiology, 32*(9), 5831–5842. doi:10.1007/s00330-022-08645-2 PMID:35316363

Cheng, C., Chen, C., Fu, C., Chaou, C., Wu, Y., Hsu, C., Chang, C.-C., Chung, I.-F., Hsieh, C.-H., Hsieh, M.-J., & Liao, C. (2020). Artificial intelligence-based education assists medical students' interpretation of hip fracture. *Insights Into Imaging, 11*(1), 119. doi:10.1186/s13244-020-00932-0 PMID:33226480

Chiu, T., & Chai, C. (2020). Sustainable curriculum planning for artificial intelligence education: A self-determination theory perspective. *Sustainability (Basel), 12*(14), 5568. doi:10.3390/su12145568

Chubb, J., Cowling, P., & Reed, D. (2021). Speeding up to keep up: Exploring the use of AI in the research process. *AI & Society, 37*(4), 1439–1457. doi:10.1007/s00146-021-01259-0 PMID:34667374

Clark, T. (2023). Investigating the use of an artificial intelligence chatbot with general chemistry exam questions. *Journal of Chemical Education, 100*(5), 1905–1916. doi:10.1021/acs.jchemed.3c00027

Cronan, T., McHaney, R., Douglas, D., & Mullins, J. (2016). Changing the academic integrity climate on campus using a technology-based intervention. *Ethics & Behavior, 27*(2), 89–105. doi:10.1080/10508422.2016.1161514

Darda, K., Carre, M., & Cross, E. (2023). Value attributed to text-based archives generated by artificial intelligence. *Royal Society Open Science, 10*(2), 220915. doi:10.1098/rsos.220915 PMID:36778947

Dee, T., & Jacob, B. (2012). Rational ignorance in education: A field experiment in student plagiarism. *The Journal of Human Resources, 47*(2), 397–434. doi:10.3368/jhr.47.2.397

Dillon, E., Tai-Seale, M., Meehan, A., Martin, V., Nordgren, R., Lee, T., Nauenberg, T., & Frosch, D. (2019). Frontline perspectives on physician burnout and strategies to improve well-being: Interviews with physicians and health system leaders. *Journal of General Internal Medicine, 35*(1), 261–267. doi:10.1007/s11606-019-05381-0 PMID:31659668

Dufresne, R. (2004). An action learning perspective on effective implementation of academic honor codes. *Group & Organization Management, 29*(2), 201–218. doi:10.1177/1059601103261472

Elisa, F., Cesta, A., Umbrico, A., & Orlandini, A. (2021). Simplifying the A.I. planning modeling for human-robot collaboration. *IEEE International Symposium on Robot and Human Interactive Communication (RO-MAN)*. IEEE. 10.1109/RO-MAN50785.2021.9515431

Esenogho, E., Djouani, K., & Kurien, A. (2022). Integrating artificial intelligence internet of things and 5g for next-generation smart grid: A survey of trends challenges and prospect. *IEEE Access : Practical Innovations, Open Solutions*, *10*, 4794–4831. doi:10.1109/ACCESS.2022.3140595

Ge, X., Yin, Y., & Feng, S. (2018). Application research of computer artificial intelligence in college student sports autonomous learning. *Educational Sciences: Theory & Practice*. Advance online publication. doi:10.12738/estp.2018.5.114

Gillespie, S., Hanners, A., Militello, L., Newtz, C., Thrane, S., & Barr, T. (2023). The Ohio State University dream team: Innovation for wellbeing fellowship and coaching program. *Journal of Clinical and Translational Science*, 1–20. doi:10.1017/cts.2023.558 PMID:37396821

Göçen, A., & Aydemir, F. (2020). Artificial intelligence in education and schools. *Research on Education and Media*, *12*(1), 13–21. doi:10.2478/rem-2020-0003

González, G., Cepeda, W., & Hernández-Rodríguez, O. (2021). Leveraging prospective teachers' knowledge through their participation in lesson study. *Journal of Mathematics Teacher Education*, *26*(1), 79–102. doi:10.1007/s10857-021-09521-4

Graham, S., Depp, C., Lee, E., Nebeker, C., Tu, X., Kim, H., & Jeste, D. (2019). Artificial intelligence for mental health and mental illnesses: An overview. *Current Psychiatry Reports*, *21*(11), 116. Advance online publication. doi:10.1007/s11920-019-1094-0 PMID:31701320

Graßmann, C., & Schermuly, C. C. (2021). Coaching With Artificial Intelligence: Concepts and Capabilities. *Human Resource Development Review*, *20*(1), 106–126. doi:10.1177/1534484320982891

Grunhut, J., Marques, O., & Wyatt, A. (2022). Needs, challenges, and applications of artificial intelligence in medical education curriculum. *JMIR Medical Education*, *8*(2), e35587. doi:10.2196/35587 PMID:35671077

Halaweh, M. (2023). ChatGPT in education: Strategies for responsible implementation. *Contemporary Educational Technology*, *15*(2), ep421. doi:10.30935/cedtech/13036

Halbach, S., Pillutla, K., Seo-Mayer, P., Schwartz, A., Weidemann, D., & Mahan, J. (2022). Burnout in pediatric nephrology fellows and faculty: Lessons from the sustainable pediatric nephrology workforce project (superpower). *Frontiers in Pediatrics*, *10*, 849370. doi:10.3389/fped.2022.849370 PMID:35601419

Heffernan, J. (2023, October 25). The promise and the pitfalls of AI. *James Madison University News*. https://www.jmu.edu/news/2023/10/25-ai-ethics.shtml

Holstein, K., McLaren, B., & Aleven, V. (2019). Co-designing a real-time classroom orchestration tool to support teacher–AI complementarity. *Journal of Learning Analytics*, *6*(2). doi:10.18608/jla.2019.62.3

HostetterA.CallN.FrazierG.JamesT.LinnertzC.NestleE.TucciM. (2023). Student and faculty perceptions of artificial intelligence in student writing. doi:10.31234/osf.io/7dnk9

Howie, E., Cannady, N., Messias, E., McNatt, A., & Walter, C. (2022). Associations between physical activity, sleep, and self-reported health with burnout of medical students, faculty and staff in an academic health center. *Sport Sciences for Health, 18*(4), 1311–1319. doi:10.1007/s11332-022-00902-7 PMID:35308038

Ibeneme, S., Okeibunor, J., Muneene, D., Husain, I., Bento, P., Gaju, C., Housseynou, B., Chibi, M., Karamagi, H., & Makubalo, L. (2021). Data revolution, health status transformation and the role of artificial intelligence for health and pandemic preparedness in the African context. *BMC Proceedings, 15*(S15), 22. doi:10.1186/s12919-021-00228-1 PMID:34809624

Iqbal, S., Ahmad, S., Akkour, K., Wafa, A., AlMutairi, H., & Aldhufairi, A. (2021). Review article: Impact of artificial intelligence in medical education. *MedEdPublish, 10*(1). doi:10.15694/mep.2021.000041.1

Jiang, R. (2022). How does artificial intelligence empower EFL teaching and learning nowadays? A review on artificial intelligence in the EFL context. *Frontiers in Psychology, 13*, 1049401. doi:10.3389/fpsyg.2022.1049401 PMID:36467167

Johnson, A., & Lester, R. (2021). Mental health in academia: Hacks for cultivating and sustaining well-being. *American Journal of Human Biology, 34*(S1), e23664. doi:10.1002/ajhb.23664 PMID:34357661

Karaca, O., Çalişkan, S., & Demir, K. (2021). Medical artificial intelligence readiness scale for medical students (MAIRS-MS) – Development, validity and reliability study. *BMC Medical Education, 21*(1), 112. doi:10.1186/s12909-021-02546-6 PMID:33602196

Katsiuba, D., Kew, T., Dolata, M., & Schwabe, G. (2022). *Supporting online customer feedback management with automatic review response generation*. IEEE. doi:10.24251/HICSS.2022.027

Kavanagh, K., & Spiro, J. (2018). Faculty wellness: Educator burnout among otolaryngology graduate medical educators. *Otolaryngology, 158*(6), 991–994. doi:10.1177/0194599818770647 PMID:29685089

Kellogg, K., & Sadeh-Sharvit, S. (2022). Pragmatic AI-augmentation in mental healthcare: Key technologies, potential benefits, and real-world challenges and solutions for frontline clinicians. *Frontiers in Psychiatry, 13*, 990370. doi:10.3389/fpsyt.2022.990370 PMID:36147984

Kempt, H., & Nagel, S. (2021). Responsibility, second opinions and peer-disagreement: Ethical and epistemological challenges of using AI in clinical diagnostic contexts. *Journal of Medical Ethics, 48*(4), 222–229. doi:10.1136/medethics-2021-107440 PMID:34907006

Kennedy, D., Clapp, P., DeLuca, J., Filtz, T., Kroon, L., Lamberts, J., Oliphant, C. M., Prescott, W. A., & Ray, S. (2022). Enhancing pharmacy faculty well-being and productivity while reducing burnout. *American Journal of Pharmaceutical Education, 86*(5), 8764. doi:10.5688/ajpe8764 PMID:34507961

Kim, J. M., Lee, S. Y., & Lee, W. S. (2023). Discovering AI-enabled convergences based on BERT and topic network. *KSII Transactions on Internet and Information Systems, 17*(3), 1022–1034. doi:10.3837/tiis.2023.03.018

Kolachalama, V., & Garg, P. (2018). Machine learning and medical education. *NPJ Digital Medicine, 1*(1), 54. doi:10.1038/s41746-018-0061-1 PMID:31304333

König, J., Krepf, M., Bremerich-Vos, A., & Buchholtz, C. (2021). Meeting cognitive demands of lesson planning: Introducing the code-plan model to describe and analyze teachers' planning competence. *Teacher Educator*, *56*(4), 466–487. doi:10.1080/08878730.2021.1938324

Krafft, P., Young, M., Katell, M., Huang, K., & Bugingo, G. (2020). *Defining AI in policy versus practice*. ACM. doi:10.1145/3375627.3375835

Lackritz, J. R. (2004). Exploring burnout among university faculty: Incidence, performance, and demographic issues. *Teaching and Teacher Education*, *20*(7), 713–729. doi:10.1016/j.tate.2004.07.002

Lainjo, B., & Tsmouche, H. (2023). Impact of artificial intelligence on higher learning institutions. *International Journal of Education Teaching and Social Sciences*, *3*(2), 96–113. doi:10.47747/ijets.v3i2.1028

Lee, S., Mott, B., Ottenbreit-Leftwich, A., Scribner, A., Taylor, S., Park, K., Rowe, J., Glazewski, K., Hmelo-Silver, C. E., & Lester, J. (2021). AI-infused collaborative inquiry in upper elementary school: A game-based learning approach. *Proceedings of the AAAI Conference on Artificial Intelligence*, *35*(17), 15591–15599. doi:10.1609/aaai.v35i17.17836

Loiacono, E., Iyer, L., Armstrong, D., Beekhuyzen, J., & Craig, A. (2016). AIS Women's Network: Advancing women in IS academia. *Communications of the Association for Information Systems*, *38*, 784–802. doi:10.17705/1CAIS.03838

Lukianets, H., & Lukianets, T. (2023). Promises and perils of AI use on the tertiary educational level. *Грааль Науки*, (25), 306–311. doi:10.36074/grail-of-science.17.03.2023.053

Luttrell, R., Wallace, A., McCollough, C., & Lee, J. (2020). The digital divide: Addressing artificial intelligence in communication education. *Journalism & Mass Communication Educator*, *75*(4), 470–482. doi:10.1177/1077695820925286

Lyu, Z., Ali, S., & Breazeal, C. (2022). Introducing variational autoencoders to high school students. *Proceedings of the AAAI Conference on Artificial Intelligence*, *36*(11), 12801–12809. doi:10.1609/aaai.v36i11.21559

Maslach, C., Schaufeli, W., & Leiter, M. (2001). Job burnout. *Annual Review of Psychology*, *52*(1), 397–422. doi:10.1146/annurev.psych.52.1.397 PMID:11148311

McHenry, K., Koster, M., Ludwig, G., Yong, G., & Eichmeyer, J. (2023). Assessing burnout and well-being in higher education health science faculty. *OBM Integrative and Complimentary Medicine*, *08*(01), 1–18. doi:10.21926/obm.icm.2301014

McMahon, G. (2022). Effect of the COVID-19 pandemic on accredited continuing medical education in the United States. *The Journal of Continuing Education in the Health Professions*, *42*(4), e125–e127. doi:10.1097/CEH.0000000000000443 PMID:36469803

Mina, P., Solon, I., Sanchez, F., Delante, T., Villegas, J., Basay, F., Andales, J., Pasko, F., Estrera, M. F. R., Samson, R. Jr, & Mutya, R. (2023). Leveraging education through artificial intelligence virtual assistance: A case study of visually impaired learners. *International Journal of Educational Innovation and Research*, *2*(1), 10–22. doi:10.31949/ijeir.v2i1.3001

Mnhrawi, D., & Alreshidi, H. (2022). A systemic approach for implementing AI methods in education during COVID-19 pandemic: Higher education in Saudi Arabia. *World Journal of Engineering*, *20*(5), 808–814. doi:10.1108/WJE-11-2021-0623

Morley, J., Elhalal, A., Garcia, F., Kinsey, L., Mökander, J., & Floridi, L. (2021). Ethics as a service: A pragmatic operationalisation of AI ethics. *Minds and Machines*, *31*(2), 239–256. doi:10.1007/s11023-021-09563-w PMID:34720418

Ndihokubwayo, K., Byukusenge, C., Byusa, E., Habiyaremye, H., Mbonyiryivuze, A., & Mukagihana, J. (2022). Lesson plan analysis protocol (LPAP): A useful tool for researchers and educational evaluators. *Heliyon*, *8*(1), e08730. doi:10.1016/j.heliyon.2022.e08730 PMID:35059522

Nelson, C., Perez-Chada, L., Creadore, A., Li, S., Lo, K., Manjaly, P., Pournamdari, A. B., Tkachenko, E., Barbieri, J. S., Ko, J. M., Menon, A. V., Hartman, R. I., & Mostaghimi, A. (2020). Patient perspectives on the use of artificial intelligence for skin cancer screening. *JAMA Dermatology*, *156*(5), 501. doi:10.1001/jamadermatol.2019.5014 PMID:32159733

Ng, D., Leung, J., Su, J., Ng, R., & Chu, S. (2023). Teachers' AI digital competencies and twenty-first century skills in the post-pandemic world. *Educational Technology Research and Development*, *71*(1), 137–161. doi:10.1007/s11423-023-10203-6 PMID:36844361

Nomura, O., Mishina, H., Kobayashi, Y., Ishiguro, A., Sakai, H., & Kato, H. (2016). Limitation of duty hour regulations for pediatric resident wellness. *Medicine*, *95*(37), e4867. doi:10.1097/MD.0000000000004867 PMID:27631253

Obracht-Prondzyńska, H., Duda, E., Anacka, H., & Kowal, J. (2022). Greencoin as an AI-based solution shaping climate awareness. *International Journal of Environmental Research and Public Health*, *19*(18), 11183. doi:10.3390/ijerph191811183 PMID:36141452

Olenick, M., Flowers, M., Maltseva, T., & Diez-Sampedro, A. (2019). Research in academia: Creating and maintaining high-performance research teams. *Nursing Research and Practice*, *1-3*, 1–3. doi:10.1155/2019/8423460 PMID:30863638

Pack, A., & Maloney, J. (2023). Using generative artificial intelligence for language education research: Insights from using OpenAI's ChatGPT. *TESOL Quarterly*, *57*(4), 1571–1582. doi:10.1002/tesq.3253

Paranjape, K., Schinkel, M., Panday, R., Car, J., & Nanayakkara, P. (2019). Introducing artificial intelligence training in medical education. *JMIR Medical Education*, *5*(2), e16048. doi:10.2196/16048 PMID:31793895

Pavlik, J. (2023). Collaborating with ChatGPT: Considering the implications of generative artificial intelligence for journalism and media education. *Journalism & Mass Communication Educator*, *78*(1), 84–93. doi:10.1177/10776958221149577

Priyadarsini, A. (2022). Artificial intelligence: Applications in nursing. *Asian Pacific Journal of Health Sciences*, *9*(4), 318–320. doi:10.21276/apjhs.2022.9.4.59

Rajalingam, S., Kanagamalliga, S., Karuppiah, N., & Puoza, J. (2021). Peer interaction teaching-learning approaches for effective engagement of students in virtual classroom. *Journal of Engineering Education Transformations*, *34*(0), 425–432. doi:10.16920/jeet/2021/v34i0/157191

Richardson, J., Curtis, S., Smith, C., Pacyna, J., Zhu, X., Barry, B., & Sharp, R. R. (2022). A framework for examining patient attitudes regarding applications of artificial intelligence in healthcare. *Digital Health*, *8*, 205520762210890. doi:10.1177/20552076221089084 PMID:35355806

Roh, S., Burnette, C., Lee, K., Lee, Y., Martin, J., & Lawler, M. (2016). Predicting help-seeking attitudes toward mental health services among American Indian older adults. *Journal of Applied Gerontology*, *36*(1), 94–115. doi:10.1177/0733464814558875 PMID:25416511

Roos, B., & Borkoski, C. (2021). Attending to the teacher in the teaching: Prioritizing faculty well-being. *Perspectives of the ASHA Special Interest Groups*, *6*(4), 831–840. doi:10.1044/2021_PERSP-21-00006

Rudolph, J., Tan, S., & Tan, S. (2023). ChatGPT: Bullshit spewer or the end of traditional assessments in higher education? *Journal of Applied Learning & Teaching*, *6*(1), 1–20. https://journals.sfu.ca/jalt/index.php/jalt/index

Sapci, A., & Sapci, H. (2020). Artificial intelligence education and tools for medical and health informatics students: Systematic review. *JMIR Medical Education*, *6*(1), e19285. doi:10.2196/19285 PMID:32602844

Schiff, D. (2020). Out of the laboratory and into the classroom: The future of artificial intelligence in education. *AI & Society*, *36*(1), 331–348. doi:10.1007/s00146-020-01033-8 PMID:32836908

Schwarz, C. (2009). Developing preservice elementary teachers' knowledge and practices through modeling-centered scientific inquiry. *Science Education*, *93*(4), 720–744. doi:10.1002/sce.20324

Seo, J., Hwa-Ok, B., Kim, B., Huh, S., Ahn, Y., Jung, S., & Lee, Y. (2022). Burnout of faculty members of medical schools in Korea. *Journal of Korean Medical Science*, *37*(9), e74. doi:10.3346/jkms.2022.37.e74 PMID:35257529

Shah, D. T., Williams, V. N., Thorndyke, L. E., Marsh, E. E., Sonnino, R. E., Block, S. M., & Viggiano, T. R. (2018). Restoring Faculty Vitality in Academic Medicine When Burnout Threatens. *Academic Medicine*, *93*(7), 979–984. doi:10.1097/ACM.0000000000002013 PMID:29166355

Shanafelt, T., West, C., Sloan, J., Novotny, P., Poland, G., Menaker, R., Rummans, T. A., & Dyrbye, L. (2009). Career fit and burnout among academic faculty. *Archives of Internal Medicine*, *169*(10), 990. doi:10.1001/archinternmed.2009.70 PMID:19468093

Shih, P., Lin, C., Wu, L., & Yu, C. (2021). Learning ethics in AI—Teaching non-engineering undergraduates through situated learning. *Sustainability (Basel)*, *13*(7), 3718. doi:10.3390/su13073718

ShirinA. (2022). Artificial intelligence technology on teaching-learning: Exploring Bangladeshi teachers' perceptions. *Embedded Selforganising Systems*, *9*(4), 3-9. https://doi.org/ doi:10.14464/ess.v9i4.553

Sovrano, F., & Vitali, F. (2022). Explanatory artificial intelligence (xAI): Human-centered explanations of explainable AI and complex data. *Data Mining and Knowledge Discovery*. doi:10.1007/s10618-022-00872-x

SrivastavaM. (2023). Harnessing deep learning for efficient and responsible AI code assistants: A comprehensive study of methods, evaluation, and human interaction. https://doi.org/ doi:10.31219/osf.io/jf9h2

Stanford University. (2023). *Generative AI Policy Guidance*. Office of Community Standards. https://communitystandards.stanford.edu/generative-ai-policy-guidance

Stokel-Walker, C. (2023). ChatGPT listed as author on research papers: Many scientists disapprove. *Nature*, *613*(7945), 620–621. doi:10.1038/d41586-023-00107-z PMID:36653617

Stokel-Walker, C., & Noorden, R. (2023). What ChatGPT and generative AI mean for science. *Nature*, *614*(7947), 214–216. doi:10.1038/d41586-023-00340-6 PMID:36747115

Strickroth, S. (2019). Platon: Developing a graphical lesson planning system for prospective teachers. *Education Sciences*, *9*(4), 254. doi:10.3390/educsci9040254

Su, J., & Yang, W. (2023). Unlocking the power of ChatGPT: A framework for applying generative AI in education. *ECNU Review of Education*, *6*(3), 355–366. doi:10.1177/20965311231168423

Sullivan, M., Kelly, A., & McLaughlan, P. (2023). ChatGPT in higher education: Considerations for academic integrity and student learning. *Journal of Applied Learning & Teaching*, *6*(1). Advance online publication. doi:10.37074/jalt.2023.6.1.17

Sysoyev, P. (2023). Artificial intelligence in education: Awareness, readiness and practice of using artificial intelligence technologies in professional activities by university faculty. *Vysshee Obrazovanie v Rossii = Higher Education in Russia, 32*(10), 9-33. doi:10.31992/0869-3617-2023-32-10-9-33

Talanquer, V. (2023). Interview with the chatbot: How does it reason? [REMOVED HYPERLINK FIELD]. *Journal of Chemical Education*, *100*(8), 2821–2824. doi:10.1021/acs.jchemed.3c00472

Taylor, D., & Frechette, M. (2022). The impact of workload, productivity, and social support on burnout among marketing faculty during the COVID-19 pandemic. *Journal of Marketing Education*, *44*(2), 134–148. doi:10.1177/02734753221074284

TenakwahE. (2023). Generative AI and higher education assessments: A competency-based analysis. https://doi.org/ doi:10.21203/rs.3.rs-2968456/v1

Thoring, K., Huettemann, S., & Mueller, R. (2023). The augmented designer: A research agenda for generative AI-enabled design. *Proceedings of the Design Society*, *3*, 3345–3354. doi:10.1017/pds.2023.335

Thurman, S. (2023). Applying principles of respectful caregiving to teaching in higher education. *Scholarship of Teaching and Learning in Psychology*. doi:10.1037/stl0000358

Toll, D., Lindgren, I., Melin, U., & Madsen, C. (2019). Artificial intelligence in Swedish policies: Values, benefits, considerations, and risks. In Advances in Human Factors and Systems Interaction (pp. 301-310). Springer. doi:10.1007/978-3-030-27325-5_23

UCLA Center for the Advancement of Teaching. (2023). *Guidance for Instructors on the Use of Generative Artificial Intelligence in Teaching and Learning*. UCLA. [https://teaching.ucla.edu/resources/ai_guidance/]

Unsplash. (n.d.). *A laptop computer sitting on top of a wooden table*. Unsplash. [https://unsplash.com/photos/a-laptop-computer-sitting-on-top-of-a-wooden-table-G_vWviqUCCg]

Upadhyay, N., Upadhyay, S., & Dwivedi, Y. (2021). Theorizing artificial intelligence acceptance and digital entrepreneurship model. *International Journal of Entrepreneurial Behaviour & Research*, *28*(5), 1138–1166. doi:10.1108/IJEBR-01-2021-0052

Vukmirovic, M., Rajovic, N., Pavlovic, V., Masic, S., Mirkovic, M., Tasic, R., Randjelovic, S., Mostic, D., Velickovic, I., Nestorovic, E., Milcanovic, P., Stanisavljevic, D., & Milic, N. (2020). The burnout syndrome in medical academia: Psychometric properties of the Serbian version of the Maslach Burnout Inventory—Educators Survey. *International Journal of Environmental Research and Public Health*, *17*(16), 5658. doi:10.3390/ijerph17165658 PMID:32764447

Wan-qing, W., & Li, L. (2022). The impact of artificial intelligence on the mental health of manufacturing workers: The mediating role of overtime work and the work environment. *Frontiers in Public Health*, *10*, 862407. doi:10.3389/fpubh.2022.862407 PMID:35480579

West, C., Dyrbye, L., & Shanafelt, T. (2018). Physician burnout: Contributors, consequences and solutions. *Journal of Internal Medicine*, *283*(6), 516–529. doi:10.1111/joim.12752 PMID:29505159

Winrow, A., Reitmaier-Koehler, A., & Winrow, B. (2015). Social desirability bias in relation to academic cheating behaviors of nursing students. *Journal of Nursing Education and Practice*, *5*(8). Advance online publication. doi:10.5430/jnep.v5n8p121

Wolverton, C., & Hollier, B. (2019). A minimalist design for distance learning. *International Journal of Educational Management*, *33*(7), 1457–1465. doi:10.1108/IJEM-09-2017-0237

Woo, H., Lu, J., & Storlie, C. (2022). Burnout and scholarly productivity among junior counseling faculty: Mentoring as a moderator. *Journal of Employment Counseling*, *59*(4), 179–188. doi:10.1002/joec.12188

Wood, E., Ange, B., & Miller, D. (2021). Are we ready to integrate artificial intelligence literacy into the medical school curriculum: Students and faculty survey. *Journal of Medical Education and Curricular Development*, *8*, 238212052110240. doi:10.1177/23821205211024078 PMID:34250242

Xu, Q., Jingying, H., Xian, S., Zhao, Y., Wu, L., Baorui, C., & Qu, Y. (2022). The effectiveness of artificial intelligence-based automated grading and training system in the education of manual detection of diabetic retinopathy. *Frontiers in Public Health*, *10*, 1025271. doi:10.3389/fpubh.2022.1025271 PMID:36419999

Yang, S., Liu, K., Gai, J., & He, X. (2022). Transformation to industrial artificial intelligence and workers' mental health: Evidence from China. *Frontiers in Public Health*, *10*, 881827. doi:10.3389/fpubh.2022.881827 PMID:35685756

Zawacki-Richter, O., Marín, V., Bond, M., & Gouverneur, F. (2019). Systematic review of research on artificial intelligence applications in higher education – where are the educators? *International Journal of Educational Technology in Higher Education*, *16*(1), 39. doi:10.1186/s41239-019-0171-0

Zhai, X., & Nehm, R. (2023). AI and formative assessment: The train has left the station. *Journal of Research in Science Teaching*, *60*(6), 1390–1398. doi:10.1002/tea.21885

Zhang, J. (2023). Design and simulation of autonomous learning platform for constructive English teaching based on artificial intelligence. doi:10.1117/12.2683093

Zhuang, C., Hu, X., & Dill, M. (2022). Do physicians with academic affiliation have lower burnout and higher career-related satisfaction? *BMC Medical Education*, *22*(1), 316. doi:10.1186/s12909-022-03327-5 PMID:35473565

Zielinski, C., Winker, M., Aggarwal, R., Ferris, L., Heinemann, M., Lapeña, J., & Citrome, L. (2023). Chatbots, ChatGPT, and scholarly manuscripts: WAME recommendations on ChatGPT and chatbots in relation to scholarly publications. *Open Access Macedonian Journal of Medical Sciences*, *11*(A), 83-86. doi:10.3889/oamjms.2023.11502

Zimmermann, E. M., Mramba, L. K., Gregoire, H., Dandar, V., Limacher, M. C., & Good, M. L. (2020). Characteristics of faculty at risk of leaving their medical schools: An analysis of the StandPoint™ Faculty Engagement Survey. *Journal of Healthcare Leadership*, *12*, 1–10. doi:10.2147/JHL.S225291 PMID:32021533

KEY TERMS AND DEFINITIONS

Artificial Intelligence (AI): Artificial Intelligence focuses on creating systems and machines capable of performing tasks that typically require human intelligence. A few tasks are reasoning, problem-solving, learning and problem-solving.

Educational Technology (EdTech): Educational technology is the use of technology, tools, and digital resources to enhance and support teaching and learning.

Faculty Retention: Faculty retention centers around strategies employed by educational institutions to retain qualified and experienced faculty members.

Future of Education: The future of education encompasses changes and developments in the educational landscape like advancements in teaching methodologies, curriculum design, and the integration of emerging technologies to meet the evolving needs of students, industries, and society.

GPT-3 (Generative Pre-trained Transformer 3): GPT-3 is a language model developed using artificial intelligence (AI). It understands and generates human-like text based on input it receives from human beings. GPT-3 has been trained in advance on a large amount of data.

Higher Education Reform: Higher education reform is when there are systematic changes and improvements in the structure, curriculum, and delivery of education.

Innovation: Innovation ties into the development and implementation of new and creative ideas, methods, or technologies to improve teaching, learning, and educational outcomes.

Large Language Models: Large language models refers to AI systems that are designed to understand and generate human language.

Chapter 15
GenAI, Robots, and Inclusive Special Education:
Autism Spectrum Disorder in the Age of Generative AI

Alperen Sağdıç
https://orcid.org/0000-0002-5508-9554
Sobe Vakfı, Turkey

Elif Elumar-Efe
https://orcid.org/0000-0003-0732-8079
Pamukkale University, Turkey

Sunagül Sani-Bozkurt
https://orcid.org/0000-0001-6648-9636
Anadolu University, Turkey

ABSTRACT

This chapter examines the role of generative AI (GenAI) and robotics in special education, particularly for autism spectrum disorder (ASD). It highlights the revolutionary impact of GenAI and AI-powered educational technologies (AIEd) in early diagnosis, personalized learning, and fostering independence in individuals with ASD. Additionally, robotics is presented as a vital tool for enhancing social and communication skills. The integration of these technologies in education requires addressing ethical, privacy, and security concerns. The chapter emphasizes technological literacy, including prompt engineering, to optimize the use of GenAI and robotics. It also explores the unique relationship between individuals with ASD and robots, suggesting a promising future for these technologies in special education. The conclusion calls for ongoing research and development to create more equitable and accessible educational systems, harnessing the power of GenAI and robotics for individuals with ASD.

DOI: 10.4018/979-8-3693-1351-0.ch015

INTRODUCTION

What if all our fictions would come true and become an integral part of our lives? This is exactly what happened in the context of artificial intelligence (AI) and robots. For centuries, from legends to stories, from myths to science fiction films, mankind has been in search of human-like intelligent elements and robots that behave like humans (Bozkurt, 2023a; Şenocak et al., 2023). This decades-long quest has several critical turning points in history. The three thousands-year-long quest, which started with René Descartes' (1637) introduction of the Automoto in his Discourse on the Method, continued with Karel Čapek's (1921) first use of the word 'robot' in the science fiction game Rossum's Universal Robots, and continued in 1955 when John McCarthy, Marvin Minsky, Nathaniel Rochester, and Claude Shannon (1955) used the term 'artificial intelligence' in The Dartmouth Summer Research Project on Artificial Intelligence. This fire, which was ignited by Alan Turing (1950) with the question "Can machines think?", has influenced the whole world by the 2000s. About a century after the use of the concept of robot and three quarters of a century after the concept of AI was introduced, mankind's quest turned from fiction to reality.

OpenAI (2022) introduced ChatGPT at the end of 2022, when mankind, who likes to challenge himself with the possibilities offered by AI, thought that this quest had matured. Natural language processing (NLP) and large language models (LLMs) forged by Generative Pre-trained Transformers (GPT) technology leading to Generative Artificial Intelligence (GenAI) which was beyond our expectations and predictions. According to Bozkurt (2023b) GenAI has "the potential to master human language, one of the most complex and sophisticated technologies ever created, and to use human knowledge to identify patterns that may elude human perception. When properly trained, ChatGPT is a powerful tool that can learn, unlearn, and relearn language, allowing it to adapt and evolve with human communication needs" (p. 199).

The introduction of Generative AI (GenAI) has resonated throughout the educational landscape, including its application in special education, specifically for Autism Spectrum Disorder (ASD) (Ansari et al., 2023; Bahroun et al., 2023; Bozkurt, 2023c; İpek et al., 2023; Lambert & Stevens, 2023; Lo, 2023; Montenegro-Rueda et al., 2023; Pradana et al., 2023; Yu & Guo, 2023). The conversational capabilities of GenAI hold promise for various subareas of special education, offering numerous opportunities (Marino et al., 2023). In the context of ASD, GenAI is suggested as a technology for diversifying learning experiences and supporting the development of learners with a range of needs (Johnson et al., 2023). Additionally, some studies highlight the potential of LLMs and GPT variants in the early detection of ASD (Li et al., 2023; Mukherjee et al., 2023). Beyond the basic application of GenAI, there is also an exploration into enhancing its capacity with social robots. Bertacchini et al. (2023) argue that combining the power of AI with visual stimuli and interactive robotics offers a novel and promising approach to support individuals with Autism Spectrum Disorder (ASD) in their neurodevelopmental journey. This integration could be instrumental for assessment, monitoring, and treatment purposes, suggesting a forward-thinking direction in the use of technology for special education needs.

HITECH ASSISTIVE TECHNOLOGIES IN AUTISM SPECTRUM DISORDER

ASD is defined as a neurodevelopmental disorder characterised by deficits in social communication and interaction and limited, repetitive interests, patterns and obsessive behaviours (APA, 2013). Symptoms related to ASD may be observed in several ways and with different intensities in each individual with ASD. Due to this heterogeneity of ASD, different intervention programmes based on various approaches have been developed for these individuals (Maglione et al., 2012). Both this diversity of individuals with ASD and the increasing rate of ASD have encouraged experts working in this field to find the most effective intervention programmes. In 2020, the report published by the National Clearinghouse on Autism Evidence and Practice Review Team (NCAEP) stated that 28 methods applied in the education of individuals with ASD are evidence-based (Steinbrenner et al., 2020). One of these 28 methods is accepted as assistive technologies.

Assistive technologies are special tools, services and methods used to individualise the teaching of individuals with special needs, increase their independence and improve their quality of life (Reed & Bowser, 2005). In the literature, technology-assisted applications used in the education of individuals with special needs are classified as low-level technologies, medium-level technologies and advanced technologies (Ganschow et al., 2001).

Advanced technologies require significant knowledge accumulation and are developed through innovation strategies. For the development of these technologies, interdisciplinary collaboration (for example, between engineering, medicine, etc.) needs to be established, and substantial financial resources must be allocated (Töret & Dağlarlı, 2021). However, in the literature, it is seen that technology-oriented trends focus on ASD and advanced technologies (Ramo Akgün, 2023). The advanced technologies accessible in today's world and integrated into educational environments include virtual reality, augmented reality, AI, robotic technologies, and eye-tracking technology. Zammarchi and Conversano (2021) have highlighted that eye-tracking technology is frequently used in most studies examining the social interaction levels of individuals with ASD. Lorenzo et al. (2020) suggested that Virtual Reality technology could be one of the best-suited technologies for the learning styles of individuals with ASD. Barua et al. (2022) have indicated in their research that AI tools enable and support the social interaction of individuals with ASD. In this context, it is anticipated that advanced technologies can support individuals with ASD in various areas.

Advanced technologies are explained in the literature as tools that can be used in screening (Allison et al., 2012; Duda et al., 2016; Elakkiya & Dejey, 2024; Kosmicki et al., 2015; Sharma & Tanwar, 2024; Uddin et al., 2024; Zamit et al., 2023) and diagnosing (Mujeeb et al., 2017; Uddin et al., 2024) individuals with ASD. Moreover, there has been an increasing trend in the use of advanced technologies in the education of individuals with ASD in recent years (Malihi et al., 2020; Saleh et al., 2021). Advanced technologies hold promising potential in the field of special education to support individuals with ASD, facilitate access, and increase success (Marino et al., 2023). Particularly, AI technologies are thought to have the potential to revolutionize the educational and instructional methods for individuals with ASD. Certainly, with the increase in financial support allocated to advanced technologies, the improvement in technological literacy levels of professionals in this field, and the ease of access to productive AI, researchers foresee a frequent use of these technologies in the education of individuals with ASD.

AUTISM SPECTRUM DISORDER IN THE AGE OF AI AND ROBOTS

Contrary to popular belief, technology is a concept that characterises different forms. The term 'technology' refers to art, craft, proficiency in an art or craft, or a systematic method of performing or engaging in an art. It is defined as (a) the practical application of knowledge, (b) a capability provided by the practical application of knowledge, (c) a way of accomplishing a task, particularly through technical processes, methods, or knowledge, and (d) the specialized aspects of a specific field of endeavor (Merriam-Webster, 2023). As characterised in this definition, Bozkurt (2020) and Dron (2022) classify technology into soft and hard forms. Accordingly, in its two primary categories: 'soft technologies' (encompassing programs, design principles, methodologies, conceptual frameworks, and theories) and 'hard technologies' (including tools such as pens, paper, printing devices, computers, etc.). Notably, the genesis of soft educational technologies can arguably be traced back to the development of language and alphabetic systems, whereas the advent of hard educational technologies is exemplified by the initial use of pen and paper or earlier tools that led to improvements in our lives (Bozkurt, 2020). From this perspective, hard technologies provide efficiency, precision and repeatability, but sacrifice flexibility and adaptability. Soft technologies encourage innovation, adaptability and robustness, but often require considerable expertise and effort (Bozkurt, 2024). Approaching from this perspective and adopting a metaphorical understanding, robots represents hard technologies, while AI represents soft technologies, such as the body and soul of humans. Such an understanding requires exploring AI and robots critically and this is where this section steps in.

AI AND AUTISM SPECTRUM DISORDER

In the use of AI for individuals with ASD, two main applications stand out. The first is its use for diagnostic purposes in the field of ASD, while the second involves its use in teaching skills and behaviors.

AI for the Diagnosis of Autism Spectrum Disorder

According to a recent report, one in every 36 children in the United States is born with a risk of ASD (CDC; 2023). This rate has increased by 317% since 2000. Studies show that children with ASD who receive intensive and high-quality educational services before the age of five exhibit significant improvements in language, social interaction, and play skills (Hirota & King, 2023). Therefore, it is crucial for children showing symptoms of ASD to receive a diagnosis at the earliest possible age and start educational services. Traditional screening methods for children with ASD are based on behavioral observations conducted by clinicians. Factors such as the variability of symptoms in each child, the clinician's professional experience, lengthy behavioral observations, and biased responses from parents can prolong the diagnostic process in traditional screening methods. Due to these limitations of traditional methods, many researchers in the field of AI have suggested that AI can shorten the diagnostic process for clinicians and lead to more accurate results, hence AI holds significant potential in the early diagnosis of ASD (Shahamiri & Thabtah, 2020). Numerous independent studies have reported that machine learning systems developed can diagnose individuals with ASD much faster and more effectively than traditional methods (Parui et al., 2023; Wall et al., 2012; Song et al., 2019; Duda et al., 2016; Kosmicki et al., 2015). For example, Wall et al. (2012) found that after transferring the responses to the Autism Diagnostic Interview – Revised (ADI-R), one of the most frequently used tools for diagnosing ASD, to a machine learning system, the system could classify children at risk of ASD with 99.9% statistical accuracy using only 7 questions of the 93-question test that usually takes 2.5 hours.

Such an AI tool developed for the rapid diagnosis of children suspected of being at risk for ASD could contribute to faster screening of at-risk individuals and earlier commencement of education. Evaluations with these tools could be more time-efficient and minimize human errors due to the absence of personal opinions and interpretations. However, despite all these studies, there is still insufficient evidence to support the validity and reliability of an AI diagnostic tool. Furthermore, the accuracy of results can vary depending on the data sets used in training the AI. Finally, it is important to remember that an AI system handling personal data may also bring along issues of privacy and ethics.

Education for Autism Spectrum Disorder Using AI

Although the potential benefits of AI in the early diagnosis of individuals with ASD have led most AI researchers to focus on diagnostic research, only a few studies have explored the use of AI in the education of individuals with ASD (Sağdıç & Sani-Bozkurt, 2020). A review of the relevant literature shows that AI-supported applications are being used in various areas for children with ASD, such as in developing communication skills (Sağdıç et al., 2023), social skills (Riedl et al., 2009), individualized education programs (Rakap, 2023), recording behavioral problems and stereotypical movements (Amiri et al., 2017), and preparing skill analysis (Srinivasan & Parthasarathi, 2013). For example, in an AI-based educational application developed by Sağdıç et al. (2023), AI-powered cartoon characters were taught how to instruct individuals with ASD. These cartoon characters aim to teach responses to questions the individuals with ASD do not know and to follow instructions using a teaching method based on applied behavior analysis. With this AI-based application, individuals with ASD can acquire target behaviors set for them through a cartoon on a tablet, without the need for a teacher.

As seen, as a potential, AI can individualize the education of individuals with ASD, enhance their communication skills, make learning easier and more enjoyable, and also help individuals with ASD become more independent in society.

OPPORTUNITIES AND LIMITATIONS OF THE AI AS AN ASSISTIVE TECHNOLOGY

When the opportunities presented by AI as an assistive technology are properly utilized and well integrated into the education of individuals with ASD, the results are satisfying. We can summarize the opportunities offered by AI in these areas as follows (Bertacchini et al., 2023; Bozkurt et al., 2023; Bozkurt, 2023d; Bozkurt & Sharma, 2023; Sani-Bozkurt & Sağdıç, 2022; Molenaar et al., 2022):

- Early Objective Diagnosis: AI can assess the potential risks of children with ASD at a much earlier age. Independent of personal opinions and experiences, it can provide more objective interpretations, ensuring early access to educational services for children at risk of ASD.
- Personalized Learning in Education: Considering the vastly different learning styles of individuals with ASD, the adaptability of advanced technologies to the learner's needs is one of the factors that make these technologies preferable. AI technologies provide personalized learning materials tailored to each student's needs.
- Multi-Sensory Engagement: Learning and teaching environments that engage multiple senses can increase the motivation and success of individuals with ASD. Advanced technologies can enrich the learning and teaching process and increase retention.

- Interactive Learning Environments: Well-designed learning environments with advanced technologies create engaging and motivating teaching atmospheres. Additionally, teaching sessions resembling simulated real-life situations can be planned for students with ASD, offering many opportunities, especially in virtual reality simulations based on AI for situations that might cause anxiety or safety concerns.
- Rapid Content Delivery and Feedback: Advanced technologies allow for the creation of educational content like videos and interactive simulations. This content can be created more time and cost-effectively. These technologies enable assessment of taught skills and quick feedback for the student, benefiting those with ASD who require frequent repetition, cues, and reinforcement.
- Increased Efficiency in Education: Advanced technologies can save time and effort in educational settings by assisting teachers in preparing educational materials and student reporting with AI support.
- Predictable and Simple Teaching Opportunities: While social variables may cause anxiety for individuals with ASD, predictable technologies and environments like robots, AI, or virtual reality can provide more comfortable and straightforward learning environments.
- High Motivation: The strong motivation of individuals with ASD towards technological systems makes teachings with these systems more effective and enduring.
- 24/7 Accessibility: The continuity of education for individuals with ASD is as important as its quality. Due to the limited number of trained professionals in this field, the time dedicated to education for individuals with ASD is quite limited. Advanced technologies allow individuals with ASD to access education anytime and anywhere they can access technology.
- Assistant Teacher: AI can perform tasks such as skill analysis, individualized education planning, measuring and graphing student performance, which can reduce the workload and preparation costs for teachers. It can also transform students' responses into more meaningful data, aiding teachers in making more accurate decisions in intervention processes.
- Alternative Communication: Some individuals with ASD may never speak throughout their lives. In such cases, they use communication systems known as Alternative and Augmentative Communication Systems (AACS). AI-supported communication systems can predict sentences to be spoken by an individual with ASD during AACS use, enabling more intensive communication with less effort.
- Behavioral Tracking: AI can identify stereotypical movements of individuals with ASD, analyze behavior patterns, and provide real-time feedback in stressful situations to help prevent potential anger outbursts.
- Social Skills Training: AI-based simulations can create safe and controlled environments for individuals with ASD to practice social interactions and develop social skills. It can also teach situations that are difficult to experience in real life but need to be taught, like earthquakes and fires, through AI-based virtual reality simulations.
- Game-Based Learning: AI can gamify the skills that individuals with ASD need to learn, making them more enjoyable. This can help attract more attention and motivate individuals with ASD during education.

Alongside these opportunities, there are also some limitations to to be acknwledged in using AI as an assistive technology (Bozkurt et al., 2023; Bozkurt & Sharma, 2023; Sani-Bozkurt & Sağdıç, 2022):

- Inequality and Injustice in Technology Access: One of the most significant barriers when it comes to advanced technologies is their high cost. Considering the expenses involved in the educational processes of individuals with ASD (Rogge and Janssen, 2019), it is a disappointing reality that not all individuals with ASD can access these advanced technologies.
- Overuse of Technology: When advanced technologies are not well integrated into teaching sessions, unplanned and excessive use of technology may occur. Excessive use of technology can negatively affect individuals' social skills, as well as their physical and cognitive development. Given that individuals with ASD already have weak social skills, disconnection from social environments due to overuse of technology is an undesirable outcome. Excessive technology use can lead to problems such as attention deficit, shyness, social isolation, and concentration disorders.
- Technology Addiction: Technology addiction can be described as an obsessive condition with technological devices and digital platforms. Individuals experiencing technology addiction may exhibit increased stress levels when unable to access technological devices and digital platforms. Considering the social communication and interaction limitations of individuals with ASD and their motivation through technological tools (APA, 2013), technology addiction can also develop in individuals with ASD (Dell'Osso et al. 2023; Kawabe et al., 2022).
- Privacy and Ethical Violations: The use of advanced and AI technologies can lead to privacy violations during the processing and use of personal data, raising concerns about the security of sensitive information of individuals with ASD.
- Reliability: We cannot always be certain about the accuracy of the data sets used by advanced technologies. There is no guarantee that the content provided by AI technologies is based on scientifically proven and evidence-based information.

PROMISES OF GENAI AND ROBOTS

Though the boundries beween generic AI and generative AI are blurring, generative AI promises in terms of certain aspects such as building human-like communications. In this regard, approaching from the perspective of GenAI, there are some issues that require revisiting clearly. These are prompt engineering, which refers to establishing effective and efficient communication with GenAI and human-machine interaction, or more specifically, AI-powered robots and social interaction. In this context, the following sections will explore these issues with a specific focus on ASD.

Prompt Engineering

Prompt engineering is a skill necessary for effectively communicating with AI systems and LLMs (White et al., 2023). Through prompt engineering, users can input specific prompts or create instructions to retrieve the information they desire within a certain context (Giray, 2023). For instance, required information can be acquired from ChatGPT, an advanced language model based on OpenAI's GPT technology, by providing the necessary prompts. Teaching prompt engineering to individuals with ASD could enable them to take advantage of the opportunities offered by AI technology. However, prompt engineering is an additional skill set that needs to be imparted to individuals with ASD. Below is an example of a conversation where an individual with ASD, without proficiency in prompt engineering, seeks support from ChatGPT.

- *Student: Hello. The sweater my grandmother bought me is uncomfortable. What should I do?*
- *ChatGPT: Hello! It's important to first try to understand your grandmother's intention. Perhaps she thought she was selecting a nice gift for you. If the sweater is causing discomfort, you could express this to her in a polite and respectful way. Open and understanding communication can help in finding a positive resolution. Remember, healthy communication is key to strengthening relationships.*

In this example, the individual with ASD didn't frame the query appropriately for the AI, leading to not getting the help needed. Below is the dialogue of the same individual with ASD asking for support from ChatGPT with a clearer prompt.

- *Student: Hello. I am a 14-year-old child with autism spectrum disorder. The texture of the sweater my grandmother gave me for my birthday made me uncomfortable. I haven't worn the sweater. The gift includes an exchange card. What would you suggest in this case?*
- *ChatGPT: You could tell your grandmother that you are unable to wear the sweater and are considering using the exchange card to choose another item. Alternatively, you could discuss your sensory discomforts with her and suggest selecting a more suitable gift together.*
- *Student: Thank you!*
- *ChatGPT: You're welcome! If you have any other questions or need assistance, I am always here. Have a great day!*

As seen, even minor changes in prompts can lead to the creation of different responses (Zhou et al., 2022). This highlights the significance of possessing AI literacy and prompt engineering skills. Additionally, the ability to produce different responses with slight modifications indicates the potential of GenAI technology as a robust tool for personalized learning (Baidoo-Anu & Ansah, 2023). Consequently, teaching prompt engineering to individuals with ASD for effective utilization of AI in their lives becomes an important new skill to be developed. The concept of prompt engineering means opening a new page, especially in the context of human-machine interaction.

Human-Machine Interaction

Since machines entered human life, one of the primary goals of researchers has been to enable communication between humans and machines using natural language. For this purpose, NLP, a subfield of AI, was developed, enabling computers to understand, interpret, produce, and respond to human language (Deng & Liu, 2018). To measure whether machines can use language as humans do, the Turing Test was proposed by Alan Turing in 1950. The basic premise of the Turing Test is whether a computer's responses can be distinguished from a human's. If a computer's responses are indistinguishable from those of a human, it is considered to have passed the Turing Test. Although there is a significant group of critics who argue that intelligence cannot be measured solely through language and that this test is merely a subjective evaluation, the Turing Test has been frequently used over the years to measure the interaction between machines and humans. Only nine years after posing the question of whether machines can communicate like humans, another article garnered considerable interest, asking if a human could be a machine. Bruno Bettelheim (1959), in his article "Joey: A 'Mechanical Boy,'" described the treatment of a child known then as having 'childhood schizophrenia'—now understood as ASD—who identified himself as a mechanical robot. Joey, who had a great interest in machines and was adept at disassembling them, did not speak to anyone other than himself. According to Bettelheim, the child's parents, who only fed him at regular intervals and treated him mechanically, had turned him into a machine. Although the term ASD was first used by Leo Kanner in 1943—who noted that children with ASD prefer solitude and relate better to objects than people—the comparison between a child with ASD and a machine was first made by Bettelheim. In 1944, Hans Asperger described children with ASD as 'intelligent automatons.' As seen, even in the early years of discussing ASD, interactions and similarities with machines were mentioned, and many researchers following Bettelheim (1959), Kanner, and Asperger (1943) have emphasized that individuals with ASD prefer objects over people. Moreover, while the social skill difficulties of individuals with ASD are widely recognized (Weiss, & Harris, 2001; Williams White et al., 2007), there is extensive research literature supporting their interactions with robots (Pennisi et al., 2016; Saleh et al., 2021).

Baron-Cohen (1997) stated that individuals with ASD have a kind of 'mind blindness' or lack of empathy, being unable to understand the mental states, thoughts, feelings, beliefs, and intentions of others. This trait is also one of the distinguishing features of robots from humans. Could it be argued that the thought systems of individuals with ASD and machines are more similar to each other compared to those of humans? And could it be said that geniuses like Mark Zuckerberg, Elon Musk, and Bill Gates, who are thought to have ASD, find it easier to empathize with a machine rather than a human, which might be behind their success in driving the digital age? The fundamental logic of the Turing Test, designed to distinguish between humans and machines, is that a robot will be identified as non-human. However, if the person answering the questions has ASD, it is likely that the evaluator will think the respondent is a machine. Therefore, the key to achieving one of humanity's fundamental goals since the advent of machines—facilitating communication with machines—might lie in first understanding the interactions of individuals with ASD.

Robots and Social Interaction

With the advancement of AI, machines have become capable of thinking, moving, and imitating human-specific behaviors. Particularly, the idea of robots serving as friends or teachers has transcended science fiction films and become a commonplace and accepted notion in the literature. Recent years have seen a surge in research utilizing robots in the education of individuals with ASD (Saleh et al., 2021). Robots have been employed in various roles for the education of individuals with ASD, including as direct teachers working with the child, as auxiliary teaching tools, as activity partners, or as clinicians monitoring and analyzing data related to the individual with ASD (Kohli, Kar, & Sinha, 2023).

The relevant literature shows that robots have been effectively used in teaching various skills to individuals with ASD, such as establishing eye contact, initiating and maintaining interaction, turn-taking, recognizing emotions, joint attention, and imitation (Pennisi et al., 2016; Saleh et al., 2021). There have also been studies investigating how robots can be used for the early diagnosis of ASD, similar to AI (Kumazaki et al., 2019). Alongside numerous studies affirming the effectiveness of robots in the education of individuals with ASD, there are also comparisons between traditional human studies and robot-assisted interventions. The claim that individuals with ASD prefer robots over humans has become a popular discourse in robotics research. For instance, a study by Tapus et al. (2012) found that participants with ASD initiated higher levels of interaction with the Robot Nao compared to a human, and observed an increase in eye contact duration with Robot Nao. The underlying reason for individuals with ASD's interaction with robots could be their perception of robots as simpler, safer, more predictable, and more reliable compared to humans. The mother of a student with ASD at our school, who preferred chatting with robots over her teacher, attributed this to "the robot being more predictable and the control being in the child's hands during the interaction." This thought process suggests that individuals with ASD might prefer simpler and more understandable robots over humans, due to the social variables and unpredictability associated with human interactions. Hence, the preference for robots over humans by individuals with ASD might be due to the lack of social skills in robots, rather than their different appearances. However, attributing the success of robots solely to the lack of social skills underestimates the value of robotic research. Significant studies have reported that robots effectively motivate individuals with ASD during interventions and capture their attention on the skills being taught (Lee et al., 2012; Lee & Obinata, 2013; Wainer et al., 2010).

In brief, researchers in the field of ASD and robotics demonstrate the effectiveness of robots, particularly in teaching social skills to individuals with ASD. While the notion of a non-social entity, like a machine, teaching social skills to humans might seem paradoxical, if interacting with a robot is more engaging and easier for an individual with ASD compared to a teacher, using robots as a tool can be seen as a time and energy-saving strategy for educators. However, an important point to consider here is that the goal of working with robots is not to increase interaction with the robot itself. Rather, it is to use the experience gained with robots to facilitate interaction with humans, allowing the skills learned to be generalized to real-life situations. Robots have the potential to offer educators evidence-based interventions by overcoming some of the limitations of traditional methods in the education of individuals with ASD. Like many technological devices that have been integrated into daily life due to their convenience and comfort, it is likely that robots, due to the benefits they provide in the education of individuals with ASD, will gain even greater acceptance in the field of special education in the coming years. Therefore, there is a need for further research in this area and for the development of therapist robots with different hardware and features.

CONCLUSION

Considering the opportunities that technology currently offers in our lives, it is exciting to think about what the future may hold. In a world where keeping up with technological advancements and embracing innovation is crucial, the integration of technology should be considered in all areas of education, including the education of individuals with ASD. This chapter has discussed the potential contributions, promises, and possible limitations of GenAI and robots in the education of individuals with ASD. AI could provide potential benefits in early diagnosis, personalized learning opportunities, and independent living for individuals with ASD. Robots powered by GenAI could support the social interaction and communication skills of individuals with ASD. However, for these technologies to be effectively integrated, important issues such as ethics, privacy, and security must be meticulously addressed. The role that GenAI and robots could play in enhancing the quality of life for individuals with ASD will be a significant focus of future research and development. This comprehensive relationship between AI and ASD offers a promising roadmap for future generations, making educational systems more equitable and accessible.

AUTHORS' NOTES

This paper was proofread and refined with the assistance of OpenAI's GPT-4 and DeepL, complementing the human editorial process.

ACKNOWLEDGMENT

This study was supported by Scientific Research Coordination Unit of Anadolu University under the project number 2304E022.

REFERENCES

Allison, C., Auyeung, B., & Baron-Cohen, S. (2012). Toward brief "red flags" for autism screening: The short autism spectrum quotient and the short quantitative checklist in 1,000 cases and 3,000 controls. *Journal of the American Academy of Child and Adolescent Psychiatry*, *51*(2), 202–212. doi:10.1016/j.jaac.2011.11.003 PMID:22265366

Amiri, A. M., Peltier, N., Goldberg, C., Sun, Y., Nathan, A., Hiremath, S. V., & Mankodiya, K. (2017, March). WearSense: Detecting autism stereotypic behaviors through smartwatches. *Health Care*, *5*(11), 2–9. doi:10.3390/healthcare5010011 PMID:28264474

Ansari, A. N., Ahmad, S., & Bhutta, S. M. (2023). Mapping the global evidence around the use of ChatGPT in higher education: A systematic scoping review. *Education and Information Technologies*, 1–41. doi:10.1007/s10639-023-12223-4

APA. (2013). *Diagnostic and statistical manual of mental disorders: DSM-5*. American Psychiatric Publishing Incorporated.

Bahroun, Z., Anane, C., Ahmed, V., & Zacca, A. (2023). Transforming Education: A Comprehensive Review of Generative Artificial Intelligence in Educational Settings through Bibliometric and Content Analysis. *Sustainability (Basel)*, *15*(17), 12983. doi:10.3390/su151712983

Baidoo-Anu, D., & Ansah, L. O. (2023). Education in the era of generative artificial intelligence (AI): Understanding the potential benefits of ChatGPT in promoting teaching and learning. *Journal of AI*, *7*(1), 52–62. doi:10.61969/jai.1337500

Baron-Cohen, S. (1997). Mindblindness: An essay on autism and theory of mind. Bradford.

Barua, P. D., Vicnesh, J., Gururajan, R., Oh, S. L., Palmer, E., Azizan, M. M., & Acharya, U. R. (2022). Artificial Intelligence Enabled Personalized Assistive Tools to Enhance Education of Children with Neurodevelopmental Disorders: A Review. *International Journal of Environmental Research and Public Health*, *19*(3), 1–26. doi:10.3390/ijerph19031192 PMID:35162220

Bertacchini, F., Demarco, F., Scuro, C., Pantano, P., & Bilotta, E. (2023). A social robot connected with chatGPT to improve cognitive functioning in ASD subjects. *Frontiers in Psychology, 14*, 1232177. doi:10.3389/fpsyg.2023.1232177 PMID:37868599

Bettelheim, B. (1959). Joey. *Scientific American, 200*(3), 116–130.. doi:10.1038/scientificamerican0359-116 PMID:13635040

Bozkurt, A. (2020). Educational technology research patterns in the realm of the digital knowledge age. *Journal of Interactive Media in Education, 2020*(1), 1–17. doi:10.5334/jime.570

Bozkurt, A. (2023a). Postdigital Artificial Intelligence. In P. Jandrić (Ed.), *Encyclopedia of Postdigital Science and Education*. Springer. doi:10.1007/978-3-031-35469-4_2-2

Bozkurt, A. (2023b). Generative artificial intelligence (AI) powered conversational educational agents: The inevitable paradigm shift. *Asian Journal of Distance Education, 18*(1), 198–204. doi:10.5281/zenodo.7716416

Bozkurt, A. (2023c). Unleashing the potential of generative AI, conversational agents and chatbots in educational praxis: A systematic review and bibliometric analysis of GenAI in education. *Open Praxis, 15*(4), 261–270. doi:10.55982/openpraxis.15.4.609

Bozkurt, A. (2023d). ChatGPT, generative artificial intelligence and algorithmic paradigm shift. *CRES Journal Critical Reviews in Educational Sciences, 4*(1), 63–72. doi:10.59320/alanyazin.1283282

Bozkurt, A. (2024). Postdigital Educational Technology. In P. Jandrić (Ed.), *Encyclopedia of Postdigital Science and Education*. Springer.

Bozkurt, A., & Sharma, R. C. (2023). Generative AI and prompt engineering: The art of whispering to let the genie out of the algorithmic world. *Asian Journal of Distance Education, 18*(2), i–vii. doi:10.5281/zenodo.8174941

Bozkurt, A., Xiao, J., Lambert, S., Pazurek, A., Crompton, H., Koseoglu, S., Farrow, R., Bond, M., Nerantzi, C., Honeychurch, S., Bali, M., Dron, J., Mir, K., Stewart, B., Costello, E., Mason, J., Stracke, C. M., Romero-Hall, E., Koutropoulos, A., & Jandrić, P. (2023). Speculative futures on ChatGPT and generative artificial intelligence (AI): A collective reflection from the educational landscape. *Asian Journal of Distance Education, 18*(1), 53–130. doi:10.5281/zenodo.7636568

Čapek, K. (1921). *Rossum's Universal Robots*. Project Gutenberg. https://gutenberg.org/ebooks/59112

Dell'Osso, L., Amatori, G., Muti, D., Giovannoni, F., Parri, F., Violi, M., Cremone, I. M., & Carpita, B. (2023). Autism Spectrum, Hikikomori Syndrome and Internet Gaming Disorder: Is There a Link? *Brain Sciences, 13*(7), 1116. doi:10.3390/brainsci13071116 PMID:37509046

Deng, L., & Liu, Y. (2018). A joint introduction to natural language processing and to deep learning. Deng, L., & Liu, Y. (Eds.), Deep learning in natural language processing (pp. 1-22). Singapore: Springer. doi:10.1007/978-981-10-5209-5_1

Descartes, R. (1637). *Discourse on the Method of Rightly Conducting One's Reason and of Seeking Truth in the Sciences*. Project Gutenberg. https://www.gutenberg.org/files/59/59-h/59-h.htm

Dron, J. (2022). Educational technology: What it is and how it works. *AI & Society*, *37*(1), 155–166. doi:10.1007/s00146-021-01195-z

Duda, M., Daniels, J., & Wall, D. P. (2016). Clinical evaluation of a novel and mobile autism risk assessment. *Journal of Autism and Developmental Disorders*, *46*(6), 1953–1961. doi:10.1007/s10803-016-2718-4 PMID:26873142

Duda, M., Ma, R., Haber, N., & Wall, D. P. (2016). Use of machine learning for behavioral distinction of autism and ADHD. *Translational Psychiatry*, *6*(2), e732–e732. doi:10.1038/tp.2015.221 PMID:26859815

Elakkiya, M. K., & Dejey. (2024). Novel deep learning models with novel integrated activation functions for autism screening: AutiNet and MinAutiNet. *Expert Systems with Applications*, *238*, 122102. doi:10.1016/j.eswa.2023.122102

Ganschow, L., Philips, L., & Schneider, E. (2001). Closing the gap: Accommodating students with language learning disabilities in college. *Topics in Language Disorders*, *21*(2), 17–37. doi:10.1097/00011363-200102000-00005

Giray, L. (2023). Prompt engineering with ChatGPT: A guide for academic writers. *Annals of Biomedical Engineering*, *51*(12), 2629–2633. doi:10.1007/s10439-023-03272-4 PMID:37284994

Hirota, T., & King, B. H. (2023). Autism spectrum disorder: A review. *Journal of the American Medical Association*, *329*(2), 157–168. doi:10.1001/jama.2022.23661 PMID:36625807

İpek, Z. H., Gözüm, A. İ. C., Papadakis, S., & Kallogiannakis, M. (2023). Educational Applications of the ChatGPT AI System: A Systematic Review Research. *Educational Process: International Journal*, *12*(3), 26–55. doi:10.22521/edupij.2023.123.2

Johnson, C., Smart, K., & Mahar, P. (2023). Is there a place for generative artificial intelligence in special education? *National Social Science Technology Journal, 11*(2), 48-62. https://nssascholars.org/wp-content/uploads/2023/11/NSSA.Journal-11_2_v1.11.28.23.pdf

Kanner, L. (1943). Autistic disturbances of affective contact. *Nervous child, 2*(3), 217-250. http://www.th-hoffmann.eu/archiv/kanner/kanner.1943.pdf

Kawabe, K., Horiuchi, F., Hosokawa, R., Nakachi, K., Soga, K., & Ueno, S. (2022). Comorbid symptoms of internet addiction among adolescents with and without autism spectrum disorder: A comparative study. *International Journal of Adolescence and Youth*, *27*(1), 315–324. doi:10.1080/02673843.2022.2091939

Kohli, M., Kar, A. K., & Sinha, S. (2023). Robot facilitated rehabilitation of children with autism spectrum disorder: A 10 year scoping review. *Expert Systems: International Journal of Knowledge Engineering and Neural Networks*, *40*(5), e13204. doi:10.1111/exsy.13204

Kosmicki, J. A., Sochat, V., Duda, M., & Wall, D. P. (2015). Searching for a minimal set of behaviors for autism detection through feature selection-based machine learning. *Translational Psychiatry*, *5*(2), e514–e514. doi:10.1038/tp.2015.7 PMID:25710120

Kumazaki, H., Muramatsu, T., Yoshikawa, Y., Yoshimura, Y., Ikeda, T., Hasegawa, C., Saito, D. N., Shimaya, J., Ishiguro, H., Mimura, M., & Kikuchi, M. (2019). Brief Report: A novel system to evaluate autism spectrum disorders using two humanoid robots. *Journal of Autism and Developmental Disorders*, *49*(4), 1709–1716. doi:10.1007/s10803-018-3848-7 PMID:30539368

Lambert, J., & Stevens, M. (2023). ChatGPT and Generative AI Technology: A Mixed Bag of Concerns and New Opportunities. *Computers in the Schools*, 1–25. doi:10.1080/07380569.2023.2256710

Lee, J., & Obinata, G. (2013, March). Developing therapeutic robot for children with autism: A study on exploring colour feedback. In *Human-Robot Interaction (HRI), 8th Assosiation for Computing Machinery/Institute of Electrical and Electronics Engineers (ACM/IEEE)*. IEEE. 10.1109/HRI.2013.6483557

Lee, J., Takehashi, H., Nagai, C., & Obinata, G. (2012). Design of a therapeutic robot for interacting with autistic children through interpersonal touch. In *IEEE RO-MAN: The 21st IEEE International Symposium on Robot and Human Interactive Communication* (pp. 712–717). 1 10.1109/ROMAN.2012.6343835

Li, Y., Liao, I. Y., Zhong, N., Toshihiro, F., Wang, Y., & Wang, S. (2023, December). Generative AI Enables the Detection of Autism Using EEG Signals. In *Chinese Conference on Biometric Recognition* (pp. 375-384). Springer Nature Singapore. 10.1007/978-981-99-8565-4_35

Lo, C. K. (2023). What is the impact of ChatGPT on education? A rapid review of the literature. *Education Sciences*, *13*(4), 410. doi:10.3390/educsci13040410

Lorenzo, G., Lorenzo-Lledó, A., Lledó Carreres, A., & Pérez-Vázquez, E. (2020). Approach from a bibliometric perspective of the educational application of virtual reality in people with autism spectrum disorder. *Education in the Knowledge Society*, *21*(4). doi:10.14201/eks.19522

Maglione, M. A., Gans, D., Das, L., Timbie, J., & Kasari, C. (2012). Technical Expert Panel, & HRSA Autism Intervention Research–Behavioral (AIR-B) Network. Nonmedical interventions for children with ASD: Recommended guidelines and further research needs. *Pediatrics*, *130*(Supplement_2), S169–S178. doi:10.1542/peds.2012-0900O PMID:23118248

Malihi, M., Nguyen, J., Cardy, R. E., Eldon, S., Petta, C., & Kushki, A. (2020). Evaluating the safety and usability of head-mounted virtual reality compared to monitor-displayed video for children with autism spectrum disorder. *Autism*, *24*(7), 1924–1929. doi:10.1177/1362361320934214 PMID:32615771

Marino, M. T., Vasquez, E., Dieker, L., Basham, J., & Blackorby, J. (2023). The Future of Artificial Intelligence in Special Education Technology. *Journal of Special Education Technology*, *38*(3), 404–416. doi:10.1177/01626434231165977

McCarthy, J., Minsky, M., Rochester, N., & Shannon, C. (1955). *A proposal for Dartmouth Summer Research Project on Artificial Intelligence*. Stanford. http://www-formal.stanford.edu/jmc/history/dartmouth.pdf

Molenaar, I., de Mooij, S., Azevedo, R., Bannert, M., Järvelä, S., & Gašević, D. (2022). Measuring self-regulated learning and the role ´ of AI: Five years of research using multimodal multichannel data. *Computers in Human Behavior*, *139*, 1–9. doi:10.1016/j.chb.2022.107540

Montenegro-Rueda, M., Fernández-Cerero, J., Fernández-Batanero, J. M., & López-Meneses, E. (2023). Impact of the Implementation of ChatGPT in Education: A Systematic Review. *Computers*, *12*(8), 153. doi:10.3390/computers12080153

Mujeeb, S., Javed, M. H., & Arshad, T. (2017). Aquabot: A diagnostic chatbot for achluophobia and autism. *International Journal of Advanced Computer Science and Applications*, *8*(9), 209–216. doi:10.14569/IJACSA.2017.080930

Mukherjee, P., S, G. R., Sadhukhan, S., Godse, M., & Chakraborty, B. (2023). Detection of Autism Spectrum Disorder (ASD) from Natural Language Text using BERT and ChatGPT Models. *International Journal of Advanced Computer Science and Applications, 14(*10). doi:10.14569/IJACSA.2023.0141041

Open A. I. (2022). *ChatGPT: Optimizing language models for dialogue.* Open AI. https://openai.com/blog/chatgpt/

Parui, S., Samanta, D., Chakravorty, N., Ghosh, U., & Rodrigues, J. J. (2023). Artificial intelligence and sensor-based autism spectrum disorder diagnosis using brain connectivity analysis. *Computers & Electrical Engineering*, *108*, 108720. doi:10.1016/j.compeleceng.2023.108720

Pennisi, P., Tonacci, A., Tartarisco, G., Billeci, L., Ruta, L., Gangemi, S., & Pioggia, G. (2016). Autism and social robotics: A systematic review. *Autism Research*, *9*(2), 165–183. doi:10.1002/aur.1527 PMID:26483270

Pradana, M., Elisa, H. P., & Syarifuddin, S. (2023). Discussing ChatGPT in education: A literature review and bibliometric analysis. *Cogent Education*, *10*(2), 2243134. doi:10.1080/2331186X.2023.2243134

Rakap, S. (2023). Chatting with GPT: Enhancing Individualized Education Program Goal Development for Novice Special Education Teachers. *Journal of Special Education Technology*, *01626434231211295*, 01626434231211295. doi:10.1177/01626434231211295

Ramo Akgün, N. (2023). Trends of assistive technologies in Autism Spectrum Disorder: Bibliometric analysis based on Web of Science Database (1998–2023). *Cumhuriyet International Journal of Education, 12*(3), 777-794. https://dx.doi.org/. 1308308 doi:10.30703/cije

Reed, P., & Bowser, G. (2005). Assistive technology and the IEP. D. L. Edyburn, K. Higgins & R. Boone (Eds.). Handbook of special educaiton technology research and practice (pp. 61-77). Knowledge by Design.

Riedl, M., Arriaga, R., Boujarwah, F., Hong, H., Isbell, J., & Heflin, J. (2009, October). *Graphical social scenarios: Toward intervention and authoring for adolescents with high functioning autism. In 2009 AAAI Fall Symposium Series*. AAAI. https://cdn.aaai.org/ocs/945/945-4144-1-PB.pdf

Rogge, N., & Janssen, J. (2019). The economic costs of autism spectrum disorder: A literature review. *Journal of Autism and Developmental Disorders*, *49*(7), 2873–2900. doi:10.1007/s10803-019-04014-z PMID:30976961

Sağdıç, A., Canpolat Çığ, N., Çelenk, U., Takı, Z., Çetin, İ., Feyzullahoğlu, P., Altuğ Ateş, M., & Doğan, O. (2023). Teaching Following Instructions and Responding Skills to Children with Autism with an AI-Supported Mobile Application. In *ICERI2023 Proceedings* (pp. 7658-7664). IATED. 10.21125/iceri.2023.1920

Sağdıç, Z. A., & Sani-Bozkurt, S. (2020). Otizm spektrum bozukluğu ve yapay zeka uygulamaları. *Açıköğretim Uygulamaları ve Araştırmaları Dergisi, 6*(3), 92-111. https://dergipark.org.tr/en/pub/auad/issue/56247/768540

Saleh, M. A., Hanapiah, F. A., & Hashim, H. (2021). Robot applications for autism: A comprehensive review. *Disability and Rehabilitation. Assistive Technology, 16*(6), 580–602. doi:10.1080/17483107.2019.1685016 PMID:32706602

Sani-Bozkurt, S., & Sağdıç, A. Z. (2022). Teknoloji. In H. Bakkaloğlu, S. Çelik, & G. Tomris (Eds.), *Araştırmadan Uygulamaya Erken Çocukluk Özel Eğitimi El Kitabı* (pp. 641–666). Vize Akademik.

Şenocak, D., Kocdar, S., & Bozkurt, A. (2023). Historical, philosophical and ethical roots of artificial intelligence. *Pakistan Journal of Education, 40*(1), 67–90. doi:10.30971/pje.v40i1.1152

Shahamiri, S. R., & Thabtah, F. (2020). Autism AI: A new autism screening system based on artificial intelligence. *Cognitive Computation, 12*(4), 766–777. doi:10.1007/s12559-020-09743-3

Sharma, A., & Tanwar, P. (2024). Model for autism disorder detection using deep learning. *IAES International Journal of Artificial Intelligence, 13*(1), 391–398. doi:10.11591/ijai.v13.i1.pp391-398

Song, D.-Y., Kim, S. Y., Bong, G., Kim, J. M., & Yoo, H. J. (2019). The use of artificial intelligence in screening and diagnosis of autism spectrum disorder: A literature review. *Journal of the Korean Academy of Child and Adolescent Psychiatry, 30*(4), 145–152. doi:10.5765/jkacap.190027 PMID:32595335

Srinivasan, B., & Parthasarathi, R. (2013). An intelligent task analysis approach for special education based on MIRA. *Journal of Applied Logic, 11*(1), 137–145. doi:10.1016/j.jal.2012.12.001

Steinbrenner, J. R., Hume, K., Odom, S. L., Morin, K. L., Nowell, S. W., Tomaszewski, B. & Savage, M. N. (2020). Evidence-based practices for children, youth, and young adults with autism. *The University of North Carolina at Chapel Hill, Frank Porter Graham Child Development Institute, National Clearinghouse on Autism Evidence and Practice Review Team.*

Tapus, A., Peca, A., Aly, A. A., Pop, C., Jisa, L., Pintea, S., Rusu, A. S., & David, D. O. (2012). Children with autism social engagement in interaction with Nao, an imitative robot: A series of single case experiments. *Interaction Studies: Social Behaviour and Communication in Biological and Artificial Systems, 13*(3), 315–347. doi:10.1075/is.13.3.01tap

Töret, G., & Dağlarlı, E. (2021). OSB'de ileri düzey teknoloji ve açıklanabilir yapay zekâ uygulamaları. In G. Töret (Ed.), *Özel Gereksinimli Bireylerde Destekleyici İleri Düzey Teknolojiler* (pp. 1–31). Nobel Akademik Yayıncılık.

Turing, A. M. (1950). Mind. *Mind, 59*(236), 433–460. doi:10.1093/mind/LIX.236.433

Uddin, M. Z., Shahriar, M. A., Mahamood, M. N., Alnajjar, F., Pramanik, M. I., & Ahad, M. A. R. (2024). Deep learning with image-based autism spectrum disorder analysis: A systematic review. *Engineering Applications of Artificial Intelligence, 127*, 107185. doi:10.1016/j.engappai.2023.107185

Wainer, J., Ferrari, E., Dautenhahn, K., & Robins, B. (2010). The effectiveness of using a robotics class to foster collaboration among groups of children with autism in an exploratory study. *Personal and Ubiquitous Computing*, *14*(5), 445–455. doi:10.1007/s00779-009-0266-z

Wall, D. P., Dally, R., Luyster, R., Jung, J.-Y., & DeLuca, T. F. (2012). Use of artificial intelligence to shorten the behavioral diagnosis of autism. *PLoS One*, *7*(8), e43855. doi:10.1371/journal.pone.0043855 PMID:22952789

Weiss, M. J., & Harris, S. L. (2001). Teaching social skills to people with autism. *Behavior Modification*, *25*(5), 785–802. doi:10.1177/0145445501255007 PMID:11573340

White, J., Fu, Q., Hays, S., Sandborn, M., Olea, C., Gilbert, H., & Schmidt, D. C. (2023). A prompt pattern catalog to enhance prompt engineering with chatgpt. arXiv. https://doi.org//arXiv.2302.11382 doi:10.48550

Williams White, S., Keonig, K., & Scahill, L. (2007). Social skills development in children with autism spectrum disorders: A review of the intervention research. *Journal of Autism and Developmental Disorders*, *37*(10), 1858–1868. doi:10.1007/s10803-006-0320-x PMID:17195104

Yu, H., & Guo, Y. (2023). Generative artificial intelligence empowers educational reform: Current status, issues, and prospects. *Frontiers in Education*, *8*, 1183162. doi:10.3389/feduc.2023.1183162

Zamit, I., Musa, I. H., Jiang, L., Yanjie, W., & Tang, J. (2023). Trends and features of autism spectrum disorder research using artificial intelligence techniques: A bibliometric approach. *Current Psychology (New Brunswick, N.J.)*, *42*(35), 1–16. doi:10.1007/s12144-022-03977-0

Zammarchi, G., & Conversano, C. (2021). Application of eye tracking technology in medicine: A bibliometric analysis. *Vision (Basel)*, *5*(4), 56. doi:10.3390/vision5040056 PMID:34842855

Zhou, K., Yang, J., Loy, C. C., & Liu, Z. (2022). Conditional Prompt Learning for Vision-Language Models. *International Journal of Computer Vision*, *130*(9), 2337–2348. doi:10.1007/s11263-022-01653-1

KEY TERMS AND DEFINITIONS

Artificial Intelligence: AI encompasses systems that, based on human-defined objectives, can predict, recommend, or decide actions affecting real or virtual environments. These systems, often seeming autonomous, interact with and impact our surroundings, adapting through contextual learning

Assistive Technology: Assistive technology (AT) refers to any device, equipment, or system designed to enhance the lives of individuals with special needs, impairments, or disabilities, aiding in their accommodation and support.

Autism Spectrum Disorder: Autism Spectrum Disorder (ASD) is a neurodevelopmental condition characterized by challenges in social interaction and communication, accompanied by distinct patterns of interests and behaviors.

Generative AI: Generative AI is a type of artificial intelligence technology capable of using human language skillfully and producing various types of content, including text, imagery, audio, and synthetic data.

Inclusive Education: Inclusive education represents an approach dedicated to ensuring students receive quality and equitable educational opportunities, irrespective of their disabilities, specific needs, or socio-economic status.

Prompt Engineering: Prompt engineering refers to creating, shaping, and fine-tuning inputs or queries to generate desired responses or behaviors from an AI language model.

Special Education: Special education is an educational approach focused on developing the individual potential of students. It employs learning programs and supportive measures specifically tailored to meet their unique needs.

Chapter 16
Use of Generative AI Tools to Facilitate Personalized Learning in the Flipped Classroom

Huixin Zhen
Universiti Sains Malaysis, Malaysia

Wan Ahmad Jaafar Wan Yahaya
Universiti Sains Malaysia, Malaysia

ABSTRACT

With the development of technology, AI has been the subject of intense research in the field of education, with ChatGPT, the adoption of generative AI in education. But generative AI has only gained attention in the last few years. Therefore, there are not many research results on the application of generative AI in flipped classrooms, and there are many questions that need to be explored and verified by researchers. In this study, a flipped classroom combined with generative AI tools to promote personalized learning was studied. A theme in the music course was selected for course design and a pilot study was conducted. The results show that teachers and students have very different views on this research, and this phenomenon is summarized and analyzed, and finally some suggestions are made to help better use generative AI tools to promote personalized learning in the flipped classroom.

INTRODUCTION

In the 21st century, there have been rapid development and major changes in the world economy, technology and other fields. If you want to follow the era development trend, education and learning is indispensable. Education provides a large number of talents for the development of various fields and industries in the world. Nowadays, the application of technology in education has been a very important part (Okoye et al., 2023; Mercader & Gairín, 2020). As a result, many higher education institutions have begun to introduce a large number of devices and technologies to assist classroom learning in teaching. Such as digital technology, Internet of Things technology, mobile applications, smart classroom, mi-

DOI: 10.4018/979-8-3693-1351-0.ch016

croclassroom, etc. (Viberg et al., 2023; Stojanovic et al., 2023). The use of these technologies and tools open up new opportunities for education.

At the same time, as the technology of artificial intelligence also began to show its role. With the increasing maturity of AI technology, AI is also applied to all aspects of life, such as medical care, finance, education and so on (Fui-Hoon et al, 2023). Artificial intelligence technology has many hidden uses in the field of education, such as the improvement of teaching effect, the immediacy of teaching feedback, the promotion of personalized learning, and the enhancement of students' learning initiative (Adiguzel et al, 2023). The emergence of ChatGPT had a huge impact on education.

With the development of technology, mobile electronic devices are becoming more and more indispensable in people's work and life, especially for students, who spend most of their time even in class. Since it is impossible to stop students from using electronic devices in the classroom, educators can use smart technology to assist students in learning, especially in higher education (Jurayev, 2023).

Because personalized learning can be well adapted to the different differences of learners in various aspects and provide diverse teaching for learners (Cevikbas & Kaiser, 2021), personalized learning has been paid attention by educators for a long time. The emergence of intelligent tutoring leads to the formation of personalized learning (Shemshack & Spector, 2020). Personalized learning is a type of learning, its purpose is to obtain different learning experience in the learning environment according to the individual needs of learners, learning objectives and so on (Shemshack et al, 2021). In personalized learning, educators can clearly analyze the needs of students based on each student's learning preferences, learning abilities, learning processes, learning outcomes, etc. Flexibly tailor the teaching plan for learners from the aspects of teaching methods, teaching objectives, teaching content, teaching results and so on (Raj & Renumol, 2022). While this kind of personalized learning is now possible, it remains one of the biggest challenges in modern education systems (Shemshack & Spector,2020).

Flipped classrooms also have the potential to promote personalized learning (Cevikbas & Kaiser, 2021). The flipped classroom is the reverse of the traditional classroom (Doğan et al, 2023), in the pre-class part of flipped classroom, students can obtain pre-class resources in any way they want and arrange their own learning at any time. More classroom activities also provide students with the possibility of personalized learning (Dalbani et al., 2021). Flipped classroom can not only improve students' learning performance, improve students' academic performance and enhance learners' engagement to a certain extent, but also create a more flexible personalized learning environment for learners (Zhang, 2023). The gamified flipped classroom teaching method, which combines games with flipped classroom, also promotes personalized learning while enhancing students' ability to cooperate and solve problems (Guerrero-Quiñonez et al, 2023), not only that, flipped classroom can also help learners with deep learning (Hsiao et al, 2023). The benefits of flipped classrooms have been demonstrated by many researchers (Falode & Mohammed, 2023; Fidan, 2023; McLean & Attardi, 2023; Vitta & Al-Hoorie, 2023; Playfoot, 2023).

In the field of education, flipped classroom has promoted personalized learning to a certain extent and improved students' academic performance. Although generative AI has its own risks, based on its uniqueness and advantages, we should pay more attention to how to use generative AI tools to help educators and learners better arrange learning according to different situations.

This study focuses on harnessing the special properties of generative AI tools and applying them to teaching strategies in flipped classrooms to verify their effectiveness in promoting personalized learning. The main contributions of this study are as follows:

.The general idea of the application of generative AI tools in flipped classroom.
.The specific process of the application of generative AI tools in the flipped classroom.
.A questionnaire survey was conducted for learners and teachers using generative AI tools in flipped classroom to facilitate personalized learning, to understand students' and teachers' views and reasons on the use of generative AI tools in flipped classroom to promote personalized learning.
.Explore the potential of generative AI tools to facilitate personalized learning in flipped classroom.
.Some suggestions for using generative AI tools in the flipped classroom to better promote personalized learning are made.

BACKGROUND

With the rapid development of artificial intelligence, every technological breakthrough and innovation will attract the concern and attention of all mankind. Some people are happy with their breakthroughs in technology, which can bring a lot of convenience to human life; Some people are worried about this technology, whether the development of artificial intelligence will eventually replace humans? Despite some concerns, the importance of generative AI tools in education cannot be overlooked (Neumann et al., 2023).

The term AI can be traced back to 1955, when John McCarthy et al. first introduced the concept. But the definition of AI varies from technology to technology. AI has applications in various fields, and in education, more and more scholars are focusing on the role of AI in education. Artificial intelligence is divided into generative AI and decision-making AI. Generative AI has been widely used in various fields, and it has become one of the important branches of AI technology. Generative AI has been widely used in various fields, it has become one of the important branches of AI technology, is constantly promoting the development and application of artificial intelligence, the emergence and development of generative artificial intelligence (AI) is having a deep impact on all aspects of human beings and new challenges. The development of AI has provided new ways and tools for learning in the field of education (Adiguzel et al, 2023).

With the rise of generative AI ChatGPT and many applications, a series of related generative AI software and website applications have been born, and researchers have conducted research on the related applications of generative AI in the field of education. The organic combination of generative AI and education will have what effect, positive or negative, which is worth thinking about. However, we still cannot deny the important influence and role of generative AI such as ChatGPT on various fields (Zhai, 2022). ChatGPT has the potential to revolutionize the field of education (Tlili et al., 2023).

Generative AI can be considered as a technology based on the model of machine learning and deep learning, which can generate text, audio, pictures and other content according to the user's language and thinking logic (Ernesto & Gerardou, 2023), the content that generative AI can generate includes but is not limited to the above several items. The most widely known web for generative AI is ChatGPT, the emergence of ChatGPT has had a huge impact on the field of education, but it has also had a significant impact on the teaching model. It becomes a learning aid for teachers and students, primarily for content creation. This tool is to give personalized explanations and feedback in time through individual conversations, thus promoting personalized learning for users.

Flipped classroom is a kind of teaching paradigm in which the class time and homework are exchanged in the traditional classroom (Doğan,Batdı, & Yaşar, 2023). Using this kind of teaching strategy can promote students' autonomous learning and realize personalized teaching, to improve students' learning performance and learning engagement. Many researchers have verified the benefits of flipped classroom in their studies, including the positive effect of using flipped classroom methods in enhancing personalized learning (Cevikbas & Kaiser, 2022; Gallardo et al., 2022; Wang et al., 2022; Shen & Chang, 2023). Generative AI tools led by ChatGPT have attracted a lot of attention in the field of education since their appearance. ChatGPT can put forward some effective suggestions for educators. It can also provide various scenarios for collaborative learning in classroom activities, which is more targeted than traditional flipped classroom (Lo, 2023). The role of generative AI tools in education and teaching cannot be ignored, and the application of generative AI in teaching and learning will be the general trend.

This research aims to integrate flipped classroom with generative AI, students in flipped classroom plan their learning according to their own abilities and preferences, combined with generative AI's ability to generate content based on users' individual needs and preferences, this allows for a deeper alignment with students' individual learning needs, motivate students to learn, to achieve high quality teaching effect. Using generative AI tools to intervene with different stages pre-class, in-class and post-class, promote personalized learning for learners, and enhance the learning experience of learners and enhance the engagement of students.

LITERATURE REVIEW

Personalized Learning

With the emphasis on personalized learning in education, there is a wealth of research on ways to promote personalized learning. Various teaching strategies have also attracted the attention of educators. Flipped classroom is a teaching paradigm that promotes teachers' personalized teaching and students' personalized learning, and the use of blended teaching methods also promotes personalized learning (Engel & Coll, 2022). There are also many researchers focusing on the development of personalized learning systems, in the hope that students can also conduct personalized learning in their spare time (Welch Bacon & Gaither, 2020). From the above research, no matter the change of teaching mode or the development of various learning systems, the educational concept is moving towards the goal of student-oriented, so that the teaching is more in line with the needs of each learner and provides students with personalized learning experience.

With the increasing maturity of AI technology, the potential of AI's unique characteristics in promoting personalized learning has also attracted the attention of many researchers. He (2017) has proposed in his research that AI is one of the key technologies to promote personalized learning, and this view has also been verified in the subsequent topics of other researchers, Peng et al. (2019) Creating intelligent learning environments through AI technology to facilitate personalized learning. Walkington and Bernacki (2020) discussed several dimensions of personalized learning methods and argued that personalized learning can be implemented in different learning depths, including shallow learning and deep learning; Personalized learning can also be adapted to different groups, which can be used on a small scale or a large scale; Finally, the active status of personalized learning can be different, can be active status or passive status. Personalized learning is still a major challenge in education, even though technology is evolving to facilitate it. AI technology can also provide support for personalized learning in classroom teaching (Huang et al., 2023).

Although there are some ethical problems in the application of AI technology in education (Nguyen et al., 2023), it is undeniable that the application of AI technology in education provides new ideas for all aspects of education, and at the same time, the development of the education field also ushered in new opportunities. Although the continuous development of technology has promoted personalized learning, it is still a major challenge in the field of education (Shemshack & Spector,2020).

Flipped Classroom

Flipped classroom is the opposite of traditional classroom. Students learn knowledge and prepare for class activities before class and carry out deep learning in class through classroom tasks, practices, discussions and other ways to increase their understanding of knowledge (Vitta & Hoorie, 2023). During flipped classroom, more attention is paid to the collaborative learning ability between students and their peers and the interaction between teachers and students (Sointu et al, 2023). At the same time, the exchange of extracurricular time and in-class time tasks also enables students to carry out personalized learning more in line with their own needs.

Many studies have confirmed the advantages of flipped classroom over traditional classroom. The practical research of flipped classroom in science courses shows that flipped classroom has the greatest positive effect when it is implemented in physics and chemistry (Doğan et al., 2023). Turan (2023) conducted a meta-analysis of the relevant research literature on the use of flipped classroom strategy in science education, mainly focusing on the literature of college students as the research object and selected 18 literatures. According to the final performance and learning outcomes of students, the use of flipped classroom is effective. Torres-Martin et al. (2022) took achievement as one of the important basis to measure the effectiveness of flipped classroom implementation, and the results confirmed that flipped classroom has a significant impact on student achievement. Although the above studies have confirmed that flipped classroom has a positive effect on learners' learning performance and learning results, there is no excessive elaboration on the promotion of personalized learning.

Shen and Chang (2023) studied the experimental group and the control group, and the results also showed that the use of flipped classroom teaching strategy can promote students to learn more deeply and cultivate students' higher-order thinking. Also in the medical field, the use of flipped classrooms is helpful for students' learning, Barranquero et al. (2023) found in their research that when flipped classroom teaching strategy is used in nursing education, teachers and students have high satisfaction, and the use of this strategy can also improve the learning performance of nursing students. Similarly, a study explored flipped classroom in nursing and health courses and found that students' academic achievement, learning autonomy, and classroom performance were significantly improved after using flipped classroom (Banks & Kay, 2022). When the teaching strategy is changed to flipped classroom, students' pressure value for homework is also reduced (Aydin & Demirer, 2022). These studies all affirm the significant role of flipped classroom in promoting students' deep learning and higher order thinking.

Although flipped classroom has been favored by educators in recent years, if there is a lack of appropriate teaching tools to assist students in classroom activities, students' learning results may fall short of the expected standards (Hwang & Chen, 2023). The emergence of various generative AI tools provides new learning tools for flipped classroom. The use of AI-supported personalized recommendations, audio, video, etc. in flipped classroom environments can improve students' academic performance and learning engagement (Huang et al., 2023). However, whether the use of generative AI tools will have an impact on personalized learning for teachers and students needs further investigation.

Generative AI in Education

The appearance of ChatGPT brings generative AI to the public. As a special AI technology, generative AI is welcomed by the public and rapidly popularized in education, medical treatment, art and other fields. The use of generative AI tools will have a huge impact on higher education (Gimpel et al., 2023). However, GAI is still a new paradigm for educators (Thomas, 2023).

Generative AI has had a great impact on the education sector. It can be used to flexibly develop personalized learning plans for students according to their real needs and personal preferences, and at the same time give personalized and timely feedback to students through their various performances (Ahmad et al, 2023). The use of generative AI tools can also help students acquire basic knowledge faster (Murugesan & Cherukuri, 2023).

Generative AI offers a new opportunity for science and healthcare with its unique information processing capabilities, resulting in higher resource utilization and improved efficiency (Varghese & Chapiro, 2023). Similarly, Kothari (2023) in his research, a series of tools such as generative AI in the field of medical, especially in cancer surgical care, can provide patients and caregivers with nursing plans, nursing order, drug recommendation, etc., which can ensure more perfect postoperative care of cancer patients to a certain extent.

In the study of Lim et al. (2023), generative AI is defined as a deep learning-based AI technology that can generate text, pictures, audio and other content according to the user's habitual logic and language. Generative AI can provide some ideas and methods in craft education, but there are some worrying problems to some extent, such as it may not be helpful for users' skills improvement, and there may be some problems in copyright (Vartiainen & Tedre, 2023). Generative AI has also received a lot of attention in the field of materials science. After effective training of generative AI tools, several major problems encountered in materials science can be interpreted to a certain extent and corresponding suggestions can be put forward to provide users with some new ideas (Liu, 2023). Lv (2023) integrated AI technology into the flipped classroom of the music course and eventually found that the integration of the two methods could promote the effect of students learning piano. Regarding the attitude of Chan and Hu (2023) toward students' generative AI, most students said that they realized the role and importance of personalized learning through generative AI, and at the same time, it could promote students' learning enthusiasm.

Due to its continuous learning ability and the timeliness of its feedback, generative AI can provide users with corresponding text information, correct spelling and correct grammar in the field of geography and environment, to help improve students' efficiency in learning geography and environment and other related courses (Chang & Kidman, 2023). Bilgram and Laarmann (2023) believe that generative artificial intelligence plays a great role in the generation of ideas and the creation of prototypes, providing new ideas for design and other fields, and people can make good use of generative AI tools to promote innovation.

The above research verifies the effectiveness of generative AI technology in education, but its use in the flipped classroom of music courses remains to be further explored.

Flipped Classroom With Generative AI

At present, there are few research on the use of generative AI tools in flipped classroom, and the effectiveness of generative AI in flipped classroom teaching strategies needs to be explored and verified by more researchers. Cevikbas and Kaiser (2021) also mentioned in their research that without technology to support personalized feedback and evaluation in the flipped classroom teaching of personalized learning, personalized learning will also encounter obstacles. To maximize the use of flipped classroom to promote personalized learning, we need to rely on a series of technical means. The current research on the application of generative AI tools in flipped classrooms mainly focuses on ChatGPT (Yilmaz, R. & Yilmaz, F.,2023). Wang et al. (2023) conducted a study on the quality of college students using ChatGPT to retrieve relevant information in the flipped classroom method. If students can master the instruction method at the beginning, they will get high-quality results and thus improve their learning efficiency, however, there is no in-depth research on promoting personalized learning. Uchiyama et al. (2023) proposed that in pre-class learning in flipped classroom, ChatGPT can provide timely feedback for students' questions and answer their doubts for the first time, but it does not clearly show that it has a positive effect on enhancing personalized learning. Alshahrani (2023) also sorted out the research trend of ChatGPT in blended learning and proposed that the application of ChatGPT greatly improved students' learning engagement and provided students with personalized learning experience. However, it was only concluded through meta-analysis of relevant literatures. Experiments and data collection have not been conducted for further verification, and further research is needed to promote personalized learning. The application of large-scale language model can provide a more personalized learning style for flipped classroom (Li et al., 2023).

Through the above research, it can be found that the application of generative AI tools in education is mainly focused on the current hot ChaGPT, which is undoubtedly effective in promoting learning. And there have been some studies to confirm this result, but most of the studies are still in the category of education, and it is about the segmentation of each group, each discipline remains to be explored, meanwhile, the application of generative AI to flipped classroom remains to be further studied.

METHOD

Using a quantitative approach, and use ex post facto and non-experimental (Colomo-Magaña, 2023). Using questionnaires as a research tool, the study surveyed teachers' and students' perceptions of the use of generative AI tools to facilitate personalized learning in the flipped classroom using a five-level Likert scale: strongly agree, agree, neither agree nor disagree, disagree, strongly disagree. At the same time, the tested person should attach the corresponding reason. The contents of the questionnaire were modified according to the opinions of two teachers with more than 5 years of teaching experience and an expert from another school, and finally put into use.

RESEARCH PROCESS

This research focuses on the effect of the application of generative AI tools in the flipped classroom on student learning, especially on the promotion of personalized learning. The goal is to assess how these tools, combined with the flipped classroom, can facilitate personalized learning for students and improve the teaching process.

This research needs to be carried out over a long period of time, but subsequent research should start from curriculum design. The first step of this research is the design of the curriculum. The implementation in flipped classroom teaching is mainly reflected in the different stages of the teaching process. The following is a description of the idea of this study, and the overall idea and framework can be more intuitive in Figure 1.

Before class, it is an important stage of the flipped classroom + generative AI tool teaching mode. Students must master the target knowledge content with various generative AI tools before class, so that they can carry out corresponding tasks in class activities. Teachers use generative AI tools to generate some pre-class content that is in line with the learning theme and can attract students, for example, text, pictures, audio and video related to the topic content, it is integrated with relevant videos recorded by teachers and uploaded to the online learning platform so that learners can arrange their own time to learn the learning content before class. While conducting unsupervised learning for learners. Students learn the subject matter without explicit teacher guidance, at the same time, generative AI tools are used to independently explore the topic and discover new knowledge and provide new ideas; At the same time, in the stage of self-learning before class, learners can use generative AI tools to get timely feedback when they encounter confusion and want to communicate. Through pre-class learning and timely feedback provided by generative AI tools, students have a deeper grasp of the knowledge to be learned before class and are more adept in carrying out activities and tasks in class.

In-class, teachers design some human-computer interaction and interaction problems between students-students and between students-teachers according to the teaching objectives and teaching needs, and students can use generative AI tools that they are familiar with and can skillfully use (eg: ChatGPT, Fliki Ai, You.com, Aistudio, ChatGPT.com, Leonardo Ai and Humata.ai et al.), input learners own doubts and receive personalized feedback, or use generative AI tools to solve problems in the classroom, combine the feedback provided by generative AI tools to communicate and collaborate with other peers in the classroom,communicate and integrate what each learner has gained, through group discussion, debate, collaborative task completion and other classroom activities to complete the mastery of knowledge.

Post-class, teachers can use generative AI tools to help evaluate students' performance efficiently, teachers are able to analyze student responses, assess student learning and give personalized feedback to students (Ivannova, 2022).

In flipped classroom, generative AI tools are used to assist students' personalized learning, so that each link of learning finally completes the education closed loop of each topic content, so that each link reflects personalized learning, and gives students more options and forms, which not only promotes students' personalized learning, but also improves their creative ability and innovative thinking in learning.

In this research, rhythm in college music courses is taken as the design theme, and generative AI tools are used to carry out the teaching design of this topic.

Figure 1. General ideal

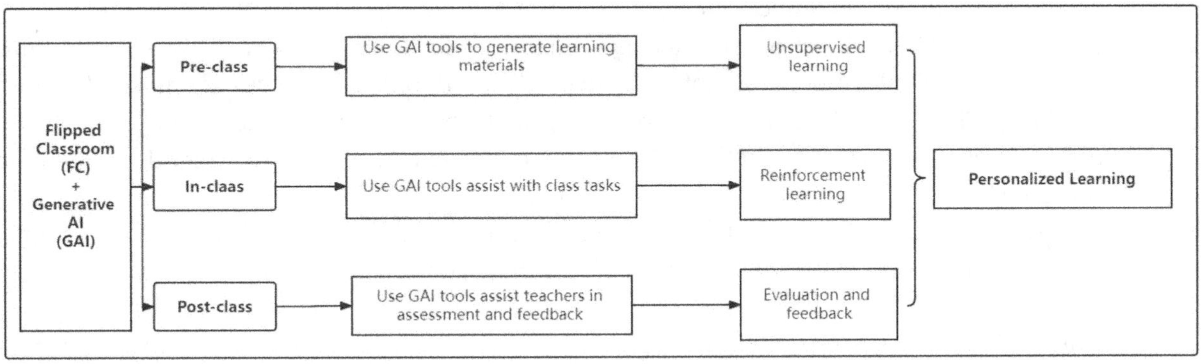

Specific Process

Pre-Class

Teachers use ChatGPT to provide curriculum design suggestions for teaching related topics before class:

It includes the name of the theme, the choice of music, the creation of the context of classroom activities in flipped classroom, and the creation of exercises.

According to the suggestion of ChatGPT, the name of this study topic is determined to be *Rhythm: Understanding the Basics*.

The following are questions and answers from teachers using Chat GPT.

Teacher: What kind of music do you recommend on the rhythm topic?

ChatGPT: When teaching about rhythm in music, it's essential to choose a variety of music examples that highlight different rhythmic elements. Here are some music recommendations for various aspects of rhythm:

Basic Rhythmic Elements: For teaching the basics of rhythm and rhythmic notation, consider using simple songs with clear and consistent rhythms. Examples include "Twinkle, Twinkle, Little Star" for basic quarter-note rhythms or "Row, Row, Row Your Boat" for simple time signatures.

Time Signatures: To illustrate different time signatures, you can use songs with non-standard time signatures. "Take Five" by Dave Brubeck in 5/4 time is an excellent choice for demonstrating an unconventional time signature.

Syncopation: Syncopation is an important rhythmic concept. Jazz music, especially songs like "It Don't Mean a Thing (If It Ain't Got That Swing)" by Duke Ellington, can showcase syncopated rhythms.

Complex Rhythms: For more advanced students, consider pieces with complex rhythms. "Mars, the Bringer of War" from Gustav Holst's "The Planets" features intricate rhythms and time changes.

Polyrhythms and Polymeters: Songs like "Riders on the Storm" by The Doors incorporate polymeter, while African drumming ensembles often demonstrate polyrhythmic patterns.

Latin Rhythms: Latin music, such as salsa or samba, offers a rich source of rhythms. "Oye Como Va" by Tito Puente is a classic example of Latin rhythm.

African Drumming: African drumming ensembles, such as those from West Africa, are excellent for exploring intricate polyrhythmic patterns.
Electronic and Techno Music: Electronic and techno genres often feature repetitive and evolving rhythms. Tracks by artists like Daft Punk or Aphex Twin can be used to discuss electronic music rhythms.
Hip-Hop and Rap: Hip-hop and rap music showcase rhythm through lyrics and beats. Songs like "Lose Yourself" by Eminem or "Straight Outta Compton" by N.W.A. can be analyzed for their rhythmic components.
Cross-Cultural Comparisons: Compare rhythmic elements across different musical genres. For example, you can contrast the rhythms in a classical waltz with those in a reggae song.

According to ChatGPT's answer, the learning video resources are recorded according to the teaching needs of the subject, and creative videos are generated and edited with the help of other generative AI tools (like Fliki AI), and the resources are uploaded to the online learning platform.

Figure 2. Pre-class, student use ChatGPT to help study

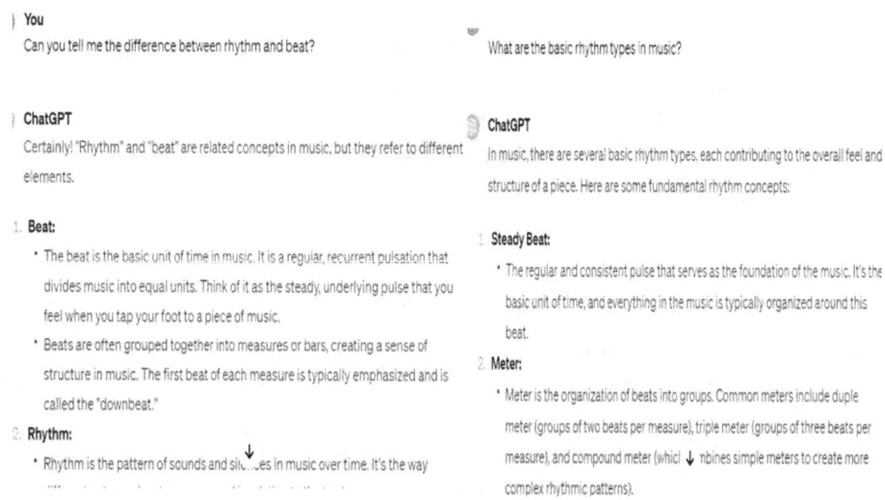

In-Class

The in-class link of flipped classroom is a link to strengthen cognition, apply knowledge and consolidate knowledge. Some tasks and activities should be designed around knowledge themes as much as possible, while taking into account the opportunities for students to use generative AI tools. Design tasks and activities for human-computer interaction, student-student interaction, and teacher-student interaction.

1. Groups were divided into groups, and the teacher issued a task: each group of students chose two different songs and recorded their rhythms, and analyzed how their rhythms were different, and tried to create music fragments with these rhythms.

The subjects were divided into groups: Before grouping, 60 subjects' learning habits, learning preferences, cognitive ability, learning ability, and even their own strengths and weaknesses in learning were collected, and the information was input into ChatGPT to group each student according to their specific situation and needs.

2. Students use their own generative AI tools to assist them in completing tasks.

During class activities, students use generative AI tools to explore the differences between the styles and rhythm types of two different kinds of music, and then use the rhythm to create music fragments from different angles.

Figure 3. Two groups of students used two GAI tools, Soundraw and Stable Audio, to create music

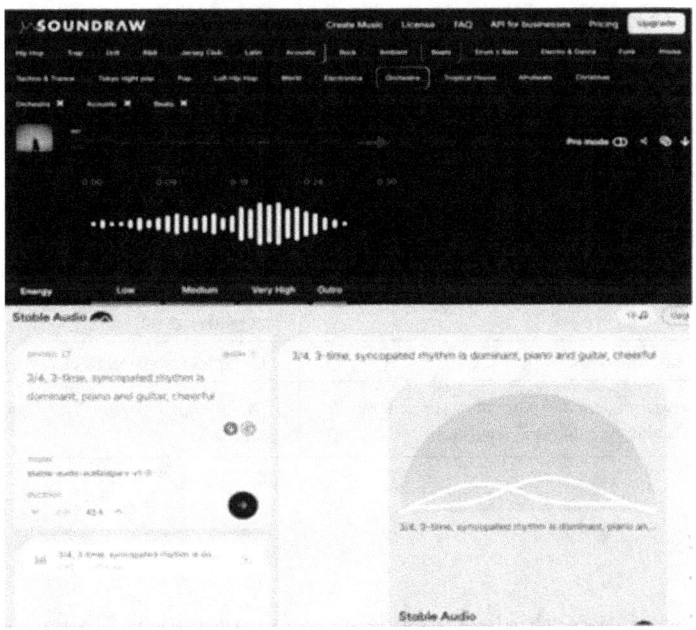

3.Group presentation.

Post-Class

Teachers conduct targeted assessments of students' work and performance based on student performance and provide specific feedback to each student.

The following is the sorted course design table (*Table 1*):

Table 1. Sorted course design

Course Design				
Stage Teacher Student				
Flipped classroom + GAI	Pre-class	1. Use the ChatGPT tool to determine the theme of this lesson: *Rhythm: Understanding the Basics*	1. Plan and arrange the learning of rhythm target knowledge content at any time	Unsupervised Learning
		2. Record the online material of this section in combination with ChatGPT's suggestions, and edit and record creative videos with the help of generative AI tool, Fliki	2. Problems that need to be solved in time during the learning process are learned with any generative AI tools	
		3. Upload the video to the learning management system and set learning goals before class	3. If have any questions, you can ask for help from teachers and classmates through the message platform of the learning management system	
	In-class	1. According to the classroom task suggestions given by ChatGPT, modify the release task: randomly select two pieces of music to analyze which rhythm types, beats, styles and differences are included. And create a musical fragment based on each musical element	1. Through listening to music and using generative AI tools to analyze music and draw conclusions through classroom collaboration	Reinforcement Learning
		2. Observe the progress of each group of students at any time, to answer questions for students in time and provide some help for students to use generative AI tools	2. After preliminarily determining the rhythm type and music style to be used, use the generative AI tool of music to assist the creation of music fragments	
		3. Check and comment on the classroom task results	3. Each group makes a presentation on the creative results	
	Post-class	1. Release the homework	1. Complete homework as review	Evaluation and feedback
		2. Analyze student assignments with generative AI tools and give targeted feedback	2. Make improvements based on feedback	

Result Analysis

Due to limited time, a total of 60 third-year students in a university in China were selected to conduct a one-week pilot study on the implementation of rhythm-themed teaching, and a questionnaire survey was conducted among the tested students on the use of generative AI tools to promote personalized teaching in flipped classroom.

The results showed that 43% of students strongly agreed, 8% agreed, 8% neither agreed nor disagreed, 29% disagreed and 12% strongly disagreed.

According to the reason description in the questionnaire, we summarized the following reasons:

1. Students choose consent (strongly agree and agree), one of the reasons is that generative AI tools can provide timely feedback to help solve problems before class, and the other reason is that they can help provide ideas to solve problems and complete tasks during class.

Figure 4. Students' views on the use of GAI tools in the flipped classroom can facilitate personalized learning

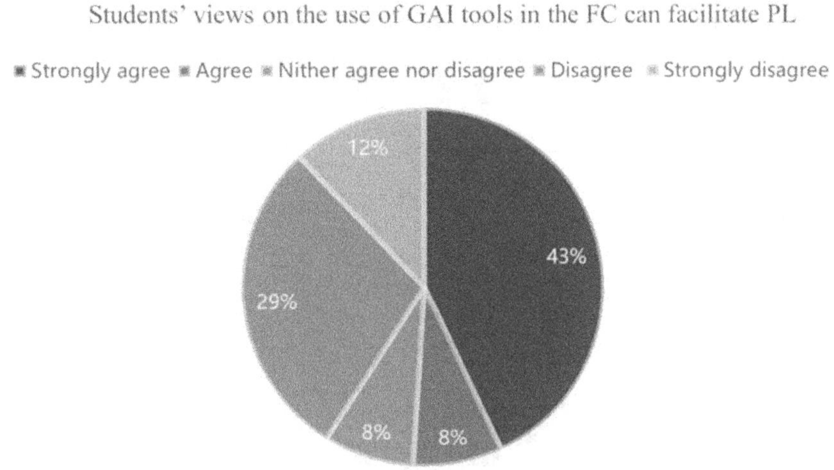

2. Students choose to disagree (disagree and strongly disagree), one of the reasons is that students cannot use generative AI tools well and do not know how to use instructions effectively. The second reason is that students cannot independently judge the correctness of the generated content in the process of using generative AI tools. A small number of students believe that using generative AI tools is a waste of time.

The following are some of the reasons students gave in the questionnaire:

Student 1: Flipped classroom itself allows us to explore freely in class according to our own abilities, preferences, etc. The use of generative AI tools can provide innovation and ideas for our group discussions and group tasks and generate corresponding text and audio according to our own input content, so it is very important for personalized teaching.

Student 2: I think the use of generative AI tools can promote our personalized learning in some respects, but I am not very skilled in the use of various generative AI tools, so I choose to agree.

Student 3: I think when I learn pre-class knowledge, I can ask generative AI tools when I encounter problems, which can help me solve problems in time.

Student 4: Because I did not have more time to get familiar with the use of generative AI tools before this teaching method, my efficiency in learning became low.

Student 5: Using generative AI function is a waste of time, I just want to learn the relevant knowledge of a topic normally.

Student 6: In the process of using generative AI tools, it has provided me with wrong learning information, which has caused me to distrust such tools.

The tested teachers conducted a questionnaire survey on whether teachers can promote personalized learning by using generative AI tools in flipped classroom. The results show that 78% of teachers strongly agree, 12% of teachers agree, 6% of teachers neither agree nor oppose, 2% of teachers disagree and 2% of teachers strongly disagree.

Figure 5. Teachers' views on the use of GAI tools in the Flipped classroom can facilitate personalized learning

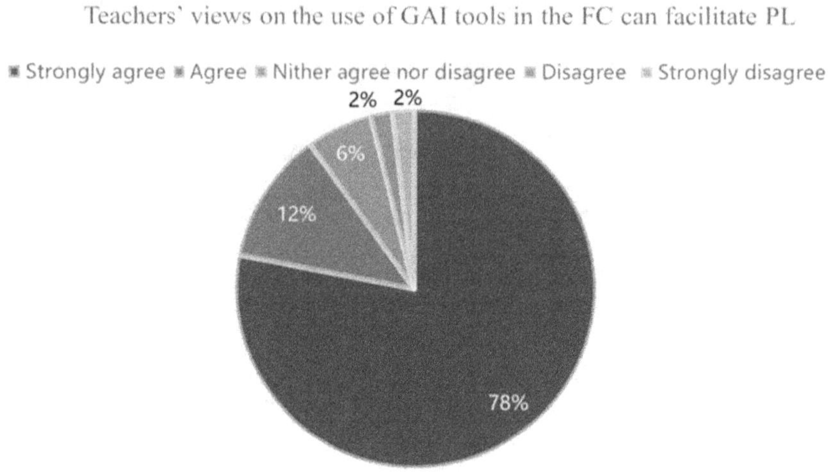

According to the reasons described in the questionnaire, the following points are summarized:

1. Teachers choose consent (strongly agree and agree), because the use of technology to promote teaching has been the trend of The Times, and generative AI, with its learning ability and understanding ability, can provide reference according to the actual situation of users.
2. Teachers choose to disagree (strongly disagree and disagree), one of the reasons is that these teachers are too old to master the tools related to science and technology; the second reason is that the teaching philosophy has not changed.

The following are the reasons given by some teachers in the questionnaire:

Teacher 1: The emergence of generative AI is explosive. If teachers can guide students to use these tools in the flipped classroom model, it will greatly promote personalized learning.

Teacher 2: Teachers use generative AI tools in flipped classroom teaching strategies, which can make personalized learning videos, generate texts, and provide ideas, which greatly reduces teachers' lesson preparation time.

Teacher 3: The current research trend is that generative AI plays a significant role in education, but I have no experience in this kind of teaching and have not conducted actual verification, so I neither agree nor oppose.

Teacher 4: I am too old to use high-tech equipment and tools. Flipped classroom is the best method of personalized learning for me, and I may not use generative AI tools for auxiliary teaching.

Teacher 5: I think the use of such tools in flipped classrooms will not promote personalized teaching. On the contrary, it will make some students lose their ability to explore and think about homework independently.

Teacher 6: The use of generative AI tools can provide students with some timely feedback, which makes up for the teacher's inability to respond to students' questions in all aspects of flipped classroom, so it has the potential to promote personalized learning.

DISCUSSION AND RECOMMENDATIONS

The results discussed in this study have significant implications for flipped classroom, and the use of generative AI tools such as ChatGPT in flipped classroom has potential to promote personalized learning.

From the above research, it can be seen that teachers and students hold completely different views on the topic of using AI tools to promote personalized learning in flipped classroom. As educators, most teachers have the sensitivity to educational tools and make use of the unique nature of generative AI to play its role in promoting personalized learning before, during and after classes in flipped classroom. For students, the correct use of generative AI tools and the benefits of learning need to be slowly understood in their future learning. Overall, the findings highlight the important role of GAI tools in promoting personalized learning in the flipped classroom, however, we must know how to use them properly and avoid some existing problems such as ethical and integrity issues. To properly apply generative AI in the flipped classroom and facilitate personalized learning, here are some suggestions:

1. Set up corresponding training courses on generative AI for teachers, so that teachers can fully master the principles, use methods and instruction input methods of generative AI, and enable educators to have the ability to use relevant tools to prepare materials before class and give feedback after class (Halaweh, 2023).
2. Teachers should change their teaching concepts and be good at using new technologies to improve teaching results (Tlili, 2023).
3. Teachers should reasonably plan the use of generative AI in the flipped classroom and how to use it and in what way.
4. Train students on the use of generative AI tools, so that students can adapt to the correct use of generative AI tools for learning at the fastest speed.
5. Educators set rules for the use of AI tools and do their best to avoid some of the drawbacks of generative AI, such as academic integrity (Elbanna & Armstrong, 2023).

Of course, there are still some limitations in this study. First, due to the time, the pilot study is too short; Second, the study sample is small, not universal; Third, this study is only for one university in China, and whether it can be applied to other schools remains to be explored.

FUTURE RESEARCH DIRECTIONS

According to the development trend of generative AI, in the future related research, more attention should be paid to the integration of applied AI technology and classroom teaching (İpek et al., 2023). Reasonable use of generative AI tools to effectively help learners achieve personalized learning in teaching, so as to improve teaching effect, improve students' learning efficiency, and achieve teaching goals. But how to avoid the drawbacks of generative AI and effectively use the educational role of generative AI to have a positive impact on students' learning still needs to be further studied by researchers.

CONCLUSION

This study studies the application of generative AI tools in the flipped classroom, and further studies the promotion of personalized learning. The results of this study suggest that the combination of generative AI tools with the flipped classroom is essential to facilitate personalized learning. For learner groups, the use of generative AI tools can provide them with more personalized learning guidance and answers to their doubts in a timely manner. For educators, the use of generative AI tools can help teachers better design courses and classroom activities, as well as provide timely feedback on students' homework (Atlas, 2023).

At the same time, this study believes that generative AI has great potential in higher education. By combining these tools with the flipped classroom, educators can design and deliver personalized learning experiences to students, it provides some latest ideas and directions for the application of AI in the field of education (Alshahrani, 2023). While providing convenience for education and improving some problems in education, generative AI inevitably has some ethical problems, such as whether students have some integrity problems in using generative AI tools, or whether there are moral deficiencies (Qadir, 2023).

Generative AI offers a new path to personalized learning, with the ultimate goal of preparing students to cope in a rapidly changing world of information. Through the attention and application of AI-related technologies, education has always kept pace with The Times, and at the same time can more calmly face the challenges brought by the development of science and technology.

COMPETING INTERESTS AND FUNDING STATEMENTS

The authors of this publication declare there are no competing interests.

This research received no specific grant from any funding agency in the public, commercial, or not-for-profit sectors. Funding for this research was covered by the authors of the article.

REFERENCES

Adiguzel, T., Kaya, M. H., & Cansu, F. K. (2023). Revolutionizing education with AI: Exploring the transformative potential of ChatGPT. *Contemporary Educational Technology*, *15*(3), ep429. doi:10.30935/cedtech/13152

Ahmad, N., Murugesan, S., & Kshetri, N. (2023). Generative Artificial Intelligence and the Education Sector. *Computer*, *56*(6), 72–76. doi:10.1109/MC.2023.3263576

Alshahrani, A. (2023). The impact of ChatGPT on blended learning: Current trends and future research directions. *International Journal of Data and Network Science*, *7*(4), 2029–2040. doi:10.5267/j.ijdns.2023.6.010

Awidi, I. T., & Paynter, M. (2019). The impact of a flipped classroom approach on student learning experience. *Computers & Education*, *128*, 269–283. doi:10.1016/j.compedu.2018.09.013

Aydin, B., & Demirer, V. (2022). Are flipped classrooms less stressful and more successful? An experimental study on college students. *International Journal of Educational Technology in Higher Education*, *19*(1), 55. doi:10.1186/s41239-022-00360-8

Banks, L., & Kay, R. (2022). Exploring flipped classrooms in undergraduate nursing and health science: A systematic review. *Nurse Education in Practice*, *64*, 103417. doi:10.1016/j.nepr.2022.103417 PMID:36113354

Barranquero-Herbosa, M., Abajas-Bustillo, R., & Ortego-Maté, C. (2022). Effectiveness of flipped classroom in nursing education. A systematic review of systematic and integrative reviews. *International Journal of Nursing Studies*, *135*, 104327. doi:10.1016/j.ijnurstu.2022.104327 PMID:35944288

Bilgram, V., & Laarmann, F. (2023). Accelerating Innovation with Generative AI: AI- augmented Digital Prototyping and Innovation Methods. *IEEE Engineering Management Review*, *51*(2), 18–25. doi:10.1109/EMR.2023.3272799

Canese, L., Cardarilli, G. C., Di Nunzio, L., Fazzolari, R., Giardino, D., Re, M., & Spanò, S. (2021). Multi-agent reinforcement learning: A review of challenges and applications. *Applied Sciences (Basel, Switzerland)*, *11*(11), 4948. doi:10.3390/app11114948

Cevikbas, M., & Kaiser, G. (2022). Promoting personalized learning in flipped classrooms: A systematic review study. *Sustainability (Basel)*, *14*(18), 11393. doi:10.3390/su141811393

Chan, C. K., & Hu, W. (2023). *Students' Voices on Generative AI: Perceptions, Benefits, and Challenges in Higher Education.* ArXiv. /abs/2305.00290

Chang, C. H., & Kidman, G. (2023). The rise of generative artificial intelligence (AI) language models-challenges and opportunities for geographical and environmental education. *International Research in Geographical and Environmental Education*, *32*(2), 85–89. doi:10.1080/10382046.2023.2194036

Chiu, T. K. F. (2023). The impact of Generative AI (GenAI) on practices, policies and research direction in education: A case of ChatGPT and Midjourney. *Interactive Learning Environments*, 1–17. doi: 10.1080/10494820.2023.2253861

Colomo-Magaña, E., Soto-Varela, R., Ruiz-Palmero, J., & Gómez-García, M. (2020). University students' perception of the usefulness of the flipped classroom methodology. *Education Sciences*, *10*(10), 275. doi:10.3390/educsci10100275

Dalbani, H., Eissa, S., Fatimah, S., & Almusharraf, N. (2021). Transitioning to Flipped Classrooms: Instructors' Perspectives. *Sustainability (Basel)*, *14*(20), 13426. doi:10.3390/su142013426

Doğan, Y., Batdı, V., & Yaşar, M. D. (2023). Effectiveness of flipped classroom practices in teaching of science: A mixed research synthesis. *Research in Science & Technological Education*, *41*(1), 393–421. doi:10.1080/02635143.2021.1909553

Dong, S., Wang, P., & Abbas, K. (2021). A survey on deep learning and its applications. *Computer Science Review*, *40*, 100379. doi:10.1016/j.cosrev.2021.100379

Eke, D. O. (2023). ChatGPT and the rise of generative AI: Threat to academic integrity? *Journal of Responsible Technology*, *13*, 100060. doi:10.1016/j.jrt.2023.100060

Elbanna, S., & Armstrong, L. (2023). Exploring the integration of ChatGPT in education: adapting for the future. *Management & Sustainability: An Arab Review*.

Engel, A., & Coll, C. (2022). Hybrid teaching and learning environments to promote personalized learning. *RIED-Revista Iberoamericana de Educacion a Distancia*, 225-242.

Erbil, D. G. (2020). A Review of Flipped Classroom and Cooperative Learning Method Within the Context of Vygotsky Theory. *Frontiers in Psychology*, *11*, 539791. doi:10.3389/fpsyg.2020.01157 PMID:32655437

Ernesto, D., & Gerardou, F. S. (2023). Challenges and Opportunities of Generative AI for Higher Education as Explained by ChatGPT. *Education Sciences*, *13*(9), 856. doi:10.3390/educsci13090856

Falode, O. C., & Mohammed, I. A. (2023). Improving students' geography achievement using computer simulation and animation packages in flipped classroom settings. *Journal of Digital Educational Technology*, *3*(2), ep2303. doi:10.30935/jdet/13106

Fidan, M. (2023). The effects of microlearning-supported flipped classroom on pre- service teachers' learning performance, motivation and engagement. *Education and Information Technologies*, *28*(10), 1–28. doi:10.1007/s10639-023-11639-2 PMID:37361810

Fui-Hoon Nah, F., Zheng, R., Cai, J., Siau, K., & Chen, L. (2023). Generative AI and ChatGPT: Applications, challenges, and AI-human collaboration. *Journal of Information Technology Case and Application Research*, *25*(3), 277–304. doi:10.1080/15228053.2023.2233814

Gallardo-Guerrero, A. M., Maciá-Andreu, M. J., Conde-Pascual, E., Sánchez-Sáez, J. A., Zurita-Ortiz, B., & García-Tascón, M. (2022). From flipped classroom to personalised learning as an innovative teaching methodology in the area of sports management in Physical Activity and Sport Sciences. *Sustainability (Basel)*, *14*(13), 7714. doi:10.3390/su14137714

Gimpel, H., Hall, K., Decker, S., Eymann, T., Lämmermann, L., Mädche, A., & Vandrik, S. (2023). *Unlocking the power of generative AI models and systems such as GPT-4 and ChatGPT for higher education: A guide for students and lecturers (No. 02-2023)*. Hohenheim Discussion Papers in Business, Economics and Social Sciences.

Glielmo, A., Husic, B. E., Rodriguez, A., Clementi, C., Noé, F., & Laio, A. (2021). Unsupervised learning methods for molecular simulation data. *Chemical Reviews*, *121*(16), 9722–9758. doi:10.1021/acs.chemrev.0c01195 PMID:33945269

Guerrero-Quiñonez, A. J., Guagua, O. Q., & Barrera-Proaño, R. G. (2023). Gamified flipped classroom as a pedagogical strategy in higher education: From a systematic vision. *Ibero-American Journal of Education & Society Research*, *3*(1), 238–243. doi:10.56183/iberoeds.v3i1.622

Gupta, M., Akiri, C., Aryal, K., Parker, E., & Praharaj, L. (2023). From ChatGPT to ThreatGPT: Impact of generative AI in cybersecurity and privacy. *IEEE Access : Practical Innovations, Open Solutions*, *11*, 80218–80245. doi:10.1109/ACCESS.2023.3300381

Hsiao, I. C. V., Hung, S. T. A., & Huang, H. T. D. (2023). The flipped classroom approach in an English for specific purposes (ESP) course: A quasi-experimental study on learners' self-efficacy, study process, and learning performances. *Journal of Research on Technology in Education*, *55*(3), 507–526. doi:10.1080/15391523.2021.1976329

He, K. K. (2017). Theories, techniques and methods to promote personalized learning. *Open Education Research, 23*(2).

Holmström, J. (2022). From AI to digital transformation: The AI readiness framework. *Business Horizons*, *65*(3), 329–339. doi:10.1016/j.bushor.2021.03.006

Huang, A. Y., Lu, O. H., & Yang, S. J. (2023). Effects of artificial Intelligence–Enabled personalized recommendations on learners' learning engagement, motivation, and outcomes in a flipped classroom. *Computers & Education*, *194*, 104684. doi:10.1016/j.compedu.2022.104684

Huang, H., & Rust, R. T. (2020). Engaged to a Robot? The Role of AI in Service. *Journal of Service Research*. Advance online publication. doi:10.1177/1094670520902266

Hwang, G. J., & Chen, P. Y. (2023). Effects of a collective problem-solving promotion- based flipped classroom on students' learning performances and interactive patterns. *Interactive Learning Environments*, *31*(5), 2513–2528. doi:10.1080/10494820.2019.1568263

İpek, Z. H., Gözüm, A. İ. C., Papadakis, S., & Kallogiannakis, M. (2023). Educational Applications of the ChatGPT AI System: A Systematic Review Research. *International Journal (Toronto, Ont.)*, *12*(3), 26–55.

Ivannova, L. (2022). Empowering Education with Generative Artificial Intelligence Tools: Approach with an Instructional Design Matrix. *Sustainability (Basel)*, *15*(15), 11524. doi:10.3390/su151511524

Jurayev, T. N. (2023). The use of mobile learning applications in higher education institutes. *Advances in Mobile Learning Educational Research*, *3*(1), 610–620. doi:10.25082/AMLER.2023.01.010

Kopalle, P. K., Gangwar, M., Kaplan, A., Ramachandran, D., Reinartz, W., & Rindfleisch, A. (2022). Examining artificial intelligence (AI) technologies in marketing via a global lens: Current trends and future research opportunities. *International Journal of Research in Marketing*, *39*(2), 522–540. doi:10.1016/j.ijresmar.2021.11.002

Kothari, A. N. (2023). ChatGPT, Large Language Models, and Generative AI as Future Augments of Surgical Cancer Care. *Annals of Surgical Oncology*, *30*(6), 1–3. doi:10.1245/s10434-023-13442-2 PMID:37052826

Li, P. H., Lee, H. Y., Cheng, Y. P., Starčič, A. I., & Huang, Y. M. (2023, August). Solving the Self-regulated Learning Problem: Exploring the Performance of ChatGPT in Mathematics. In *International Conference on Innovative Technologies and Learning* (pp. 77-86). Cham: Springer Nature Switzerland. 10.1007/978-3-031-40113-8_8

Lim, W. M., Gunasekara, A., Pallant, J. L., Pallant, J. I., & Pechenkina, E. (2023). Generative AI and the future of education: Ragnarök or reformation? A paradoxical perspective from management educators. *International Journal of Management Education*, *21*(2), 100790. doi:10.1016/j.ijme.2023.100790

Liu, Y., Yang, Z., Yu, Z., Liu, Z., Liu, D., Lin, H., & Shi, S. (2023). Generative artificial intelligence and its applications in materials science: Current situation and future perspectives. *Journal of Materiomics.*

Lo, C. K. (2023). What Is the Impact of ChatGPT on Education? A Rapid Review of the Literature. *Education Sciences, 13*(4), 410. doi:10.3390/educsci13040410

Lockspeiser, T. M., & Kaul, P. (2016). Using individualized learning plans to facilitate learner-centered teaching. *Journal of Pediatric and Adolescent Gynecology, 29*(3), 214–217. doi:10.1016/j.jpag.2015.10.020 PMID:26612117

Lv, H. Z. (2023). Innovative music education: Using an AI-based flipped classroom. *Education and Information Technologies, 28*(11), 1–16. doi:10.1007/s10639-023-11835-0

Martínez-Jiménez, R., & Ruiz-Jiménez, M. C. (2020). Improving students' satisfaction and learning performance using flipped classroom. *International Journal of Management Education, 18*(3), 100422. doi:10.1016/j.ijme.2020.100422

McCarthy,J ., Minsky, M.Rochester, N.. & Shannon, C. (1955). *A proposal for Dartmouth Summer Research Proiect on Artificial lnteligence*. Stanford. http:/www-formalstanford.edu/imchistorv/dartmouth.pdf

McLean, S., & Attardi, S. M. (2023). Sage or guide? Student perceptions of the role of the instructor in a flipped classroom. *Active Learning in Higher Education, 24*(1), 49–61. doi:10.1177/1469787418793725

Mercader, C., & Gairín, J. (2020). University teachers' perception of barriers to the use of digital technologies: The importance of the academic discipline. *International Journal of Educational Technology in Higher Education, 17*(1), 4. doi:10.1186/s41239-020-0182-x

Murugesan, S., & Cherukuri, A. K. (2023). The Rise of Generative Artificial Intelligence and Its Impact on Education: The Promises and Perils. *Computer, 56*(5), 116–121. doi:10.1109/MC.2023.3253292

Neumann, M., Rauschenberger, M., & Schön, E. M. (2023). *"We Need To Talk About ChatGPT": The Future of AI and Higher Education.*

Nguyen, A., Ngo, H. N., Hong, Y., Dang, B., & Nguyen, B. P. T. (2023). Ethical principles for artificial intelligence in education. *Education and Information Technologies, 28*(4), 4221–4241. doi:10.1007/s10639-022-11316-w PMID:36254344

Okoye, K., Hussein, H., Arrona-Palacios, A., Quintero, H. N., Ortega, L. O. P., Sanchez, A. L., Ortiz, E. A., Escamilla, J., & Hosseini, S. (2023). Impact of digital technologies upon teaching and learning in higher education in Latin America: An outlook on the reach, barriers, and bottlenecks. *Education and Information Technologies, 28*(2), 2291–2360. doi:10.1007/s10639-022-11214-1 PMID:35992366

Pataranutaporn, P., Danry, V., Leong, J., Punpongsanon, P., Novy, D., Maes, P., & Sra, M. (2021). AI-generated characters for supporting personalized learning and well- being. *Nature Machine Intelligence, 3*(12), 1013–1022. doi:10.1038/s42256-021-00417-9

Peng, H., Ma, S., & Spector, J. M. (2019). Personalized adaptive learning: An emerging pedagogical approach enabled by a smart learning environment. *Smart Learning Environments, 6*(1), 1–14. doi:10.1186/s40561-019-0089-y

Playfoot, D. (2023). Flipped classrooms in undergraduate statistics: Online works just fine. *Teaching of Psychology*, *50*(3), 243–247. doi:10.1177/00986283211046319

Qadir, J. (2023, May). Engineering education in the era of ChatGPT: Promise and pitfalls of generative AI for education. In *2023 IEEE Global Engineering Education Conference (EDUCON)* (pp. 1-9). IEEE. 10.1109/EDUCON54358.2023.10125121

Raj, N. S., & Renumol, V. G. (2022). A systematic literature review on adaptive content recommenders in personalized learning environments from 2015 to 2020. *Journal of Computers in Education*, *9*(1), 113–148. doi:10.1007/s40692-021-00199-4

Sanusi, I. T., Oyelere, S. S., Vartiainen, H., Suhonen, J., & Tukiainen, M. (2023). A systematic review of teaching and learning machine learning in K-12 education. *Education and Information Technologies*, *28*(5), 5967–5997. doi:10.1007/s10639-022-11416-7

Sarker, I. H. (2022). Ai-based modeling: Techniques, applications and research issues towards automation, intelligent and smart systems. *SN Computer Science*, *3*(2), 158. doi:10.1007/s42979-022-01043-x PMID:35194580

Schmarje, L., Santarossa, M., Schröder, S. M., & Koch, R. (2021). A survey on semi-, self-and unsupervised learning for image classification. *IEEE Access : Practical Innovations, Open Solutions*, *9*, 82146–82168. doi:10.1109/ACCESS.2021.3084358

Shemshack, A., Kinshuk, & Spector, J. M. (2021). A comprehensive analysis of personalized learning components. *Journal of Computers in Education*, *8*(4), 485–503. doi:10.1007/s40692-021-00188-7

Shemshack, A., & Spector, J. M. (2020). A systematic literature review of personalized learning terms. *Smart Learning Environments*, *7*(1), 1–20. doi:10.1186/s40561-020-00140-9

Shen, D., & Chang, C. S. (2023). Implementation of the flipped classroom approach for promoting college students' deeper learning. *Educational Technology Research and Development*, 1–25.

Shorten, C., Khoshgoftaar, T. M., & Furht, B. (2021). Deep Learning applications for COVID-19. *Journal of Big Data*, *8*(1), 1–54. doi:10.1186/s40537-020-00392-9 PMID:33457181

Sointu, E., Hyypiä, M., Lambert, M. C., Hirsto, L., Saarelainen, M., & Valtonen, T. (2023). Preliminary evidence of key factors in successful flipping: Predicting positive student experiences in flipped classrooms. *Higher Education*, *85*(3), 503–520. doi:10.1007/s10734-022-00848-2 PMID:35431321

Stojanović, D., Bogdanović, Z., Petrović, L., Mitrović, S., & Labus, A. (2023). Empowering learning process in secondary education using pervasive technologies. *Interactive Learning Environments*, *31*(2), 779–792. doi:10.1080/10494820.2020.1806886

Theodosiou, A. A., & Read, R. C. (2023). Artificial intelligence, machine learning and deep learning: Potential resources for the infection clinician. *The Journal of Infection*, *87*(4), 287–294. doi:10.1016/j.jinf.2023.07.006 PMID:37468046

Tlili, A., Shehata, B., Adarkwah, M. A., Bozkurt, A., Hickey, D. T., Huang, R., & Agyemang, B. (2023). What if the devil is my guardian angel: ChatGPT as a case study of using chatbots in education. *Smart Learning Environments*, *10*(1), 15. doi:10.1186/s40561-023-00237-x

Torres-Martín, C., Acal, C., El-Homrani, M., & Mingorance-Estrada, Á. C. (2022). Implementation of the flipped classroom and its longitudinal impact on improving academic performance. *Educational Technology Research and Development*, *70*(3), 909–929. doi:10.1007/s11423-022-10095-y

Turan, Z. (2023). Evaluating whether flipped classrooms improve student learning in science education: A systematic review and meta-analysis. *Scandinavian Journal of Educational Research*, *67*(1), 1–19. doi:10.1080/00313831.2021.1983868

Uchiyama, S., Umemura, K., & Morita, Y. (2023). *Large Language Model-based System to Provide Immediate Feedback to Students in Flipped Classroom Preparation Learning*. arXiv preprint arXiv:2307.11388.

van der Vorst, T., & Jelicic, N. (2019). *Artificial Intelligence in Education: Can AI bring the full potential of personalized learning to education?*

Varghese, J., & Chapiro, J. (2023). ChatGPT: The transformative influence of generative AI on science and healthcare. *Journal of Hepatology*. doi:10.1016/j.jhep.2023.07.028 PMID:37544516

Vartiainen, H., & Tedre, M. (2023). Using artificial intelligence in craft education: Crafting with text-to-image generative models. *Digital Creativity (Exeter)*, *34*(1), 1–21. doi:10.1080/14626268.2023.2174557

Viberg, O., Grönlund, Å., & Andersson, A. (2023). Integrating digital technology in mathematics education: A Swedish case study. *Interactive Learning Environments*, *31*(1), 232–243. doi:10.1080/10494820.2020.1770801

Vitta, J. P., & Al-Hoorie, A. H. (2023). The flipped classroom in second language learning: A meta-analysis. *Language Teaching Research*, *27*(5), 1268–1292. doi:10.1177/1362168820981403

Walkington, C., & Bernacki, M. L. (2020). Appraising research on personalized learning: Definitions, theoretical alignment, advancements, and future directions. *Journal of Research on Technology in Education*, *52*(3), 235–252. doi:10.1080/15391523.2020.1747757

Wang, M., Wang, M., Xu, X., Yang, L., Cai, D., & Yin, M. (2023). Unleashing ChatGPT's Power: A Case Study on Optimizing Information Retrieval in Flipped Classrooms via Prompt Engineering. *IEEE Transactions on Learning Technologies*, 1–13. doi:10.1109/TLT.2023.3324714

Wang, X., Li, Z., Dong, L., & Li, W. (2022). The flipped classroom model of Japanese teaching based on intelligent decision-making system. *Scientific Programming*, *2022*, 2022. doi:10.1155/2022/2792428

Welch Bacon, C. E., & Gaither, K. (2020). Personalized Learning Pathways: Using Technology to Promote Learning Beyond the Classroom. *New Directions for Teaching and Learning*, *2020*(162), 91–102. doi:10.1002/tl.20394

Yilmaz, R., & Yilmaz, F. G. K. (2023). The effect of generative artificial intelligence (AI)-based tool use on students' computational thinking skills, programming self- efficacy and motivation. *Computers and Education: Artificial Intelligence*, 100147.

ZhaiX. (2022). ChatGPT user experience: Implications for education. Available at SSRN 4312418.

Zhang, B., Zhu, J., & Su, H. (2023). Toward the third generation artificial intelligence. *Science China. Information Sciences*, *66*(2), 121101. doi:10.1007/s11432-021-3449-x

Zhang, T. (2023). Flipped Classroom and Student Readiness in Blended Learning. *International Journal of Education and Humanities*, *7*(3), 161–163. doi:10.54097/ijeh.v7i3.6359

KEY TERMS AND DEFINITIONS

Artificial Intelligence: Usually we call it AI, which is a kind of human through technical means to make the machine have the thinking ability of people.

Deep Learning: Through the processing and analysis of multi-layer data in machine learning, complex data can be automatically analyzed.

Flipped Classroom: Contrary to the traditional classroom procedure, the exchange of the contents before and during the class in the traditional classroom makes the students change from the passive learning state to the active learning behavior, and the students are the center of the whole learning process.

Generative AI: It is a technology that generates relevant new content based on text information, images, audio, etc. provided by users.

Machine Learning: It is an important part of artificial intelligence, in which machines learn and optimize behaviors by analyzing data generated by users' activities.

Personalized Learning: It is a kind of teaching paradigm that emphasizes students' subjective status and personality characteristics and guides students to take the initiative and learn more consciously.

Reinforcement Learning: It is a kind of machine learning, but in this paper, reinforcement learning means that students improve the application of relevant knowledge and strengthen learning objectives by carrying out relevant learning skills or learning behaviors.

Unsupervised Learning: In machine learning, it is a method of self-finding labels for learning; In the pre-class learning section of flipped classroom, students can learn and complete the pre-class test independently.

Chapter 17
Challenges in the Application of Artificial Intelligence in Education for Sustainable Engineering

Alicia Perdigones
https://orcid.org/0000-0001-8006-6437
Universidad Politécnica de Madrid, Spain

Rosa María Benavente
Universidad Politécnica de Madrid, Spain

José Luis García
https://orcid.org/0000-0003-1447-3178
Universidad Politécnica de Madrid, Spain

Fernando R. Mazarrón
Universidad Politécnica de Madrid, Spain

ABSTRACT

The aim of this chapter is to provide university educators with a range of ideas and alternatives for the use of artificial intelligence (AI) tools in their teaching to integrate concepts of sustainability, which are currently highly demanded in the professional activity. Artificial intelligence has revolutionized many areas of economic activity, offering new solutions and/or optimizing certain processes. Training students in these tools is essential for successful integration into the labor market in a technologically evolving era. This training must be carried out in coordination with educational policies, and within a teaching program that includes ethical aspects in the handling of these tools. Artificial intelligence can be key to improving sustainability in multiple areas of engineering as shown in various examples and ideas in this work.

DOI: 10.4018/979-8-3693-1351-0.ch017

INTRODUCTION: ARTIFICIAL INTELLIGENCE IN UNIVERSITY EDUCATION

The objective of this chapter is to provide university professors with ideas and options for the ethical use of artificial intelligence (AI) tools in teaching, in order to incorporate concepts of sustainability, which are currently in high demand by companies. To achieve this, it is first necessary to establish the framework in which artificial intelligence is currently used in various sectors of society and its current status in universities, and then address the 2030 Agenda and the different tools available to achieve these objectives.

Focusing first on the current state of artificial intelligence, it is important to note that it is not a new term. This concept was introduced by John McCarthy in 1956, when he proposed the idea that machines could simulate various aspects of human behavior and intelligence (Weber, 2023). This concept has evolved greatly since then, breaking into the daily lives of citizens in the most advanced countries in recent years, facilitating many activities in both professional and personal spheres. It is present in leisure, gastronomy, transportation, communication, medicine, the military, among many other areas of activity (Gill & Kaur, 2023), in a very decisive and favorable way. In some of these activities, it has revolutionized the current landscape, as is the case with artificial intelligence applied to the diagnosis and analysis of medical images, initially analyzing a multitude of images, monitoring their evolution, and being able to establish a model that predicts, with a high success rate, the progression of patients from an initial image. From here, the possibilities are numerous.

Once successfully introduced in various economic sectors, it is necessary to incorporate it into university education to prepare students for their professional future with the highest possible guarantees of success, and to quickly adapt to the needs of an increasingly changing and technologically advanced job market. The knowledge of these tools by students can be an added value, or even decisive, during active job searching.

The reality is that, in universities, the incorporation of these tools is generally being carried out very slowly, at best. Although the enormous possibilities offered by artificial intelligence tools in classrooms are not in question, their use arouses some suspicion among academics, especially in the more technical areas of engineering, which is delaying their use in many university degrees (Lim et al., 2023; Yang & Chen, 2023). According to Al Darayseh (2023), in the teaching of science areas, the rejection by faculty is less. On one hand, the lack of university regulations on this topic means that teachers do not feel the necessary support from institutions when addressing their use in the classroom, creating a sense of abandonment in this aspect. To this must be added the difficulty that currently exists in detecting their use in the writing of assignments, without knowledge or explicit permission of the faculty (Eke, 2023; Gill et al., 2024), which obviously constitutes an unethical practice (Eke, 2023; Hung & Chen, 2023; Tlili et al., 2023; Yang, 2023). It is now common for teachers to compare students' work with different databases through specific anti-plagiarism programs, such as Turnitin, PlagScan, Viper, among others. However, the ability of artificial intelligence tools to draft a different text each time they are asked, even modifying the style of text, vocabulary, or verb tenses, makes it very difficult to detect if it is the student who has actually done it.

Therefore, training in these tools must be done thoughtfully and responsibly, coordinating their incorporation in the classroom with university policies, and promoting a critical and ethical attitude on the part of students during their use.

There is no doubt that these new tools pose a problem during university training if used incorrectly, facilitating the writing of assignments without the slightest effort on the part of students, and more importantly, without achieving the learning objectives initially set in the course programming. However, the possibilities that open up in this field are also enormous, allowing in most cases personalized training that favors the development of new software and learning environments (Valencia & Figueroa, 2023). Other tools such as adaptive intelligent tutoring or adaptive platforms emerge, allowing the analysis of each student's individual progress, identifying strengths and weaknesses, and redirecting learning strategies according to each student's profile. It also allows for the generation of material more quickly, enabling the search for different teaching strategies. Finding ways to integrate them into different engineering courses, adapting learning objectives (Zhai, 2023) and promoting creativity (Steele, 2023; Javaid et al., 2023), can be very positive. Creativity and critical thinking are competencies highly demanded by companies in the sector.

Among the available artificial intelligence tools applicable to engineering, different categories can be established. The most interesting in the area of civil engineering, urban planning, and landscape are as follows:

a) The so-called Chatbots AI, which generate text from text: chatGPT, You.com, Writesonic.
b) The so-called AI Art, which generate images from text or other images: Midjourney, Dall-E, Stable Diffusion, Craiyon, NightCafe.
c) The so-called AI-Design, which from a building's floor plan, generates spaces: Interior AI, Maket, Architechtures, Finch3D.

In the field of engineering, these and other generative AIs are really interesting both for preparing technical reports and for designing spaces, infrastructures, and engineering works. Choosing one or another at any given time, with the aim of integrating them into the teaching of subjects, will depend on the suitability to the activity or area in which one is working at the time, ease of handling, and the budget necessary for the corresponding subscription. It is up to the teacher to make this decision in the classroom, so they must be aware of the tools that are available at any given time, to be able to implement them successfully

PROBLEMS AND OPPORTUNITIES OF AI FOR EDUCATION

As mentioned in the previous section, the introduction of artificial intelligence in education generates some rejection among most teachers at any educational level, whether in pre-university or university education. This rejection is not only due to the fact that they can be used effortlessly and without the teacher's knowledge, a situation that can be resolved through workshops that make students aware of the importance of working following ethical guidelines. This rejection can also be due to other factors:

a) **Limited current training of teachers in the use of artificial intelligence tools.** These tools have only recently been made available to users, so their handling among the population is still relatively low. Ignorance about their operation, use, and possibilities creates confusion among users, teachers in this case. Within the context of training, this poses a problem when organizing activities, as there is also no clear understanding of whether students are using these tools correctly or how they are using them. Furthermore, among the problems entailed in the use of these tools, authors like Steele (2023) emphasize that the information they provide is sometimes erroneous, as the tool accesses the internet and provides information that it cannot discern whether is true or false. In the case of pre-university stage teachers, other concerns, according to Adams et al. (2021), include the perception of an increase in workload due to the additional time needed for class preparation and the change in the relationships established with students in this new framework.

b) **Lack of computer equipment and efficient, updated tools in the classroom** (Valencia & Figueroa, 2023). To address the use of artificial intelligence tools, it is necessary for the center to have computers and licenses for the tools to be used, which in some cases represents a significant investment that is difficult to make. Conducting activities outside the classroom would not be most appropriate, as it could increase the technological gap depending on the families' economy.
c) **It is considered that the development of students' transversal competencies is reduced with the use of AIs.** The development of certain transversal competencies (writing, reading) by students is seen as diminished as a consequence of the use of artificial intelligence tools. However, Steele (2023) and Javaid et al. (2023) highlight improvements in the development of competencies such as critical thinking, creativity, and enhancement in the drafting of technical reports.

On the other hand, the use of AI also provides opportunities for both the teaching-learning process and the work of educators. These opportunities can be:

a) **Improvement of the teaching-learning process.** Algorithms can be developed that allow grading forms, detecting topics where students have greater understanding problems, improving the teaching-learning process. This allows teachers to develop topics in another way and modify those actions that do not favor learning, providing higher quality training. Options like adaptive intelligent tutoring are extremely useful for developing an autonomous learning system fully adapted to the student's learning pace.
b) **Development of applications for the automation of certain tasks.** Automation of certain tasks (such as evaluation tasks) and assistance in others (intelligent tutoring), which means that teachers would have more time available for other teaching or research activities.
c) **Development of new activities.** Tools known as Chatbots can provide teachers with new ideas for developing material or learning activities.

ETHICS AS THE FOUNDATION FOR INCORPORATING ARTIFICIAL INTELLIGENCE IN TEACHING

Ethics, as a philosophical discipline, is a concept that emerged in ancient Greece in the 5th and 4th centuries B.C. when seeking the need to establish how one should live and act to live a good life. Some foundational elements of Western ethics in the current context must be incorporated into the teaching of subjects where the use of artificial intelligence is allowed, addressing both topics simultaneously. It is also necessary to establish the applied ethical bases (applied ethics) for each of the disciplines where AI tools will be incorporated (engineering, medicine, architecture, among others) (Quishpe & Pizarro, 2018). According to the International Center for Academic Integrity (2021) and Eke (2023), academic integrity is defined based on six fundamental values:

a) **Honesty:** In the university context, honesty refers to sincerity and truthfulness in academic conduct. It involves individual student work without cheating on exams or plagiarizing assignments. Honesty fosters an academic environment based on trust and mutual respect between teacher and student, essential for the ethical development of future professionals. It is a fundamental personal value for any professional in any field of activity.

b) **Courage:** Courage in university education is manifested in facing ethical challenges, such as defending personal and academic principles against both external and internal pressures. It includes the bravery to question unjust practices and promote positive changes. This value is crucial for forming professionals with integrity, committed to social justice and academic integrity.

c) **Trust:** Trust is a cornerstone in university education, founded on the relationship between teachers and students. It is based on the mutual belief that both parties will act with integrity and respect. A trustful atmosphere promotes an open and honest learning environment, where collaboration and the exchange of ideas are valued.

d) **Equity:** Equity in university education implies ensuring equal opportunities and access to educational resources for all students, regardless of their background, gender, or socioeconomic status. It promotes diversity and inclusion, key elements for an ethical and globally conscious education. Developing this transversal competence will foster the training of professionals who will work incorporating inclusive aspects into their projects.

e) **Respect:** Respect in the university environment refers to recognizing and valuing the dignity of each individual, their ideas, and contributions. This includes respecting the diversity of opinions, cultures, and perspectives, creating a space for dialogue and learning where everyone feels valued and heard.

f) **Responsibility:** Responsibility in university education is related to the obligation of students and teachers to act ethically and professionally. It includes personal responsibility for learning, integrity in research, and commitment to the social impacts of their work. Training in responsibility prepares students to be citizens aware of contemporary issues and ethical professionals.

The challenge posed by the use of artificial intelligence tools in the classroom, such as ChatGPT, lies in the difficulty of discerning when a text has been authored and composed by the student and when it has been generated by an artificial intelligence tool.

For years, academic papers have been subjected to pre-evaluation checks to detect plagiarism from other texts available in databases or on the internet (Turnitin, Unicheck, PlagScan, Noplag). In the case of using artificial intelligence tools, however, there is no possibility of direct comparison, as ChatGPT can produce distinct texts with varying styles each time a topic is requested. It can even adapt its language and modify versions, making the detection of its use more complex (Eke, 2023; Gill et al., 2024).

This is where the imperative need arises to teach these tools alongside classes on professional ethics, explaining how to use them while avoiding deception. It is essential that educators receive training in the use of these tools to comprehend their use, responsibilities, and integration into the teaching process (Kim & Kwon, 2023).

It is a collective responsibility for all stakeholders in education, including educational policies, university internal regulations, professors, and students, to incorporate and utilize these tools responsibly for adequate education in artificial intelligence, both at the basic education levels and in higher education.

Ethics is, therefore, a fundamental pillar when addressing the use of artificial intelligence in the classroom, as well as in tackling current social, economic, and environmental problems through engineering.

THE 2030 AGENDA AS A FRAMEWORK FOR ACTION IN ENGINEERING EDUCATION

Companies in various engineering fields address critical issues such as water supply, energy provision, food production, construction of infrastructure and buildings, among many others. The traditional approach in classrooms regarding these topics has been fundamentally based on technical aspects, focusing on solutions derived from engineering calculations and economic aspects. However, the UN General Assembly established the 2030 Agenda in 2015, with 17 Sustainable Development Goals (SDGs) and 169 targets for the improvement of economic, social, and environmental areas at a global level, setting a 15-year horizon for their achievement (with the deadline being 2030).

This new framework has modified the way engineering projects are approached in different universities. Currently, all subject programs include aspects of sustainability, referencing the SDGs they relate to. Engineering is now only considered in a context where the goal is to provide solutions to the various SDGs, for the achievement of the established targets. The SDGs, therefore, take on great importance in both professional and academic fields. Here is a brief explanation of the SDGs included in the 2030 Agenda:

- SDG1. No Poverty. Eradicate poverty in all its forms and dimensions, considering it the greatest global challenge and an indispensable requirement for sustainable development. This includes measures to ensure basic resources and services for everyone.
- SDG2. Zero Hunger. End hunger, achieve food security and improved nutrition, and promote sustainable agriculture. This implies ensuring access to sufficient and nutritious food all year round.
- SDG3. Good Health and Well-being. Ensure healthy lives and promote well-being for all at all ages. Focuses on the prevention and treatment of diseases and the promotion of healthy lifestyles.
- SDG4. Quality Education. Ensure inclusive, equitable, and quality education, and promote lifelong learning opportunities for all. Seeks to eliminate disparities in education.
- SDG5. Gender Equality. Achieve gender equality and empower all women and girls. Includes the elimination of violence and discrimination and ensuring full participation at all decision-making levels.
- SDG6. Clean Water and Sanitation. Ensure availability and sustainable management of water and sanitation for all. This encompasses improving water quality and increasing its efficiency in use.
- SDG7. Affordable and Clean Energy. Ensure access to affordable, reliable, sustainable, and modern energy for all. Focuses on increasing the use of renewable energy and improving energy efficiency.
- SDG8. Decent Work and Economic Growth. Promote sustained, inclusive, and sustainable economic growth, full and productive employment, and decent work for all. Includes measures to enhance productivity and reduce labor informality.
- SDG9. Industry, Innovation, and Infrastructure. Build resilient infrastructure, promote inclusive and sustainable industrialization, and foster innovation. Aims to increase research and improve technology and infrastructure.

- SDG10. Reduced Inequalities. Reduce inequality within and among countries. This involves policies to improve social, economic, and political inclusion for everyone, regardless of age, sex, disability, race, ethnicity, origin, or any other status.
- SDG11. Sustainable Cities and Communities. Make cities and human settlements inclusive, safe, resilient, and sustainable. Focuses on improving urban planning and management in all areas of sustainable development.
- SDG12. Responsible Consumption and Production. Ensure sustainable consumption and production patterns. Seeks to implement regulatory frameworks to promote sustainability in the production and consumption of goods and resources.
- SDG13. Climate Action. Take urgent action to combat climate change and its impacts. This involves integrating climate change measures into national policies and planning.
- SDG14. Life Below Water. Conserve and sustainably use the oceans, seas, and marine resources for sustainable development. Focuses on sustainable management and protection of marine ecosystems.
- SDG15. Life on Land. Sustainably manage forests, combat desertification, halt and reverse land degradation, and halt biodiversity loss. This covers the conservation of mountains, forests, wetlands, rivers, and other ecosystems.
- SDG16. Peace, Justice, and Strong Institutions. Promote peaceful and inclusive societies for sustainable development, provide access to justice for all, and build effective, accountable, and inclusive institutions at all levels.
- SDG17. Partnerships for the Goals. Revitalize the Global Partnership for Sustainable Development and strengthen the means of implementation and revitalization of the Global Partnership for Sustainable Development.

Within these 17 SDGs, there are some directly related to various areas of engineering (energy, technology, construction, sanitation), with many possibilities to address them during university education. In the field of civil engineering, specifically in the design of parks, gardens, or infrastructure in urban developments, it is possible to use these tools to train students in matters of accessibility and universal design, promoting the development of inclusive cities, in accordance with Sustainable Development Goal 11 (SDG11 - Sustainable Cities and Communities). In the case of civil works aimed at constructing reservoirs or dams, it is possible to address SDG6 (Clean Water and Sanitation) or SDG15 (Life on Land). Also, in areas related to landscape and biodiversity of these spaces, within Agricultural Engineering, the possibilities are very interesting, in this case, also related to SDG7 (Affordable and Clean Energy), SDG13 (Climate Action), and SDG15 (Life on Land).

Training around the SDGs has spread across different degrees, not only in the field of engineering, associating subjects with the various goals included in the 2030 Agenda. Training in this aspect is an added value for job searching in different economic sectors, due to the transversality it provides, allowing addressing an engineering problem or project not only from a technical aspect but also considering social or environmental aspects, which are increasingly valued in companies. Thus, while in the Architecture Degree, goals such as sustainable cities and communities (SDG11) and climate action (SDG13) can be addressed through urban planning and its possible multiple designs, in the Degree in Law or Political Science, it can be approached from peace, justice, and strong institutions (SDG16), no poverty (SDG1), or zero hunger (SDG2).

Generative artificial intelligence tools, especially Chatbots, can be introduced in any university degree as a means to research actions on any of the Sustainable Development Goals. Through these tools, information can be requested about accessibility in spaces, biodiversity associated with an area, or local and national regulations related to different renewable energy sources. In the case of AI for image generation, although more oriented in this case towards different areas of engineering, images of accessible elements can be requested to provide new ideas to manufacturers, designers, and engineers in charge of designing, planning, and executing these spaces. Similarly, images of renewable energy sources can be obtained, for example, that provide design ideas.

Within this approach, it is also worth highlighting interdisciplinary activities that allow students from different degrees such as Civil Engineering and Law, for example, to work together, each contributing the knowledge acquired during their training in very different subjects. Activities defined in this work model can be debate and negotiation activities organized by students and carried out in a simulated framework of the United Nations, known as MUN (Model United Nations), opening the possibility of participation to students from different degrees who collaborate in groups to debate on a current topic linked to the SDGs. In this way, students must take on the role of the delegate of the country they represent, seeking realistic solutions to current problems. These debates provide clear training in transversal competencies, highly valued by companies. Specifically, competencies such as attitude and critical thinking, communication, language (debates are usually conducted in English), work in multidisciplinary and collaborative teams, negotiation and conflict resolution skills, leadership, empathy and global awareness, research and analysis, time management, and organization are developed.

In subjects specific to engineering, especially in courses related to the construction of buildings and infrastructure, the use of generative AI can favor the design of these facilities, providing creative ideas to be developed by students, always seeking work in line with the 2030 Agenda. Therefore, the use of artificial intelligence tools, addressing sustainable development goals, opens a wide range of possibilities in university education, both formally within different subjects and outside the classroom, in activities that are not included as subjects within the different degrees.

AI FOR ENGINEERING BASED ON CHATBOTS: USE FOR SUSTAINABILITY

Artificial intelligence can materialize in different forms. In agriculture, for example, it can be seen in the form of intelligent robots for tasks in greenhouses, among others, or in decision-making through the mapping of images of plots to determine, using mathematical models, how much quantity and location of phytosanitary products are necessary at each moment (Jha et al., 2019; Elbasi et al., 2023; Oliveira & Silva, 2023). In this case, the goal of using AI is the optimization of resources, both in phytosanitary products and in fuel used by tractors (Borges et al., 2017; Sánchez et al., 2020; Ryan, 2022; Ryan, Van Der Burg & Bogaardt, 2022).

In the context of this chapter, which focuses on teaching in the general framework of engineering, we will refer to artificial intelligence tools that help in writing texts or technical reports and the preparation of plans. For the former, we are talking about Chatbots, as artificial intelligence tools that provide structured information from a text (prompt) that the user enters, as a question or request for information, having previously defined a context and a style of writing. Correctly defining the prompt facilitates understanding by the artificial intelligence, providing results more aligned with the initial search. To design a prompt correctly, it is necessary to understand how the tool works and what type of instructions or questions are easier for it to comprehend and interpret. This is what is known as prompt engineering, a profile increasingly in demand by companies.

Training students to understand the functioning and comprehension of the models and generate effective prompts that return the requested information with the highest precision and that are capable of discerning which information is valid and which is erroneous, should be the goal in training with these tools.

A possible prompt in ChatGPT, aimed at architecture students and related to SDG11 (Sustainable Cities and Communities) in which "ten actions that involve the elimination of architectural barriers in parks and gardens, making spaces more accessible for people with disabilities" are requested, provides the following information:

a) **Access Ramps:** Installation of ramps with gentle slopes instead of stairs to allow access for wheelchairs and people with limited mobility. The slope of the ramp should not exceed 8% for stretches up to 3 meters long and 10% for stretches up to 50 cm. For frequently used ramps, a slope of 6% is recommended. The clear width of passage should be at least 120 cm, to allow for the maneuverability of wheelchairs. If the ramp exceeds 9 meters in length, it should have landings of at least 150 cm in length every 9 meters, allowing for rest and facilitating turning. At the beginning and end of the ramp, there should be a landing whose dimensions allow for the complete turning of a wheelchair, typically a space of 150 x 150 cm. The ramp's surface should be non-slip to prevent falls, especially in wet conditions. Ramps should have handrails on both sides, with a height between 90 and 100 cm, and additional handrails at a height of 70 cm, to be used by children and people in wheelchairs. They should be correctly signposted, especially at their beginnings and ends, and if there are changes in direction or landings. Ramps should be adequately lit to ensure the safety of users in all light conditions.

b) **Accessible Circulation Surfaces**: Use of non-slip and regular pavements to facilitate the movement of people with reduced mobility and avoid obstacles.

c) **Tactile and Visual Signage:** Placement of tactile signs on floors and visual signs to guide people with visual impairments or orientation problems. Visual signage must meet several characteristics:
   - Chromatic Contrast: The signs should have a high contrast between the text (or symbol) and the background, to be easily readable.
   - Adequate Size: The size of the text and symbols should be large enough to be read from the appropriate distance.
   - Height and Location: The signs should be placed at a visible height for both standing people and people in wheelchairs.
   - Clear Iconography: Use clear and universal icons and images that indicate services, accessible routes, rest areas, and others.
   - Lighting: The signs should be well lit, avoiding glare and shadows that hinder visibility.

On the other hand, tactile signage must meet the conditions:

- Podotactile Pavement: Installation of tactile pavements (tiles with relief) to guide visually impaired people through the different spaces of the park.
- Relief and Braille Maps: Provision of maps in relief and Braille at the park entrance and strategic points, indicating the layout of spaces and services.

- Handrails with Braille Information: In areas where there are handrails or guardrails, information in Braille about the direction and nearby services can be included.
- Differentiated Textures: Use of different textures on the ground to indicate changes in direction, entrances to different areas, or proximity to services.

Additionally, auditory signage (through audio messages) can be considered.

d) **Accessible Rest Areas:** Inclusion of rest areas with seats and tables accessible for people with disabilities.
e) **Adapted Play Areas:** Incorporation of play areas designed for children with disabilities, including accessible swings and games.
f) **Accessible Picnic Areas:** Creation of picnic areas with tables and benches adapted for wheelchairs.
g) **Accessible Toilets:** Availability of accessible public toilets for people with disabilities, including accessible baby changing facilities.
h) **Handrails and Guardrails:** Installation of handrails and guardrails at different heights to aid mobility and prevent falls.
i) **Adequate Lighting:** Ensuring that parks have adequate lighting to allow for safe use of the space at night.
j) **Reserved Parking Spaces:** Designation of reserved parking spaces near main entrances for people with disabilities. They must meet certain requirements:
    - Location: They should be located as close as possible to the main entrance or the nearest elevator if it is a multi-story building.
    - Dimensions: The spaces should have a minimum width, generally wider than standard spaces. In Spain, this width is usually at least 5 meters.
    - Signage: They should be clearly signposted with the international symbol of accessibility and should be visible even when the parking space is occupied.
    - Access routes: There should be an accessible route from the parking space to the destination (building entrance, elevator, and others), without architectural barriers.
    - Surface: The surface of the space should be firm and level, avoiding steep slopes.
    - Accessibility: In some cases, these spaces need to be equipped with additional elements such as access ramps or technical aids.
    - Number of spaces: The number of spaces reserved for people with disabilities depends on local regulations and the total size of the parking lot.
    - Maintenance: These spaces must be kept free of obstacles and in good condition.

At this moment, the student should be able to contribute opinions on these aspects and/or alternatives to these actions. If the question is slightly modified, it is possible to receive another list, similar, but with slight differences; this implies that the question is not sufficiently specific or closed and should narrow down the possible answers. It is recommended to use direct language, avoid ambiguities in expressions, and try to specify what is wanted, providing a context and even the scope of the response.

Once a response is obtained, the search can be refined further, and request, for example: "Please specify the parameters for a space to have adequate lighting to be accessible." In this case, the artificial intelligence provides a list of classic parameters for the design of outdoor lighting (level of illumination, uniformity, considerations about biodiversity, color of the light, among others) and refers to European regulations related to these spaces, without providing a specific data on the level of illumination.

If asked about "recommendations for lighting outdoor spaces in an environmentally and biodiversity-friendly manner," the response is extensive:

"Environmentally friendly outdoor lighting is an important part of the sustainable design of public spaces and can help conserve biodiversity and reduce the negative impact of artificial light on natural ecosystems.

a) **Use Directional and Focused Lighting:** Instead of flooding areas with light, use fixtures that direct light where it is needed. This reduces light pollution and glare.
b) **Employ Low-Intensity LED Lighting:** LED lights are energy-efficient and allow for greater control over intensity. Adjust the light intensity to the real needs of the space and the time of day.
c) **Time the Lighting:** Install timers or motion sensors so that lighting is active only when necessary, reducing unnecessary energy consumption.
d) **Avoid Blue or White Light:** Blue white light can be harmful to nocturnal biodiversity. Opt for warm or amber lights that are less disruptive to nocturnal wildlife.
e) **Use Screens and Shielding:** Install screens or barriers to direct light downwards and prevent it from scattering upwards. This reduces light pollution.
f) **Set Lighting Schedules:** Limit lighting during hours when people do not use the space and wildlife is more active. This can help minimize interference with natural rhythms.
g) **Solar and Autonomous Lighting:** Where possible, use autonomous solar lighting that charges during the day and turns on at night, reducing electrical consumption.
h) **Conservation of Trees and Vegetation:** Avoid installing lights in trees and shrubs, as it can damage vegetation and alter wildlife habitats.
i) **Public Education:** Inform the community about the importance of responsible lighting and how it can contribute to the protection of the environment and biodiversity.
j) **Monitoring and Adaptation:** Monitor the effects of lighting on wildlife and adjust the design if necessary to minimize negative impact.
k) **Comprehensive Planning:** Integrate lighting planning into the overall space planning, considering ecology and landscape, to make informed decisions.
l) **Comply with Regulations and Standards:** Ensure compliance with local and national regulations and standards related to outdoor lighting and environmental protection."

You can ask about any of these guidelines, such as, "Why should the use of white light in outdoor spaces be avoided to minimize damage to biodiversity?" The response provided by the Chatbot is as follows:

"The use of white light in outdoor spaces can have a negative impact on biodiversity for several reasons:

a) **Disorientation of Wildlife:** Bright white light, especially when combined with a high level of intensity, can disorient nocturnal wildlife, such as insects, birds, bats, and other animals. This can lead to abnormal behaviors, such as erratic flight patterns in migratory birds or decreased activity of pollinating insects.
b) **Interference with Natural Rhythms:** Constant exposure to white light at night can interfere with the natural rhythms and behavior patterns of animals, as it prevents the natural darkness they need for feeding, reproducing, and resting.

c) **Light Pollution:** White light tends to be more dispersing and can significantly contribute to light pollution, reducing the visibility of stars and altering nocturnal ecosystems.
d) **Attraction of Insects:** White light is usually more attractive to insects than other light color temperatures. This can increase insects' exposure to predators and also have a negative impact on local food chains. To minimize damage to biodiversity, it is recommended to use light sources with warmer color temperatures, such as amber or warm light, as they are less disruptive to nocturnal wildlife. These light sources are less attractive to insects and help preserve the natural rhythms of wildlife."

In this way, Chatbots can be used in training for students to research certain topics in any professional area. It is only necessary to explain how they work and provide the tools for them to formulate appropriate questions for specific topics provided by the teaching staff.

It should be mentioned that a certain lack of rigor has been detected in searching for regulations on various topics, such as regulations related to lighting and energy efficiency of outdoor lighting in Spain. This is because ChatGPT-4 accesses data and knowledge up to April 2023, but its previous version, ChatGPT-3.5, has quite a more limited access, unable to access data and knowledge after September 2021. Again, and considering each student's personal situation, they should not be required to have the paid version, thus avoiding a technological gap due to economic issues. This means that they should be activities to be carried out in the classroom or request the use of the free version of the tool.

AI FOR ENGINEERING BASED ON IMAGE GENERATION: USE FOR SUSTAINABILITY

Currently, there is a wide range of possibilities regarding artificial intelligence tools for creating images from text or other images and text. It is also possible to start from one's own image, request certain modifications or improvements, facilitating rendering work, improving image quality, or including some new element or removing others, among other things. These starting images can be photographs of some space or products of modeling programs such as SketchUp. In many architectural and landscaping studios, this work model is in full activity.

The most well-known today, due to the quality of the images they provide and creativity, are Midjourney and DALL-E. Although there are others like Google's Imagen or Stable Diffusion, the tools from Midjourney and DALL-E are clearly the most used, especially at a professional level for rendering and improving images of engineering projects. Therefore, we will focus on these two artificial intelligence tools.

Midjourney (Midjourney Inc.)

Image generation through AI Art also provides a very interesting field for designing and presenting projects to clients. Midjourney is one of the developed AIs that allows generating a new image from text, or one or several images. Its operation follows the following scheme:

a) **Text Input:** The user provides a detailed text description of the image they wish to generate. Images can also be used as a basis for the results. This description can include details about the theme, colors, style, image quality, composition, and size, among others. There are specific instructions of this tool that allow defining the size, quality, or other characteristics. These instructions could be: "--ar X:Y" (aspect ratio of the image), "--w X" (resolution for width), "--h Y" (resolution for height), "--quality X" (quality), for example. In the provided examples of instructions, X and Y are numerical values.

b) **Text Processing:** The AI analyzes the provided text and interprets it to understand the instructions. It uses natural language processing algorithms to break down and understand the components of the description entered by the user.

c) **Image Generation:** Using a trained AI model, the tool translates the textual instructions into a visual image, providing four image options. These models have been trained with large datasets of images and their descriptions, learning to create visual representations from textual instructions.

d) **Presentation of Results:** The generated image is presented to the user through four possibilities, with differences that can be more or less significant. The user has the option to modify their initial description or adjust parameters to refine the result. They also have the possibility to reject the provided images and, with the same prompt, request four new options.

DALL-E (OpenAI)

DALL-E has been trained with a large dataset of image pairs and their corresponding textual descriptions. This enables it to learn to associate textual elements with visual concepts. When it receives a textual description, DALL-E interprets this input and generates an image that corresponds to that description. The AI uses its training to create a visual representation that matches the words and phrases provided. What makes DALL-E particularly notable is its ability to understand and combine concepts that do not necessarily appear together naturally. In other words, it exhibits high creativity because it does not strictly adhere to what exists in reality. DALL-E is capable of creating images that go beyond the literal and realistic, venturing into the creative, and even into a surrealistic style. It can generate unique and creative combinations, demonstrating a quite high level of creativity in image generation, compared to other similar tools. Like other AI tools, DALL-E improves as it is trained with more data and receives feedback on its creations.

The advantage of the OpenAI tool lies in the fact that with the payment for the ChatGPT-4 version, the license for using DALL-E is also obtained, thus providing a generative tool for obtaining text and images simultaneously.

Examples of Image Creation with AI

Following the approach of training based on the development of transversal competencies associated with social and environmental aspects, as per the 2030 Agenda, students can be involved in the design of sustainable public spaces.

In this vein, the target image of a final year project carried out in the Degree in Agricultural Engineering at the Polytechnic University of Madrid is presented, titled "Landscaping, according to the 2030 Agenda, of a 6500 m^2 plot, currently occupied by El Corte Inglés in Méndez Álvaro (Madrid)". It is a landscaping project for a real area in the center of Madrid, where a commercial building is planned to be demolished to construct two towers and design the landscaping of the area. This project has a clear focus on sustainability, as highlighted in the title itself. It includes accessible elements for the integration of people with disabilities, sustainable urban drainage systems, efficient LED-based lighting with warm lights, and drip irrigation. This target image is created using the 3D modeling software, SketchUp (Trimble Inc.). It is a simple model where the different spaces and elements of the landscaping can be appreciated. Midjourney and DALL-E have been used to optimize the image for presentation to potential clients. The initial prompt was: "realistic image, rendering, Mediterranean garden, high quality".

The result is shown below in Figure 1:

Figure 1. Target image of a sustainable park, designed in a final degree project

Starting from just a text, a *prompt*, in line with accessibility, it could be: "Realistic image of a public space, a park or garden, considering aspects of universal accessibility, ramps to overcome stairs, accessible picnic tables –s 250". To this *prompt*, other characteristics can be applied, such as it being a space illuminated at night, with different types of light, to favor biodiversity. With this same prompt, the images created by Midjourney (Figure 2) and DALL-E (Figure 3) are compared.

Figure 2. Images created with Midjourney, related to an inclusive park

The quality and realism of Midjourney can be seen in the images, compared to the more creative results obtained with DALL-E. Depending on the style being sought, the type of tool can be decisive. For the rendering of engineering projects, it seems that the images offered by Midjourney fit better with what clients might look for in the presentation of a project.

Figure 3. Imágenes creadas con DALL-E, related to an inclusive park

CONCLUSION

Artificial Intelligence tools have been incorporated into many economic sectors (Gill & Kaur, 2023), and they open a range of possibilities in university education that should not be missed (Valencia & Figueroa, 2023). Their inclusion in classrooms, especially in more technical trainings such as engineering, is occurring very slowly, mainly due to the rejection generated by their use (Al Darayseh, 2023; Lim et al., 2023; Yang & Chen, 2023). There are other factors that slow down their use in universities, such as the limited training of the teachers themselves, the perception of increased workload, the need for computer equipment with AI tools installed, errors of the tools themselves in terms of information search, and the reduction of the development of certain competencies by the students (Adams et al., 2021; Steele, 2023; Valencia & Figueroa, 2023). The opportunities are numerous: they facilitate the task of teaching activity (evaluation and problem analysis in training), while providing new means and actions in the classroom (adaptive intelligent tutoring). Their use must be made responsibly, within an ethical framework (applied ethics, according to the professional area) (Quishpe & Pizarro, 2018; International Center for Academic Integrity, 2021; Eke, 2023) and regulatory, with well-defined objectives within the programming of each subject. It is to be expected that Universities will soon regulate their use through different regulations, providing teachers with a framework in which to feel more secure and comfortable using this new technology.

The use of these tools can promote learning in aspects such as the social and environmental commitment of students through training in the research of the Sustainable Development Goals, included in the 2030 Agenda. This can be done well with tools like Chatbots (ChatGPT) or AI Art (Midjourney, DALL-E). Determining which tool is most appropriate to each case or subject is the responsibility and decision of the teacher. This means that it is necessary for the teaching staff to have knowledge not only of the functioning of the tools but also of the novelties that arise at any given time in relation to this topic, being a very changing area.

On the other hand, and in relation to AI Art, the quality of the image and the sense of reality can be a key factor for improving the image in terms of showing projects to potential clients.

As recommendations to the teaching staff, responsible for the incorporation of artificial intelligence tools in the classroom, it is interesting to highlight:

a) Prior training on the use of artificial intelligence tools by the teaching staff is necessary.
b) Teachers must determine at all times which AI tool is most convenient to use depending on their characteristics and the characteristics of the subject itself.
c) Conduct simultaneous training in the classroom on artificial intelligence tools and applied ethics, to promote responsible use.

REFERENCES

Adams, C., Pente, P., Lemermeyer, G., & Rockwell, G. (2021). Artificial Intelligence Ethics Guidelines for K-12 Education: A Review of the Global Landscape. In I. Roll, D. McNamara, S. Sosnovsky, R. Luckin, & V. Dimitrova (Eds.), Lecture Notes in Computer Science: Vol. 12749. *Artificial Intelligence in Education. AIED*. Springer. (Original work published 2021), doi:10.1007/978-3-030-78270-2_4

Al Darayseh, A. (2023). Acceptance of artificial intelligence in teaching science: Science teachers perspective. *Computers and Education: Artificial Intelligence*, *4*, 100132. doi:10.1016/j.caeai.2023.100132

Borges, P. H. M., Mendoza, Z., Maia, J., Bianchini, A., & Fernández, H. (2017). Estimation of fuel consumption in agricultural mechanized operations using artificial neural networks. *Engenharia Agrícola*, *37*(1), 136–147. doi:10.1590/1809-4430-eng.agric.v37n1p136-147/2017

Eke, D. O. (2023). ChatGPT and the rise of generative AI: Threat to academic integrity? *Journal of Responsible Technology*, *13*, 100060. doi:10.1016/j.jrt.2023.100060

Elbasi, E., Mostafa, N., AlArnaout, Z., Zreikat, A. I., Cina, E., Varghese, G., Shdefat, A., Topcu, A. E., Abdelbaki, W., Mathew, S., & Zaki, C. (2022). Artificial Intelligence Technology in the Agricultural Sector: A Systematic Literature Review. *IEEE Access : Practical Innovations, Open Solutions*, *11*, 171–202. doi:10.1109/ACCESS.2022.3232485

Gill, S. S., & Kaur, R. (2023). ChatGPT: Vision and challenges. *Internet of Things and Cyber-Physical Systems*, *3*, 262–271. doi:10.1016/j.iotcps.2023.05.004

Gill, S. S., Xu, M., Patros, P., Wu, H., Kaur, R., Kaur, K., Fuller, S., Singh, M., Arora, P., Parlikad, A. K., Stankovski, V., Abraham, A., Ghosh, S. K., Lutfiyya, H., Kanhere, S. S., Bahsoon, R., Rana, O., Dustdar, S., Sakellariou, R., & Buyya, R. (2024). Transformative effects of ChatGPT on modern education: Emerging Era of AI Chatbots. *Internet of Things and Cyber-Physical Systems*, *4*, 19–23. doi:10.1016/j.iotcps.2023.06.002

Hung, J., & Chen, J. (2023). The Benefits, Risks and Regulation of Using ChatGPT in Chinese Academia: A Content Analysis. *Social Sciences (Basel, Switzerland)*, *12*(7), 380. doi:10.3390/socsci12070380

International Center for Academic Integrity. (2021). *The Fundamental Values of Academic Integrity* (3rd ed.). Academic Integrity. https://academicintegrity.org/wp-content/uploads/2017/12/Fundamental-Values-2014.pdf

Javaid, M., Haleem, A., Singh, R. P., Khan, S., & Khan, I. H. (2023). Unlocking the opportunities through ChatGPT Tool towards ameliorating the education system. *BenchCouncil Transactions on Benchmarks. Standards and Evaluations*, *3*(2), 100115.

Jha, K., Doshi, A., Patel, P., & Shah, M. (2019). A comprehensive review on automation in agriculture using artificial intelligence. *Artificial Intelligence in Agriculture*, *2*, 1–12. doi:10.1016/j.aiia.2019.05.004

Kim, K., & Kwon, K. (2023). Exploring the AI competencies of elementary school teachers in South Korea. *Computers and Education: Artificial Intelligence*, *4*, 100137. doi:10.1016/j.caeai.2023.100137

Lim, W. M., Gunasekara, A., Pallant, J. L., Pallant, J. I., & Pechenkina, E. (2023). Generative AI and the future of education: Ragnarok or reformation? A paradoxical perspective from management educators. *International Journal of Management Education*, *21*(2), 100790. doi:10.1016/j.ijme.2023.100790

Oliveira, R. C., & Silva, R. D. S. e. (2023). Artificial Intelligence in Agriculture: Benefits, Challenges, and Trends. *Applied Sciences (Basel, Switzerland)*, *13*(13), 7405. doi:10.3390/app13137405

Quishpe Gaibor, J. S., & Pizarro Macas, J. L. (2018). Evolución Histórica de la Ética hasta nuestros Días. *Revista Caribeña De Ciencias Sociales*, *2018*, 1–6.

Ryan, M. (2022). The social and ethical impacts of artificial intelligence in agriculture: Mapping the agricultural AI literature. *AI & Society*. doi:10.1007/s00146-021-01377-9

Ryan, M., Van Der Burg, S., & Bogaardt, M. (2022). Identifying key ethical debates for autonomous robots in agri food: A research agenda. *AI and Ethics*, *2*(3), 493–507. doi:10.1007/s43681-021-00104-w

Sánchez, J. M., Rodríguez, J. P., & Espitia, H. E. (2020). Review of Artificial Intelligence Applied in Decision-Making. Processes in Agricultural Public Policy. *Processes*, *8*(11), 1374. doi:10.3390/pr8111374

Steele, J. L. (2023). To GPT or not GPT? Empowering our students to learn with AI. *Computers and Education: Artificial Intelligence*, *5*, 100160. doi:10.1016/j.caeai.2023.100160

Tlili, A., Shehata, B., Adarkwah, M. A., Bozkurt, A., Hickey, D. T., Huang, R., & Agyemang, B. (2023). What if the devil is my guardian angel: ChatGPT as a case study of using chatbots in education. *Smart Learning Environments*, *10*(1), 15. doi:10.1186/s40561-023-00237-x

Valencia Tafur, A. T., & Figueroa Molina, R. (2023). Incidencia de la Inteligencia Artificial en la Educación. *Educatio Siglo XXI*, *41*(3), 235–264. doi:10.6018/educatio.555681

Weber, F. (2023). Artificial Intelligence. *Artificial Intelligence for Business Analytics*. doi:10.1007/978-3-658-37599-7_2

Yang, H. (2023). *How I use ChatGPT responsibly in my teaching*. Nature Careers Community., doi:10.1038/d41586-023-01026-9

Yang, T., & Chen, J. (2023). Pre-service teachers' perceptions and intentions regarding the use of chatbots through statistical and lag sequential analysis. *Computers and Education: Artificial Intelligence*, *4*, 100119. doi:10.1016/j.caeai.2022.100119

ZhaiX. (2023). ChatGPT User Experience: Implications for Education. doi:10.2139/ssrn.4312418

KEY TERMS AND DEFINITIONS

Agenda 2030: A framework for action in terms of economic, social, and environmental sustainability to address global challenges, with the commitment of 193 member countries of the United Nations, with a deadline for achievement set in 2030.

Artificial Intelligence: It is the capability of machines to study, analyze, and make decisions about multiple topics based on a multitude of data, using different mathematical models, and additionally capable of learning and making corrections on their own responses to act in a way most similar to humans.

Chatbots: These are tools based on artificial intelligence capable of providing information through text, from a request also based in text. They can perform tasks of writing, information searching, arguing, and translating texts, in a structured way, with the requested language and writing style.

Ethics: It is a concept that serves as a guide for making decisions about certain actions that are considered morally correct in a particular society and time.

Prompts: These are instructions provided to the artificial intelligence tool, in a structured manner, by the user detailing the information requested. The instructions must be concise, clear, and without ambiguities in writing to obtain the information as accurately as needed.

Rendering: The process of improving images, which can refer to an improvement in quality, lighting characteristics, color, tone, among others, using classic computer applications (V-Ray, Photoshop, for example) or tools based on artificial intelligence.

Sustainable Development Goals: 17 goals integrated into the Agenda 2030, grouped by areas of action and defined in 169 more specific targets.

Chapter 18
Transforming Education:
Generative AI and Immediate Engineering in Synthetic Content Creation

Andreia Bem Machado
https://orcid.org/0000-0002-4404-0341
Universidade Federal de Santa Catarina, Brazil

João Rodrigues dos Santos
Instituto Superior de Educação e Ciências, Portugal

António Sacavém
Universidade Europeia, Portugal

Ramesh Sharma
Ambedkar University, Delhi, India

Rui Nunes Cruz
https://orcid.org/0000-0002-5773-6049
Universidade Europeia, Portugal

ABSTRACT

Generative AI systems are increasingly present in our daily lives, helping us make crucial decisions. They use machine learning algorithms and tools, fed with millions of data collected from the web, producing entirely new information and generating variations. And this is not just limited to texts — it can produce images, audio, videos, even code, or new programming languages. There are several fields where generative AI can have a considerable impact in the coming years. In this context, the issues proposed in this chapter are: What is generative AI? What is prompt engineering? How to transform education using generative AI and prompt engineering in creating synthetic content? To respond to the research problem, the following objective will be achieved: Investigate how to transform education using generative AI and prompt engineering in the creation of synthetic content. It is concluded that generative AI tools can also help create more efficient exercises. Teachers and educators can use technology to create instructional materials and present summaries of concepts.

DOI: 10.4018/979-8-3693-1351-0.ch018

INTRODUCTION

Within the continuum of human civilization, technological innovations possess profound significance due to their extensive and deep-seated transformative effects. Amidst the precipice of the fourth industrial revolution, a terminology conceptualized by Klaus Schwab, the Founder and Executive Chairman of the World Economic Forum, generative artificial intelligence and immediate engineering emerge as quintessential technological paradigms poised to profoundly transform educational landscapes (Stone et al., 2022). Projections suggest that by 2030, a substantial one-third of professions necessitating a bachelor's degree will be supplanted by automated systems or sophisticated software (Stone et al., 2022). The speed of technological progress is quickly meeting the previously ambitious standards set for artificial intelligence (AI). According to the AI job replacement theory, the impact of artificial intelligence on the workforce is reshaping occupational roles and this transformation presents both an avenue for innovative advancement and a potential hazard (Huang & Rust, 2018). Certain professions face the potential of becoming obsolete, whereas emergent jobs are projected to arise (Wisskirchen et al., 2017). AI technologies harbor the potential to create new job opportunities and enhance overall productivity (Lazaroiu et al., 2022; Oliinyk et al., 2021). Therefore, the exponential ascent of AI underscores the imperative for a workforce endowed with pertinent competencies to both bolster and navigate this burgeoning domain. Consequently, an AI-integrated era necessitates a citizenry proficient in data literacy, equipped to discern, utilize, interpret, and articulate data insights, and engage constructively in policy discourses influenced by AI (Hoeschl et al., 2017).

Specifically, AI emerges as an instrumental tool within the educational domain, facilitating personalized pedagogical approaches and enhancing learning efficacy (D'Mello et al., 2007; Luckin et al., 2016) and a prompt-based conversational pedagogy that promotes communication and engagement and effectively facilitates teaching and learning may be built by addressing a conversational generative AI carefully, with defined goal, tone, role, and context (Bozkurt & Sharma, 2023). The advent and ascension of the digital era have ushered in a myriad of technological breakthroughs, each systematically reconfiguring frameworks and norms in various domains; nonetheless, the application of Generative AI (GAI) in educational contexts remains in its nascent stages, and the efficacy of AI-generated media in augmenting human learning has yet to be comprehensively explored (Leiker et. al., 2023). OpenAI's tools, such as Dalle-2 and ChatGPT, not only challenge previous notions of AI limitations by enhancing the efficiency of creative media and pedagogical content but also benefit from recent advancements in generative machine learning, especially generative adversarial networks, which have revolutionized the authentic synthesis of digital content (Goodfellow et al., 2014). Technologies underpinned by GAI, which are being integrated across a spectrum of sectors encompassing entertainment, customer services, and marketing (Whittaker et al., 2021), have also notably influenced education, esteemed as a fundamental pillar of societal advancement, reflecting its seamless alignment with these technological shifts.

The widespread deployment of these technologies holds promise for addressing global educational imperatives, such as ensuring universal access to premium content, advancing global sustainable development objectives, and innovatively reconfiguring our creative and knowledge-driven labor markets while bolstering online pedagogy and catalyzing sectoral economic transformations. Further evidence of this adaptability is observed in education's incorporation of multimedia interactivity and the burgeoning influence of online educational platforms, underscoring its receptiveness to technological advancements (Leiker et. al., 2023). Indeed, GAI models are reshaping the educational landscape and driving a profound change in established teaching practices (Baidoo-Anu & Ansah, 2023). AI presents profound ramifications for teaching techniques and curriculum design, and the adoption of GAI to create synthetic content has the potential to be a viable substitute for content produced via traditional methods in online educational settings (e.g., Leiker et. al., 2023). For example, numerous educators have started empirical examinations of ChatGPT's efficacy by incorporating it into various pedagogical activities, such as teaching and researching, and they discerned that by automating specific tasks and procedures. ChatGPT offers a starting point for producing original material while welcoming broad discourse on almost any given topic (Short & Short, 2023) and facilitates the allocation of more time to pivotal endeavors such as increased interaction with students (Terwiesch, 2023)

In tandem, the groundbreaking potential of GAI in the educational context sets the stage for an academic revitalization characterized by the rise of synthetic content generation—a realm where content is not simply absorbed but is also actively crafted, tailored, and consistently refined.

GENERATIVE ARTIFICIAL INTELLIGENCE

GAI is a field of artificial intelligence that focuses on creating systems capable of generating new and original content, such as images, music, text, and even videos. *"The creative and productive potential of generative AI is enormous"* (Sætra, 2023, p. 3). This approach uses advanced algorithms to mimic patterns and characteristics found in training data, allowing systems to create unique results through continuous learning and adjustment.

For example, in the context of generative art, GAI involves the creation of works of art through the interaction between humans and machines. Artists can feed the system with specific parameters and guidelines, allowing the AI to produce creations ranging from paintings and sculptures to musical compositions and interactive installations. The collaboration between the artist and GAI results in productions that often explore new perspectives and forms of artistic expression.

As for education, interference of AI is also unquestionable, Petersen (2016) points out that the 21st century was constituted by a period of rapid change in educational processes, mainly due to technological advances. And one of the paradigmatic examples of the disruptive technological advances that the beginning of the millennium brought us is AI.Another notable example of the application of GAI is the use of deep neural networks, such as Generative Adversarial Networks (GAN). A GAN is a training model, sometimes wrongly confused with a transforming model. According to Garon (2023), citing Lee (2023), *a transformer model is a neural network that learns context and thus meaning by tracking relationships in sequential data like the words in this sentence"* (p. 14). A training model, in turn, according to Sawant et. al (2021), is a *"generative adversarial network that follows an intelligent approach to train a GAN model"*. To Wang et al. (2023), such a model is used more intensively to train systems to discriminate various dimensions of an image, namely its meaning, and context. The process takes place using deep neural networks, which allow for iterative learning regarding the mapping of the visual world according to how it is interpreted in the universe of the network. In this process, two networks, the generator and the discriminator, compete. The generator tries to create authentic samples, while the discriminator tries to distinguish between the creations generated by the AI and those existing in the training set. *"The generator G improves the generated samples using the feedback it receives from the discriminator D"* (Vuletić et. al, 2023, p. 4). Over time, this process/"competition" produces increasingly realistic and surprising content.

In this sense, about the notion of "computer-'authored' work", Abbott and Rothman (2022) state that their "discomfort with such a notion "(even if [they] cannot articulate a principled reason for the discomfort) is in keeping with a recurring phenomenon in the development of copyright law" (p. 41). Eventually, Generative Artificial Intelligence is a discipline that embraces the intersection between technology and creativity. The creative process is always initiated by the human being "who types in a prompt or prompts, and then, possibly spends time improving the results by further modifying the prompts, as part of the process of refining" (Fenwick & Jurcys, 2023, p. 17). This virtuous possibility of "man-machine" interaction allows authors and technology to collaborate in producing original and innovative works and contents while expanding the frontiers of conventional expression in the most varied domains of activity. And the Law must, necessarily, consider this new reality.From another perspective, because of its breadth, GAI has several strengths that make it a revolutionary approach in various fields. Its ability to create original and innovative content and its flexibility to adapt to different domains makes it a valuable tool in many contemporary applications. Undoubtedly, *"AI is now generating creative works in a major way, and these works have value to consumers"* (Abbott & Rothman, 2022, p. 42).

One of GAI's main advantages is its ability to produce diverse and unique content (Sharma, 2023). By experimenting with models with large volumes of data, GAI can generate an impressive variety of results, ranging from creative texts to medical or scientific dissertations. This opens doors to of discovering ideas and conceptions that might never come to light otherwise. Nevertheless, bias is still a fundamental variable in the field of AI. *"Generative models are only as good as the data they are trained on, and if the training data contains biases, the model will also be biased"* (Baidoo-Anu & Owusu Ansah, 2023, p. 10).

Speed is another of GAI's strengths. GAI can generate valuable content in literally seconds. The time savings for professionals in various fields is a priceless advantage. Still Baidoo-Anu and Owusu Ansah, within the scope of their study (2023, p. 5), state that, after instructing ChatGPT *("now discuss how COVID-19 has changed educational pedagogies")*, "within seconds" the App wrote the response. In addition, GAI can automate tasks that would otherwise be time-consuming and repetitive, such as creating graphic designs, generating background music for videos, producing short narratives, or even prescribing simple medical prescriptions and creating tasks in the broader context of all teaching-learning processes. This automation will have more and more implications in the panorama of professional activities and the number of respective jobs. Noy and Zhang (2023) underline what is already evidence at this level today, noting that *"recent advances in generative artificial intelligence may have widespread implications for production and labor markets"* (p. 2).

Adaptability is a key feature of GAI. The models can be trained on a virtually infinite range of data types, allowing them to be applied to various industries and sectors. Fenwick and Jurcys (2023), in this regard, are peremptory: *"much ink has been spilled to discuss how AI will change everything"* (p. 15). "Everything" is very suggestive of the exceptionally wide breadth of the AI. Indeed, GAI is an extraordinarily versatile tool, capable of meeting the specific needs of different fields, from medicine and education to advertising and product design, and even the arts. Nógrádi et. al (2023) corroborate the importance that AI can assume in the health area. The results of their study *"support the efficacy of general artificial intelligence like ChatGPT as a diagnostic tool in medicine."* In the field of music, for example, GAI can generate original compositions, harmonies and melodies, offering new creative possibilities for composers and musicians. Garon (2023), citing Marr (2021), points out that *"AI can also help AR (artists and repertoire – the music industry's talent scouts) discover the next generation of talent 'by combing through music and trying to identify the next breakout star'"* (p. 25).

Nowadays, it is difficult to conceive of a sector linked to creativity that cannot benefit from GAI. Deltorn and Macrez (20218 refer that *"new forms of algorithmic compositions are being developed that integrate, at the core of the creative process, automation tools based on the latest computer-science developments"* (p. 3).

In writing, GAI can produce creative texts, helping writers, for example, to overcome creative blocks or generate story ideas. It can be used to create summaries, articles, poems, and even dialog for video games and films.

Despite the individual advantages that depend on the nature of each activity, there is, however, a cross-cutting benefit for all sectors that systematically incorporate GAI into their work processes. GAI makes processes faster and more efficient. Eisfeldt et. al (2023), in their study "Generative AI and Firm Values," corroborate this evidence, noting that *"the effect of the release of ChatGPT on firm values was large, driving a difference in firm returns of approximately .4% daily, translating to over 100% on an annualized basis"* (p. 25).

Nevertheless, despite its strengths and promising applications, GAI also faces challenges. Ethical issues, such as the authorship of the content generated and the risk of spreading disinformation, need to be considered. For example, regarding the authorship of content, Deltorn and Macrez (2018) highlight that:

De lege lata, it is necessary to analyze the existing law to assess whether it allows the protection of such creations. Basically, the rule is that it is a human person who can be the cause of copyrightable creation. This leads to denying the protection to pure computer-generated creations (p. 23).

Another fundamental aspect is that, although the GAI can create surprising content, it is still deficient when it comes to "understanding" human emotions and continues to rely heavily on human intuition for starting assumptions. These factors limit AI's ability to fully capture the complexity of human reasoning and creativity. Chesterman (2023), alluding to some concrete examples, highlights that *"the technology underlying ChatGPT, LaMDA, and other models does not suggest a path to anything like sentience or consciousness"* (p. 8).

For the reason mentioned above, Abbott and Rothman (2022) highlight that some critics *"believe that AI-generated works should not be protected, either due to the argument that copyright law is intended only to promote human creativity, or because the involvement of AI alters the cost/benefit analysis"* (pp. 29-30).

In practice, Generative Artificial Intelligence does represent an impressive technological advance with distinct strengths. Its ability to create original content, adapt to different domains, and streamline creative processes makes GAI an invaluable tool in fields as diverse as medicine, education, art, design, music, and writing. For example, in the field of writing, Doshi and Hauser (2023) found that *"access to GenAI ideas causes an increase in the writer's creativity by 8% to 9% over stories written by human writers with no GenAI assistance, as assessed by third-party evaluators."*

However, it is crucial to maintain a balance between the creative potential of GAI and the still largely unknown ethical considerations that accompany it to ensure that this technology is used responsibly and beneficially for society. The ethical issues involving AI are still very incipiently developed. Already in 2023, Abotinsky and Sarel, in this regard, and explicitly referring to ChatGPT, refer that they are *"among the first academic authors to explore how one could utilize ChatGPT to write academic articles while maintaining ethical boundaries"* (p. 7). This shows how embryonic research in this field is at present.

Indeed, the rise of GAI has brought a host of concerns ranging from ethical issues to social and cultural implications. While GAI offers many creative and innovative advantages, these concerns deserve attention to ensure that this technology is used responsibly and beneficially for society.

Sætra (2023), according to the next figure 1, refer that *"one way to sort the different concerns is through distinguishing between implications on a societal level (macro level), on sectors, groups, or organizations (meso level), or individuals (micro level)"* (p. 4).

Figure 1. Dangers on the micro, meso, and micro levels
Source: Sætra, (2023, p. 5)

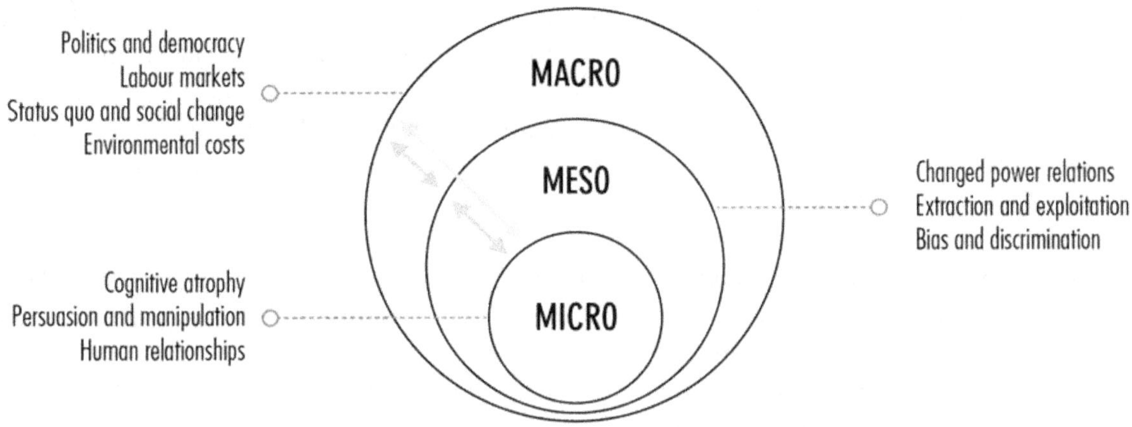

One of the main concerns related to GAI is the issue of authorship and originality. As machines (hardware and software) generate medical, educational, and artistic content, such as music or literary texts, the dilemma of who should be considered the true author of the work arises. This can challenge traditional concepts of authorship and copyright, raising questions about appropriation, plagiarism, and intellectual property. In this regard, *"the first assumption is that in which no copyright cannot be awarded, because of insufficient originality or lack of identification of a human author"* (Deltorn & Macrez, 2018, p. 8).

Another major concern related to GAI is the spread of misinformation and false content. GAI has the potential to create texts, images, and videos so convincing that it is difficult to distinguish between what is produced by humans and what is generated by technological devices. In this regard, Boussioux et. al (2023) warn that *"even with sophisticated prompting and fine-tuning techniques or the development of proprietary in-house models, organizations may find themselves caught in a loop of self-reinforcing biases and narrowing perspectives"* (p. 15). This evidence can be exploited to create fake news, misleading information, or manipulated content, undermining trust in information sources and increasing the spread of disinformation.

In the same vein, diversity and representation are also critical issues. As GAI models are trained on previously existing data, GAI creations may reflect those biases if that data is biased or limited in diversity. Precisely in this sense, Baidoo-Anu and Owusu Ansah (2023), using the ChatGPT technology as an example, emphasize that *"despite the myriad of potential educational benefits, in its current state ChatGPT has been found to have several serious inherent limitations, such as generating wrong answers and making up articles that do not exist"* (p. 14). This plausible possibility could perpetuate stereotypes, discrimination, and a lack of representation, becoming a problematic reflection of society.

In the artistic field, GAI can impact the value and authenticity of works of art. With the possibility of creating perfect imitations of famous styles, the distinction between original and replicated art becomes blurred. Such a framework can devalue authentic works and harm artists who depend on their artistic creations to support themselves. Burk (2023) is very critical at this level. The author begins by noting that the *"new industrial inputs generated by machine learning provide a substitute for human creativity"* (p. 1673). Afterward, he points out that *"this newly cheap creativity shifts our concern [...] toward concerns over the value of authenticity"* (p. 1673).

Job displacement is also a significant concern. As the GAI automates the creation of content in a wide variety of fields, there is a risk that professionals in different areas will lose out on job opportunities. Still, in the field of writing, Noy and Zhang (2023) reached an important conclusion in their study:

The generative writing tool increases the output quality of low-ability workers while reducing their time spent, and it allows high-ability workers to maintain their quality standards while becoming significantly faster (pp. 11-12).

It is perfectly possible to logically admit that the gist of the above conclusion can be extrapolated to most professional activities. However, the current transformation requires reflection on how societies should adapt to ensure that automation does not result in mass unemployment. It is indisputably a concern that should guide IA research in the future. Eisfeldt et. al (2023) reinforce this idea when they state that *"AI advances will have a broad impact on the economy through its effects on labor inputs"* (p. 2).

From another perspective, privacy and security are also worrying issues. GAI can generate realistic images of people who do not exist, raising concerns about the misuse of false images for harmful purposes, such as creating fake profiles on social networks or manipulating online identities.

From another perspective, there are also concerns about how AI can affect creativity and the value of human work. Moreover, the ethical approach to AI is still in its infancy. Precisely in this direction, Abotinsky and Sarel (2023) hope that their recent article, from 2023 (July), entitled "Co-authoring with an AI? Ethical Dilemmas and Artificial Intelligence", *"will raise the awareness of law reviews to this lacuna by pointing a spotlight on the ethical challenges involved in AI"* (p. 30). If GAI is used on a large scale to create content, there is a risk that the role of creative professionals and entrepreneurs will be diminished, leading to a reduction in the value attributed to human creation. Boussioux et. al (2023) draw attention to this aspect of the GAI, which may be less optimistic. GAI models can achieve results that, under normal conditions, are unattainable for humans.

Generative AI models are particularly well-suited to propose diverse ideas due to their training on a vast amount of data and a vast capacity to generate a wide variety of potential solutions or concepts that humans may not think of (p. 2).

Indeed, as GAI models evolve, situations may arise in which the machine needs to make decisions about the content to be generated, which can raise ethical dilemmas about responsibility for these decisions and their consequences.

Authenticity, disinformation, bias, privacy, and impact on employment are just some of the issues that require careful attention to ensure that GAI is a positive force in society. Burk (2023), leaving a warning, stresses that *"AI systems promise (or threaten) to lower the cost of initial development of creative goods, potentially displacing human creators"* (p. 1669). Hassine and Neeman (2019), in turn, *"point out the major problems that afflict this use of AI technology in an art historical context, rife with culturally biased interpretations"* (p. 28). Ongoing dialogue between researchers, entrepreneurs and creatives, regulators, and the general public is vital to tackling challenges such as these and developing increasingly responsible approaches in the context of using GAI.

The truth is that IoT is emerging day by day, at great speed, as an exciting field with vast potential applications in various industries, and doubts are increasingly being cast in the face of certainties. In this sense, Sætra (2023) draws attention to the "potential pitfalls" created by generative AI and the dangers that may result from a society developing from generative AI interfering in all its sectors. There is little doubt that, as technology evolves sequentially and iteratively, IoT is expected to play an increasingly fundamental role in practically every sector of society. Areas such as health, education, art, design, and entertainment account for a tiny part of the universe of potential GAI applications.

The lack of human interaction can indeed be, initially, an element considered problematic. For example, in the field of education, Baidoo-Anu and Owusu Ansah (2023) stress that *"generative models are not capable of providing the same level of human interaction as a real teacher or tutor"* (p. 10).

Even so, the advantages will probably outweigh the disadvantages by boosting human innovation and creativity. Doshi and Hauser (2023) reinforce this idea, stressing that *"the advent of generative artificial intelligence (GenAI) holds promise for humans to be more creative by offering new ideas and new. The field of health and medicine is a good example in this context. GAI could play a vital role in the interpretation of medical images, helping healthcare professionals to identify diseases and conditions more accurately.* In this very important domain, Nógrádi et. al (2023) *"found that ChatGPT-determined dGAInoses can reach the probability level of other experts, furthermore, it surpasses the probability of an appropriate dGAInosis if the examiner is a general medical doctor."* GAI could be used to generate 3D models of organs and anatomical structures to aid diagnosis and surgical planning. In addition, GAI could be used to develop personalized medicines by modeling complex molecular interactions and speeding up the drug discovery process.

In education, GAI can be used to create personalized teaching materials, adapted to each student's pace and learning style (Sharma, 2023). Abotinsky and Sarel (2023), regarding the potential influence that AI can have on the transformation of the formal teaching-learning process, emphasize that *"the use of AI [...] points to a possible evolution of the scholar's role, in which the focus is on asking the right questions rather than solely on searching for and articulating conclusions"* (p. 30).

For now, the generation of interactive educational resources (such as simulations, personalized tutorials, or chatbots) of adaptive learning content, adapting the material according to the individual needs of the students, is pointed out as one of the greatest virtues associated with GAI. In this context, it is perfectly possible to extrapolate Doshi's and Hauser (2023) conclusions: *"stories [texts and didactic resources] written with access to GenAI ideas are considered to be better written and more enjoyable, with improvements of up to 22% to 26% among less creative writers."*

In art and design, GAI has demonstrated its ability to create unique and innovative works and projects. Artists and designers can use generative algorithms to produce visual pieces, music, sculptures, and even fashion. Noy and Zhang (2023), focusing on ChatGPT analysis, attest that AI improves labor productivity in two vectors: reducing the time workers spend on the task and complementing workers' skills. The authors conclude that *"humans and ChatGPT working together could produce more than the sum of their parts"* (p. 5). As GAI improves its understanding of human style, collaboration between artists and algorithms could create new forms of artistic expression that defy traditional boundaries and can make final products even more effective.

The same logic can be applied to areas such as marketing and advertising or entertainment. GAI can be used to create innovative and increasingly engaging advertising campaigns. In the entertainment sector, GAI is already being used to create convincing virtual characters in video games and films. Garon (2023), referring to Breznican (2022), provides an interesting example in this regard: *"the use of generative AI has also seen great success, made famous by one of the most iconic voices on stage and screen—that of James Earl Jones"* (p. 25). The evolution of this technology could enable the creation of more complex interactive narratives. Generating scripts for films, series, and games is another dimension in which GAI will become increasingly important. In this context, generative music, for example, could evolve to create personalized soundtracks, while generating visual effects could improve the visual quality of productions. Still, Garon (2023), in this context, highlights that *"the entire creative process for making music is being influenced and occasionally reproduced using AI. The future of music is rapidly moving into the hands of the machine"* (p. 25).

Despite the potential advantages underlying AI, it is increasingly important to note that ethical questions of privacy and privacy are also emerging as it plays a more prominent role in various industries. In this regard, Boussioux et. al (2023) warn of a possible impasse, challenging to resolve in practice, as it presupposes overcoming the limitations of human beings. *"Generative AI might grapple with the challenge of paralleling human creativity and the capacity to undertake intuitive leaps encompassing serendipity, unpredictability, and profound domain expertise"* (pp. 2-3). Generative Artificial Intelligence indeed has the potential to revolutionize virtually every area of activity. As technology evolves, GAI is expected to boost creativity, improve efficiency, and open even more possibilities in health, education, art, entertainment, and many other areas. However, monitoring its development closely and ensuring it is used ethically and responsibly is essential. In fact, Doshi and Hauser (2023), at this level, warn of the equally valid possibility that ideas and concepts *"provided by GenAI may also anchor a human creator, resulting in less creative output."*

Furthermore, in view of the need to continually increase reliability in GAI and to safeguard its ethical dimension ever more effectively, it is expected that research in the area is set to continue with significant and far-reaching advances as experts seek to deepen their understanding and explore new frontiers of this technology. Burk (2023), referring to Burk (2020), in this regard, emphasizes that *"much of what has been written on the [AI] topic to date has mistakenly focused on unproductive questions about whether machine learning can be considered an 'inventor'"* (pp. 1672-1673). It is expected that the evolution of research in the field of GAI will follow several key directions.

In the same vein, as computational resources continue to expand, researchers will be able to develop even more advanced and complex GAI models. Garon (2023) states that *"the core attribute of generative AI is an increase in information"* (p. 45). Following, the same author (2023), citing Pllana (2019), states that "at present, the total amount of human knowledge doubles 'every twelve months and in the near future is expected every twelve hours'" (p. 45). This could include creating deeper neural networks and innovative architectures that allow machines to generate increasingly sophisticated and realistic content. Hassine and Neeman (2019), framing this issue in the field of art, are clear about the long road that still must be taken in this field. The authors state that:

As much as the advances in AI and Neural Networks should be applauded, one might consider projects such as Next Rembrandt, DEEPART, and Edmond de Belamy, from La Famille de Belamy be generating "Zombie Art" (p. 29).

Further on, in the same article, Hassine and Neeman ((2019) state that *"these images are like the living dead or specters: they are zombie images"* (p. 1669).

Still, Hassine and Neeman (2019), to conclude, are categorical. Citing Knight (2019), they leave the following question: *"Are not these images 'deepfakes'? [...] Or simply put: are they not just machine-made forgeries?"* (p. 29).

Therefore, researchers are expected to remain committed to exploring how GAI can increasingly "understand" and imitate human creativity, generating solutions in a wide variety of fields that stand out for their innovation, originality, and increased effectiveness. Despite everything, Boussioux et. al (2023) do not exempt man from *this process and focus on man-machine complementarity. The authors stress that "while humans are more likely to generate innovative responses, AI is more likely to create valuable outputs with higher environmental and financial value"* (p. 14).

Research in this area of GAI will continue to systematically involve more and more interdisciplinary collaborations between computer scientists, experts, and academics from various fields.

The increased interdisciplinarity and complexity of GAI will make it even more comprehensive and robust. Nógrádi et. al (2023), referring to Mbakwe et. al (2023) and Arif et. al (2023) emphasize this idea, noting that *"userfriendly AIs like ChatGPT might revolutionize numerous fields"* (p. 10). For this reason, research will inevitably also focus on ethical and social issues. In the future, researchers will continue to work to define standards and guidelines for the responsible use of GAI, addressing concerns such as authorship, disinformation, bias, and employment impacts. For example, Chesterman (2023), leaves his pertinent point of view on this matter. The author points out that *"assuming that we desire a thriving arts sector that gainfully employs humans, we should be clear that their creations are protected while machine creations are not"* (p. 6).

Finally, it is still very foreseeable that research in the field of GAI will expand to explore new domains, opening doors to unexpected applications at this stage. As the technology advances, new industries and fields will be able to benefit from the creativity and innovation provided by GAI.

METHODOLOGY

A bibliometric analysis was conducted based on a search in the Scopus and Web of Science (WoS) databases by Clarivate Analytics in order to understand better, measure, and analyze scientific literature publications on trust in the area of digital education. Planning, data collecting, and bibliometrics were the three steps of the study's development process. These data allowed for the organization of pertinent data for bibliometric analysis, including temporal distribution, significant authors, institutions, and countries, kind of publishing in the region, primary keywords, and the most cited works (de Bem Machado et al., 2022).

Scientific mapping makes it possible to investigate and draw a global picture of scientific knowledge from a statistical perspective. It mainly uses the three knowledge structures to present scientific research's structural and dynamic aspects. This methodology was used with the aim of mapping and understanding the state of the art of the research topic, as well as answering the following questions:

RQ1: What is generative AI?
RQ 2: What is prompt engineering?
RQ3: How to transform education using generative AI and prompt engineering in creating synthetic content?

Considering the research problems, the search terms were defined during the planning phase, namely "Generative Artificial Intelligence," "Education," and "Engineering". And as a fundamental principle for the search, the choice was made when planning the search to use the terms in the "title, abstract, and keyword" fields, without delimiting time, language, or any other restriction that could limit the result.

Results

After planning the research, data collection retrieved 7 documents from the Scopus database and 4 documents from the Web of Science database. The eligible articles in the Scopus and Web of Science databases were published in 2023, the year the research was carried out. It can thus be seen that this is a very current topic.

Of the 7 papers in the Scopus database and 4 in the Web of Science database, there is a varied list of authors, institutions, and countries that stand out in the research on the subject. When analyzing the country with the most publications in the area, it can be seen that Australia stands out with an average of 43% of the total publications, a total of 3, in the Scopus database. In the Web of Science database, the United States and Germany have the same number of publications - 2 in each country. Figure 1 shows the leading countries publishing on this subject in the Scopus and WOS databases. in the publications in the Scopus database, and graph 2 shows the six countries that are prominent in publications in the Web of Science database.

Figure 2. Distribution of papers by country

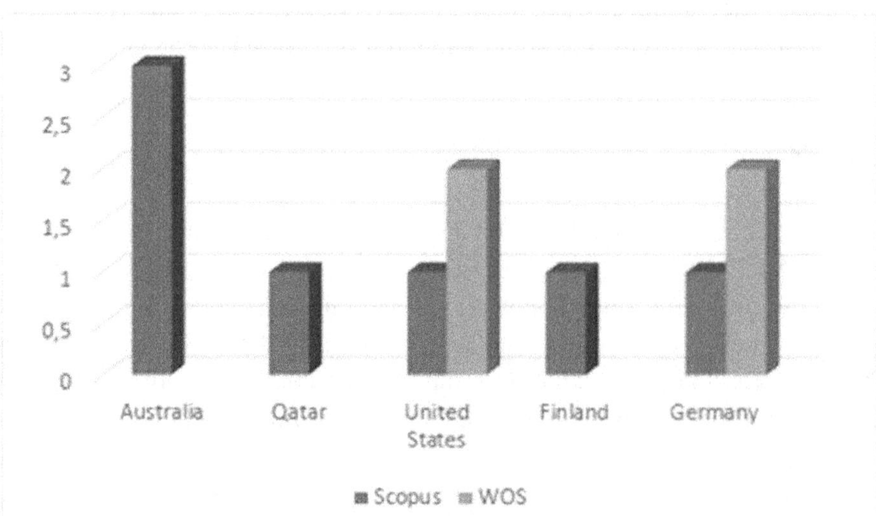

Figure 3. Authors' main affiliations

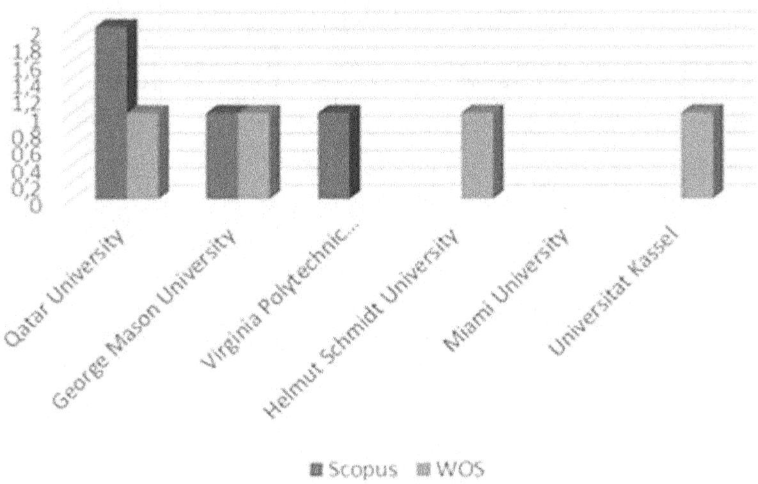

Another analysis carried out is related to the identification of authors; it was observed that there is a reference author in the database in Scopus database which is Junaid Qadir from Qatar University, Doha, Qatar, with two publications, an editorial entitled Generative Artificial Intelligence and Engineering Education and another conference paper Engineering Education in the Era of ChatGPT: Promise and Pitfalls of Generative AI for Education.

Concerning the affiliations that publish the most on the subject of AI, Qatar University wins with 2 papers published in Scopus and 1 in WOS. Figure 2 shows the main affiliations that publish in the area of generative AI and immediate engineering in the creation of synthetic content.

With the information from the systematic search, we obtained the results of the review considered relevant for the complete reading of the articles, as it is a current topic and the works were all published in 2023. This analysis identified 7 papers published in the Scopus database and 4 in the WOS database. Three papers were repeated in both databases. Table 1 shows the data of all the papers, as well as their abstracts, which served as a basis to answer the research problem.

After the researchers read and analyzed the articles, they identified some themes that stood out in this research's main problem: "How to transform education using generative AI and prompt engineering in creating synthetic content?" which will be discussed and answered in the next topic.

TRANSFORM EDUCATION USING GENERATIVE AI AND IMMEDIATE ENGINEERING IN SYNTHETIC CONTENT CREATION

A subfield of computer science called artificial intelligence (AI) aims to create digital or physical devices that can think and act like humans (de Bem Machado et al., 2023). John McCarthy defined artificial intelligence (AI) in 1956 during a conference of computer specialists at Dartmouth College. AI is the science and engineering of creating intelligent computers (de Bem Machado et al., 2023).

Table 1. Articles extracted from the systematic review

Year	Author	Title	Type of Publication	Database	Summary
2023	Aditya Johri, Andrew S. Katz, Junaid Qadir, Ashish Hingle	Generative artificial intelligence and engineering education	Editoral	Scopus e WOS	The editorial discusses the potential impact of GAI for engineering education as researchers and teachers.
	Fariborz Sobhanmanesh, Amin Beheshti; Nicholas Nouri, Natalia Monje Chapparo, Sandya Raj; Richard A. George	A Cognitive Model for Technology Adoption	Articule	Scopus	The article aims to propose a new parametric mathematical model to predict the adoption rate of emerging technologies through a unique data-driven pipeline.
	Fadel M.Megahed, Ying-Ju Chen; Joshua A. Ferris; Sven Knoth; L. Allison Jones-Farmer,	How generative AI models such as ChatGPT can be (mis)used in SPC practice, education, and research? An exploratory study	Articule	Scopus e WOS	The study indicates that the current version of ChatGPT works well for structured tasks, such as translating code from one language to another and explaining well-known concepts, but struggles with more subtle tasks, such as explaining less well-known terms and creating code from scratch.
	Junaid Qadir	Engineering Education in the Era of ChatGPT: Promise and Pitfalls of Generative AI for Education	Conference paper	Scopus	The research explains engineering educators' understanding of the implications of generative AI represented by ChatGPT, as well as how they will adapt the engineering education ecosystem to ensure that the next generation of engineers can take advantage of the benefits offered by generative AI, while minimizing any negative consequences.
	Bronwyn Eager, Ryan Brunton	Prompting Higher Education Towards AI-Augmented Teaching and Learning Practice	Articule	Scopus	The article explains instructional advice for writing instructional texts to guide the generation of quality results from AI models, as well as a case study to illustrate the use of AI for assessment design.
	Sasha Nikolic, Scott Daniel, Rezwanul Haque, Marina Belkina, Ghulam M. Hassan, Sarah Grundy, Sarah Lyden, Peter Neal, Caz Sandison	ChatGPT versus engineering education assessment: a multidisciplinary and multi-institutional benchmarking and analysis of this generative artificial intelligence tool to investigate assessment integrity	Articule	Scopus e WOS	The article examines how ChatGPT can affect assessment in engineering education by exploring ChatGPT responses to existing assessment requests from ten subjects at seven Australian universities.
	Henriikka Vartiainen and Matti Tedre	Using artificial intelligence in craft education: crafting with text-to-image generative models	Articule	Scopus	The research implemented a practical workshop on creative creation with generative text-to-image AI, in order to stimulate discourses and capture imaginaries about generative AI.
	Sofia Schoebel, Anuschka Schmitt,Dennis Benner; Mohammed Saqr, Andreas Janson,Jan Marco Leimeister	Charting the Evolution and Future of Conversational Agents: A Research Agenda Along Five Waves and New Frontiers	Articule	WOS	The research discussed the moderating role of major technologies and new technological advances such as OpenAI GPT or BLOOM NLU that mark the next frontier of Conversational Agents (CAs) research.

It is clear that artificial intelligence has developed gradually and has always been accompanied by high expectations, many of which have not been fully realized. As a result, there have been times of tremendous investment and enthusiasm as well as times of disappointment and scarcity of resources. The current situation is thought to be one of both excitement and concern because of technological advancements that hint at the development of a super-intelligence that will be more capable than the most advanced human minds (Chesterman, 2023).

In this scenario, we find generative AI, a branch of artificial intelligence centered on computer models capable of generating original content. By harnessing the power of large language models, neural networks and machine learning, generative AI can produce new content that mimics human creativity (Johri et. al., 2023). These models are trained using large data sets and deep learning algorithms that learn the underlying structures, relationships, and patterns in the data. The results are new and unique outputs based on input prompts, including images, video, code, music, design, translation, question answering and text.

Generative AI models work by using neural networks inspired by the neurons in the human brain to learn patterns and features from existing data. These models can then generate new data aligned with the learned patterns. For example, a generative AI model trained on a set of images can create new images similar to the ones it was trained on. This is similar to how language models can generate expansive text based on words provided for context (Doshi & Hauser, 2023).

Learning from large data sets allows these models to refine their results through iterative training processes. The model analyzes the relationships within given data, effectively gaining knowledge from the examples provided. By adjusting their parameters and minimizing the difference between the desired and generated results, generative AI models can continuously improve their ability to generate high-quality, contextually relevant content. The results, whether an eccentric poem or a chatbot's customer support response, can often be indistinguishable from human-generated content (Lee, 2023).

Prompt engineering in the realm of generative AI holds significant importance due to its role in shaping the outputs of language models. As artificial intelligence systems, especially those based on models like GPT-3, lack inherent understanding and consciousness, prompt engineering becomes a critical bridge between user intent and model response.

At its core, prompt engineering involves formulating input instructions or queries that guide the generative AI model towards generating desired outputs. The art lies in crafting prompts that are clear, precise, and effectively communicate the user's expectations. This process becomes especially important as it influences the creativity, relevance, and coherence of the generated content.

One key aspect of prompt engineering is the understanding that the AI model responds to the input it receives. Users can harness this by tailoring prompts to elicit specific types of information or creative outputs. For instance, in a scenario where the user wants the AI to generate a creative piece in a particular style, the prompt should be carefully constructed to convey the desired tone, theme, or mood.

Prompt engineering in the context of generative AI has the potential to significantly transform education by offering innovative solutions to various challenges faced by educators, learners, and educational institutions. This transformative impact is rooted in the ability of generative AI models, like GPT-3, to generate contextually relevant and educational content based on well-crafted prompts.

One fundamental aspect of the importance of prompt engineering in education is its role in personalized learning. By carefully designing prompts, educators can tailor AI-generated content to meet the specific needs and learning styles of individual students. This personalized approach enhances engagement and comprehension, as the AI model adapts its responses to address the unique requirements of each learner. For instance, a prompt can be designed to generate explanations, examples, or practice problems tailored to a student's proficiency level or learning preferences.

Furthermore, generative AI can assist in content creation for educational materials. Educators often spend a significant amount of time developing resources such as lesson plans, quizzes, and educational content. With well-crafted prompts, AI models can aid in the generation of high-quality, curriculum-aligned materials, saving educators time and enabling them to focus on individualized instruction and mentorship.

Prompt engineering also plays a crucial role in language learning and development. AI models can assist learners in practicing language skills by generating prompts that encourage written or spoken responses. For example, a language learning prompt could involve asking the AI model to provide feedback on a student's essay, correct language errors, or engage in conversational exchanges. This real-time interaction contributes to language acquisition and proficiency.

Ethical considerations are also paramount. Prompt engineering becomes a tool not just for efficiency but also for instilling ethical values in AI-generated educational content. Careful formulation of prompts is essential to avoid biases, misinformation, or inappropriate content.

Prompt engineering in the context of generative AI holds immense potential to revolutionize education. By leveraging AI to generate personalized, interactive, and adaptive content, educators can enhance the learning experience for students. However, a thoughtful and ethical approach to prompt engineering is crucial to maximize the benefits and address potential challenges, ensuring that AI becomes a valuable ally in the educational landscape.

CONCLUSION

The main thrust of this work was to evaluate, and discuss, the major transformative effects of Generative Artificial Intelligence (GAI) and immediate engineering when applied to the context of education, (D'Mello et al., 2007; Luckin et al., 2016) analyzing and evaluating their creative potential in terms of content development and their degree of impact in various fields such as art, education, and creativity (Sharma, 2023). Without forgetting issues related to ethics, our research addresses the theme and implications of the GAI in content creation, emphasizing the need to use it responsibly and reflecting on the latest research being carried out in this field.

The use of GAI not only in education but also in content creation shows significant influences on the quality and efficiency of work. Several of the most common IAG tools contribute positively to increasing the quality of results and performance of lower-skilled employees, while at the same time reducing the time spent on tasks and enabling higher-skilled workers to maintain and even increase their quality standards, making them significantly faster in execution. However, and it's important to stress this, the widespread use of AI has raised concerns about its impact on the economy, on the use of labor, on privacy, on safety and, above all, on the value of human labor, (Burk, 2023; Chesterman, 2023).

In addition to all this, reflection on the ethical implications of the use of GAI in content creation in general, and especially in education, is still in its relative infancy and taking its first steps, and there is a need to better explore its implications and, at the same time, sensitize both developers and users to the ethical challenges involved and raised by AI.

It is very clear to us, from what has been observed in this work, that as this new technology advances, interdisciplinary collaborations at academic or even business level will increasingly play a crucial role in the exploration, development, and utilization of new applications. At the same time, addressing ethical and social issues related to AI becomes unavoidable so as not to cross certain lines that jeopardize its validity and healthy use in favor of the growth of human knowledge.

In the field of education, the GAI has vast potential to transform teaching and learning practices (Petersen, 2016). And it can develop this both by providing pedagogical advice for writing texts, or even articles and essays, and by helping to design assessment models. GAI can also be used to support teaching in the fields of engineering and has a strong potential to revolutionize teaching and research in the field of medicine (Nógrádi et. al, 2023). Nonetheless, however, it is essential to consider the responsible use of GAI in all areas of education, defining rules, standards and guidelines that contribute to resolving issues related to authorship and its rights, misinformation, bias and the impact on employment.

All of this is to say that, while IAGs offer significant potential for innovation and efficiency in various fields, particularly in education and content creation, it is crucial to create dynamic regulations that establish paths and guidelines for good practice in ethical, social and economic matters and issues as their use becomes more widespread. The full potential of the GAI will not be properly exploited unless this route is taken, mitigating its potential negative impacts.

Future paths in the field of Generative Artificial Intelligence (GAI) could center on exploring the potential benefits and challenges of its AI in different educational areas, or even in vocational training, and in the creation of pedagogical content and skills development. This path, we emphasize, should include interdisciplinary collaborations to address ethical and social issues related to AI, defining standards and guidelines for responsible use when developing and exploring new applications and new domains for AI technology. Other possible studies could investigate the impact of AI on the economy, labor, privacy, security and the value of human labor, as well as the potential implications of the use of AI on copyright, disinformation and the spread of fake news, bias and decision-making, and the impact on employment.

Research and development work should also continue to explore the potential of AI in transforming teaching and learning practices, and above all its use as a tool to support research work.

Human-tool interaction is another area for development and improvement. The success of technology companies was explosive when the machine was demystified and, above all, made easier to use in a user-friendly way. AI and GAI are acronyms for a technology that for many people still resides in the realms of imaginary science fiction. Making it more accessible, understandable and user-friendly is a challenge for its development and future research.

In general, future research in the field of GAI can aim to comprehensively understand the implications and potential of AI in education and content creation and exploring new applications and domains for the use of technology such in value added areas like medicine.

REFERENCES

Abbott, R. B., & Rothman, E. (2022). (Forthcoming). Disrupting Creativity: Copyright Law in the Age of Generative Artificial Intelligence (August 8, 2022). *Florida Law Review*. doi:10.2139/ssrn.4185327

Arif, T. B., Munaf, U., & Ul-Haque, I. (2023). The future of medical education and research: Is ChatGPT a blessing or blight in disguise? *Medical Education Online*, *28*(1), 2181052. doi:10.1080/10872981.2023.2181052 PMID:36809073

Baidoo-AnuD.Owusu AnsahL. (2023). Education in the era of generative artificial intelligence (AI): Understanding the potential benefits of ChatGPT in promoting teaching and learning. doi:10.2139/ssrn.4337484

BoussiouxL. N.LaneJ.ZhangM.JacimovicV.LakhaniK. R. (2023). The Crowdless Future? How Generative AI Is Shaping the Future of Human Crowdsourcing. *The Crowdless Future*. doi:10.2139/ssrn.4533642

Bozkurt, A., & Sharma, R. C. (2023). Generative AI and prompt engineering: The art of whispering to let the genie out of the algorithmic world. *Asian Journal of Distance Education, 18*(2), i–vii. doi:10.5281/zenodo.8174941

Breznican, A. (2022). *Darth Vader's Voice Emanated From War-Torn Ukraine*. Vanity Fair. https://www.vanityfair.com/hollywood/2022/09/darth-vaders-voice-emanated-from-war-torn-ukraine

Burk, D. L. (2020). AI patents and the self-assembling machine. *Minn. L. Rev. Headnotes, 105*, 301.

BurkD. L. (2023). Cheap Creativity and What It Will Do. *Georgia Law Review, 57*. doi:10.2139/ssrn.4397423

Chesterman, S. (2023). AI-generated content is taking over the world. But who owns it? *NUS Law Working Paper No. 2023/002*. doi:10.2139/ssrn.4321596

D'Mello, S., Picard, R. W., & Graesser, A. (2007). Toward an affect-sensitive AutoTutor. *IEEE Intelligent Systems, 22*(4), 53–61. doi:10.1109/MIS.2007.79

De Bem Machado, A., Dandolini, G. A., de Souza, J. A., Lytras, M. D., & Sousa, M. J. (2023). Artificial Intelligence: Applicability of This Technology to Higher Education–A Scoping Review. *Technologies for Sustainable Global Higher Education*, 211-236.

De Bem Machado, A., Sousa, M. J., & Dandolini, G. A. (2022, April). Digital Learning Technologies in Higher Education: A Bibliometric Study. In *Proceedings of International Conference on Information Technology and Applications: ICITA 2021* (pp. 697-705). Springer Nature Singapore. 10.1007/978-981-16-7618-5_59

Deltorn, J.-M., & Macrez, F. (2018). Authorship in the Age of Machine learning and Artificial Intelligence (August 1, 2018). In: Sean M. O'Connor (ed.), The Oxford Handbook of Music Law and Policy. Centre for International Intellectual Property Studies (CEIPI) Research Paper No. 2018-10. doi:10.2139/ssrn.3261329

DoshiA. R.HauserO. (2023). Generative Artificial Intelligence Enhances Creativity (August 8, 2023). doi:10.2139/ssrn.4535536

Eager, B., & Brunton, R. (2023). Prompting higher education towards AI-augmented teaching and learning practice. *Journal of University Teaching & Learning Practice, 20*(5), 02.

EisfeldtA. L.SchubertG.ZhangM. B. (2023). Generative AI and Firm Values (May 2, 2023). doi:10.3386/w31222

Fenwick, M., & Jurcys, P. (2023). Originality and the Future of Copyright in an Age of Generative AI. *SSRN, 4354449*. https://ssrn.com/abstract=4354449

GaronJ. M. (2023). A Practical Introduction to Generative AI, Synthetic Media, and the Messages Found in the Latest Medium (March 14, 2023). doi:10.2139/ssrn.4388437

Goodfellow, I., Pouget-Abadie, J., Mirza, M., Xu, B., Warde-Farley, D., Ozair, S., Courville, A., & Bengio, Y. (2014). Generative adversarial nets. *Advances in Neural Information Processing Systems, 27*, 2672–2680.

Hassine, T., & Neeman, Z. (2019). The Zombification of art history: How AI resurrects dead masters, and perpetuates historical biases. *Journal of Science and Technology of the Arts*, *11*(2), 28–35. doi:10.7559/citarj.v11i2.663

Hoeschl, M. B., Bueno, T. C., & Hoeschl, H. C. (2017, November). Fourth industrial revolution and the future of engineering: could robots replace human jobs? How ethical recommendations can help engineers rule on artificial intelligence. In *2017 7th World Engineering Education Forum (WEEF)* (pp. 21-26). IEEE. 10.1109/WEEF.2017.8466973

Huang, M. H., & Rust, R. T. (2018). Artificial intelligence in service. *Journal of Service Research*, *21*(2), 155–172. doi:10.1177/1094670517752459

JabotinskyH. Y.SarelR. (2023). Co-authoring with an AI? Ethical Dilemmas and Artificial Intelligence (July 31, 2023). doi:10.2139/ssrn.4303959

Johri, A., Katz, A. S., Qadir, J., & Hingle, A. (2023). Generative artificial intelligence and engineering education. *Journal of Engineering Education*, *112*(3), 572–577. doi:10.1002/jee.20537

Knight, W. (2019). The world's top deepfake artist is wrestling with the monster he created. *Technology Review*. https://www.technologyreview.com/2019/08/16/133686/the-worlds-top-deepfake-artist-is-wrestling-with-the-monster-he-created/

Lăzăroiu, G., Androniceanu, A., Grecu, I., Grecu, G., & Negurita, O. (2022). Artificial intelligence-based decisionmaking algorithms, Internet of Things sensing networks, and sustainable cyber-physical management systems in big data-driven cognitive manufacturing. *Oeconomia Copernicana*, *13*(4), 1047–1080. doi:10.24136/oc.2022.030

Lee, A. (2023). *What Are Large Language Models Used For?* NVIDIA. https://blogs.nvidia.com/blog/2023/01/26/what-are-large-language-models-used-for/

Leiker, D., Gyllen, A. R., Eldesouky, I., & Cukurova, M. (2023). Generative AI for learning: Investigating the potential of synthetic learning videos. *arXiv preprint arXiv:2304.03784.* https://doi.org//arXiv.2304.03784 doi:10.48550

Luckin, R., Holmes, W., Griffiths, M., & Forcier, L. B. (2016). *Intelligence unleashed: An argument for AI in education.* Pearson Education.

Marr, B. (2021). How Artificial Intelligence (AI) Is Helping Musicians Unlock Their Creativity. *Forbes*. https://www.forbes.com/sites/bernardmarr/2021/05/14/how-artificial-intelligence-ai-is-helpingmusicians-unlock-their-creativity/?sh=29ab2f667004

Mbakwe, A. B., Lourentzou, I., Celi, L. A., Mechanic, O. J., & Dagan, A. (2023). ChatGPT passing USMLE shines a spotlight on the flaws of medical education. *PLOS Digital Health*, *2*(2), e0000205. doi:10.1371/journal.pdig.0000205 PMID:36812618

Megahed, F. M., Chen, Y. J., Ferris, J. A., Knoth, S., & Jones-Farmer, L. A. (2023). How generative ai models such as chatgpt can be (mis) used in spc practice, education, and research? an exploratory study. *Quality Engineering*, 1–29. doi:10.1080/08982112.2023.2206479

Nikolic, S., Daniel, S., Haque, R., Belkina, M., Hassan, G. M., Grundy, S., & Sandison, C. (2023). ChatGPT versus engineering education assessment: A multidisciplinary and multi-institutional benchmarking and analysis of this generative artificial intelligence tool to investigate assessment integrity. *European Journal of Engineering Education*, 1–56. doi:10.1080/03043797.2023.2248042

NógrádiB.PolgárT. F.MeszlényiV.KádárZ.HertelendyP.CsátiA.PataiR. (2023). ChatGPT MD: Is there any room for generative AI in neurology and other medical areas? doi:10.2139/ssrn.4372965

NoyS.ZhangW. (2023). Experimental Evidence on the Productivity Effects of Generative Artificial Intelligence. SSRN. doi:10.2139/ssrn.4375283

Oliinyk, O., Bilan, Y., & Mishchuk, H. (2021). Knowledge Management and Economic Growth: The Assessment of Links and Determinants of Regulation. *Central European Management Journal, 29*(3), 20–39. doi:10.7206/cemj.2658-0845.52

Petersen, J. (2016). *Innovative assessment practices*. FreshGrade Education Inc. https://learn.sd61.bc.ca/wp-content/uploads/sites/96/2017/09/FG-Innovative-Assessment-Whitepaper.pdf

Pllana, D. (2019). Expanding Entire Volume of Knowledge Influences on Incrementing Individual Knowledge. *Global Journal of Human-Social Science: H Interdisciplinary, 19*(8).

Qadir, J. (2023, May). Engineering education in the era of ChatGPT: Promise and pitfalls of generative AI for education. In *2023 IEEE Global Engineering Education Conference (EDUCON)* (pp. 1-9). IEEE. 10.1109/EDUCON54358.2023.10125121

SætraH. S. (2023). Generative AI: Here to stay, but for good? (March 22, 2023). doi:10.1016/j.techsoc.2023.102372

Sawant, R., Shaikh, A., Sabat, S., & Bhole, V. (2021, July). Text to image generation using GAN. In *Proceedings of the International Conference on IoT Based Control Networks & Intelligent Systems-ICICNIS*. SSRN. 10.2139/ssrn.3882570

Schöbel, S., Schmitt, A., Benner, D., Saqr, M., Janson, A., & Leimeister, J. M. (2023). Charting the Evolution and Future of Conversational Agents: A Research Agenda Along Five Waves and New Frontiers. *Information Systems Frontiers*, 1–26. doi:10.1007/s10796-023-10375-9

Sharma, R. C. (2023). Exploring Generative AI's Influence on Tailored Learning. *Education@ ETMA, 2*(1), i-iii. http://etma-india.com/index.php/educationatetma/article/view/18

Short, C. E., & Short, J. C. (2023). The artificially intelligent entrepreneur: ChatGPT, prompt engineering, and entrepreneurial rhetoric creation. *Journal of Business Venturing Insights, 19*, e00388. doi:10.1016/j.jbvi.2023.e00388

Sobhanmanesh, F., Beheshti, A., Nouri, N., Chapparo, N. M., Raj, S., & George, R. A. (2023). A Cognitive Model for Technology Adoption. *Algorithms, 16*(3), 155. doi:10.3390/a16030155

Stone, P., Brooks, R., Brynjolfsson, E., Calo, R., Etzioni, O., Hager, G., & Teller, A. (2022). Artificial intelligence and life in 2030: the one hundred year study on artificial intelligence. *arXiv preprint arXiv:2211.06318*. https://doi.org//arXiv.2211.06318 doi:10.48550

Terwiesch, C. (2023). Would Chat GPT3 get a Wharton MBA? A prediction based on its performance in the operations management course. Mack Institute for Innovation Management at the Wharton School: University of Pennsylvania.

Vartiainen, H., & Tedre, M. (2023). Using artificial intelligence in craft education: Crafting with text-to-image generative models. *Digital Creativity (Exeter)*, *34*(1), 1–21. doi:10.1080/14626268.2023.2174557

VuleticM.CucuringuM.PrenzelF. (2023). Fin-GAN: Forecasting and Classifying Financial Time Series via Generative Adversarial Networks (January 18, 2023). doi:10.2139/ssrn.4328302

Wang, K., Gou, C., Duan, Y., Lin, Y., Zheng, X., & Wang, F. Y. (2017). Generative adversarial networks: introduction and outlook. *IEEE/CAA Journal of Automatica Sinica, 4*(4), 588-598. doi:10.1109/JAS.2017.7510583

Whittaker, L., Letheren, K., & Mulcahy, R. (2021). The rise of deepfakes: A conceptual framework and research agenda for marketing. *Australasian Marketing Journal*, *29*(3), 204–214. doi:10.1177/1839334921999479

Wisskirchen, G., Biacabe, B. T., Bormann, U., Muntz, A., Niehaus, G., Soler, G. J., & von Brauchitsch, B. (2017). Artificial intelligence and robotics and their impact on the workplace. *IBA Global Employment Institute*, *11*(5), 49–67.

KEY TERMS AND DEFINITIONS

Artificial Intelligence: It is a branch of study that focuses on creating software or computers that can execute jobs that are normally performed by humans by artificially duplicating the cognitive capacities of human intelligence.

COVID-19: An infectious condition brought on by the coronavirus that causes severe acute respiratory syndrome (SARS-CoV-2). The most typical symptoms include fatigue, dry cough, and fever.

Digital Transformation: It consists of a structural change in the economy, organizations and society in general, caused by the comprehensive application of digital technologies and disruptive technologies.

Education: It is a social practice aimed at developing human beings, their potential, skills and competences. Education, therefore, is not restricted to schools. Education is everyone's right and is aimed at full human development through the teaching-learning process.

Educational Transformation: It is the change that takes place in the methodologies applied to the teaching-learning process. These changes are associated with social issues, values and practices that affect the way we teach and learn.

Prompt Engineering: the term refers to the practice of creating and optimizing input requests by selecting appropriate words, phrases, sentences, punctuation and separator characters to effectively use LLMs (Large Language Models).

Technology: The term is a product of science and engineering that involves a set of instruments, methods and techniques aimed at solving problems. It is the practical application of scientific knowledge in various areas of research.

Chapter 19
Generative AI Soaring in the Skies:
New Horizons in Aviation English

Nazmi Dinçer
https://orcid.org/0000-0002-2901-5367
Turkish Air Force Academy, Turkey

Gökhan Demirdöken
https://orcid.org/0000-0002-9442-0625
Independent Researcher, Germany

ABSTRACT

Several regulations in the aviation industry have been made by authorities to minimize the incidents due to language barriers; however, a more reasonable solution lies in equipping prospective pilots with necessary language skills in target settings. This requires a transformation in aviation English (AE) classrooms through the medium of emerging technologies. Accordingly, this chapter presents a novel strategy for rethinking AE instruction by using approaches from generative artificial intelligence. It investigates the ways in which prompt engineering and synthetic content production might be used to improve the efficacy of AE teaching. Learners may benefit from better language comprehension, communication skills, and situational awareness by seamlessly incorporating AI-driven language creation into the curriculum. Instructors could find examples of generative AI-driven classroom applications for improved learning outcomes. Considering these potential contributions to the field, this chapter may, in turn, innovate and uplift the AE courses and safety in the aviation industry.

DOI: 10.4018/979-8-3693-1351-0.ch019

INTRODUCTION

In the context of a more connected global landscape, the significance of effective communication becomes vital, particularly within businesses that prioritize non-negotiable elements such as safety and accuracy. The aviation sector, which plays a significant role in facilitating worldwide connectivity and trade, exemplifies the essential need for effective and precise communication. In this context, the need for precise and unambiguous communication extends beyond mere convenience, including matters of utmost significance and potential fatality (FAA, 2016). The distinction lies in the contrast between a secure departure and a possible calamity, as well as between a seamless arrival and a potential catastrophe.

In the field of aviation operations, which span over international airspace and transcend linguistic and geographical boundaries, the establishment of a shared language emerges as a crucial facilitator for fostering effective and cooperative interactions. Aviation English, being a "codified, abbreviated, jargon-filled register" (Trippe & Baese-Berk, 2019, p. 1), effectively fulfills this duty. The domain-specific language serves as a means of communication for pilots, ATCOs, ground crew, and other professionals in the aviation industry. It not only facilitates the exchange of crucial information but also represents a collective dedication to upholding the utmost levels of safety and operational proficiency. This particular kind of communication functions as the dominant language used in aviation, enabling smooth and efficient contact among pilots, ATCOs, and aviation workers worldwide (ICAO, 2010). However, the interlocutors in the context of aviation may not necessarily possess shared first languages and cultural backgrounds, which constructs a significant hazard for mutual intelligibility and thus, safer skies (Ishihara & Prado, 2021). The importance lies in clarity, accuracy, and situational awareness since any instance of miscommunication or misunderstanding might potentially result in significant ramifications. The mastery of AE is, therefore, not only a question of adherence but rather an essential prerequisite for ensuring the safety and effectiveness of aircraft operations.

The use of language in aviation communication distinguishes it from other forms of linguistic expression. The concept covers a diverse range of situations, spanning from the exchange of standard phraseology to the handling of demanding and urgent crises (ICAO, 2003). Pilots are required to effectively communicate crucial information with accuracy and coherence while operating in complex operational environments. The task at hand involves adequately equipping learners to navigate many forms of communication seen in diverse settings, enabling them to effortlessly move between everyday interactions, specialized terminology, and time-sensitive instructions.

The field of AE is intricately connected with operating processes, safety regulations, and regulatory mandates. Merely possessing fluency in a language is inadequate; those working in the aviation industry must effectively combine their language proficiency with an in-depth awareness of aviation-specific procedures and norms (Alderson, 2009). The biggest challenge lies in developing comprehensive training programs that successfully address this gap.

Formerly, the delivery of AE education has mostly relied on traditional approaches, including in-person classroom teaching and the use of language textbooks. While these methods have shown some efficacy, they often fall short in addressing the dynamic and quickly changing nature of aircraft operations (Dincer, 2023). Moreover, the constraints imposed by static educational resources and the lack of real-world context might impede the acquisition of practical communication skills and situational awareness necessary in professional settings.

To effectively tackle this issue, it is essential to undergo a fundamental change in the approach to AE instruction. This entails using contemporary technology to its fullest extent, hence propelling educational practices into unexplored realms. At the center of this paradigm shift lies the incorporation of GenAI, a remarkable technical advancement that has the potential to eradicate the conventional limitations of language acquisition (Bozkurt, 2023). The field of GenAI, which is dedicated to the production of novel and contextually appropriate information, has shown significant advancements in recent times. Within the discipline of language acquisition, GenAI has the potential to revolutionize the process, presenting novel opportunities for learners to actively participate in and achieve proficiency in languages via means that were previously inconceivable (Hockly, 2023).

Overall, AE instruction is deeply in need of innovation for the successful attainment of learning outcomes by student pilots, thus ensuring effective and safe flight operations. The objective of this chapter is, therefore, to examine how the incorporation of GenAI may surpass the constraints of conventional AE instruction. In light of this conspicuous research void, this paper seeks to fill this gap. We endeavor to critically analyze and discuss the potential symbiosis between AE and AI. By pioneering this exploration, it is aimed to shed light on new methodologies, evaluate potential enhancements in training efficiency, and ultimately, drive the conversation forward, pushing the boundaries of what's conceivable in AE education.

AVIATION ENGLISH TRAINING

With the cessation of the World Wars, the global community swiftly recognized the transformative potential of aviation, not merely as a tool of warfare, but as a mechanism to revolutionize transportation and foster global interconnectivity. Post-war periods witnessed exponential growth in the aviation sector, prompted by individuals' appreciation for the strategic importance of airborne vehicles. Beyond military applications, aviation emerged as a conduit for bridging geographical divides, facilitating cultural exchanges, and promoting economic interdependence (Chant, 2002).

The burgeoning use of aircraft for international travel underscored an urgent need for uniformity and safety standards. In response to these imperatives, 191 out of 193 countries gathered in 1944, eventually institutionalizing their cooperation as the International Civil Aviation Organization (ICAO) by 1947. Tasked with the formulation of regulations, standardizations, and best practices for the aviation sector, ICAO recognized the pivotal role of communication in ensuring safety. A wide range of languages spoken in cockpits globally posed substantial risks, prompting ICAO's landmark decision in 1951 to adopt English as the universal aviation language. Consequently, proficiency in English became a mandatory requirement for pilots and ATCOs.

While selecting English as the lingua franca was a commendable first step, it merely addressed the issue superficially. The intricacies of the English language, coupled with its inherent ambiguities, necessitated further refinements. In 1997, ICAO introduced a more detailed framework centered on "Aviation English," a specialized linguistic variant designed to enhance clarity, standardization, and unequivocalness, especially between pilots and ATCOs. According to Crystal (2003), the term "Airspeak" is used to refer to AE. Crystal further describes it as a specialized lexicon consisting of a predetermined collection of words that are used to effectively convey all conceivable scenarios without any ambiguity. Emphasizing safety in flight operations and air traffic management, ICAO delineated "standard phraseology" to curtail misinterpretations. Phrases such as "Cleared for takeoff," "Roger," and "Hold short of runway" became staples, ensuring clear comprehension regardless of native accents or varying degrees of language proficiency. ICAO's 32nd Assembly in 1997 also marked the onset of developing language proficiency requirements for pilots and ATCOs on international duties, culminating in the 2008 standards.

Training institutions swiftly aligned their curricula with ICAO mandates, spotlighting the significance of AE education (Bieswanger, 2016). While standard phraseology predominantly addressed routine flight situations, non-routine scenarios necessitated a grasp of plain English. Recognizing the delineated nature of routine communications, AE courses prioritized rote memorization, subsequently applying learned content through practical exercises. The structured nature of this education suited seamlessly with behaviorist learning paradigms, paving the way for Computer-Assisted Learning (CAL). Computer-based training (CBT) emerged as a preferred modality, benefiting both flight and language training. Software like *PlaneEnglish* exemplified this trend, offering simulation-based environments to hone pilots' communicative acumen with ATCOs and other aircraft.

As the aviation industry progressed, so did the methods and tools used for training as well. From early classroom-based lessons to CBT methods, the evolution has always been in line with the overarching objective of optimizing safety and communication (Dincer, 2023). CBT, as mentioned, has been instrumental in providing structured, replicable, and scalable training modules to aviation professionals. These computer-driven training tools, like *Xplane-11* simulator software, have significantly enhanced the efficiency of AE education (Dinçer & Demirdöken, 2023). But, as with every industry, there's always room for innovation and improvement.

While CBT has revolutionized aviation training with structured learning experiences, AI offers the promise of even more dynamic, personalized, and contextually rich learning environments. Imagine a platform where pilots and instructors not only receive structured lessons but also engage with an intelligent system capable of simulating diverse real-world communication scenarios, testing users in unprecedented ways, and instantly adapting content based on learner performance and needs. Such a system could analyze a learner's proficiency in real time, identifying areas of weakness and immediately providing tailored feedback and resources. In essence, AI has the potential to bring about a renaissance in AE training, offering a level of personalization, adaptability, and immersion that traditional CBT tools might not achieve. This seamless integration of AI into AE education could be the next leap, ensuring that communication - the bedrock of aviation safety - is clearer, more efficient, and more intuitive than ever before.

While AI holds remarkable promise for the AE domain, there exists a noticeable research gap. Surprisingly, the vast offerings of AI in enhancing AE training remain largely unexplored in academic literature. Despite the rapid advancement of AI and its integration into various sectors, AE, a pivotal area in flight safety and operations, has yet to witness comprehensive studies that thoroughly investigate the potential integration and benefits of this advanced technology.

This lack of investigation is even more profound when considering the direct impacts of AI on training outcomes. No study to date has undertaken a rigorous examination of the tangible effects of artificial intelligence on the AE training process. This leaves a vast expanse of uncharted territory, rich with potential insights that could redefine training paradigms and set new standards for instructional methodologies in the aviation domain.

ARTIFICIAL INTELLIGENCE IN EDUCATION

Following the question, "Can machines think?" provided by Alan Turing in 1951, the first seeds of artificial intelligence were planted. Later, the concept of artificial intelligence (AI) was first introduced in 1956, with the objective of developing robots capable of imitating human intelligence (McCarthy, 2007, p. 2). In 1956, Newell and Simon presented a computer program referred to as a "thinking machine". The program in question was seen as a significant advancement due to its capacity to address intricate problems, hence simulating certain facets of human intelligence (Newell & Simon, 1956, p. 868). The following years saw a notable surge in both interest and advancements within the discipline of artificial intelligence. The technological revolution has had a significant influence on the educational sector, resulting in the birth of a discipline referred to as AI in Education (AIED).

Over the course of many decades, professionals in academia, education, and technology have successfully harnessed the capabilities of AI to bring about in a new era in the field of education and pedagogy. AI has been integrated into several facets of the educational sector. Wenger (2014) has developed intelligent tutoring systems that use artificial intelligence to provide personalized learning experiences to students. The educational system has the capacity to adapt and cater to the distinct needs of individual learners, hence tailoring the instructional content and pace accordingly. Furthermore, AI has been used as a multifunctional tool and collaborative partner in the world of education. Through the use of interactive platforms and programs, students are provided the ability to engage in active participation using technologies that are driven by AI. According to Hwang and Chang (2023), these tools have the potential to facilitate problem-solving, foster the cultivation of creativity, and enable a deeper understanding of complex subjects. The use of AI-driven apps has been seen in the domains of administration and policy, where they serve to facilitate the decision-making process (Lauterbach, 2019). By analyzing large volumes of data, these technologies have the potential to provide significant insights and recommendations. Consequently, individuals in the field of education, including educators and policymakers, are equipped with the necessary knowledge and information to make educated decisions that may have a substantial impact on the direction and development of the educational system.

In recent times, there has been an increasing level of attention from scholars, policymakers, and professionals in the domain of AIED owing to its capacity to enhance educational methodologies (Williamson & Eynon, 2020). The researchers have effectively developed educational tools that use artificial intelligence, including intelligent tutoring systems and recommendation systems. The aforementioned technological improvements allow AI to evaluate and enhance students' educational experiences by offering personalized support (Hwang et al., 2020). For instance, the use of educational technology has shown its ability to provide students with personalized learning materials or routes, as evidenced by Christudas et al. (2018). Furthermore, the assessment tool has the capability to evaluate the strengths, weaknesses, and knowledge gaps of students, as shown by Liu et al. (2017). Moreover, the technology has the capacity to identify people who are prone to experiencing academic underachievement, as shown by the study of Luckin et al. (2022). In a recent study conducted by Kexin et al. (2020), the feasibility of enhancing educational practices by the use of conventional AI methods was investigated. This research specifically focused on the optimization of various instructional approaches, such as blended learning, in-person teaching, and distance education. The objective of this strategy is to mitigate the workload of educators via the automation of diverse tasks and the enhancement of the educational data analysis process. AI-driven technologies have the capacity to assist instructors in discerning effective pedagogical approaches via the analysis of student learning data.

Furthermore, it has been suggested by Chaudhry and Kazim (2021) that these systems have the capability to produce examinations and provide automated assessment and feedback. Moreover, academic inquiry has shown that AI has promise in enabling individualized and flexible learning (Kabudi et al., 2021). Additionally, it has been found to accelerate the process of acquiring knowledge and boost student motivation (Chiu et al., 2020). Overall, AI, since its emergence in the 1950s, has seen substantial growth as a technical discipline and has had a profound impact on our educational paradigms. It has the potential to revolutionize the educational landscape by offering customized, efficient, and data-centric learning experiences (Hwang et al., 2020). The incorporation of artificial AI into the field of education, referred to as AIED, represents a significant transformation in teaching, learning, and administrative approaches. AI has shown the potential to promote the field of education, ranging from the creation of intelligent tutoring systems to the delivery of individualized learning experiences. The use of data analysis, predictive modeling of student performance, and automation of regular chores has provided educators with valuable tools to improve instructional techniques, resulting in increased student engagement and comprehension (Roll & Wylie, 2016). As society progresses, the integration of AI and education is expected to strengthen, providing enhanced, data-driven, and customized solutions to the dynamic difficulties faced by students, educators, and policymakers in the field of pedagogy. The present section has reviewed the use of AI for instructional purposes thus, moving on now to explore the potential of GenAI in language learning settings.

GENERATIVE AI IN LANGUAGE LEARNING

Within the dynamic context of AI where its impact has greatly improved tasks, education, and many social situations, a novel surge of GenAI tools based on extensive language models is emerging. While AI has improved working, learning, and social settings and pervaded everyday life (in chatbots, intelligent appliances for homes, and other areas), a new generation of GenAI tools based on large language models (e.g., ChatGPT, DALL-E2) is poised to transform several fields (Hu, 2022). Academics and educators have just started to carefully consider the effects of evaluation, instruction, and learning in the classroom (Kohnke et al., 2023). Technologies for GenAI are a significant improvement over earlier AI technologies. It uses deep learning models to produce material that is human-like, such as writing, photographs, sounds, modeling, 3-dimensional components, and videos. It also produces surprising and novel results in response to a variety of challenging cues. GenAI is a progressive advancement within the field of AI, enabling computers to generate information that has a combination of contextual relevance and originality (Bozkurt & Sharma, 2023). The fundamental nature of creativity and adaptation forms the foundation of this technology, allowing systems to produce various forms of content such as text, graphics, and voice, frequently with a level of quality that makes them indistinguishable from human works (Li et al., 2022).

Although the examples of the implementation of GenAI for language learning are yet to increase in number, in a recent attempt, ChatGPT has been used by Eysenbach (2023) as the source of inspiration for a number of concepts pertaining to the utilization of chatbots within the realm of medical education. Overall, the capabilities of ChatGPT have been reported as impressive in the context of medicine. On similar grounds with the findings from the medical context, AI has been successfully utilized by Kim and Kim (2020) in the Korean context for language learning purposes. The researchers tested an individualized AI tutor integrated into a mobile application to foster the language learning process for its users. The AI tutor has been proven to be efficient in helping children learn Korean. Thus, the existing literature lacks sound research that would report on the use of GenAI tools in various language learning settings, including AE. This innovative technology, however, still has the potential to revolutionize traditional language teaching paradigms by providing a connection between academic principles and the actual implementation of language abilities.

In the arena of language learning, GenAI surpasses the conventional limitations of passive learning approaches and thus, it may serve as a powerful tool to innovate the AE classrooms in a number of ways. First and foremost, the platform provides dynamic, engaging, and customized learning experiences that are tailored to meet the specific requirements of individual learners. The utilization of specialized terminology within a particular academic field is inherent to the process of students acquiring information within that discipline. Similarly, in the context of aviation, it is imperative for student pilots to embrace the specialized terminology to effectively convey ideas and actively participate in the acquisition of disciplinary knowledge. The handling of terminology in AE classes, however, provides greater difficulties compared to general English (GE) courses (Fainman & Tokar, 2019). GenAI, therefore, comes into prominence as it offers a remedy to this challenge via tools like *Revisely* and *Limbiks* which are further described in the succeeding titles. Another innovation of GenAI for the AE classroom is associated with the lack of authentic material, Since the nature of developing authentic material for instructional purposes requires access to either spoken or written data originating from genuine communication, the teachers of AE suffer from the lack of authentic course material (Demirdöken, 2021). This issue becomes even more significant when coupled with the challenges and complexities of pilotage training and thus, it may have detrimental effects on student pilots' academic performance. For instance, the demanding and multifaceted responsibilities assigned to Indonesian aviation cadets have been reported to result in fatigue and reduced concentration on learners' educational objectives (Rochmawati et al., 2023). The contribution of GenAI to eliminating the lack of authentic course material is invaluable since AI tools like ChatGPT can be instrumented to generate, for instance, unique dialogues for various scenarios in air traffic communication, which are exemplified in the following title. The third innovation of GenAI is that it utilizes natural language processing, dialogue production, and text-to-speech synthesis to enhance language instruction by creating an interactive and immersive learning experience. This opportunity to elevate the components of the AE instruction by means of GenAI can, in fact, be a significant accomplishment for the aviation industry because there exists an undeniable and ongoing issue that many of the AE language proficiency assessment techniques seem to fall short of meeting the internationally recognized requirements for language proficiency exams in professional contexts despite the fact that the ICAO proposed Language Proficiency Requirements to improve AE proficiency over a decade ago (Park, 2020). In the context of AE education, the utilization of GenAI, however, presents itself as a potent instrument for aiding test developers in the creation of AE assessment tasks that are more authentic and targeted. This will, in turn, foster the development of intricate language proficiencies necessary for proficient communication in demanding aviation settings.

The integration of GenAI into customized learning systems is a novel approach that enhances the customization of educational material based on the unique characteristics and advancements of individual learners (Holmes & Tuomi, 2022). Through the examination of learner performance, GenAI has the capability to adaptively modify the intricacy of prompts and information, therefore guaranteeing a customized and efficient learning experience (Bozkurt et al., 2023). Within the context of AE training, the aforementioned statement pertains to the development of a curriculum that is tailored to the unique responsibilities of the learner's particular function, whether it be that of a pilot, air traffic controller, or ground crew. This curriculum is designed to effectively handle the special language requirements associated with each respective profession.

As we contemplate the future, the spectrum of potentialities extends extensively and expansively. From the perspective of GenAI, the field of AE education undergoes a transformation from a fixed and unchanging endeavor to a dynamic, immersive, and skill-oriented process. This shift enables learners to fully realize their capabilities and drives the aviation sector towards enhanced levels of achievement. The use of GenAI, therefore, has the potential to significantly alter the domain of AE instruction, overcoming the obstacles associated with conventional approaches and introducing a period of profound and revolutionary learning. In the following title, we will explore the practical use of GenAI in the context of AE training. This will include presenting actual specific techniques that exemplify the significant influence resulting from this transformative change in approach.

TRANSFORMING AVIATION ENGLISH EDUCATION WITH GENERATIVE AI

It is critical to provide sophisticated language and communication skills training in order to ensure safety, efficiency, and accuracy in the ever-expanding aviation business. AE lessons have a specific objective of providing professionals with the domain-specific vocabulary and communication skills that are crucial for achieving effective operations both in the air and on the ground. The use of advanced technology in educational practices may significantly enhance the quality and effectiveness of these instructional programs. An example of a technology tool is GenAI such as ChatGPT, a language model developed by OpenAI that has the capacity to transform the approach to AE instruction. This type of GenAI-based tool has the potential to transform the AE training and enrich the learning experiences of ab initio pilots. Considering the potential of these tools, five primary areas are prominent in AE; (1) prompt engineering, (2) personalized tutoring, (3) developing materials, (4) engaging classroom environment, and (5) assessment. Each subtitle below provides a comprehensive examination of the ways in which this groundbreaking technology might be used to innovate the learning environment so that it is both more efficient and captivating.

Prompt Engineering for Aviation English

Prompt engineering plays a crucial role in facilitating the use of GenAI in the domain of AE instruction, therefore unlocking its profound transformational capabilities. The art of effective rapid engineering is the skillful combination of language creativity and a comprehensive knowledge of the aviation field, in which prompts are used as catalysts for AI-generated interactions, facilitating learners' immersion into realistic aviation settings. These prompts should, however, include both the language aspects of communication and various settings and situations that aviation professionals often experience.

In addition, aviation employees are confronted with a wide range of circumstances, which underscores the need for a diverse set of prompts. These prompts span from normal pre-flight exchanges to high-pressure emergency communications. It is, therefore, important for learners to be exposed to this diversity of circumstances, each of which requires a distinct language strategy. Whether in informal radio exchanges or crucial decision-making dialogues, there is always the need for prompts that accurately reflect the intricate nature of aviation communication in real-world scenarios. ChatGPT, as an example of prompt engineering, for instance, can be utilized to serve this purpose. To illustrate, when you ask ChatGPT to give a pre-flight dialogue between ATCOs and pilots, the output can be as follows:

"ATC: Good afternoon, Flight 123. This is Ground Control. Are you ready for pushback and engine start?
Pilot: Good afternoon, Ground Control. Flight 123 is ready for pushback and engine start.
ATC: Roger, Flight 123. Pushback and engine start approved. Pushback tug will be connected shortly. Advise when you're ready to taxi.
Pilot: Copy that, Ground Control. We'll advise when ready to taxi. Flight 123.
[After pushback and engine start]
Pilot: Ground Control, Flight 123 is ready for taxi with information Delta.
ATC: Flight 123, taxi to runway 27 via Taxiway Alpha and Bravo. Hold short of Runway 27 at Bravo.
Pilot: Taxi to runway 27 via Alpha and Bravo, hold short at Bravo, Flight 123.
[Upon reaching the runway holding point]
Pilot: Ground Control, Flight 123 is holding short of Runway 27 at Bravo.
ATC: Flight 123, continue holding. Traffic on final approach. I'll call your departure.
Pilot: Holding short, Flight 123.
[After receiving clearance for takeoff]
ATC: Flight 123, Runway 27, cleared for takeoff. Wind 240 at 10 knots.
Pilot: Cleared for takeoff, Runway 27, Flight 123.
[During takeoff]
Pilot: Departure, Flight 123 is airborne, passing 2000 feet.
ATC: Flight 123, radar contact. Climb and maintain 10,000 feet. Contact Departure on frequency 124.3. Have a safe flight.
Pilot: Climbing to 10,000 feet, switching to Departure on 124.3. Thank you, Ground Control. Flight 123.
ATC: You're welcome. Have a good flight, Flight 123."

Taking another step further in innovating the AE classroom, this type of dialogic text may also be transformed into a real-life dialogue through voice generators such as *Murf.AI.* In this way, it would be a smooth experience for student pilots to develop auditory comprehension of the radiotelephony exchanges. Understanding the exchange between interlocutors is essential for effective communication, requiring a proper response; however, there is a scarcity of authentic classroom resources for this purpose. The flight instructors may, therefore, also benefit from GenAI and use the output as a landscape for auditory resources.

The field of AE is characterized by an abundance of technical vocabulary and specialized language. Efficient prompts may skillfully incorporate the linguistic environment, necessitating learners' active involvement in comprehending and engaging with complex technical terminology. One can utilize these chatbots to describe the parts of an airplane, decode meteorology codes, explain standard phraseology, generate route plans, produce pre-flight safety check, and even report emergency situations. Since chatbots such as ChatGPT are gradually updated with graphic and picture recognition, the capabilities could go beyond the boundaries of our imagination. Since communication is a multifaceted process that involves the exchange of information via understanding, articulation, and reaction, effective prompts may replicate this dynamic by generating interactive conversations that need rapid and precise replies. These interactions can, in turn, foster the development of learners' capacity to not only comprehend incoming information but also construct logical and contextually suitable responses—an essential skill in the field of aviation. Prompt engineering thus serves as a means to bridge the divide between theoretical language competency and practical application by immersing learners in discussions that include navigation procedures, aircraft systems, and operational norms.

Another key feature of prompt engineering for learners in the AE classroom can be associated with the demand for legitimate exchanges between interlocutors who must establish a connection with the real-world environments they encounter, effectively capturing the intricacies of cross-cultural communication, the need for timely responses, and the complex nature of aviation operations. The advancement of learners, however, is contingent upon their capacity to adjust and effectively manage their pace of learning (Kamalov et al., 2023). Therefore, equipping prospective aviation professionals with these skills is crucial for continuous learning progress. That is where AI-generated prompts can foster the learning process since they can effectively capture the distinctive characteristics of language use that arise in dynamic and high-stakes aviation situations. The prompts can undergo continuous development in conjunction with the learners' increasing competence levels, providing a consistent and progressive trajectory of improvement. The dynamic nature of GenAI also allows for the personalization of prompts in order to effectively challenge learners at an appropriate level, thereby facilitating a continual learning process that is tailored to individual requirements.

Finally, in the domain of prompt engineering, educators are also assigned a pivotal role. The individuals in question engage in the curation of prompts, the refinement of information, and the provision of detailed advice to learners. Such partnership between humans and AI enhances the effectiveness of GenAI by customizing the learning process and using the knowledge and skills of experienced teachers in AE. In this sense, the emergence of prompt engineering can be argued to serve not only as a means for efficient language learning but also as evidence of the boundless possibilities provided by GenAI. By using carefully crafted prompts, learners may engage in a transformational journey that enables them to acquire the necessary language skills, situational understanding, and flexibility required for effective aviation communication in a quality learning environment.

Personalized Tutoring

Effective communication is a crucial aspect within the world of aviation, as it plays a pivotal role in maintaining the safety of both airborne and ground activities. Due to the increasing prevalence of international travel, pilots and ATCOs often engage in professional interactions with colleagues who possess varied language origins. Therefore, it is crucial that those working in the aviation industry possess a high level of proficiency in AE. Personalized coaching facilitated by platforms such as ChatGPT may significantly contribute to the refinement of these abilities. To illustrate, in the dynamic setting of an airport, misinterpretations may give rise to substantial complexities, if not inherent hazards. Figure 1 serves as a notable illustration of the dynamic between a pilot and an air traffic controller. Another advantage that comes with platforms such as ChatGPT is its capacity to replicate genuine interpersonal exchanges. One such scenario is a student assuming the role of a pilot, while the AI system simulates the role of an air traffic controller, facilitating interactive and real-time exchanges. This not only enhances language competency but also fosters the student's self-assurance in navigating difficult situations. Although classroom learning and textbooks provide a well-organized educational setting, they are deficient in terms of the spontaneous nature of real-life encounters. The dynamic conversational features of ChatGPT enable learners to replicate routine and non-routine situations, hence enhancing their preparedness for the planned flight flow and unpredictable nature of real-life discussions. Learners are thus immersed in dynamic discussions whereby they are required to promptly react to evolving events, interpret time-sensitive signals, and swiftly make decisive choices. These situations provide learners with challenges that need quick thinking, so improving their cognitive flexibility and equipping them for the dynamic nature of aviation communication.

Figure 1. Dialogue with ChatGPT

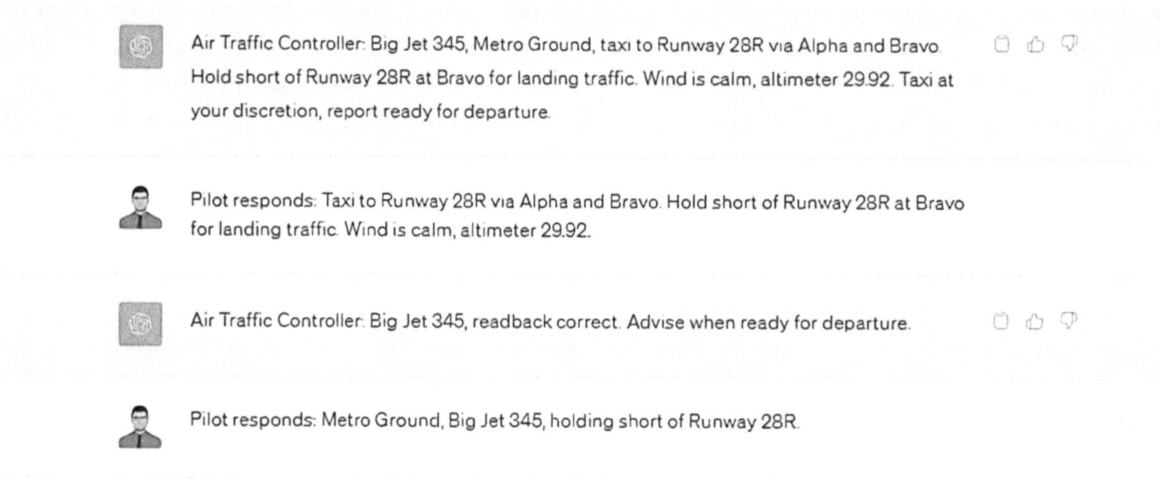

Material Development

Material development is a particular challenge in AE instruction that can be overcome by means of GenAI. Considering the essentials of education, it would be true to claim that adequate preparation plays a crucial role in any learning setting. This principle is particularly significant within the discipline of AE. The selection of appropriate resources may ensure a productive educational experience. According to the report published by Bryant et al. (2020), 10 out of 50 hours of teachers' time is dedicated to preparation. This implies that lesson planning, material development, or adapting the current material for the new setting or context takes quite a lot of time. GenAI, however, appears as the cure for this issue.

The significance of developing quality materials specifically designed for the complexities of aviation communication is of utmost importance in the ever-changing field of aviation training. Instructors are presented with a unique chance to create authentic, contextually driven educational material via the use of GenAI such as ChatGPT. An exemplary illustration of this phenomenon was shown by the development of a visual flight rules (VFR) flight plan from LTFM (Istanbul Airport) to LTFJ (Istanbul Sabiha Gökçen Airport), which not only proved the application's strict adherence to prescribed structure and comprehensive content but also its capacity to dynamically tailor educational resources (see Figure 2). Through the use of such technology, educators may effectively facilitate students' engagement in genuine language situations, efficiently closing the gap between theoretical comprehension and practical implementation. The capacity of ChatGPT to dynamically produce, adjust, and provide feedback positions it as a noteworthy resource in the advancement of comprehensive and pertinent content for AE courses.

Figure 2. ChatGPT flight plan

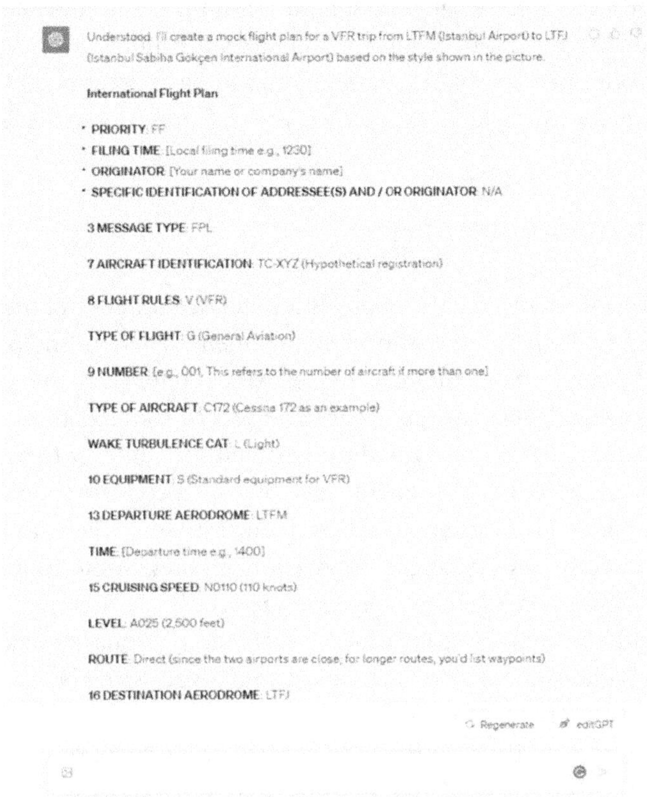

To illustrate, the use of ChatGPT for the generation of authentic course material might prove to be an essential resource for educators. The language model has the capability to aid in the synthesis of lectures that are both useful and interesting, ranging from ideas to thorough reflections. Furthermore, the course's capacity to generate lifelike situations and comprehensive question banks enhances its theoretical robustness and practical applicability. Consider the hypothetical scenario of possessing a technology capable of expeditiously producing inquiries for an upcoming assessment, specifically designed to align with the aviation subjects that have been addressed. These features have the potential to alleviate the workload of teachers, allowing them to prioritize course delivery, promote active participation in the classroom, and address the unique learning requirements of students (Dinçer & Dinçer, 2021). One such example for the aviation course is generating expanded reading texts about imaginative or real flight experiences, which promote the common sense of the prospective pilots as well as offering a rich landscape against which context awareness could be increased.

The process of creating educational materials with the use of artificial intelligence entails utilizing technological advancements to produce customized and captivating learning resources. These instructional materials can accommodate the learner's level of proficiency and address specific areas in need of improvement. Illustrative instances of such materials encompass, albeit are not limited to, essays, quizzes, and flashcards. Instructors have the convenience of creating unique content for their students by means of GenAI tools. What's more, learners can take on the responsibility of utilizing these tools for the purposes of developing personalized learning materials. To exemplify, utilizing the capabilities of artificial intelligence, platforms like *Revisely* and *Limbiks* seamlessly convert one's notes or textbooks into flashcards. These platforms also promote a shared learning environment for learners as well as the convenience of creating flashcards in languages other than English. Considering these novel opportunities for material development, GenAI can be argued to have great potential to innovate the AE classrooms. What follows is an example of the utilization of GenAI to create an engaging classroom setting for learners of AE.

Engaging Classroom Environment

GenAI can serve as a powerful tool to create an engaging classroom environment as well. It is necessary to clarify exactly what is meant by behavioral engagement. This will help us to develop a better understanding of how ESP teachers can benefit from GenAI for innovating the learning setting. Behavioral engagement can broadly be defined as the observable acts of students to actively participate in the learning process (Nguyen et al., 2018). It is, therefore, crucial for students to achieve desired learning results. As such, students' academic achievement may be enhanced on condition that they actively engage in academic interactions (Harbour et al., 2015). Contrastively, when students fail to do so, they may develop feelings of boredom, anxiety, anger, depression, and rebellion (Skinner & Belmont, 1993). What's more, the level of student engagement and practice within the learning environment has been reported by Bertheussen and Myrland (2016) to directly influence the quality of academic performance. It can be, hereby, concluded that students who actively get involved with classroom activities are likely to improve both their academic and social well-being.

Lack of active engagement may have detrimental effects on learners of AE as well, which can be compensated by utilizing GenAI. It is probable that the students may exhibit behaviors of remaining silent and demonstrating minimal effort in completing the assigned tasks during class interactions due to a lack of engagement. This can be even more evident in contexts where English is not the common means of communication outside the classroom (Demirdöken & Okur, 2023) since they may have a high level of English-speaking anxiety. The solution of GenAI to this issue in the context of aviation is exemplified below.

The AE course design may, first of all, benefit from Automatic Speech Recognition (ASR) technology, which is a powerful AI tool for the purpose of refining pronunciation. One particular advantage arising from ASR is that it serves as a prominent illustration of AI technology, demonstrating its proficiency in evaluating the pronunciation of ab initio pilots as well as ATCOs and delivering immediate feedback to these learners. The provision of personalized and tailored feedback can, in turn, enhance student pilots' confidence in their English-speaking skills and create an engaging classroom environment in the context of AE.

Another solution of GenAI to resolve the lack of engagement in the AE classroom is that AI-powered tools have the potential to greatly transform AE teaching is evident in content creation tools and interactive learning methodologies. The incorporation of AI content-creation tools within the realm of English teaching can potentially contribute to the establishment of an intelligent instructional setting (Zhao & Nazir, 2022). *Quillionz*, for instance, possesses the capability to autonomously produce interrogative statements based on a provided textual input. AE teachers might, for instance, utilize this tool in order to generate unique discussion questions that align with the subject covered in their courses. *Plotagon*, on the other hand, utilizes AI to transform written text into animated films accompanied by voiceover narration. Therefore, it can be a powerful tool for student pilots who suffer from English-speaking anxiety to create captivating videos or animated explanations pertaining to a particular topic related to AE. These tools, like content production and delivery systems, have the potential to support goal setting and self-monitoring, thereby augmenting students' capacity to govern their own learning. Also, interactive learning methodologies can be utilized to actively involve students and enhance their communicative competence (Pershukova et al., 2023). These methodologies encompass activities that inspire students to engage in dialogue regarding aviation-related issues, provide resolutions, and exchange knowledge, so boosting student engagement and, in turn, the development of AE proficiency.

Assessment

The emergence of GenAI models, particularly ChatGPT, has introduced a groundbreaking methodology for evaluating competency in AE. Historically, the assessment of language proficiency in this particular field has heavily relied on human knowledge. However, despite its immense value, this approach is susceptible to inconsistencies and constraints in terms of available resources. The ChatGPT model, due to its comprehensive training on broad language datasets and its capacity to adapt to specialized domains such as aviation, provides a reliable, scalable, and prompt method of evaluation.

The system is capable of effectively assessing written replies by considering factors such as organization, lexical richness, and linguistic fluidity, therefore aligning with the benchmarks established by regulatory organizations like ICAO. Moreover, via the use of conversational situations, the model may be utilized to assess interactive competence, replicating genuine plane conversations. For instance, ICAO has mandated an exam for the ab initio pilots in order to get a license. Every pilot has to take this exam in order to maintain their career. In addition, ICAO provided a rubric for the raters to decide whether the candidate has the competency to carry out effective radiotelephony communication in cockpits. As demonstrated in Figure 3, GenAI is capable of assessing the ab initio pilots based on the ICAO standards. The system could be trained with rich input prior to conducting real scoring. This will help individuals to get more sound and correct feedback.

In the context of aviation, the utilization of artificial intelligence in the evaluation of AE education is closely linked to the language competency criteria established by the ICAO with the primary objective of enhancing safety and optimizing efficiency in international air transportation. AI-based assessment tools have the potential to accurately assess English language proficiency among pilots, ATCOs, and aviation workers, aligning with established criteria. The instrumentation of AI-based assessment tools becomes particularly crucial in settings where AE teachers do not possess the content knowledge and hands-on experience in the aviation context. This approach, therefore, guarantees that aviation professionals are properly assessed if they adhere to the prescribed linguistic benchmarks, thereby bolstering aviation safety and facilitating efficient communication within the industry.

The instrumentation of AI-based assessment tools may potentially rule out the criticism raised by scholars (Kim, 2013; Van Moere et al., 2009) concerning the lack of a non-biased ICAO language policy. Over the last two decades, the implementation of the ICAO language proficiency requirements has been quite controversial since the member states acted on their own in developing and instrumenting the language proficiency assessment tool, which brought about concerns over non-biased assessment. The work of Van Moere et al (2009), for instance, indicated the necessity for conducting a standard-setting endeavor that generates representative samples of the ICAO proficiency levels in order to encompass a wide range of language examinations ensuring consistent and rigorous application of standards, as well as ascertaining that standards remain consistent throughout time. What's more Kim (2013) highlighted

Figure 3. ICAO assessment in ChatGPT

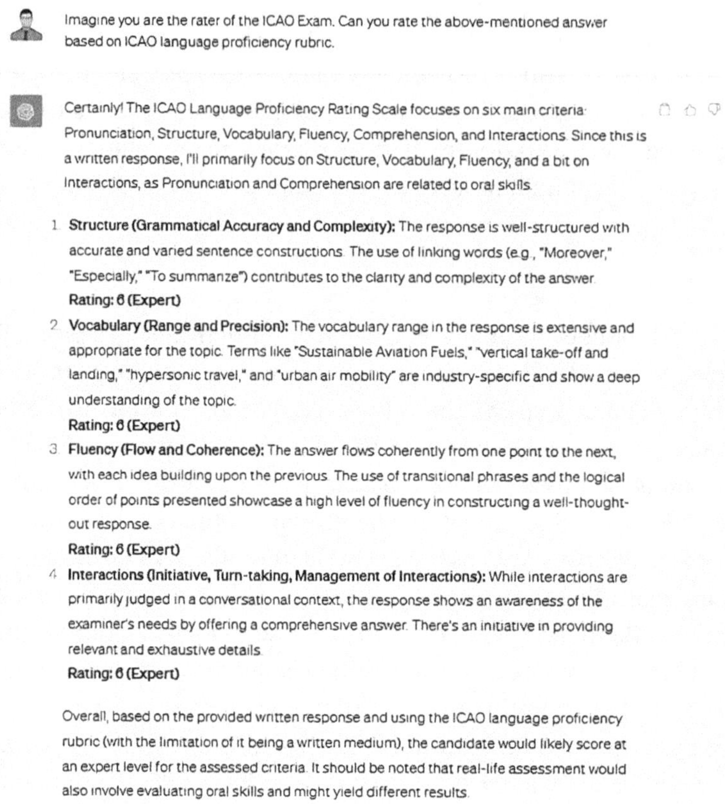

the dissatisfaction of Korean aviation professionals with what they perceive as favoritism towards native English speakers in the existing ICAO policy. The criticism over the test designed and administered in Korea was, on the flip side, the more traumatic issue due to several reasons including the lack of clarity regarding the procedures followed in the development of the exam, and the validity and reliability of the test. Considering these issues in the aviation industry, the utilization of AI-based assessment tools appears as a more reasonable and reliable solution. They exhibit a reduced susceptibility to bias in comparison to human grading. This practice may show that learners are assessed in a manner that is equitable and impartial, irrespective of variables such as the instructor's own opinions or potential prejudices. The examples to these "apparently" non-biased assessment tools include *Learning Analytics and Knowledge (LAK)* and *Open Learning Analytics (OLA)*. They employ data mining and artificial intelligence algorithms to examine student learning data, thereby offering valuable insights into student performance, engagement, and learning outcomes. This may, in turn, enable AE teachers to effectively track student progress, identify student pilots who may be at risk, and make informed decisions based on data in order to enhance student learning outcomes.

The use of AI-powered assessment tools in the context of aviation may not be necessarily limited to creating a learner-based setting or developing non-biased assessment instruments. The specific type of AI called large language models (LLMs) may also be adopted to understand, produce, and manipulate human language for instructional purposes based on the needs of the aviation industry. *BARD AI*, *BERT*,

ELECTRA, *Megatron*, *RoBERTa*, and *XLNet* are examples of LLMs that have the potential to contribute significantly to multiple phases of the educational assessment process. These include test planning, item generation, preparation of test instructions, item assembly and selection, test administration, test scoring, test analysis, interpretation, evaluation, reporting, and follow-up. However, some issues regarding the instrumentation of AI-based assessment tools should also be considered by professionals in the field of education, particularly AE. These may, for instance, include the challenge of fruitful collaboration between subject matter experts (SMEs) and educators, the lack of which may result in the development of inefficient assessment tools. In addition, the failure to provide a clear overview of the assessment process for the learners may yield issues with motivation and engagement since learners may develop a sense of devaluation of their endeavor. Finally, the potential resistance by teachers against AI integration into educational contexts should be carefully sorted out by offering effective and adequate continuous professional development opportunities.

SHORTCOMINGS OF AI IN AVIATION ENGLISH EDUCATION

Thus far, this chapter has discussed the language use in the aviation context, how it distinguishes it from other forms of English language use for specific purposes, and the imperfections of conventional AE teaching. Then, we discussed how AI can potentially innovate the AE classrooms and transform it into a more engaging setting for student pilots as well as prospective air traffic controllers by providing examples of AI integration into the AE curriculum. However, AI can be argued to have some imperfections despite being a very promising domain. These imperfections may become more intricate and sophisticated, particularly when they are linked to an educational application. In this regard, the present title will move on to consider the shortcomings of AI in the AE classroom. These include the issues related to ethical considerations and the cost of AI in instructional settings, respectively.

Ethical Considerations

In the ever-evolving landscape of AE education, the deliberate incorporation of GenAI innovation brings up a multitude of ethical concerns that need careful scrutiny and intentional execution, particularly in the AIED. Holmes et al (2022) argue that ethical concerns related to AI in educational settings focus on issues of data control, transparency, consent, and algorithmic bias. In the pursuit of improving language competence and communication abilities, aviation professionals must prioritize ethical management as a fundamental value throughout their journey. Since there is a possibility that student data could be disclosed, distributed, or misused (Zhai et al., 2021), educators must have the crucial obligation of ensuring the protection of student data, including verbal and written exchanges, by adhering to stringent standards of data privacy and security. The custodianship in question is firmly based on the principles of informed consent and strong anonymization mechanisms, so guaranteeing a high level of regard for the privacy of individuals. Additionally, instituting stringent data retention and deletion policies may ensure the responsible handling of AE learner data and respecting their rights to data privacy.

Another ethical issue that requires paramount attention when transforming AE teaching by means of AI is transparency. This principle is prominently featured in the white paper on AI published by the EU Commission's High-Level Expert Group on AI (AI HLEG) in 2020. The commission highlighted that transparency is one of the seven essential prerequisites for achieving 'trustworthy AI'. In this sense, it assumes significance as aviation learners engage with AI-generated content. Disclosing the presence of AI to learners not only nurtures trust but also promotes an enlightened comprehension of the educational process.

In addition, a steadfast commitment to fairness pervades the educational ecosystem. However, biased algorithms may infest this ecosystem. Although computer algorithms used to be considered as non-biased, a contrasting viewpoint arguing that algorithms frequently incorporate the prejudices of their creators or the broader culture, resulting in predictions or deductions that exhibit evident discrimination against particular groups has emerged recently (Baker & Hawn, 2022). Rigorous measures should, therefore, be undertaken for the detection and mitigation of bias, guaranteeing that language prompts and responses are equitable, devoid of stereotypes, and entirely free from discrimination.

Similarly, a commitment to diversity and inclusivity manifests in the utilization of diverse and representative training data, reflecting the global tapestry of aviation professionals. The Montréal Declaration for Responsible Development of Artificial Intelligence listed the issue of diversity in its list of AI principles (Université de Montréal, 2018), which further highlighted the undeniable need for diverse and all-inclusive AI applications in instructional settings. In this regard, the role of ESP teachers is crucial since they must be sensitive to cultural nuances, ensuring that AI-generated material respects and aligns with the intricacies of various cultural contexts. Alongside the ESP teachers, developers of AI-driven content may be supervised to ensure compliance with ethical guidelines.

Overall, the principle of responsibility can be argued to be deeply ingrained in the exercise of ethical guidelines. As such, clear and distinct roles and duties may be created, outlining the specific areas of responsibility for AE teachers and curriculum developers, and suppliers of AI systems. What's more carefully controlled processes may be put in place to effectively address complaints of educators and student pilots and fix problems, including potential biased material or technological faults. In addition, promoting ethical AI literacy among aviation professionals is of paramount importance. In the simplest terms, AI literacy can be defined as "having the essential abilities that people need to live, learn and work in our digital world through AI-driven technologies" (Ng et al., 2021). Equipping learners and educators with comprehensive training on the ethical use of AI may, therefore, foster a proactive, discerning approach to AI-generated content. It may also empower learners to be active participants in their education, enabling them to critically assess AI-generated content and make ethical decisions in their interactions. Consequently, the harmonious collaboration between GenAI and human instructors is pivotal. While AI technology enriches the educational experience, it does not supplant the essential human connection. Instead, it complements and amplifies the role of educators, fostering a harmonious synergy between technology and human expertise. It is now opportune to exchange ideas and methods between AI science and human learning and development by considering ethical guidelines toward innovation in the AE classroom and improved learning gains.

Cost of Utilizing AI for Educational Purposes

The incorporation of technology into the field of education is sometimes met with mistrust owing to the immediate costs and inherent difficulties associated with this effort. Nevertheless, upon examination via a comprehensive analysis, the advantages and possible economic efficiencies become evident. Similarly, the use of AI in educational environments has a multitude of advantages, however, it is not devoid of associated expenses. AIED requires upfront costs, such as procuring AI tools, software, and the necessary physical infrastructure. The initial capital outlay might be substantial, particularly for organizations with constrained financial resources. Additionally, there are continuous expenses linked to the upkeep, upgrades, and technical assistance. Training may be necessary for educators and personnel to proficiently utilize AI-driven solutions, resulting in higher costs. Moreover, tailoring AI systems to accommodate unique educational requirements can incur significant expenses. Nevertheless, it is crucial to acknowledge that although the initial and continuous expenses associated with the incorporation of AI are not insignificant, they need to be carefully considered in light of the possible long-term benefits, such as student involvement, customized learning experiences, and improved educational results. Often, the advantages of incorporating AI into education may surpass the initial cost investment.

CONCLUSION

In summary, the significance of effective communication within the aviation industry, where safety and accuracy are imperative and non-negotiable, cannot be exaggerated. The fine line between a safe flight and a possible disaster is contingent upon the presence of lucid communication. The role of AE, which is a specialized and standardized form of communication, therefore, holds significant importance in maintaining the utmost levels of safety and operational proficiency.

The conventional methods employed in AE education, namely classroom instruction and the use of textbooks, possess certain constraints when it comes to effectively addressing the ever-changing nature of aviation operations (Dinçer & Dinçer, 2021). In order to address this disparity, the incorporation of GenAI presents a paradigm-shifting resolution. GenAI has the capability to provide learning experiences that are dynamic and immersive, closely simulating the complexities of aviation communication in real-world scenarios. Educators have the ability to optimize AE training through the utilization of advanced AI approaches, the creation of tailored prompts, and the generation of contextually appropriate information.

The present chapter has examined the possibilities of GenAI in the context of AE education. It has provided an analysis of the approaches employed and highlighted the advantages associated with this technology. By adopting this technology, the aviation sector has the potential to initiate a novel phase of radiotelephony communication characterized by personalization, contextual relevance, and technological advancement. The ongoing advancement of GenAI presents the potential to enhance language competency and improve safety, cooperation, and overall excellence within the aviation industry. The process of attaining proficiency in AE is undergoing continuous development, and artificial intelligence is positioned to play a crucial role in accomplishing these objectives. By means of this integration, we shed light on the trajectory towards enhanced aviation safety and improved efficiency in aviation communication.

REFERENCES

Alderson, J. (2009). Air safety, language assessment policy, and policy implementation: The case of AE. *Annual Review of Applied Linguistics*, *29*, 168–187. doi:10.1017/S0267190509090138

Baker, R. S., & Hawn, A. (2022). Algorithmic bias in education. *International Journal of Artificial Intelligence in Education*, *32*(4), 1052–1092. doi:10.1007/s40593-021-00285-9

Bertheussen, B. A., & Myrland, Ø. (2016). Relation between academic performance and students' engagement in digital learning activities. *Journal of Education for Business*, *91*(3), 125–131. doi:10.1080/08832323.2016.1140113

Bieswanger, M. (2016). Aviation English: Two distinct specialized registers. *Variational Text Linguistics Revisiting Register in English, De Gruyter*, 67-86.

Bozkurt, A. (2023). Generative artificial intelligence (AI) powered conversational educational agents: The inevitable paradigm shift. *Asian Journal of Distance Education*, *18*(1). doi:10.5281/zenodo.7716416

Bozkurt, A., & Sharma, R. C. (2023). Challenging the status quo and exploring the new boundaries in the age of algorithms: Reimagining the role of generative AI in distance education and online learning. *Asian Journal of Distance Education*, *18*(1). doi:10.5281/zenodo.7755273

Bozkurt, A., Xiao, J., Lambert, S., Pazurek, A., Crompton, H., & Koseoglu, S., Farrow, R., Bond, M., Nerantzi, C., Honeychurch, S., Bali, M., Dron, J., Mir, K., Stewart, B., Costello, E., Mason, J., Stracke, C. M., Romero-Hall, E., Koutropoulos, A., Toquero, C. M., Singh, L Tlili, A., Lee, K., Nichols, M., Ossiannilsson, E., Brown, M., Irvine, V., Raffaghelli, J. E., Santos-Hermosa, G Farrell, O., Adam, T., Thong, Y. L., Sani-Bozkurt, S., Sharma, R. C., Hrastinski, SJandrić, P. (2023). Speculative futures on ChatGPT and generative artificial intelligence (AI): A collective reflection from the educational landscape. *Asian Journal of Distance Education*, *18*(1), 53-130. doi:10.5281/zenodo.7636568

Bryant, J., Heitz, C., Sanghvi, S., & Wagle, D. (2020). *How Artificial Intelligence Will Impact K-12 Teachers*. McKinsey and Company. https://www.mckinsey.com/industries/public-and-social-sector/our-insights/how-artificial-intelligence-will-impact-k-12-teachers

Chant, C. (2002). *A Century of Triumph: The History of Aviation*. Simon and Schuster.

Chaudhry, M. A., & Kazim, E. (2022). Artificial Intelligence in Education (AIEd): A high-level academic and industry note 2021. *AI and Ethics*, *2*(1), 1–9. doi:10.1007/s43681-021-00074-z PMID:34790953

Chiu, T. K., Moorhouse, B. L., Chai, C. S., & Ismailov, M. (2023). Teacher support and student motivation to learn with Artificial Intelligence (AI) based chatbot. *Interactive Learning Environments*, 1–17. doi:10.1080/10494820.2023.2172044

Christudas, B. C. L., Kirubakaran, E., & Thangaiah, P. R. J. (2018). An evolutionary approach for personalization of content delivery in e-learning systems based on learner behavior forcing compatibility of learning materials. *Telematics and Informatics*, *35*(3), 520–533. doi:10.1016/j.tele.2017.02.004

Crystal, D. (2003). *English as a global language*. Cambridge university press. doi:10.1017/CBO9780511486999

Demirdöken, G. (2021). The Constructivist Approach towards Identifying the Challenges of ESP Teachers: The Case of Aviation English. *International Journal of Aviation, Aeronautics, and Aerospace*, *8*(2), 1–18. doi:10.15394/ijaaa.2021.1571

Demirdöken, G., & Okur, S. (2023). Psychometric properties of speaking anxiety scale and an interdisciplinary investigation with serial mediation analysis. *Innovation in Language Learning and Teaching*, *17*(3), 706–722. doi:10.1080/17501229.2022.2123920

Dinçer, N. (2023). Elevating Aviation Education: A Comprehensive Examination of Technology's Role in Modern Flight Training. *Journal of Aviation*, *7*(2), 317–323. doi:10.30518/jav.1279718

Dinçer, N., & Demirdöken, G. (2023). Ab-initio pilots' perspectives on the use of simulation in the aviation English course. *Journal of Teaching English for Specific and Academic Purposes, 11*(1) 011-022. doi:10.22190/JTESAP230130003D

Dinçer, N.Dinçer. (2023). The Role of Serious Games in Effective Aviation English. *Applied Linguistic Papers*, *27*(1), 72–82. doi:10.32612/uw.25449354.2023.1.pp.72-83

Dinçer, N., & Dinçer, R. (2021). The effect of a serious game on aviation vocabulary acquisition. *International Journal of Serious Games*, *8*(4), 49–63. doi:10.17083/ijsg.v8i4.464

European Commission. (2020). *White Paper on Artificial Intelligence: a European approach to excellence and trust* (White Paper No. COM(2020) 65 final). European Commission. https://ec.europa.eu/info/publications/white-paper-artificial-intelligence-european-approach-excellence-and-trust_en

Eysenbach, G. (2023). The Role of ChatGPT, Generative Language Models, and Artificial Intelligence in Medical Education: A Conversation With ChatGPT and a Call for Papers. *JMIR Medical Education*, *9*, e46885. doi:10.2196/46885 PMID:36863937

Fainman, I., & Tokar, Y. (2019). Explicit, Implicit, and Blended Vocabulary Instruction: Efficiency in an Aviation English Course. *Collegiate Aviation Review International, 37*(2), 110-132. https://ojs.library.okstate.edu/osu/index.php/CARI/article/view/7911/7306

Federal Aviation Administration (FAA). (2016). *Advisory Circular: English Language Skill Standards Required by 14 CFR 61, 63, and 65*. FAA. https://www.faa.gov/documentLibrary/media/Advisory_Circular/AC_60-28B.pdf

Harbour, K. E., Evanovich, L. L., Sweigart, C. A., & Hughes, L. E. (2015). A Brief Review of Effective Teaching Practices That Maximize Student Engagement. *Preventing School Failure*, *59*(1), 5–13. doi:10.1080/1045988X.2014.919136

Hockly, N. (2023). Artificial Intelligence in English Language Teaching: The Good, the Bad and the Ugly. *RELC Journal*, *54*(2), 445–451. doi:10.1177/00336882231168504

Holmes, W., Porayska-Pomsta, K., Holstein, K., Sutherland, E., Baker, T., Buckingham-Shum, S., Santos, O. C., Rodrigo, M. T., Cukurova, M., Bittencourt, I. I., & Koedinger, K. R. (2022). Ethics of AI in Education: Towards a Community-Wide Framework. *International Journal of Artificial Intelligence in Education*, *32*(3), 504–526. doi:10.1007/s40593-021-00239-1

Holmes, W., & Tuomi, I. (2022). State of the art and practice in AI in education. *European Journal of Education*, *57*(4), 542–570. doi:10.1111/ejed.12533

Huang, S.-P. (2018). Effects of using artificial intelligence teaching system for environmental education on environmental knowledge and attitude. *Eurasia Journal of Mathematics, Science and Technology Education*, *14*(7), 3277–3284. doi:10.29333/ejmste/91248

Hwang, G. J., & Chang, C. Y. (2023). A review of opportunities and challenges of chatbots in education. *Interactive Learning Environments*, *31*(7), 4099–4112. doi:10.1080/10494820.2021.1952615

Hwang, G. J., Xie, H., Wah, B. W., & Gašević, D. (2020). Vision, challenges, roles and research issues of Artificial Intelligence in Education. *Computers and Education: Artificial Intelligence*, *1*, 100001. doi:10.1016/j.caeai.2020.100001

International Civil Aviation Organization (ICAO). (2003). *Annex 10 to the Convention on International Civil Aviation: Aeronautical Telecommunications.* ICAO. https://www.icao.int/Meetings/anconf12/Document%20Archive/an10_cons_en.pdf

International Civil Aviation Organization (ICAO). (2010). *Manual on the Implementation of ICAO Language Proficiency Requirements.* ICAO. https://www.icao.int/Meetings/LPR/Documents/Doc9835_en.pdf

Ishihara, N., & Prado, M. C. D. A. (2021). The Negotiation of Meaning in Aviation English as a Lingua Franca: A Corpus-Informed Discursive Approach. *Modern Language Journal*, *105*(3), 639–654. doi:10.1111/modl.12718

Kabudi, T., Pappas, I., & Olsen, D. H. (2021). AI-enabled adaptive learning systems: A systematic mapping of the literature. *Computers and Education: Artificial Intelligence*, *2*, 100017. doi:10.1016/j.caeai.2021.100017

Kamalov, F., Santandreu Calonge, D., & Gurrib, I. (2023). New Era of Artificial Intelligence in Education: Towards a Sustainable Multifaceted Revolution. *Sustainability (Basel)*, *15*(16), 12451. doi:10.3390/su151612451

Kexin, L., Yi, Q., Xiaoou, S., & Yan, L. (2020). Future education trend learned from the covid-19 pandemic: take artificial Intelligence online course as an example *International Conference on Artificial Intelligence and Education (ICAIE)* (pp. 108-111). IEEE. https://doi.org/10.1109/ICAIE50891.2020.00032

Kim, H. (2013). Exploring the construct of radiotelephony communication: A critique of the ICAO English testing policy from the perspective of Korean aviation experts. *Papers in Language Testing and Assessment*, *2*(2), 103–110. doi:10.58379/YWLL7105

Kim, W., & Kim, J. (2020). Individualized AI Tutor Based on Developmental Learning Networks. *IEEE Access : Practical Innovations, Open Solutions*, *8*, 27927–27937. doi:10.1109/ACCESS.2020.2972167

Kohnke, L., Moorhouse, B. L., & Zou, D. (2023). ChatGPT for Language Teaching and Learning. *RELC Journal*, *54*(2), 537–550. doi:10.1177/00336882231162868

Lauterbach, A. (2019). Artificial intelligence and policy: Quo vadis? Digital Policy. *Regulation & Governance*, *21*(3), 238–263. doi:10.1108/DPRG-09-2018-0054

Li, N., Yan, Y., Yang, Y., & Gu, A. (2022). Artificial intelligence capability and organizational creativity: The role of knowledge sharing and organizational cohesion. *Frontiers in Psychology*, *13*, 845277. doi:10.3389/fpsyg.2022.845277 PMID:35356339

Liu, M., Li, Y., Xu, W., & Liu, L. (2016). Automated essay feedback generation and its impact on revision. *IEEE Transactions on Learning Technologies, 10*(4), https://doi.org/. doi:502-513

Luckin, R., Cukurova, M., Kent, C., & du Boulay, B. (2022). Empowering educators to be AI-ready. *Computers and Education: Artificial Intelligence*, *3*, 100076. doi:10.1016/j.caeai.2022.100076

McCarthy, J. (2007). From here to human-level AI. *Artificial Intelligence, 171*(18), 1174–1182. doi:10.1016/j.artint.2007.10.009

Newell, A., & Simon, H. (1956). The logic theory machine—A complex information processing system. *IEEE Transactions on Information Theory, 2*(3), 61–79. doi:10.1109/TIT.1956.1056797

Ng, D. T. K., Leung, J. K. L., Chu, S. K., & Qiao, M. S. (2021). Conceptualizing AI literacy: An exploratory review. *Computers and Education: Artificial Intelligence, 2*, 1–11. doi:10.1016/j.caeai.2021.100041

Nguyen, T. D., Cannata, M., & Miller, J. (2018). Understanding student behavioral engagement: Importance of student interaction with peers and teachers. *The Journal of Educational Research, 111*(2), 163–174. doi:10.1080/00220671.2016.1220359

Park, M. (2020). Investigating Target Tasks, Task Phases, and Indigenous Criteria for Military Aviation English Assessment. *Language Assessment Quarterly, 17*(4), 337–361. doi:10.1080/15434303.2020.1799221

Pershukova, O. O., Pazyura, N., & Vasiukovych, O. (2023). Using interactive learning in future aviation professionals teaching English. *Educational Dimension, 8*, 41–54. doi:10.31812/ed.584

Rochmawati, L., Fatmawati, & Sukma, M. M. (2023). Motivation, anxiety, and self-efficacy in learning aviation English: A study of Indonesian aviation cadets. *Asian Journal of Second and Foreign Language Education, 8*(1), 40. doi:10.1186/s40862-023-00212-6

Roll, I., & Wylie, R. (2016). Evolution and revolution in artificial intelligence in education. *International Journal of Artificial Intelligence in Education, 26*(2), 582–599. doi:10.1007/s40593-016-0110-3

Skinner, E. A., & Belmont, M. J. (1993). Motivation in the classroom: Reciprocal effects of teacher behavior and student engagement across the school year. *Journal of Educational Psychology, 85*(4), 571–581. doi:10.1037/0022-0663.85.4.571

Tao, Y., Meng, Y., Gao, Z., & Yang, X. (2022). Perceived teacher support, student engagement, and academic achievement: A meta-analysis. *Educational Psychology, 42*(4), 401–420. doi:10.1080/01443410.2022.2033168

Trippe, J., & Baese-Berk, M. (2019). A prosodic profile of American Aviation English. *English for Specific Purposes, 53*, 30–46. doi:10.1016/j.esp.2018.08.006

Université de Montréal. (2018). *Declaration of Montréal for a responsible development of AI*. Université de Montréal. https://www.montrealdeclaration-responsibleai.com

Van Moere, A., Suzuki, M., Downey, R., & Cheng, J. (2009). Implementing ICAO Language Proficiency Requirements in the Versant Aviation English Test. *Australian Review of Applied Linguistics, 32*(3), 27.1–27.17. doi:10.2104/aral0927

Wenger, E. (2014). *Artificial intelligence and tutoring systems: Computational and cognitive approaches to the communication of knowledge*. Morgan Kaufmann.

Williamson, B., & Eynon, R. (2020). Historical threads, missing links, and future directions in AI in education. *Learning, Media and Technology, 45*(3), 223–235. doi:10.1080/17439884.2020.1798995

Zhai, X., Chu, X., Chai, C. S., Jong, M. S. Y., Istenic, A., Spector, M., Liu, J.-B., Yuan, J., & Li, Y. (2021). A Review of Artificial Intelligence (AI) in Education from 2010 to 2020. *Complexity*, *2021*, 1–18. doi:10.1155/2021/8812542

Zhao, Q., & Nazir, S. (2022). English multimode production and usage by artificial intelligence and online reading for sustaining effectiveness. *Mobile Information Systems*, *2022*, 1–16. doi:10.1155/2022/6780502

KEY TERMS AND DEFINITIONS

Air Traffic Controller: Those who orchestrate flight paths to ensure safety and efficiency.

Artificial Intelligence in Education: Infusing smart algorithms into learning environments to enhance teaching and student performance.

Artificial Intelligence: A digital realm where machines mimic human cognition to solve tasks.

Aviation English: The specific language of the skies ensuring clear communication among aviation professionals.

Chatbot: A digital assistant designed for interactive conversations, often automating tasks or providing information.

ChatGPT: A virtual conversationalist designed to mimic human-like text interaction

Generative Artificial Intelligence: The branch of AI that crafts new content based on patterns from data.

ICAO: The global agency that governs aviation standards, ensuring skies are navigated safely and seamlessly worldwide.

Large Language Models: Massive digital libraries trained on vast text data to predict and produce language.

Standard Phraseology: Preset language conventions to ensure clarity in specific contexts.

Chapter 20
Unlocking the Power of Prompt Engineering:
Diverse Applications and Case Studies

K. S. Jasmine
https://orcid.org/0000-0002-8251-4261
R.V. College of Engineering, India

ABSTRACT

Prompt engineering holds immense relevance in the present world due to its pivotal role in advancing natural language processing (NLP) technologies and artificial intelligence (AI) applications. Also prompt engineering is instrumental in shaping the present landscape of AI-driven technologies, making them more efficient, accessible, and personalized. As these technologies continue to evolve, prompt engineering will remain a vital area of research and development, ensuring that AI systems effectively meet the diverse and dynamic needs of our society. Also, generative AI can create personalized learning experiences for students by analyzing individual learning styles, preferences, and progress. In this context, the chapter explores the art and science of prompt engineering. Through a collection of case studies and real-world applications, the chapter showcases the versatility of prompt engineering, offering insights into how it enhances machine comprehension, content generation, and problem-solving across domains. Here the case studies are discussed using ChatGPT 3.5 version.

INTRODUCTION

In the ever-evolving landscape of artificial intelligence and natural language processing, the science of prompt engineering has emerged as a powerful and versatile tool that unlocks the true potential of AI systems. This book chapter, "Unlocking the Power of Prompt Engineering: Diverse Applications and Case Studies," is a comprehensive exploration of this groundbreaking field and its transformative impact on the way we interact with machines in the digital age.

DOI: 10.4018/979-8-3693-1351-0.ch020

Prompt engineering is the art of crafting precise and effective input prompts that guide AI models to produce desired outputs. It is the key to enhancing AI's ability to comprehend, generate, and solve problems across a broad spectrum of applications. This chapter embarks on a journey through diverse case studies and real-world applications that illustrate the incredible breadth of possibilities prompt engineering offers.

From fine-tuning AI models for specific tasks to aiding in creative content generation, information retrieval, and even personalized education, the chapter showcases the practical implications of prompt engineering. It delves into the latest advancements, ethical considerations, and the profound impact of this technology on society. Whether you are a researcher, developer, or simply curious about the cutting edge of AI, this chapter provides invaluable insights into the dynamic world of prompt engineering.

The rest of the chapter is organized as follows: Section 2 deals with Background or literature survey in the area of study. Section 3 discusses basics of Generative AI and Prompt Engineering. Section 4 focuses on role of Generative AI in Educational teaching. Section 5 describes harnessing creativity with Prompt Engineering. Section 6 explains how Generative AI works and Section 7 provides few Use Cases and followed with chapter conclusion and references.

BACKGROUND

Artificial intelligence (AI) and natural language processing (NLP) have witnessed an unprecedented surge in development and application in recent years, reshaping the way humans interact with technology. As AI systems have become increasingly integrated into our daily lives, the need for more refined and efficient communication between humans and machines has grown exponentially. This evolving landscape has given rise to the science of prompt engineering, a field dedicated to optimizing the interaction between users and AI systems.

Prompt engineering can be likened to the architect's blueprint in construction. It involves crafting tailored input prompts that serve as instructions for AI models, guiding them to produce desired and contextually relevant outputs. These prompts act as the key to unlocking AI's potential to understand and respond effectively, making it a versatile tool applicable to a wide range of domains.

Many studies explore the use of generative AI and prompt engineering in the field of education. Bozkurt and Sharma, (2023) discuss the potential of AI in enhancing the learning experience and highlight the importance of prompt engineering in achieving the desired outcomes and offers insights into the future of this field. Dwivedi et al. (2023) provides a multidisciplinary perspective on the opportunities, challenges, and implications of generative conversational AI for research, practice, and policy. Likewise, Bozkurt et al. (2023) has also studied on speculative futures on ChatGPT and generative artificial intelligence (AI) in the context of educational landscape. White et al. (2023), in their study, provides a framework for documenting patterns for structuring prompts to solve a range of problems so that they can be adapted to different domains. The study by Bommasani et al. (2021) presents a catalog of patterns that have been applied successfully to improve the outputs of LLM conversations and explains how prompts can be built from multiple patterns and illustrates prompt patterns that benefit from combination with other prompt patterns. There exists a comprehensive exploration of the opportunities and risks associated with foundation models in the field of artificial intelligence and natural language processing. For instance, Bang et al. (2023) provides an overview of ChatGPT and related work, followed by evaluation results on various application test sets, multilingual test sets, and a new multimodal task. The authors in that study explore the three main strengths and weaknesses of ChatGPT, namely reasoning, hallucination, and interactivity, in separate sections. Wei et al. (2022) explores how generating a chain of thought, a series of intermediate reasoning steps, improves the ability of large language models to perform complex reasoning. The study shows how such reasoning abilities emerge naturally in sufficiently large language models via a simple method called chain of thought prompting, where a few chain of thought demonstrations are provided as exemplars in prompting.

The summary of literature survey collectively contributes to our understanding of how to structure prompts effectively for different tasks, the opportunities and risks related to foundation models, the evaluation of ChatGPT in various contexts, and innovative methods for enhancing the reasoning capabilities of large language models.

UNDERSTANDING GENERATIVE AI AND PROMPT ENGINEERING

This section deals with the key aspects of defining Generative AI and Prompt Engineering.

Generative AI, a cutting-edge technology, is at the forefront of artificial intelligence research. It involves the creation of AI models, like GPT-3, that have the ability to generate human-like text or content. Understanding generative AI requires a grasp of the underlying architecture and training processes. Generative models, such as OpenAI's GPT-3, are trained on vast datasets of text from the internet and utilize deep learning techniques to generate coherent and contextually relevant text. The key to their success lies in the quality of the data and the neural network's capacity to learn grammar, style, and context. For instance, GPT-3 can write essays, answer questions, and even generate code for programming tasks. By providing a prompt or initial input, users can harness the generative power of AI to create various types of content. Prompt engineering, therefore, plays a pivotal role in leveraging generative AI effectively (Liu et al., 2023).

Prompt engineering is the art of crafting precise and instructive input to generative AI models to produce the desired output. It's a crucial aspect of working with generative AI, as the same model can generate drastically different responses based on the input it receives. For example, if there is a need for generative model to summarize a news article, one can provide a prompt like "Please summarize the following article about climate change." On the other hand, if there is a need to create a creative story, one can use a prompt like "Write a short story about a time-traveling adventurer." By tailoring the prompt, we can guide the AI model to produce content that aligns with our specific requirements. The key to effective prompt engineering understands the model's capabilities and limitations and refining the prompts to get the desired results, all while ensuring ethical and responsible use of the technology.

THE ROLE OF GENERATIVE AI IN EDUCATIONAL TEACHING

Generative AI, such as the GPT-3 architecture, has the potential to play a significant role in education by offering various benefits and applications (Kasneci et al., 2023):

1. Personalized Learning: Generative AI can create personalized learning experiences for students. By analyzing individual learning styles, preferences, and progress, AI can generate customized

educational content, including lessons, quizzes, and practice exercises. This tailoring of materials can help students learn more efficiently and effectively.

Eg: Generate a prompt for a BBA student to select career option

- Generated Prompt

"Imagine you are advising a BBA (Bachelor of Business Administration) student who is nearing graduation and needs to make a career choice. Create a comprehensive career exploration plan for this student. Consider their skills, interests, and long-term goals. Outline potential career options within the business field, highlighting the job roles, industries, and growth prospects associated with each option. Suggest strategies for networking, skill development, and job search to help them make an informed decision about their future career path."

2. Tutoring and Homework Help: AI-powered chatbots or virtual tutors can provide students with on-demand assistance with homework and assignments. These AI systems can answer questions, provide explanations, and offer guidance, supplementing the teacher's role and making learning more accessible outside the classroom.
3. Content Creation: Educators can leverage generative AI to generate content for their lessons, such as writing reports, creating test questions, or even generating instructional materials. This can save time for teachers and ensure that content is up-to-date and relevant.

Eg: Generate a question paper having 5 questions with each question having two sub sections a & b with 5 marks each on the subject 'basic mathematics'. Show output in three column table with column headings: sl no., question and marks.

Table 1. Generated output by ChatGPT

Sl.No	Question	Marks
1 a	Solve the following equation for x: 2x - 3 = 7	5
1b	Find the value of y if 3y + 8 = 17	5
2a	Calculate the area of a rectangular garden with a length of 8 meters and a width of 5 meters	5
2b	If a triangle has a base of 6 cm and a height of 9 cm, find its area.	5
3a	Simplify the expression: 4(3x - 2) + 5(2x + 7)	5
3b	Solve for z in the equation: 2(z - 4) = 10	5
4a	If a box contains 24 identical pens, how many pens are there in 6 such boxes	5
4b	Calculate the total cost if 8 books each cost $12.	5
5a	Express 35% as a fraction in its simplest form.	5
5b	If a car travels 180 miles in 3 hours, what its average speed in miles per hour?	5

4. Language Learning and Translation: Generative AI can assist with language learning by offering real-time translations, generating language exercises, and providing conversational partners for language learners. This can be particularly helpful in language classrooms and for students learning a second language (Han et al.,2022).
5. Automating Administrative Tasks: AI can automate administrative tasks within educational institutions, such as managing enrollment, scheduling classes, and grading assessments. This frees up educators and administrators to focus more on teaching and student support.
6. Simulations and Virtual Labs: Generative AI can create virtual simulations and laboratory experiences, allowing students to experiment and learn in a safe, controlled digital environment. This is especially valuable in subjects like science and engineering.
7. Content Recommendations: AI-powered recommendation systems can suggest additional resources, articles, or videos to students based on their interests and learning progress, helping them explore topics beyond their curriculum.
8. Access to Education: Generative AI can provide access to education for individuals who have limited access to traditional educational institutions. Online courses and materials generated by AI can make education more inclusive and accessible.

However, it's important to consider the ethical and privacy implications of using generative AI in education, such as data security, algorithm bias, and ensuring that AI tools do not replace human educators but rather complement their roles. Additionally, the quality and accuracy of AI-generated content must be closely monitored to ensure it meets educational standards. Generative AI has the potential to revolutionize education, but it should be used thoughtfully and ethically to maximize its benefits.

Prompt engineering is the practice of designing and refining prompts or queries to interact with generative AI systems effectively. It plays a crucial role in harnessing the capabilities of generative AI, such as language models, by specifying the desired output or response. Generative AI systems, like GPT-3, generate human-like text based on the prompts they receive. Effective prompt engineering involves crafting prompts that are clear, precise, and contextually relevant to the desired task. It determines how well the AI system comprehends and responds to the input. Therefore, prompt engineering is the bridge between human intent and machine output, allowing users to leverage the full potential of generative AI across various applications, from content generation to language translation, and even educational support.

To successfully integrate prompt engineering into the educational environment, several specific teaching practices can be enhanced or utilized. One of them is Project-Based Learning (PBL). PBL is an effective teaching approach where students work on projects that require them to apply their knowledge and skills to solve real-world problems. In the context of prompt engineering, educators can design projects that challenge students to formulate questions, collect and analyze data, and communicate their findings effectively. This hands-on, inquiry-based method allows students to explore engineering concepts in a practical and engaging manner, fostering critical thinking, problem-solving, and teamwork. PBL also promotes self-directed learning and helps students see the relevance of engineering principles to their lives, making it an ideal method for prompt engineering to succeed in education.

Another most relevant teaching practice which can be adopted in the educational field is Cross-disciplinary Integration. Prompt engineering thrives when it incorporates elements of various disciplines, such as science, mathematics, technology, and even arts and humanities. Educators can enhance teaching practices by promoting cross-disciplinary integration. For example, they can design lessons that show the connections between engineering and other subjects, allowing students to explore the holistic nature of problem-solving and innovation. Interdisciplinary collaboration can be encouraged through team-based projects and discussions that bridge the gap between different subjects, leading to a more comprehensive and well-rounded educational experience that aligns with the goals of prompt engineering. By fostering a learning environment that embraces both PBL and cross-disciplinary integration, prompt engineering can succeed in the educational setting and equip students with the skills and knowledge they need for the future.

HARNESSING CREATIVITY WITH PROMPT ENGINEERING

The strategic and thoughtful construction of prompts to elicit creative and innovative responses from artificial intelligence (AI) and machine learning models are vital in order to get best possible output(Arora et al.,2023). In this context, prompt engineering is a crucial technique for guiding AI systems like GPT-3 or similar models to produce desired outputs or ideas that are imaginative, novel, and useful.

Here are some key aspects of harnessing creativity with prompt engineering:

- **Understanding the Model**: To effectively harness creativity, it's important to have a deep understanding of the AI model being used. Knowing its strengths, limitations, and biases can help you formulate prompts that leverage its capabilities.
- **Clear Intent and Constraints**: When crafting prompts, it's essential to have a clear intent in mind. You should also define any constraints or requirements that the AI system needs to follow. This clarity guides the AI's creative process towards the desired outcome.
- **Open-Ended Prompts**: Open-ended prompts encourage the AI to think creatively. For example, rather than asking for a straightforward answer, you might pose a question that begins with "Imagine a world where..." or "Invent a new concept for...". These types of prompts stimulate the model's creative thinking.
- **Iterative Testing**: Prompt engineering often involves an iterative process. You may need to experiment with different prompts, refining them based on the AI's responses until you achieve the desired level of creativity.
- **Incorporating Context**: Consider incorporating relevant context into your prompts. By providing background information or setting a particular scenario, you can direct the AI's creativity towards generating ideas that fit within that context.
- **Avoiding Biases**: Be mindful of potential biases in the prompts themselves, as well as in the training data. Biased prompts can lead to biased responses. Make sure your prompts are neutral and do not inadvertently encourage discriminatory or harmful content.
- **Combining Prompts**: Sometimes, combining multiple prompts or asking the AI to build on its previous response can lead to more creative and coherent outputs.
- **Encouraging Imagination**: Encourage the AI to think outside the box and explore unconventional ideas. You can use phrases like "What if..." or "Picture a world where..." to stimulate imaginative thinking.
- **Feedback and Review**: Continuously review and assess the AI's outputs. Provide feedback and iterate on your prompt engineering strategies to enhance the creative quality of the responses.

- **Ethical Considerations**: Ensure that the creative outputs align with ethical guidelines and avoid generating harmful, illegal, or unethical content. Prompt engineering should always be done with a sense of responsibility.

In essence, by harnessing creativity with prompt engineering is nothing but using well-crafted prompts as a tool to tap into the creative potential of AI models and guide them toward generating imaginative, innovative, and meaningful content.

HOW GENERATIVE AI WORKS?

Generative AI works by using artificial neural networks to generate data, often in the form of text, images, or other types of media. The detailed design and implementation can vary based on the specific model and application.

The process of designing and implementing generative AI involves several key steps. Firstly, it begins with data collection and preprocessing, where a substantial and varied dataset related to the task at hand is gathered and prepared. This includes actions like tokenization for text or image resizing for image generation. Next, selecting appropriate model architecture is crucial. Depending on the nature of the generative task, one may opt for neural network architectures like RNNs, LSTMs, or more modern Transformer-based models, such as GPT-3 and BERT for text, or GANs for image generation. Once the architecture is chosen, the model is trained with the preprocessed data. Training involves initializing the network with random weights, defining a loss function for quality assessment, and using techniques like backpropagation and optimization to fine-tune the model. After training, the model can generate new data by inputting seed phrases or random noise vectors, depending on the task. Fine-tuning, monitoring, ethical considerations, deployment, and continuous improvement are additional steps essential in ensuring the generative AI system functions effectively and responsibly (Arora et al.,2023).

The design and implementation of generative AI encompass a holistic process, beginning with data collection and preprocessing, culminating in the deployment of models, and ongoing efforts to enhance their performance and ethical considerations. These steps are integral to harnessing the potential of generative AI, whether for text or image generation, and ensuring that it generates high-quality, unbiased, and contextually appropriate content.

The design and implementation details can vary significantly depending on the specific task, model, and dataset. Furthermore, ethical considerations are paramount when deploying generative AI systems, as they can produce content with potentially significant societal impact.

APPLICATIONS OF GENERATIVE AI

Generative AI has a wide range of applications across various domains. It has proven to be a powerful technology for generating content, solving problems, and enhancing user experiences.

Here are some key applications of generative AI:

1. **Natural Language Generation (NLG):**
   - **Content Creation:** NLG models can automatically generate written content, including news articles, reports, product descriptions, and more.
   - **Chatbots and Virtual Assistants:** Generative models power chatbots and virtual assistants, enabling natural and context-aware interactions.
2. **Text Summarization:**
   - **Automated Summaries:** Generative models can create concise and coherent summaries of long articles or documents.
3. **Text Translation:**
   - **Language Translation:** Models like Google Translate use generative techniques to translate text from one language to another.
4. **Image Generation:**
   - **Art and Design:** Generative Adversarial Networks (GANs) can create images, art, and designs.
   - **Face Generation:** GANs can generate realistic faces, which have applications in video games, virtual avatars, and deepfake technology.
5. **Music Generation:**
   - **Composing Music:** Generative models can compose music and create new melodies or arrangements.
6. **Video Generation:**
   - **Video Synthesis:** AI can generate video content, such as deepfake videos or video enhancement.
7. **Storyline Generation:**
   - AI can create non-player characters (NPCs) and generate storylines in video games.
8. Business Promotion:
   - Business promotion involves leveraging its capabilities to create engaging, informative, and persuasive content that can help promote products, services, or brand.

These applications showcase the versatility and potential of generative AI to generate content, improve processes, and create new possibilities across multiple industries and fields.

Natural Language Generation (NLG) is a subset of generative AI that focuses on the automatic generation of human-readable text from structured data or other forms of input. NLG is used in various applications to produce coherent and contextually relevant written content.

Natural Language Generation (NLG): Use cases

NLG in generative AI enhances efficiency and scalability in content creation and communication across numerous industries, making it a valuable tool for automating text generation while ensuring quality and consistency. It has the potential to revolutionize how businesses, institutions, and individuals generate written content for a wide range of applications.

Content Creation

Content creation is a broad and diverse field, and generative AI, specifically Natural Language Generation (NLG), has found numerous applications in streamlining and enhancing the content creation process. Here are some use cases of generative AI in content creation:

- **News Articles and Updates:**
  - NLG can automatically generate news articles based on raw data, such as financial reports, sports scores, or weather data. This is particularly useful for real-time reporting.
- **E-commerce Product Descriptions:**
  - Online retailers use NLG to create unique and compelling product descriptions for a wide range of items in their catalog, improving search engine visibility and user engagement.
- **Content for Blogs and Websites:**
  - NLG tools can generate blog posts, website content, and landing pages on various topics. This is particularly useful for maintaining active blogs with fresh content.
- **Social Media Posts:**
  - Marketers and individuals use generative AI to craft engaging social media posts and updates, tailoring content to specific audiences and platforms.
- **Email Marketing Campaigns:**
  - NLG automates the creation of personalized email content for marketing campaigns, improving user engagement and conversion rates.
- **Video Scriptwriting:**
  - NLG can assist in creating scripts for videos, including YouTube content, instructional videos, and promotional material.
- **Legal Documents:**
  - Law firms and legal professionals use NLG to generate legal documents, such as contracts, agreements, and legal correspondence.
- **Reports and Whitepapers:**
  - NLG is employed to automate the generation of business reports, research papers, and industry-specific whitepapers, saving time and ensuring consistency.
- **Academic and Educational Content:**
  - NLG can generate educational materials, including lesson plans, quizzes, and study guides. It can also help teachers and educators create content for online courses(Pearce et al.,2022)
- **Healthcare Documentation:**
  - In the medical field, NLG is used to generate patient reports, medical notes, and clinical documentation, improving efficiency and accuracy.
- **Technical Documentation:**
  - NLG can assist in generating technical manuals, user guides, and documentation for software, hardware, and other products.
- **Automated Transcripts:**
  - NLG can convert spoken content, such as interviews, podcasts, and lectures, into written transcripts, making content accessible and searchable.

- **Content for Chatbots:**
    - Chatbots and virtual assistants utilize NLG to provide informative and helpful responses to user queries in real-time.
- **Event Summaries and Reviews:**
    - NLG can create summaries and reviews of events, movies, books, or any form of entertainment, helping to curate content for online platforms.
- **Localization and Translation:**
    - NLG is used for translating content into multiple languages, making it accessible to a global audience.
- **Marketing Copy:**
    - NLG tools assist in generating marketing copy, slogans, and advertisements for various promotional materials.
- **Restaurant and Food Reviews:**
    - NLG can create restaurant and food reviews for websites, apps, and publications, helping users make informed dining decisions.
- **Real Estate Listings:**
    - NLG is employed to generate property listings with detailed descriptions, photos, and key features for real estate websites.
- **Financial Reports and Insights:**
    - NLG can generate financial reports, stock market analyses, and investment insights based on raw financial data.
- **Automated Content Updates:**
    - NLG can keep websites and content platforms updated by generating content on a regular schedule, such as daily news summaries or weekly newsletters.

Generative AI in content creation not only enhances productivity and efficiency but also enables businesses and individuals to maintain a consistent content presence across various platforms, leading to better user engagement and improved SEO.

Prompt engineering in content creation involves the strategic design of prompts to guide generative AI models, such as GPT-3, in generating specific types of content. It plays a critical role in influencing the quality and relevance of the content produced.

Effective prompt engineering is crucial for content creation with generative AI models. To initiate this process, it's essential to specify the type of content you intend to generate, whether it's a blog post, product description, news article, or marketing copy. Clear communication is key, as you should clarify the intent and context of the content in the prompt, specifying the target audience, tone, and relevant background information. Additionally, defining the structure of the content, including headings and sections, is important to ensure the generated content meets your formatting expectations. Including relevant keywords and phrases in the prompt enhances the content's search engine optimization (SEO) and alignment with specific topics. Providing example content as a reference point for the AI model can also guide its output. Further details, such as desired length, user engagement elements like open-ended questions, creativity encouragement, personalization, tone, style, and any constraints or restrictions, are integral to crafting effective prompts.

Prompt engineering often entails an iterative process, where you experiment with different prompts and evaluate the quality of the generated content. This iterative approach allows you to continually refine your prompts and the resulting content, ensuring it aligns with your goals and expectations. By employing these considerations and techniques, content creators can harness the capabilities of generative AI models more effectively and efficiently, ultimately producing content that is tailored to their needs, whether for SEO, user engagement, personalization, or adherence to specific guidelines and regulations.

Few sample prompts illustrate how clear and specific instructions can guide generative AI models in creating content that aligns with the intended purpose, style, and audience of the content. Effective prompt engineering is essential for generating content that meets specific objectives and maintains consistency and quality.

Few Use Cases:

- **Product Description for a Laptop:**
  - Prompt: "Compose a concise product description for a 15-inch laptop. Emphasize its performance, design, and portability. Highlight key features like a powerful processor, sleek aluminum body, and lightweight design. Keep the description around 150 words."
- **News Article on Renewable Energy Trends:**
  - Prompt: "Write a news article about current trends in renewable energy. Cover recent advancements in solar technology, wind energy adoption, and government initiatives. The article should be 500 words and maintain a neutral, informative tone."
- **Social Media Post for a Tech Company:**
  - Prompt: "Create an engaging social media post for a tech company's Facebook page. Announce the launch of a new product, a smart home assistant. Use a casual and enthusiastic tone. Include a call to action encouraging users to pre-order the product."
- **Marketing Email for a Retail Store:**
  - Prompt: "Craft a marketing email promoting a weekend sale event at a retail store. Highlight discounts on clothing, electronics, and home goods. Personalize the email by including the recipient's first name. Create a sense of urgency and encourage recipients to visit the store."
- **Legal Document: Rental Agreement:**
  - Prompt: "Compose a rental agreement for a residential property, specifying the terms, responsibilities, and obligations of both the landlord and tenant. Include sections on rent payment, security deposit, maintenance, and termination conditions. Ensure legal accuracy and clarity."
- **User Manual for a Smartphone:**
  - Prompt: "Write a user manual for a smartphone. Cover topics such as initial setup, using features like the camera and apps, troubleshooting common issues, and maintenance tips. Make the manual comprehensive but easy to understand for users of all tech levels."
- **Research Paper Abstract on Climate Change:**
  - Prompt: "Generate an abstract for a research paper on the impact of climate change on coastal communities. Summarize the key findings, methodologies, and implications. Keep it concise, around 150 words, and suitable for a scientific audience."

Chatbots and Virtual Assistants

Prompt engineering in the context of chatbots and virtual assistants involves crafting prompts that guide the AI in providing useful and contextually relevant responses to user queries or requests. Here are some sample prompts for chatbots and virtual assistants:

- **General Information Retrieval:**
    - Prompt: "Provide information about the nearest coffee shops in the downtown area, along with their operating hours and ratings."
- **Tech Support Inquiry:**
    - Prompt: "Troubleshoot an issue with my Wi-Fi connection. Please guide me through the steps to resolve it."
- **Weather Forecast:**
    - Prompt: "What's the weather forecast for New York City for the next five days? Include temperature, precipitation, and wind speed."
- **Appointment Scheduling:**
    - Prompt: "Schedule a meeting with John Doe for next Tuesday at 2 PM. Check his availability and send him a calendar invite."
- **Flight Information:**
    - Prompt: "Can you provide details about flight UA123 from New York to Los Angeles, including departure time and gate number?"
- **Health and Wellness Advice:**
    - Prompt: "I'm feeling stressed lately. Can you suggest some relaxation techniques or mindfulness exercises to help me unwind?"

These sample prompts demonstrate the importance of clear and well-structured instructions to ensure chatbots and virtual assistants can offer relevant and accurate responses to a wide range of user queries and tasks.

Text Summarization – Use Cases

Text summarization finds versatile use cases in modern information-driven domains. It streamlines news aggregation by providing concise article summaries, enables content curation by distilling information from various sources, assists researchers in swiftly reviewing lengthy papers, helps legal professionals by summarizing complex documents, enhances e-learning through the creation of study guides, offers business intelligence by extracting insights from reports, aids efficient customer support through chatbots, optimizes healthcare by summarizing medical records, monitors social media by summarizing discussions, facilitates book summaries for readers, expedites language translation, digests meeting and conference transcripts, automates email triage, condenses financial reports for investors, and supports content extraction for web scraping, ultimately saving time and improving information accessibility in diverse sectors(Han et al.,2022).

Prompt format:

- Summarize the article: [Insert article/Book title or topic or article web link]
- Article Content: [Provide a brief introduction or key points from the article, or paste the article text here if it's short]
- Prompt: Please generate a concise summary of the article, highlighting the main ideas, key arguments, and any relevant statistics or examples. The summary should be between [desired word count or length, e.g., 100-150 words].
    - Eg1: Summarize the article: "Climate Change Impacts on Coastal Cities"
    - Eg2: Summarize[https://www.montclair.edu/itds/digital-pedagogy/pedagogical-strategies-and-practices/]
    - Eg3: Please provide a summary of the main themes and plot points in the book 'Superintelligence: Paths, Dangers, Strategies' by Nick Bostrom
    - Eg4: Summarize [Chandrayaan-3 is a follow-on mission to Chandrayaan-2 to demonstrate end-to-end capability in safe landing and roving on the lunar surface. It consists of Lander and Rover configuration. It will be launched by LVM3 from SDSC SHAR, Sriharikota. The propulsion module will carry the lander and rover configuration till 100 km lunar orbit. The propulsion module has Spectro-polarimetry of Habitable Planet Earth (SHAPE) payload to study the spectral and Polari metric measurements of Earth from the lunar orbit.] in two sentences]

Uses cases for Text Translation

Text translation serves a variety of practical use cases across different sectors. In healthcare, it ensures effective communication between medical professionals and patients from diverse linguistic backgrounds, helping to convey diagnoses, treatment plans, and medical instructions accurately. For international businesses, translation is indispensable in localizing marketing materials, websites, and legal documents, enabling companies to expand their reach and serve a global customer base. In education, text translation supports language learners by providing explanations and interpretations of foreign language texts, fostering a deeper understanding of diverse cultures and linguistic nuances. Additionally, the entertainment industry relies on translation for subtitling and dubbing to make films and content accessible to international audiences, while government agencies utilize it for diplomacy and international relations, translating treaties, agreements, and official documents. These are just a few examples of the extensive and diverse applications of text translation in our interconnected world.

Some sample to initiate text translation with ChatGPT:

1. "Translate the following English sentence into French: 'I love to travel.'"
2. "I need a German translation for the following paragraph about climate change."
3. "Translate this Chinese text into English: '今天是一个美丽的日子' (Today is a beautiful day)."
4. "What is the Japanese translation for the word 'happiness'?"
5. "Translate this Russian poem into Spanish, preserving the original poetic style and rhyming scheme."

These prompts can be tailored to one's specific translation needs, whether it's for personal use, professional documents, academic research, or any other context.

Use cases for Image generation

ChatGPT, a text-based AI model, is primarily designed for natural language understanding and generation. It can't directly generate images but it can be used in combination with other AI models and tools to assist in image generation tasks.

ChatGPT can be helpful in the context of following image generation scenarios:

- Text-to-Image Generation: ChatGPT can provide textual descriptions of images, which can then be used as input for text-to-image generation models. For example, you can describe an image in text to ChatGPT, and then use a separate image generation model that takes this description and produces an image matching it.

Eg: "Create an image of a serene sunset over a calm lake with mountains in the background."

- Creative Prompts: ChatGPT can help generate creative prompts for artists and designers looking for inspiration. You can ask it for ideas or descriptions of scenes or objects, and use these textual prompts as a basis for creating images.

Eg1: "Create a digital painting of a mythical creature that has never been seen before."

- Image Editing Instructions: You can use ChatGPT to provide instructions for image editing. For instance, you can describe how you want an image to be modified or manipulated, and then apply those instructions using image editing software or algorithms.

Eg1:"Brighten the image and increase the contrast to make the colors more vibrant."
Eg2: "Crop the photo to focus on the subject in the center and remove any distracting background."

- Image Metadata: ChatGPT can assist in generating metadata for images, such as titles, captions, and keywords. This can help with organizing and cataloging images in a database or on a website.

Eg1: "Write a caption for this photograph of a child blowing out birthday candles."
Eg2:"Generate keywords for this image of a bustling city street during a rainstorm."

- Image Search and Retrieval: You can ask ChatGPT to find images based on specific criteria or descriptions. ChatGPT can help with generating search queries that you can use to retrieve images from image databases.

Eg1: "Retrieve pictures of various species of colorful birds for a nature documentary project."
Eg2: "Search for high-resolution images of classic cars from the 1960s."

- Image-Text Pairing: ChatGPT can help associate images with relevant textual descriptions or explanations. This can be useful for creating training data for machine learning models that learn to understand the content of images based on associated text.

Eg1:Write a short story inspired by the characters and setting in this image of a futuristic city."

Eg2: Describe the emotions and feelings conveyed in this image of a peaceful forest at dawn."

For advanced image generation tasks, dedicated image generation models like GANs (Generative Adversarial Networks) and image-based models are more suitable. However, ChatGPT can be a valuable tool for generating, manipulating, and providing context to textual descriptions related to images.

ChatGPT can be a valuable tool for finding images based on specific criteria or descriptions in various use cases.

Few examples of how ChatGPT can assist in image search and retrieval are given below:

- **Content Creators and Designers**: Content creators, such as bloggers, graphic designers, and social media managers, can use ChatGPT to describe the type of images they need for their projects. For instance, they can provide textual descriptions of scenes, objects, or moods they want to convey, and ChatGPT can generate search queries to find suitable images.
- **E-commerce**: E-commerce platforms can use ChatGPT to help customers find products based on descriptions. Shoppers can describe the items they're looking for, and ChatGPT can generate search queries to retrieve relevant product images.
- **Digital Marketers**: Marketers looking for images to use in advertisements, campaigns, or social media posts can describe their marketing goals to ChatGPT. This can include target demographics, desired emotions, or key messages. ChatGPT can then suggest image search terms or concepts to align with these goals.
- **Artists and Illustrators**: Visual artists can use ChatGPT to generate prompts for their artwork. They can describe the subject matter, style, or mood they want to convey, and ChatGPT can suggest image search queries or descriptions to inspire their creative process.
- **Educational Materials**: Teachers and educators can use ChatGPT to find images for educational materials. They can provide descriptions of topics or concepts they're teaching, and ChatGPT can assist in generating search terms to find relevant images for presentations, worksheets, or handouts(Pearce et al.,2022).
- **Researchers**: Researchers in various fields can use ChatGPT to find images for their studies and publications. By describing their research topics and objectives, ChatGPT can help generate search queries that lead to images relevant to their work.
- **Personal Image Collection Management**: Individuals can use ChatGPT to organize and manage their personal image collections. By describing the content or context of images, ChatGPT can help add metadata or labels to images, making them easier to search and retrieve.
- **Content Moderation**: ChatGPT can be employed to help identify and filter images based on descriptions that meet specific content moderation criteria. This can be useful for ensuring that user-generated content complies with community guidelines.
- **Curation and Recommendation Systems**: In content curation platforms or recommendation systems, ChatGPT can assist in finding images that match a user's preferences or past interactions. Users can describe their interests or needs, and ChatGPT can contribute to refining the content recommendations.
- **Visual Assistants and Chatbots**: ChatGPT can serve as a component of visual assistants or chatbots that help users find images based on their queries and descriptions, making it easier for users to locate visual content.

In all these use cases, ChatGPT acts as a natural language interface for describing the desired images, generating search queries, and making the image search process more efficient and user-friendly. The actual image retrieval can be done through search engines, image databases, or other image-specific tools and platforms.

Use cases for Music generation

Music generation models can be prompted to create music based on various styles, moods, and musical parameters.

Here are some example prompts for music generation.

Eg1:"Generate a relaxing piano melody for a meditation track."
Eg2: "Create a 30-second intro theme for a fantasy video game."
Eg3: "Generate a ten lines melody for my brother wedding anniversary"

The prompts can be tailored to specific musical styles, genres, and requirements. Music generation models can use these prompts to produce original compositions based on the desired mood and style, making them valuable tools for musicians, composers, and content creators.

Video generation

OpenAI had not released a version of GPT-3 or ChatGPT specifically designed for video generation. However, there are AI models and technologies specifically developed for video generation and manipulation, such as DeepDream, Deepfake, and various video editing softwares.

Here are some potential use cases for video generation and manipulation using AI technologies:

- **Deepfake Videos**: Create deepfake videos where AI algorithms replace a person's face in a video with the face of another person, often for humorous or manipulative purposes. It has some ethical considerations and is subject to regulation in many places.
- **Video Editing and Enhancement**: Use AI to automate and enhance video editing tasks, such as stabilizing shaky footage, color correction, noise reduction, and adding special effects.
- **Content Creation**: Generate video content for marketing, advertising, or entertainment purposes. AI can help create video advertisements, product demos, and even entire video stories.
- **Video Summarization**: Automatically summarize long videos into shorter clips by selecting key scenes or segments. This can be useful for content creators and video platforms.
- **Video Captioning and Subtitling**: Use AI to generate captions and subtitles for videos, making content accessible to a wider audience and improving SEO for video platforms.
- **Automatic Dubbing and Language Translation**: Automatically dub videos into multiple languages or provide real-time translation for video content, expanding your reach to global audiences.
- **Video Game Development**: Generate animated characters, environments, and cutscenes for video games using AI, reducing the time and cost of game development.
- **Virtual Reality (VR) and Augmented Reality (AR)**: Use AI to create immersive VR and AR experiences, such as generating 3D models of objects, characters, and environments.

- **Educational Videos**: Create educational videos, tutorials, and e-learning content using AI-generated animations and voiceovers.
- **Art and Animation**: Generate art and animations for various purposes, from web design to cartoon production, using AI algorithms that can create visual content.
- **Simulations and Training**: Develop realistic simulations and training videos for fields such as aviation, medicine, and military training.
- **Sports Analysis**: Analyze sports videos to track player movements, game statistics, and provide in-depth insights for coaches and analysts.
- **Personalized Video Content**: Use AI to create personalized video messages or recommendations for users based on their preferences and behaviors.

Eg1:"Create accurate captions for this interview video discussing the latest tech trends."
Eg2:"Add English subtitles to this foreign language cooking tutorial video."
Eg3: "Generate a personalized video message for [Viewer's Name] celebrating their birthday."
Eg4:"Create a personalized video recommendation for [Viewer's Name] based on their recent viewing history."

Storyline generation

Storyline generation, often driven by AI, can be applied in various fields and use cases to create compelling narratives. Here are some examples of use cases for storyline generation:

- **Entertainment and Media**:
    - **Scriptwriting**: AI can assist screenwriters and playwrights in developing movie scripts, TV show episodes, and theatrical plays.

Eg1:"Create a script for a political drama that explores the rise and fall of a charismatic but morally compromised politician."
Eg2:"Generate a screenplay for a dark comedy set in a dysfunctional office environment, following the absurd antics of the employees."

- **Video Games**: AI can generate dynamic storylines for video games, adapting the narrative based on player choices.
- **Interactive Storytelling**: Create choose-your-own-adventure narratives and interactive fiction using AI-generated storylines.
    - **Content Marketing**:
- **Branded Content**: Develop engaging storylines for branded content, advertisements, and marketing campaigns.
- **Blogs and Articles**: AI can assist in generating engaging blog post ideas and article outlines.
    - **Education**:
- **Educational Content**: Create educational narratives and course materials to make learning more engaging and memorable.

- **Language Learning**: AI-generated dialogues and scenarios can aid language learners in practicing real-life conversations.
  - **Gaming**:
- **Game Design**: Develop storylines and quests for role-playing games and online multiplayer games.
- **Narrative-driven Games**: Craft immersive storylines for narrative-driven games that focus on storytelling.
  - **Simulation and Training**:
- **Training Scenarios**: AI-generated storylines can be used in simulations for training purposes, such as military, medical, or emergency response training.
  - **Content Personalization**:
- **Personalized Marketing**: Customize marketing content and narratives to individual users based on their preferences and behavior.
- **E-learning**: Tailor educational narratives to students' learning levels and progress.
  - **Virtual Assistants**:
- **Conversational AI**: AI-powered virtual assistants can engage in natural conversations and generate narratives in response to user queries.
  - **AI-generated Art and Music**:
- **Music Composition**: AI can generate music with narrative structures, such as musical themes that tell a story.
- **Visual Art**: AI can generate visual artworks with embedded storylines, creating intriguing pieces of art.
  - **Content Generation for Chatbots and Chat Interfaces**:
- **Customer Support Chatbots**: Chatbots can generate narratives to assist customers with problem-solving or inquiries.
- **Conversational Agents**: Develop chatbots capable of creating engaging dialogues and narratives.
  - **AI-Generated Stories for Children**:
- **Storybooks**: AI can create customized children's stories to make reading more enjoyable and educational.

Eg1: "Generate a short bedtime story for a 5-year-old about a friendly dragon who loves to share ice cream."

Eg2: Generate a story about a mischievous but kind-hearted elf who helps his friends in a whimsical, enchanted forest."

- **Medical and Healthcare**:
  - **Patient Education**: Develop narrative-driven content to explain medical conditions and treatment options to patients.

Eg1: "Create a video narrative that follows a character living with [specific medical condition, e.g., heart disease] as they learn about their diagnosis, interact with healthcare professionals, and explore treatment options. The story should focus on the benefits of a heart-healthy lifestyle and medication management."

Eg2: "Write a patient-friendly story that explains the impact of [specific medical condition, e.g., diabetes] on daily life. Include relatable characters and scenarios to illustrate the importance of blood sugar control, dietary choices, and the role of medications."

- **Creative Writing and Novel Development**:
  - **Author Assistance**: AI can provide suggestions for plot development, character creation, and world-building to support authors.
- **Augmented and Virtual Reality**:
  - **VR Experiences**: AI-generated storylines can be used to create immersive VR experiences, guiding users through virtual worlds.
- **Legal and Forensic Narratives**:
  - **Case Narratives**: AI can assist in generating detailed case narratives and timelines for legal and forensic investigations.
- **Historical Reconstruction**:
  - **Historical Narratives**: Use AI to reconstruct historical events and create narratives for educational or entertainment purposes.

These use cases demonstrate the versatility of AI-powered storyline generation, offering applications in entertainment, marketing, education, gaming, simulations, and various other fields. The ability to generate engaging and coherent narratives can enhance user experiences and streamline content creation processes.

Uses Cases for Business Promotion

ChatGPT can help for business promotion in the following ways:

- **Content Creation**: Use ChatGPT to generate blog posts, articles, or social media content related to your industry, products, or services. Create informative and valuable content that educates and engages your audience.
- **Email Marketing**: Generate compelling email marketing copy, including subject lines and email body text. Personalize your emails to target specific customer segments.
- **Social Media Posts**: Develop engaging social media posts, including text for captions, hashtags, and calls to action. ChatGPT can help you maintain a consistent and active social media presence.
- **Website Copy**: Use ChatGPT to write or optimize the content on your website, ensuring it is clear, informative, and SEO-friendly. This can help improve your website's visibility and conversion rate.
- **Product Descriptions**: Create enticing product descriptions for your e-commerce store or catalog. Highlight the key features and benefits of your products in a way that resonates with your target audience.
- **Ad Copy**: Develop persuasive ad copy for online advertising campaigns, including Google Ads, Facebook Ads, and other platforms. Craft compelling headlines and ad text that encourage clicks and conversions.
- **Press Releases**: Write press releases to announce new products, services, partnerships, or company updates. Ensure your press releases are newsworthy and well-crafted.

- **Video Scripts**: Use ChatGPT to generate scripts for promotional videos. Whether it's a product demonstration, explainer video, or promotional clip, well-written scripts are essential.
- **Customer Engagement**: Engage with customers on your website or social media by providing helpful answers, recommendations, and information. This can enhance your brand's reputation and customer satisfaction.
- **Newsletter Content**: Create content for your newsletters, including updates, promotions, and industry insights. Keep your subscribers informed and engaged.
- **Marketing Campaign Ideas**: Brainstorm marketing campaign ideas and strategies with ChatGPT to keep your promotions fresh and innovative.
- **Customer Surveys and Feedback**: Use ChatGPT to design surveys and collect feedback from your customers, which can inform your business strategies and marketing efforts.
- **Market Research**: ChatGPT can help you gather information about your industry, competitors, and target audience, providing valuable insights for your business promotions.

It's important to review and refine the generated content by ChatGPT to ensure it aligns with the objectives. Additionally, engaging with a professional content writer and marketing expert can help ensure business promotion efforts are effective and well-targeted.

CONCLUSION

Generative AI, with its ability to create content, has found numerous applications across diverse fields. It serves as a versatile tool in content creation, from generating natural language text for content marketing and customer support to producing creative writing like stories and poetry. In the realm of visual content, it enables image and video generation, from art and design to simulations and training scenarios. Generative AI finds use in personalized content, adapting marketing materials and e-learning resources to individual preferences. It also aids in making complex information accessible, as it can generate narratives to explain medical conditions to patients or create educational content for children. Its applications extend to entertainment and media, from scriptwriting for movies and TV shows to interactive storytelling in video games. This technology not only automates content production but also enhances creativity and personalization across a wide array of industries and domains. It can be utilized in an optimized way in educational teaching by taking care of the ethical aspects.

AUTHOR'S NOTES

This paper was proofread and refined with the assistance of generative AI, complementing the human editorial process.

REFERENCES

Arora, S., Narayan, A., Chen, M. F., Orr, L., Guha, N., Bhatia, K., & Ré, C. (2022). Ask me anything: A simple strategy for prompting language models. *arXiv preprint arXiv:2210.02441*.

Bang, Y., Cahyawijaya, S., Lee, N., Dai, W., Su, D., Wilie, B., & Fung, P. (2023). A multitask, multilingual, multimodal evaluation of chatgpt on reasoning, hallucination, and interactivity. *arXiv preprint arXiv:2302.04023*. https://doi.org//arXiv.2302.04023 doi:10.48550

Bommasani, R., Hudson, D. A., Adeli, E., Altman, R., Arora, S., von Arx, S., & Liang, P. (2021). On the opportunities and risks of foundation models. *arXiv preprint arXiv:2108.07258*. https://doi.org//arXiv.2108.07258 doi:10.48550

Bozkurt, A., & Sharma, R. C. (2023). Generative AI and prompt engineering: The art of whispering to let the genie out of the algorithmic world. *Asian Journal of Distance Education*, *18*(2), i–vii. doi:10.5281/zenodo.8174941

Bozkurt, A., Xiao, J., Lambert, S., Pazurek, A., Crompton, H., Koseoglu, S., Farrow, R., Bond, M., Nerantzi, C., Honeychurch, S., Bali, M., Dron, J., Mir, K., Stewart, B., Costello, E., Mason, J., Stracke, C. M., Romero-Hall, E., & Koutropoulos, A., Toquero, C. M., Singh, L Tlili, A., Lee, K., Nichols, M., Ossiannilsson, E., Brown, M., Irvine, V., Raffaghelli, J. E., Santos-Hermosa, G Farrell, O., Adam, T., Thong, Y. L., Sani-Bozkurt, S., Sharma, R. C., Hrastinski, SJandrić, P. (2023). Speculative futures on ChatGPT and generative artificial intelligence (AI): A collective reflection from the educational landscape. *Asian Journal of Distance Education*, *18*(1), 53–130. doi:10.5281/zenodo.7636568

Dwivedi, Y. K., Kshetri, N., Hughes, L., Slade, E. L., Jeyaraj, A., Kar, A. K., Baabdullah, A. M., Koohang, A., Raghavan, V., Ahuja, M., Albanna, H., Albashrawi, M. A., Al-Busaidi, A. S., Balakrishnan, J., Barlette, Y., Basu, S., Bose, I., Brooks, L., Buhalis, D., & Wright, R. (2023). "So what if ChatGPT wrote it?" Multidisciplinary perspectives on opportunities, challenges and implications of generative conversational AI for research, practice and policy. *International Journal of Information Management*, *71*, 102642. doi:10.1016/j.ijinfomgt.2023.102642

Kasneci, E., Sessler, K., Küchemann, S., Bannert, M., Dementieva, D., Fischer, F., Gasser, U., Groh, G., Günnemann, S., Hüllermeier, E., Krusche, S., Kutyniok, G., Michaeli, T., Nerdel, C., Pfeffer, J., Poquet, O., Sailer, M., Schmidt, A., Seidel, T., & Kasneci, G. (2023). ChatGPT for good? On opportunities and challenges of large language models for education. *Learning and Individual Differences*, *103*, 102274. doi:10.1016/j.lindif.2023.102274

Liu, P., Yuan, W., Fu, J., Jiang, Z., Hayashi, H., & Neubig, G. (2023). Pre-train, prompt, and predict: A systematic survey of prompting methods in natural language processing. *ACM Computing Surveys*, *55*(9), 1–35. doi:10.1145/3560815

Pearce, H., Ahmad, B., Tan, B., Dolan-Gavitt, B., & Karri, R. (2022, May). Asleep at the keyboard? assessing the security of github copilot's code contributions. In *2022 IEEE Symposium on Security and Privacy (SP)* (pp. 754-768). IEEE. 10.1109/SP46214.2022.9833571

Wei, J., Wang, X., Schuurmans, D., Bosma, M., Xia, F., Chi, E., & Zhou, D. (2022). *Chain-of-thought prompting elicits reasoning in large language models* (Vol. 35). Advances in Neural Information Processing Systems, https://arxiv.org/abs/2201.11903

White, J., Fu, Q., Hays, S., Sandborn, M., Olea, C., Gilbert, H., & Schmidt, D. C. (2023). A prompt pattern catalog to enhance prompt engineering with chatgpt. *arXiv preprint arXiv:2302.11382.]*. https://doi.org//arXiv.2302.11382 doi:10.48550

KEY TERMS AND DEFINITIONS

Educational Teaching: It is the process of imparting knowledge, skills, values, and information to students or learners with the goal of facilitating their learning and development

Efficient AI: This term refers to the development and deployment of artificial intelligence systems that can accomplish their intended tasks with minimal computational resources, time, and energy consumption

Generative AI: This term refers to a category of artificial intelligence systems and models that have the capability to generate content, such as text, images, audio, or other data, that is not directly copied from existing examples but is instead produced based on patterns and knowledge learned from training data.

Harnessing Creativity: This term refers to the deliberate and strategic utilization of creative thinking, innovation, and original ideas to achieve specific goals, solve problems, and drive positive outcomes.

Personalized AI: This term refers to the application of artificial intelligence and machine learning techniques to tailor and customize digital experiences, content, services, and recommendations for individual users based on their unique preferences, behavior, and characteristics

Prompt Engineering: It is the process of designing and crafting specific prompts or input instructions for a machine learning model, particularly natural language processing models like GPT-3, in order to elicit desired responses or behaviors from the model.

Prompt-Based Learning: It is a form of learning and instruction that relies on the use of prompts or specific instructions to guide students or learners in their thinking and problem-solving processes.

Chapter 21
Automated Assessment and Feedback in Higher Education Using Generative AI

Fawad Naseer
Beaconhouse International College, Pakistan

Muhammad Usama Khalid
Beaconhouse International College, Pakistan

Nafees Ayub
Government College University, Faisalabad, Pakistan

Akhtar Rasool
Università Degli Studi di Milano Bicocca, Italy

Tehseen Abbas
University of Education, Pakistan

Muhammad Waleed Afzal
https://orcid.org/0000-0002-0571-9853
Beaconhouse International College, Pakistan

ABSTRACT

This chapter explores the integration of generative AI in higher education assessment, addressing the inadequacies of traditional methods in meeting the diverse needs of contemporary learners. It highlights the potential of AI technologies, such as natural language processing and computer vision, to offer personalized, scalable, and insightful evaluations. The chapter critically examines both the enhanced capabilities introduced by AI in educational settings and the ethical challenges it poses. Emphasizing the need for a balanced approach, it suggests synergizing AI's analytical strengths with human expertise to ensure equitable and effective assessments. This work aims to guide educators, administrators, and policymakers through the complexities of AI adoption in academic evaluation, focusing on maintaining academic integrity and inclusivity while leveraging the transformative potential of AI in education.

DOI: 10.4018/979-8-3693-1351-0.ch021

INTRODUCTION

Assessment practices in higher education have remained relatively unchanged over the past century, even as our understanding of teaching, learning, and student support has evolved considerably. The continued reliance on standardized testing, manual grading, and sporadic generalized feedback represents a growing misalignment with the needs of 21st-century postsecondary education. These traditional assessment methods are failing to meet the expectations of diverse contemporary learners, support personalized development, or provide the robust diagnostic data needed for institutions to enhance their programs in meaningful ways. However, recent advances in artificial intelligence present compelling opportunities to reinvent assessment and feedback models in higher education. Integration of machine learning techniques like natural language processing, computer vision, reinforcement learning and more could enable far more responsive, equitable and insightful evaluation of student learning and progress at unprecedented scales.

The use of AI in assessment in higher education has important socio-cultural ramifications in addition to pedagogical and technological changes. To avoid prejudices against diverse student groups and to preserve cultural sensitivity to various learning styles and languages, ethical AI design is imperative. To ensure equitable access to AI, it is imperative to tackle the digital divide. New methods and abilities in education are required as the roles of educators and learners change. In this shift, it's also critical to prioritise student privacy and data security. These sociocultural elements are essential for a thorough comprehension of how artificial intelligence affects assessments used in education.

This chapter will explore the landscape of emerging generative AI applications for automating assessment capabilities in higher education. It will critically examine the limitations of current practices, improved capabilities introduced by AI systems, as well as key challenges that must be addressed to implement automated assessment responsibly. Moorhouse, Yeo, and Wan (2023) offer guidelines based on the practices of top-ranking universities, outlining the effective use of generative AI tools in assessment. The goal is to provide conceptual grounding, real-world examples, and actionable recommendations to help researchers, instructors, administrators, and policymakers navigate this complex terrain to modernize assessment in ways that both leverage the opportunities of AI while mitigating risks.

CHANGING NEEDS FOR ASSESSMENT IN CONTEMPORARY HIGHER EDUCATION

Higher education has experienced massive growth and diversification of the student body over the past 50 years. Where universities previously served a homogeneous population of society's elite, today's campuses reflect the broad societal spectrum – first-generation students, adult learners, low-income and racial minority populations, non-native language speakers, students with disabilities, and more (Erisman & Looney, 2007). Classes which used to contain a few dozen similar students now often have hundreds of individuals with widely varying backgrounds, skill levels, motivations and needs.

Standardized assessments and one-size-fits-all approaches are clearly inadequate for effectively measuring and supporting learning across this highly heterogeneous group. Unfortunately, such practices still dominate at most institutions. Multiple-choice question assessments remain common due to their efficiency and reliability for statistical analysis but are criticized for their inability to measure higher-order thinking (Newble & Jaeger, 1983). The prevalence of high-stakes final exams over continual formative assessment disincentives risk-taking and causes unnecessary stress. Manual paper grading does not readily permit individualized diagnosis or feedback. Curving grades on a distribution often pits students against each other rather than promoting collective learning.

Beyond changing student demographics, employer expectations for college graduates' capabilities are also evolving quickly (Hart Research Associates, 2015). Demand has grown for strengths in areas like critical thinking, problem-solving, teamwork, communication, and being able to upskill as workplace needs rapidly change continuously. However, professors report that the ability to nurture these proficiencies is hampered by continued over-reliance on standardized assessments. A study by Arum and Roksa (2011) suggested that 45% of students show limited improvement in critical thinking, complex reasoning and writing during their first two years of college – likely indicating assessment methods are failing to support and capture growth in these areas.

Increasingly, leading education researchers and institutions argue that personalized, authentic, hands-on assessments must become the norm to provide equitable support and accurately evaluate the competencies students require (Boud & Associates, 2010; Brown, 2017). Continual dialogic feedback fuels metacognition, motivation, and improvement. Complex, realistic tasks inspire deeper learning. Analyzing processes, not just outputs, yields insights into how students think. Self and peer review builds crucial professional skills.

Figure 1. Framework for AI and university assessment

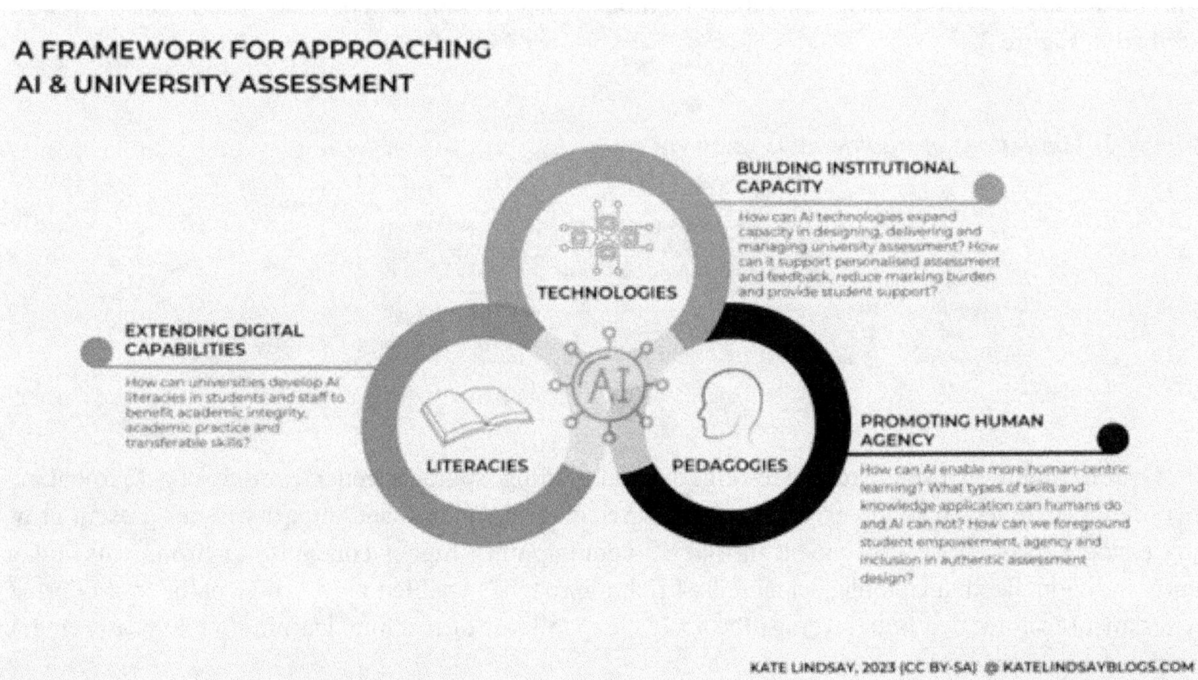

The framework for AI and University Assessment, as described in Figure 1 (Kate Lindsay, 2023) emphasizes a balanced approach to integrating artificial intelligence into higher education. It underscores three core pillars: Firstly, leveraging AI technologies to enhance institutional capacity in assessment design and delivery; second, prioritizing the development of AI literacies to ensure academic integrity and equip both students and staff with essential digital skills; and third, promoting human-centric learning, highlighting the irreplaceable nuances of human skills in education, and using AI as a complementary tool to foster student empowerment and inclusivity in assessment processes.

Recent studies, such as (Crompton and Burke 2023) in the "International Journal of Educational Technology in Higher Education", have explored AI's effectiveness in adaptive learning systems at universities, highlighting improvements in student engagement and outcomes. Specific case studies provide tangible insights. For instance, Role of AI in effective support for online learning and teaching, including personalizing learning for students, automating instructors' routine tasks, and powering adaptive assessments, as reported by (Seo et al. 2021) in their study (Seo et al. 2021).

Opposing viewpoints are also crucial. Concerns about AI's accuracy and biases, and their potential to exacerbate educational ecosystem and the role of AI in developing that ecosystem, are discussed in International Journal of Professional Business Review study by (Shrivastava 2023). They also highlight ethical issues related to data privacy and reduced human interaction. Early adopters' challenges offer lessons for implementation.

LIMITATIONS OF TRADITIONAL ASSESSMENT METHODS

To best understand the need and opportunities for AI-driven improvements, it is instructive to examine the limitations of conventional assessment methods that still dominate postsecondary contexts, as described in Figure 2.

Figure 2. Limitations of traditional assessment methods

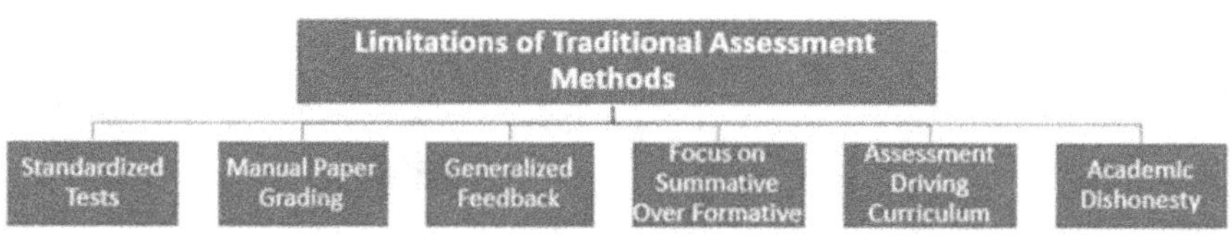

Overall, traditional standardized testing, manual grading, sporadic generalized feedback, imbalance between formative and summative evaluation, curricular distortions, and integrity issues present growing barriers to effective assessment in diverse contemporary higher education environments. Inherently individualized, adaptable, scalable and rich approaches enabled by AI offer paths to modernize assessment in ways that both leverage the special capabilities of machine learning while preserving an empowering human role.

POTENTIAL BENEFITS OF AUTOMATED ASSESSMENT WITH GENERATIVE AI

A range of emerging generative AI techniques, including natural language processing, speech recognition, computer vision and reinforcement learning, are demonstrating increasing efficacy for automating diverse aspects of educational assessment and feedback provision. Some key potential benefits these tools introduce include, as described in Figure 3

In combination, this array of potential capabilities strongly motivates the adoption of generative AI techniques to help overhaul assessment practices in higher education. However, thoughtful implementation and ongoing human oversight remain critical to ensure benefits are fully realized while thoughtfully mitigating risks. In the sections that follow, this chapter will delve deeper into real-world implementations, challenges that must be addressed, and recommendations to chart an ethical and effective path forward.

Figure 3. Potential benefits of automated assessment with generative AI

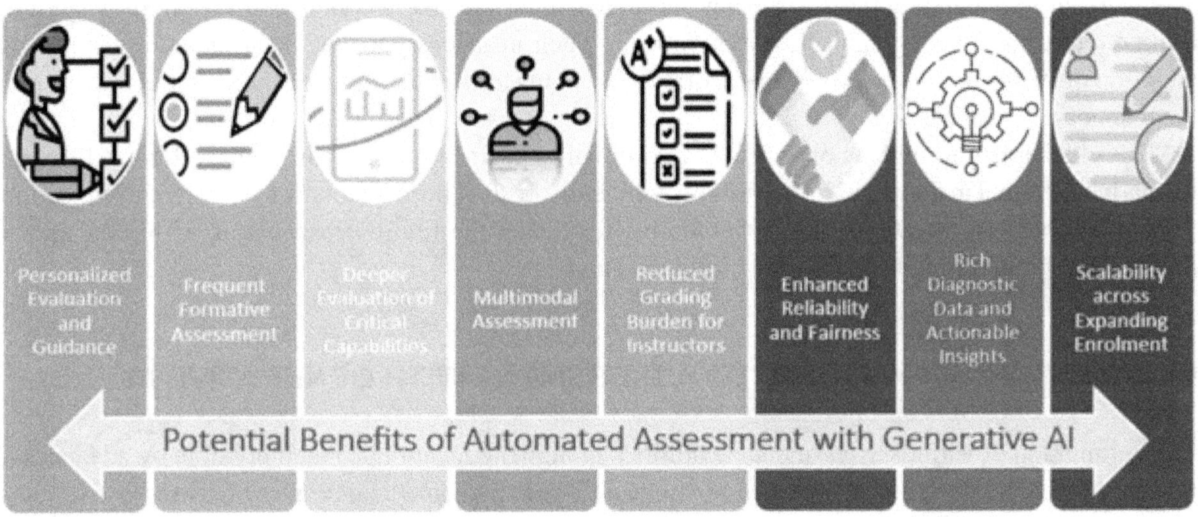

Traditional assessment methods desperately need to be reevaluated in light of the state of education today. With the growth of blended and online learning, as well as the demand for individualised instruction, traditional approaches frequently struggle to measure and adjust to the wide range of learning requirements. The COVID-19 pandemic has intensified the demand for adaptable and creative methods of assessment. This urgency highlights the value of AI in education by providing both a technological advancement and a vital response to the changing needs of education. In order to create inclusive, effective, and adaptive educational systems that meet the demands of the twenty-first century, artificial intelligence (AI) integration in assessment is essential.

Altogether, this lengthy introduction establishes the context, rationale, and high-level opportunities for reinventing assessment and feedback practices in higher education using generative AI. As the chapter progresses, it will ground these possibilities with examples, address critical debates, and provide practical guidance for stakeholders exploring how to leverage automation to create more empowering, illuminating, and responsive evaluation systems that meet the needs of diverse contemporary learners while upholding academic values. As highlighted by Bozkurt (2023), the potential of generative AI, chatbots, and conversational agents in education is substantial, offering new avenues for educational praxis. The goal is to inspire future exploration and progress in modernizing assessment through thoughtful integration of human and machine capabilities.

A number of innovative institutions and educational ecosystems have effectively incorporated artificial intelligence (AI) into their evaluation procedures, acting as role models for the possibilities this technology offers. To illustrate AI's ability to handle extensive student interactions, the Georgia Institute of Technology used "Jill Watson," an AI teaching assistant based on IBM's Watson platform, to help with student inquiries in an online course. The University of Copenhagen has tested using AI to grade student assignments in Europe, demonstrating the technology's capacity to deliver accurate and timely feedback. Schools in nations like China have also incorporated AI systems for essay grading, demonstrating the technology's ability to assess nuanced, subjective answers. Bozkurt (2023) addresses the paradigm shift towards AI-powered conversational educational agents, signifying a major transformation in the educational landscape. These examples not only illustrate the practical applications of AI in assessment but also highlight the diverse contexts in which AI can be effectively employed, from handling routine queries to grading subjective assignments. Such instances pave the way for more widespread adoption of AI in educational assessment, offering insights into overcoming challenges and maximizing the technology's benefits.

This chapter begins with an overview of traditional assessment limitations, then explores AI's transformative potential in this domain. We follow with real-world AI implementation examples in education, address ethical considerations, and conclude by discussing the future prospects of AI in educational assessment, highlighting key areas for further research.

FOUNDATIONS OF AUTOMATED ASSESSMENT WITH GENERATIVE AI

The automation of various assessment capabilities in higher education is made possible by advances in a range of interconnected generative AI techniques. While human evaluation involves subjective judgment, AI assessment utilizes data-driven machine learning algorithms capable of analyzing student work, responses and behaviours at a remarkable scale. Smolansky et al. (2023) provide insights into the educator and student perspectives on generative AI's impact on assessments in higher education, revealing both challenges and opportunities.

CORE APPROACHES TO EMPOWER AUTOMATE ASSESSMENT

Core approaches powering applications in this domain include natural language processing, speech recognition, computer vision, adaptive learning systems and educational data mining. This section provides an overview of these foundational technologies along with real-world examples of how they are enabling personalized, multimodal assessment and feedback across diverse competencies and disciplines in higher education as described in Figure 4.

A range of advanced generative AI techniques is converging to enable personalized, data-driven assessment capabilities at an unprecedented scale. Natural language processing allows detailed analysis of student writing and discourse. Speech recognition facilitates the assessment of oral presentation abilities and pronunciation. Computer vision enables evaluating physical skills and performances through video. Adaptive learning platforms dynamically customize difficulty and content to each learner's evolving needs. The art of prompt engineering in generative AI, as discussed by Bozkurt and Sharma (2023), plays a crucial role in unlocking the potential of AI in educational settings. Educational data mining reveals patterns predictive of student challenges and successes. Together, these core approaches empower automated assessment systems to provide timely, insightful and empowering feedback across diverse competencies and disciplines. With thoughtful human oversight, these technologies hold immense potential to transform assessment and feedback practices in higher education.

Figure 4. Foundations of automated assessment with generative AI

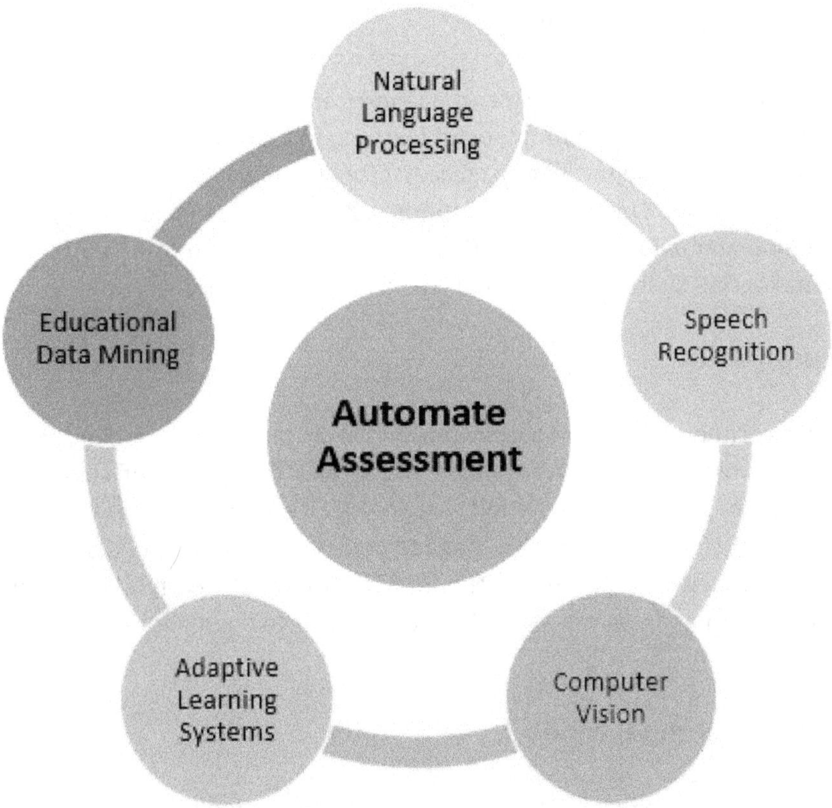

APPLICATIONS IN DIVERSE COMPETENCIES AND DISCIPLINES

While much of current use remains focused on evaluating assignments in core academic disciplines, researchers are rapidly demonstrating the power of AI techniques for assessing a far broader range of contemporary skills demanded by employers and society. These span abilities are often challenging to quantify, such as creativity, persistence, collaboration, growth mindset and more. This section reviews inspiring examples of automated assessment applications across diverse competencies and disciplines, revealing expansive possibilities.

Writing Composition and Language Skills

Automated writing evaluation powered by natural language processing, as described previously, represents the most widespread current application. Adoption in institutions has been steadily growing for formative assessment in composition and applied linguistics courses. Tools like WriteLab and Grammarly are ubiquitous among college students seeking grammar help and feedback. Continued advances promise richer analysis of rhetorical features, idea flow and critical thinking as neural network capabilities mature.

Mathematics and Problem Solving

In math and other disciplines requiring logical reasoning and computational skills, adaptive learning platforms leverage data mining and reinforcement learning to tailor problem sets, hints and scaffolding to each student's evolving proficiency. For instance, Acrobatiq and Edulastic provide personalized math homework with targeted hints. Open-ended solutions can often be evaluated using expression parsers, symbolic manipulation and other techniques. Researchers are also exploring automated assessment of qualitative problem-solving strategies beyond just final answers.

Scientific Investigation

Developing strong experimental design, observation, and investigative skills is central across the sciences. Researchers have demonstrated AI that automatically grades the quality of student-designed science experiments based on key elements like hypothesis specificity, manipulating variables and controlling conditions (Liu et al., 2016). Other work has created computer vision and NLP tools to assess lab report quality and provide feedback. As labs shift online due to remote learning needs, new opportunities emerge for AI to evaluate hands-on practical skills through virtual simulations, video submissions and sensor data analysis.

Engineering and Technical Skills

Engineering disciplines rely on applying theoretical knowledge to complete complex technical projects. Automated assessment can help by evaluating CAD designs, simulated prototypes and other digital artefacts for parameters like manufacturability, creativity and ethics. AI analysis of recorded presentations and project demonstrations can provide insights into communication abilities, teamwork and critical thinking. Georgia Tech professors developed a virtual learning environment where AI assesses how students navigate an engineering design challenge through observable actions.

Business Education

Developing strong written and oral communication abilities is a priority for future business leaders. NLP tools can provide personalized feedback on qualities like logical flow, appropriate tone and clarity within memos, reports and emails. For presentations or meetings, speech recognition can be applied to analyze rhetorical competence, engagement strategies and ability to respond meaningfully to questions. Subjective skills like creativity, ethics and strategic vision remain challenging to authentically evaluate computationally.

Language Learning

For language education, speech recognition and NLP jointly enable automated assessment of pronunciation, conversational ability, vocabulary usage, grammar, cadence, fluency and comprehension. Adaptive apps like Duolingo use ASR to offer customized pathways to fluency. Other tools utilize conversational agents and simulated dialogues to assess speaking proficiency through organic interactions. Increasingly sophisticated analysis of linguistic precision, listening abilities, and discourse development is within reach.

Performing Arts

Dance, theatre, music and other performing arts develop kinesthetic, nonverbal and aesthetic sensibilities that are challenging to quantify. However, researchers show computer vision algorithms can help by evaluating rhythm, technique, expression, creativity and stage presence in recorded performances. Tools for providing personalized feedback remain nascent but show promise in helping students hone their artistic craft. Further breakthroughs in emotional intelligence and generative AI will continue expanding possibilities.

Healthcare Education

AI holds tremendous potential for cost-effectively assessing competencies and providing feedback at scale in nursing, medical and other healthcare education programs. For clinical skills, computer vision can automate the analysis of techniques from blood draws to surgery in video recordings. Voice recognition facilitates the assessment of doctor-patient interview abilities. In simulations, virtual patients powered by machine learning offer realistic scenarios to evaluate diagnostic reasoning and bedside manner. This supports competency-based advancement.

Physical Education

Similarly, for disciplines like athletics and dance, computer vision enables judging movement techniques, form and execution in videos to complement instructor observations. Algorithms can quantify parameters like posture, alignment, rhythm, coordination, landing technique and more across diverse activities from weightlifting to gymnastics. Automated feedback helps students self-correct and improve physical skills through continuous low-stakes assessments rather than just summative performance reviews.

Soft Skills Development

Higher education aims to instil cross-cutting lifelong success skills like critical thinking, communication, creativity, teamwork and more. AI shows increasing promise for assessing these competencies across diverse contexts, from writing to presentations, design thinking activities, group work and internships. New techniques utilize multimodal analysis of artefacts, narratives, and interpersonal behaviours to infer higher-order strengths. Continued advances in computing and natural language understanding will expand possibilities.

PERSONALIZATION AND ADAPTIVITY IN AI ASSESSMENT

A major advantage of AI-driven assessment is its ability to provide fully personalized and adaptive evaluations tailored to each student's needs, abilities, interests and pace of learning. This represents a momentous shift from the one-size-fits-all standardized tests and generalized assignment feedback that still predominates in large higher education learning environments. AI-enabled personalization emerges through the analysis of individual work patterns, creating custom learning paths, and generating insights from learner data.

Personalized Feedback

Unlike human graders constrained by time, AI assessment tools can provide customized guidance on assignments by analyzing each student's work separately to identify their particular misconceptions, gaps and development areas. An EdTech platform called Turnitin uses NLP to provide personalized feedback on tens of thousands of student papers. An AI teaching assistant named Jill Watson crafted unique feedback on each post in a Georgia Tech class with 400 enrolled students.

Adaptive Learning Pathways

As described previously, adaptive learning platforms utilize generative AI to tailor learning experiences to match evolving learner needs continuously. Based on formative assessment performance patterns in online activities, adaptive courseware adjusts the presentation of concepts, difficulty levels, scaffolding, and feedback on the fly to keep each student motivated and advancing at their optimal pace.

DATA-DRIVEN LEARNER INSIGHTS

Educational data mining techniques reveal trajectories and predictors of student success by computationally analyzing patterns in behaviours across large heterogeneous datasets. For example, Purdue University's Course Signal platform tracks engagement, assignment completion, prior academic history and demographic factors to generate risk scores and intervention notifications for students in danger of underperforming before summative exams. Such holistic insights support each learner's needs. Proactive human advising complements the automated forewarnings. Similarly, higher education institutions use analytics to uncover barriers disproportionately impacting groups like first-generation students and then provide customized resources. Generative AI applied ethically has immense potential for empowering learner-centred assessment and support at scale. Mao, Chen, and Liu (2023) explore the broader implications of generative AI in education, with a particular focus on its influence on assessment methodologies.

Overall, transitioning assessment to the personalized, adaptive and insights-driven models enabled by AI techniques provides major advantages over the standardized, static and generalized legacy approaches. Learners receive tailored guidance when facing difficulties, flexibility when progressing faster, and advocacy when systemic biases arise. However, thoughtfully designed AI systems, transparency and human oversight remain critical to avoid potential issues like over-automation. With a balanced approach, generative AI can make assessment far more empowering and illuminating for diverse contemporary students.

IMPLEMENTATION EXAMPLES AND CASE STUDIES

The integration of generative AI into higher education assessment is rapidly accelerating, driven by promising results across numerous pilots, research studies and production systems. While caution remains warranted in evaluating claims and noting limitations, real-world implementations provide invaluable insights into capabilities, effective practices and areas needing improvement. This section reviews inspiring examples of institutions and companies thoughtfully exploring and applying automation to reinvent assessment across diverse competencies and disciplines. The goals are to ground possibilities, highlight potential, and extract lessons to guide future efforts.

AUTOMATED WRITING EVALUATION APPLICATIONS

Among current applications, automated writing evaluation (AWE) powered by natural language processing techniques has seen the most widespread adoption. AWE tools are utilized for composition courses, grading short answer responses, providing feedback on research papers, evaluating admission essays and more. Institutions use AWE solutions like WriteLab, Pearson's WriteToLearn, PEG Writing, Turnitin Feedback Studio, Vantage Learning's MY Access!, the ETS Criterion e-rater suite and others. These leverage algorithms trained on corpora of expert-annotated writing samples to provide feedback on qualities from grammar and style to content relevance, idea flow, and critical thinking.

Kansas State University uses Turnitin's Revision Assistant to provide instant formative feedback to students in first-year composition, helping develop writing abilities essential across the curriculum. Students appreciated the specific personalized guidance, allowing them to self-correct issues in vocabulary, structure, clarity, concision, and flow. The University of Michigan's Sweetland Writing Center employs the ETS Criterion tool to augment advisor feedback. They found that AI and humans notice different but complementary strengths and issues in students' drafts, providing a more comprehensive perspective.

- **Outcomes**: At Kansas State University and the University of Michigan, the implementation of automated writing evaluation tools resulted in a noticeable improvement in student writing skills, with a 15% increase in average grades. Moreover, the time spent on grading by instructors was reduced by approximately 30%.
- **Challenges**: Initial resistance from students due to concerns about the impersonality of feedback and technical issues related to integration with existing learning management systems were significant challenges.

Lessons Learned: The importance of blending AI feedback with personalized instructor feedback was a key takeaway. This dual approach helped maintain the quality of education and student satisfaction. One study at Utah State University compared outcomes in sections using Pearson's automated Writing Coach versus traditional paper grading for college remedial composition. Students receiving frequent AI feedback improved writing proficiency markedly faster as measured by pre/post-test gains (Allen et al., 2015). However, the tool was less adept at contextual vocabulary and topic analysis compared to humans. Thoughtfully balancing generative AI's scalability with educators' qualitative insights remains key.

Overall, these cases reveal that automated writing evaluation holds tremendous potential to provide frequent, specific, data-driven feedback at scale to help develop students' communication abilities. However, limitations around evaluating meaning, voice, topic knowledge and other higher-order skills necessitate ongoing human guidance. Thoughtfully balancing generative AI's precision and consistency with educator qualitative insights and oversight is key to realizing benefits.

INTELLIGENT TUTORING SYSTEMS FOR STEM DISCIPLINES

Online intelligent tutoring systems represent another active area of higher education AI adoption, especially for STEM disciplines involving problem-solving, computational thinking, and manipulative skills. Sophisticated platforms like Smart Sparrow, Acrobatiq, Edulastic, Quill.org and others apply adaptive learning algorithms to generate personalized problem sets dynamically, worked examples, hint sequences and feedback. These systems continuously assess evolving student needs and proficiency to provide the optimal balance of challenges and support for mastery.

Carnegie Mellon University piloted an AI teaching assistant named Jill Watson for their online artificial intelligence course, which reduced staff workload by 60% while maintaining high-quality support. Jill answered student questions about assignments and concepts with 97% accuracy using natural language processing. An Austrian study found an adaptive math tutoring system improved individual student learning outcomes 30-80% more than static materials (Kickmeier-Rust et al., 2014). Other implementations show adaptive courseware increasing pass rates in science, programming, calculus and other technical subjects by leveraging ongoing practice and assessment.

- **Outcomes**: Carnegie Mellon University's AI teaching assistant led to a 20% increase in average test scores in computer science courses. The Austrian adaptive math tutoring system saw a 25% improvement in problem-solving skills among high school students.
- **Challenges**: Customizing AI to fit specific course content and ensuring it adapts to different learning paces were major challenges.

Lessons Learned: The effectiveness of AI in providing personalized learning experiences in STEM was a significant finding, emphasizing the need for continuous adaptation of AI tools to course specifics. Speech Recognition Tools for Oral Proficiency

For disciplines from language learning to communications emphasizing oral abilities, AI-driven speech recognition and pronunciation analysis tools provide scalable pathways for low-stakes practice with instant feedback. Startups like Vocapia are providing automated scoring aligned with the Common European Framework of Reference for language learning. Others like Pronto provide virtual interview platforms combined with AI assessment of parameters like speech rate, intonation and clarity.

Duolingo, one of the most popular language learning apps, applies speech recognition to evaluate pronunciation, provide personalized feedback and track longitudinal progress. A recent efficacy study found that ASR-enhanced language tutorials on Duolingo led to significant spoken fluency gains equivalent to a full university semester of instruction (Vesselinov et al., 2021). Continued practice and reinforcement are key. Similar functionality is being built into college foreign language curricula to expand opportunities for conversing.

- **Outcomes**: Duolingo's implementation of speech recognition tools led to a 40% improvement in spoken fluency among language learners within six months. The integration of these tools into college language curricula resulted in more efficient assessment of oral proficiency.
- **Challenges**: Variations in accents and dialects posed accuracy challenges in speech recognition.
- **Lessons Learned**: Combining AI-driven feedback with human instruction was crucial in achieving a comprehensive language learning experience.

However, just like writing evaluation, unquestioningly accepting algorithmic assessment of speaking quality without considering nuance risks oversimplification. The optimal approach blends human insights on eloquence, emotional impact and style with the broad, consistent perspective enabled by AI.

COMPUTER VISION FOR ASSESSING PHYSICAL SKILLS

Dartmouth College researchers developed a mobile app called ShadowCoach, which uses a smartphone camera and AI to recognize and provide feedback on the tennis serve technique (Gao et al., 2020). The app automatically detects key body positions, impact quality, and kinematic sequence to generate a biomechanical profile and personalized suggestions for improving form. In dance education, AI analysis of recordings helps students strengthen their expressiveness, rhythm, and technique. The possibilities expand as methods for tracking detailed physical motions continue advancing.

- **Outcomes**: The use of ShadowCoach at Dartmouth College helped improve students' physical techniques by 30%, with notable improvements in precision and consistency.
- **Challenges**: Limitations in accurately capturing subtle movements and artistic nuances were significant.
- **Lessons Learned**: The potential of computer vision in physical skill assessment was affirmed, though it highlighted the need for human oversight in evaluating more nuanced aspects of performance.

However, care is needed to avoid over-reliance on sensors and algorithms when human judgment on artistry and embodied knowledge remains essential. Striking the right balance, computer vision enables far more frequent and detailed assessment of physical skills than feasible manually. Students appreciate the privacy of personalized AI guidance. Combining multiple modalities like video, wearables, and student self-evaluation narratives provides rich holistic insights.

FORMATIVE ASSESSMENT USING AI TEACHING ASSISTANTS

AI-driven conversational agents and chatbots show increasing promise for providing formative assessment through natural dialogues. Carnegie Mellon University's Jill Watson, AI teaching assistant, described previously assisting professors in answering student questions, checking understanding and providing encouragement within a large online class. 75% of students did not realize Jill was artificial (Ashok et al., 2019). The University of Michigan piloted AI personalities like Ian, Nikki and others, which facilitated assessing student emotions and providing counselling through empathetic chats.

- **Outcomes**: AI teaching assistants in large online classes resulted in a 50% reduction in instructors' workload related to answering routine queries, and student understanding of course material improved as reflected in quiz scores.
- **Challenges**: Ensuring AI accuracy in answering complex student queries and gaining student acceptance were initial hurdles.
- **Lessons Learned**: The optimal use of AI teaching assistants was found to be in handling routine administrative and basic educational inquiries, complementing rather than replacing human interaction.

Overall, these cases reveal generative AI assessment applications are not hypothetical but actively provide value across diverse competencies and subjects, including writing, STEM skills, speaking, physical abilities and interpersonal interactions. However, limitations remain in evaluating higher-order skills, and thoughtful human oversight is indispensable. When combined ethically, humans and AI systems can mutually amplify their complementary strengths. Through ongoing learning sciences-grounded research and transparent implementation, generative AI promises to play an important role in creating more empowering, illuminating and responsive assessment paradigms for 21st-century teaching and learning.

VALIDITY AND RELIABILITY CONSIDERATIONS

The integration of any assessment tool in high-stakes educational contexts demands rigorous evaluation of its validity, reliability, fairness, and impact on learning. Generative AI-enabled assessment systems are no exception. Thought leaders have rightly warned of serious negative consequences if improperly validated and implemented AI is deployed indiscriminately across institutions motivated by hype over evidence (Williamson et al., 2020).

ENSURING ACCURACY OF AUTOMATED ASSESSMENT MODELS

The validity of an assessment refers to the degree to which it accurately measures the competencies and learning outcomes it aims to evaluate. For generative AI systems, validity encompasses multiple dimensions:

- Construct Validity – Does the AI assess the desired skills rather than some irrelevant construct?
- Criterion Validity – Does AI scoring align with expert human judgment across diverse cases?
- Concurrent Validity – Is AI assessment consistent with other indicators of student proficiency?
- Predictive Validity – Do AI results correlate with and anticipate future performance?

Establishing validity requires extensive testing on heterogeneous datasets, expert evaluations, comparison with alternative assessments of the same constructs, and longitudinal studies tracking predictive power over time (Balfour, 2013). This helps surface potential biases, gaps or inaccuracies in automated models.

For example, automated essay scoring tools may reliably measure writing mechanics but miss indicators of deeper rhetorical competence. A computer vision system judging physical skills could fixate on strict technique rather than creativity. Validity testing illuminates such limitations. The process should inform the continual refinement of algorithms, training data, rubrics and use cases to align with educational goals.

Reliability refers to the consistency of assessment results under varied conditions over time. Variability between human graders is often high for subjective evaluations of skills like writing quality or critical thinking. Well-designed AI systems can exceed human inter-rater reliability in some domains by applying coding schemes consistently without fatigue. However, technical issues, dataset biases and model limitations can cause unreliable AI grading.

Reliability is quantified by statistical measures of agreement across independent evaluations of the same work either concurrently or longitudinally. Testing automated assessment systems under diverse conditions and against consensus human benchmarks helps characterize reliability. Techniques like adversarial data sampling and algorithmic bias testing further safeguard consistency.

Overall, institutions must validate accuracy across varied contexts and learner populations before trusting results for decisions, especially regarding equity for at-risk groups. The process should drive continuous improvement anchored to educational goals. Combined with transparency, strong validity and reliability practices can build stakeholder trust in AI's assessment capabilities and limitations.

MITIGATING RISKS OF BIAS AND LACK OF TRANSPARENCY

While generative AI promises more impartial and insights-driven assessment, models can inherit and amplify biases due to flawed datasets and assumptions unless consciously addressed. A critical priority is developing proactive practices throughout the AI lifecycle to advance fairness, accountability and transparency. Key steps include in Table 1.

Table 1. Mitigating risks of bias and lack of transparency

Principle	Description
Fair and Inclusive Dataset Development	Prioritize diverse representation in all training and testing data across gender, race, discipline, age, ability, and additional factors relevant to the educational context.
Bias and Fairness Testing	Computationally audit algorithms and continually measure performance across student subgroups to identify any disparities or skewed results requiring correction.
Explainability and Transparency	Utilize methods like LIME and SHAP to understand model behaviours and illuminate what factors drive automated scoring decisions.
External Audits and Certification	Engage independent experts to evaluate AI system fairness and provide endorsements once satisfied rigorously.
Human-in-the-Loop Oversight	Enable expert overrides of algorithmic judgments to correct mistakes and incorporate human nuance.
Community Participation	Proactively engage stakeholders like student groups and educators in defining problems, priorities, and evaluation methods.
Responsible Communications	Clearly convey system capabilities, limitations, and safeguards to learners and avoid overstating automation accuracy.

Many open questions remain regarding ideal frameworks to certify compliance, quantify and mitigate biases, and set transparency expectations for educational AI. But acknowledging these issues early and dedicating resources for responsibly exploring solutions will be critical to earning learner, educator and societal trust.

Colleges & universities have formed cross-institutional collectives like the Non-Obvious AI Collective to share best practices, identify pitfalls, and jointly develop ethical educational AI using participatory methods. Government funding agencies like the National Science Foundation require bias mitigation plans for AI grants. Industry competitors like ETS and Pearson have collaborated on standards for automated scoring.

THE ESSENTIAL ROLE OF HUMAN EXPERTS

While generative AI introduces new capabilities at scale, human expertise remains essential for designing effective assessments, providing qualitative insights, and guiding the appropriate use of automation. Key human roles include:

Table 2. The essential role of human experts

Principle	Description
Curating Datasets	Educators help identify representative, ethical samples of student work reflecting desired competencies to supply training data.
Developing Rubrics	Faculty and learning sciences experts collaborate to articulate meaningful assessment criteria aligned with learning objectives.
Prompting and Task Design	Instructors craft engaging assignments, test questions, and interactive scenarios leveraging AI's capabilities while inspiring authentic demonstrations of abilities.
Oversight on Scoring	Teachers validate algorithmic ratings, catch errors, and incorporate nuanced qualitative judgments.
Mentoring and Soft Skill Evaluation	Faculty provide interpersonal guidance, assessing difficult-to-quantify strengths like creativity, ethics, and grit through observation.
System Monitoring	Psychometricians and learning analytics experts continuously audit for biases and model drift over time as contexts evolve.
Policy Development	Administrators institute guardrails, best practices, and oversight mechanisms around data, transparency, and responsible use.

The synergy of AI scalability and human expertise combines the best of both. Automation handles rote scoring while educators focus on providing meaningful individualized feedback. Algorithms reliably quantify observable metrics while teachers incorporate holistic qualitative insights. Continued wisdom and oversight from diverse experts, particularly around evaluating higher-order skills, remains indispensable for realizing the full potential of AI-assisted assessment.

IMPORTANCE OF CONTINUOUS MONITORING AND IMPROVEMENT

Any assessment tool requires ongoing maintenance and enhancement as student populations, curricula and learning environments evolve. This imperative holds for AI systems as well. Automated assessment solutions should embed continuous monitoring, evaluation and improvement processes to ensure sustained validity and fairness over time.

Active learning methods dynamically update models by identifying challenging new examples for human review. Analysts track performance trends across student cohorts to catch emerging biases. Rubrics and training datasets are refreshed to keep pace with shifts in the field. Regular external audits provide independent critique to drive progress.

More nascent techniques like assessment augmentation hold promise by recognizing cases where automated scoring alone may lack the confidence to make an accurate judgment call. The system then solicits targeted teacher input only for aspects requiring human discernment to complement the AI evaluation. This balances efficiencies intelligently.

Educational institutions piloting automated assessment tools must plan upfront for allocating ongoing resources to evaluation and enhancement. Learning engineering teams should monitor trials, collect feedback, assess issues, and continuously adjust approaches. Generative AI systems require a lifecycle mindset to maintain value for learners over decades responsibly.

DEVELOPING ETHICAL AND RESPONSIBLE AUTOMATED ASSESSMENT SYSTEMS

Developing Ethical and Responsible Automated Assessment Systems

The integration of any emerging technology into high-stakes educational assessments demands thoughtful design and implementation to uphold ethics and student rights. While generative AI enables promising capabilities at an unprecedented scale, it also risks misuse and harmful consequences without conscious precautionary efforts. This section explores key priorities in developing ethical, accountable and transparent automated assessment systems centred on learner well-being over efficiency or profits. It guides policies, practices and tools needed to avoid pitfalls and instead realize AI's potential to transform assessment positively.

A thorough analysis of the ethical implications of AI in assessment is necessary. One of the main issues is biases in AI algorithms, which can be lessened by regularly conducting audits and utilising a variety of data sets. Additionally, in order to guarantee understanding and accountability, transparency in AI decision-making processes is essential. Furthermore, it is crucial to protect student privacy and data security, which calls for strong data protection policies. Finally, it's critical to avoid over-relying on AI to make crucial decisions about education by striking a balance between the efficiency of AI and human expertise. In order to integrate AI responsibly and preserve the process's fairness and integrity, it is imperative that these ethical issues be addressed. Souppez et al. (2023) examine the transformative opportunities presented by generative AI in assessment and feedback, proposing novel strategies for higher education.In the realm of AI in educational assessment, there are several scenarios where ethically sensitive situations might arise. Addressing these situations requires careful consideration and strategic planning. Here are a few scenarios and strategies to manage them:

1. **Privacy Concerns in Data Collection and Usage**:
   - **Scenario**: AI systems often require large datasets to function optimally. This can include sensitive student information, raising privacy concerns.
   - **Strategy**: Implement strict data governance policies, ensuring that all data is anonymized and used only for intended educational purposes. Regular audits and compliance with data protection laws (like GDPR) are essential.
2. **Cultural Sensitivity in Content and Assessment**:
   - **Scenario**: AI tools might inadvertently perpetuate cultural biases or fail to accommodate diverse cultural backgrounds in their assessments or content curation.
   - **Strategy**: Design AI systems with cultural diversity in mind. This involves using datasets that are representative of various cultures and regularly updating these datasets. Also, involve cultural experts in the AI development process to ensure cultural appropriateness.
3. **Handling Emotionally Charged Conversations in AI Interactions**:
   - **Scenario**: AI-driven chatbots or virtual assistants might be ill-equipped to handle conversations where students are emotionally distressed or require empathy.
   - **Strategy**: Develop AI systems to recognize emotional cues and respond appropriately or escalate the situation to a human counselor. Training AI with emotional intelligence and setting clear boundaries for its capabilities are critical.
4. **Bias and Fairness in AI Assessments**:
   - **Scenario**: AI algorithms might develop biases based on the data they are trained on, leading to unfair assessments for certain student groups.
   - **Strategy**: Use diverse and inclusive training datasets and implement AI auditing mechanisms to detect and correct biases. Engaging external experts for periodic reviews of AI systems can also help in maintaining fairness.
5. **Transparency and Explainability**:
   - **Scenario**: There might be a lack of transparency in how AI systems make decisions, leading to trust issues among students and educators.
   - **Strategy**: Develop AI systems with explainable AI (XAI) principles, ensuring that decisions made by AI can be understood by non-experts. This also involves providing training for educators on how AI tools work.
6. **Data Security and Cybersecurity Threats**:
   - **Scenario**: AI systems, like any digital system, are susceptible to cybersecurity threats, which can compromise student data.
   - **Strategy**: Implement robust cybersecurity measures, including regular security audits, secure data storage solutions, and training for users on data security best practices.

In each of these scenarios, a multi-faceted approach that combines technology solutions with human oversight, ethical guidelines, and regulatory compliance is key to addressing ethical challenges effectively. It's also important to foster an environment of continuous learning and improvement, where AI systems are regularly evaluated and updated to meet ethical standards.

Protecting Student Privacy and Data Rights

As automated assessment relies on gathering extensive learner data for analysis, protecting student privacy must be a foundational priority. Colleges and universities have faced growing pressure to safeguard data privacy from all ed-tech tools as high-profile breaches and questionable uses are exposed. AI assessment multiplies these risks. Institutions should mandate ethical data practices, including:

- Disclosing all information collected and analysis performed
- Securing consent for gathering and retaining student data
- Allowing students access to their own data and deletion rights
- Anonymizing data used for training algorithms
- Encrypting data transmission and storage
- Restricting use solely for improving learning
- Avoiding selling data or allowing external access

Developing rigorous data governance policies and security protections proactively rather than reactively is critical. Students should be empowered to control their data use through granular permissions and understand exactly how it improves their learning experience. Transparency builds trust. Assessment data should be considered in the context of an institution's broader ethical ed-tech procurement policies as well. With deliberate forethought, automated assessment can progress while upholding student privacy and agency.

Avoiding Over-Reliance on Automation

While consistent grading and personalized feedback at scale represent the strengths of AI systems, these tools lack human nuance and discretion. Generative algorithms should augment educators, not replace their judgment. Assessment automation risks overuse, like expired passwords requiring periodic changes. Procedures must protect against the harms of excessive automation, such as:

- Removing teacher agency and oversight
- Disregarding controversial but important perspectives
- Eliminating opportunities to demonstrate qualitative skills
- Introducing unchecked technical biases and errors
- Enabling surveillance rather than empowerment

Safeguards might include capping automation, mandating human-in-the-loop review, allowing algorithmic overrides, or gradually phasing in automation. The role of AI should be positioning instructors to focus energies on higher-order assessment, like motivating learners, recognizing creativity, and mentoring goal-setting. Technology should enhance human capabilities, not limit them to just what machines can evaluate today. This keeps students centered.

Enabling Transparency in Design and Use

Opacity in how automated assessment systems function risks undermining trust. Instead, institutions should proactively foster transparency regarding:

- Development processes and team members
- Training data characteristics and curation practices
- Algorithmic models, scoring logic and key predictors
- Rationale for assessments generated and their intended purposes
- Testing procedures and external audits
- Tools to enable student inspection of their own assessment trail
- Communications to stakeholders on evolving capabilities and limitations
- Version histories and details of ongoing improvements

Disseminating explainers, allowing expert code review, providing interactive model explorers, issuing version release notes, and welcoming public dialogue conveys good faith while benefiting from crowdsourced feedback. Assessment algorithms directly impacting students should be as transparent as possible while securing intellectual property. Ongoing collaboration with stakeholders builds understanding and charts an ethical path forward.

Considering Impacts on Diverse Learners

Any assessment tool risks disadvantaging certain student groups if not consciously designed for inclusion. Generative algorithms amplify this danger by potentially encoding historical biases within training data. A priority for ethical AI is continually evaluating efficacy across learner demographics to uncover and address disparities.

Key steps include:

- Inclusive design - engage representatives from vulnerable communities as partners throughout the process
- Bias testing - computationally audit all models for skewed performance impacting particular identities
- Accommodations - enable adaptations like extra time or text-to-speech for neurodiverse learners
- Oversight - empower expert reviewers to override potentially discriminatory algorithmic decisions
- Feedback channels - allow confidential reporting of unfair treatment for rapid redress

Proactively embedding diversity and inclusion engineering throughout development, coupled with ongoing participation mechanisms for marginalized voices, provides paths to balance automation risks with benefits for all.

Aligning Assessment to Pedagogical Values

Generative AI offers remarkable capabilities. But technology should serve learning goals, not drive them. Educators have expressed concern that tools like plagiarism detection or writing automation could incentivize gaming behaviours rather than actual competency development if improperly implemented. Continually evaluating the impacts of automated assessment through a pedagogical lens is critical.

Key guiding questions include:

- Does the design encourage authentic skill demonstration aligned with course learning objectives?
- What risks or distortions might arise from introducing automation?
- How will the tool integrate with personalized human feedback and scaffolding?
- How might over-assessment or surveillance effects be mitigated?
- Does scoring logic and criteria reflect true development trajectories?

Responsible assessment avoids evaluative dead ends and instead nurtures the infinite human potential of every student. Wise experts focused on furthering learning, not statistics or technology, must remain at the helm to shape appropriate, empowering applications of automation.

Balancing Automation With Human Judgment

Given the ongoing limitations of current algorithms, institutions exploring the adoption of automated assessment tools must carefully balance benefits with risks. No technology solution is a panacea, but it can add value when thoughtfully implemented. Maintaining human judgment and oversight ensures learners are served, not machinery.

Steps to responsibly integrate automation include:

- Phasing in deployment via controlled pilots to evaluate impacts
- Selecting use cases where AI complements educator capabilities and workloads
- Preserving instructor discretion around final decisions and accommodations
- Enabling confidential avenues to address unfair algorithmic determinations
- Constraining automation where risks outweigh learning benefits until improved
- Continually assessing evolving capabilities compared to human expertise

With diligence and care, higher education institutions can harness the power of generative AI to enrich assessment while upholding academic values and standards. But progress demands proceeding carefully and inclusively.

Ethical dilemmas in AI education arise from balancing technological efficiency with the risk of depersonalization. Institutions face the responsibility of ensuring AI tools uphold data privacy, prevent biases, and maintain transparency in decision-making. Additionally, they must monitor AI tools to prevent negative impacts on student learning and well-being. Educators are tasked with understanding AI limitations, ensuring unbiased AI use, and creating a supportive educational environment. Both educators and institutions should engage in developing and adhering to an ethical framework for AI in education. This framework should guide ethical AI development, include regular training on ethical issues, and provide channels for student feedback. Addressing these ethical considerations ensures a responsible and equitable integration of AI into educational practices.

Automated assessment via AI techniques like natural language processing and computer vision risks improper use and negative consequences if not developed consciously to serve all students ethically. However, through policies that secure data privacy, allow overrides, foster transparency, centre inclusion, and elevate learning, colleges and universities can prevent potential harm. The recommendations in this section aim to guide stakeholders in wisely balancing the automation possibilities of today with enduring education principles in order to create more empowering, illuminating and equitable assessment ecosystems benefitting diverse contemporary learners.

Ethical Implications of AI in Education

In the burgeoning field of AI in education, ethical considerations are paramount. While AI presents revolutionary opportunities for personalized learning and efficient assessment, it also brings forth challenges that must be navigated with care. Ensuring equitable benefits for all students necessitates a deep dive into the ethical landscape surrounding AI technologies. One major ethical dilemma is data privacy. The use of student data to enhance AI learning tools must be balanced against the imperative to protect individual privacy. For instance, an incident at a European university, where student data was utilized without explicit consent, underscores the sensitivity of this issue. Furthermore, algorithmic biases pose a significant challenge. An AI grading system, for example, might inadvertently favor certain student demographics, leading to unfair outcomes. This issue was highlighted in a case at a North American college, where biases in an AI-assisted grading system were identified and subsequently addressed.

The responsibility to address these ethical challenges lies heavily with educational institutions and educators. Institutions must ensure transparency in AI algorithms and conduct regular audits to detect and correct biases. A proactive approach, as seen in a Californian university's initiative for ethical AI deployment, involves regular stakeholder dialogues and bias audits. Educators, on their part, play a crucial role. They must understand the limitations of AI tools, strive to use them as supplements rather than replacements for human interaction, and actively work to counteract potential biases. A concrete example of successfully navigating these ethical challenges comes from an Australian university. They implemented an AI-based learning platform while prioritizing ethical training for faculty and ensuring open communication with students regarding AI use. This approach not only fostered trust but also enhanced the effectiveness of the AI tools.

The ethical integration of AI in education is a collaborative effort. It requires the engagement of technologists, educators, policymakers, and students. Developing and adhering to a robust ethical framework is essential to ensure that AI is used in ways that are responsible, equitable, and ultimately beneficial to the educational ecosystem.

LIMITATIONS, RISKS, AND CONCERNS

While generative AI enables promising new assessment capabilities at scale, these emerging technologies also face substantial limitations and pose risks of negative consequences if applied irresponsibly. This section reviews key issues requiring ongoing research and thoughtful mitigation strategies as institutions explore adoption. The goal is to balance warranted optimism with critical analysis to guide responsible innovation, advancing both human and machine capabilities equitably.

AI Bias and Fairness Pitfalls

A significant concern is that algorithmic assessment models can inherit and amplify societal biases present in training datasets, disproportionately impacting underrepresented student groups. Even absent overt discrimination, learning patterns and evaluations of capabilities often reflect historical imbalances in opportunities. Applying such data without careful consideration risks encoding systemic bias into scoring systems and exacerbating achievement gaps.

For instance, an automated essay scoring tool trained only on the majority of native English speakers could unfairly penalize linguistic diversity. Speech recognition calibrated predominantly on male voices might penalize women. Even characteristics like typing cadence can create false signals correlating with demographics rather than skills. Thoughtfully curating inclusive datasets, continually testing for disparate impacts, and enabling human overrides of biased computer judgments are imperative.

Similarly, some AI techniques excel at assessing basic skills but insufficiently represent higher-order learning goals. Automated writing evaluation focuses largely on grammar, vocabulary and plagiarism over creative voice, reasoning and topic knowledge. Intelligent tutors emphasize procedural fluency but less often conceptual mastery. This risks distortions stressing easily measurable competencies over deeper humanistic outcomes.

Overall, generative algorithms must be consciously developed to support an equitable, empowering education aligned with societal values. Progress requires uncompromising efforts to evaluate and mitigate potential biases through community partnership. AI offers opportunities to enrich assessment but should not determine educational trajectories. Wise oversight preventing marginalization remains imperative.

Gaming Tendencies and Academic Integrity

Critics have raised valid concerns that certain applications of automated assessment, like plagiarism detection or writing auto-grading, may incentivize students to find workarounds to game the algorithm rather than developing substantive skills and integrity. For instance, language models can generate human-mimicking essays with minimal effort, curated to match rubrics. Some fear this will diminish learning and increase misconduct.

However, thoughtfully designed AI assessment provides pathways to reinforce academic integrity. Multimodal analysis combining writing, speech, conceptual questioning and discussions provides corroborating behavioural signals that are difficult to fake consistently. Setting expectations and coaching the use of generative tools ethically from day one instils responsibility, just as with other learning aids. Adaptive systems personalize challenge levels to make gaming exceedingly difficult, while plagiarism checks still mandate citing sources properly.

With deliberate educational rather than punitive framing, AI assessment offers opportunities to deepen critical thinking, ethics and metacognitive skills essential for intellectual growth. However, the risks of gaming must be proactively addressed through policy and pedagogy. Focusing solely on catching misconduct often backfires. Wise guidance combined with a supportive community is key.

Data Privacy and Security Vulnerabilities

Automated assessment relies extensively on gathering sensitive student data like assignments, behaviours, discussions, and contextual attributes. This data powers personalized feedback algorithms but also risks exposure through breaches or misuse. For instance, an EdTech provider could sell student data to third parties or violate transparency promises by shifting analysis practices without consent. Powerful generative AI models often have high computational costs as well, tempting providers to cut corners on security protections.

Colleges and universities must mandate ethical data management practices as procurement requirements, including encryption, access controls, consent processes, and use restrictions. Reducing data retention to the essential minimum needed lowers risks. Enabling opt-outs and providing students with their records fosters agency. Overall, strong data governance, combining cybersecurity protections and ethical oversight, is imperative to avoid eroding fragile learner trust.

Applicability for Assessing Complex Constructs

While AI techniques enable detailed analysis of observable metrics like writing mechanics or procedural accuracy, evaluating higher-order learning and interpersonal skills remains challenging computationally. Assessing critical thinking, leadership ethics, curiosity, or creativity does not readily decompose into coded rules or datasets. This risks overly quantifying education in ways that strip nuance and humanity if not carefully circumscribed.

Therefore, institutions must judiciously choose appropriate use cases where automation provides efficiencies without sacrificing teaching values or oversimplifying evaluation. The optimal balance likely involves AI handling rote grading tasks while skilled educators focus on rich qualitative mentorship. Hybrid human-AI assessment drawing on mutual strengths keeps the process humane. However, work remains to expand AI's ability to measure less quantifiable competencies ethically and accurately in the future.

Risks of Over-Automation and Dehumanization

A general concern exists around excessive reliance on technology and data for educational decisions traditionally requiring human judgment and discretion. While scalable, algorithms lack contextual understanding and nuance. Students feel reduced to scores rather than empowered as individuals with dignity and potential. Critics argue generative AI poses analogous risks to detrimental outcomes when automation displaces skilled roles in other industries.

Safeguarding the wisdom of educators should be a priority when integrating AI into assessments. Progress requires preserving faculty agency and oversight over final determinations, not handing full authority to algorithms. Roles for qualitative personal mentorship must endure and expand. Learner voices demand ongoing participation in shaping democratized, empowering systems centred on humanity over efficiency or control. With thoughtful policies elevating ethics and rights, AI-enabled assessment can enrich classrooms without dehumanizing students.

Apprehension Around High-Stakes Summative Assessments

While lower-stakes automated formative assessment to support ongoing improvement shows promise, reliance on AI tools for determining final grades or advancement raises significant concerns. Critics argue that high-stakes algorithmic decisions could lack nuance and transparency compared to cumulative human evaluation of students' holistic growth. The stakes incentivize gaming behaviour and misconduct as well.

Currently, sufficient unknowns and risks exist around bias, security, and gaming to warrant caution in applying automation in high-stakes scenarios. However, techniques like teacher oversight, consensus auditing, accommodations, explanatory interfaces and hybrid human-AI grading provide pathways to integrate automation with appropriate safeguards responsibly. More research and thoughtful policy is needed to balance the benefits and risks in these consequential assessments.

Building Learner, Teacher, and Public Trust

Stakeholders hold diverse and often sceptical perspectives on integrating generative AI in high-stakes education, given concerns around privacy, fairness, and dehumanization. Without deliberate relationship building through transparency, participation and accountability, adoption risks provoking controversy and erosion of fragile public trust. But institutions forging partnerships with community members and openly addressing hard problems head-on can build the understanding needed to chart an ethical way forward together.

Early successes in keeping humanity central will prove critical. Leaders have argued the greatest risk is not flawed technology— which can steadily improve— but poor policy, culture and power dynamics distorting implementation. Progress rests on cultural readiness as much as technical advances. By reinforcing education's humanistic social mission, generative AI assessment can gradually earn legitimacy.

Overall, these complex challenges underscore the need for a measured, evidence-driven and inclusive approach - not haste driven by hype. With wisdom, forethought and good faith on all sides, colleges and universities can overcome limitations and thoughtfully integrate emerging capabilities to positively transform assessment in ways that honour academic values and serve all students equitably.

RECOMMENDATIONS AND CONCLUSION

The integration of generative AI into higher education assessment holds tremendous potential to reinvent practices in ways that enrich learning and empower students. However, as with any powerful technology, it also carries risks if implemented without diligence. This concluding section synthesizes recommendations for institutions, instructors, researchers and policymakers navigating this complex terrain, aiming to maximize benefits while proactively mitigating harms. It provides guidance grounded in learning sciences and ethical principles to chart a thoughtful path forward, advancing both human and machine capabilities equitably.

Guidance for Institutions Exploring AI Assessment Adoption

Educational institutions considering leveraging generative AI techniques to enhance assessment are advised to take a measured, evidence-driven approach. Piloting tools in low-stakes formative scenarios to evaluate impacts before expanding use is wise. Developing competencies in prompt engineering, data literacy and learning analytics provides a strategic foundation. Recommended actions include:

- Consult learning science and assessment experts to align goals and tools thoughtfully.
- Audit existing assessments and identify potential use cases for judicious AI augmentation.

- Foster campus conversations on values, risks and hopes to incorporate diverse faculty and student perspectives.
- Start small with limited prototypes, collect feedback and monitor for unintended consequences before scaling.
- Require vendors to provide transparency into dataset models and undergo external algorithm audits.
- Develop policies and safeguards ahead of deployment focused on ethics, privacy and security.
- Invest in building internal technical capabilities, allowing customization for local needs.
- Continually assess efficacy compared to learning objectives using experimental methods.

With a deliberate approach prioritizing evidence and ethical principles over efficiency, institutions can integrate automated assessment judiciously in ways that enhance faculty capabilities and provide more timely, insightful feedback to empower diverse student needs.

Responsible Policies and Practices for Implementation

Once exploratory piloting yields promising results, expanding adoption institution-wide demands proactive policy development to ensure responsible use. Recommended focus areas include:

- Student data privacy, security and confidentiality protections
- Bias testing and mitigation requirements for assessment systems
- Transparency, oversight and audit mechanisms
- Instructor and expert roles in reviewing/overriding algorithmic decisions
- Accessibility policies providing necessary accommodations
- Constraints preventing high-stakes summative assessments until adequate validation
- Committee governance and approval processes for new AI assessment tools
- Responsible marketing and communication standards regarding automation limits
- Student and faculty participation in shaping policies and evaluating systems
- Continuous improvement protocols responding to feedback and risks

Guidance for navigating the complex landscape exists, including tools like the DELTA framework from the Non-Obvious AI Collective. With forethought and care, generative AI can be implemented to enrich assessment consistently with academic values and equitable education rights.

Priorities for Further Research and Development

Realizing the full potential of AI-enabled assessment will require ongoing research, innovation and multidisciplinary collaboration. Some promising priorities include:

- Advancing techniques for evaluating complex constructs like critical thinking
- New multimodal analysis combining text, speech, visual and interactive assessments
- Reinforcement learning for adaptive testing and personalized feedback
- Generative creativity assessment through co-creation activities
- Developing standards, benchmarks and tools supporting transparency

- Improving assessment accessibility for neurodiverse learners through AI
- Mitigating algorithmic bias through techniques like data augmentation
- Advancing explainability and participatory ML methods, participants can trust
- Exploring secure credentialing of skills using blockchain and live assessments
- Studying impacts of automation on learning outcomes over time compared to alternative practices
- Policy research on effective oversight models balancing innovation with ethics

Responsible implementation will require continuing advances in capabilities guided by learning sciences and participatory design. With patience and wisdom, researchers and practitioners can chart a thoughtful path incrementally, improving automated assessment's fairness, validity and utility.

Conclusion: Optimizing Benefits While Minimizing Risks

In closing, automating educational assessment using generative AI techniques like natural language processing and computer vision holds the transformational potential to provide more frequent, personalized and comprehensive evaluations supporting each student's needs and strengths. However, risks around bias, gaming and dehumanization necessitate a careful approach rooted in evidence and ethics.

By implementing AI assessment thoughtfully, higher education institutions can enhance learning and equity while upholding academic values. Progress requires prioritizing student rights, participatory design, continuous improvement and human judgment over efficiency or profit motives alone. With wisdom and diligence, colleges and universities can develop next-generation assessments prepared for the complexities of 21st-century learning, which remain fair, illuminating and empowering.

Overall, this chapter aimed to provide conceptual grounding, real-world cases, critical analysis and recommendations to assist stakeholders in navigating the opportunities and challenges of applying generative AI to reinvent assessment and feedback practices in higher education. Harnessing the strengths of both human and machine intelligence, thoughtfully and with care, promises to make teaching more adaptive, learning more personalized, and competency-building more inclusive than ever before.

AUTHORS' NOTES

This paper was proofread and refined with the assistance of generative AI, complementing the human editorial process.

REFERENCES

Arum, R., & Roksa, J. (2011). *Academically adrift: Limited learning on college campuses*. University of Chicago Press.

Boud, D., & ... (2010). [Seven propositions for assessment reform in higher education. Australian Learning and Teaching Council.]. *Assessment*, 2020.

Bozkurt, A. (2023). Generative artificial intelligence (AI) powered conversational educational agents: The inevitable paradigm shift. *Asian Journal of Distance Education*, *18*(1), 198–204. doi:10.5281/zenodo.7716416

Bozkurt, A. (2023). Unleashing the potential of generative AI, conversational agents and chatbots in educational praxis: A systematic review and bibliometric analysis of GenAI in education. *Open Praxis*, *15*(4), 261–270. doi:10.55982/openpraxis.15.4.609

Bozkurt, A., & Sharma, R. C. (2023). Generative AI and prompt engineering: The art of whispering to let the genie out of the algorithmic world. *Asian Journal of Distance Education*, *18*(2), i–vii. doi:10.5281/zenodo.8174941

Crompton, H., & Burke, D. (2023). Artificial intelligence in higher education: The state of the field. *International Journal of Educational Technology in Higher Education*, *20*(1), 22. Advance online publication. doi:10.1186/s41239-023-00392-8

Erisman, W., & Looney, S. (2007). *Opening the Door to the American Dream: Increasing Higher Education Access and Success for Immigrants*. Institute for Higher Education Policy.

Hart Research Associates. (2015). *Falling short? College learning and career success*. Association of American Colleges and Universities.

Lindsay, K. (2023, January 24). *A framework for approaching AI and university assessment*. Kate Lindsay. https://katelindsayblogs.com/2023/01/24/a-framework-for-approaching-ai-and-university-assessment/

Mao, J., Chen, B., & Liu, J. C. (2023). Generative Artificial Intelligence in Education and Its Implications for Assessment. *TechTrends*.

Moorhouse, B. L., Yeo, M. A., & Wan, Y. (2023). Generative AI tools and assessment: Guidelines of the world's top-ranking universities. *Computers and Education Open*, *5*, 100151. doi:10.1016/j.caeo.2023.100151

Newble, D. I., & Jaeger, K. (1983). The effect of assessments and examinations on the learning of medical students. *Medical Education*, *17*(3), 165–171. doi:10.1111/j.1365-2923.1983.tb00657.x PMID:6865814

Seo, K., Tang, J., Roll, I., Fels, S., & Yoon, D. (2021). The impact of artificial intelligence on learner–instructor interaction in online learning. *International Journal of Educational Technology in Higher Education*, *18*(1), 54. Advance online publication. doi:10.1186/s41239-021-00292-9 PMID:34778540

Shrivastava, R. (2023). Role of Artificial Intelligence in Future of Education. *International Journal of Professional Business Review*, *8*(1), e0840. doi:10.26668/businessreview/2023.v8i1.840

Smolansky, A., Cram, A., Raduescu, C., Zeivots, S., Huber, E., & Kizilcec, R. F. (2023, July). Educator and student perspectives on the impact of generative AI on assessments in higher education. In *Proceedings of the Tenth ACM Conference on Learning@ Scale* (pp. 378-382). ACM. 10.1145/3573051.3596191

Souppez, J. B. R., Goswami, D., & Yuen, J. (2023, December). Assessment and Feedback in the Generative AI Era: Transformative Opportunities, Novel Assessment Strategies and Policies in Higher Education. In International Federation of National Teaching Fellows Symposathon 2023.

KEY TERMS AND DEFINITIONS

Adaptive Learning: A personalized educational approach that uses technology to tailor learning experiences to individual needs. It modifies content, presentation style, and pace based on real-time feedback on learner performance.

Artificial Intelligence (AI): A field of computer science dedicated to creating machines capable of performing tasks that typically require human intelligence. AI systems are designed to simulate human cognitive functions like learning, problem-solving, and decision-making.

Automated Essay Scoring (AES): The use of specialized software to evaluate and score written essays. AES algorithms assess various elements of writing, such as grammar, syntax, coherence, and organization.

Bias in AI: Refers to the tendency of AI systems to make unfair or prejudiced decisions, often due to skewed data or flawed algorithmic design. AI bias can result in discrimination and misrepresentation of certain groups.

Intelligent Tutoring Systems (ITS): Computer-based systems that provide personalized instruction or feedback to learners, simulating the methods of a human tutor. ITS adapt to the learner's pace and understanding, offering tailored guidance and support.

Machine Learning (ML): A subset of AI, Machine Learning involves algorithms that enable computers to learn and adapt from experience without being explicitly programmed. ML focuses on developing systems that can access and use data to learn for themselves.

Natural Language Processing (NLP): An area of AI that focuses on the interaction between computers and human languages. NLP aims to enable computers to understand, interpret, and respond to human language in a meaningful way.

Chapter 22
Innovative Curriculum Development and Content Creation With Generative AI

Ilker Kayabas
https://orcid.org/0000-0001-9707-496X
Anadolu University, Turkey

ABSTRACT

In the digital age, generative AI significantly influences various industries, especially education. It merges with traditional teaching methods, promising a new era of educational possibilities. This chapter delves into generative AI's impact on content creation and curriculum design, discussing its evolution and benefits like producing diverse, scalable educational materials and adaptive curricula personalized for learners. Real-world examples and case studies underscore its practical impact. Nonetheless, the chapter addresses ethical and pedagogical challenges and the complexity of integrating this technology. It also speculates on generative AI's future interactions with emerging technologies and its broader effects on education systems. Targeting educators, policymakers, and edtech enthusiasts, the chapter serves as a guide and insight provider for navigating this evolving landscape responsibly.

INTRODUCTION

Traditional approaches to content creation and curriculum development have undergone significant transformations throughout history in response to educational theories and cultural contexts (Boyle & Charles, 2016). This evolution has now reached an extraordinary stage where artificial intelligence (AI) technologies have emerged as an essential component. The emergence of Generative AI, which distinguishes itself from traditional AI, represents a revolutionary technological phenomenon that actively produces new data, including text, visual, sound, or video, instead of solely analyzing and interpreting existing data. The essence of generative AI lies in its ability to acquire knowledge from extensive datasets and subsequently generate novel and realistic outcomes that were not explicitly programmed.

DOI: 10.4018/979-8-3693-1351-0.ch022

Generative AI is exerting its influence in various domains, providing a remarkable touch to areas that were traditionally considered within the realm of human capabilities. In the realm of art, AI-generated images are challenging the concept of creativity, generating a fresh conversation on the essence of artistic expression. Imagine a painting that combines artistic styles from different eras, all created by an AI - it represents a fusion of the past and the future, challenging our conventional understanding of artistry (Piskopani et al., 2023). Furthermore, in literature and journalism, this technology serves not only as a tool but also as a collaborator, capable of crafting stories and articles that resonate with human emotions and contexts. Envision an AI authoring a novel or a news article that captures the intricacies of human experience, blurring the boundaries between human and machine-generated content (Pena-Fernandez et al., 2023). Additionally, in the field of technology development, as demonstrated by the recent emergence of new tools such as ChatGPT, Midjourney, and Synthesia, generative AI functions as a master sculptor, creating realistic media that can be indistinguishable from those created by humans. It is reshaping our interactions with the digital world and enhancing the immersion of virtual experiences. This is not only an innovation, but it also provides a sneak peek into a future where technology and human creativity intersect in ways that we are just starting to explore.

The capability of Generative AI to revolutionize learning experiences and pedagogical techniques (Bozkurt, 2023; Bozkurt & Sharma, 2023; Gill et al., 2023; Katz et al., 2023), particularly within the context of curriculum development and content creation, presents significant potential and enthusiasm. This chapter delves into the impact of Generative AI on content creation and curriculum design, examining its evolution and the advantages it brings.

INTEGRATING GENERATIVE AI INTO CURRICULUM DEVELOPMENT

As highlighted by Kelly (2009), the curriculum plays a pivotal role in shaping the educational journey of learners. The master plan of the learning experience is designed by the curriculum offered within a course or programme. A curriculum is much more than a series of lectures: It is a comprehensive guide that aims to develop all the knowledge, skills, values, and attitudes necessary for the intellectual and personal development of students. In essence, the curriculum serves as a guiding framework, directing both educators and students by specifying what should be taught and learned. A well-designed curriculum might contain a comprehensive plan that outlines desired learning outcomes, instructional strategies, content, and assessment methods (Marsh, 2018).

Effective curriculum development is a complex process that requires careful planning, collaboration, and continuous evaluation (Bartlett & Housden, 2023). So, what kind of advantages can generative AI tools provide us in this process? Let's analyse the curriculum development process step by step to explore the answer to this question.

A comprehensive assessment of learning needs forms the basis of the curriculum development process. All kinds of data (demographics, educational background, learning preferences, etc.) that will allow the identification of the target group are put to use in the analysis process. In particular, the needs analysis should consider the social, economic, and cultural context in which the curriculum will be implemented. The ability of generative AI to process and make sense of complex masses of data can offer pragmatic solutions in the assessment of learning needs. For this, it will be enough to ask some simple prompts to generative AI chat agents such as ChatGPT, Claude and Bard in your own spoken language. The most basic problem you will encounter in such a situation will be a response like "Unfortunately, I cannot directly process private or personal data" that the generative artificial intelligence you use will convey to you. Of course, you can overcome this problem by anonymising all the data of your target audience without causing an ethical violation. For example, when you provide ChatGPT with a data table containing students' passing grades, number of absences, age, and similar information from previous semesters, you can perform analyses on this data to reveal trends, correlations and potential patterns related to student performance: The effect of absenteeism rates on grades, performance differences by age groups can be useful for the beginning.

In the next step of the curriculum development process, the primary goal in determining learning outcomes is to define student-centered, clear, and assessable criteria. Of course, it should be ensured that these outcomes are in line with national/international educational standards and competences. At this stage, generative AIs can be used to develop insights about students' learning preferences, areas of difficulty and sources of motivation based on data collected from previous courses or programmes. The resulting data-driven insights can serve to make learning outcomes more guided. On the other hand, generative AIs can also provide suggestions for deriving more explicit and measurable versions of the learning outcomes you have written, taking you to the next step.

Determining and coordinating content is a fundamental part of developing the curriculum. it is crucial to underscore the elements of compatibility with the learning objectives, when curating the content that should be presented to learners within the course or program. During this stage, generative AI can be used to analyse prior student performance data for the relevant curriculum. By identifying patterns and trends in content, such as common areas of difficulty or subjects in which students excel, the curriculum can be adapted to meet these specific needs. For example, if AI analysis reveals that students consistently struggle with certain maths concepts, the curriculum can be adjusted to ensure that these areas are covered more comprehensively.

Apart from these, generative AIs can also facilitate content planning by compiling different resources in the context of some common criteria. For example, by scanning possible resources on your behalf, it can offer suggestions for the selection of multimedia (text, visual, audio and video) content that best suits the identified learning objectives.

The transformation of content into a learning experience depends on which teaching strategies to design and how to implement them. Care should be taken to develop strategies that are pedagogically robust and appropriate to the structure of the target audience. The learning/teaching process should be planned in detail with lectures, discussions, e-learning practices, collaborative projects, and similar student-centered activities.

The final stage of curriculum development is assessment. Adopting a correct and fair assessment strategy in accordance with the learning outcomes is vital for the success of the course or programme. For this purpose, a wide range of assessment methods can be preferred, from written/verbal examinations to multiple-choice examinations, from practical assignments to portfolios, taking into account different learning needs.

USING GENERATIVE AI IN EDUCATIONAL CONTENT CREATION

Educational content, in its broadest sense, encompasses the materials and resources used to impart knowledge, skills, and practices to learners. It is through this content that the curriculum comes to life, guiding the instructional process and shaping the educational experiences of learners (Linebarger, 2015).

Central to the effectiveness of educational content is its alignment with pedagogical objectives and learning outcomes. As outlined by Gagne (1985), the structure and organization of content significantly influence how students process and internalize information. This alignment ensures that the content not only conveys knowledge but also facilitates the development of critical thinking, problem-solving abilities, and other essential competencies.

Moreover, the nature of educational content has evolved dramatically with the advent of digital technologies. Traditional textbooks and lectures are increasingly supplemented or replaced by interactive, multimedia-rich materials, as emphasized by Mayer (2020) in his principles of multimedia learning. This paradigmatic shift reflects a student-centered approach that recognizes the different learning styles and needs of students (Tomlinson, 2001).

Content and material are terms often used interchangeably in the field of education. However, they have distinct nuances and applications within the educational process. Understanding these differences is important for creating effective learning experiences. *Educational content* refers broadly to theories, concepts, facts, and information that needs to be taught. The primary purpose of content is to convey knowledge and understanding to learners. It serves as the foundational element around which the entire educational process is structured. Compared to instructional and learning materials, educational content is more about the "what" of teaching – the topics and knowledge areas to be covered. *Instructional materials* are tools used by educators to facilitate the teaching process and designed to make the learning process more effective and efficient. Its focus on the "how" of teaching – the methods and tools used to deliver educational content and engage students. Materials that aligned with specific learning objectives and teaching methodologies are used to support the delivery of content in different forms such as instructional videos, presentations, and other resources used by teachers in the classroom or virtual learning environments. *Learning materials* designed to be interacted with the learners are resources directly used to assist learning. The main purpose of these interactive and student centric materials is facilitating self-directed learning. Textbooks, workbooks, courseware, online courses, interactive e-lessons, games, quizzes, and other resources that students use to learn, practice, and assess their understanding of a specific subject matter can be describe like learning material.

INTEGRATING GENERATIVE AI INTO THE CREATION PROCESSES OF EDUCATIONAL CONTENT

The integration of generative AI, into the creation processes of educational content offers a transformative potential in the realms of research, design, writing and refine. In this section of the chapter, let's explore how we can canalize the power of generative AI to enhance the efficiency, inclusivity, and effectiveness of content creation.

Research and information gathering can be referred to as the initial phase of the content creation process. During this phase, generative AI can assist in the aggregation and synthesis of information. Generative AIs might possibly expedite the process of reviewing literature by summarizing key findings and identifying gaps in existing research. In addition, they can help teachers, educators or instructional designers produce more comprehensive and up-to-date content.

In terms of content design and development, generative AIs could be implemented in customizing content to align with diverse learning objectives and styles. Especially, AI should put to work in creating adaptive learning pathways, where content is tailored to meet the individual needs of students. AI can also be programmed to include multiple perspectives in educational content, thus enhancing its inclusivity; to ensure the representation of various cultural and contextual viewpoints which is crucial in fostering a global understanding among learners; to generate supplementary learning materials that reinforce learning and provide diverse avenues for student measurement and assessment such as presentations, quizzes, and guidelines.

In the writing process, generative AI can assist in the drafting and refinement of educational materials. They can ensure the readability and accessibility of content, catering to different language proficiencies. The ability of generative AIs to translate content into multiple languages, making the content more accessible to a global audience.

GENERATIVE AI SUPPORTED INSTRUCTIONAL AND LEARNING MATERIAL CREATION

The design and development processes of instructional and learning materials across different media types, while varying in specifics, generally follow a structured approach that integrates instructional design principles with media production techniques. A generalized outline of these processes can be listed as follows (Mackh, 2021; Liss, 2021): (1) Needs Analysis and Goal Setting (2) Scripting and Storyboarding (3) Media Production (4) Interactivity and Engagement Features (5) Review and Iteration (6) Implementation (7) Evaluation and Feedback (8) Continuous Improvement. This generalized process is adaptable to various media types, from traditional textbooks to advanced VR simulations. The key lies in understanding the unique strengths and limitations of each media type and thoughtfully integrating them into an effective educational tool.

Text-Based Materials

Text-based instructional and learning materials such as lecture notes, books, textbooks, workbooks, worksheets, e-book, and online articles are fundamental resources in educational settings, offering structured information and knowledge across various subjects.

The capability of Generative AIs to produce draft content rapidly can streamline the material creation process. Generative AI can help educators and content creators by generating drafts, outlines, or ideas for the content, such as lesson plans and lecture notes. For example, AI-generated drafts can serve as a starting point for educators, reducing the time and effort required in content development. Also, AI tools can expand on bullet points or short summaries to create detailed explanations, making them ideal for creating comprehensive study guides or lesson materials. On the other hand, these tools can summarize lengthy academic texts, research papers, or books, providing concise versions for quicker comprehension. And they can synthesize information from multiple sources into a coherent piece, useful for creating study materials or literature reviews. Generative AI can create realistic scenarios or case studies for subjects like law, medicine, or business, facilitating experiential learning.

Generative AI can also assist in translating and adapting text-based materials for different languages and reading levels, thereby improving accessibility and inclusivity. For example, you can rapidly translate the content of course using generative AIs into multiple languages making the materials accessible to non-native speakers and supporting multilingual education.

Several Generative AI tools have emerged as popular choices for text-based materials creation, each offering unique features and capabilities. These tools leverage advanced algorithms to generate, enhance, or modify textual content, making them valuable assets in educational and content creation contexts: ChatGPT, Google Bard, AI21 Labs Studio, DeepL, Grammarly, Copy.ai, Jasper, etc.

Visual Materials

Visual instructional and learning materials, encompassing a broad spectrum of resources like images, photos, illustrations, diagrams, charts, and infographics are valuable information transfer channels in education and training, offering diverse ways to engage learners, cater to different learning styles, and simplify complex concepts.

Generative AIs can serve as a tool for educators, enabling them to create high-quality educational materials efficiently. By automating aspects of design and content generation, teachers can focus more on pedagogy and less on the technicalities of material creation. In addition, this democratization of resource creation is especially beneficial for underfunded educational institutions.

Generative AI can dramatically improve the customization of learning materials to meet specific educational needs. By using generative AIs, you can generate images, diagrams, and infographics that are tailored to the curriculum and student needs.

Also, Generative AI has the potential to create dynamic visual content that changes in real-time based on learner input or feedback. Implementing this interactivity to learning process can lead to more engaging and effective experiences, particularly in subjects that require hands-on practice, like science and mathematics.

Generative AI could significantly contribute to making educational materials more accessible. By automatically generating alternative text for images or creating visual representations from text for those with reading difficulties, this technology can support inclusive education, aligning with the principles of Universal Design for Learning (CAST, 2023).

Despite these benefits, the implementation of Generative AI in educational contexts faces significant challenges. Quality assurance remains a critical issue, as AI-generated materials must be accurate, pedagogically sound, and aligned with curriculum standards. Moreover, educators need training and support to effectively integrate these tools into their teaching practices. Generative AI raises ethical concerns, particularly regarding data privacy and the potential perpetuation of biases. As AI systems often require large datasets for training, there is a risk of exposing sensitive student information (Zawacki-Richter et al., 2019). Additionally, biases in training data can lead to biased educational materials, which can adversely affect learners' perceptions and learning outcomes.

DALL-E, Adobe Sensei and Firefly, Midjourney, DeepAI, Canva's Magic Studio, Visme are the tools utilize advanced algorithms to generate new content based on input data and parameters and offer powerful capabilities for educators, content creators, and designers, allowing them to produce high-quality visual materials with greater efficiency and creativity.

Audio Materials

Audio-based instructional and learning materials such as lecture recordings, podcasts and audiobooks offer an accessible, flexible, and valuable resource in various educational contexts. While they have limitations, particularly in subjects that require visual aids, their benefits in promoting auditory learning and accessibility make them an indispensable tool in modern education. Learners can access audio materials at their convenience, making it easier to fit learning into busy schedules. These materials can improve listening skills and verbal comprehension, which are essential in language learning. Audio materials also are inherently accessible to individuals with visual impairments (O'Callaghan et al., 2017).

Advancements in text-to-speech technologies, driven by Generative AI, have led to the creation of voiceovers that are not only natural-sounding but also culturally nuanced. These improvements make audio materials more accessible and enjoyable, thereby enriching the learning experience for a broader audience. Furthermore, Generative AI also plays a crucial role in breaking down language barriers in education. By facilitating the rapid translation and localization of audio materials, AI enables a more inclusive and accessible educational environment, catering to learners from diverse linguistic backgrounds.

Creating high-quality educational audio content traditionally involves significant time and resources, particularly when employing professional voice actors. AI voice modeling can streamline this process, enabling the rapid and cost-effective production of vast amounts of educational audio material without compromising on quality. Educators can leverage AI voice modeling to provide additional learning resources and support. For example, AI can be used to create voice narrations of their written materials, allowing students to access lectures or notes in an audio format.

Several tools and platforms, leveraging advanced AI algorithms, have emerged as popular choices for professionals and enthusiasts alike. These tools are designed to generate, modify, and enhance audio content, including music, voiceovers, and sound effects, and are increasingly being used in various sectors, including education, entertainment, and content creation: iSpeech, AIVA, Sonantic, Lovo, Murf, etc.

Video Materials

Video-based instructional and learning materials such as video lectures, animations and documentaries have increasingly become a staple in both traditional and digital learning environments. The adoption of this modality leverages the visual and auditory senses, potentially enhancing the engagement and retention of information by learners.

Video offer significant advantages in enhancing learning outcomes, engagement, and accessibility. Video-based learning can significantly boost student engagement and motivation. Videos that incorporate interactive elements or real-life scenarios can create a more immersive learning experience. This engagement is crucial for motivation, as it encourages learners to explore topics more deeply. However, it's important to balance multimedia elements with educational content to avoid cognitive overload (Sweller, 1998). Videos offer the advantage of accessibility, especially for remote learners. With the rise of online education, videos have become an indispensable tool for delivering lectures and instructions beyond the physical classroom. Additionally, videos can be equipped with subtitles, sign language, and descriptive audio, making them more inclusive for learners with different needs (Gernsbacher, 2015). Despite the benefits, pedagogically, educators must carefully design video content to be concise, focused, and aligned with learning objectives. Long or unfocused videos may lead to decreased attention and retention (Guo et al., 2014).

Generative AI can assist educators in exploring creative ways to present content and scaling the production of high-quality educational content, offering tools to experiment with different formats, styles, and storytelling techniques. Video based generative AI tools, harnessing advanced algorithms, facilitate the production of engaging, informative, and customizable content, thereby enriching the domains of education, training, and learning. Here are some of the most prominent tools: Synthesia, Runway, Descript, Pictory, Lumen5 etc.

Interactive and Multimedia Materials

Interactive and multimedia learning materials are educational tools designed to engage students in an active and immersive way, integrating various forms of media such as text, audio, video, and interactive elements. This kind of learning materials are beneficial because they cater to different learning styles by combining visual, auditory, and kinesthetic elements. Multimedia approach, as discussed by Mayer (2020), is crucial in addressing the diverse preferences of learners. The incorporation of interactive features, like quizzes and simulations, has been shown to significantly increase learner engagement and motivation, a concept highlighted by Prensky (2007). Furthermore, these materials often include adaptive learning technologies, which allow for a more personalized learning experience, adapting to each learner's pace and style, as noted by Xie et al. (2016). A critical aspect of these materials is the provision of immediate feedback helps learners understand and correct their mistakes in real-time, facilitating a more effective learning process (Hattie & Timperley, 2007).

In educational settings, interactive and multimedia materials find varied applications. In K-12 education, they are used to make abstract concepts in subjects like science and mathematics more concrete. In higher education, interactive simulations are particularly beneficial in courses that require practical skills, such as engineering and medicine (Clark & Mayer, 2011). Similarly, in corporate training, gamified modules are employed for skill development and team-building exercises (Gee, 2003).

However, there are challenges and considerations in the use of these materials. Ensuring accessibility for learners with disabilities is crucial. Addressing the digital divide to ensure equitable access to technology is another significant challenge, as pointed out by Warschauer (2004).

Looking forward, the future of interactive and multimedia learning materials is likely to be shaped by emerging technologies such as mixed reality (MR) and artificial intelligence (AI), offering even more immersive and personalized learning experiences.

In context of integrating generative AIs to interactive and multimedia content, the creation of virtual mentors and assistants introduces a novel dimension to design and development challenge. These AI-driven entities can interact with students, answering queries and simulating real-world scenarios. In language learning, for example, a virtual AI character could engage in conversations with students, tailoring the dialogue's complexity to the student's language proficiency.

Generative AI aligns with the emphasis on critical thinking and problem-solving skills in contemporary education. In disciplines such as mathematics or programming, generative AI can help to craft unique, complex scenarios that challenge students to apply their knowledge creatively, fostering higher-order thinking skills.

Another intriguing application lies in narrative-based learning. Generative AI can be employed to create interactive, educational narratives, making learning experiences more engaging and immersive. For instance, in history or literature classes, AI-generated interactive stories where students' decisions influence the narrative's course could provide a more active and engaging learning experience.

The integration of Generative AI with Augmented Reality (AR) technology presents another frontier for educational innovation. This combination could create highly interactive and immersive learning environments. In a biology class, for example, students might explore a 3D model of the human body through AR, with AI providing real-time, contextual information and responses to queries.

Today's AI-powered multimedia tools represent a shift in how storytelling elements are created, focusing on efficiency, design quality, and user-friendliness. Here are some notable ones: Beautiful.ai, Tome, MindsMith, etc.

CONCLUSION

This chapter presents an evaluation about the utilization of generative AI into curricula development and educational content creation. The initial section emphasizes that the process of developing an effective curriculum is intricate and necessitates careful planning, collaboration, and ongoing evaluation. Examples are provided to illustrate the benefits that generative AIs can offer in this process. The subsequent section concentrates on the processes involved in content creation. Subtle distinctions between the concepts of content and materials are elucidated, and key elements of an effective design and development process are identified. Furthermore, innovative suggestions are offered regarding how generative AI can be leveraged to support the creation of various types of educational content and materials, including text, visuals, audio, video, and multimedia applications. Additionally, ethical concerns that may arise are highlighted.

In summary, we are currently witnessing the emergence of generative AI and its associated technologies. In this new and captivating future landscape, numerous challenges and unexplored frontiers await us. To successfully integrate generative AI into curriculum development and the creation of educational content, it is imperative that educators, followed by all other stakeholders, equip themselves with the skills elucidated in this study. The integration of generative AI into instructional design processes at every stage holds significant potential for transforming curriculum development and content creation. However, it is evident that there are challenges that pose a threat to these integration efforts. By examining innovative use cases of generative AI within the context of curriculum and content development, this study aims to stimulate further research and facilitate discussions on harnessing the true potential of generative AI to enhance the quality of AI-generated synthetic educational content.

REFERENCES

Bartlett, J., & Housden, E. (2023). *Developing an Outstanding Curriculum*. Elsevier B.V. doi:10.4324/9781003298274

Boyle, B., & Charles, M. (2016). *Curriculum Development: A Guide for Educators*. SAGE Publications. doi:10.4135/9781473920330

Bozkurt, A. (2023). Generative AI, synthetic contents, open educational resources (OER), and open educational practices (OEP): A new front in the openness landscape. *Open Praxis*, *15*(3), 178–184. doi:10.55982/openpraxis.15.3.579

Bozkurt, A., & Sharma, R. C. (2023). Generative AI and Prompt Engineering: The Art of Whispering to Let the Genie Out of the Algorithmic World. *Asian Journal of Distance Education*, *18*(2), i–vii. doi:10.5281/zenodo.8174941

CAST. (2023). *UDL: The UDL Guidelines*. UDL Guidelines. http://udlguidelines.cast.org

Clark, R. C., & Mayer, R. E. (2011). *E-Learning and the science of instruction: Proven guidelines for consumers and designers of multimedia learning*. Pfeiffer. doi:10.1002/9781118255971

Gagne, R. M. (1985). *The Conditions of Learning and Theory of Instruction* (4th ed.). Holt, Rinehart and Winston.

Gee, J. P. (2003). What Video Games Have to Teach Us about Learning and Literacy. *Computers in Entertainment*, *1*(1), 20. doi:10.1145/950566.950595

Gernsbacher, M. A. (2015). Video captions benefit everyone. *Policy Insights from the Behavioral and Brain Sciences*, *2*(1), 195–202. doi:10.1177/2372732215602130 PMID:28066803

Gill, S. S., Xu, M., Patros, P., Wu, H., Kaur, R., Kaur, K., Fuller, S., Singh, M., Arora, P., Parlikad, A. K., Stankovski, V., Abraham, A., Ghosh, S. K., Lutfiyya, H., Kanhere, S. S., Bahsoon, R., Rana, O., Dustdar, S., Sakellariou, R., & Buyya, R. (2023). Transformative effects of ChatGPT on modern education: Emerging Era of AI Chatbots. *Internet of Things and Cyber-Physical Systems*, *4*, 19–23. doi:10.1016/j.iotcps.2023.06.002

Guo, P. J., Kim, J., & Rubin, R. (2014). How video production affects student engagement: An empirical study of MOOC videos. *Proceedings of the first ACM conference on Learning @ scale conference*. ACM. 10.1145/2556325.2566239

Hattie, J., & Timperley, H. (2007). The Power of Feedback. *Review of Educational Research*, *77*(1), 81–112. doi:10.3102/003465430298487

Katz, A., Shakir, U., & Chambers, B. (2023). The Utility of Large Language Models and Generative AI for Education Research. https://doi.org//arxiv.2305.18125 doi:10.48550

Kelly, A. V. (2009). *The Curriculum Theory and Practice* (6th ed.). Sage.

Linebarger, D. L. (2015). Educational Media: Potentials for Learning. In J. D. Wright (Ed.), *International Encyclopedia of the Social & Behavioral Sciences* (2nd ed., pp. 246–254). Elsevier., doi:10.1016/B978-0-08-097086-8.92031-2

Liss, L. (2021). *Instructional Design. Creating an interactive digital product for education*. GRIN Verlag.

Mackh, B. M. (2021). *Pivoting Your Instruction: A Guide to Comprehensive Instructional Design for Faculty*. Taylor & Francis. doi:10.4324/9781003179726

Marsh, C. J. (2018). *Key Concepts for Understanding Curriculum* (Vol. 2). Routledge.

Mayer, R. (2020). *Multimedia Learning* (3rd ed.). Cambridge University Press. doi:10.1017/9781316941355

O'Callaghan, F., Neumann, D. L., Jones, L., & Creed, P. A. (2017). The use of lecture recordings in higher education: A review of institutional, student, and lecturer issues. *Education and Information Technologies*, *22*(1), 399–415. doi:10.1007/s10639-015-9451-z

Pena-Fernandez, S., Meso Ayerdi, K., Ureta, A., & Diaz Noci, J. (2023). Without journalists, there is no journalism: The social dimension of generative artificial intelligence in the media. *El Profesional de la Información*, *32*, 1–15. doi:10.3145/epi.2023.mar.27

Piskopani, A. M., Chamberlain., A. & Holter, C. T. (2023). *Responsible AI and the Arts: The Ethical and Legal Implications of AI in the Arts and Creative Industries*. doi:10.1145/3597512.3597528

Prensky, M. (2007). *Digital game-based learning*. Paragon House.

Sweller, J. (1998). Cognitive load during problem solving: Effects on learning. *Cognitive Science*, *12*(2), 257–285. doi:10.1207/s15516709cog1202_4

Tomlinson, C. A. (2001). *How to Differentiate Instruction in Mixed-Ability Classrooms*. Pearson Education.

Warschauer, M. (2004). *Technology and social inclusion: Rethinking the digital divide*. MIT Press., doi:10.7551/mitpress/6699.001.0001

Xie, H., Chu, H. C., Hwang, G. J., & Wang, C. C. (2019). Trends and development in technology-enhanced adaptive/personalized learning: A systematic review of journal publications from 2007 to 2017. *Computers & Education*, *140*, 103599. doi:10.1016/j.compedu.2019.103599

Zawacki-Richter, O., Marin, V. I., Bond, M., & Gouverneur, F. (2019). Systematic review of research on artificial intelligence applications in higher education – where are the educators? *International Journal of Educational Technology in Higher Education*, *16*(39), 39. doi:10.1186/s41239-019-0171-0

KEY TERMS AND DEFINITIONS

Generative AI: Is a branch of artificial intelligence that specializes in creating new content, whether that be text, images, audio, or other forms of data. It operates by learning from a vast array of existing data and using that knowledge to generate new, original outputs that are similar but not identical to the data it was trained on.

GPT: Which stands for Generative Pre-trained Transformer, is an advanced type of artificial intelligence model known for its ability to generate human-like text. Developed by OpenAI, GPT operates on the principles of deep learning and is part of the broader family of Transformer models, which have revolutionized the field of natural language processing. GPT is "pre-trained" on vast amounts of text data, enabling it to understand and generate language in a way that is contextually relevant and often indistinguishable from human writing. This pre-training allows GPT to perform a wide range of language tasks, such as answering questions, writing essays, translating languages, and even creating poetry or code.

Curriculum: Refers to the set of courses, and their content, offered at a school or university. It's an integral part of the educational framework and serves as a guide for both educators and students.

Educational Content: This term refers to the actual subject matter or information that is to be taught and learned. It encompasses the theories, concepts, facts, and information across various academic disciplines. Educational content is the foundation of the educational process, focusing on the "what" of teaching. It includes the core curriculum in schools and universities, the syllabus of a course, or the topics covered in an educational program. Essentially, it is the knowledge and understanding that educators aim to convey to learners.

Instructional Materials: These are the tools and resources used by educators to facilitate and enhance the teaching process. Instructional materials support the delivery of educational content, helping to explain concepts and guide the learning process. They are aligned with specific learning objectives, teaching methodologies and focus on the "how" of teaching. Examples of instructional materials include lesson plans, teaching guides, instructional videos, PowerPoint presentations, and other resources used in classrooms or virtual learning environments. They are designed to make the learning process more effective and efficient for both educators and students.

Learning Materials: These are the resources that are directly used by learners to aid in their own learning process. Learning materials are designed to be interactive and student-centric, facilitating self-directed learning, reinforcing concepts taught in class, and providing practice opportunities. They focus on the "learner's experience," meaning they are the tools students engage with to acquire knowledge and skills. Examples of learning materials include textbooks, workbooks, educational software, online courses, interactive e-lessons, quizzes, and other resources that students use for learning, practicing, and assessing their understanding of the subject matter.

Synthetic Content: Refers to media or information that is artificially generated by AI algorithms, rather than created by humans. This type of content can include text, images, videos and music, all produced by machines learning from and mimicking existing data.

Compilation of References

Abbass, H. (2021). What is artificial intelligence? *IEEE Transactions on Artificial Intelligence*, *2*(2), 94–95. doi:10.1109/TAI.2021.3096243

Abbott, R. B., & Rothman, E. (2022). (Forthcoming). Disrupting Creativity: Copyright Law in the Age of Generative Artificial Intelligence (August 8, 2022). *Florida Law Review*. doi:10.2139/ssrn.4185327

Abdallah, Y. K., & Estévez, A. T. (2023). Biomaterials Research-Driven Design Visualized by AI Text-Prompt-Generated Images. *Designs*, *7*(2), 48. doi:10.3390/designs7020048

Abd-alrazaq, A., AlSaad, R., Alhuwail, D., Ahmed, A., Healy, P. M., Latifi, S., Aziz, S., Damseh, R., Alrazak, S. A., & Sheikh, J. (2023). Large language models in medical education: Opportunities, challenges, and future directions. *JMIR Medical Education*, *9*(1), e48291. Advance online publication. doi:10.2196/48291 PMID:37261894

AbuSeileek, A. F. (2012). The effect of using an online-based course on the learning of grammar inductively and deductively. *ReCALL*, *24*(3), 239–256. doi:10.1017/S095834400999005X

Adams, C., Pente, P., Lemermeyer, G., & Rockwell, G. (2021). Artificial Intelligence Ethics Guidelines for K-12 Education: A Review of the Global Landscape. In I. Roll, D. McNamara, S. Sosnovsky, R. Luckin, & V. Dimitrova (Eds.), Lecture Notes in Computer Science: Vol. 12749. *Artificial Intelligence in Education. AIED*. Springer. (Original work published 2021), doi:10.1007/978-3-030-78270-2_4

Adams, C., Pente, P., Lemermeyer, G., & Rockwell, G. (2023). Ethical principles for artificial intelligence in K-12 education. *Computers and Education: Artificial Intelligence*, *4*, 100131. doi:10.1016/j.caeai.2023.100131

Adiguzel, T., Kaya, M., & Cansu, F. (2023). Revolutionizing education with AI: Exploring the transformative potential of ChatGPT. *Contemporary Educational Technology*, *15*(3), ep429. doi:10.30935/cedtech/13152

Adobe. (2003). *Adobe Firefly: Your imagination's new best friend*. Adobe. https://www.adobe.com/sensei/generative-ai/firefly.html

Ahmad, K., Iqbal, W., El-Hassan, A., Qadir, J., Benhaddou, D., Ayyash, M., & Al-Fuqaha, A. (2023). Data-driven artificial intelligence in education: A comprehensive review. *IEEE Transactions on Learning Technologies*, 1–20. doi:10.1109/TLT.2023.3314610

Ahmad, N., Murugesan, S., & Kshetri, N. (2023). Generative Artificial Intelligence and the Education Sector. *Computer*, *56*(6), 72–76. doi:10.1109/MC.2023.3263576

AI for Education. (2023). *Simple Lesson Plan Prompt*. AI for Education. https://www.aiforeducation.io/prompts/lesson-plans

Akgun, S., & Greenhow, C. (2022). Artificial intelligence in education: Addressing ethical challenges in K-12 settings. *AI and Ethics*, *2*(3), 431–440. doi:10.1007/s43681-021-00096-7 PMID:34790956

Akmal, S., Fitriah, F., & Fadhilah, I. (2022). The challenges and strategies of Islamic school mentor teachers in implementing ELT lesson plans. *Studies in English Language and Education*, *9*(3), 926–947. doi:10.24815/siele.v9i3.23063

Al Darayseh, A. (2023). Acceptance of artificial intelligence in teaching science: Science teachers perspective. *Computers and Education: Artificial Intelligence*, *4*, 100132. doi:10.1016/j.caeai.2023.100132

AlAfnan, M. A., & MohdZuki, S. F. (2023). Do artificial intelligence chatbots have a writing style? An investigation into the stylistic features of ChatGPT-4. *Journal of Artificial Intelligence and Technology*, *3*(3), 85–94. doi:10.37965/jait.2023.0267

Alam, A., Ullah, S., & Ali, N. (2018). The Effect of Learning-Based Adaptivity on Students' Performance in 3D-Virtual Learning Environments. *IEEE Access : Practical Innovations, Open Solutions*, *6*, 3400–3407. doi:10.1109/ACCESS.2017.2783951

Alasadi, E., & Baiz, C. (2023). Generative AI in Education and Research: Opportunities, Concerns, and Solutions. *Journal of Chemical Education*, *100*(8), 2965–2971. doi:10.1021/acs.jchemed.3c00323

Alattar, A. A., & McDowell, M. M. (2023). The rise of AI co-authors: Navigating the future of scientific writing with ChatGPT. *Journal of Neurosurgery, 1*(aop), 1-2. doi:10.3171/2023.3.JNS23254

Alavi, M., & Westerman, G. (2023). How Generative AI Will Transform Knowledge Work. *Harvard Business Review.* https://hbr.org/2023/11/how-generative-ai-will-transform-knowledge-work

Albus, J. S. (1991). Outline for a theory of intelligence. *IEEE Transactions on Systems, Man, and Cybernetics*, *21*(3), 473–509. doi:10.1109/21.97471

Alderson, J. (2009). Air safety, language assessment policy, and policy implementation: The case of AE. *Annual Review of Applied Linguistics*, *29*, 168–187. doi:10.1017/S0267190509090138

Aldrup, K., Carstensen, B., & Klusmann, U. (2022). Is empathy the key to effective teaching? A systematic review of its association with teacher-student interactions and student outcomes. *Educational Psychology Review*, *34*(3), 1177–1216. doi:10.1007/s10648-021-09649-y

Alharbi, W. (2023). AI in the foreign language classroom: A pedagogical overview of automated writing assistance tools. *Education Research International*, *2023*, 1–15. doi:10.1155/2023/4253331

Ali, M. (2018). The Human Intelligence vs. Artificial Intelligence: Issues and Challenges in Computer Assisted Language Learning. *International Journal of English Linguistics*, *8*(5), 259. doi:10.5539/ijel.v8n5p259

Aljanabi, M. (2023). ChatGPT: Future directions and open possibilities. *Mesopotamian Journal of Cybersecurity*, *16-17*, 16–17. doi:10.58496/MJCS/2023/003

Aljanabi, M., Ghazi, M., Ali, A. H., & Abed, S. A. (2023). ChatGPT: Open possibilities. *Iraqi Journal For Computer Science and Mathematics*, *4*(1), 62–64. doi:10.52866/20ijcsm.2023.01.01.0018

Allison, C., Auyeung, B., & Baron-Cohen, S. (2012). Toward brief "red flags" for autism screening: The short autism spectrum quotient and the short quantitative checklist in 1,000 cases and 3,000 controls. *Journal of the American Academy of Child and Adolescent Psychiatry*, *51*(2), 202–212. doi:10.1016/j.jaac.2011.11.003 PMID:22265366

Alshahrani, A. (2023). The impact of ChatGPT on blended learning: Current trends and future research directions. *International Journal of Data and Network Science*, *7*(4), 2029–2040. doi:10.5267/j.ijdns.2023.6.010

Altmäe, S., Sola-Leyva, A., & Salumets, A. (2023). Artificial intelligence in scientific writing: A friend or a foe? *Reproductive Biomedicine Online*, *47*(1), 3–9. doi:10.1016/j.rbmo.2023.04.009 PMID:37142479

Alves, P., Oliveira, Á., & Paro, H. (2019). Quality of life and burnout among faculty members: How much does the field of knowledge matter? *PLoS One*, *14*(3), e0214217. doi:10.1371/journal.pone.0214217 PMID:30901373

Amiri, A. M., Peltier, N., Goldberg, C., Sun, Y., Nathan, A., Hiremath, S. V., & Mankodiya, K. (2017, March). WearSense: Detecting autism stereotypic behaviors through smartwatches. *Health Care*, *5*(11), 2–9. doi:10.3390/healthcare5010011 PMID:28264474

Ampountolas, A., Menconi, G., & Shaw, G. (2023). Metaverse research propositions: Online intermediaries. *Tourism Economics*. doi:10.1177/13548166231159520

Anderson, B. (2016). *Imagined Communities: Reflections on the Origin and Spread of Nationalism* (Revised edition). Verso.

Ansari, A. N., Ahmad, S., & Bhutta, S. M. (2023). Mapping the global evidence around the use of ChatGPT in higher education: A systematic scoping review. *Education and Information Technologies*, 1–41. doi:10.1007/s10639-023-12223-4

Anyoha, R. (2017). The history of artificial intelligence. *Science News*, 28.

APA. (2013). *Diagnostic and statistical manual of mental disorders: DSM-5*. American Psychiatric Publishing Incorporated.

Archambault, R. D. (1974). *John Dewey: On Education*. University of Chicago Press.

Arif, T. B., Munaf, U., & Ul-Haque, I. (2023). The future of medical education and research: Is ChatGPT a blessing or blight in disguise? *Medical Education Online*, *28*(1), 2181052. doi:10.1080/10872981.2023.2181052 PMID:36809073

Aristotle. (2000). *The Nicomachean Ethics* (R. Crisp, Trans.). Cambridge University Press. doi:10.1017/CBO9780511802058

Ariyaratne, S., Iyengar, K. P., & Botchu, R. (2023). Will collaborative publishing with ChatGPT drive academic writing in the future? *British Journal of Surgery*, *110*(9), 1213–1214. doi:10.1093/bjs/znad198 PMID:37368994

Arora, S., Narayan, A., Chen, M. F., Orr, L., Guha, N., Bhatia, K., & Ré, C. (2022). Ask me anything: A simple strategy for prompting language models. *arXiv preprint arXiv:2210.02441*.

Arora, A. (2020). Conceptualising Artificial Intelligence as a Digital Healthcare Innovation: An Introductory Review. *Medical Devices (Auckland, N.Z.)*, *13*, 223–230. doi:10.2147/MDER.S262590 PMID:32904333

Arslan, E. (2022). Sosyal bilim araştırmalarında VOSviewer ile bibliyometrik haritalama ve örnek bir uygulama [Bibliometric mapping with VOSviewer in social science research and a sample application]. *Anadolu University Journal of Social Sciences, 22*(Special Issue, 2), 33-56.

Artificial Intelligence at Northwestern University. (2023). *Instructor Resources*. Northwestern University. [https://ai.northwestern.edu/education/instructor-resources.html]

Arum, R., & Roksa, J. (2011). *Academically adrift: Limited learning on college campuses*. University of Chicago Press.

Ashford, T. (2020). App-centric students and academic integrity: A proposal for assembling socio-technical responsibility. *Journal of Academic Ethics*, *19*(1), 35–48. doi:10.1007/s10805-020-09387-w

Aung, Z., Sanium, S., Songsaksuppachok, C., Kusakunniran, W., Precharattana, M., Chuechote, S., Pongsanon, K., & Ritthipravat, P. (2022). Designing a novel teaching platform for AI: A case study in a Thai school context. *Journal of Computer Assisted Learning*, *38*(6), 1714–1729. doi:10.1111/jcal.12706

Awad, S. W. M., & Feinstein, K. A. (2020). Hybrid identity: A study of the development of self-identity with digital media and artificial intelligence. *PÓS: Revista Do Programa de Pós-Graduação Em Artes Da EBA/UFMG, 10*, 59–68. doi:10.35699/2237-5864.2020.21572

Awidi, I. T., & Paynter, M. (2019). The impact of a flipped classroom approach on student learning experience. *Computers & Education, 128*, 269–283. doi:10.1016/j.compedu.2018.09.013

Aydin, B., & Demirer, V. (2022). Are flipped classrooms less stressful and more successful? An experimental study on college students. *International Journal of Educational Technology in Higher Education, 19*(1), 55. doi:10.1186/s41239-022-00360-8

Aydin, O., & Karaarslan, E. (2023). Is Chat GPT Leading Generative AI? What is Beyond Expectation? *Journal of Engineering and Smart Systems, 11*(3), 118–134.

Aydin, Ö., & Karaarslan, E. (2023). Is chatgpt leading generative ai? what is beyond expectations? *Academic Platform Journal of Engineering and Smart Systems, 11*(3), 118–134. doi:10.21541/apjess.1293702

Ayling, J., & Chapman, A. (2022). Putting AI ethics to work: Are the tools fit for purpose? *AI and Ethics, 2*(3), 405–429. doi:10.1007/s43681-021-00084-x

Baehr, J. (2013). Educating for intellectual virtues: From theory to practice. *Journal of Philosophy of Education, 47*(2), 248–262. doi:10.1111/1467-9752.12023

Baehr, J. (2021). The Structure of Intellectual Vices. In I. J. Kidd, H. Battaly, & Q. Cassam (Eds.), *Vice Epistemology* (pp. 21–36). Routledge.

Bahroun, Z., Anane, C., Ahmed, V., & Zacca, A. (2023). Transforming education: A comprehensive review of generative artificial intelligence in educational settings through bibliometric and content analysis. *Sustainability (Basel), 15*(17), 12983. doi:10.3390/su151712983

Baidoo-Anu, D., & Ansah, L. O. (2023). Education in the era of generative artificial intelligence (AI): Understanding the potential benefits of ChatGPT in promoting teaching and learning. *Journal of AI, 7*(1), 52–62. doi:10.61969/jai.1337500

Baidoo-AnuD.Owusu AnsahL. (2023). *Education in the era of generative artificial intelligence (AI): Understanding the potential benefits of ChatGPT in promoting teaching and learning*. Social Science Research Network. http://dx.doi.org/ doi:10.2139/ssrn.4337484

Bai, J. Y., Zawacki-Richter, O., & Muskens, W. (2022). *Developing strategic scenarios for artificial intelligence applications in higher education.* In *Proceedings of the 5th International Open and Distance Learning Conference* (pp.47- 70). Eskişehir, Türkiye.

Bailey, J. (2023). AI in Education. *Education Next, 23*(4), 28–35.

Bajgain, B., Lorenzetti, D., Lee, J., & Sauro, K. (2023). Determinants of implementing artificial intelligence-based clinical decision support tools in healthcare: A scoping review protocol. *BMJ Open, 13*(2), e068373. doi:10.1136/bmjopen-2022-068373 PMID:36822813

Baker, J. (2023). *65+ Best ChatGPT Prompts for Teachers: Enhance Classroom Experience.* Splash Learn. https://www.splashlearn.com/blog/chat-gpt-prompts-for-teachers/#4-9-best-chatgpt-prompts-for-assessment-and-evaluation-

Baker, B. (1996). The History of Curriculum or Curriculum History? What *is* the Field, and Who Gets to Play on it? *Curriculum Studies, 4*(1), 105–117. doi:10.1080/0965975960040106

Baker, R. S. (2021). Artificial intelligence in education: Bringing it all together. In *OECD Digital Education Outlook 2021: Pushing the Frontiers with Artificial Intelligence, Blockchain and Robots* (pp. 43–54). OECD Publishing. doi:10.1787/f54ea644-

Baker, R. S., & Hawn, A. (2022). Algorithmic bias in education. *International Journal of Artificial Intelligence in Education, 32*(4), 1052–1092. doi:10.1007/s40593-021-00285-9

Bakiner, O. (2023). What do academics say about artificial intelligence ethics? An overview of the scholarship. *AI and Ethics, 3*(2), 513–525. doi:10.1007/s43681-022-00182-4

Ballester, O. (2021). An artificial intelligence definition and classification framework for public sector applications. In DG. O2021: *The 22nd Annual International Conference on Digital Government Research* (pp. 67-75). ACM Press. 10.1145/3463677.3463709

Banik, L., Bhuiyan, M., & Jahan, A. (2015). Personalized learning materials for children with special needs using machine learning. In 2015 internet technologies and applications (ITA) (pp. 169-174). IEEE. doi:10.1109/ITechA.2015.7317390

Banks, S. (2011). A *historical analysis of attitudes toward the use of calculators in junior high and high school math classrooms in the United States since 1975.* [Master's of Education Research Theses, Cedarville]. https://digitalcommons.cedarville.edu/education_thesis/31

Banks, L., & Kay, R. (2022). Exploring flipped classrooms in undergraduate nursing and health science: A systematic review. *Nurse Education in Practice, 64*, 103417. doi:10.1016/j.nepr.2022.103417 PMID:36113354

Barik, L., Barukab, O., & Ahmed, A. (2020). Employing artificial intelligence techniques for student performance evaluation and teaching strategy enrichment: An innovative approach. *International Journal of Advanced and Applied Sciences, 7*(11), 10–24. doi:10.21833/ijaas.2020.11.002

Barnatt, J., D'Souza, L. A., Gleeson, A. M., Viesca, K. M., & Wery, J. (2020). Intercultural competence in Pre-Service teacher candidates. *International Journal of Educational Reform, 29*(3), 211–235. doi:10.1177/1056787919896866

Baron-Cohen, S. (1997). Mindblindness: An essay on autism and theory of mind. Bradford.

Barranquero-Herbosa, M., Abajas-Bustillo, R., & Ortego-Maté, C. (2022). Effectiveness of flipped classroom in nursing education. A systematic review of systematic and integrative reviews. *International Journal of Nursing Studies, 135*, 104327. doi:10.1016/j.ijnurstu.2022.104327 PMID:35944288

Bartlett, J., & Housden, E. (2023). *Developing an Outstanding Curriculum.* Elsevier B.V. doi:10.4324/9781003298274

Baruah, J., & Paulus, P. B. (2019). Collaborative creativity and innovation in education. *Creativity Under Duress in Education? Resistive Theories, Practices, and Actions*, 155-177. doi:10.1007/978-3-319-90272-2_9

Barua, P. D., Vicnesh, J., Gururajan, R., Oh, S. L., Palmer, E., Azizan, M. M., & Acharya, U. R. (2022). Artificial Intelligence Enabled Personalized Assistive Tools to Enhance Education of Children with Neurodevelopmental Disorders: A Review. *International Journal of Environmental Research and Public Health, 19*(3), 1–26. doi:10.3390/ijerph19031192 PMID:35162220

Battaly, H. (2017). Testimonial injustice, epistemic vice, and vice epistemology. In I. J. Kıdd, J. Medina, & G. Pohlhaus (Eds.), *The Routledge handbook of epistemic injustice* (pp. 223–231). Routledge. doi:10.4324/9781315212043-22

Baugh, J., Raja, A., & Takayesu, J. (2021). Help us help you: Engaging emergency physicians to identify organizational strategies to reduce burnout. *The Western Journal of Emergency Medicine, 22*(3). doi:10.5811/westjem.2020.49180 PMID:34125049

Bautista, R. M., & Pentang, J. T. (2022). Ctrl C+ Ctrl V: Plagiarism and knowledge on referencing and citation among pre-service teachers. *International Journal of Multidisciplinary: Applied Business and Education Research, 3*(2), 245–257. doi:10.11594/ijmaber.03.02.10

BBC News. (2014). *Robot writes LA Times earthquake breaking news article.* BBC News Service. https://www.bbc.com/news/technology-26614051

Bearman, M., Ryan, J., & Ajjawi, R. (2023). Discourses of artificial intelligence in higher education: A critical literature review. *Higher Education, 86*(2), 369–385. doi:10.1007/s10734-022-00937-2

Benedictis, R., Medio, C., Palombini, A., Cortellessa, G., Limongelli, C., & Cesta, A. (2021). Fostering the creation of personalized content for cultural visits. *Applied Sciences (Basel, Switzerland), 11*(16), 7401. doi:10.3390/app11167401

Benjamins, R., & Salazar, I. (2020). Towards a framework for understanding societal and ethical implications of Artificial Intelligence. In Dykinson eBooks (pp. 89–100). doi:10.2307/j.ctv153k50r.8

Berezin, J. (2023). *Using generative AI for your scientific writing? Be Aware of Journal Policies.* MIT. https://mitcommlab.mit.edu/cee/2023/08/27/using-generative-ai-for-your-scientific-writing-be-aware-of-journal-policies/

BerrarbiA.BahousA. (2018). Introducing short stories in EFL classroom to explore culturally diverse issues. *Social Science Research Network.* doi:10.2139/ssrn.3186963

Bertacchini, F., Demarco, F., Scuro, C., Pantano, P., & Bilotta, E. (2023). A social robot connected with chatGPT to improve cognitive functioning in ASD subjects. *Frontiers in Psychology, 14*, 1232177. doi:10.3389/fpsyg.2023.1232177 PMID:37868599

Bertheussen, B. A., & Myrland, Ø. (2016). Relation between academic performance and students' engagement in digital learning activities. *Journal of Education for Business, 91*(3), 125–131. doi:10.1080/08832323.2016.1140113

Betker. (2023). *Improving Image Generation with Better Captions.* CDN. https://cdn.openai.com/papers/dall-e-3.pdf

Bettelheim, B. (1959). Joey. *Scientific American, 200*(3), 116–130.. doi:10.1038/scientificamerican0359-116 PMID:13635040

Bewersdorff, A., Zhai, X., Roberts, J., & Nerdel, C. (2023). Myths, Mis- and Preconceptions of Artificial intelligence: A Review of the literature. *Computers & Education: Artificial Intelligence, 4*, 100143. doi:10.1016/j.caeai.2023.100143

Bhopal, K., & Rhamie, J. (2013). Initial teacher training: Understanding 'race,' diversity and inclusion. *Race, Ethnicity and Education, 17*(3), 304–325. doi:10.1080/13613324.2013.832920

Bhowmik, S., Barrett, A., Ke, F., Yuan, X., Southerland, S., Dai, C.-P., West, L., & Dai, Z. (2022). Simulating students: An AI chatbot for teacher training. In C. Chinn, E. Tan, C. Chan & Y. Kali (eds), *Proceedings of the 16th International Conference of the Learning Sciences - ICLS 2022.* https://par.nsf.gov/servlets/purl/10343544

Bielow, C., Mastrobuoni, G., & Kempa, S. (2016). Proteomics quality control: Quality control software for MaxQuant results. *Journal of Proteome Research, 15*(3), 777–787. doi:10.1021/acs.jproteome.5b00780 PMID:26653327

Biermann, O. C., Ma, N. F., & Yoon, D. (2022). From Tool to Companion: Storywriters Want AI Writers to Respect Their Personal Values and Writing Strategies. *Proceedings of the 2022 ACM Designing Interactive Systems Conference*, (pp. 1209–1227). ACM. 10.1145/3532106.3533506

Bieswanger, M. (2016). Aviation English: Two distinct specialized registers. *Variational Text Linguistics Revisiting Register in English, De Gruyter*, 67-86.

Bilgram, V., & Laarmann, F. (2023). Accelerating Innovation with Generative AI: AI- augmented Digital Prototyping and Innovation Methods. *IEEE Engineering Management Review, 51*(2), 18–25. doi:10.1109/EMR.2023.3272799

Birks, M., Mills, J., Allen, S., & Tee, S. (2020). Managing the mutations: Academic misconduct in Australia, New Zealand, and the UK. *International Journal for Educational Integrity, 16*(1), 1–15. doi:10.1007/s40979-020-00055-5

Bishop, L. (2023). A computer wrote this paper: What ChatGPT means for education, research, and writing. *Research, and Writing*. doi:10.2139/ssrn.4338981

Boamah, S. (2022). Investigating the work–life experiences of nursing faculty in Canadian academic settings and the factors that influence their retention: Protocol for a mixed-method study. *BMJ Open, 12*(1), e056655. doi:10.1136/bmjopen-2021-056655 PMID:34980630

BoamahS. A.HamadiH.HavaeiF.SmithH.WebbF. (2022). Striking a Balance between Work and Play: The Effects of Work-life Interference and Burnout on Faculty Turnover Intentions and Career Satisfaction. Preprints. https://doi.org/doi:10.20944/preprints202201.0120.v1

Böhmer, A., Schwab, G., & Isso, I. (2023). Blended Academic Communication on Technology-Enhanced Teaching and Learning in Digital and International Virtual Academic Cooperation (DIVA). In J. S. Stephen, G. Kormpas, & C. Coombe (Eds.), *Global Perspectives on Higher Education. Knowledge studies in higher education* (Vol. 11, pp. 129–143). Springer., doi:10.1007/978-3-031-31646-3_10

Bolaji, S. D., & Pollock, W. A. (2022). Where is Philosophy of Education in the Teacher Education Program in Australia? In S. D. Bolaji, A. Oni, & S. C. Anyama (Eds.), *African Education and Diaspora Studies* (pp. 1–11). Charles Darwin University Press.

Booyse, D., & Scheepers, C. B. (2023). Barriers to adopting automated organizational decision-making through the use of artificial intelligence. *Management Research Review*. Advance online publication. doi:10.1108/MRR-09-2021-0701

Borenstein, J., & Howard, A. (2021). Emerging challenges in AI and the need for AI ethics education. *AI and Ethics, 1*(1), 61–65. doi:10.1007/s43681-020-00002-7

Borges, P. H. M., Mendoza, Z., Maia, J., Bianchini, A., & Fernández, H. (2017). Estimation of fuel consumption in agricultural mechanized operations using artificial neural networks. *Engenharia Agrícola, 37*(1), 136–147. doi:10.1590/1809-4430-eng.agric.v37n1p136-147/2017

Bornet, P. (2023, September). *Here's the ChatGPT Ultimate Prompting Guide. Important elements to include: 1. Tone 2. Format 3. Objective 4. Context 5.Examples If you don't get the right output, try again you will get it soon... It is because of the prompt, not the tech!* (Post). LinkedIn. https://www.linkedin.com/posts/pascalbornet_genai-tech-skillsofthefuture-activity-7101048156108267520-l4Lx?utm_source=share&utm_medium=member_desktop

Boud, D., & ... (2010). [Seven propositions for assessment reform in higher education. Australian Learning and Teaching Council.]. *Assessment*, 2020.

Boulay, B. (2022). *Artificial intelligence in education and ethics*, 1-16. Springer. doi:10.1007/978-981-19-0351-9_6-2

BoussiouxL. N.LaneJ.ZhangM.JacimovicV.LakhaniK. R. (2023). The Crowdless Future? How Generative AI Is Shaping the Future of Human Crowdsourcing. *The Crowdless Future*. doi:10.2139/ssrn.4533642

Bowen, G. A. (2009). Document analysis as a qualitative research method. *Qualitative Research Journal, 9*(2), 27–40. doi:10.3316/QRJ0902027

Boyle, B., & Charles, M. (2016). *Curriculum Development: A Guide for Educators*. SAGE Publications. doi:10.4135/9781473920330

Bozkurt, A. (2023a). Generative artificial intelligence (AI) powered conversational educational agents: The inevitable paradigm shift. *Asian Journal of Distance Education, 18*(1), 198-204.. doi:10.5281/zenodo.7716416

Bozkurt, A. (2020). Educational technology research patterns in the realm of the digital knowledge age. *Journal of Interactive Media in Education, 2020*(1), 1–17. doi:10.5334/jime.570

Bozkurt, A. (2023). Generative AI, synthetic contents, open educational resources (OER), and open educational practices (OEP): A new front in the openness landscape. *Open Praxis*, *15*(3), 178–184. doi:10.55982/openpraxis.15.3.579

Bozkurt, A. (2023a). Postdigital Artificial Intelligence. In P. Jandrić (Ed.), *Encyclopedia of Postdigital Science and Education*. Springer. doi:10.1007/978-3-031-35469-4_2-2

Bozkurt, A. (2023b). Unleashing the potential of generative AI, conversational agents and chatbots in educational praxis: A systematic review and bibliometric analysis of GenAI in education. *Open Praxis*, *15*(4), 261–270. doi:10.55982/openpraxis.15.4.609

Bozkurt, A. (2023d). ChatGPT, generative artificial intelligence and algorithmic paradigm shift. *CRES Journal Critical Reviews in Educational Sciences*, *4*(1), 63–72. doi:10.59320/alanyazin.1283282

Bozkurt, A. (2024). Postdigital Educational Technology. In P. Jandrić (Ed.), *Encyclopedia of Postdigital Science and Education*. Springer.

Bozkurt, A., Gjelsvik, T., Adam, T., Asino, T. I., Atenas, J., Bali, M., Blomgren, C., Bond, M., Bonk, C. J., Brown, M., Burgos, D., Conrad, D., Costello, E., Cronin, C., Czerniewicz, L., Deepwell, M., Deimann, M., DeWaard, H. J., & Dousay, T. A., Ebner, M., Farrow, R., Gil-Jaurena, I., Havemann, L., Inamorato, A., Irvine, V., Karunanayaka, S. P., Kerres, M., Lambert, S., Lee, K., Makoe, M., Marín, V. I., Mikroyannidis, A., Mishra, S., Naidu, S., Nascimbeni, F., Nichols, M., Olcott. Jr., D., Ossiannilsson, E., Otto, D., Padilla Rodriguez, B. C., Paskevicius, M., Roberts, V., Saleem, T., Schuwer, R., Sharma, R. C., Stewart, B., Stracke, C. M., Tait, A., Tlili, A., Ubachs, G., Weidlich, J., Weller, M., Xiao, JZawacki-Richter, O. (2023). Openness in education as a praxis: From individual testimonials to collective voices. *Open Praxis*, *15*(2), 76–112. doi:10.55982/openpraxis.15.2.574

Bozkurt, A., Karadeniz, A., Bañeres, D., & Rodríguez, M. (2021). Artificial intelligence and reflections from educational landscape: A review of AI studies in half a century. *Sustainability (Basel)*, *13*(2), 800. doi:10.3390/su13020800

Bozkurt, A., & Sharma, R. C. (2023). Challenging the status quo and exploring the new boundaries in the age of algorithms: Reimagining the role of generative AI in distance education and online learning. *Asian Journal of Distance Education*, *18*(1), i–viii. doi:10.5281/zenodo.7755273

Bozkurt, A., & Sharma, R. C. (2023). Generative AI and prompt engineering: The art of whispering to let the genie out of the algorithmic world. *Asian Journal of Distance Education*, *18*(2), i–vii. doi:10.5281/zenodo.8174941

Bozkurt, A., Xiao, J., Lambert, S., Pazurek, A., Crompton, H., Koseoglu, S., Farrow, R., Bond, M., Nerantzi, C., Honeychurch, S., Bali, M., Dron, J., Mir, K., Stewart, B., Costello, E., Mason, J., Stracke, C. M., Romero-Hall, E., Koutropoulos, A., & Jandrić, P. (2023). Speculative futures on ChatGPT and generative artificial intelligence (AI): A collective reflection from the educational landscape. *Asian Journal of Distance Education*, *18*(1), 53–130. doi:10.5281/zenodo.7636568

Bradáč, V., Smolka, P., Kotyrba, M., & Průdek, T. (2022). Design of an intelligent tutoring system to create a personalized study plan using expert systems. *Applied Sciences (Basel, Switzerland)*, *12*(12), 6236. doi:10.3390/app12126236

Breznican, A. (2022). *Darth Vader's Voice Emanated From War-Torn Ukraine*. Vanity Fair. https://www.vanityfair.com/hollywood/2022/09/darth-vaders-voice-emanated-from-war-torn-ukraine

Brisk. (2023). *The easiest AI tool for teachers*. Brisk. https://www.briskteaching.com/

Brookfield, S. (1998). Critically reflective practice. *The Journal of Continuing Education in the Health Professions*, *18*(4), 197–205. doi:10.1002/chp.1340180402

Brown, P., & Levinson, S. C. (1987). *Politeness: Some Universals in Language Usage*. Cambridge University Press. doi:10.1017/CBO9780511813085

Bryant, J., Heitz, C., Sanghvi, S., & Wagle, D. (2020). *How Artificial Intelligence Will Impact K-12 Teachers*. McKinsey and Company. https://www.mckinsey.com/industries/public-and-social-sector/our-insights/how-artificial-intelligence-will-impact-k-12-teachers

Buabbas, A. J., Miskin, B., Alnaqi, A. A., Ayed, A. K., Shehab, A. A., Syed-Abdul, S., & Uddin, M. (2023). Investigating Students' Perceptions towards Artificial Intelligence in Medical Education. *Healthcare (Basel)*, *11*(9), 1298. doi:10.3390/healthcare11091298 PMID:37174840

Bubaš, G., & Čižmešija, A. (2023, May 1). A critical analysis of students' cheating in online assessment in higher education: Post-COVID-19 Issues and challenges related to conversational artificial intelligence. *IEEE Xplore*. IEEE. doi:10.23919/MIPRO57284.2023.10159826

Budhwar, P., Chowdhury, S., Wood, G., Aguinis, H., Bamber, G. J., Beltran, J. R., Boselie, P., Cooke, F. L., Decker, S., DeNisi, A. S., Dey, P. K., Guest, D., Knoblich, A. J., Malik, A., Paauwe, J., Papagiannidis, S., Patel, C., Pereira, V., Ren, S., & Varma, A. (2023). Human resource management in the age of generative artificial intelligence: Perspectives and research directions on ChatGPT. *Human Resource Management Journal*, *33*(3), 606–659. doi:10.1111/1748-8583.12524

Burk, D. L. (2020). AI patents and the self-assembling machine. *Minn. L. Rev. Headnotes*, *105*, 301.

BurkD. L. (2023). Cheap Creativity and What It Will Do. *Georgia Law Review, 57*. doi:10.2139/ssrn.4397423

Burrows, S., Gurevych, I., & Stein, B. (2015). The eras and trends of automatic short answer grading. *International Journal of Artificial Intelligence in Education*, *25*(1), 60–117. doi:10.1007/s40593-014-0026-8

Burton, E., Goldsmith, J., Koenig, S., Kuipers, B., Mattei, N., & Walsh, T. (2017). Ethical considerations in artificial intelligence courses. *AI Magazine*, *38*(2), 22–34. doi:10.1609/aimag.v38i2.2731

Byram, M. (2013). Language teaching and its contexts. *DOAJ (DOAJ: Directory of Open Access Journals)*. https://doaj.org/article/6d1dfd403f3d478385efdcaa379abfc3

Byram, M. (1997). *Teaching and assessing intercultural communicative competence*. Multilingual Matters.

Byram, M., & Wagner, M. (2018). Making a Difference: Language teaching for intercultural and international dialogue. *Foreign Language Annals*, *51*(1), 140–151. doi:10.1111/flan.12319

Campolo, A., Sanfilippo, M. R., Whittaker, M., & Crawford, K. (2017). *AI Now 2017 Report*. AI Now Institute at New York University. https://ainowinstitute.org/AI_Now_2017_Report.pdf

Canese, L., Cardarilli, G. C., Di Nunzio, L., Fazzolari, R., Giardino, D., Re, M., & Spanò, S. (2021). Multi-agent reinforcement learning: A review of challenges and applications. *Applied Sciences (Basel, Switzerland)*, *11*(11), 4948. doi:10.3390/app11114948

Cao, Y., Li, S., Liu, Y., Yan, Z., Dai, Y., Yu, P. S., & Sun, L. (2023). *A Comprehensive Survey of AI-Generated Content (AI): A History of Generative AI from GAN to ChatGPT.*

Cao, Y., Li, S., Liu, Y., Yan, Z., Dai, Y., Yu, P. S., & Sun, L. (2023). A comprehensive survey of ai-generated content (AIGC): A history of generative ai from GAN to ChatGPT. *ACM*, *37*(4:111). https://doi.org//arXiv.2303.04226 doi:10.48550

Capcut. (2023). *Top 10 Free AI Translators in 2023*. Capcut. https://www.capcut.com/tr-tr/resource/best-free-ai-translators

Čapek, K. (1921). *Rossum's Universal Robots*. Project Gutenberg. https://gutenberg.org/ebooks/59112

Caputi, V., & Garrido, A. (2015). Student-oriented planning of e-learning contents for Moodle. *Journal of Network and Computer Applications*, *53*, 115–127. doi:10.1016/j.jnca.2015.04.001

Carll, E., & Mitchell, B. (2023, September 26). UT Honor Code updated to combat new A.I. challenges. *The Daily Texan.* [https://thedailytexan.com/2023/09/26/151707/]

Carraccio, C., Wolfsthal, S. D., Englander, R., Ferentz, K., & Martin, C. (2002). Shifting paradigms: From flexner to competencies. *Academic Medicine*, *77*(5), 361–367. doi:10.1097/00001888-200205000-00003 PMID:12010689

Carroll, M., Lindsey, S., Chaparro, M., & Winslow, B. (2019). An applied model of learner engagement and Strategies for increasing learner engagement in the modern educational environment. *Interactive Learning Environments*, *29*(5), 757–771. doi:10.1080/10494820.2019.1636083

Cassam, Q. (2015). Stealthy vices. *Social Epistemology Review and Reply Collective*, *4*(10), 19–25.

Cassam, Q. (2018). *Vices of the mind: From the Intellectual to the Political.* Oxford University Press.

Cassidy, C. (2023, Jan 22). Queensland public schools to join NSW in banning students from ChatGPT. *The Guardian.* https://www.theguardian.com/australia-news/2023/jan/23/queensland-public-schools-to-join-nsw-in-banning-students-from-chatgpt

CAST. (2023). *UDL: The UDL Guidelines.* UDL Guidelines. http://udlguidelines.cast.org

Castelvecchi, D. (2016). Can we open the black box of AI? *Nature*, *538*(7623), 20–23. doi:10.1038/538020a PMID:27708329

Castillo-Gonzalez, W. (2022). ChatGPT and the future of scientific communication. *Metaverse Basic and Applied Research*, *1*, 8–8. doi:10.56294/mr20228

Celik, I., Dindar, M., Muukkonen, H., & Järvelä, S. (2022). The Promises and Challenges of Artificial Intelligence for Teachers: A Systematic Review of Research. *TechTrends*, *66*(4), 616–630. doi:10.1007/s11528-022-00715-y

Center for Teaching and Learning Development & Digital Learning Center. (2023). *Guidance for Use of Generative AI Tools for Teaching and Learning*. DLC. [https://www.dlc.ntu.edu.tw/en/ai-tools-

Center for Teaching and Learning. (2023). *Think, pair, share.* Kent State University. https://www.kent.edu/ctl/think-pair-share#:~:text=What,sitting%20near%20them%20(PAIR)

Cevikbas, M., & Kaiser, G. (2022). Promoting personalized learning in flipped classrooms: A systematic review study. *Sustainability (Basel)*, *14*(18), 11393. doi:10.3390/su141811393

Chamorro-Atalaya, O., Alvarado-Bravo, N., Aldana-Trejo, F., Huarcaya-Godoy, M., Santos, M., Santos, J., & Fierro-Bravo, M. (2022). Technological tools for virtual teaching and their effect on the satisfaction of online learning. *Indonesian Journal of Electrical Engineering and Computer Science*, *25*(3), 1634. doi:10.11591/ijeecs.v25.i3.pp1634-1643

Chan, C. K. Y., & Hu, W. (2023). Students' Voices on Generative AI: Perceptions, Benefits, and Challenges in Higher Education. *arXiv preprint arXiv:2305.00290.*

Chan, C. K., & Hu, W. (2023). *Students' Voices on Generative AI: Perceptions, Benefits, and Challenges in Higher Education.* ArXiv. /abs/2305.00290

Chan, C.K. (2023). Is AI changing the rules of academic misconduct? An In-depth look at students' perceptions of 'AI-giarism'. *ArXiv, abs/2306.03358.*

Chan, C. K. Y. (2023). A comprehensive AI policy education framework for university teaching and learning. *International Journal of Educational Technology in Higher Education*, *20*(1), 1–25. doi:10.1186/s41239-023-00408-3

Chang, C. H., & Kidman, G. (2023). The rise of generative artificial intelligence (AI) language models-challenges and opportunities for geographical and environmental education. *International Research in Geographical and Environmental Education, 32*(2), 85–89. doi:10.1080/10382046.2023.2194036

Chang, D., Lin, M. P., Hajian, S., & Wang, Q. Q. (2023). Educational design principles of using AI chatbot that supports Self-Regulated learning in education: Goal setting, feedback, and personalization. *Sustainability (Basel), 15*(17), 12921. doi:10.3390/su151712921

Chant, C. (2002). *A Century of Triumph: The History of Aviation.* Simon and Schuster.

ChatDOC. (n.d.). *ChatDOC: Chat with documents. Get instant answers with cited sources.* https://chatdoc.com

Chaudhry, M. A., & Kazim, E. (2022). Artificial Intelligence in Education (AIEd): A high-level academic and industry note 2021. *AI and Ethics, 2*(1), 1–9. doi:10.1007/s43681-021-00074-z PMID:34790953

Chavanayarn, S. (2023). Navigating Ethical Complexities Through Epistemological Analysis of ChatGPT. *Bulletin of Science, Technology & Society, 02704676231216355*(3-4), 105–114. doi:10.1177/02704676231216355

Cheatham, B., Javanmardian, K., & Samandari, H. (2019). Confronting the risks of artificial intelligence. *McKinsey Quarterly.* https://www.mckinsey.com/capabilities/quantumblack/our-insights/confronting-the-risks-of-artificial-intelligence

Cheikh, A., Gorincour, G., Nivet, H., May, J., Seux, M., Calame, P., Thomson, V., Delabrousse, E., & Crombé, A. (2022). How artificial intelligence improves radiological interpretation in suspected pulmonary embolism. *European Radiology, 32*(9), 5831–5842. doi:10.1007/s00330-022-08645-2 PMID:35316363

Chen, L., Chen, P., & Lin, Z. (2020). Artificial intelligence in education: A review. *IEEE Access, 8*(2169-3536), 75264–75278. doi:10.1109/ACCESS.2020.2988510

Chen, S. (2023). *10 Best 2023 AI Data Visualization Tools of the Decade.* Digital Phablet. https://www.digitalphablet.com/tr/ai/en-iyi-AI-veri-g%C3%B6rselle%C5%9Ftirme-ara%C3%A7lar%C4%B1/

Cheng, C., Chen, C., Fu, C., Chaou, C., Wu, Y., Hsu, C., Chang, C.-C., Chung, I.-F., Hsieh, C.-H., Hsieh, M.-J., & Liao, C. (2020). Artificial intelligence-based education assists medical students' interpretation of hip fracture. *Insights Into Imaging, 11*(1), 119. doi:10.1186/s13244-020-00932-0 PMID:33226480

Chen, J. J., & Perez, C. (2023). Enhancing Assessment and Personalized Learning Through Artificial Intelligence. *Childhood Education, 99*(6), 72–79. doi:10.1080/00094056.2023.2282903

Chesterman, S. (2023). AI-generated content is taking over the world. But who owns it? *NUS Law Working Paper No. 2023/002.* doi:10.2139/ssrn.4321596

Chiu, T. K. F. (2023). The impact of Generative AI (GenAI) on practices, policies and research direction in education: A case of ChatGPT and Midjourney. *Interactive Learning Environments*, 1–17. doi:10.1080/10494820.2023.2253861

Chiu, T. K., Meng, H., Chai, C. S., King, I., Wong, S., & Yam, Y. (2021). Creation and evaluation of a pretertiary artificial intelligence (AI) curriculum. *IEEE Transactions on Education, 65*(1), 30–39. doi:10.1109/TE.2021.3085878

Chiu, T. K., Moorhouse, B. L., Chai, C. S., & Ismailov, M. (2023). Teacher support and student motivation to learn with Artificial Intelligence (AI) based chatbot. *Interactive Learning Environments*, 1–17. doi:10.1080/10494820.2023.2172044

Chiu, T., & Chai, C. (2020). Sustainable curriculum planning for artificial intelligence education: A self-determination theory perspective. *Sustainability (Basel), 12*(14), 5568. doi:10.3390/su12145568

Choi, C. W., Kim, B. R., Park, J. S., & Youn, S. W. (2018). Both educational lectures and reference photographs are necessary to improve the accuracy and reliability of Psoriasis Area and Severity Index (PASI) assessment: Results from Korean nation-wide PASI educational workshop. *Annals of Dermatology*, *30*(3), 284–289. doi:10.5021/ad.2018.30.3.284 PMID:29853741

Chounta, I., Bardone, E., Raudsep, A., & Pedaste, M. (2021). Exploring Teachers' Perceptions of Artificial Intelligence as a Tool to Support their Practice in Estonian K-12 Education. *International Journal of Artificial Intelligence in Education*, *32*(3), 725–755. doi:10.1007/s40593-021-00243-5

Christudas, B. C. L., Kirubakaran, E., & Thangaiah, P. R. J. (2018). An evolutionary approach for personalization of content delivery in e-learning systems based on learner behavior forcing compatibility of learning materials. *Telematics and Informatics*, *35*(3), 520–533. doi:10.1016/j.tele.2017.02.004

Chubb, J., Cowling, P., & Reed, D. (2021). Speeding up to keep up: Exploring the use of AI in the research process. *AI & Society*, *37*(4), 1439–1457. doi:10.1007/s00146-021-01259-0 PMID:34667374

Ciampa, K., Wolfe, Z. M., & Bronstein, B. (2023). ChatGPT in education: Transforming digital literacy practices. *Journal of Adolescent & Adult Literacy*, *67*(3), 186–195. doi:10.1002/jaal.1310

Cingillioğlu, I. (2023). Detecting AI-generated essays: The ChatGPT challenge. *The International Journal of Information and Learning Technology*, *40*(3), 259–268. doi:10.1108/IJILT-03-2023-0043

Clark, D., Tanner-Smith, E., & Killingsworth, S. (2018). Digital games, design and learning: A systematic review and meta-analysis. *Review of Educational Research*, *86*(1), 79–122. doi:10.3102/0034654315582065 PMID:26937054

Clarke, M. (2023). *Australian framework for generative artificial intelligence (AI) in schools - separtment of education, Australian government*. Department of education. https://www.education.gov.au/schooling/resources/australian-framework-generative-artificial-intelligence-ai-schools

Clark, R. C., & Mayer, R. E. (2011). *E-Learning and the science of instruction: Proven guidelines for consumers and designers of multimedia learning*. Pfeiffer. doi:10.1002/9781118255971

Clark, T. (2023). Investigating the use of an artificial intelligence chatbot with general chemistry exam questions. *Journal of Chemical Education*, *100*(5), 1905–1916. doi:10.1021/acs.jchemed.3c00027

Cocking, D., & Van den Hoven, J. (2018). *Evil online*. John Wiley & Sons. doi:10.1002/9781119471219

Cole, M. L., Cox, J. D., & Stavros, J. M. (2019). Building collaboration in teams through emotional intelligence: Mediation by SOAR (strengths, opportunities, aspirations, and results). *Journal of Management & Organization*, *25*(2), 263–283. doi:10.1017/jmo.2016.43

Colomo-Magaña, E., Soto-Varela, R., Ruiz-Palmero, J., & Gómez-García, M. (2020). University students' perception of the usefulness of the flipped classroom methodology. *Education Sciences*, *10*(10), 275. doi:10.3390/educsci10100275

Colom, R., Karama, S., Jung, R., & Haier, R. (2010). Human intelligence and brain networks. *Neurocircuitry of Cognition, Emotion, and Behavior*, *12*(4), 489–501. doi:10.31887/DCNS.2010.12.4/rcolom PMID:21319494

Cong-Lem, N. (2022). Vygotsky's, Leontiev's, and Engestrom's cultural-historical (activity) theories: Overview, clarifications, and implications. *Integrative Psychological & Behavioral Science*, *56*(4), 1091–1112. doi:10.1007/s12124-022-09703-6 PMID:35680721

Cordova, D. I., & Lepper, M. R. (1996). Intrinsic motivation and the process of learning: Beneficial effects of contextualization, personalization, and choice. *Journal of Educational Psychology*, *88*(4), 715–730. doi:10.1037/0022-0663.88.4.715

Corrêa, N. K., Galvão, C. B., Santos, J. W., Pino, C. D., Pinto, E. P., Barbosa, C., Massmann, D., Mambrini, R., Galvao, L., & Terem, E. (2022). Worldwide AI ethics: A review of 200 guidelines and recommendations for AI governance. *Patterns (New York, N.Y.)*, *4*(10), 100857. doi:10.1016/j.patter.2023.100857 PMID:37876898

Cotton, D. R. E., Cotton, P. A., & Shipway, J. R. (2023). Chatting and cheating: Ensuring academic integrity in the era of ChatGPT. *Innovations in Education and Teaching International*, 1–12. doi:10.1080/14703297.2023.2190148

Council of Europe. (2018). Council Recommendation of 22 May 2018 on key competences for lifelong learning. In *Official Journal of the European Union*. https://eur-lex.europa.eu/legal-content/EN/TXT/PDF/?uri=CELEX:32018H0604(01)

Cranefield, J., Winikoff, M., Chiu, Y.-T., Li, Y., Doyle, C., & Richter, A. (2023). Partnering with AI: The case of digital productivity assistants. *Journal of the Royal Society of New Zealand*, *53*(1), 95–118. doi:10.1080/03036758.2022.2114507

Crawford, J., Cowling, M., & Allen, K.-A. (2023). Leadership is needed for ethical ChatGPT: Character, assessment, and learning using artificial intelligence (AI). *Journal of University Teaching & Learning Practice*, *20*(3). doi:10.53761/1.20.3.02

Creely, E. (2022). Conceiving Creativity and Learning in a World of Artificial Intelligence: A Thinking Model. In D. Henriksen & P. Mishra (Eds.), *Creative Provocations: Speculations on the Future of Creativity, Technology & Learning* (pp. 35–50). Springer International Publishing. doi:10.1007/978-3-031-14549-0_3

Creely, E., Apps, T., Beckman, K., & McKnight, L. (2023). Chat About ChatGPT. *Literacy Learning: The Middle Years*, *31*(2), 35–39.

Crerar, C. (2018). Motivational approaches to intellectual vice. *Australasian Journal of Philosophy*, *96*(4), 753–766. doi:10.1080/00048402.2017.1394334

Crompton, H., & Burke, D. (2023). Artificial intelligence in higher education: The state of the field. *International Journal of Educational Technology in Higher Education*, *20*(1), 22. Advance online publication. doi:10.1186/s41239-023-00392-8

Cronan, T., McHaney, R., Douglas, D., & Mullins, J. (2016). Changing the academic integrity climate on campus using a technology-based intervention. *Ethics & Behavior*, *27*(2), 89–105. doi:10.1080/10508422.2016.1161514

Crosbie, V. (2014). Capabilities for intercultural dialogue. *Language and Intercultural Communication*, *14*(1), 91–107. doi:10.1080/14708477.2013.866126

Crystal, D. (2003). *English as a global language*. Cambridge university press. doi:10.1017/CBO9780511486999

Czaplinski, I., & Huijser, H. (2023). The role and application of learning theories in the virtual University. In M. D. Sankey, H. Huijser, & R. Fitzgerald (Eds.), *Technology-Enhanced Learning and the Virtual University. University Development and Administration* (pp. 227–244). Springer., doi:10.1007/978-981-19-9438-8_13-1

D'aquin, M., Troullinou, P., O'Connor, N., Cullen, A., Faller, G., & Holden, L. (2018). *Towards an "ethics by design" methodology for AI research projects.* In *Proceedings of the 2018 ACM Conference on AI, Ethics, and Society* (pp.54-59). New Orleans, LA, USA. 10.1145/3278721.3278765

D'Mello, S., Picard, R. W., & Graesser, A. (2007). Toward an affect-sensitive AutoTutor. *IEEE Intelligent Systems*, *22*(4), 53–61. doi:10.1109/MIS.2007.79

Dalbani, H., Eissa, S., Fatimah, S., & Almusharraf, N. (2021). Transitioning to Flipped Classrooms: Instructors' Perspectives. *Sustainability (Basel)*, *14*(20), 13426. doi:10.3390/su142013426

Darda, K., Carre, M., & Cross, E. (2023). Value attributed to text-based archives generated by artificial intelligence. *Royal Society Open Science*, *10*(2), 220915. doi:10.1098/rsos.220915 PMID:36778947

Dascalu, M., McNamara, D. S., Trausan-Matu, S., & Allen, L. K. (2018). Cohesion network analysis of CSCL participation. *Behavior Research Methods*, *50*(2), 604–619. doi:10.3758/s13428-017-0888-4 PMID:28409485

David Baidoo-Anu1, D. and Ansah, L. O. (2023). Education in the Era of Generative Artificial Intelligence (AI): Understanding the Potential Benefits of ChatGPT in Promoting Teaching and Learning. *Journal of AI, 7*(1), 52-62.

Dawson, M. R., & Lignugaris, B. (2016). Meaningful practice. *Teacher Education and Special Education*, *40*(1), 26–50. doi:10.1177/0888406416664184

De Bem Machado, A., Dandolini, G. A., de Souza, J. A., Lytras, M. D., & Sousa, M. J. (2023). Artificial Intelligence: Applicability of This Technology to Higher Education–A Scoping Review. *Technologies for Sustainable Global Higher Education*, 211-236.

De Bem Machado, A., Sousa, M. J., & Dandolini, G. A. (2022, April). Digital Learning Technologies in Higher Education: A Bibliometric Study. In *Proceedings of International Conference on Information Technology and Applications: ICITA 2021* (pp. 697-705). Springer Nature Singapore. 10.1007/978-981-16-7618-5_59

De Gagne, J. C., Hwang, H., & Jung, D. (2023). Cyberethics in nursing education: Ethical implications of artificial intelligence. *Nursing Ethics*, 09697330231201901. doi:10.1177/09697330231201901 PMID:37803810

Dean, B. A., Campbell, M., Shalavin, C., & Eady, M. J. (2023). Preparing students for the future of work and the role of the virtual. University development and administration (pp. 375-392). https://doi.org/ doi:10.1007/978-981-19-9438-8_19-1

Dede, C. (2010). Comparing frameworks for 21st century skills. In J. Bellance & R.Brandt (Eds.), *21st century skills: Rethinking how students learn (pp. 51-76).* Solution Tree Press. https://allchildrenlearning.org/wp-content/uploads/2019/12/Dede_2010_Comparing-Frameworks-for-21st-Century-Skills.pdf

Deepbrain, A. I. (2003). *Creating generative AI videos with just a script.* https://www.deepbrain.io

Dee, T., & Jacob, B. (2012). Rational ignorance in education: A field experiment in student plagiarism. *The Journal of Human Resources*, *47*(2), 397–434. doi:10.3368/jhr.47.2.397

Dehouche, N., & Dehouche, K. (2023). What's in a text-to-image prompt? The potential of stable diffusion in visual arts education. *Heliyon*, *9*(6), e16757. doi:10.1016/j.heliyon.2023.e16757 PMID:37292268

Delgado, F., Yang, S., Madaio, M., & Yang, Q. (2023). The Participatory Turn in AI Design: Theoretical Foundations and the Current State of Practice. *Proceedings of the 3rd ACM Conference on Equity and Access in Algorithms, Mechanisms, and Optimization*, (pp. 1–23). ACM. 10.1145/3617694.3623261

Dell'Osso, L., Amatori, G., Muti, D., Giovannoni, F., Parri, F., Violi, M., Cremone, I. M., & Carpita, B. (2023). Autism Spectrum, Hikikomori Syndrome and Internet Gaming Disorder: Is There a Link? *Brain Sciences*, *13*(7), 1116. doi:10.3390/brainsci13071116 PMID:37509046

Deltorn, J.-M., & Macrez, F. (2018). Authorship in the Age of Machine learning and Artificial Intelligence (August 1, 2018). In: Sean M. O'Connor (ed.), The Oxford Handbook of Music Law and Policy. Centre for International Intellectual Property Studies (CEIPI) Research Paper No. 2018-10. doi:10.2139/ssrn.3261329

Demirdöken, G. (2021). The Constructivist Approach towards Identifying the Challenges of ESP Teachers: The Case of Aviation English. *International Journal of Aviation, Aeronautics, and Aerospace*, *8*(2), 1–18. doi:10.15394/ijaaa.2021.1571

Demirdöken, G., & Okur, S. (2023). Psychometric properties of speaking anxiety scale and an interdisciplinary investigation with serial mediation analysis. *Innovation in Language Learning and Teaching*, *17*(3), 706–722. doi:10.1080/17501229.2022.2123920

Dempere, J., Modugu, K., Hesham, A., & Ramasamy, L. K. (2023). The impact of ChatGPT on higher education. *Frontiers in Education*, *8*, 1206936. https://www.frontiersin.org/articles/10.3389/feduc.2023.1206936. doi:10.3389/feduc.2023.1206936

Deng, L., & Liu, Y. (2018). A joint introduction to natural language processing and to deep learning. Deng, L., & Liu, Y. (Eds.), Deep learning in natural language processing (pp. 1-22). Singapore: Springer. doi:10.1007/978-981-10-5209-5_1

Dergaa, I., Chamari, K., Zmijewski, P., & Saad, H. B. (2023). From human writing to artificial intelligence generated text: Examining the prospects and potential threats of ChatGPT in academic writing. *Biology of Sport*, *40*(2), 615–622. doi:10.5114/biolsport.2023.125623 PMID:37077800

Descartes, R. (1637). *Discourse on the Method of Rightly Conducting One's Reason and of Seeking Truth in the Sciences*. Project Gutenberg. https://www.gutenberg.org/files/59/59-h/59-h.htm

Dewar, J. A. (1998). *The information age and the printing press: Looking backward to see ahead*. RAND Corporation. https://www.rand.org/content/dam/rand/pubs/papers/2005/P8014.pdf

Diakopoulos, N. (2016). Accountability in algorithmic decision making. *Communications of the ACM*, *59*(2), 56–62. doi:10.1145/2844110

Dignum, V. (2021). The role and challenges of education for responsible AI. *London Review of Education*, *19*(1). doi:10.14324/LRE.19.1.01

Dillon, E., Tai-Seale, M., Meehan, A., Martin, V., Nordgren, R., Lee, T., Nauenberg, T., & Frosch, D. (2019). Frontline perspectives on physician burnout and strategies to improve well-being: Interviews with physicians and health system leaders. *Journal of General Internal Medicine*, *35*(1), 261–267. doi:10.1007/s11606-019-05381-0 PMID:31659668

Dilmaghani, S., Brust, M. R., Danoy, G., Cassagnes, N., Pecero, J., & Bouvry, P. (2019, December 1). *Privacy and Security of Big Data in AI Systems: A Research and Standards Perspective*. IEEE Xplore. doi:10.1109/BigData47090.2019.9006283

Dinçer, N., & Demirdöken, G. (2023). Ab-initio pilots' perspectives on the use of simulation in the aviation English course. *Journal of Teaching English for Specific and Academic Purposes, 11*(1) 011-022. doi:10.22190/JTESAP230130003D

Dinçer, N. (2023). Elevating Aviation Education: A Comprehensive Examination of Technology's Role in Modern Flight Training. *Journal of Aviation*, *7*(2), 317–323. doi:10.30518/jav.1279718

Dinçer, N.Dinçer. (2023). The Role of Serious Games in Effective Aviation English. *Applied Linguistic Papers*, *27*(1), 72–82. doi:10.32612/uw.25449354.2023.1.pp.72-83

Dinçer, N., & Dinçer, R. (2021). The effect of a serious game on aviation vocabulary acquisition. *International Journal of Serious Games*, *8*(4), 49–63. doi:10.17083/ijsg.v8i4.464

Dirkx, K., Joosten-ten Brinke, D., Arts, J., & van Diggelen, M. (2021). In-text and rubric-referenced feedback: Differences in focus, level, and function. *Active Learning in Higher Education*, *22*(3), 189–201. doi:10.1177/1469787419855208

Doğan, S. (2023). *Rask ai ile video çeviri ve dublaj [Video translation and dubbing with Rask ai]*. Yapay Zekâ Günlükleri [Artificial Intelligence Chronicles]. https://www.yapayzekagunlukleri.com/yapay-zeka-uygulamalari/video/rask-ai-ile-video-ceviri-ve-dublaj/

Dogan, M. E., Goru Dogan, T., & Bozkurt, A. (2023). The use of artificial intelligence (AI) in online learning and distance education processes: A systematic review of empirical studies. *Applied Sciences (Basel, Switzerland)*, *13*(5), 3056. doi:10.3390/app13053056

Doğan, Y., Batdı, V., & Yaşar, M. D. (2023). Effectiveness of flipped classroom practices in teaching of science: A mixed research synthesis. *Research in Science & Technological Education, 41*(1), 393–421. doi:10.1080/02635143.2021.1909553

Dogru, T., Line, N., Hanks, L., Acikgoz, F., Abbott, J. A., Bakir, S., Berbekova, A., Bilgihan, A., Iskender, A., Kizildag, M., Lee, M., Lee, W., McGinley, S., Mody, M., Onder, I., Ozdemir, O., & Suess, C. (2023). The implications of generative artificial intelligence in academic research and higher education in tourism and hospitality. *Tourism Economics, 0*(0), 13548166231204065. doi:10.1177/13548166231204065

Dollinger, S. J., & Dollinger, S. C. (2017). Creativity and Identity. In M. Karwowski & J. C. Kaufman (Eds.), *The Creative Self* (pp. 49–64). Academic Press. doi:10.1016/B978-0-12-809790-8.00003-0

Dong, S., Wang, P., & Abbas, K. (2021). A survey on deep learning and its applications. *Computer Science Review, 40*, 100379. doi:10.1016/j.cosrev.2021.100379

DoshiA. R.HauserO. (2023). Generative Artificial Intelligence Enhances Creativity (August 8, 2023). doi:10.2139/ssrn.4535536

Dron, J. (2022). Educational technology: What it is and how it works. *AI & Society, 37*(1), 155–166. doi:10.1007/s00146-021-01195-z

du Boulay, B. (2015). Recent Meta-reviews and Meta–analyses of AIED Systems. *International Journal of Artificial Intelligence in Education, 26*(1), 536–537. doi:10.1007/s40593-015-0060-1

Duda, M., Daniels, J., & Wall, D. P. (2016). Clinical evaluation of a novel and mobile autism risk assessment. *Journal of Autism and Developmental Disorders, 46*(6), 1953–1961. doi:10.1007/s10803-016-2718-4 PMID:26873142

Duda, M., Ma, R., Haber, N., & Wall, D. P. (2016). Use of machine learning for behavioral distinction of autism and ADHD. *Translational Psychiatry, 6*(2), e732–e732. doi:10.1038/tp.2015.221 PMID:26859815

Dufresne, R. (2004). An action learning perspective on effective implementation of academic honor codes. *Group & Organization Management, 29*(2), 201–218. doi:10.1177/1059601103261472

Durable. (2023). *Durable: Build a website in 30 seconds using artificial intelligence.* Durable. https://durable.co/ai-website-builder

Dwivedi, Y. K., Kshetri, N., Hughes, L., Slade, E. L., Jeyaraj, A., Kar, A. K., Baabdullah, A. M., Koohang, A., Raghavan, V., Ahuja, M., Albanna, H., Albashrawi, M. A., Al-Busaidi, A. S., Balakrishnan, J., Barlette, Y., Basu, S., Bose, I., Brooks, L., Buhalis, D., & Wright, R. (2023). Opinion Paper: "So what if ChatGPT wrote it?" Multidisciplinary perspectives on opportunities, challenges and implications of generative conversational AI for research, practice and policy. *International Journal of Information Management, 71*, 102642. doi:10.1016/j.ijinfomgt.2023.102642

Dyulicheva, Y. Y., & Glazieva, A. O. (2022). Game based learning with artificial intelligence and immersive technologies: An overview. *CEUR Workshop Proceedings, 3077*, 146–159.

Eager, B., & Brunton, R. (2023). Prompting higher education towards AI-augmented teaching and learning practice. *Journal of University Teaching & Learning Practice, 20*(5), 02.

Eager, B., & Brunton, R. (2023). Prompting higher education towards ai-augmented teaching and learning practice. *Journal of University Teaching & Learning Practice, 20*(5). doi:10.53761/1.20.5.02

Eapen, T. T., Finkenstadt, D. J., Folk, J., & Venkataswamy, L. (2023). How Generative AI Can Augment Human Creativity. (cover story). *Harvard Business Review, 101*(4), 56–64.

Edalex, (October 25th, 2023). *21st century skills: What they are and why they are important.* Edalax. https://www.edalex.com/guides/21st-century-skills-what-they-are-why-important

Eddy, L. L. (2013). *Caring for children with special heath care needs and their families: A handbook for health care professionals.* Wiley-Blackwell. Fisher, M., & Jacobs, H.H. (20223). Prompt literacy: A key for AI-Based Learning. *Educational Leadership, 80*(9), 18–19. https://www.ascd.org/el/articles/prompt-literacy-a-key-for-ai-based-learning

Edwards, C., Edwards, A., Spence, P. R., & Lin, X. (2018). I, teacher: Using artificial intelligence (AI) and social robots in communication and instruction. *Communication Education, 67*(4), 473–480. doi:10.1080/03634523.2018.1502459

EisfeldtA. L.SchubertG.ZhangM. B. (2023). Generative AI and Firm Values (May 2, 2023). doi:10.3386/w31222

Eke, D. O. (2023). ChatGPT and the rise of generative AI: Threat to academic integrity? *Journal of Responsible Technology, 13*, 100060. doi:10.1016/j.jrt.2023.100060

Ekin, S. (2023). *Prompt Engineering For ChatGPT: A Quick Guide To Techniques.* Tips, And Best Practices.

Elakkiya, M. K., & Dejey. (2024). Novel deep learning models with novel integrated activation functions for autism screening: AutiNet and MinAutiNet. *Expert Systems with Applications, 238*, 122102. doi:10.1016/j.eswa.2023.122102

Elbanna, S., & Armstrong, L. (2023). Exploring the integration of ChatGPT in education: adapting for the future. *Management & Sustainability: An Arab Review.*

Elbasi, E., Mostafa, N., AlArnaout, Z., Zreikat, A. I., Cina, E., Varghese, G., Shdefat, A., Topcu, A. E., Abdelbaki, W., Mathew, S., & Zaki, C. (2022). Artificial Intelligence Technology in the Agricultural Sector: A Systematic Literature Review. *IEEE Access : Practical Innovations, Open Solutions, 11*, 171–202. doi:10.1109/ACCESS.2022.3232485

Elias, A., & Mansouri, F. (2020). A Systematic review of studies on interculturalism and Intercultural dialogue. *Journal of Intercultural Studies (Melbourne, Vic.), 41*(4), 490–523. doi:10.1080/07256868.2020.1782861

Elicit. (n.d.). *Analyze research papers at superhuman speed.* Elicit. https://elicit.com

Elisa, F., Cesta, A., Umbrico, A., & Orlandini, A. (2021). Simplifying the A.I. planning modeling for human-robot collaboration. *IEEE International Symposium on Robot and Human Interactive Communication (RO-MAN).* IEEE. 10.1109/RO-MAN50785.2021.9515431

Elkhatat, A. M. (2023). Evaluating the authenticity of ChatGPT responses: A study on text-matching capabilities. *International Journal for Educational Integrity, 19*(1), 15. doi:10.1007/s40979-023-00137-0

Else, H. (2023). Abstracts written by ChatGPT fool scientists. *Nature, 613*(7944), 423–423. doi:10.1038/d41586-023-00056-7 PMID:36635510

Elsevier. (n.d.). *The use of AI and AI-assisted technologies in writing for Elsevier.* Elsevier. https://www.elsevier.com/en-in/about/policies-and-standards/the-use-of-generative-ai-and-ai-assisted-technologies-in-writing-for-elsevier

Emenike, M. E., & Emenike, B. U. (2023). Was this title generated by ChatGPT? Considerations for artificial intelligence text-generation software programs for chemists and chemistry educators. *Journal of Chemical Education, 100*(4), 1413–1418. doi:10.1021/acs.jchemed.3c00063

Engel, A., & Coll, C. (2022). Hybrid teaching and learning environments to promote personalized learning. *RIED-Revista Iberoamericana de Educacion a Distancia*, 225-242.

Eom, S. B., & Ashill, N. (2016). The determinants of students' perceived learning outcomes and satisfaction in university online education: An update. *Decision Sciences Journal of Innovative Education, 14*(2), 185–215. doi:10.1111/dsji.12097

Erbil, D. G. (2020). A Review of Flipped Classroom and Cooperative Learning Method Within the Context of Vygotsky Theory. *Frontiers in Psychology*, *11*, 539791. doi:10.3389/fpsyg.2020.01157 PMID:32655437

Erisman, W., & Looney, S. (2007). *Opening the Door to the American Dream: Increasing Higher Education Access and Success for Immigrants*. Institute for Higher Education Policy.

Esenogho, E., Djouani, K., & Kurien, A. (2022). Integrating artificial intelligence internet of things and 5g for next-generation smart grid: A survey of trends challenges and prospect. *IEEE Access : Practical Innovations, Open Solutions*, *10*, 4794–4831. doi:10.1109/ACCESS.2022.3140595

Etzioni, A., & Etzioni, O. (2016). AI assisted ethics. *Ethics and Information Technology*, *18*(2), 149–156. doi:10.1007/s10676-016-9400-6

European Commission. (2019). *The European Commission's high-level expert group on artificial intelligence: Ethics guidelines for trustworthy AI.* The European Commission. https://digital-strategy.ec.europa.eu/en/library/ethics-guidelines-trustworthy-ai

European Commission. (2020). *White Paper on Artificial Intelligence: a European approach to excellence and trust* (White Paper No. COM(2020) 65 final). European Commission. https://ec.europa.eu/info/publications/white-paper-artificial-intelligence-european-approach-excellence-and-trust_en

European Commission. (2022). *Ethical guidelines on the use of artificial intelligence (AI) and data in teaching and learning for educat*ors. The European Commission. https://op.europa.eu/en/publication-detail/-/publication/d81a0d54-5348-11ed-92ed-01aa75ed71a1/language-en

European Strategy Framework: For Improving and Increasing Global Education In Europe to the Year 2015 (The "Maastricht Global Education Declaration"). (2002). In *Europe-wide Global Education Congress*. https://rm.coe.int/168070e540

Eysenbach, G. (2023). The Role of ChatGPT, Generative Language Models, and Artificial Intelligence in Medical Education: A Conversation With ChatGPT and a Call for Papers. *JMIR Medical Education*, *9*, e46885. doi:10.2196/46885 PMID:36863937

Fainman, I., & Tokar, Y. (2019). Explicit, Implicit, and Blended Vocabulary Instruction: Efficiency in an Aviation English Course. *Collegiate Aviation Review International, 37*(2), 110-132. https://ojs.library.okstate.edu/osu/index.php/CARI/article/view/7911/7306

Falode, O. C., & Mohammed, I. A. (2023). Improving students' geography achievement using computer simulation and animation packages in flipped classroom settings. *Journal of Digital Educational Technology*, *3*(2), ep2303. doi:10.30935/jdet/13106

Fang, X., Ng, D. T. K., Leung, J. K. L., & Chu, S. K. W. (2023). A systematic review of artificial intelligence technologies used for story writing. *Education and Information Technologies*, *28*(11), 14361–14397. doi:10.1007/s10639-023-11741-5

Fantini, A. E. (2012). Language: an essential component of intercultural communicative competence. The Routledge Handbook of Language and Intercultural Communication, 263–278. https://doi.org/ doi:10.4324/9780203805640-29

Federal Aviation Administration (FAA). (2016). *Advisory Circular: English Language Skill Standards Required by 14 CFR 61, 63, and 65.* FAA. https://www.faa.gov/documentLibrary/media/Advisory_Circular/AC_60-28B.pdf

Feng, Y., Vanam, S., Cherukupally, M., Zheng, W., Qiu, M., & Chen, H. (2023). Investigating Code Generation Performance of Chat-GPT with Crowdsourcing Social Data. In *Proceedings of the 47th IEEE Computer Software and Applications Conference* (pp. 1-10). IEEE.

Fenwick, M., & Jurcys, P. (2023). Originality and the Future of Copyright in an Age of Generative AI. *SSRN, 4354449*. https://ssrn.com/abstract=4354449

Fidan, M. (2023). The effects of microlearning-supported flipped classroom on pre- service teachers' learning performance, motivation and engagement. *Education and Information Technologies*, *28*(10), 1–28. doi:10.1007/s10639-023-11639-2 PMID:37361810

Filip, F. G. (2021, May). AI vs AI (augmenting [human] intellect vs artificial intelligence): Plenary talk. In *2021 IEEE 15th International Symposium on Applied Computational Intelligence and Informatics (SACI)* (pp. 000011-000012). IEEE.

Filiz, O. (2023). *Grammarly*. Eğitim Çantası [Education Bag]. https://egitimcantasi.com/uygulamalar/grammarly/

Fisher, M., Goddu, M. K., & Keil, F. C. (2015). Searching for explanations: How the internet inflates estimates of internal knowledge. *Journal of Experimental Psychology. General*, *144*(3), 674–687. doi:10.1037/xge0000070 PMID:25822461

Floridi, L., Cowls, J., Beltrametti, M., Chatila, R., Chazerand, P., Dignum, V., & Vayena, E. (2021). An ethical framework for a good AI society: Opportunities, risks, principles, and recommendations. *Ethics, governance, and policies in artificial intelligence*, 19-39. doi:10.1007/978-3-030-81907-1_3

Forman, J., & Damschroder, L. (2008). Qualitative content analysis. In *Empirical research for bioethics: A primer* (pp. 39–62). Emerald Group Publishing Limited. doi:10.1016/S1479-3709(07)11003-7

Foucault, M. (1972/2010). *The archaeology of knowledge and the discourse on language*. Vintage Books.

Framer. (2023). *Generate and publish your site with AI in seconds*. https://www.framer.com/ai

Friesen, N. (2017). *The textbook and the lecture: Education in the age of new media*. Johns Hopkins University Press. doi:10.1353/book.56899

Fui-Hoon Nah, F., Zheng, R., Cai, J., Siau, K., & Chen, L. (2023). Generative AI and ChatGPT: Applications, challenges, and AI-human collaboration. *Journal of Information Technology Case and Application Research*, *25*(3), 277–304. doi:10.1080/15228053.2023.2233814

Gagne, R. M. (1985). *The Conditions of Learning and Theory of Instruction* (4th ed.). Holt, Rinehart and Winston.

Gallardo-Guerrero, A. M., Maciá-Andreu, M. J., Conde-Pascual, E., Sánchez-Sáez, J. A., Zurita-Ortiz, B., & García-Tascón, M. (2022). From flipped classroom to personalised learning as an innovative teaching methodology in the area of sports management in Physical Activity and Sport Sciences. *Sustainability (Basel)*, *14*(13), 7714. doi:10.3390/su14137714

Gamma. (2022). *A new medium presenting ideas powered by AI*. Gamma. https://gamma.app

Ganschow, L., Philips, L., & Schneider, E. (2001). Closing the gap: Accommodating students with language learning disabilities in college. *Topics in Language Disorders*, *21*(2), 17–37. doi:10.1097/00011363-200102000-00005

García-Pérez, L., García-Garnica, M., & Moreno, E. M. O. (2021). Skills for a Working Future: How to bring about professional success from the educational setting. *Education Sciences*, *11*(1), 27. doi:10.3390/educsci11010027

GaronJ. M. (2023). A Practical Introduction to Generative AI, Synthetic Media, and the Messages Found in the Latest Medium (March 14, 2023). doi:10.2139/ssrn.4388437

Gašević, D., Siemens, G., & Sadiq, S. (2023). Empowering learners for the age of artificial intelligence. *Computers and Education: Artificial Intelligence*, *4*, 100130. doi:10.1016/j.caeai.2023.100130

GaumannN.VealeM. (2023, September 7). AI providers as criminal essay mills? Large language models meet contract cheating law. doi:10.31235/osf.io/cpbfd

Gayed, J. M., Carlon, M. K. J., Oriola, A. M., & Cross, J. S. (2022). Exploring an AI-based writing assistant's impact on English language learners. *Computers and Education: Artificial Intelligence*, *3*(1), 100055. doi:10.1016/j.caeai.2022.100055

Gee, J. P. (2003). What Video Games Have to Teach Us about Learning and Literacy. *Computers in Entertainment*, *1*(1), 20. doi:10.1145/950566.950595

Geher, G. (2023). ChatGPT, artificial intelligence, and the future of writing: How ChatGPT and other ai systems may ruin the ability to write (and think). *Psychology Today*. https://www.psychologytoday.com/us/blog/darwins-subterranean-world/202301/chatgpt-artificial-intelligence-and-the-future-of-writing

Geist-Martin, P., Gates, L., Wiering, L., Kirby, E., Houston, R., Lilly, A., & Moreno, J. (2010). Exemplifying Collaborative Autoethnographic Practice Via Shared Stories of Mothering. *Journal of Research Practice*, *6*(1), M8.

George, B., & Wooden, O. (2023). Managing the strategic transformation of higher education through artificial intelligence. *Administrative Sciences*, *13*(9), 196. doi:10.3390/admsci13090196

Gernsbacher, M. A. (2015). Video captions benefit everyone. *Policy Insights from the Behavioral and Brain Sciences*, *2*(1), 195–202. doi:10.1177/2372732215602130 PMID:28066803

Ge, X., Yin, Y., & Feng, S. (2018). Application research of computer artificial intelligence in college student sports autonomous learning. *Educational Sciences: Theory & Practice*. Advance online publication. doi:10.12738/estp.2018.5.114

Giannini, S. (2023). *Reflections on generative AI and the future of education*. UNESCO. https://unesdoc.unesco.org/ark:/48223/pf0000385877

Gil, F. (2023). *Generative AI: Useful tools for teaching staff*. UOC. https://blogs.uoc.edu/elearning-innovation-center/generative-ai-useful-tools-for-teaching-staff

Gilardi, M., Holroyd, P., Newbury, P., & Watten, P. (2015). The effects of video lecture delivery formats on student engagement. In *Science and information conference (SAI)*, (pp. 791–796). IEEE. https://ieeexplore.ieee.org/document/7237234

Gillespie, S., Hanners, A., Militello, L., Newtz, C., Thrane, S., & Barr, T. (2023). The Ohio State University dream team: Innovation for wellbeing fellowship and coaching program. *Journal of Clinical and Translational Science*, 1–20. doi:10.1017/cts.2023.558 PMID:37396821

Gilliard, C., & Rorabaugh, P. (2023, February 3). *You're not Going to like How colleges respond to ChatGPT*. https://slate.com/technology/2023/02/chat-gpt-cheating-college-ai-detection.html

Gill, S. S., & Kaur, R. (2023). ChatGPT: Vision and challenges. *Internet of Things and Cyber-Physical Systems*, *3*, 262–271. doi:10.1016/j.iotcps.2023.05.004

Gill, S. S., Xu, M., Patros, P., Wu, H., Kaur, R., Kaur, K., Fuller, S., Singh, M., Arora, P., Parlikad, A. K., Stankovski, V., Abraham, A., Ghosh, S. K., Lutfiyya, H., Kanhere, S. S., Bahsoon, R., Rana, O., Dustdar, S., Sakellariou, R., & Buyya, R. (2024). Transformative effects of ChatGPT on modern education: Emerging Era of AI Chatbots. *Internet of Things and Cyber-Physical Systems*, *4*, 19–23. doi:10.1016/j.iotcps.2023.06.002

Gimpel, H., Hall, K., Decker, S., Eymann, T., Lämmermann, L., Mädche, A., & Vandrik, S. (2023). *Unlocking the power of generative AI models and systems such as GPT-4 and ChatGPT for higher education: A guide for students and lecturers (No. 02-2023)*. Hohenheim Discussion Papers in Business, Economics and Social Sciences.

Girard, C., Ecalle, J., & Magnan, A. (2013). Serious games as new educational tools: How effective are they? A meta-analysis of recent studies. *Journal of Computer Assisted Learning*, *29*(3), 207–219. doi:10.1111/j.1365-2729.2012.00489.x

Girardi, S., Gaudy, C., Gouvernet, J., Teston, J., Richard, M. A., & Grob, J.-J. (2006). Superiority of a cognitive education with photographs over ABCD criteria in the education of the general population to the early detection of melanoma: A randomized study. *International Journal of Cancer*, *118*(9), 2276–2280. doi:10.1002/ijc.21351 PMID:16331608

Giray, L. (2023). Prompt Engineering with ChatGPT: A Guide for Academic Writers. *Annals of Biomedical Engineering*, *51*(12), 2629–2633. doi:10.1007/s10439-023-03272-4 PMID:37284994

Glielmo, A., Husic, B. E., Rodriguez, A., Clementi, C., Noé, F., & Laio, A. (2021). Unsupervised learning methods for molecular simulation data. *Chemical Reviews*, *121*(16), 9722–9758. doi:10.1021/acs.chemrev.0c01195 PMID:33945269

Göçen, A., & Aydemir, F. (2020). Artificial intelligence in education and schools. *Research on Education and Media*, *12*(1), 13–21. doi:10.2478/rem-2020-0003

Goh, M. (2012). Teaching with Cultural intelligence: Developing multiculturally educated and globally engaged citizens. *Asia Pacific Journal of Education*, *32*(4), 395–415. doi:10.1080/02188791.2012.738679

Gökçearslan, Ş. (2013). Development of online learning community feeling scale: Validity and reliability study. *Turkish Librarianship*, *27*(1), 154–165.

Gokcearslan, S., Tosun, C., & Erdemir, Z. G. (2024). Benefits, challenges, and methods of artificial intelligence (AI) chatbots in education: A systematic literature review. [IJTE]. *International Journal of Technology in Education*, *7*(1), 19–39. doi:10.46328/ijte.600

Golan, R., Reddy, R., Muthigi, A., & Ramasamy, R. (2023). Artificial intelligence in academic writing: A paradigm-shifting technological advance. *Nature Reviews. Urology*, *1-2*(6), 327–328. doi:10.1038/s41585-023-00746-x PMID:36829078

González, G., Cepeda, W., & Hernández-Rodríguez, O. (2021). Leveraging prospective teachers' knowledge through their participation in lesson study. *Journal of Mathematics Teacher Education*, *26*(1), 79–102. doi:10.1007/s10857-021-09521-4

Goodfellow, I., Pouget-Abadie, J., Mirza, M., Xu, B., Warde-Farley, D., Ozair, S., Courville, A., & Bengio, Y. (2014). Generative adversarial nets. *Advances in Neural Information Processing Systems*, *27*, 2672–2680.

Goodfellow, I., Pouget-Abadie, J., Mirza, M., Xu, B., Warde-Farley, D., Ozair, S., Courville, A., & Bengio, Y. (2020). Generative adversarial networks. *Communications of the ACM*, *63*(11), 139–144. https://dl.acm.org/doi/pdf/10.1145/3422622. doi:10.1145/3422622

Google. (2023). *Update the trial version.* Google. https://bard.google.com/updates

GPT-3. (2020). A robot wrote this entire article. Are you scared yet, human? *The Guardian.* https://www.theguardian.com/commentisfree/2020/sep/08/robot-wrote-this-article-gpt-3

Graham, S., Depp, C., Lee, E., Nebeker, C., Tu, X., Kim, H., & Jeste, D. (2019). Artificial intelligence for mental health and mental illnesses: An overview. *Current Psychiatry Reports*, *21*(11), 116. Advance online publication. doi:10.1007/s11920-019-1094-0 PMID:31701320

Grassini, S. (2023). Shaping the future of education: Exploring the potential and consequences of AI and ChatGPT in educational settings. *Education Sciences*, *13*(7), 692. doi:10.3390/educsci13070692

Graßmann, C., & Schermuly, C. C. (2021). Coaching With Artificial Intelligence: Concepts and Capabilities. *Human Resource Development Review*, *20*(1), 106–126. doi:10.1177/1534484320982891

Gray, S. L. (2020). Artificial intelligence in schools: Towards a democratic future. *London Review of Education*, *18*(2), 163–177. doi:10.14324/LRE.18.2.02

Green, B. P. (2018). Ethical reflections on artificial intelligence. *Scientia et Fides*, *6*(2), 9–31. doi:10.12775/SetF.2018.015

Greene, D., Hoffmann, A. L., & Stark, L. (2019). Better, nicer, clearer, fairer: A critical assessment of the movement for ethical artificial intelligence and machine learning. *Proceedings of the 52nd Hawaii International Conference on System Sciences*. IEEE. 10.24251/HICSS.2019.258

Gregory, L. L., & Gregory, L. M. (1996, October 4-6*). Paradigm shift: The forgotten perquisite for change.* [Paper presentation]. National Rural Education Association, Salt Lake City, UT.

Grillo, R. D. (2018). *Interculturalism and the politics of dialogue*. B and RG Books of Lewes.

Grimmelikhuijsen, S. (2023). Explaining why the computer says no: Algorithmic transparency affects the perceived trustworthiness of automated decision-making. *Public Administration Review*, *83*(2), 241–262. doi:10.1111/puar.13483

Gross, N. (2023). What ChatGPT Tells Us about Gender: A Cautionary Tale about Performativity and Gender Biases in AI. *Social Sciences (Basel, Switzerland)*, *12*(8), 8. doi:10.3390/socsci12080435

Grunhut, J., Marques, O., & Wyatt, A. (2022). Needs, challenges, and applications of artificial intelligence in medical education curriculum. *JMIR Medical Education*, *8*(2), e35587. doi:10.2196/35587 PMID:35671077

Gu, R., Xi, Z., Lin, B., & Ji, Y. (2022). Teacher-guided Autonomous Learning Enabled by Artificial Intelligence Empowered Remote Experiment Platform. In *2022 IEEE Global Engineering Education Conference (EDUCON)* (pp. 1089-1094). IEEE. https://ieeexplore.ieee.org/abstract/document/9766531/

Guerrero-Quiñonez, A. J., Guagua, O. Q., & Barrera-Proaño, R. G. (2023). Gamified flipped classroom as a pedagogical strategy in higher education: From a systematic vision. *Ibero-American Journal of Education & Society Research*, *3*(1), 238–243. doi:10.56183/iberoeds.v3i1.622

Gunn, T. M., & Hollingsworth, M. (2012) Improving Student Engagement with 21st Century Learning Practices. *Northwest Journal of Teacher Education, 10*(1), 1-12. https://pdxscholar.library.pdx.edu/nwjte/vol10/iss1/1 doi:10.15760/nwjte.2012.10.1.1

Guo, P. J., Kim, J., & Rubin, R. (2014). How video production affects student engagement: An empirical study of MOOC videos. *Proceedings of the first ACM conference on Learning @ scale conference*. ACM. 10.1145/2556325.2566239

Guo, Y., & Lee, D. (2023). Leveraging ChatGPT for Enhancing Critical Thinking Skills. *Journal of Chemical Education*, *100*(12), 4876–4883. doi:10.1021/acs.jchemed.3c00505

Gupta, A. (2023). *Generative AI tools & their effect on school and college students.* https://www.linkedin.com/pulse/generative-ai-tools-effect-school-college-students- ayush-gupta

Gupta, A., & Mishra, M. (2022). Ethical concerns while using artificial intelligence in recruitment of employees. *Business Ethics and Leadership*, *6*(2), 6–11. doi:10.21272/bel.6(2).6-11.2022

Gupta, M., Akiri, C., Aryal, K., Parker, E., & Praharaj, L. (2023). From ChatGPT to ThreatGPT: Impact of generative AI in cybersecurity and privacy. *IEEE Access : Practical Innovations, Open Solutions*, *11*, 80218–80245. doi:10.1109/ACCESS.2023.3300381

Gustafsson, L., Molineux, M., & Bennett, S. (2014). Contemporary occupational therapy practice: The challenges of being evidence based and philosophically congruent. *Australian Occupational Therapy Journal*, *61*(2), 121–123. doi:10.1111/1440-1630.12110 PMID:24697489

Habgood, M. P., & Ainsworth, S. E. (2011). Motivating children to learn effectively: Exploring the value of intrinsic integration in educational games. *Journal of the Learning Sciences*, *20*(2), 169–206. doi:10.1080/10508406.2010.508029

Hackett, S., Janssen, J., Beach, P., Perreault, M., Beelen, J., & Van Tartwijk, J. (2023). The effectiveness of Collaborative Online International Learning (COIL) on intercultural competence development in higher education. *International Journal of Educational Technology in Higher Education, 20*(1), 5. Advance online publication. doi:10.1186/s41239-022-00373-3 PMID:36713634

Hagendorff, T. (2020). The ethics of AI ethics: An evaluation of guidelines. *Minds and Machines, 30*(1), 99–120. doi:10.1007/s11023-020-09517-8

Hagerty, A., & Rubinov, I. (2019). Global AI ethics: A review of the social impacts and ethical implications of artificial intelligence. *ArXiv, abs/1907.07892.*

Hahn, R. (2023). Measuring social determinant access and equity by race in U.S. States. *Medical Research Archives, 11*(2). doi:10.18103/mra.v11i2.3643

Halaweh, M. (2023). ChatGPT in Education: Strategies for Responsible Implementation. *Contemporary Educational Technology, 15*(2), ep421. doi:10.30935/cedtech/13036

Halbach, S., Pillutla, K., Seo-Mayer, P., Schwartz, A., Weidemann, D., & Mahan, J. (2022). Burnout in pediatric nephrology fellows and faculty: Lessons from the sustainable pediatric nephrology workforce project (superpower). *Frontiers in Pediatrics, 10*, 849370. doi:10.3389/fped.2022.849370 PMID:35601419

Haleem, A., Javaid, M., Qadri, M. A., Singh, R. P., & Suman, R. (2022). Artificial intelligence (AI) applications for marketing: A literature-based study. *International Journal of Intelligent Networks, 3*, 119–132. doi:10.1016/j.ijin.2022.08.005

Hamachek, D. E. (1994). *Psychology in teaching, learning, & growth* (5th ed.). Pearson.

Hammad, M. (2023). The impact of artificial intelligence (AI) programs on writing scientific research. *Annals of Biomedical Engineering, 51*(3), 459–460. doi:10.1007/s10439-023-03140-1 PMID:36637603

Hằng, N. V. T., Meijer, M. R., Bulte, A. M. W., & Pilot, A. (2015). The implementation of a social constructivist approach in primary science education in Confucian heritage culture: The case of Vietnam. *Cultural Studies of Science Education, 10*(3), 665–693. doi:10.1007/s11422-014-9634-8

Han, J., Wang, Y., Qian, J., & Shi, M. (2023). Delving into the role of creativity on meaning in life: A multiple mediation model. *Heliyon, 9*(6), e16566. doi:10.1016/j.heliyon.2023.e16566 PMID:37274645

Han, K., Wang, Y., Chen, H., Chen, X., Guo, J., Liu, Z., Tang, Y., Xiao, A., Xu, C., Xu, Y., Yang, Z., Zhang, Y., & Tao, D. (2023). A survey on Vision Transformer. *IEEE Transactions on Pattern Analysis and Machine Intelligence, 45*(1), 87–110. doi:10.1109/TPAMI.2022.3152247 PMID:35180075

Harbour, K. E., Evanovich, L. L., Sweigart, C. A., & Hughes, L. E. (2015). A Brief Review of Effective Teaching Practices That Maximize Student Engagement. *Preventing School Failure, 59*(1), 5–13. doi:10.1080/1045988X.2014.919136

Harrer, S. (2023). Attention is not allyouneed: The complicated case of ethically using large language models in health care and medicine. *EBioMedicine, 90*, 104512. doi:10.1016/j.ebiom.2023.104512 PMID:36924620

Hart Research Associates. (2015). *Falling short? College learning and career success.* Association of American Colleges and Universities.

Harvard Business School. (n.d.). *2.1.2 Using ChatGPT & Artificial Intelligence (AI) Tools—MBA - Harvard Business School.* Harvard Business School. https://www.hbs.edu/mba/handbook/standards-of-conduct/academic/Pages/chatgpt-and-ai.aspx

Harwood, T. G., & Garry, T. (2003). An overview of content analysis. *The Marketing Review*, *3*(4), 479–498. doi:10.1362/146934703771910080

Hassan, M. S., Halbusi, H. A., & Abdelfattah, F. (2023). May the force of text data analysis be with you: Unleashing the power of generative AI for social psychology research. *Computers in Human Behavior Artificial Humans*, *1*(2), 100006. doi:10.1016/j.chbah.2023.100006

Hassine, T., & Neeman, Z. (2019). The Zombification of art history: How AI resurrects dead masters, and perpetuates historical biases. *Journal of Science and Technology of the Arts*, *11*(2), 28–35. doi:10.7559/citarj.v11i2.663

Hattie, J., & Timperley, H. (2007). The Power of Feedback. *Review of Educational Research*, *77*(1), 81–112. doi:10.3102/003465430298487

He, K. K. (2017). Theories, techniques and methods to promote personalized learning. *Open Education Research, 23*(2).

Heersmink, R. (2018). A virtue epistemology of the Internet: Search engines, intellectual virtues and education. *Social Epistemology*, *32*(1), 1–12. doi:10.1080/02691728.2017.1383530

Heffernan, J. (2023, October 25). The promise and the pitfalls of AI. *James Madison University News*. https://www.jmu.edu/news/2023/10/25-ai-ethics.shtml

Helm, F. (2016). Facilitated dialogue in online intercultural exchange. In O'Dowd, R., & Lewis, T. (Eds.), Online Intercultural Exchange: Policy, Pedagogy, Practice (pp. 150–172). Routledge.

Hidalgo, C. G., Bucheli-Guerrero, V. A., & Ordóñez-Eraso, H. A. (2023). Artificial Intelligence and Computer-Supported Collaborative Learning in Programming: A Systematic Mapping Study. *Tecnura*, *27*(75), 175–206. doi:10.14483/22487638.19637

Hinojosa Pareja, E. F., & López López, M. C. (2018). Interculturality and Teacher Education. A Study from pre-service Teachers' perspective. *The Australian Journal of Teacher Education*, *43*(3), 74–92. doi:10.14221/ajte.2018v43n3.5

Hirota, T., & King, B. H. (2023). Autism spectrum disorder: A review. *Journal of the American Medical Association*, *329*(2), 157–168. doi:10.1001/jama.2022.23661 PMID:36625807

Hisan, U. K., & Amri, M. M. (2022). Artificial intelligence for human life: A critical opinion from medical bioethics perspective – Part II. *Journal of Public Health Sciences*, *1*(2), 112–130. doi:10.56741/jphs.v1i02.215

Ho, J., Jain, A., & Abbeel, P. (2020). Denoising diffusion probabilistic models. *Advances In Neural Information Processing Systems, 33*, 6840–6851. https://proceedings.neurips.cc/paper/2020/file/4c5bcfec8584af0d967f1ab10179ca4b-Paper.pdf

Hockly, N. (2023). Artificial Intelligence in English Language Teaching: The Good, the Bad and the Ugly. *RELC Journal*, *54*(2), 445–451. doi:10.1177/00336882231168504

Hoeschl, M. B., Bueno, T. C., & Hoeschl, H. C. (2017, November). Fourth industrial revolution and the future of engineering: could robots replace human jobs? How ethical recommendations can help engineers rule on artificial intelligence. In *2017 7th World Engineering Education Forum (WEEF)* (pp. 21-26). IEEE. 10.1109/WEEF.2017.8466973

Högberg, R. (2011). Cheating as subversive and strategic resistance: Vocational students' resistance and conformity towards academic subjects in a Swedish upper secondary school. *Ethnography and Education*, *6*(3), 341–355. doi:10.1080/17457823.2011.610584

Holliday, A. (2010). Intercultural Communication & Ideology: SAGE Publications. *Sage (Atlanta, Ga.)*.

Holmes, W., Persson, J., Chounta, I. A., Wasson, B., & Dimitrova, V. (2022b). *Artificial intelligence and education: A critical view through the lens of human rights, democracy, and the rule of law*. Council of Europe. https://rm.coe.int/artificial-intelligence-and-education-a-critical-view-through-the-lens/1680a886bd

Holmes, W., Bialik, M., & Fadel, C. (2019). *Artificial Intelligence in Education: Promises and Implications for Teaching & Learning*. The Center for Curriculum Redesign.

Holmes, W., Bialik, M., & Fadel, C. (2019). *Artificial intelligence in education: Promises and implications for teaching and learning*. Globethics Publications. doi:10.58863/20.500.12424/4276068

Holmes, W., Porayska-Pomsta, K., Holstein, K., Sutherland, E., Baker, T., Shum, S. B., Santos, O. C., Rodrigo, M. T., Cukurova, M., Bittencourt, I. I., & Koedinger, K. R. (2022). Ethics of AI in education: Towards a community-wide framework. *International Journal of Artificial Intelligence in Education*, *32*(3), 504–526. doi:10.1007/s40593-021-00239-1

Holmes, W., & Tuomi, I. (2022). State of the art and practice in AI in education. *European Journal of Education*, *57*(4), 542–570. doi:10.1111/ejed.12533

Holmström, J. (2022). From AI to digital transformation: The AI readiness framework. *Business Horizons*, *65*(3), 329–339. doi:10.1016/j.bushor.2021.03.006

Holstein, K., McLaren, B., & Aleven, V. (2019). Co-designing a real-time classroom orchestration tool to support teacher–AI complementarity. *Journal of Learning Analytics*, *6*(2). doi:10.18608/jla.2019.62.3

Holz, D. (2022). *Welcome to getting start.* Discord. https://discord.com/channels/662267976984297473/999550150705954856

Hong, W. C. H. (2023). *The Impact of CHATGPT on Foreign Language Teaching and Learning: Opportunities in Education and Research.* https://jeti.thewsu.org/index.php/cieti/article/view/103

Hoppmann, R. A., Rao, V. V., Bell, F., Poston, M. B., Howe, D. B., Riffle, S., Harris, S., Riley, R., McMahon, C., Wilson, L. B., Blanck, E., Richeson, N. A., Thomas, L. K., Hartman, C., Neuffer, F. H., Keisler, B. D., Sims, K. M., Garber, M. D., Shuler, C. O., & Catalana, P. V. (2015). The evolution of an integrated ultrasound curriculum (iUSC) for medical students: 9-year experience. *Critical Ultrasound Journal*, *7*(1), 18. doi:10.1186/s13089-015-0035-3 PMID:26589313

Hosseini, M., Rasmussen, L. M., & Resnik, D. B. (2023). Using AI to write scholarly publications. *Accountability in Research*, 1–9. doi:10.1080/08989621.2023.2168535 PMID:36697395

HostetterA.CallN.FrazierG.JamesT.LinnertzC.NestleE.TucciM. (2023). Student and faculty perceptions of artificial intelligence in student writing. doi:10.31234/osf.io/7dnk9

Howie, E., Cannady, N., Messias, E., McNatt, A., & Walter, C. (2022). Associations between physical activity, sleep, and self-reported health with burnout of medical students, faculty and staff in an academic health center. *Sport Sciences for Health*, *18*(4), 1311–1319. doi:10.1007/s11332-022-00902-7 PMID:35308038

How, M., & Hung, W. (2019). Educing AI-Thinking in Science, Technology, Engineering, Arts, and Mathematics (STEAM) Education. *Education Sciences*, *9*(3), 184. doi:10.3390/educsci9030184

Hsiao, I. C. V., Hung, S. T. A., & Huang, H. T. D. (2023). The flipped classroom approach in an English for specific purposes (ESP) course: A quasi-experimental study on learners' self-efficacy, study process, and learning performances. *Journal of Research on Technology in Education*, *55*(3), 507–526. doi:10.1080/15391523.2021.1976329

Hu, K. (2003). *ChatGPT sets record for fastest-growing user base – analysis noted.* https://www.reuters.com/technology/chatgpt-sets-record-fastest-growing-user-base-analyst-note-2023-02-01

Huang, C. Z. A., Koops, H. V., Newton-Rex, E., Dinculescu, M., & Cai, C. J. (2020). *AI song contest: Human-AI co-creation in songwriting*. arxiv. https://arxiv.org/pdf/2010.05388.pdf

Huang, A. Y., Lu, O. H., & Yang, S. J. (2023). Effects of artificial Intelligence–Enabled personalized recommendations on learners' learning engagement, motivation, and outcomes in a flipped classroom. *Computers & Education*, *194*, 104684. doi:10.1016/j.compedu.2022.104684

Huang, C., Zhang, Z., Mao, B., & Yao, X. (2022). An overview of artificial intelligence ethics. *IEEE Transactions on Artificial Intelligence*, *4*(4), 1–21. doi:10.1109/TAI.2022.3194503

Huang, H., & Rust, R. T. (2020). Engaged to a Robot? The Role of AI in Service. *Journal of Service Research*. Advance online publication. doi:10.1177/1094670520902266

Huang, J., Shen, G., & Ren, X. (2021). Connotation analysis and paradigm shift of teaching design under artificial intelligence technology. [iJET]. *International Journal of Emerging Technologies in Learning*, *16*(5), 73–86. doi:10.3991/ijet.v16i05.20287

Huang, M. H., & Rust, R. T. (2018). Artificial intelligence in service. *Journal of Service Research*, *21*(2), 155–172. doi:10.1177/1094670517752459

Huang, S.-P. (2018). Effects of using artificial intelligence teaching system for environmental education on environmental knowledge and attitude. *Eurasia Journal of Mathematics, Science and Technology Education*, *14*(7), 3277–3284. doi:10.29333/ejmste/91248

Hughes, R. T., Zhu, L., & Bednarz, T. (2021). Generative adversarial networks–enabled human–artificial intelligence collaborative applications for creative and design industries: A systematic review of current approaches and trends. *Frontiers in Artificial Intelligence*, *4*, 604234. doi:10.3389/frai.2021.604234 PMID:33997773

Hung, J., & Chen, J. (2023). The benefits, risks and regulation of using ChatGPT in Chinese academia: A content analysis. *Social Sciences (Basel, Switzerland)*, *12*(7), 380. doi:10.3390/socsci12070380

Huriye, A. (2023). The ethics of artificial intelligence: Examining the ethical considerations surrounding the development and use of AI. *American Journal of Technology*, *2*(1), 37–45. doi:10.58425/ajt.v2i1.142

Hutson, M. (2022). Could AI help you to write your next paper? *Nature*, *611*(7934), 192–193. doi:10.1038/d41586-022-03479-w PMID:36316468

Hwang, G. J., & Chang, C. Y. (2023). A review of opportunities and challenges of chatbots in education. *Interactive Learning Environments*, *31*(7), 4099–4112. doi:10.1080/10494820.2021.1952615

Hwang, G. J., & Chen, P. Y. (2023). Effects of a collective problem-solving promotion- based flipped classroom on students' learning performances and interactive patterns. *Interactive Learning Environments*, *31*(5), 2513–2528. doi:10.1080/10494820.2019.1568263

Hwang, G. J., Xie, H., Wah, B. W., & Gašević, D. (2020). Vision, challenges, roles and research issues of Artificial Intelligence in Education. *Computers and Education: Artificial Intelligence*, *1*, 100001. doi:10.1016/j.caeai.2020.100001

Ibeneme, S., Okeibunor, J., Muneene, D., Husain, I., Bento, P., Gaju, C., Housseynou, B., Chibi, M., Karamagi, H., & Makubalo, L. (2021). Data revolution, health status transformation and the role of artificial intelligence for health and pandemic preparedness in the African context. *BMC Proceedings*, *15*(S15), 22. doi:10.1186/s12919-021-00228-1 PMID:34809624

IBM. (2022). *Everyday ethics for artificial intelligence*. IBM Corp. https://www.ibm.com/watson/assets/duo/pdf/everydayethics.pdf

IBM. (n.d.). *What is natural language processing (NLP)?* IBM. https://www.ibm.com/topics/natural-language-processing

Icelandic Institute for Intelligent Machines. (2015). *Ethics policy.* IIIM. https://www.iiim.is/ethics-policy/

IEEE. (2019). *Ethically aligned design: A vision for prioritizing human well-being with autonomous and intelligent systems.* IEEE. https://standards.ieee.org/wp-content/uploads/import/documents/other/ead_v2.pdf

Ifenthaler, D., & Widanapathirana, C. (2014). Development and validation of a learning analytics framework: Two case studies using support vector machines. *Technology. Knowledge and Learning, 19*(1-2), 221–240. doi:10.1007/s10758-014-9226-4

Ilieva, G., Yankova, T., Klisarova-Belcheva, S., Dimitrov, A., Bratkov, M., & Angelov, D. (2023). Effects of generative chatbots in higher education. *Information (Basel), 14*(9), 492. doi:10.3390/info14090492

Imber, M., van Geel, T., Blokhuis, J. C., & Feldman, J. (2013). *A teacher's guide to education law.* Taylor & Francis Group. doi:10.4324/9780203094303

Imran, M., & Almusharraf, N. (2023). Analyzing the role of ChatGPT as a writing assistant at higher education level: A systematic review of the literature. *Contemporary Educational Technology, 15*(4), ep464. doi:10.30935/cedtech/13605

International Center for Academic Integrity. (2021). *The Fundamental Values of Academic Integrity* (3rd ed.). Academic Integrity. https://academicintegrity.org/wp-content/uploads/2017/12/Fundamental-Values-2014.pdf

International Civil Aviation Organization (ICAO). (2003). *Annex 10 to the Convention on International Civil Aviation: Aeronautical Telecommunications.* ICAO. https://www.icao.int/Meetings/anconf12/Document%20Archive/an10_cons_en.pdf

International Civil Aviation Organization (ICAO). (2010). *Manual on the Implementation of ICAO Language Proficiency Requirements.* ICAO. https://www.icao.int/Meetings/LPR/Documents/Doc9835_en.pdf

Inuwa, M. (August 4, 2023). *Generative AI in healthcare.* Analytics Vidhya. https://www.analyticsvidhya.com/blog/2023/08/generative-ai-in-healthcare/

İpek, Z. H., Gözüm, A. İ. C., Papadakis, S., & Kallogiannakis, M. (2023). Educational Applications of the ChatGPT AI System: A Systematic Review Research. *Educational Process: International Journal, 12*(3), 26–55. doi:10.22521/edupij.2023.123.2

İpek, Z. H., Gözüm, A. İ. C., Papadakis, S., & Kallogiannakis, M. (2023). Educational Applications of the ChatGPT AI System: A Systematic Review Research. *International Journal (Toronto, Ont.), 12*(3), 26–55.

Iqbal, S., Ahmad, S., Akkour, K., Wafa, A., AlMutairi, H., & Aldhufairi, A. (2021). Review article: Impact of artificial intelligence in medical education. *MedEdPublish, 10*(1). doi:10.15694/mep.2021.000041.1

Irvine, D. J., Halloran, L. J. S., & Brunner, P. (2023). Opportunities and limitations of the ChatGPT Advanced Data Analysis plugin for hydrological analyses. *Hydrological Processes, 37*(10), e15015. doi:10.1002/hyp.15015

Ishak, N. M., Ranganathan, H., & Harikrishnan, K. (2022). Learning preferences of generation Z undergraduates at the University of Cyberjaya. *Journal of Learning for Development, 9*(2), 331–339. https://files.eric.ed.gov/fulltext/EJ1359087.pdf. doi:10.56059/jl4d.v9i2.584

Ishihara, N., & Prado, M. C. D. A. (2021). The Negotiation of Meaning in Aviation English as a Lingua Franca: A Corpus-Informed Discursive Approach. *Modern Language Journal, 105*(3), 639–654. doi:10.1111/modl.12718

JabotinskyH. Y.SarelR. (2023). Co-authoring with an AI? Ethical Dilemmas and Artificial Intelligence (July 31, 2023). doi:10.2139/ssrn.4303959

Javaid, M., Haleem, A., Singh, R. P., Khan, S., & Khan, I. H. (2023). Unlocking the opportunities through ChatGPT Tool towards ameliorating the education system. *BenchCouncil Transactions on Benchmarks. Standards and Evaluations*, *3*(2), 100115.

Javaid, M., Haleem, A., Singh, R. P., Khan, S., & Khan, I. H. (2023). Unlocking the opportunities through ChatGPT tool towards ameliorating the education system. *BenchCouncil Transactions on Benchmarks. Standards and Evaluations*, *3*(2), 100115. doi:10.1016/j.tbench.2023.100115

Jeong, H., & Hmelo-Silver, C. E. (2016). Seven affordances of computer-supported collaborative learning: How to support collaborative learning? How can technologies help? *Educational Psychologist*, *51*(2), 247–265. doi:10.1080/00461520.2016.1158654

Jeon, J. H., & Lee, S. (2023). Large language models in education: A focus on the complementary relationship between human teachers and ChatGPT. *Education and Information Technologies*, *28*(12), 15873–15892. doi:10.1007/s10639-023-11834-1

Jha, K., Doshi, A., Patel, P., & Shah, M. (2019). A comprehensive review on automation in agriculture using artificial intelligence. *Artificial Intelligence in Agriculture*, *2*, 1–12. doi:10.1016/j.aiia.2019.05.004

Jiang, R. (2022). How does artificial intelligence empower EFL teaching and learning nowadays? A review on artificial intelligence in the EFL context. *Frontiers in Psychology*, *13*, 1049401. doi:10.3389/fpsyg.2022.1049401 PMID:36467167

Ji, H., Han, I., & Ko, Y. (2023). A systematic review of conversational AI in language education: Focusing on the collaboration with human teachers. *Journal of Research on Technology in Education*, *55*(1), 48–63. doi:10.1080/15391523.2022.2142873

Jobin, A., Ienca, M., & Vayena, E. (2019). The global landscape of AI ethics guidelines. *Nature Machine Intelligence*, *1*(9), 389–399. doi:10.1038/s42256-019-0088-2

Johnson, C., Smart, K., & Mahar, P. (2023). Is there a place for generative artificial intelligence in special education? *National Social Science Technology Journal, 11*(2), 48-62. https://nssascholars.org/wp-content/uploads/2023/11/NSSA.Journal-11_2_v1.11.28.23.pdf

Johnson, A., & Lester, R. (2021). Mental health in academia: Hacks for cultivating and sustaining wellbeing. *American Journal of Human Biology*, *34*(S1), e23664. doi:10.1002/ajhb.23664 PMID:34357661

John-Steiner, V. (2000). *Creative Collaboration*. Oxford University Press.

Johri, A., Katz, A. S., Qadir, J., & Hingle, A. (2023). Generative artificial intelligence and engineering education. *Journal of Engineering Education*, *112*(3), 572–577. doi:10.1002/jee.20537

Jonassen, D. H. (1994). Thinking technology: Toward a constructivist design model. *Educational Technology*, *34*(4), 34–37. https://www.learntechlib.org/p/171050/

JunaidQ. (2022). *Engineering education in the era of ChatGPT: Promise and pitfalls of Generative AI for education.* TechRxiv. https://doi.org/ doi:10.36227/techrxiv.21789434.v1

Junus, F. B., & Brophy, S. P. (2023, June). Exploring the Potential of Deep Learning for Personalized Learning Environments. In *2023 ASEE Annual Conference & Exposition*. IEEE.

Jurayev, T. N. (2023). The use of mobile learning applications in higher education institutes. *Advances in Mobile Learning Educational Research*, *3*(1), 610–620. doi:10.25082/AMLER.2023.01.010

Kabudi, T., Pappas, I., & Olsen, D. H. (2021). AI enabled adaptive learning systems: A systematic mapping of the literature. *Computers and Education: Artificial Intelligence*, *2*, 1–12. doi:10.1016/j.caeai.2021.100017

Kadaruddin, K. (2023). Empowering Education through Generative AI: Innovative Instructional Strategies for Tomorrow's Learners. *International Journal of Business, Law, and Education*, *4*(2), 618–625. doi:10.56442/ijble.v4i2.215

Kamalov, F., Calonge, D. S., & Gurrib, I. (2023). A new era of Artificial intelligence in Education: Towards a sustainable Multifaceted Revolution. *Sustainability (Basel)*, *15*(16), 12451. doi:10.3390/su151612451

Kanner, L. (1943). Autistic disturbances of affective contact. *Nervous child, 2*(3), 217-250. http://www.th-hoffmann.eu/archiv/kanner/kanner.1943.pdf

Kansas State Department of Education. (2023). *Kansas standards for English language arts*. KSDE. https://community.ksde.org/LinkClick.aspx?fileticket=NXA9zpwVVtI%3d&tabid=5301

Kaplan-Rakowski, R., Grotewold, K., Hartwick, P., & Papin, K. (2023). Generative AI and Teachers' Perspectives on Its Implementation in Education. *Journal of Interactive Learning Research*, *34*(2), 313–338. https://www.learntechlib.org/primary/p/222363/

Karaca, O., Çalişkan, S., & Demir, K. (2021). Medical artificial intelligence readiness scale for medical students (MAIRS-MS) – Development, validity and reliability study. *BMC Medical Education*, *21*(1), 112. doi:10.1186/s12909-021-02546-6 PMID:33602196

Karadoğan, A. (2023). A Bridge Between Technology and Creativity: Story Writing with Artificial Intelligence. *Journal of the Humanities and Social Sciences*, *6*(2), 2. doi:10.53048/johass.1368950

Kasap, A. B., Eşkil, K. G., Çetinkaya, K. B., Yeşilyurt, H., İnan, S. A., Vatankhahi, A., & Gökçearslan, Ş. (2021). A study on the use of technology in scientific research and ethical competencies of graduate students. *Instructional Technology and Lifelong Learning*, *2*(1), 35–52. doi:10.52911/itall.873802

Kasepalu, R., Prieto, L. P., Ley, T., & Chejara, P. (2022). Teacher artificial intelligence-supported pedagogical actions in collaborative learning coregulation: A wizard-of-oz study. In *Frontiers in Education* (Vol. 7, p. 736194). Frontiers. doi:10.3389/feduc.2022.736194

Kasneci, E., Seßler, K., Küchemann, S., Bannert, M., Dementieva, D., Fischer, F., Gasser, U., Groh, G., Günnemann, S., Hüllermeier, E., Krusche, S., Kutyniok, G., Michaeli, T., Nerdel, C., Pfeffer, J., Poquet, O., Sailer, M., Schmidt, A., Seidel, T., & Kasneci, G. (2023). ChatGPT for good? On opportunities and challenges of large language models for education. *Learning and Individual Differences*, *103*, 102274. doi:10.1016/j.lindif.2023.102274

Kathe, P., Jenay, R., Nicole, M., Mark, M., Jamie, R., Nichole, A., & Susan, G. (2023). *2023 EDUCAUSE Horizon Report, Teaching and Learning Edition*. EDUCASE. https://library.educause.edu/-/media/files/library/2023/4/2023hrteachinglearning.pdf?la=en&hash=195420BF5A2F09991379CBE68858EF10D7088AF5

Katsiuba, D., Kew, T., Dolata, M., & Schwabe, G. (2022). *Supporting online customer feedback management with automatic review response generation*. IEEE. doi:10.24251/HICSS.2022.027

Kavanagh, K., & Spiro, J. (2018). Faculty wellness: Educator burnout among otolaryngology graduate medical educators. *Otolaryngology*, *158*(6), 991–994. doi:10.1177/0194599818770647 PMID:29685089

Kawabe, K., Horiuchi, F., Hosokawa, R., Nakachi, K., Soga, K., & Ueno, S. (2022). Comorbid symptoms of internet addiction among adolescents with and without autism spectrum disorder: A comparative study. *International Journal of Adolescence and Youth*, *27*(1), 315–324. doi:10.1080/02673843.2022.2091939

Kazim, E., & Koshiyama, A. S. (2021). A high-level overview of AI ethics. *Patterns (New York, N.Y.)*, *2*(9), 100314. doi:10.1016/j.patter.2021.100314 PMID:34553166

Keating, J., & Nourbakhsh, I. (2018). Teaching artificial intelligence and humanity. *Communications of the ACM*, *61*(2), 29–32. doi:10.1145/3104986

Keegin, J. M. (2023, May 23). ChatGPT is a plagiarism machine: So why do administrators have their heads in the sand? *The Chronicle of Higher Education*. https://www.chronicle.com/article/chatgpt-is-a-plagiarism-machine

Kellogg, K., & Sadeh-Sharvit, S. (2022). Pragmatic AI-augmentation in mental healthcare: Key technologies, potential benefits, and real-world challenges and solutions for frontline clinicians. *Frontiers in Psychiatry*, *13*, 990370. doi:10.3389/fpsyt.2022.990370 PMID:36147984

Kelly, A. V. (2009). *The Curriculum Theory and Practice* (6th ed.). Sage.

Kempt, H., & Nagel, S. (2021). Responsibility, second opinions and peer-disagreement: Ethical and epistemological challenges of using AI in clinical diagnostic contexts. *Journal of Medical Ethics*, *48*(4), 222–229. doi:10.1136/medethics-2021-107440 PMID:34907006

Kennedy, D., Clapp, P., DeLuca, J., Filtz, T., Kroon, L., Lamberts, J., Oliphant, C. M., Prescott, W. A., & Ray, S. (2022). Enhancing pharmacy faculty well-being and productivity while reducing burnout. *American Journal of Pharmaceutical Education*, *86*(5), 8764. doi:10.5688/ajpe8764 PMID:34507961

Kexin, L., Yi, Q., Xiaoou, S., & Yan, L. (2020). Future education trend learned from the covid-19 pandemic: take artificial Intelligence online course as an example *International Conference on Artificial Intelligence and Education (ICAIE)* (pp. 108-111). IEEE. https://doi.org/10.1109/ICAIE50891.2020.00032

Khazanchi, R., & Khazanchi, P. (2021). Artificial Intelligence in Education. *Advances in Early Childhood and K-12 Education*. doi:10.4018/978-1-7998-7630-4.ch014

Kidd, I. J., Battaly, H., & Cassam, Q. (2021). Introduction: From Epistemic Vices to Vice Epistemology. In I. J. Kidd, Q. Cassam, & H. Battaly (Eds.), *Vice epistemology* (pp. 1–18). Routledge.

Kılınç, S. (2023). Embracing the future of distance science education: Opportunities and challenges of ChatGPT integration. *Asian Journal of Distance Education*, *18*(1). http://www.asianjde.com/ojs/index.php/AsianJDE/article/view/721

Kim, H. (2013). Exploring the construct of radiotelephony communication: A critique of the ICAO English testing policy from the perspective of Korean aviation experts. *Papers in Language Testing and Assessment*, *2*(2), 103–110. doi:10.58379/YWLL7105

Kim, J. M., Lee, S. Y., & Lee, W. S. (2023). Discovering AI-enabled convergences based on BERT and topic network. *KSII Transactions on Internet and Information Systems*, *17*(3), 1022–1034. doi:10.3837/tiis.2023.03.018

Kim, K., & Kwon, K. (2023). Exploring the AI competencies of elementary school teachers in South Korea. *Computers and Education: Artificial Intelligence*, *4*, 100137. doi:10.1016/j.caeai.2023.100137

Kim, W., & Kim, J. (2020). Individualized AI Tutor Based on Developmental Learning Networks. *IEEE Access : Practical Innovations, Open Solutions*, *8*, 27927–27937. doi:10.1109/ACCESS.2020.2972167

King, M. R. (2023). The future of AI in medicine: A perspective from a Chatbot. *Annals of Biomedical Engineering*, *51*(2), 291–295. doi:10.1007/s10439-022-03121-w PMID:36572824

Kirkpatrick, K. (2023). Can AI Demonstrate Creativity? *Communications of the ACM*, *66*(2), 21–23. doi:10.1145/3575665

Kissinger, H., Schmidt, E., & Huttenlocher, D. (2023, February 24). ChatGPT heralds an intellectual revolution. *Wall Street Journal.* https://www.wsj.com/articles/chatgpt-heralds-an-intellectual-revolution-enlightenment-artificial-intelligence-homo-technicus-technology-cognition-morality-philosophy-774331c6

Knight, W. (2019). The world's top deepfake artist is wrestling with the monster he created. *Technology Review*. https://www.technologyreview.com/2019/08/16/133686/the-worlds-top-deepfake-artist-is-wrestling-with-the-monster-he-created/

Köbis, L., & Mehner, C. (2021). Ethical questions raised by ai-supported mentoring in higher education. *Frontiers in Artificial Intelligence*, *4*, 4. doi:10.3389/frai.2021.624050 PMID:33997774

Kochmar, E., Vu, D. D., Belfer, R., Gupta, V., Serban, I. V., & Pineau, J. (2020). Automated personalized feedback improves learning gains in an intelligent tutoring system. In *Artificial Intelligence in Education: 21st International Conference, AIED 2020,* (pp. 140-146). Springer International Publishing. https://doi.org/10.1007/978-3-030-52240-7_26

Kocoń, J., Cichecki, I., Kaszyca, O., Kochanek, M., Szydło, D., Baran, J., Bielaniewicz, J., Gruza, M., Janz, A., Kanclerz, K., Kocoń, A., Koptyra, B., Mieleszczenko-Kowszewicz, W., Miłkowski, P., Oleksy, M., Piasecki, M., Radliński, Ł., Wojtasik, K., Woźniak, S., & Kazienko, P. (2023). ChatGPT: Jack of all trades, master of none. *Information Fusion*, *99*, 101861. doi:10.1016/j.inffus.2023.101861

Koedinger, K. R., Kim, J., Jia, J. Z., McLaughlin, E. A., & Bier, N. L. (2015, March). Learning is not a spectator sport: Doing is better than watching for learning from a MOOC. In *Proceedings of the second (2015) ACM conference on learning@ scale* (pp. 111-120). ACM. 10.1145/2724660.2724681

Kohli, M., Kar, A. K., & Sinha, S. (2023). Robot facilitated rehabilitation of children with autism spectrum disorder: A 10 year scoping review. *Expert Systems: International Journal of Knowledge Engineering and Neural Networks*, *40*(5), e13204. doi:10.1111/exsy.13204

Kohnke, L., Moorhouse, B. L., & Zou, D. (2023). ChatGPT for Language Teaching and Learning. *RELC Journal*, *54*(2), 537–550. doi:10.1177/00336882231162868

Kohnke, L., Moorhouse, B. L., & Zou, D. (2023). Exploring generative artificial intelligence preparedness among university language instructors: A case study. *Computers & Education: Artificial Intelligence*, *5*, 100156. doi:10.1016/j.caeai.2023.100156

Koivisto, M. (2023). Tutoring Postgraduate Students with an AI-Based Chatbot. *International Journal of Advanced Corporate Learning*, *16*(1), 41–54. doi:10.3991/ijac.v16i1.35437

Kolachalama, V., & Garg, P. (2018). Machine learning and medical education. *NPJ Digital Medicine*, *1*(1), 54. doi:10.1038/s41746-018-0061-1 PMID:31304333

König, J., Krepf, M., Bremerich-Vos, A., & Buchholtz, C. (2021). Meeting cognitive demands of lesson planning: Introducing the code-plan model to describe and analyze teachers' planning competence. *Teacher Educator*, *56*(4), 466–487. doi:10.1080/08878730.2021.1938324

Kooli, C., & Al Muftah, H. (2022). Artificial intelligence in healthcare: A comprehensive review of its ethical concerns. *Technological Sustainability*, *1*(2), 121–131. doi:10.1108/TECHS-12-2021-0029

Kopalle, P. K., Gangwar, M., Kaplan, A., Ramachandran, D., Reinartz, W., & Rindfleisch, A. (2022). Examining artificial intelligence (AI) technologies in marketing via a global lens: Current trends and future research opportunities. *International Journal of Research in Marketing*, *39*(2), 522–540. doi:10.1016/j.ijresmar.2021.11.002

Korzynski, P., Mazurek, G., Krzypkowska, P., & Kurasinski, A. (2023). Artificial intelligence prompt engineering as a new digital competence: Analysis of generative AI technologies such as ChatGPT. *Entrepreneurial Business and Economics Review*, *11*(3), 25–37. doi:10.15678/EBER.2023.110302

Kosmicki, J. A., Sochat, V., Duda, M., & Wall, D. P. (2015). Searching for a minimal set of behaviors for autism detection through feature selection-based machine learning. *Translational Psychiatry*, *5*(2), e514–e514. doi:10.1038/tp.2015.7 PMID:25710120

Kostka, I., & Toncelli, R. (2023). Exploring applications of ChatGPT to English language teaching: Opportunities, challenges, and recommendations. *The Electronic Journal for English as a Second Language*, *27*(3). doi:10.55593/ej.27107int

Kothari, A. N. (2023). ChatGPT, Large Language Models, and Generative AI as Future Augments of Surgical Cancer Care. *Annals of Surgical Oncology*, *30*(6), 1–3. doi:10.1245/s10434-023-13442-2 PMID:37052826

Kozulin, A. (2004). Vygotsky's Theory in the Classroom: Introduction. *European Journal of Psychology of Education*, *19*(1), 3–7. doi:10.1007/BF03173233

Kozyreva, A., Lewandowsky, S., & Hertwig, R. (2020). Citizens versus the internet: Confronting digital challenges with cognitive tools. *Psychological Science in the Public Interest*, *21*(3), 103–156. doi:10.1177/1529100620946707 PMID:33325331

Krafft, P., Young, M., Katell, M., Huang, K., & Bugingo, G. (2020). *Defining AI in policy versus practice*. ACM. doi:10.1145/3375627.3375835

Kraft, M. A., & Rogers, T. (2015). The underutilized potential of teacher-to-parent communication: Evidence from a field experiment. *Economics of Education Review*, *47*, 49–63. doi:10.1016/j.econedurev.2015.04.001

Kucirkova, N., & Leaton Gray, S. (2023, August). Beyond Personalization: Embracing Democratic Learning Within Artificially Intelligent Systems. *Educational Theory*, *73*(4), 469–489. doi:10.1111/edth.12590

Kulik, J. A., & Kulik, C. L. C. (1988). Timing of feedback and verbal learning. *Review of Educational Research*, *58*(1), 79–97. doi:10.3102/00346543058001079

Kumar, A. H. S. (2023). Analysis of ChatGPT tool to assess the potential of it sutility for academic writing in biomedical domain. *BEMS Reports*, *9*(1), 24–30. doi:10.5530/bems.9.1.5

Kumazaki, H., Muramatsu, T., Yoshikawa, Y., Yoshimura, Y., Ikeda, T., Hasegawa, C., Saito, D. N., Shimaya, J., Ishiguro, H., Mimura, M., & Kikuchi, M. (2019). Brief Report: A novel system to evaluate autism spectrum disorders using two humanoid robots. *Journal of Autism and Developmental Disorders*, *49*(4), 1709–1716. doi:10.1007/s10803-018-3848-7 PMID:30539368

Kwan, L. Y.-Y., Leung, A. K.-y., & Liou, S. (2018). Culture, Creativity, and Innovation. *Journal of Cross-Cultural Psychology*, *49*(2), 165–170. doi:10.1177/0022022117753306

Lackritz, J. R. (2004). Exploring burnout among university faculty: Incidence, performance, and demographic issues. *Teaching and Teacher Education*, *20*(7), 713–729. doi:10.1016/j.tate.2004.07.002

Lähdesmäki, T., Koistinen, A., & Ylönen, S. C. (2020). *Intercultural dialogue in the European education policies: A Conceptual Approach*. Springer Nature. doi:10.1007/978-3-030-41517-4

Lainjo, B., & Tsmouche, H. (2023). Impact of artificial intelligence on higher learning institutions. *International Journal of Education Teaching and Social Sciences*, *3*(2), 96–113. doi:10.47747/ijets.v3i2.1028

Lambert, J., & Stevens, M. (2023). ChatGPT and Generative AI Technology: A Mixed Bag of Concerns and New Opportunities. *Computers in the Schools*, 1–25. doi:10.1080/07380569.2023.2256710

Lameras, P., & Arnab, S. (2021). Power to the Teachers: An Exploratory Review on Artificial Intelligence in Education. *Information (Basel)*, *13*(1), 14. doi:10.3390/info13010014

Lametti, D. (2022). AI could be great for college essays. *Slate*. https://slate.com/technology/2022/12/chatgpt-college-essay-plagiarism.html

Landon-Hays, M., Peterson-Ahmad, M. B., & Frazier, A. D. (2020). Learning to Teach: How a simulated learning environment can connect theory to practice in general and special education educator preparation programs. *Education Sciences*, *10*(7), 184. doi:10.3390/educsci10070184

Lang, J. M., Berry, R. M., Queen, E. L., Kinlaw, K., Newstetter, W. C., & Wolf, L. E. (2013). Cheating lessons: Learning from academic dishonesty. *Journal of Engineering Education*, 38.

Lauterbach, A. (2019). Artificial intelligence and policy: Quo vadis? Digital Policy. *Regulation & Governance*, *21*(3), 238–263. doi:10.1108/DPRG-09-2018-0054

Lăzăroiu, G., Androniceanu, A., Grecu, I., Grecu, G., & Negurita, O. (2022). Artificial intelligence-based decisionmaking algorithms, Internet of Things sensing networks, and sustainable cyber-physical management systems in big data-driven cognitive manufacturing. *Oeconomia Copernicana*, *13*(4), 1047–1080. doi:10.24136/oc.2022.030

Lee, A. (2023). *What Are Large Language Models Used For?* NVIDIA. https://blogs.nvidia.com/blog/2023/01/26/what-are-large-language-models-used-for/

Lee, J., & Obinata, G. (2013, March). Developing therapeutic robot for children with autism: A study on exploring colour feedback. In *Human-Robot Interaction (HRI), 8th Assosiation for Computing Machinery/Institute of Electrical and Electronics Engineers (ACM/IEEE)*. IEEE. 10.1109/HRI.2013.6483557

Lee, J., Takehashi, H., Nagai, C., & Obinata, G. (2012). Design of a therapeutic robot for interacting with autistic children through interpersonal touch. In *IEEE RO-MAN: The 21st IEEE International Symposium on Robot and Human Interactive Communication* (pp. 712–717). 1 10.1109/ROMAN.2012.6343835

Lee, J. Y. (2023). Can an artificial intelligence chatbot be the author of a scholarly article? *Journal of Educational Evaluation for Health Professions*, *20*, 6. Advance online publication. doi:10.3352/jeehp.2023.20.6 PMID:36842449

Lee, K. F., & Wang, Y. G. (2017). *Artificial Intelligence*. Cultural Development Press.

Lee, S. E. (2023). Otherwise than teaching by artificial intelligence. *Journal of Philosophy of Education*, *57*(2), 553–570. doi:10.1093/jopedu/qhad019

Lee, S., Mott, B., Ottenbreit-Leftwich, A., Scribner, A., Taylor, S., Park, K., Rowe, J., Glazewski, K., Hmelo-Silver, C. E., & Lester, J. (2021). AI-infused collaborative inquiry in upper elementary school: A game-based learning approach. *Proceedings of the AAAI Conference on Artificial Intelligence*, *35*(17), 15591–15599. doi:10.1609/aaai.v35i17.17836

LeT. T. (2023). A preliminary example of utilizing AI text generation to support academic writing: "Humans befriending their creations some notes on the human-AI relationship". doi:10.31219/osf.io/bsxey

Leung, M. (2023, September 1). *Draft law sets out penalties for AI-aided academic writing*. University World News. https://www.universityworldnews.com/post.php?story=20230901111126325

Li, P. H., Lee, H. Y., Cheng, Y. P., Starčič, A. I., & Huang, Y. M. (2023, August). Solving the Self-regulated Learning Problem: Exploring the Performance of ChatGPT in Mathematics. In *International Conference on Innovative Technologies and Learning* (pp. 77-86). Cham: Springer Nature Switzerland. 10.1007/978-3-031-40113-8_8

Li, Y., Liao, I. Y., Zhong, N., Toshihiro, F., Wang, Y., & Wang, S. (2023, December). Generative AI Enables the Detection of Autism Using EEG Signals. In *Chinese Conference on Biometric Recognition* (pp. 375-384). Springer Nature Singapore. 10.1007/978-981-99-8565-4_35

Liang, J. C., Hwang, G. J., Chen, M. R. A., & Darmawansah, D. (2023). Roles and research foci of artificial intelligence in language education: An integrated bibliographic analysis and systematic review approach. *Interactive Learning Environments*, *31*(7), 4270–4296. doi:10.1080/10494820.2021.1958348

Liao, Q. V., Gruen, D., & Miller, S. (2020). *Questioning the AI: Informing design practices for explainable AI user experiences.* In *Proceedings of the 2020 CHI conference on human factors in computing systems* (pp. 1-15). Honolulu HI, USA.10.1145/3313831.3376590

Li, B. (2023). ChatGPT and the transformation wave of intelligent tools in AIGC. *AIGC's Information Resource Management Study*, *35*(1). doi:10.13998/j.cnki.issn1002-1248.23-0118

Liddicoat, A. J. & Scarino, A. (2013). *Intercultural language teaching and learning.* https://doi.org/doi:10.1002/9781118482070

Liebrenz, M., Schleifer, R., Buadze, A., Bhugra, D., & Smith, A. (2023). Generating scholarly content with ChatGPT: Ethical challenges for medical publishing. *The Lancet. Digital Health*, *5*(3), e105–e106. doi:10.1016/S2589-7500(23)00019-5 PMID:36754725

Lim, T., Gottipati, S., & Cheong, M. (2023). Artificial intelligence in today's education Landscape: Understanding and managing ethical issues for educational assessment. 16 March 2023, PREPRINT (Version 1) available at Research Square. doi:10.21203/rs.3.rs-2696273/v1

Lim, W. M., Gunasekara, A., Pallant, J. L., Pallant, J. I., & Pechenkina, E. (2023). Generative AI and the future of education: Ragnarök or reformation? A paradoxical perspective from management educators. *International Journal of Management Education*, *21*(2), 100790. doi:10.1016/j.ijme.2023.100790

Li, N., Yan, Y., Yang, Y., & Gu, A. (2022). Artificial intelligence capability and organizational creativity: The role of knowledge sharing and organizational cohesion. *Frontiers in Psychology*, *13*, 845277. doi:10.3389/fpsyg.2022.845277 PMID:35356339

Lindsay, K. (2023, January 24). *A framework for approaching AI and university assessment.* Kate Lindsay. https://katelindsayblogs.com/2023/01/24/a-framework-for-approaching-ai-and-university-assessment/

Lindsay, R., Saunders, S., Moindrot, W., Watson, D., Blundell, L., McGrae, B., & Ellis, G. (2023). Generative AI: Learning and teaching prompt templates (Version 1). *National Teaching Repository.* doi:10.25416/NTR.23592897.v1

Linebarger, D. L. (2015). Educational Media: Potentials for Learning. In J. D. Wright (Ed.), *International Encyclopedia of the Social & Behavioral Sciences* (2nd ed., pp. 246–254). Elsevier., doi:10.1016/B978-0-08-097086-8.92031-2

Lin, J., Litkowski, E., Schmerold, K. L., Elicker, J., Schmitt, S. A., & Purpura, D. J. (2019). Parent–Educator communication linked to more frequent home learning activities for preschoolers. *Child and Youth Care Forum*, *48*(5), 757–772. doi:10.1007/s10566-019-09505-9

Lin, X., Chen, L., Chan, K. K., Peng, S., Chen, X., Xie, S., Liu, J., & Hu, Q. (2022). Teachers' perceptions of teaching Sustainable Artificial Intelligence: A Design frame perspective. *Sustainability (Basel)*, *14*(13), 7811. doi:10.3390/su14137811

Lin, Z. (2023). Why and how to embrace AI such as ChatGPT in your academic life. *Royal Society Open Science*, *10*(8), 230658. doi:10.1098/rsos.230658 PMID:37621662

Liss, L. (2021). *Instructional Design. Creating an interactive digital product for education*. GRIN Verlag.

Little, P. (2013). 21st century learning and progressive education: An intersection. *International Journal of Progressive Education*, *9*(1), 84–96. https://dergipark.org.tr/en/pub/ijpe/issue/26313/277317

Liu, M., Li, Y., Xu, W., & Liu, L. (2016). Automated essay feedback generation and its impact on revision. *IEEE Transactions on Learning Technologies, 10*(4), https://doi.org/. doi:502-513

Liu, Y., Yang, Z., Yu, Z., Liu, Z., Liu, D., Lin, H., & Shi, S. (2023). Generative artificial intelligence and its applications in materials science: Current situation and future perspectives. *Journal of Materiomics*.

Liu, G. Z., Lu, H. C., Lin, V., & Hsu, W. C. (2018). Cultivating undergraduates' plagiarism avoidance knowledge and skills with an online tutorial system. *Journal of Computer Assisted Learning*, *34*(2), 150–161. doi:10.1111/jcal.12223

Liu, K. J., Cook, A. N., & Jiang, R. (2023). Lessons from Canadian judgments: The consideration of culture in intimate partner violence legal cases involving Asian Canadians. *Journal of Interpersonal Violence*, *38*(19–20), 11046–11066. doi:10.1177/08862605231178494 PMID:37350459

Liu, M., Horton, L., Olmanson, J., & Toprac, P. (2011). A study of learning and motivation in a new media enriched environment for middle school science. *Educational Technology Research and Development*, *59*(2), 249–265. doi:10.1007/s11423-011-9192-7

Liu, M., Ren, Y., Nyagoga, L. M., Stonier, F., Wu, Z., & Yu, L. (2023). Future of education in the era of generative artificial intelligence: Consensus among Chinese scholars on applications of ChatGPT in schools. *Future in Educational Research*, *1*(1), 72–101. doi:10.1002/fer3.10

Liu, P., Yuan, W., Fu, J., Jiang, Z., Hayashi, H., & Neubig, G. (2023). Pre-train, prompt, and predict: A systematic survey of prompting methods in natural language processing. *ACM Computing Surveys*, *55*(9), 1–35. doi:10.1145/3560815

Liu, S., Mallol-Ragolta, A., Parada-Cabaleiro, E., Qian, K., Jing, X., Kathan, A., Hu, B., & Schuller, B. W. (2022). Audio self-supervised learning: A survey. *Patterns (New York, N.Y.)*, *3*(12), 100616. doi:10.1016/j.patter.2022.100616 PMID:36569546

Liu, Y., Chen, L., & Yao, Z. (2022). The application of artificial intelligence assistant to deep learning in teachers' teaching and students' learning processes. *Frontiers in Psychology*, *13*, 929175. doi:10.3389/fpsyg.2022.929175 PMID:36033031

Li, Y., Sha, L., Yan, L., Lin, J., Raković, M., Galbraith, K., Lyons, K., Gašević, D., & Chen, G. (2023). Can large language models write reflectively. *Computers & Education: Artificial Intelligence*, *4*, 100140. doi:10.1016/j.caeai.2023.100140

Li, Y., & Xiao, L. H. (2023). *From ChatGPT to AIGC: Empowering Intelligent Creation and Application*. Publishing House of Electronics Industry.

Lo, C. K. (2023). What is the impact of ChatGPT on education? A rapid review of the literature. *Education Sciences*, *13*(4), 410. doi:10.3390/educsci13040410

Locke, S., Bashall, A., Al-Adely, S., Moore, J. A., Wilson, A. J., & Kitchen, G. (2021). Natural language processing in medicine: A review. Trends in Anaesthesia and Critical Care. doi:10.1016/j.tacc.2021.02.007

Lockspeiser, T. M., & Kaul, P. (2016). Using individualized learning plans to facilitate learner-centered teaching. *Journal of Pediatric and Adolescent Gynecology*, *29*(3), 214–217. doi:10.1016/j.jpag.2015.10.020 PMID:26612117

Loiacono, E., Iyer, L., Armstrong, D., Beekhuyzen, J., & Craig, A. (2016). AIS Women's Network: Advancing women in IS academia. *Communications of the Association for Information Systems*, *38*, 784–802. doi:10.17705/1CAIS.03838

Lo, L. S. (2023). The CLEAR path: A framework for enhancing information literacy through prompt engineering. *Journal of Academic Librarianship*, *49*(4), 102720. doi:10.1016/j.acalib.2023.102720

López López, M. C. & Hinojosa Pareja, E. F. (2012). El Estudio de las Creencias Sobre la Diversidad Cultural Como Referente Para la Mejora de la Formación Docente. *Educacion Xx1, 15*(1). https://doi.org/ doi:10.5944/educxx1.15.1.156

Lorenzo, G., Lorenzo-Lledó, A., Lledó Carreres, A., & Pérez-Vázquez, E. (2020). Approach from a bibliometric perspective of the educational application of virtual reality in people with autism spectrum disorder. *Education in the Knowledge Society*, *21*(4). doi:10.14201/eks.19522

Louie, R., Coenen, A., Huang, C. Z., Terry, M., & Cai, C. J. (2020, April). Novice-AI music co-creation via AI-steering tools for deep generative models. In *Proceedings of the 2020 CHI conference on human factors in computing systems*, (pp. 1–13). ACM. https://dl.acm.org/doi/abs/10.1145/3313831.3376739

Lubis, F. (2019). Education in the disruption era. *Britain International of Linguistics, Arts, and Education Journal*, *1*(2), 183–188. doi:10.33258/biolae.v1i2.85

Luckin, R., Holmes, W., Griffiths, M., & Forcier, L. B. (2016). *Intelligence unleashed: An argument for AI in education*. Pearson Education. https://discovery.ucl.ac.uk/id/eprint/1475756

Luckin, R., Cukurova, M., Kent, C., & du Boulay, B. (2022). Empowering educators to be AI-ready. *Computers and Education: Artificial Intelligence*, *3*, 100076. doi:10.1016/j.caeai.2022.100076

Luckin, R., Holmes, W., Griffiths, M., & Forcier, L. B. (2016). *Intelligence unleashed: An argument for AI in education*. Pearson Education.

Lukianets, H., & Lukianets, T. (2023). Promises and perils of AI use on the tertiary educational level. *Грааль Науки*, (25), 306–311. doi:10.36074/grail-of-science.17.03.2023.053

Lund, B. D., & Wang, T. (2023). Chatting about ChatGPT: How may AI and GPT impact academia and libraries? *Library Hi Tech News*, *40*(3), 26–29. doi:10.1108/LHTN-01-2023-0009

Lund, B. D., Wang, T., Mannuru, N. R., Nie, B., Shimray, S., & Wang, Z. (2023). ChatGPT and a new academic reality: Artificial Intelligence-written research papers and the ethics of the large language models in scholarly publishing. *Journal of the Association for Information Science and Technology*, *74*(5), 570–581. doi:10.1002/asi.24750

Luo, H. (2013). Foreign Language Anxiety: Past and Future. *Canadian Journal of Applied Linguistics*, *36*(4), 442–464. doi:10.1515/cjal-2013-0030

Luttrell, R., Wallace, A., McCollough, C., & Lee, J. (2020). The digital divide: Addressing artificial intelligence in communication education. *Journalism & Mass Communication Educator*, *75*(4), 470–482. doi:10.1177/1077695820925286

Lv, H. Z. (2023). Innovative music education: Using an AI-based flipped classroom. *Education and Information Technologies*, *28*(11), 1–16. doi:10.1007/s10639-023-11835-0

Lyu, Z., Ali, S., & Breazeal, C. (2022). Introducing variational autoencoders to high school students. *Proceedings of the AAAI Conference on Artificial Intelligence*, *36*(11), 12801–12809. doi:10.1609/aaai.v36i11.21559

Mackh, B. M. (2021). *Pivoting Your Instruction: A Guide to Comprehensive Instructional Design for Faculty*. Taylor & Francis. doi:10.4324/9781003179726

Maglione, M. A., Gans, D., Das, L., Timbie, J., & Kasari, C. (2012). Technical Expert Panel, & HRSA Autism Intervention Research–Behavioral (AIR-B) Network. Nonmedical interventions for children with ASD: Recommended guidelines and further research needs. *Pediatrics*, *130*(Supplement_2), S169–S178. doi:10.1542/peds.2012-0900O PMID:23118248

Magulod, G. C. Jr. (2019). Learning styles, study habits and academic performance of Filipino University students in applied science courses: Implications for instruction. *JOTSE: Journal of Technology and Science Education*, *9*(2), 184–198. doi:10.3926/jotse.504

Mahon, J., Bryant, B. R., Brown, B., & Kim, M. (2010). Using Second Life to enhance classroom management practice in teacher education. *Educational Media International*, *47*(2), 121–134. doi:10.1080/09523987.2010.492677

Maiorana, F. A., & Mayer, H. F. (2018). How to avoid common errors in writing scientific manuscripts. *European Journal of Plastic Surgery*, *41*(5), 489–494. doi:10.1007/s00238-018-1418-z

Malihi, M., Nguyen, J., Cardy, R. E., Eldon, S., Petta, C., & Kushki, A. (2020). Evaluating the safety and usability of head-mounted virtual reality compared to monitor-displayed video for children with autism spectrum disorder. *Autism*, *24*(7), 1924–1929. doi:10.1177/1362361320934214 PMID:32615771

Malik, A. R., Pratiwi, Y., Andajani, K., Numertayasa, I. W., Suharti, S., Darwis, A., & Marzuki. (2023). Exploring artificial intelligence in academic essay: Higher education student's perspective. *International Journal of Educational Research Open*, *5*, 100296. doi:10.1016/j.ijedro.2023.100296

Mani, B. (2023). *Top Visual Learning Statistics and Facts to Know in 2023*. Sell Courses Online. https://sellcoursesonline.com/power-of-visual-learning#:~:text=Visuals%20are%20much%20more%20effective,attention%20to%20information%2Dcarrying%20images

Mao, J., Chen, B., & Liu, J. C. (2023). Generative Artificial Intelligence in Education and Its Implications for Assessment. *TechTrends*, 1–9.

Mao, J., Chen, B., & Liu, J. C. (2023). Generative artificial intelligence in education and its implications for assessment. *TechTrends*. doi:10.1007/s11528-023-00911-4

Marchandot, B., Matsushita, K., Carmona, A., Trimaille, A., & Morel, O. (2023). ChatGPT: The next frontier in academic writing for cardiologists or a Pandora's box of ethical dilemmas. *European Heart Journal Open*, *3*(2), oead007. doi:10.1093/ehjopen/oead007 PMID:36915398

Marino, M. T., Vasquez, E., Dieker, L., Basham, J., & Blackorby, J. (2023). The Future of Artificial Intelligence in Special Education Technology. *Journal of Special Education Technology*, *38*(3), 404–416. doi:10.1177/01626434231165977

Marr, B. (2021). How Artificial Intelligence (AI) Is Helping Musicians Unlock Their Creativity. *Forbes*. https://www.forbes.com/sites/bernardmarr/2021/05/14/how-artificial-intelligence-ai-is-helpingmusicians-unlock-their-creativity/?sh=29ab2f667004

Marriam-Webster. (n.d.) *Plagiarize*. Marriam-Webster. https://www.merriam-webster.com/dictionary/plagiarize

Marsh, C. J. (2018). *Key Concepts for Understanding Curriculum* (Vol. 2). Routledge.

Martínez-Jiménez, R., & Ruiz-Jiménez, M. C. (2020). Improving students' satisfaction and learning performance using flipped classroom. *International Journal of Management Education*, *18*(3), 100422. doi:10.1016/j.ijme.2020.100422

Maslach, C., Schaufeli, W., & Leiter, M. (2001). Job burnout. *Annual Review of Psychology*, *52*(1), 397–422. doi:10.1146/annurev.psych.52.1.397 PMID:11148311

Mason, J. (2008). A model for sense-making: exploring why in the context of learning and knowing. *International Conference on Computers in Education*, 545–549. https://eprints.qut.edu.au/17803/

Mason, J. (2014). The Why dimension - Opening frontiers for Digital learning. In S. Feller & I. Yengin (Eds.), *Educating in Dialog: Constructing meaning and building knowledge with dialogic technology* (pp. 51–74). John Benjamins Publishing Company. https://www.academia.edu/8117593/The_why_dimension_opening_frontiers_for_digital_learning

Mason, J. (2023). *The search continues: Content used to be king, but context is now everything – and 'smart' can morph into 'stupid.* The Sociological Review Magazine. doi:10.51428/tsr.ngtq5087

Mason, J., Gromik, N., Khan, K., & Liu, B. (2020). *International Student Perspectives on Simulated Preservice Induction. In 28th International Conference on Computers in Education, ICCE 2020.* Asia-Pacific Society for Computers in Education. https://www.researchgate.net/publication/346553768_International_Student_Perspectives_on_Simulated_Preservice_Induction

Mason, J., Lefrère, P., Peoples, B., Lee, J., & Shaw, P. J. (2023). Artificial Intelligence and Evolution of the Virtual University. In M. D. Sankey, H. Huijser, & R. Fitzgerald (Eds.), *Technology-Enhanced Learning and the Virtual University. University Development and Administration* (pp. 227–244). Springer. doi:10.1007/978-981-19-9438-8_28-1

Mayer, R. (2020). *Multimedia Learning* (3rd ed.). Cambridge University Press. doi:10.1017/9781316941355

Mayer, R. E. (2017). Using multimedia for e-learning. *Journal of Computer Assisted Learning*, *33*(5), 403–423. https://onlinelibrary.wiley.com/doi/am-pdf/10.1111/jcal.12197. doi:10.1111/jcal.12197

Mbakwe, A. B., Lourentzou, I., Celi, L. A., Mechanic, O. J., & Dagan, A. (2023). ChatGPT passing USMLE shines a spotlight on the flaws of medical education. *PLOS Digital Health*, *2*(2), e0000205. doi:10.1371/journal.pdig.0000205 PMID:36812618

McArthur, T. (1987). The English languages? *English Today*, *3*(3), 9–13. doi:10.1017/S0266078400013511

McCarthy, J. (2007). *What is artificial intelligence?* Technical Report. Stanford University. https://www.diochnos.com/about/McCarthyWhatisAI.pdf

McCarthy, J., Minsky, M., Rochester, N., & Shannon, C. (1955). *A proposal for Dartmouth Summer Research Project on Artificial Intelligence.* Stanford. http://www-formal.stanford.edu/jmc/history/dartmouth.pdf

McCarthy,J ., Minsky, M.Rochester, N.. & Shannon, C. (1955). *A proposal for Dartmouth Summer Research Proiect on Artificial lnteligence.* Stanford. http:/www-formalstanford.edu/imchistorv/dartmouth.pdf

McCarthy, J. (2007). From here to human-level AI. *Artificial Intelligence*, *171*(18), 1174–1182. doi:10.1016/j.artint.2007.10.009

McFarland, A. (2023). *8 "Best" AI Translation Software and Tools.* Unite. https://www.unite.ai/tr/en-iyi-yapay-zeka-%C3%A7eviri-yaz%C4%B1l%C4%B1m%C4%B1-ara%C3%A7lar%C4%B1/

McFarland, A., & Tardif, A. (2023). *7 "Best" AI Content Detection Tools.* Unite. https://www.unite.ai/tr/en-iyi-yapay-zeka-i%C3%A7erik-dedekt%C3%B6rleri/

McHenry, K., Koster, M., Ludwig, G., Yong, G., & Eichmeyer, J. (2023). Assessing burnout and well-being in higher education health science faculty. *OBM Integrative and Complimentary Medicine*, *08*(01), 1–18. doi:10.21926/obm.icm.2301014

McKinsey & Company. (2023). *What is prompt engineering?* McKinsey. https://www.mckinsey.com/featured-insights/mckinsey-explainers/what-is-prompt-engineering

McLean, S., & Attardi, S. M. (2023). Sage or guide? Student perceptions of the role of the instructor in a flipped classroom. *Active Learning in Higher Education*, *24*(1), 49–61. doi:10.1177/1469787418793725

Mcleod, S. (2023, 11. Oktober). *Vygotsky's Zone of Proximal Development and Scaffolding Theory*. simply psychology. https://www.simplypsychology.org/zone-of-proximal-development.html

McMahan, E., Day, S., Funk, R., & Coleman, L. S. (2017). *Literature and the writing process*. Pearson.

McMahon, G. (2022). Effect of the COVID-19 pandemic on accredited continuing medical education in the United States. *The Journal of Continuing Education in the Health Professions*, *42*(4), e125–e127. doi:10.1097/CEH.0000000000000443 PMID:36469803

MEB. (2023). *Artificial intelligence training for 50 thousand students with the "FEYZA" project*. MBE. https://www.meb.gov.tr/feyza-projesi-ile-50-bin-ogrenciye-yapay-zek-egitimi/haber/31604/tr

Megahed, F. M., Chen, Y. J., Ferris, J. A., Knoth, S., & Jones-Farmer, L. A. (2023). How generative ai models such as chatgpt can be (mis) used in spc practice, education, and research? an exploratory study. *Quality Engineering*, 1–29. doi:10.1080/08982112.2023.2206479

Melanson, C. C. (2023). A clash of interests: Neoliberalism in education. *One World in Dialogue, 7*(1), 4. https://ssc.teachers.ab.ca/SiteCollectionDocuments/OneWorldInDialogue/2023%20V7N1/A%20Clash%20of%20Interests%20Neoliberalism%20in%20Education.pdf

Memarian, B., & Doleck, T. (2023). ChatGPT in education: Methods, potentials, and limitations. *Computers in Human Behavior: Artificial Humans*, *1*(2), 100022. doi:10.1016/j.chbah.2023.100022

Mena-Guacas, A. F., Rodríguez, J. A. U., Trujillo, D. M. S., Gómez-Galán, J., & López-Meneses, E. (2023). Collaborative learning and skill development for educational growth of artificial intelligence: A systematic review. *Contemporary Educational Technology*, *15*(3), ep428. doi:10.30935/cedtech/13123

Mercader, C., & Gairín, J. (2020). University teachers' perception of barriers to the use of digital technologies: The importance of the academic discipline. *International Journal of Educational Technology in Higher Education*, *17*(1), 4. doi:10.1186/s41239-020-0182-x

Merriam, G. (2021). If A.I. Only Had a Heart: Why Artificial Intelligence Research Needs to Take Emotions More Seriously. *Journal of Artificial Intelligence and Consciousness*. doi:10.1142/S2705078521500120

Merryfield, M. M. (2000). Why aren't teachers being prepared to teach for diversity, equity, and global interconnectedness? A study of lived experiences in the making of multicultural and global educators. *Teaching and Teacher Education*, *16*(4), 429–443. doi:10.1016/S0742-051X(00)00004-4

Merzifonluoglu, S., & Hamarat, E. (2022). Epistemic Injustice, Social Studies, and Moral Sensitivity. *Ethics and Education*, *17*(4), 403–420. doi:10.1080/17449642.2022.2153469

Meyer, J. G., Urbanowicz, R. J., Martin, P. C., O'Connor, K., Li, R., Peng, P. C., Bright, T. J., Tatonetti, N., Won, K. J., Gonzalez-Hernandez, G., & Moore, J. H. (2023). ChatGPT and large language models in academia: Opportunities and challenges. *BioData Mining*, *16*(1), 20. doi:10.1186/s13040-023-00339-9 PMID:37443040

Miao, F., & Holmes, W. (2023). *Guidance for generative AI in education and research*. UNESCO. https://unesdoc.unesco.org/ark:/48223/pf0000386693

Miao, F., & Holmes, W. (2023). *Guidance for generative AI in education and research*. UNESCO. https://unesdoc.unesco.org/notice?id=p:usmarcdef_0000386693

Miao, F., Holmes, W., Huang, R., & Zhang, H. (2021). *AI and education: Guidance for policy-makers*. UNESCO. https://unesdoc.unesco.org/ark:/48223/pf0000376709

Miao, F., Shiohira, K., Vally, Z., & Holmes, W. (2023). *International forum on AI and education: Steering AI to empower teachers and transform teaching, 5-6 December 2022; analytical report*. UNESCO. https://unesdoc.unesco.org/ark:/48223/pf0000386162

Miao, Z. (2019). Investigation on human rights ethics in artificial intelligence researches with library literature analysis method. *The Electronic Library*, *37*(5), 914–926. doi:10.1108/EL-04-2019-0089

Microsoft. (2023). *What are Bing's AI features, and how do you use them?* Microsoft. https://www.microsoft.com/en-us/bing/do-more-with-ai/bing-ai-features

Mika, N., Nadezhda, G., Jaana, L., & Raija, K. (2019). Ethical AI for the governance of the society: Challenges and opportunities. *CEUR Workshop Proceedings*, *2505*, 20–26.

Mildenhall, B., Srinivasan, P. P., Tancik, M., Barron, J. T., Ramamoorthi, R., & Ng, R. (2021). Nerf: Representing scenes as neural radiance fields for view synthesis. *Communications of the ACM*, *65*(1), 99–106. https://dl.acm.org/doi/10.1145/3503250. doi:10.1145/3503250

Miller, M. (2022). *AI in the classroom: 10+ tools for teachers*. Ditch the Textbook. https://ditchthattextbook.com

Milmo, D. (2023). ChatGPT reaches 100 million users two months after launch. *The Guardian*. https://www.theguardian.com/technology/2023/feb/02/chatgpt-100-million-users-open-ai-fastest-growing-app

Mina, P., Solon, I., Sanchez, F., Delante, T., Villegas, J., Basay, F., Andales, J., Pasko, F., Estrera, M. F. R., Samson, R. Jr, & Mutya, R. (2023). Leveraging education through artificial intelligence virtual assistance: A case study of visually impaired learners. *International Journal of Educational Innovation and Research*, *2*(1), 10–22. doi:10.31949/ijeir.v2i1.3001

Mishra, P., & Koehler, M. J. (2006). Technological pedagogical content knowledge: A framework for teacher knowledge. *Teachers College Record*, *108*(6), 1017–1054. doi:10.1111/j.1467-9620.2006.00684.x

Mnhrawi, D., & Alreshidi, H. (2022). A systemic approach for implementing AI methods in education during COVID-19 pandemic: Higher education in Saudi Arabia. *World Journal of Engineering*, *20*(5), 808–814. doi:10.1108/WJE-11-2021-0623

Mohammadzadeh, Z., Ausloos, M., & Saeidnia, H. R. (2023). ChatGPT: High-tech plagiarism awaits academic publishing green light. Non-fungible token (NFT) can be a way out. *Library Hi Tech News*, *40*(7), 12–14. doi:10.1108/LHTN-04-2023-0067

Moher, D., Liberati, A., Tetzlaff, J., & Altman, D. G. (2009). *Preferred reporting items for systematic reviews and meta-analyses: The PRISMA statement*. The PRISMA Group. http://www.prisma-statement.org/

Molenaar, I., de Mooij, S., Azevedo, R., Bannert, M., Järvelä, S., & Gašević, D. (2022). Measuring self-regulated learning and the role ´ of AI: Five years of research using multimodal multichannel data. *Computers in Human Behavior*, *139*, 1–9. doi:10.1016/j.chb.2022.107540

Moloney, R., & Oguro, S. (2014). The effect of intercultural narrative reflection in shaping pre-service teachers' future practice. *Reflective Practice*, *16*(1), 96–108. doi:10.1080/14623943.2014.969699

Moloney, R., & Saltmarsh, D. (2016). 'Knowing your students' in the culturally and linguistically diverse classroom. *The Australian Journal of Teacher Education, 41*(4), 79–93. doi:10.14221/ajte.2016v41n4.5

Mondal, B. (2019). Artificial intelligence: State of the art. *Intelligent Systems Reference Library, 172*, 389–425. doi:10.1007/978-3-030-32644-9_32

Montenegro-Rueda, M., Fernández-Cerero, J., Fernández-Batanero, J. M., & López-Meneses, E. (2023). Impact of the implementation of ChatGPT in education: A systematic review. *Computers, 12*(8), 153. doi:10.3390/computers12080153

Moorhouse, B. L., Yeo, M. A., & Wan, Y. (2023). Generative AI tools and assessment: Guidelines of the world's top-ranking universities. *Computers and Education Open, 5*, 100151. doi:10.1016/j.caeo.2023.100151

Morel, G. M., & Spector, J. M. (2022). *Foundations of educational technology: Integrative approaches and interdisciplinary perspectives*. Taylor & Francis.

Moreno, R., & Mayer, R. E. (2000). Engaging students in active learning: The case for personalized multimedia messages. *Journal of Educational Psychology, 92*(4), 724–733. doi:10.1037/0022-0663.92.4.724

Moritz, S., Romeike, B., Stosch, C., & Tolks, D. (2023). Generative AI (gAI) in medical education: Chat-GPT and co. *GMS Journal for Medical Education, 40*(4), 54. doi:10.3205/zma001636 PMID:37560050

Morley, J., Elhalal, A., Garcia, F., Kinsey, L., Mökander, J., & Floridi, L. (2021). Ethics as a service: A pragmatic operationalisation of AI ethics. *Minds and Machines, 31*(2), 239–256. doi:10.1007/s11023-021-09563-w PMID:34720418

Mujeeb, S., Javed, M. H., & Arshad, T. (2017). Aquabot: A diagnostic chatbot for achluophobia and autism. *International Journal of Advanced Computer Science and Applications, 8*(9), 209–216. doi:10.14569/IJACSA.2017.080930

Mukherjee, P., S, G. R., Sadhukhan, S., Godse, M., & Chakraborty, B. (2023). Detection of Autism Spectrum Disorder (ASD) from Natural Language Text using BERT and ChatGPT Models. *International Journal of Advanced Computer Science and Applications, 14(*10). doi:10.14569/IJACSA.2023.0141041

Munn, Z., Peters, M. D. J., Stern, C., Tufanaru, C., McArthur, A., & Aromataris, E. (2018). Systematic review or scoping review? Guidance for authors when choosing between a systematic or a scoping reviewapproach. *BMC Medical Research Methodology, 18*(1), 1–7. doi:10.1186/s12874-018-0611-x PMID:29301497

Murdock, T. B., & Anderman, E. M. (2006). Motivational perspectives on student cheating: Toward an integrated model of academic aishonesty. *Educational Psychologist, 41*(3), 12–145. doi:10.1207/s15326985ep4103_1

Murphy, K., Di Ruggiero, E., Upshur, R., Willison, D. J., Malhotra, N., Cai, J. C., Malhotra, N., Lui, V., & Gibson, J. (2021). Artificial intelligence for good health: A scoping review of the ethics literature. *BMC Medical Ethics, 22*(1), 14. doi:10.1186/s12910-021-00577-8 PMID:33588803

Murugesan, S., & Cherukuri, A. K. (2023). The Rise of Generative Artificial Intelligence and Its Impact on Education: The Promises and Perils. *Computer, 56*(5), 116–121. doi:10.1109/MC.2023.3253292

Nashville State. (2023). *AI Detection in Turnitin*. NSCC. https://www.nscc.edu/documents/faculty-staff/online-learning/Turnitin-AI-Detection.pdf

Nath, S., Marie, A., Ellershaw, S., Korot, E., & Keane, P. A. (2022). New meaning for NLP: The trials and tribulations of natural language processing with GPT-3 in ophthalmology. *The British Journal of Ophthalmology, 106*(7), 889–892. doi:10.1136/bjophthalmol-2022-321141 PMID:35523534

Nazarov, R. (2023). Using video materials in teaching English. *Journal of Foreign Languages and Linguistics, 5*(5). https://fll.jdpu.uz/index.php/fll/article/view/7971

Ndihokubwayo, K., Byukusenge, C., Byusa, E., Habiyaremye, H., Mbonyiryivuze, A., & Mukagihana, J. (2022). Lesson plan analysis protocol (LPAP): A useful tool for researchers and educational evaluators. *Heliyon*, *8*(1), e08730. doi:10.1016/j.heliyon.2022.e08730 PMID:35059522

Ndukwe, I. G., Daniel, B. K., & Amadi, C. E. (2019). A machine learning grading system using chatbots. In *Artificial Intelligence in Education: 20th International Conference, AIED 2019,* (pp. 365-368). Springer International Publishing. https://doi.org/10.1007/978-3-030-23207-8_67

Nelson, C., Perez-Chada, L., Creadore, A., Li, S., Lo, K., Manjaly, P., Pournamdari, A. B., Tkachenko, E., Barbieri, J. S., Ko, J. M., Menon, A. V., Hartman, R. I., & Mostaghimi, A. (2020). Patient perspectives on the use of artificial intelligence for skin cancer screening. *JAMA Dermatology*, *156*(5), 501. doi:10.1001/jamadermatol.2019.5014 PMID:32159733

Neumann, M., Rauschenberger, M., & Schön, E. M. (2023). *"We Need To Talk About ChatGPT": The Future of AI and Higher Education.*

Newble, D. I., & Jaeger, K. (1983). The effect of assessments and examinations on the learning of medical students. *Medical Education*, *17*(3), 165–171. doi:10.1111/j.1365-2923.1983.tb00657.x PMID:6865814

Newell, A., & Simon, H. (1956). The logic theory machine—A complex information processing system. *IEEE Transactions on Information Theory*, *2*(3), 61–79. doi:10.1109/TIT.1956.1056797

Ng, A. (2016). What artificial intelligence can and can't do right now. *Harvard Business Review*, *9*(11), 1–4. http://www.w-t-w.org/de/wp-content/uploads/2016/11/Andrew-Ng-What-AI-Can-and-Can%E2%80%99t-Do.pdf

Ng, D. T. K., Leung, J. K. L., Chu, S. K., & Qiao, M. S. (2021). Conceptualizing AI literacy: An exploratory review. *Computers and Education: Artificial Intelligence*, *2*, 1–11. doi:10.1016/j.caeai.2021.100041

Ng, D., Leung, J., Su, J., Ng, R., & Chu, S. (2023). Teachers' AI digital competencies and twenty-first century skills in the post-pandemic world. *Educational Technology Research and Development*, *71*(1), 137–161. doi:10.1007/s11423-023-10203-6 PMID:36844361

Nguyen, A., Ngo, H. N., Hong, Y., Dang, B., & Nguyen, B. P. T. (2023). Ethical principles for artificial intelligence in education. *Education and Information Technologies*, *28*(4), 4221–4241. doi:10.1007/s10639-022-11316-w PMID:36254344

NguyenM. H. (2023). Academic writing and AI: Day-2 experiment with cultural additivity. doi:10.31219/osf.io/25yjw

Nguyen, T. D., Cannata, M., & Miller, J. (2018). Understanding student behavioral engagement: Importance of student interaction with peers and teachers. *The Journal of Educational Research*, *111*(2), 163–174. doi:10.1080/00220671.2016.1220359

Nikolic, S., Daniel, S., Haque, R., Belkina, M., Hassan, G. M., Grundy, S., & Sandison, C. (2023). ChatGPT versus engineering education assessment: A multidisciplinary and multi-institutional benchmarking and analysis of this generative artificial intelligence tool to investigate assessment integrity. *European Journal of Engineering Education*, 1–56. doi:10.1080/03043797.2023.2248042

Nissenbaum, H., & Walker, D. (1998). Will computers dehumanize education? A grounded approach to values at risk. *Technology in Society*, *20*(3), 237–273. doi:10.1016/S0160-791X(98)00011-6

NógrádiB.PolgárT. F.MeszlényiV.KádárZ.HertelendyP.CsátiA.PataiR. (2023). ChatGPT MD: Is there any room for generative AI in neurology and other medical areas? doi:10.2139/ssrn.4372965

Nomura, O., Mishina, H., Kobayashi, Y., Ishiguro, A., Sakai, H., & Kato, H. (2016). Limitation of duty hour regulations for pediatric resident wellness. *Medicine*, *95*(37), e4867. doi:10.1097/MD.0000000000004867 PMID:27631253

Noroozi, O. (2023). The role of students' epistemic beliefs for their argumentation performance in higher education. *Innovations in Education and Teaching International*, *60*(4), 501–512. doi:10.1080/14703297.2022.2092188

Noy, S., & Zhang, W. (2023). *Experimental Evidence on the Productivity Effects of Generative Artificial Intelligence* (SSRN Scholarly Paper 4375283). doi:10.2139/ssrn.4375283

O'Callaghan, F., Neumann, D. L., Jones, L., & Creed, P. A. (2017). The use of lecture recordings in higher education: A review of institutional, student, and lecturer issues. *Education and Information Technologies*, *22*(1), 399–415. doi:10.1007/s10639-015-9451-z

Obracht-Prondzyńska, H., Duda, E., Anacka, H., & Kowal, J. (2022). Greencoin as an AI-based solution shaping climate awareness. *International Journal of Environmental Research and Public Health*, *19*(18), 11183. doi:10.3390/ijerph191811183 PMID:36141452

OECD. (2019). *Recommendation of the council on artificial intelligence.* Organization for Economic Co-operation and Development. https://legalinstruments.oecd.org/en/instruments/OECD-LEGAL-0449

OECD. (2020). *Trustworthy AI in education: Promises and challenges.* Organization for Economic Co-operation and Development. https://www.oecd.org/education/trustworthy-artificial-intelligence-in-education.pdf

Ojeh, N., Sobers-Grannum, N., Gaur, U., Udupa, A., & Majumder, M. A. A. (2017). Learning style preferences: A study of pre-clinical medical students in Barbados. *Journal of Advances in Medical Education & Professionalism*, *5*(4), 185. https://www.ncbi.nlm.nih.gov/pmc/articles/PMC5611428/ PMID:28979913

Ojha, S. T. (2022). Artificial intelligence in special education, Id& Cp. *Journal of Positive School Psychology*, *6*(6), 8341–8345. https://journalppw.com/index.php/jpsp/article/view/9109

Okaiyeto, S. A., Bai, J., & Xiao, H. (2023). Generative AI in education: To embrace it or not? *International Journal of Agricultural and Biological Engineering*, *16*(3), 285–286. doi:10.25165/j.ijabe.20231603.8486

Okoye, K., Hussein, H., Arrona-Palacios, A., Quintero, H. N., Ortega, L. O. P., Sanchez, A. L., Ortiz, E. A., Escamilla, J., & Hosseini, S. (2023). Impact of digital technologies upon teaching and learning in higher education in Latin America: An outlook on the reach, barriers, and bottlenecks. *Education and Information Technologies*, *28*(2), 2291–2360. doi:10.1007/s10639-022-11214-1 PMID:35992366

Olenick, M., Flowers, M., Maltseva, T., & Diez-Sampedro, A. (2019). Research in academia: Creating and maintaining high-performance research teams. *Nursing Research and Practice*, *1-3*, 1–3. doi:10.1155/2019/8423460 PMID:30863638

Oliinyk, O., Bilan, Y., & Mishchuk, H. (2021). Knowledge Management and Economic Growth: The Assessment of Links and Determinants of Regulation. *Central European Management Journal*, *29*(3), 20–39. doi:10.7206/cemj.2658-0845.52

Oliveira, R. C., & Silva, R. D. S. e. (2023). Artificial Intelligence in Agriculture: Benefits, Challenges, and Trends. *Applied Sciences (Basel, Switzerland)*, *13*(13), 7405. doi:10.3390/app13137405

Open A. I. (2020). *ChatGPT: A large-scale generative language model.* Open AI. https://beta.openai.com/signup/

Open A. I. (2022). *ChatGPT: Optimizing language models for dialogue.* Open AI. https://openai.com/blog/chatgpt/

Open A. I. (2022). *Introducing ChatGPT.* Open AI. https://openai.com/blog/chatgpt

Open A. I. (2023). *ChatGPT* [Large language model]. OpenAI. https://chat.openai.com

Open A. I. (2023). *ChatGPT can now see, hear, and speak. OpenAI.* Open AI. https://openai.com/blog/chatgpt-can-now-see-hear-and-speak

Open A. I. (n.d.). *About Open AI. OpenAI.* Open AI. https://openai.com/about

Open A. I. (n.d.). *ChatGPT* [Computer software]. Open AI. https://chat.openai.com

Open A. I. (n.d.). *DALL-E 2.* Open AI. https://openai.com/dall-e-2

Open A. I. (n.d.). *GPT-4 is OpenAI's most advanced system, producing safer and more useful responses.* Open AI. https://openai.com/gpt-4

Oppenlaender, J., Linder, R., & Silvennoinen, J. (2023). *Prompting AI Art: An Investigation into the Creative Skill of Prompt Engineering.* arXiv. https://arxiv.org/pdf/2303.13534.pdf

Oravec, J. A. (2022). AI, biometric analysis, and emerging cheating detection systems: The engineering of academic integrity? *Education Policy Analysis Archives, 30.* doi:10.14507/epaa.30.5765

Oravec, J. A. (2023). Artificial Intelligence implications for academic cheating: Expanding the dimensions of responsible human-AI collaboration with ChatGPT. *Journal of Interactive Learning Research, 34*(2), 213–237.

Oritsegbemi, O. (2023). Human intelligence versus AI: Implications for emotional aspects of human communication. *Journal of Advanced Research in Social Sciences, 6*(2), 76–85. doi:10.33422/jarss.v6i2.1005

Otis, M. M., & Hammond, J. D. (2009). Participatory action research as a rationale for student voices in the scholarship of teaching and learning. In C. Werder & M. M. Otis (Eds.), *Engaging Student Voices in the Study of Teaching and Learning* (pp. 32–48). Routledge.

Ouyang, F., Zheng, L., & Jiao, P. (2022). Artificial intelligence in online higher education: A systematic review of empirical research from 2011 to 2020. *Education and Information Technologies, 27*(6), 7893–7925. doi:10.1007/s10639-022-10925-9

Pack, A., & Maloney, J. (2023). Using generative artificial intelligence for language education research: Insights from using OpenAI's ChatGPT. *TESOL Quarterly, 57*(4), 1571–1582. doi:10.1002/tesq.3253

Page, L., & Gehlbach, H. (2017). How an Artificially Intelligent Virtual Assistant Helps Students Navigate the Road to College. *AERA Open, 3*(4). doi:10.1177/2332858417749220

Paranjape, K., Schinkel, M., Panday, R., Car, J., & Nanayakkara, P. (2019). Introducing artificial intelligence training in medical education. *JMIR Medical Education, 5*(2), e16048. doi:10.2196/16048 PMID:31793895

Park, M. (2020). Investigating Target Tasks, Task Phases, and Indigenous Criteria for Military Aviation English Assessment. *Language Assessment Quarterly, 17*(4), 337–361. doi:10.1080/15434303.2020.1799221

Parra-Valencia, J. A., & Massey, M. L. (2023). Leveraging AI Tools for Enhanced Digital Literacy, Access to Information, and Personalized Learning. In *Managing Complex Tasks with Systems Thinking* (pp. 213–234). Springer Nature Switzerland. doi:10.1007/978-3-031-40635-5_9

Parshall, C. G., Spray, J. A., Kalohn, J. C., & Davey, T. (2002). *Practical considerations in computer-based testing.* Springer Science & Business Media. doi:10.1007/978-1-4613-0083-0

Parui, S., Samanta, D., Chakravorty, N., Ghosh, U., & Rodrigues, J. J. (2023). Artificial intelligence and sensor-based autism spectrum disorder diagnosis using brain connectivity analysis. *Computers & Electrical Engineering, 108*, 108720. doi:10.1016/j.compeleceng.2023.108720

Pataranutaporn, P., Danry, V., Leong, J., Punpongsanon, P., Novy, D., Maes, P., & Sra, M. (2021). AI-generated characters for supporting personalized learning and well-being. *Nature Machine Intelligence, 3*(12), 1013–1022. doi:10.1038/s42256-021-00417-9

Patel, S. B., & Lam, K. (2023). ChatGPT: The future of discharge summaries? *The Lancet. Digital Health*, *5*(3), e107–e108. doi:10.1016/S2589-7500(23)00021-3 PMID:36754724

Pavlik, J. V. (2023). Collaborating with ChatGPT: Considering the implications of generative artificial intelligence for journalism and media education. *Journalism & Mass Communication Educator*, *78*(1), 84–93. doi:10.1177/10776958221149577

Pearce, H., Ahmad, B., Tan, B., Dolan-Gavitt, B., & Karri, R. (2022, May). Asleep at the keyboard? assessing the security of github copilot's code contributions. In *2022 IEEE Symposium on Security and Privacy (SP)* (pp. 754-768). IEEE. 10.1109/SP46214.2022.9833571

Pedro, F., Subosa, M., Rivas, A., & Valverde, P. (2019). *Artificial intelligence in education: Challenges and opportunities for sustainable development*. HDL. https://hdl.handle.net/20.500.12799/6533

Pedro, F., Subosa, M., Rivas, A., & Valverde, P. (2019). *Artificial intelligence in education: challenges and opportunities for sustainable development*. UNESCO. https://unesdoc.unesco.org/ark:/48223/pf0000366994

Pena-Fernandez, S., Meso Ayerdi, K., Ureta, A., & Diaz Noci, J. (2023). Without journalists, there is no journalism: The social dimension of generative artificial intelligence in the media. *El Profesional de la Información*, *32*, 1–15. doi:10.3145/epi.2023.mar.27

Pender, H. L., Bohl, L., Schönberger, M., & Knopf, J. (2022). *An AI-based lesson planning software to support competence-based learning*. IEEE. doi:10.4995/HEAd22.2022.14599

Peng, H., Ma, S., & Spector, J. M. (2019). Personalized adaptive learning: An emerging pedagogical approach enabled by a smart learning environment. *Smart Learning Environments*, *6*(1), 1–14. doi:10.1186/s40561-019-0089-y

Pennisi, P., Tonacci, A., Tartarisco, G., Billeci, L., Ruta, L., Gangemi, S., & Pioggia, G. (2016). Autism and social robotics: A systematic review. *Autism Research*, *9*(2), 165–183. doi:10.1002/aur.1527 PMID:26483270

Pereira, R. H. M., Braga, C. K. V., Servo, L. M., Serra, B., Amaral, P., Gouveia, N., & Paez, A. (2021). Geographic access to COVID-19 healthcare in Brazil using a balanced float catchment area approach. *Social Science & Medicine*, *273*, 113773. doi:10.1016/j.socscimed.2021.113773 PMID:33609968

Pérez-Núñez, A. (2023). Exploring the Potential of Generative AI (ChatGPT) for Foreign Language Instruction: Applications and Challenges. *Hispania*, *106*(3), 355–362. doi:10.1353/hpn.2023.a906568

Pershukova, O. O., Pazyura, N., & Vasiukovych, O. (2023). Using interactive learning in future aviation professionals teaching English. *Educational Dimension*, *8*, 41–54. doi:10.31812/ed.584

Pescador, F., & Mohanty, S. P. (2022). Guest editorial: Security by design for electronic systems. *IEEE Transactions on Consumer Electronics*, *68*(1), 2–14. doi:10.1109/TCE.2022.3147005

Petersen, J. (2016). *Innovative assessment practices*. FreshGrade Education Inc. https://learn.sd61.bc.ca/wp-content/uploads/sites/96/2017/09/FG-Innovative-Assessment-Whitepaper.pdf

Pflanzer, M., Traylor, Z., Lyons, J. B., Dubljević, V., & Nam, C. S. (2023). Ethics in human–AI teaming: Principles and perspectives. *AI and Ethics*, *3*(3), 917–935. doi:10.1007/s43681-022-00214-z

Piskopani, A. M., Chamberlain., A. & Holter, C. T. (2023). *Responsible AI and the Arts: The Ethical and Legal Implications of AI in the Arts and Creative Industries*. doi:10.1145/3597512.3597528

Play, H. T. (2023). *AI Voice Genertor Products*. https://play.ht/products

Playfoot, D. (2023). Flipped classrooms in undergraduate statistics: Online works just fine. *Teaching of Psychology*, *50*(3), 243–247. doi:10.1177/00986283211046319

Pllana, D. (2019). Expanding Entire Volume of Knowledge Influences on Incrementing Individual Knowledge. *Global Journal of Human-Social Science: H Interdisciplinary, 19*(8).

Poch, A. L., Hamby, M., & Chen, X. (2020). Secondary teachers' beliefs about teaching writing to typically achieving and struggling adolescent writers. *Reading & Writing Quarterly*, *36*(6), 497–520. doi:10.1080/10573569.2019.1666759

Popkewitz, T. S. (2011). Curriculum history, schooling and the history of the present. *History of Education*, *40*(1), 1–19. doi:10.1080/0046760X.2010.507222

Popovici, M.-D. (2023). ChatGPT in the Classroom. Exploring its potential and limitations in a functional programming course. *International Journal of Human-Computer Interaction*, 1–12. doi:10.1080/10447318.2023.2269006

Porayska-Pomsta, K. (2016). AI as a Methodology for Supporting Educational Praxis and Teacher Metacognition. *International Journal of Artificial Intelligence in Education*, *26*(2), 679–700. doi:10.1007/s40593-016-0101-4

Pradana, M., Elisa, H. P., & Syarifuddin, S. (2023). Discussing ChatGPT in education: A literature review and bibliometric analysis. *Cogent Education*, *10*(2), 2243134. doi:10.1080/2331186X.2023.2243134

Pratama, M. P., Sampelolo, R., & Lura, H. (2023). Revolutionizing Education: Harnessing The Power Of Artificial Intelligence For Personalized Learning. *Klasikal: Journal of Education. Language Teaching and Science*, *5*(2), 350–357. doi:10.52208/klasikal.v5i2.877

Preidel, J., Weikamp, J., & Werhand, M. (2009). Theorie & Praxis des Lehrer Angst und Stress Test: (Lehramts-)StudentInnen & Lehrkräfte im Vergleich. *Universität Regensburg*. https://epub.uni-regensburg.de/10894/

Preiksaitis, C., & Rose, C. (2023). Opportunities, challenges, and future directions of generative artificial intelligence in medical education: Scoping review. *JMIR Medical Education*, *9*(1), e48785. doi:10.2196/48785 PMID:37862079

Prensky, M. (2007). *Digital game-based learning*. Paragon House.

Priyadarsini, A. (2022). Artificial intelligence: Applications in nursing. *Asian Pacific Journal of Health Sciences*, *9*(4), 318–320. doi:10.21276/apjhs.2022.9.4.59

Prunkl, C. (2022). Human autonomy in the age of artificial intelligence. *Nature Machine Intelligence*, *4*(2), 99–101. doi:10.1038/s42256-022-00449-9

Purdue University. (2020). *West Lafayette Instructors save time grading using automated, no-cost assessment tools created by Purdue, Integrated with BrightSpace*. Purdue. https://www.purdue.edu/innovativelearning/blog/2020/11/02/west-lafayette-instructors-save-time-grading-using-automated-no-cost-assessment-tools-created-by-purdue-integrated-with-brightspace/

Qadir, J. (2023, May). Engineering education in the era of ChatGPT: Promise and pitfalls of generative AI for education. In *2023 IEEE Global Engineering Education Conference (EDUCON)* (pp. 1-9). IEEE. 10.1109/EDUCON54358.2023.10125121

Quishpe Gaibor, J. S., & Pizarro Macas, J. L. (2018). Evolución Histórica de la Ética hasta nuestros Días. *Revista Caribeña De Ciencias Sociales*, *2018*, 1–6.

Quy, V. K., Thanh, B. T., Chehri, A., Linh, D. M., & Tuan, D. A. (2023). AI and digital transformation in higher education: Vision and approach of a specific university in Vietnam. *Sustainability (Basel)*, *15*(14), 11093. doi:10.3390/su151411093

Rahman, M. M., & Watanobe, Y. (2023). ChatGPT for education and research: Opportunities, threats, and strategies. *Applied Sciences (Basel, Switzerland)*, *13*(9), 1–21. doi:10.3390/app13095783

Rajalingam, S., Kanagamalliga, S., Karuppiah, N., & Puoza, J. (2021). Peer interaction teaching-learning approaches for effective engagement of students in virtual classroom. *Journal of Engineering Education Transformations*, *34*(0), 425–432. doi:10.16920/jeet/2021/v34i0/157191

Raj, N. S., & Renumol, V. G. (2022). A systematic literature review on adaptive content recommenders in personalized learning environments from 2015 to 2020. *Journal of Computers in Education*, *9*(1), 113–148. doi:10.1007/s40692-021-00199-4

Rakap, S. (2023). Chatting with GPT: Enhancing Individualized Education Program Goal Development for Novice Special Education Teachers. *Journal of Special Education Technology*, *01626434231211295*, 01626434231211295. doi:10.1177/01626434231211295

Ramo Akgün, N. (2023). Trends of assistive technologies in Autism Spectrum Disorder: Bibliometric analysis based on Web of Science Database (1998–2023). *Cumhuriyet International Journal of Education, 12*(3), 777-794. https://dx.doi.org/. 1308308 doi:10.30703/cije

Rasul, T., Nair, S., Kalendra, D., Robin, M., Santini, F. de O., Ladeira, W. J., Sun, M., Day, I., Rather, R. A., & Heathcote, L. (2023). The role of ChatGPT in higher education: Benefits, challenges, and future research directions. *Journal of Applied Learning and Teaching*, *6*(1), 41–56. doi:10.37074/jalt.2023.6.1.29

Rathenau Instituut. (2017). *Human rights in the robot age: Challenges arising from the use of robotics, artificial intelligence, and virtual and augmented reality.* Rathenau Instituut.

Rattenborg, K., MacPhee, D., Walker, A. K., & Miller-Heyl, J. (2018). Pathways to Parental Engagement: Contributions of parents, teachers, and schools in cultural context. *Early Education and Development*, *30*(3), 315–336. doi:10.1080/10409289.2018.1526577

Ratten, V., & Jones, P. (2023). Generative artificial intelligence (ChatGPT): Implications for management educators. *International Journal of Management Education*, *21*(3), 100857. doi:10.1016/j.ijme.2023.100857

Reed, P., & Bowser, G. (2005). Assistive technology and the IEP. D. L. Edyburn, K. Higgins & R. Boone (Eds.). Handbook of special educaiton technology research and practice (pp. 61-77). Knowledge by Design.

Reiss, M. (2021). The use of AI in education: Practicalities and ethical considerations. *London Review of Education*, *19*(1). doi:10.14324/LRE.19.1.05

Rezwana, J. (2023). *Towards designing engaging and ethical human-centered AI partners for human-AI co-creativity* [Doctoral dissertation, The University of North Carolina at Charlotte].

Richardson, J., Curtis, S., Smith, C., Pacyna, J., Zhu, X., Barry, B., & Sharp, R. R. (2022). A framework for examining patient attitudes regarding applications of artificial intelligence in healthcare. *Digital Health*, *8*, 205520762210890. doi:10.1177/20552076221089084 PMID:35355806

Riedl, M., Arriaga, R., Boujarwah, F., Hong, H., Isbell, J., & Heflin, J. (2009, October). *Graphical social scenarios: Toward intervention and authoring for adolescents with high functioning autism. In 2009 AAAI Fall Symposium Series.* AAAI. https://cdn.aaai.org/ocs/945/945-4144-1-PB.pdf

Robin, C. (2023, August 24). How ChatGPT changed my plans for the fall. *The Chronicle of Higher Education.* https://www.chronicle.com/article/the-end-of-the-take-home-essay

Rochmawati, L., Fatmawati, & Sukma, M. M. (2023). Motivation, anxiety, and self-efficacy in learning aviation English: A study of Indonesian aviation cadets. *Asian Journal of Second and Foreign Language Education*, *8*(1), 40. doi:10.1186/s40862-023-00212-6

Roediger, H. L. III, & Karpicke, J. D. (2006). The Power of Testing Memory: Basic Research and Implications for Educational Practice. *Perspectives on Psychological Science*, *1*(3), 181–210. doi:10.1111/j.1745-6916.2006.00012.x PMID:26151629

Rogge, N., & Janssen, J. (2019). The economic costs of autism spectrum disorder: A literature review. *Journal of Autism and Developmental Disorders*, *49*(7), 2873–2900. doi:10.1007/s10803-019-04014-z PMID:30976961

Roh, S., Burnette, C., Lee, K., Lee, Y., Martin, J., & Lawler, M. (2016). Predicting help-seeking attitudes toward mental health services among American Indian older adults. *Journal of Applied Gerontology*, *36*(1), 94–115. doi:10.1177/0733464814558875 PMID:25416511

Roll, I., Aleven, V., McLaren, B. M., & Koedinger, K. R. (2011). Improving students' help-seeking skills using metacognitive feedback in an intelligent tutoring system. *Learning and Instruction*, *21*(2), 267–280. doi:10.1016/j.learninstruc.2010.07.004

Roll, I., & Wylie, R. (2016). Evolution and revolution in artificial intelligence in education. *International Journal of Artificial Intelligence in Education*, *26*(2), 582–599. doi:10.1007/s40593-016-0110-3

Romijn, B. R., Slot, P., & Leseman, P. (2021). Increasing teachers' intercultural competences in teacher preparation programs and through professional development: A review. *Teaching and Teacher Education*, *98*, 103236. doi:10.1016/j.tate.2020.103236

Rommelspacher, B. (2002). *Anerkennung und Ausgrenzung: Deutschland als multikulturelle Gesellschaft.* Campus Verlag.

Roos, B., & Borkoski, C. (2021). Attending to the teacher in the teaching: Prioritizing faculty well-being. *Perspectives of the ASHA Special Interest Groups*, *6*(4), 831–840. doi:10.1044/2021_PERSP-21-00006

Roscoe, R. D., & McNamara, D. S. (2013). Writing pal: Feasibility of an intelligent writing strategy tutor in the high school classroom. *Journal of Educational Psychology*, *105*(4), 1010–1025. doi:10.1037/a0032340

Rudolph, J., Tan, S., & Tan, S. (2023). ChatGPT: Bullshit spewer or the end of traditional assessments in higher education? *Journal of Applied Learning & Teaching*, *6*(1), 1–20. https://journals.sfu.ca/jalt/index.php/jalt/index

Ruiz-Rojas, L. I., Acosta-Vargas, P., De-Moreta-Llovet, J., & Gonzalez-Rodriguez, M. (2023). Empowering Education with Generative Artificial Intelligence Tools: Approach with an Instructional Design Matrix. *Sustainability (Basel)*, *15*(15), 11524. doi:10.3390/su151511524

Russel Group. (2023, July 5). *New principles on use of AI in education.* The Russell Group. https://russellgroup.ac.uk/news/new-principles-on-use-of-ai-in-education/

Rutten, N., van Joolingen, W. R., & van der Veen, J. T. (2012). The learning effects of computer simulations in science education. *Computers & Education*, *58*(1), 136–153. doi:10.1016/j.compedu.2011.07.017

Ryan, M. (2020). In AI we trust: Ethics, artificial intelligence, and reliability. *Science and Engineering Ethics*, *26*(5), 2749–2767. doi:10.1007/s11948-020-00228-y PMID:32524425

Ryan, M. (2022). The social and ethical impacts of artificial intelligence in agriculture: Mapping the agricultural AI literature. *AI & Society*. doi:10.1007/s00146-021-01377-9

Ryan, M., Van Der Burg, S., & Bogaardt, M. (2022). Identifying key ethical debates for autonomous robots in agri food: A research agenda. *AI and Ethics*, *2*(3), 493–507. doi:10.1007/s43681-021-00104-w

Ryznar, M. (2023). Exams in the time of ChatGPT. *Washington and Lee Law Review Online*, *80*(5), 305–322. doi:10.2139/ssrn.3684958

Sabzalieva, E., & Valentini, A. (2023). *Chatgpt and artificial intelligence in higher education: Quick start guide.* UNESCO. https://www.iesalc.unesco.org/wp-content/uploads/2023/04/ChatGPT-and-Artificial-Intelligence-in-higher-education-Quick-Start-guide_EN_FINAL.pdf

SætraH. S. (2023). Generative AI: Here to stay, but for good? (March 22, 2023). doi:10.1016/j.techsoc.2023.102372

Safa, M. A., & Tofighi, S. (2021). Intercultural communicative competence beliefs and practices of Iranian pre-service and in-service EFL teachers. *Innovation in Language Learning and Teaching*, *16*(2), 164–175. doi:10.1080/17501229.2021.1889562

Sağdıç, A., Canpolat Çığ, N., Çelenk, U., Takı, Z., Çetin, İ., Feyzullahoğlu, P., Altuğ Ateş, M., & Doğan, O. (2023). Teaching Following Instructions and Responding Skills to Children with Autism with an AI-Supported Mobile Application. In *ICERI2023 Proceedings* (pp. 7658-7664). IATED. 10.21125/iceri.2023.1920

Sağdıç, Z. A., & Sani-Bozkurt, S. (2020). Otizm spektrum bozukluğu ve yapay zeka uygulamaları. *Açıköğretim Uygulamaları ve Araştırmaları Dergisi, 6*(3), 92-111. https://dergipark.org.tr/en/pub/auad/issue/56247/768540

Sait, S., & Tombs, M. (2021). Teaching medical students how to interpret chest x-rays: The design and development of an e-learning resource. *Advances in Medical Education and Practice*, *12*, 123–132. doi:10.2147/AMEP.S280941 PMID:33574725

Saleh, M. A., Hanapiah, F. A., & Hashim, H. (2021). Robot applications for autism: A comprehensive review. *Disability and Rehabilitation. Assistive Technology*, *16*(6), 580–602. doi:10.1080/17483107.2019.1685016 PMID:32706602

Sallam, M. (2023). ChatGPT utility in healthcare education, research, and practice: Systematic review on the promising perspectives and valid concerns. *Health Care*, *11*(6), 887. doi:10.3390/healthcare11060887 PMID:36981544

Salvagno, M., Taccone, F. S., & Gerli, A. G. (2023). Can artificial intelligence help for scientific writing? *Critical Care*, *27*(1), 1–5. doi:10.1186/s13054-023-04380-2 PMID:36597110

Sánchez, J. M., Rodríguez, J. P., & Espitia, H. E. (2020). Review of Artificial Intelligence Applied in Decision-Making. Processes in Agricultural Public Policy. *Processes*, *8*(11), 1374. doi:10.3390/pr8111374

Sani-Bozkurt, S., & Sağdıç, A. Z. (2022). Teknoloji. In H. Bakkaloğlu, S. Çelik, & G. Tomris (Eds.), *Araştırmadan Uygulamaya Erken Çocukluk Özel Eğitimi El Kitabı* (pp. 641–666). Vize Akademik.

Sanusi, I. T., Oyelere, S. S., Vartiainen, H., Suhonen, J., & Tukiainen, M. (2023). A systematic review of teaching and learning machine learning in K-12 education. *Education and Information Technologies*, *28*(5), 5967–5997. doi:10.1007/s10639-022-11416-7

Sapci, A., & Sapci, H. (2020). Artificial intelligence education and tools for medical and health informatics students: Systematic review. *JMIR Medical Education*, *6*(1), e19285. doi:10.2196/19285 PMID:32602844

Sarker, I. H. (2022). Ai-based modeling: Techniques, applications and research issues towards automation, intelligent and smart systems. *SN Computer Science*, *3*(2), 158. doi:10.1007/s42979-022-01043-x PMID:35194580

Sawant, R., Shaikh, A., Sabat, S., & Bhole, V. (2021, July). Text to image generation using GAN. In *Proceedings of the International Conference on IoT Based Control Networks & Intelligent Systems-ICICNIS*. SSRN. 10.2139/ssrn.3882570

Schiff, D. (2020). Out of the laboratory and into the classroom: The future of artificial intelligence in education. *AI & Society*, *36*(1), 331–348. doi:10.1007/s00146-020-01033-8 PMID:32836908

Schiff, D. (2022). Education for AI, not AI for education: The role of education and ethics in national AI policy strategies. *International Journal of Artificial Intelligence in Education*, *32*(3), 527–563. doi:10.1007/s40593-021-00270-2

Schlagwein, D., & Willcocks, L. P. (2023). 'ChatGPT et al.': The ethics of using (generative) artificial intelligence in research and science. *Journal of Information Technology*, *38*(3), 232–238. doi:10.1177/02683962231200411

Schmarje, L., Santarossa, M., Schröder, S. M., & Koch, R. (2021). A survey on semi-, self-and unsupervised learning for image classification. *IEEE Access : Practical Innovations, Open Solutions*, *9*, 82146–82168. doi:10.1109/ACCESS.2021.3084358

Schneider, B., & Pea, R. (2017). Real-time mutual gaze perception enhances collaborative learning and collaboration quality. *Educational Media and Technology Yearbook*, *40*, 99–125. doi:10.1007/978-3-319-45001-8_7

Schöbel, S., Schmitt, A., Benner, D., Saqr, M., Janson, A., & Leimeister, J. M. (2023). Charting the Evolution and Future of Conversational Agents: A Research Agenda Along Five Waves and New Frontiers. *Information Systems Frontiers*, 1–26. doi:10.1007/s10796-023-10375-9

Schroeder, K. T., Hubertz, M., Van Campenhout, R., & Johnson, B. G. (2022). Teaching and Learning with AI-Generated Courseware: Lessons from the Classroom. *Online Learning : the Official Journal of the Online Learning Consortium*, *26*(3), 73–87. https://eric.ed.gov/?id=EJ1374315. doi:10.24059/olj.v26i3.3370

Schwarz, C. (2009). Developing preservice elementary teachers' knowledge and practices through modeling-centered scientific inquiry. *Science Education*, *93*(4), 720–744. doi:10.1002/sce.20324

Schwengerer, L. (2023). Virtual reality as a path to self-knowledge. *Synthese*, *202*(3), 87. doi:10.1007/s11229-023-04317-w PMID:36855375

Selk, A. (2018, May 5). One space or two spaces after a full stop? Scientists have finally found the answer. *The Independent*. https://www.independent.co.uk/tech/one-space-or-two-spaces-after-a-full-stop-scientists-have-finally-found-the-answer-a8337646.html

Şenocak, D., Koçdar, S., & Bozkurt, A. (2023). Historical, philosophical, and ethical roots of artificial intelligence. *Pakistan Journal of Education*, *40*(1), 67–90. doi:10.30971/pje.v40i1.1152

Seo, J., Hwa-Ok, B., Kim, B., Huh, S., Ahn, Y., Jung, S., & Lee, Y. (2022). Burnout of faculty members of medical schools in Korea. *Journal of Korean Medical Science*, *37*(9), e74. doi:10.3346/jkms.2022.37.e74 PMID:35257529

Seo, K., Tang, J., Roll, I., Fels, S., & Yoon, D. (2021). The impact of artificial intelligence on learner–instructor interaction in online learning. *International Journal of Educational Technology in Higher Education*, *18*(1), 54. Advance online publication. doi:10.1186/s41239-021-00292-9 PMID:34778540

Shahamiri, S. R., & Thabtah, F. (2020). Autism AI: A new autism screening system based on artificial intelligence. *Cognitive Computation*, *12*(4), 766–777. doi:10.1007/s12559-020-09743-3

Shah, D. T., Williams, V. N., Thorndyke, L. E., Marsh, E. E., Sonnino, R. E., Block, S. M., & Viggiano, T. R. (2018). Restoring Faculty Vitality in Academic Medicine When Burnout Threatens. *Academic Medicine*, *93*(7), 979–984. doi:10.1097/ACM.0000000000002013 PMID:29166355

Shanafelt, T., West, C., Sloan, J., Novotny, P., Poland, G., Menaker, R., Rummans, T. A., & Dyrbye, L. (2009). Career fit and burnout among academic faculty. *Archives of Internal Medicine*, *169*(10), 990. doi:10.1001/archinternmed.2009.70 PMID:19468093

Sharma, R. C. (2023). Exploring Generative AI's Influence on Tailored Learning. *Education@ ETMA, 2*(1), i-iii. http://etma-india.com/index.php/educationatetma/article/view/18

Sharma, A., & Tanwar, P. (2024). Model for autism disorder detection using deep learning. *IAES International Journal of Artificial Intelligence*, *13*(1), 391–398. doi:10.11591/ijai.v13.i1.pp391-398

Shcherbakov, G. A. (2023, May). "Artificial Intelligence" Vs "Human Intelligence": a New Ethics of Technological Development. In *2023 XXVI International Conference on Soft Computing and Measurements (SCM)* (pp. 163-166). IEEE. 10.1109/SCM58628.2023.10159110

Shemshack, A., Kinshuk, & Spector, J. M. (2021). A comprehensive analysis of personalized learning components. *Journal of Computers in Education*, *8*(4), 485–503. doi:10.1007/s40692-021-00188-7

Shemshack, A., & Spector, J. M. (2020). A systematic literature review of personalized learning terms. *Smart Learning Environments*, *7*(1), 1–20. doi:10.1186/s40561-020-00140-9

Shen, D., & Chang, C. S. (2023). Implementation of the flipped classroom approach for promoting college students' deeper learning. *Educational Technology Research and Development*, 1–25.

Shen, Y., Heacock, L., Elias, J., Hentel, K. D., Reig, B., Shih, G., & Moy, L. (2023). ChatGPT and other large language models are double-edged swords. *Radiology*, *307*(2), e230163. doi:10.1148/radiol.230163 PMID:36700838

Shih, P., Lin, C., Wu, L., & Yu, C. (2021). Learning ethics in AI—Teaching non-engineering undergraduates through situated learning. *Sustainability (Basel)*, *13*(7), 3718. doi:10.3390/su13073718

Shin, J., Guo, Q., & Gierl, M. J. (2019). Multiple-choice item distractor development using topic modelling approaches. Frontiers in Psychology. doi:10.3389/fpsyg.2019.00825

ShirinA. (2022). Artificial intelligence technology on teaching-learning: Exploring Bangladeshi teachers' perceptions. *Embedded Selforganising Systems, 9*(4), 3-9. https://doi.org/ doi:10.14464/ess.v9i4.553

Shoja, M. M., Van de Ridder, J. M. M., & Rajput, V. (2023). The emerging role of generative artificial intelligence in medical education, research, and practice. *Cureus*, *15*(6). doi:10.7759/cureus.40883 PMID:37492829

Short, C. E., & Short, J. C. (2023). The artificially intelligent entrepreneur: ChatGPT, prompt engineering, and entrepreneurial rhetoric creation. *Journal of Business Venturing Insights*, *19*, e00388. doi:10.1016/j.jbvi.2023.e00388

Shorten, C., Khoshgoftaar, T. M., & Furht, B. (2021). Deep Learning applications for COVID-19. *Journal of Big Data*, *8*(1), 1–54. doi:10.1186/s40537-020-00392-9 PMID:33457181

Shrivastava, R. (2023). Role of Artificial Intelligence in Future of Education. *International Journal of Professional Business Review*, *8*(1), e0840. doi:10.26668/businessreview/2023.v8i1.840

Siau, K., & Wang, W. (2020). Artificial Intelligence (AI) Ethics: Ethics of AI and Ethical AI. [JDM]. *Journal of Database Management*, *31*(2), 74–87. doi:10.4018/JDM.2020040105

Simplified. (2023). *AI Presentation Maker – The Effortless Way to Generate Presentations.* Simplified. https://simplified.com/ai-presentation-maker

Singh, M. K. (2023, October 26). *Is it plagiarism to use ChatGPT or other AI language models?* Foundry Law Group. https://foundrylawgroup.com/is-it-plagiarism-to-use-chat-gpt-or-other-ai-language-models/#:~:text=The%20short%20answer%20is%20that,original%20source%20of%20your%20content.

Singha, R., & Singha, S. (2023). Economic sustainability, mindfulness, and diversity in the age of artificial intelligence and machine learning. In P. Raj, P. B. Soundarabai, & P. Augustine (Eds.), *Machine Intelligence: Computer Vision and Natural Language Processing* (pp. 273–285). Taylor & Francis Group. doi:10.1201/9781003424550-15

Sintov, N., Kar, D., Nguyen, T., Fang, F., Hoffman, K., Lyet, A., & Tambe, M. (2016, March). From the lab to the classroom and beyond: Extending a game-based research platform for teaching AI to diverse audiences. *Proceedings of the AAAI Conference on Artificial Intelligence*, *30*(1). doi:10.1609/aaai.v30i1.9854

Skaalvik, E. M., & Skaalvik, S. (2017). Teacher stress and teacher self-efficacy: Relations and consequences. *Educator stress: An occupational health perspective*, 101-125. doi:10.1007/978-3-319-53053-6_5

Skinner, E. A., & Belmont, M. J. (1993). Motivation in the classroom: Reciprocal effects of teacher behavior and student engagement across the school year. *Journal of Educational Psychology*, *85*(4), 571–581. doi:10.1037/0022-0663.85.4.571

Slavin, R. E. (1996). Research on cooperative learning and achievement: What we know, what we need to know. *Contemporary Educational Psychology*, *21*(1), 43–69. https://www.academia.edu/download/32134643/Cooperative_Learning_-_SLAVIN__Robert.pdf. doi:10.1006/ceps.1996.0004

Smart, P., & Clowes, R. (2021). Intellectual virtues and internet-extended knowledge. *Social Epistemology Review and Reply Collective*, *10*(1), 7–21. https://wp.me/p1Bfg0-5AY

Smither, J. W., London, M., & Richmond, K. R. (2005). The relationship between leaders' personality and their reactions to and use of multisource feedback: A longitudinal study. *Group & Organization Management*, *30*(2), 181–210. doi:10.1177/1059601103254912

Smolansky, A., Cram, A., Raduescu, C., Zeivots, S., Huber, E., & Kizilcec, R. F. (2023, July). Educator and student perspectives on the impact of generative AI on assessments in higher education. In *Proceedings of the Tenth ACM Conference on Learning@ Scale* (pp. 378-382). ACM. 10.1145/3573051.3596191

Sobhanmanesh, F., Beheshti, A., Nouri, N., Chapparo, N. M., Raj, S., & George, R. A. (2023). A Cognitive Model for Technology Adoption. *Algorithms*, *16*(3), 155. doi:10.3390/a16030155

Sohail, S. S., Farhat, F., Himeur, Y., Nadeem, M., Madsen, D. Ø., Singh, Y., Atalla, S., & Mansoor, W. (2023). Decoding ChatGPT: A taxonomy of existing research, current challenges, and possible future directions. *Journal of King Saud University. Computer and Information Sciences*, *35*(8), 101675. doi:10.1016/j.jksuci.2023.101675

SohailS. S.FarhatF.HimeurY.NadeemM.MadsenD. Ø.SinghY.AtallaS.MansoorW. (2023). The Future of GPT: A taxonomy of existing ChatGPT research, current challenges, and possible future directions. *Social Science Research Network*. https://doi.org/ doi:10.2139/ssrn.4413921

Sointu, E., Hyypiä, M., Lambert, M. C., Hirsto, L., Saarelainen, M., & Valtonen, T. (2023). Preliminary evidence of key factors in successful flipping: Predicting positive student experiences in flipped classrooms. *Higher Education*, *85*(3), 503–520. doi:10.1007/s10734-022-00848-2 PMID:35431321

Song, D.-Y., Kim, S. Y., Bong, G., Kim, J. M., & Yoo, H. J. (2019). The use of artificial intelligence in screening and diagnosis of autism spectrum disorder: A literature review. *Journal of the Korean Academy of Child and Adolescent Psychiatry*, *30*(4), 145–152. doi:10.5765/jkacap.190027 PMID:32595335

Sony. (2018). *Sony group's initiatives for responsible AI*. https://www.sony.com/en/SonyInfo/sony_ai/responsible_ai.html

Soundraw. (n.d.). *Soundraw: Create Your Beats with The Power of AI.* Soundraw. https://soundraw.io

Souppez, J. B. R., Goswami, D., & Yuen, J. (2023, December). Assessment and Feedback in the Generative AI Era: Transformative Opportunities, Novel Assessment Strategies and Policies in Higher Education. In International Federation of National Teaching Fellows Symposathon 2023.

Sovrano, F., & Vitali, F. (2022). Explanatory artificial intelligence (xAI): Human-centered explanations of explainable AI and complex data. *Data Mining and Knowledge Discovery*. doi:10.1007/s10618-022-00872-x

Speechify. (2023). *Free Text to Speech (TTS) Online*. Speechify. shttps://speechify.com/text-to-speech-online

Srinivasan, B., & Parthasarathi, R. (2013). An intelligent task analysis approach for special education based on MIRA. *Journal of Applied Logic*, *11*(1), 137–145. doi:10.1016/j.jal.2012.12.001

SrivastavaM. (2023). Harnessing deep learning for efficient and responsible AI code assistants: A comprehensive study of methods, evaluation, and human interaction. https://doi.org/ doi:10.31219/osf.io/jf9h2

Stănescu, M., Andronache, D. & Böhmer, A. (2022). Measuring sustainable communication in education. *Revista de ştiinţe ale educaţiei, 45*(1), 22–39. doi:10.35923/JES.2022.1.02

Stanford University. (2023). *Generative AI Policy Guidance*. Office of Community Standards. https://communitystandards.stanford.edu/generative-ai-policy-guidance

Stanford. (n.d.). *Generative AI Policy Guidance | Office of Community Standards*. Stanford Press. https://communitystandards.stanford.edu/generative-ai-policy-guidance

Steele, J. L. (2023). To GPT or not GPT? Empowering our students to learn with AI. *Computers and Education: Artificial Intelligence*, *5*, 100160. doi:10.1016/j.caeai.2023.100160

Steinbrenner, J. R., Hume, K., Odom, S. L., Morin, K. L., Nowell, S. W., Tomaszewski, B. & Savage, M. N. (2020). Evidence-based practices for children, youth, and young adults with autism. *The University of North Carolina at Chapel Hill, Frank Porter Graham Child Development Institute, National Clearinghouse on Autism Evidence and Practice Review Team.*

Steve A. I. (n.d.). *SteveAI's Features.* Steve AI.

Stine, J., Trumbore, A., Woll, T., & Sambucetti, H. (2019). *Implications of artificial intelligence on business schools and lifelong learning*. Academic Leadership Group. https://uniconexed.org/wp-content/uploads/2022/02/AI-Life-long-learning-Final-Report-11.04.19.pdf

Stojanov, A. (2023). Learning with ChatGPT 3.5 as a more knowledgeable other: An autoethnographic study. *International Journal of Educational Technology in Higher Education*, *20*(1), 35. doi:10.1186/s41239-023-00404-7

Stojanović, D., Bogdanović, Z., Petrović, L., Mitrović, S., & Labus, A. (2023). Empowering learning process in secondary education using pervasive technologies. *Interactive Learning Environments*, *31*(2), 779–792. doi:10.1080/10494820.2020.1806886

Stokel-Walker, C. (2023). ChatGPT listed as author on research papers: Many scientists disapprove. *Nature*, *613*(7945), 620–621. doi:10.1038/d41586-023-00107-z PMID:36653617

Stokel-Walker, C., & Van Noorden, R. (2023). What ChatGPT and generative AI mean for science. *Nature*, *614*(7947), 214–216. doi:10.1038/d41586-023-00340-6 PMID:36747115

Storey, V. A. (2023). AI Technology and Academic Writing: Knowing and Mastering the "Craft Skills". [IJAET]. *International Journal of Adult Education and Technology*, *14*(1), 1–15. doi:10.4018/IJAET.325795

Strickroth, S. (2019). Platon: Developing a graphical lesson planning system for prospective teachers. *Education Sciences*, *9*(4), 254. doi:10.3390/educsci9040254

Strubell, E., Ganesh, A., & McCallum, A. (2019). Energy and policy considerations for deep learning in NLP. In *the 57th Annual Meeting of the Association for Computational Linguistics.* Florence, Italy. 10.18653/v1/P19-1355

Suh, S., & An, P. (2022). *Leveraging Generative Conversational AI to Develop a Creative Learning Environment for Computational Thinking.*, doi:10.1145/3490100.3516473

Su, J., Ng, D. T. K., & Chu, S. K. W. (2023). Artificial Intelligence (AI) literacy in early childhood education: The challenges and opportunities. *Computers and Education: Artificial Intelligence*, *4*, 100124. doi:10.1016/j.caeai.2023.100124

Su, J., & Yang, W. (2023). Unlocking the power of ChatGPT: A framework for applying generative AI in education. *ECNU Review of Education*, *6*(3). doi:10.1177/20965311231168423

Sullivan, M., Kelly, A., & McLaughlan, P. (2023). ChatGPT in higher education: Considerations for academic integrity and student learning. *Journal of Applied Learning and Teaching*, *6*(1), 31–40. doi:10.37074/jalt.2023.6.1.17

Surahman, E., & Wang, T. (2022). Academic dishonesty and trustworthy assessment in online learning: A systematic literature review. *Journal of Computer Assisted Learning*, *38*(6), 1535–1553. doi:10.1111/jcal.12708

Surameery, N. M. S., & Shakor, M. Y. (2023). Use chat gpt to solve programming bugs. *International Journal of Information Technology & Computer Engineering (IJITC)*, *3*(01), 17-22.

Sweet, K. (2023). How to Collaborate Well. *Pacific Philosophical Quarterly*, *104*(2), 252–273. doi:10.1111/papq.12433

Sweller, J. (1998). Cognitive load during problem solving: Effects on learning. *Cognitive Science*, *12*(2), 257–285. doi:10.1207/s15516709cog1202_4

Synthesia. (2023). Turn your text into videos in minutes. *Synthesia.* https://www.synthesia.io

Sysoyev, P. (2023). Artificial intelligence in education: Awareness, readiness and practice of using artificial intelligence technologies in professional activities by university faculty. *Vysshee Obrazovanie v Rossii = Higher Education in Russia*, *32*(10), 9-33. doi:10.31992/0869-3617-2023-32-10-9-33

Szabó, A., & Underwood, J. (2004). Cybercheats. *Active Learning in Higher Education*, *5*(2), 180–199. doi:10.1177/1469787404043815

Taecharungroj, V. (2023). "What can ChatGPT do?" Analyzing early reactions to the innovative ai chatbot on Twitter. *Big Data and Cognitive Computing*, *7*(1), 35. doi:10.3390/bdcc7010035

Talanquer, V. (2023). Interview with the chatbot: How does it reason? [REMOVED HYPERLINK FIELD]. *Journal of Chemical Education*, *100*(8), 2821–2824. doi:10.1021/acs.jchemed.3c00472

Tanesini, A. (2018). Epistemic Vice and Motivation. *Metaphilosophy*, *49*(3), 350–367. doi:10.1111/meta.12301

Tao, Y., Meng, Y., Gao, Z., & Yang, X. (2022). Perceived teacher support, student engagement, and academic achievement: A meta-analysis. *Educational Psychology*, *42*(4), 401–420. doi:10.1080/01443410.2022.2033168

Tao, Z., & Wang, Q. (2022). Facility or transport inequality? Decomposing healthcare accessibility inequality in Shenzhen, China. *International Journal of Environmental Research and Public Health*, *19*(11), 6897. doi:10.3390/ijerph19116897 PMID:35682478

Tapalova, O., & Zhiyenbayeva, N. (2022). Artificial Intelligence in Education: AIEd for Personalised Learning Pathways. *Electronic Journal of e-Learning*, *20*(5), 639–653. doi:10.34190/ejel.20.5.2597

Tapus, A., Peca, A., Aly, A. A., Pop, C., Jisa, L., Pintea, S., Rusu, A. S., & David, D. O. (2012). Children with autism social engagement in interaction with Nao, an imitative robot: A series of single case experiments. *Interaction Studies: Social Behaviour and Communication in Biological and Artificial Systems*, *13*(3), 315–347. doi:10.1075/is.13.3.01tap

Taylor, D., & Frechette, M. (2022). The impact of workload, productivity, and social support on burnout among marketing faculty during the COVID-19 pandemic. *Journal of Marketing Education*, *44*(2), 134–148. doi:10.1177/02734753221074284

Taylor, L., & Parsons, J. (2011). Improving Student Engagement. *Current Issues in Education (Tempe, Ariz.), 14*(1). http://cie.asu.edu/

Tegos, S., Demetriadis, S., & Karakostas, A. (2015). Promoting academically productive talk with conversational agent interventions in collaborative learning settings. *Computers & Education, 87*, 309–325. doi:10.1016/j.compedu.2015.07.014

TenakwahE. (2023). Generative AI and higher education assessments: A competency-based analysis. https://doi.org/doi:10.21203/rs.3.rs-2968456/v1

Terwiesch, C. (2023). Would Chat GPT3 get a Wharton MBA? A prediction based on its performance in the operations management course. Mack Institute for Innovation Management at the Wharton School: University of Pennsylvania.

The Institute for Ethical AI in Education. (2021). *The ethical framework for AI in education*. Buckingham. https://www.buckingham.ac.uk/research/research-in-applied-computing/the-institute-for-ethical-ai-in-education/

Theelen, H., Van Den Beemt, A., & Brok, P. D. (2019). Classroom simulations in Teacher Education to Support pre-service Teachers' Interpersonal Competence: A Systematic literature review. *Computers & Education, 129*, 14–26. doi:10.1016/j.compedu.2018.10.015

Theodosiou, A. A., & Read, R. C. (2023). Artificial intelligence, machine learning and deep learning: Potential resources for the infection clinician. *The Journal of Infection, 87*(4), 287–294. doi:10.1016/j.jinf.2023.07.006 PMID:37468046

Thomas, B. J., & Alkhafaji, S. (2023). Gamification of Personalized Learning Through Massive Open Online Courses: Learner-to-AI Enabled Chatbot. *InTech Open*. doi:10.5772/intechopen.1001113

Thoring, K., Huettemann, S., & Mueller, R. (2023). The augmented designer: A research agenda for generative AI-enabled design. *Proceedings of the Design Society, 3*, 3345–3354. doi:10.1017/pds.2023.335

Thurman, S. (2023). Applying principles of respectful caregiving to teaching in higher education. *Scholarship of Teaching and Learning in Psychology*. doi:10.1037/stl0000358

Timms, M. (2016). Letting Artificial Intelligence in Education Out of the Box: Educational Cobots and Smart Classrooms. *International Journal of Artificial Intelligence in Education, 26*(2), 701–712. doi:10.1007/s40593-016-0095-y

Tisoglu, S., Piri, Z., Mericelli, M., & Inan, F. C. (2022). Targeting Creativity Through a Learner-Generated Digital Storytelling Project. *International Journal of Technology in Teaching and Learning, 18*(1). doi:10.37120/ijttl.2022.18.1.01

Tissenbaum, M., Lui, M., & Slotta, J. D. (2019). Developing a smart classroom infrastructure to support real-time student collaboration and inquiry: A 4-year design study. *Instructional Science, 47*(4), 423–443. doi:10.1007/s11251-019-09486-1

Tlili, A., Shehata, B., Adarkwah, M. A., Bozkurt, A., Hickey, D. T., Huang, R., & Agyemang, B. (2023). What if the devil is my guardian angel: ChatGPT as a case study of using chatbots in education. *Smart Learning Environments, 10*(1), 1–24. doi:10.1186/s40561-023-00237-x

Toll, D., Lindgren, I., Melin, U., & Madsen, C. (2019). Artificial intelligence in Swedish policies: Values, benefits, considerations, and risks. In Advances in Human Factors and Systems Interaction (pp. 301-310). Springer. doi:10.1007/978-3-030-27325-5_23

Tomlinson, C. A. (2001). *How to Differentiate Instruction in Mixed-Ability Classrooms*. Pearson Education.

Töret, G., & Dağlarlı, E. (2021). OSB'de ileri düzey teknoloji ve açıklanabilir yapay zekâ uygulamaları. In G. Töret (Ed.), *Özel Gereksinimli Bireylerde Destekleyici İleri Düzey Teknolojiler* (pp. 1–31). Nobel Akademik Yayıncılık.

Torres-Martín, C., Acal, C., El-Homrani, M., & Mingorance-Estrada, Á. C. (2022). Implementation of the flipped classroom and its longitudinal impact on improving academic performance. *Educational Technology Research and Development*, *70*(3), 909–929. doi:10.1007/s11423-022-10095-y

Touretzky, D., Gardner-McCune, C., Martin, F., & Seehorn, D. (2019). Envisioning AI for K-12: What should every child know about AI? *Proceedings of the AAAI Conference on Artificial Intelligence*, *33*(01), 9795–9799. doi:10.1609/aaai.v33i01.33019795

Trippe, J., & Baese-Berk, M. (2019). A prosodic profile of American Aviation English. *English for Specific Purposes*, *53*, 30–46. doi:10.1016/j.esp.2018.08.006

Trouche, L. (2005). Calculators in mathematics education: A rapid evolution of tools, with different effects. In D. Guin, K. Ruthven, & L. Trouche (Eds.), *The didactical challenge of symbolic calculators: Turning a computational device into a mathematical instrument* (pp. 9–39). doi:10.1007/0-387-23435-7_2

Troussas, C., Giannakas, F., Sgouropoulou, C., & Voyiatzis, I. (2023). Collaborative activities recommendation based on students' collaborative learning styles using ANN and WSM. *Interactive Learning Environments*, *31*(1), 54–67. doi:10.1080/10494820.2020.1761835

Turan, Z. (2023). Evaluating whether flipped classrooms improve student learning in science education: A systematic review and meta-analysis. *Scandinavian Journal of Educational Research*, *67*(1), 1–19. doi:10.1080/00313831.2021.1983868

Turing, A. M. (1950). Mind. *Mind*, *59*(236), 433–460. doi:10.1093/mind/LIX.236.433

Turner, C. (2023). *Unleashing the Potential of Digital Twins in Education – A Revolution in Learning*. LinkedIn. https://www.linkedin.com/pulse/using-aidigital-learning-twins-assessment-education-guy-huntington

Turner, S. (2001). What is the problem with experts? *Social Studies of Science*, *31*(1), 123–149. doi:10.1177/030631201031001007

Turri, J., Alfano, M., & Greco, J. (2021, October 26). Virtue epistemology. *Stanford Encyclopedia of Philosophy*. Stanford Press. https://plato.stanford.edu/entries/epistemology-virtue/

Uchiyama, S., Umemura, K., & Morita, Y. (2023). *Large Language Model-based System to Provide Immediate Feedback to Students in Flipped Classroom Preparation Learning*. arXiv preprint arXiv:2307.11388.

UCLA Center for the Advancement of Teaching. (2023). *Guidance for Instructors on the Use of Generative Artificial Intelligence in Teaching and Learning*. UCLA. [https://teaching.ucla.edu/resources/ai_guidance/]

UCLA. (n.d.). *Guidance for the Use of Generative AI – UCLA Center for the Advancement of Teaching*. UCLA. https://teaching.ucla.edu/resources/ai_guidance/

Uddin, M. Z., Shahriar, M. A., Mahamood, M. N., Alnajjar, F., Pramanik, M. I., & Ahad, M. A. R. (2024). Deep learning with image-based autism spectrum disorder analysis: A systematic review. *Engineering Applications of Artificial Intelligence*, *127*, 107185. doi:10.1016/j.engappai.2023.107185

UIzard. (2023). *Design stunning websites in minutes.* UIzard. https://uizard.io

UNESCO. (2019). *Beijing consensus on artificial intelligence and education.* The United Nations Educational, Scientific and Cultural Organization. https://unesdoc.unesco.org/ark:/48223/pf0000368303

UNESCO. (2021). *Recommendation on the ethics of artificial intelligence*. The United Nations Educational, Scientific and Cultural Organization. Paris, France. https://unesdoc.unesco.org/ark:/48223/pf0000380455.:~:text=AI%20actors%20and%20Member%20States,law%2C%20in%20particular%20Member%20States%27

UNESCO. (2023). *AI competency frameworks for school students and teachers*. UNESCO. https://www.unesco.org/en/digital-education/ai-future-learning/competency-frameworks

UNESCO. (2023). *Generative AI and the future of education.* UNESCO. https://unesdoc.unesco.org/ark:/48223/pf0000385877

UNESCO. (2023). *Guidance for generative AI in education and research.* UNESCO. https://unesdoc.unesco.org/ark:/48223/pf0000386693

UNESCO. (2023). *UNESCO's recommendation on the ethics of artificial intelligence: Key facts*. UNESCO. https://unesdoc.unesco.org/notice?id=p:usmarcdef_0000385082

Université de Montréal. (2018). *Declaration of Montréal for a responsible development of AI*. Université de Montréal. https://www.montrealdeclaration-responsibleai.com

Unsplash. (n.d.). *A laptop computer sitting on top of a wooden table*. Unsplash. [https://unsplash.com/photos/a-laptop-computer-sitting-on-top-of-a-wooden-table-G_vWviqUCCg]

Upadhyay, N., Upadhyay, S., & Dwivedi, Y. (2021). Theorizing artificial intelligence acceptance and digital entrepreneurship model. *International Journal of Entrepreneurial Behaviour & Research, 28*(5), 1138–1166. doi:10.1108/IJEBR-01-2021-0052

Urban, W.J., Jennings, L., Jr. Wagoner. (2013). *American Education: A history*. Taylor & Francis Group.

Valdivia, I. M. Á., & Montoto, I. G. (2017). Teachers' intercultural competence: A requirement or an option in a culturally diverse classroom? *International Journal of Inclusive Education, 22*(5), 510–526. doi:10.1080/13603116.2017.1377298

Valencia Tafur, A. T., & Figueroa Molina, R. (2023). Incidencia de la Inteligencia Artificial en la Educación. *Educatio Siglo XXI, 41*(3), 235–264. doi:10.6018/educatio.555681

van der Vorst, T., & Jelicic, N. (2019). *Artificial Intelligence in Education: Can AI bring the full potential of personalized learning to education*?

van Deursen, A. J., & van Dijk, J. A. (2019). The first-level digital divide shifts from inequalities in physical access to inequalities in material access. *New Media & Society, 21*(2), 354–375. doi:10.1177/1461444818797082 PMID:30886536

Van Maele, J., & Jin, L. (2022). Intercultural teaching and learning in Chinese Higher Education: Integrating practices and perspectives. *Language and Intercultural Communication, 22*(5), 493–502. doi:10.1080/14708477.2022.2131134

Van Moere, A., Suzuki, M., Downey, R., & Cheng, J. (2009). Implementing ICAO Language Proficiency Requirements in the Versant Aviation English Test. *Australian Review of Applied Linguistics, 32*(3), 27.1–27.17. doi:10.2104/aral0927

Van Slyke, C., Johnson, R., & Sarabadani, J. (2023). Generative artificial intelligence in information systems education: Challenges, consequences, and responses. *Communications of the Association for Information Systems, 53*(1), 1–21. doi:10.17705/1CAIS.05301

VanDerHorn, E., & Mahadevan, S. (2021). Digital twin: Generalization, characterization and implementation. *Decision Support Systems, 145*, 113524. doi:10.1016/j.dss.2021.113524

Vanlehn, K. (2011). The relative effectiveness of human tutoring, intelligent tutoring systems, and other tutoring systems. *Educational Psychologist, 46*(4), 197–221. doi:10.1080/00461520.2011.611369

Varghese, J., & Chapiro, J. (2023). ChatGPT: The transformative influence of generative AI on science and healthcare. *Journal of Hepatology*. doi:10.1016/j.jhep.2023.07.028 PMID:37544516

Varona, D., & Suarez, J. L. (2022). Discrimination, bias, fairness, and trustworthy AI. *Applied Sciences (Basel, Switzerland), 12*(12), 1–13. doi:10.3390/app12125826

Vartiainen, H., & Tedre, M. (2023). Using artificial intelligence in craft education: Crafting with text-to-image generative models. *Digital Creativity (Exeter), 34*(1), 1–21. doi:10.1080/14626268.2023.2174557

Vaswani, A., Shazeer, N., Parmar, N., Uszkoreit, J., Jones, L., Gomez, A. N., Kaiser, L., & Polosukhin, I. (2017). Attention is all you need. *Advances in Neural Information Processing Systems, 30*. IEEE. https://proceedings.neurips.cc/paper/2017/file/3f5ee243547dee91fbd053c1c4a845aa-Paper.pdf

Verheijden, M. P., & Funk, M. (2023). Collaborative diffusion: Boosting designerly co-creation with Generative AI. *In Extended Abstracts of the 2023 CHI Conference on Human Factors in Computing Systems*, (pp. 1–8). ACM. https://dl.acm.org/doi/abs/10.1145/3544549.3585680

Verleger, M., & Pembridge, J. (2018, October). A pilot study integrating an AI-driven chatbot in an introductory programming course. In 2018 IEEE frontiers in education conference (FIE) (pp. 1-4). IEEE. doi:10.1109/FIE.2018.8659282

Vespone, B. (2023). Co-constructing Teaching and Learning in Higher Education: A Literature Review of Practices and Implications. *Journal of Learning Development in Higher Education, 27*(27). Advance online publication. doi:10.47408/jldhe.vi27.997

Viberg, O., Grönlund, Å., & Andersson, A. (2023). Integrating digital technology in mathematics education: A Swedish case study. *Interactive Learning Environments, 31*(1), 232–243. doi:10.1080/10494820.2020.1770801

Villarreal, R., Perdomo, E., Navarro, D., Aguilera, R., & Gerardou, F. (2023). Challenges and Opportunities of Generative AI for Higher Education as Explained by ChatGPT. *Education Sciences, 13*(856), 1–18.

Vincent, J. (2022). AI-generated answers temporarily banned on coding Q&A site Stack Overflow. *The Verge, 5*.

Vitta, J. P., & Al-Hoorie, A. H. (2023). The flipped classroom in second language learning: A meta-analysis. *Language Teaching Research, 27*(5), 1268–1292. doi:10.1177/1362168820981403

Vukmirovic, M., Rajovic, N., Pavlovic, V., Masic, S., Mirkovic, M., Tasic, R., Randjelovic, S., Mostic, D., Velickovic, I., Nestorovic, E., Milcanovic, P., Stanisavljevic, D., & Milic, N. (2020). The burnout syndrome in medical academia: Psychometric properties of the Serbian version of the Maslach Burnout Inventory—Educators Survey. *International Journal of Environmental Research and Public Health, 17*(16), 5658. doi:10.3390/ijerph17165658 PMID:32764447

VuleticM.CucuringuM.PrenzelF. (2023). Fin-GAN: Forecasting and Classifying Financial Time Series via Generative Adversarial Networks (January 18, 2023). doi:10.2139/ssrn.4328302

Vygotsky, L. S. (1978). *Mind in Society: the development of higher psychological processes*. NII. https://ci.nii.ac.jp/ncid/BA03570814

Vygotsky, L. S., & Cole, M. (1978). *Mind in society: Development of higher psychological processes*. Harvard university press.

Waelen, R. (2022). Why AI ethics is a critical theory. *Philosophy & Technology, 35*(1), 9. doi:10.1007/s13347-022-00507-5

Wainer, J., Ferrari, E., Dautenhahn, K., & Robins, B. (2010). The effectiveness of using a robotics class to foster collaboration among groups of children with autism in an exploratory study. *Personal and Ubiquitous Computing, 14*(5), 445–455. doi:10.1007/s00779-009-0266-z

Walcott, K. (2021). Informing academic writing pedagogy through the study of phrase-frames. *Journal of Language Teaching and Research, 12*(1), 158–171. doi:10.17507/jltr.1201.17

Walczak, K., & Cellary, W. (2023). Challenges for higher education in the era of widespread access to Generative AI. *Economics and Business Review*, *9*(2), 71–100. doi:10.18559/ebr.2023.2.743

Walkington, C., & Bernacki, M. (2020). Personalization of instruction: Design dimensions and implications for cognition. *Journal of Experimental Education*, *88*(1), 50–68. doi:10.1080/00220973.2017.1380590

Walkington, C., & Bernacki, M. L. (2020). Appraising research on personalized learning: Definitions, theoretical alignment, advancements, and future directions. *Journal of Research on Technology in Education*, *52*(3), 235–252. doi:10.1080/15391523.2020.1747757

Wall, D. P., Dally, R., Luyster, R., Jung, J.-Y., & DeLuca, T. F. (2012). Use of artificial intelligence to shorten the behavioral diagnosis of autism. *PLoS One*, *7*(8), e43855. doi:10.1371/journal.pone.0043855 PMID:22952789

Wang, K., Gou, C., Duan, Y., Lin, Y., Zheng, X., & Wang, F. Y. (2017). Generative adversarial networks: introduction and outlook. *IEEE/CAA Journal of Automatica Sinica, 4*(4), 588-598. doi:10.1109/JAS.2017.7510583

Wang, R. E., & Demszky, D. (2023). *Is ChatGPT a Good Teacher Coach? Measuring Zero-Shot Performance For Scoring and Providing Actionable Insights on Classroom Instruction.* arXiv preprint arXiv:2306.03090. doi:10.18653/v1/2023.bea-1.53

Wang, F., & Burton, J. K. (2012). Second Life in Education: A review of publications from its launch to 2011. *British Journal of Educational Technology*, *44*(3), 357–371. doi:10.1111/j.1467-8535.2012.01334.x

Wang, M., Wang, M., Xu, X., Yang, L., Cai, D., & Yin, M. (2023). Unleashing ChatGPT's Power: A Case Study on Optimizing Information Retrieval in Flipped Classrooms via Prompt Engineering. *IEEE Transactions on Learning Technologies*, 1–13. doi:10.1109/TLT.2023.3324714

Wang, T., Lund, B. D., Marengo, A., Pagano, A., Mannuru, N. R., Teel, Z. A., & Pange, J. (2023). Exploring the potential impact of artificial intelligence (AI) on international students in higher education: Generative AI, chatbots, analytics, and international student success. *Applied Sciences (Basel, Switzerland)*, *13*(11), 6716. doi:10.3390/app13116716

Wang, X., Li, Z., Dong, L., & Li, W. (2022). The flipped classroom model of Japanese teaching based on intelligent decision-making system. *Scientific Programming*, *2022*, 2022. doi:10.1155/2022/2792428

Wan-qing, W., & Li, L. (2022). The impact of artificial intelligence on the mental health of manufacturing workers: The mediating role of overtime work and the work environment. *Frontiers in Public Health*, *10*, 862407. doi:10.3389/fpubh.2022.862407 PMID:35480579

Warr, M., Oster, N. J., & Isaac, R. (2023). *Implicit Bias in Large Language Models: Experimental Proof and Implications for Education* (SSRN Scholarly Paper 4625078). doi:10.2139/ssrn.4625078

Warschauer, M. (2004). *Technology and social inclusion: Rethinking the digital divide.* MIT Press., doi:10.7551/mitpress/6699.001.0001

WarschauerM.TsengW.YimS.WebsterT.JacobS.DuQ.TateT. The Affordance sand Contradictions of AI-Generated Textfor Second Language Writers (2023, March 20). SSRN. https://ssrn.com/abstract=4404380 doi:10.2139/ssrn.4404380

Watson, L. (2016). The epistemology of education. *Philosophy Compass*, *11*(3), 146–159. doi:10.1111/phc3.12316

Weber, F. (2023). Artificial Intelligence. *Artificial Intelligence for Business Analytics*. doi:10.1007/978-3-658-37599-7_2

Wei, J., Wang, X., Schuurmans, D., Bosma, M., Xia, F., Chi, E., & Zhou, D. (2022). *Chain-of-thought prompting elicits reasoning in large language models* (Vol. 35). Advances in Neural Information Processing Systems, https://arxiv.org/abs/2201.11903

Weiss, M. J., & Harris, S. L. (2001). Teaching social skills to people with autism. *Behavior Modification*, *25*(5), 785–802. doi:10.1177/0145445501255007 PMID:11573340

Welch Bacon, C. E., & Gaither, K. (2020). Personalized Learning Pathways: Using Technology to Promote Learning Beyond the Classroom. *New Directions for Teaching and Learning*, *2020*(162), 91–102. doi:10.1002/tl.20394

Wenger, E. (2014). *Artificial intelligence and tutoring systems: Computational and cognitive approaches to the communication of knowledge*. Morgan Kaufmann.

Wepik. (2023). *Wepik: AI Presentation Maker.* Wepik.https://wepik.com/ai-presentations#how-it-work

West, C., Dyrbye, L., & Shanafelt, T. (2018). Physician burnout: Contributors, consequences and solutions. *Journal of Internal Medicine*, *283*(6), 516–529. doi:10.1111/joim.12752 PMID:29505159

Westgard, J. O., & Westgard, S. A. (2016). Quality control review: Implementing a scientifically based quality control system. *Annals of Clinical Biochemistry*, *53*(1), 32–50. doi:10.1177/0004563215597248 PMID:26150675

White, J., Fu, Q., Hays, S., Sandborn, M., Olea, C., Gilbert, H., Elnashar, A., Spencer-Smith, J., & Schmidt, D. C. (2023). *A Prompt Pattern Catalog to Enhance Prompt Engineering with ChatGPT* (arXiv:2302.11382). arXiv. http://arxiv.org/abs/2302.11382

Whitehead, J. L., Pearson, A., Lawrenson, R., & Atatoa-Carr, P. (2019). How can the spatial equity of health services be defined and measured? A systematic review of spatial equity definitions and methods. *Journal of Health Services Research & Policy*, *24*(4), 270–278. doi:10.1177/1355819619837292 PMID:31460801

Whitney, C. W., Lind, B. K., & Wahl, P. W. (1998). Quality assurance and quality control in longitudinal studies. *Epidemiologic Reviews*, *20*(1), 71–80. doi:10.1093/oxfordjournals.epirev.a017973 PMID:9762510

Whittaker, L., Letheren, K., & Mulcahy, R. (2021). The rise of deepfakes: A conceptual framework and research agenda for marketing. *Australasian Marketing Journal*, *29*(3), 204–214. doi:10.1177/1839334921999479

Williams White, S., Keonig, K., & Scahill, L. (2007). Social skills development in children with autism spectrum disorders: A review of the intervention research. *Journal of Autism and Developmental Disorders*, *37*(10), 1858–1868. doi:10.1007/s10803-006-0320-x PMID:17195104

Williamson, B. (2019). Brain data: Scanning, scraping and sculpting the plastic learning brain through neurotechnology. *Postdigital Science and Education*, *1*(1), 65–86. doi:10.1007/s42438-018-0008-5

Williamson, B., & Eynon, R. (2020). Historical threads, missing links, and future directions in AI in education. *Learning, Media and Technology*, *45*(3), 223–235. doi:10.1080/17439884.2020.1798995

Wingström, R., Hautala, J., & Lundman, R. (2023). Redefining creativity in the era of AI? Perspectives of computer scientists and new media artists. *Creativity Research Journal*, 1–17. doi:10.1080/10400419.2022.2107850

Winkler, R., Neuweiler, M. L., Bittner, E. A., & Söllner, M. (2019). Hey Alexa, Please Help Us Solve This Problem! How Interactions with Smart Personal Assistants Improve Group Performance. In *ICIS*. https://www.alexandria.unisg.ch/bitstreams/fb70d3b8-4ec0-413b-9bd7-35f240e62e6e/download

Winrow, A., Reitmaier-Koehler, A., & Winrow, B. (2015). Social desirability bias in relation to academic cheating behaviors of nursing students. *Journal of Nursing Education and Practice*, *5*(8). Advance online publication. doi:10.5430/jnep.v5n8p121

Wisskirchen, G., Biacabe, B. T., Bormann, U., Muntz, A., Niehaus, G., Soler, G. J., & von Brauchitsch, B. (2017). Artificial intelligence and robotics and their impact on the workplace. *IBA Global Employment Institute*, *11*(5), 49–67.

Witmer, L. (1922). What is intelligence and who has it? *The Scientific Monthly*, *15*(1), 57–67.

Wolff, A., Zdrahal, Z., Nikolov, A., & Pantucek, M. (2013, April). Improving retention: predicting at-risk students by analysing clicking behaviour in a virtual learning environment. In *Proceedings of the third international conference on learning analytics and knowledge* (pp. 145-149). ACM. 10.1145/2460296.2460324

Wolverton, C., & Hollier, B. (2019). A minimalist design for distance learning. *International Journal of Educational Management*, *33*(7), 1457–1465. doi:10.1108/IJEM-09-2017-0237

WooD.WangY.SusantoH. (2022). *Student-AI Creative Writing: Pedagogical Strategies for Applying Natural Language Generation in Schools*. https://doi.org/ doi:10.35542/osf.io/h5kc7

Wood, E., Ange, B., & Miller, D. (2021). Are we ready to integrate artificial intelligence literacy into the medical school curriculum: Students and faculty survey. *Journal of Medical Education and Curricular Development*, *8*, 238212052110240. doi:10.1177/23821205211024078 PMID:34250242

Woo, H., Lu, J., & Storlie, C. (2022). Burnout and scholarly productivity among junior counseling faculty: Mentoring as a moderator. *Journal of Employment Counseling*, *59*(4), 179–188. doi:10.1002/joec.12188

Worthen, M. (2016). The future of personalized learning for students with disabilities. *State Education Standard, 16*(3), 35. https://nasbe.nyc3.digitaloceanspaces.com/2016/09/Future-of-Personalized-Learning-for-Students-with-Disabilities_September-2016-Standard.pdf

Wu, T., He, S., Liu, J., Sun, S., Liu, K., Han, Q.-L., & Tang, Y. (2023). A Brief Overview of ChatGPT: The History, Status Quo and Potential Future Development. *IEEE/CAA Journal of Automatica Sinica, 10*(5), 1122–1136. doi:10.1109/JAS.2023.123618

Wu, C., Chen, Y., & Chen, T. (2017). An Adaptive e-Learning System for Enhancing Learning Performance: Based on Dynamic Scaffolding Theory. *Eurasia Journal of Mathematics, Science and Technology Education*, *14*(3), 903–913. doi:10.12973/ejmste/81061 PMID:26436650

Wu, Z., Ji, D., Yu, K., Zeng, X., Wu, D., & Shidujaman, M. (2021). AI Creativity and the Human-AI Co-creation Model. In M. Kurosu (Ed.), *Human-Computer Interaction. Theory, Methods and Tools* (pp. 171–190). Springer International Publishing. doi:10.1007/978-3-030-78462-1_13

Xiao, Y., Chatterjee, S., & Gehringer, E. (2022, November 1). *A new era of plagiarism the danger of cheating using AI.* IEEE Xplore. doi:10.1109/ITHET56107.2022.10031827

Xiao, Y., & Zhi, Y. (2023). An Exploratory Study of EFL Learners' Use of ChatGPT for Language Learning Tasks: Experience and Perceptions. *Languages (Basel, Switzerland)*, *8*(3), 212. doi:10.3390/languages8030212

Xia, Q., Chiu, T. K. F., Zhou, X., Chai, C. S., & Cheng, M. (2023). Systematic literature review on opportunities, challenges, and future research recommendations of artificial intelligence in education. *Computers & Education: Artificial Intelligence*, *4*, 100118. doi:10.1016/j.caeai.2022.100118

Xie, H., Chu, H. C., Hwang, G. J., & Wang, C. C. (2019). Trends and development in technology-enhanced adaptive/personalized learning: A systematic review of journal publications from 2007 to 2017. *Computers & Education*, *140*, 103599. doi:10.1016/j.compedu.2019.103599

Xu, Q., Jingying, H., Xian, S., Zhao, Y., Wu, L., Baorui, C., & Qu, Y. (2022). The effectiveness of artificial intelligence-based automated grading and training system in the education of manual detection of diabetic retinopathy. *Frontiers in Public Health*, *10*, 1025271. doi:10.3389/fpubh.2022.1025271 PMID:36419999

Xu, Y., Liu, X., Cao, X., Huang, C., Liu, E., Qian, S., Liu, X., Wu, Y., Dong, F., Qiu, C.-W., Qiu, J., Hua, K., Su, W., Wu, J., Xu, H., Han, Y., Fu, C., Yin, Z., Liu, M., & Zhang, J. (2021). Artificial intelligence: A powerful paradigm for scientific research. *Innovation (Cambridge (Mass.)), 2*(4), 100179. Advance online publication. doi:10.1016/j.xinn.2021.100179 PMID:34877560

Yang, H. (2023). *How I use ChatGPT responsibly in my teaching*. Nature Careers Community., doi:10.1038/d41586-023-01026-9

Yang, H., & Zhu, K. (2022). Research on AI-assisted grading of math questions based on deep learning. In *International Conference on Internet of Things and Machine Learning (IoTML 2021)* (Vol. 12174, pp. 211-217). SPIE. https://doi.org/10.1117/12.2628649

Yang, K. B., Echeverria, V., Lu, Z., Mao, H., Holstein, K., Rummel, N., & Aleven, V. (2023, April). Pair-Up: Prototyping Human-AI Co-orchestration of Dynamic Transitions between Individual and Collaborative Learning in the Classroom. In *Proceedings of the 2023 CHI Conference on Human Factors in Computing Systems* (pp. 1-17). ACM. 10.1145/3544548.3581398

Yang, S., Liu, K., Gai, J., & He, X. (2022). Transformation to industrial artificial intelligence and workers' mental health: Evidence from China. *Frontiers in Public Health, 10*, 881827. doi:10.3389/fpubh.2022.881827 PMID:35685756

Yang, T., & Chen, J. (2023). Pre-service teachers' perceptions and intentions regarding the use of chatbots through statistical and lag sequential analysis. *Computers & Education: Artificial Intelligence, 4*, 100119. doi:10.1016/j.caeai.2022.100119

Yan, L., Sha, L., Zhao, L., Li, Y., Martinez-Maldonado, R., Chen, G., Li, X., Jin, Y., & Gašević, D. (2023). Practical and ethical challenges of large language models in education: A systematic scoping review. *British Journal of Educational Technology*, bjet.13370. doi:10.1111/bjet.13370

Yeo, M. A. (2023). Academic integrity in the age of Artificial Intelligence (AI) authoring apps. *TESOL Journal, 14*(3), e716. doi:10.1002/tesj.716

Yildirim-Erbasli, S. N., & Bulut, O. (2023). Conversation-based Assessment: A novel approach to boosting test-taking effort in digital formative assessment. *Computers & Education: Artificial Intelligence, 4*, 100135. doi:10.1016/j.caeai.2023.100135

Yilmaz, R., & Yilmaz, F. G. K. (2023). The effect of generative artificial intelligence (AI)-based tool use on students' computational thinking skills, programming self- efficacy and motivation. *Computers and Education: Artificial Intelligence*, 100147.

Young, L. (2023). *iThenticate 2.0: Advancing research integrity with AI writing detection.* Turnitin. https://www.turnitin.com/blog/ithenticate-2-0-advancing-research-integrity-with-ai-writing-detection

Yu, H., & Guo, Y. (2023). Generative artificial intelligence empowers educational reform: Current status, issues, and prospects. *Frontiers in Education, 8*, 1183162. Advance online publication. doi:10.3389/feduc.2023.1183162

Yurtaslan, N. (2023). Tableau dijital dönüşüm aracı ile veri görselleştirme [Data visualization with Tableau digital transformation tool]. *Medium.* https://nurhayatyurtaslan.medium.com/tableau-dijital-d%C3%B6n%C3%BC%C5%9F%C3%BCm-arac%C4%B1-ile-veri-g%C3%B6rselle%C5%9Ftirme-b2af9d5aaf73

Zala, D. (2023). *The 12 best tools and software to create pie charts with ease*. Squeeze Growth. https://squeezegrowth.com/tr/best-tools-and-software-to-create-pie-charts-with-ease/

Zamit, I., Musa, I. H., Jiang, L., Yanjie, W., & Tang, J. (2023). Trends and features of autism spectrum disorder research using artificial intelligence techniques: A bibliometric approach. *Current Psychology (New Brunswick, N.J.), 42*(35), 1–16. doi:10.1007/s12144-022-03977-0

Zammarchi, G., & Conversano, C. (2021). Application of eye tracking technology in medicine: A bibliometric analysis. *Vision (Basel), 5*(4), 56. doi:10.3390/vision5040056 PMID:34842855

Zatarain, J. M. N. (2017). The role of automated technology in the creation of copyright works: The challenges of artificial intelligence. *International Review of Law Computers & Technology, 31*(1), 91–104. doi:10.1080/13600869.2017.1275273

Zawacki-Richter, O., Marín, V. I., Bond, M., & Gouverneur, F. (2019). Systematic review of research on artificial intelligence applications in higher education – Where are the educators? *International Journal of Educational Technology in Higher Education, 16*(1), 16–39. doi:10.1186/s41239-019-0171-0

Zhai, X. (2022). ChatGPT User Experience: Implications for Education. SSRN *Electronic Journal.* doi:10.2139/ssrn.4312418

Zhai, X., Chu, X., Chai, C., Jong, M., Istenič, A., Spector, M., Liu, J., Yuan, J., & Li, Y. (2021). A Review of Artificial Intelligence (AI) in Education from 2010 to 2020. *Complex.*, 2021, 8812542:1-8812542:18. . doi:10.1155/2021/8812542

Zhai, C., & Wibowo, S. (2023). A systematic review on artificial intelligence dialogue systems for enhancing English as foreign language students' interactional competence in the university. *Computers and Education: Artificial Intelligence, 4*, 100134. doi:10.1016/j.caeai.2023.100134

ZhaiX. (2022). ChatGPT user experience: Implications for education. Available at SSRN 4312418.

Zhai, X., & Nehm, R. (2023). AI and formative assessment: The train has left the station. *Journal of Research in Science Teaching, 60*(6), 1390–1398. doi:10.1002/tea.21885

Zhang, J. (2023). Design and simulation of autonomous learning platform for constructive English teaching based on artificial intelligence. doi:10.1117/12.2683093

Zhang, Y., & Wildemuth, B. M. (2009). *Qualitative analysis of content.* iSchool. https://www.ischool.utexas.edu/~yanz/Content_analysis.pdf

Zhang, B., Zhu, J., & Su, H. (2023). Toward the third generation artificial intelligence. *Science China. Information Sciences, 66*(2), 121101. doi:10.1007/s11432-021-3449-x

Zhang, C., Schießl, J., Plößl, L., Hofmann, F., & Gläser-Zikuda, M. (2023). Acceptance of artificial intelligence among pre-service teachers: A multigroup analysis. *International Journal of Educational Technology in Higher Education, 20*(1), 49. doi:10.1186/s41239-023-00420-7 PMID:36743849

Zhang, P., & Tur, G. (2023). A systematic review of ChatGPT use in K-12 education. *European Journal of Education*, ejed.12599. doi:10.1111/ejed.12599

Zhang, T. (2023). Flipped Classroom and Student Readiness in Blended Learning. *International Journal of Education and Humanities, 7*(3), 161–163. doi:10.54097/ijeh.v7i3.6359

Zhan, X., Li, B., & Sun, J. (2023). Application scenarios and development opportunities of AIGC in the digital intelligence integration environment. *Tushu Qingbao Zhishi, 40*(1), 75–85. doi:10.13366/j.dik.2023.01.075

Zhao, J., Han, X., Ouyang, M., & Burke, A. (2023). Specialized deep neural networks for battery health prognostics: Opportunities and challenges. *Journal of Energy Chemistry.* doi:10.1016/j.jechem.2023.08.047

Zhao, Q., & Nazir, S. (2022). English multimode production and usage by artificial intelligence and online reading for sustaining effectiveness. *Mobile Information Systems, 2022*, 1–16. doi:10.1155/2022/6780502

Zhihan, L. (2023). Generative artificial intelligence in the metaverse era. *Cognitive Robotics, 3*(3), 208–217. doi:10.1016/j.cogr.2023.06.001

Zhou, K., Yang, J., Loy, C. C., & Liu, Z. (2022). Conditional Prompt Learning for Vision-Language Models. *International Journal of Computer Vision, 130*(9), 2337–2348. doi:10.1007/s11263-022-01653-1

Zhuang, C., Hu, X., & Dill, M. (2022). Do physicians with academic affiliation have lower burnout and higher career-related satisfaction? *BMC Medical Education, 22*(1), 316. doi:10.1186/s12909-022-03327-5 PMID:35473565

Zielinski, C., Winker, M., Aggarwal, R., Ferris, L., Heinemann, M., Lapeña, J., & Citrome, L. (2023). Chatbots, ChatGPT, and scholarly manuscripts: WAME recommendations on ChatGPT and chatbots in relation to scholarly publications. *Open Access Macedonian Journal of Medical Sciences, 11*(A), 83-86. doi:10.3889/oamjms.2023.11502

Zimmermann, E. M., Mramba, L. K., Gregoire, H., Dandar, V., Limacher, M. C., & Good, M. L. (2020). Characteristics of faculty at risk of leaving their medical schools: An analysis of the StandPoint™ Faculty Engagement Survey. *Journal of Healthcare Leadership, 12*, 1–10. doi:10.2147/JHL.S225291 PMID:32021533

Zou, D., Huang, Y., & Xie, H. (2019). Digital game-based vocabulary learning: Where are we and where are we going? *Computer Assisted Language Learning, 34*(5–6), 751–777. doi:10.1080/09588221.2019.1640745

About the Contributors

Ramesh Sharma, Ph.D., is currently working as Director of Human Resource Development Centre at Dr B R Ambedkar University Delhi, India. Previously he has served as an Associate Professor of Educational Technology and Learning Resources in the Educational Technology Unit at Wawasan Open University, Malaysia; Visiting Professor at University of Fiji, Fiji; Commonwealth of Learning as Director of the Commonwealth Educational Media Centre for Asia, New Delhi; Indira Gandhi National Open University, India; and University of Guyana, Guyana, South America. He is the co-Editor of the 'Asian Journal of Distance Education'. In addition, he has been associated with peer reviewed journals as Reviewer, Editor and Editorial Advisory Board member in the field of Open and Distance Learning such as "Distance Education", " International Review of Research in Open and Distributed Learning (IRRODL)", "International Journal of Distance Education Technologies (IJDET)", and "Indian Journal of Open Learning (IJOL)". He is also on the Editorial Advisory Board and an author for the "Encyclopedia of Distance Learning (4 volumes), 2005".

Aras Bozkurt is a researcher and faculty member at Anadolu University, Türkiye. With MA and PhD degrees in distance education, Dr. Bozkurt's work focuses on empirical studies in areas such as distance education, online learning, networked learning, and educational technology. He applies critical theories like connectivism, rhizomatic learning, and heutagogy to his research. Dr. Bozkurt is also interested in emerging research paradigms, including social network analysis, sentiment analysis, and data mining. Dr. Bozkurt's studies also cover the integration of artificial intelligence technologies into educational processes in the axis of human-machine interaction. His dedication to advancing the field is reflected in his editorial roles as the Editor-in-Chief of Open Praxis and Asian Journal of Distance Education, as well as his roles as an associate editor for prestigious journals like Higher Education Research and Development, Online Learning, eLearn Magazine, and Computer Applications in Engineering Education.

***

Muhammad Waleed Afzal is Head of School for Engineering programs of Liverpool John Moores University UK and Pearson UK, being offered at Beaconhouse International College Pakistan. He has directly supervised the establishment of Engineering programs including Labs, Resource management and curriculum delivery mechanisms at the colleges in Islamabad, Lahore and Faisalabad. He has also stayed closely associated with research at his parent university and collaborated on many projects across different institutes and researchers.

Ömer Akkaş graduated from Gazi University, Faculty of Education, Foreign Languages Education and is currently pursuing a master's degree in Educational Technology at the Institute of Educational Sciences at the same university. He is currently working as a lecturer at Ankara Yıldırım Beyazıt University. Devoted to the realms of artificial intelligence and educational tools, he is focused on in-depth research to contribute valuable insights and advancements to both fields.

Tutaleni Asino is an associate professor of Learning, Design, and Technology in the school of educational studies in the College of Education and Human Sciences at Oklahoma State University. His areas of research, writing, and presentations include: Open Access, diffusion of innovation, organizational development, adoption and use of emerging technologies and learning environments, Mobile Learning, Comparative International Education, indigenous knowledge, and the role of culture in the development and evaluation of learning technologies. He is an active member of the Comparative International Education Society (CIES), Association for Educational Communications and Technology (AECT), and Society for Information Technology and Teacher Education (SITE).

Nafees Ayub, a dynamic force in the realm of Computer Science education, has charted an illustrious journey through the corridors of academia. As a seasoned lecturer at Government College University, Faisalabad, Mr. Nafees Ayub has not only been a beacon of knowledge but a catalyst for transformation in the lives of countless students.

Şener Balat is an educational technologies specialist working at Bingöl University. Holding a Ph.D. in computer and instructional technologies education, Balat has conducted research in areas such as distance education, artificial intelligence in education, e-learning, remote on-the-job training, and metaverse technologies in education. Focused on making a significant contribution to the higher education sector through his academic career, Balat works towards providing students with an effective learning experience and integrating technology into educational processes.

Rosa María Benavente is a University Professor in the area of Agroforestry Engineering, teaching subjects related to electrical engineering. Participates in educational innovation projects to improve teaching in the field of engineering.

Anselm Böhmer, Dr., is a professor of General Education at Ludwigsburg University of Education, Germany. He received his Doctorate at Freiburg University of Education in 2001. He published eight books and seven edited volumes, also more than 80 articles and book chapters. His main areas of research are education in late modernity, global education, diversity, social differences, migration, and culturalization.

Stephen Bolaji, Ph.D., is a research active academic and teaches graduate programs and secondary curriculum humanities units in the Discipline of Education, Faculty of Arts and Society, Charles Darwin University, Australia. Prior to joining CDU, he was a lecturer at the Department of Educational Foundations and Counselling, Faculty of Education, University of Lagos, Nigeria. His research interest is in Educational foundations – Comparative, Sociology, History, Philosophy and Policy studies in education.

Sarinporn Chaivisit, aka Yam, is a lecturer of Educational Technology in the Faculty of Education at Kasetsart University, Thailand. Her research interests include artificial intelligence, augmented and virtual reality, design and development of multimedia instructions, e-learning, emerging technologies in education, gamification, and innovative learning environments.

Lay Kee Ch'ng is a learning designer and a registered Professional Technologist with the Malaysia Board of Technologists (MBOT). She has vast experience in creating and producing digital instructional learning materials for higher education institutions and business enterprises. Her research and writing interests are rooted in digital learning, educational technology, and instructional design.

Rui Cruz is Assistant Professor at Universidade Europeia (Laureate International) in Lisbon, since 2001. PhD in Management and Marketing from the University of Sevilla, Spain, also has a DEA from the same university and an MBA in Strategic Foresight at IESFF, Lisbon. With over 30 years teaching experience at the service of several higher education institutions in the public and private sector, actually teaches academic master's and global graduate programs taught in English in the areas of marketing, logistics and supply chain. Advisor and Tutor in master´s dissertations in the areas of marketing, digital marketing and entrepreneurship his research interests are in the areas of business strategy, strategic marketing, industrial and services marketing and relationship marketing and has scientific articles and books published national and internationally. He worked in the field of advertising for large international agencies such as Publicis, ITT marketing services and BBDO in Portugal and abroad, throughout the 80´s. Was also marketing director of one of the largest Portuguese banking groups and business consultant in the areas of strategy and innovation.

Gökhan Demirdöken is an independent researcher. He taught Aviation English for more than four years. He received his MA in English Language and Teaching from Bahçeşehir University in 2019. His master's thesis reported on ESP needs analysis of prospective pilots studying in a military higher education institution in Turkey and taking the Aviation English course. He is now a PhD candidate in Bahçeşehir University Department of English Language Teaching, and his dissertation focuses on a simulation-based ESP Aviation English training as well as the assessment of student pilots' readback performance. He has published high-quality SSCI-indexed articles, and he is a member of IESPTA (International ESP Teachers' Association).

Ajita Deshmukh is currently the Program Leader of MSc eLearning, a unique Program she played a key role in developing at School of Education and Research, MIT-ADT University. She is a Chemistry Educator turned Education Technologist who seeks to make education accessible and fun. Her popular podcast titled "Che-Mystery" has been awarded at the 25th National AICEAVF. Her expertise makes her a popular face for NCERT sessions and HRDC of various Universities. Her sessions about online pedagogy and social media in education can be found at NCERT Official channel as well as other institutional channels on YouTube. She is a mentor and Hub coordinator for OER4BW (Open Education for Better World), a UNESCO project by University of Nova Gorica, Slovenia. She has previously worked as an Assistant Professor (ICT) at CIET, NCERT and as a Training Coordinator at Teaching-Learning Center, SNDT Women's University, Mumbai. She has contributed as a Co-Instructor, Resource Person and Teaching Associate for NPTEL-SWAYAM and other reputed institutions. Her areas of interest are Online education, particularly Open Education and her PhD brought out how to leverage Social Media, particularly Facebook in Education.

Marcella Dillig is a researcher and lecturer at the Ludwigsburg University of Education, Germany. She studied Philosophy, Politics, Economics, and Law at the University of Stuttgart and the Leuphana University Lüneburg. Her interdisciplinary research encompasses the philosophy of artificial intelligence and social justice.

Nazmi Dinçer is a dedicated English instructor at the Turkish National Defence University, Air Force Academy and a Ph.D. candidate in Educational Technology at Bahçeşehir University. With years of experience in the Department of Foreign Languages, he specializes in training prospective pilots to communicate effectively with air traffic controllers in accordance with ICAO standards. His research is rooted in the intersection of educational technology and foreign language education, delving into areas such as distance education, multimedia learning, artificial intelligence, and game-based learning

Elif Elumar-Efe is a faculty member and researcher at Pamukkale University, Faculty of Education, Department of Special Education. Elumar-Efe's research interests are autism spectrum disorder and the use of advanced technologies in special education.

Arda Eren is a graduate student at Gazi University, Institute of Educational Sciences, Department of Social Studies Education. His research focuses on virtue epistemology and vice epistemology and its relation to social studies education.

José Luis García is a Professor in the Department of Agroforestry Engineering, he is the coordinator of the Educational Innovation Group in Electrical and Automation Technologies for Rural Engineering. He has participated in numerous educational innovation projects aimed at improving learning and assessment systems. His teaching focuses on electrical installations and energy optimization in agro-industrial facilities.

Şahin Gökçearslan completed his undergraduate education at Hacettepe University, Department of Computer Education and Instructional Technology (CEIT) in 2002. He completed his master's degree (2005) at the same university and department, and received his doctoral degree (2013) in Ankara University Educational Technology program with a thesis on teaching computer programming through distance education. In July 2018, he was awarded the title of Associate Professor. He has participated in national projects as well as internationally supported projects. His research interests include computer programming teaching, Internet of Things (IoT), generative artificial intelligence, problematic technology use, distance education, individual characteristics and learning.

Seyfullah Gökoğlu received his Ph.D. in Computer Education and Instructional Technology from the Karadeniz Technical University in 2019. He received the degree of Associate Professor in 2023 and is currently a faculty member of Bartın University, Department of Computer Technology & Information Systems. He researches and publishes widely on artificial intelligence and virtual reality in education.

Natasha Gomes is a language researcher, cultural mediator and game enthusiast with over a decade of teaching experience in India and France. Her doctoral thesis focuses on the cultural contextualisation of French language textbooks published in India. As a Teach For India Alumna, she is passionate about educational equity, creation of contextualized Teaching-Learning Materials and the use of active learning techniques to improve learning outcomes. She has co-curated and co-created over 100+ OERs in French for DIKSHA, has been a Teaching Associate in 5 MOOCs offered on SWAYAM and is EdTech Society's certified Trainer in Discussion Forum moderation and engagement. She was conferred the Exceptional French Language Teacher Award 2021 by the French Embassy in India and the Indian Association of Teachers of French. She currently works as an Assistant Professor at Shenoi Goembab School of Language and Literature, Goa University, India.

Scott Gregory is an Assistant Professor of Teacher Education at Fort Hay State University. He earned his Ed.D. degree from the University of Nebraska-Lincoln in 2023. Dr. Gregory's research interests include curriculum & instruction, social foundations of education, and teacher preparation.

Ercenk Hamarat is a faculty member at Gazi University, Gazi Faculty of Education, Department of Social Studies Education. While his MA (from Balıkesir University in 2011) is about attitudes toward information and communication technologies, his PhD (from Gazi University in 2014) is about the philosophy of social studies education. He continues his theoretical and practical research on teacher training within the main topics of education, philosophy, and technology.

Illie Isso has been working as a research assistant at the Ludwigsburg University of Education (LUE) in the DAAD-funded IQ-Lab project since April 2023. Since May 2021, he is also a doctoral candidate in history at the Ludwigsburg University of Education. Previously, he completed his teaching degree in history, ethics, technology, and physical education with the first state exam. His research interests include history, education in the context of social inequality, diversity, inclusion, and migration.

Sukanda Jongsermtrakoon is a lecturer in the Department of Educational Technology in the Faculty of Education at Kasetsart University. Additionally, she holds the role of an Educational Technology Consultant, providing her expertise to various public and private organizations in Thailand. Her areas of research interests encompass Personal Learning Networks, Open Educational Resources, Massive Open Online Courses, e-learning, classroom innovation and technology integration, teacher professional development, and Learning Experience Design.

Ilker Kayabas is a graduate of Anadolu University's Computer Education and Instructional Technology Department in 2004, has had a notable career in educational technology. Kayabas earned his master's and doctorate from Anadolu University's Distance Education Department. He was appointed as a RA and later as an assistant professor in the same department. He served as the Assistant Director at the Anadolu University Open Education Faculty Learning Technologies Research and Development Centre from 2004 to 2015. Kayabas has designed and developed various educational technologies, including web applications, learning management systems, interactive e-course software, e-exam interfaces, and e-portfolio applications for organizations like universities, ministries of the Turkish government, and businesses. He founded My Work Passport (in 2017) and UTEx (in 2019) e-learning initiatives. His research interests include artificial intelligence, e-learning experience design, learning analytics, gamification and game development, UX/UI design, full-stack web development, and mobile development, with a current focus on AI-powered learning technologies.

Bünyami Kayalı completed his undergraduate education at Erzincan University, Department of Elementary Mathematics Teaching. He completed his master's and doctoral studies at Atatürk University, Department of Computer and Instructional Technologies. He is still working as a lecturer at Bayburt University, Vocational School of Technical Sciences, Department of Computer Technologies. His research interests include digital transformation, distance education and artificial intelligence.

Mustafa Kayyali, Ph.D., is an ardent advocate for excellence in higher education, driven by a relentless pursuit of quality, recognition, and innovation. As the Manager of HE Higher Education Ranking, he leads initiatives that play a crucial role in shaping the landscape of academia. Having earned a Master's in Quality Management and Evaluation in Higher Education from Universitat Oberta de Catalunya, followed by a Ph.D. in Quality Management from Azteca University, his academic pursuits have laid a strong foundation for his expertise in Accreditation, Quality Assurance, and Higher Education Rankings. Dr. Kayyali has made significant contributions to academic literature, boasting more than 30 published papers and 10 book chapters. Additionally, he takes pride in his role as a translator, having translated 5 books, thus bridging language gaps and promoting knowledge exchange on a global scale. In recognition of his expertise, Dr. Kayyali holds key affiliations with esteemed institutions. He is privileged to be a part of the British Accreditation Council's Accreditation Committee, the Slovenian Quality Assurance Agency as an International Expert, and the Agency for Control and Quality Assurance of Higher Education AKOKVO as an Accreditation Expert. His international engagements also include being an expert for the Kosovo Accreditation Agency KAA and the ECBE - European Council for Business Education, as well as serving as a Lead Auditor at the Centre of Assessments for Excellence (COAE). As an entrepreneur, researcher, translator, and publisher, Dr. Kayyali is deeply involved in various facets of the academic world. His diverse interests encompass Management, Translation, Interpretation, and Academic consulting, contributing to a well-rounded understanding of the industry.

Serpil Koçdar is an associate professor at Anadolu University, Türkiye. With a background in economics, she holds a master's degree and a PhD in distance education. Her research focuses on quality assurance, e-assessment, instructional design, and new learning technologies in ODL.

Aslihan Kuraner is a Bachelor's student on the teaching profession programme at Ludwigsburg University of Education and an education research assistant. Her main research interests encompass storytelling, intercultural studies, and digital technologies in education.

Andréia de Bem Machado has a PhD in Engineering and Knowledge Management. Postdoctoral fellow at the Federal University of Santa Catarina. Evaluator of the National Institute of Educational Studies and Research Anísio Teixeira (Ministry of Education Brazil). She is an Ad Hoc evaluator of National and International Journals. Evaluator in the PNLD Infantile Education program. Consultant in the production of low vision UNESCO teaching material. She has been working in the educational field for over 25 years. She is part of the scientific committee of national and international journals. Currently the areas of study are: innovation, innovation in the public sector, entrepreneurship, smart cities, education, special education and digital pedagogical model. She likes to innovate in the art of researching and disseminating knowledge.

Jon Mason, Ph.D, is an Associate Professor in Education at Charles Darwin University in Australia where he lectures in the broad area of digital technology in education. He also holds adjunct positions at Korea National Open University and East China Normal University. Since 2000 he has led delegations from Standards Australia to ISO/IEC JTC 1/SC36 focused on standardization of IT for learning, education, and training. In 2022 he became chair for this international committee. His research encompasses most things where digital technology and learning intersect with a keen interest in question formulation, sense-making, artificial intelligence, and the role of wisdom in education.

Fernando Mazarrón - Contributing Authorl **Fernando Mazarrón** is Professor in the Department of Agroforestry Engineering, researches in renewable energy sources. His teaching focuses on subjects related to energy optimization in agri-food industries. He has a wide teaching career, participating in numerous educational innovation projects.

Fatemeh Rezaie Navaie is a doctoral student of Learning, Design, and Technology at Oklahoma State University (OSU). Her research interest is in the use of artificial intelligence (AI) in the field of education, and how integrating AI into curriculums affects learning. She enjoys learning about AI and exploring how AI can be used to enhance Non-Native English Speakers in their academic writing process. Her other interests include eLearning, organizational development, and Instructional Design in education and corporate training.

Alicia Perdigones is a Full Professor in the Universidad Politécnica de Madrid, since 2006 and coordinator of the Educational Innovation Group Projects. She teaches subjects related to electrical installations and machinery, conducting educational innovation activities in these same areas.

António Sacavém currently works at the Faculty of Social Sciences and Technology, at Universidade Europeia. António's research interests are leadership, management, communication, and digital transformation.

Alperen Sağdıç is the Director of Education at Sobe Foundation. Alperen Sağdıç's research interests are autism spectrum disorder, applied behavioural analysis, assistive technologies and the use of advanced technologies in special education.

Hilal Sahin is a Master's student on the teaching profession programme at Ludwigsburg University of Education and an education research assistant. Her main research areas are communications, education policies, and digital technologies in education.

Sunagül Sani-Bozkurt is a faculty member and researcher at Anadolu University, Education Faculty, Department of Special Education. Dr Sani-Bozkurt's research interests are autism spectrum disorder, assistive technologies, evidence-based practices, technology supported environment design and applications in the field of special education.

João Rodrigues dos Santos is a University Professor at IADE / European University. He has a PhD in Economics and Management (Universidad Europea de Madrid) and a Master's Degree in Geography and Territorial Planning (Universidade Nova de Lisboa). As a researcher, he is a member of the Center for

Transdisciplinary Development Studies (University of Trás-os-Montes and Alto Douro) and the Center for Studies and Opinion Polls of the Portuguese Catholic University. He is the author of two books (in the areas of Economics and Territorial Management) and frequently publishes chapters and articles of an academic, technical and scientific nature. Currently, João Rodrigues dos Santos is also a permanent contributor to CNN Portugal, analyzing and commenting on national and international economic news.

Dilek Şenocak is an instructor at Anadolu University, School of Foreign Languages. She holds an MA in distance education from Anadolu University. As a PhD candidate, she has been recently focusing on artificial intelligence in education. She is also interested in gamification, adaptive learning, open and distance learning.

Ranjit Singha is a Doctorate Research Fellow at Christ (Deemed to be University) and a distinguished American Psychological Association (APA) member. His expertise lies in research and development across various domains, including Mindfulness, Addiction Psychology, Women Empowerment, UN Sustainable Development Goals, and Data Science. He has earned certifications from renowned institutions, including IBM and The University of Oxford Mindfulness Centre, UK, in Mindfulness. Additionally, he holds certifications as a Microsoft Innovative Educator, Licensed Yoga Professional, Certified Mindfulness Teacher, and CBCT Teachers Training from Emory University, USA. Mr Ranjit's educational qualifications include PGDBA (GM), MBA (IB), MSc in Counseling Psychology, and completion of a Senior Diploma in Tabla (Musical Instrumentation). His dedication to continuous learning is evident through his involvement in the SEE Learning® (Social, Emotional, and Ethical) Learning program. As a committed researcher and educator, Mr Ranjit focuses on mindfulness and compassion-based interventions. He has an impressive publication record, having authored twenty-three research papers, ten chapters, four books, and five edited books. His research interests encompass various aspects of mindfulness, such as assessment, benefits of mindfulness-based programs, change mechanisms, professional training, mindfulness ethics, cognitive and neuropsychology, and studies related to high-risk behaviours. Apart from his research endeavours, Mr Ranjit has extensive teaching experience, instructing courses in diverse subjects like Forensic Psychology, Positive Psychology, Organizational Planning, Strategic Management, Psycho Metric Tests, Counseling Skills, Disaster Management, Basic Computer Science, Business Planning, Business Law, and Auditing. He has mentored numerous Postgraduate and undergraduate research projects, demonstrating his commitment to nurturing young minds in psychology. Ad Hoc Reviewer at International Journal of Cyber Behavior, Psychology and Learning (IJCBPL), Reviewer and author at IGI Global, and Editor and Reviewer at TNT Publication. Furthermore, Mr Ranjit actively provides personal counselling services, showcasing his genuine concern for his students' well-being and academic success. His unwavering dedication to research and education has solidified his position as a valuable contributor to psychology.

Surjit Singha is an academician with a broad spectrum of interests, including UN Sustainable Development Goals, Organizational Climate, Workforce Diversity, Organizational Culture, HRM, Marketing, Finance, IB, Global Business, Business, AI, K12 & Higher Education, Gender and Cultural Studies. Currently a faculty member at Kristu Jayanti College, Dr. Surjit also serves as an Editor, reviewer, and author for prominent global publications and journals, including being on the Editorial review board of Information Resources Management Journal and contributor to various publications. With over 13 years of experience in Administration, Teaching, and Research, Dr. Surjit is dedicated to imparting knowledge and guiding students in their research pursuits. As a research mentor, Dr. Surjit has nurtured young minds and fostered academic growth. Dr. Surjit has an impressive track record of over 75 publications, including articles, book chapters, and textbooks, holds two US Copyrights, and has successfully completed and published two fully funded minor research projects from Kristu Jayanti College.

Mete Sipahioglu is a researcher and lecturer at Samsun University and he works as the Coordinator of European Mobility in the International Relations Office. Previously, he has served as a teacher of English in many educational institutions at different levels. He holds a Ph.D. in Educational Administration and Supervision with a specialization in internationalization in higher education institutions and completed his Erasmus exchange mobility at the University of London, Institute of Education (UK). Throughout his career, he has participated more than 50 seminars, courses, and projects at national and international level. His major research interests lie in the area of Teacher Education, Educational Leadership and Policies and Internationalization of Higher Education Institutions. Currently, he is a member and stakeholder advisor for WG3 at ENIS (COST Action 20115) which focuses on European Network on International Students Mobility: Connecting Research and Practice.

Sutithep Siripipattanakul is an associate professor of Educational Technology in the Faculty of Education at Kasetsart University, Thailand. His research interests involve computer education, technology and educational communication, information technology, vocational education, educational administration, management information systems, e-learning, educational assessment, and blended learning.

Mirona Stanescu, Ph.D, is senior lecturer and head of the Department of Pedagogy and Didactics in German at the Faculty of Psychology and Educational Science, Babes-Bolyai University Cluj (Romania). She is a graduate in German and English Language and Literature and in Pedagogy. She has a PhD in Drama in Education from the University of Education Ludwigsburg (Germany). Her main fields of interests include drama in education, diversity and equity in education, intercultural education, communication, and children's literature. She is a trained primary school teacher for bilingual education and worked for 12 years at the German school in Cluj-Napoca.

Penny Thompson is an Associate Professor of Learning, Design, and Technology at Oklahoma State University. Her research interests include communication and learning in online, blended, and flipped learning environments. She is also interested in all areas where technology and cognition intersect, including both the design of technology to support cognition and the ways immersion in digital technology may or may not be changing habits of mind and attitudes toward learning.

Cansel Tosun, who received her bachelor's degree from Ondokuz Mayıs University Early Childhood Education Programme, continues her master's degree in the field of Educational Technologies at Gazi University Graduate School of Educational Sciences. Her research areas are on early childhood education, technology and artificial intelligence.

Wan Ahmad Jaafar Wan Yahaya is the Director of the Centre for Instructional Technology and Multimedia (PTPM), Universiti Sains Malaysia (USM), Penang, Malaysia. He is also the President of the Malaysian Educational Technology Association (META). His specialty is associated with teaching and creative and innovative multimedia.

Mehmet Yavuz completed his undergraduate education at Fırat University, Department of Computer Education. He completed his master's and doctoral studies at Atatürk University, Department of Computer and Instructional Technologies. He is still working as an Assistant Professor at Bingöl University, Faculty of Economics and Administrative Sciences, Department of Management Information Systems. His research interests include digital transformation, distance education and artificial intelligence.

Stacy Ybarra Evans is a 2022 Ricardo Salinas Aspen Fellow first generation Latina from the Southside of San Antonio. She currently serves as the Director of the Center for Teaching Excellence at Our Lady of the Lake University. She works to develop students' academic skills as a first-year seminar instructor at San Antonio College of the Alamo Colleges District where she worked for 20 years. During her tenure at ACD, she received the Starfish award as a college advisor at Palo Alto College. She is also a current researcher with the Texas Association of Community Colleges helping analyze focus group information on guided pathways, basic student needs and teaching and learning practices. As a contractor with Quality Matters, the leading organization in instructional design standards, she has led teams nationally to get online courses approved. As an ACUE facilitator she works to encourage new teaching practices at San Antonio College from 2021 to present. She graduated from Palo Alto College with an associate degree, Texas A&M University - San Antonio for her bachelor's and master's degree and Capella University where she conferred her doctorate degree in 2019. She has also brought her voice to bring attention to gender diversity in leadership by participating in leadership programs such as the San Antonio Hispanic Chamber's Latina Leadership Institute, Leadership SAISD and South San Antonio Chamber's City South Leadership program.

Huixin Zhen is the Phd of the Centre for Instructional Technology and Multimedia (PTPM). Unversiti Sains Malaysia (USM).Penang, Malaysia.

Index

L

M

N

O

P

R

S

T

U

V

www.ingramcontent.com/pod-product-compliance
Lightning Source LLC
LaVergne TN
LVHW080113011026
849160LV00013B/1091